CYBERCRIMINOLOGY

CYBERCRIMINOLOGY

Marie-Helen Maras

NEW YORK   OXFORD
OXFORD UNIVERSITY PRESS

Oxford University Press is a department of the University of Oxford.
It furthers the University's objective of excellence in research, scholarship,
and education by publishing worldwide. Oxford is a registered trademark
of Oxford University Press in the UK and certain other countries.

Published in the United States of America by Oxford University Press
198 Madison Avenue, New York, NY 10016, United States of America.

© 2017 by Oxford University Press

Library of Congress Cataloging-in-Publication Data

CIP data is on file at the Library of Congress
ISBN number: 978-0-19-027844-1

9 8 7 6 5 4 3 2 1

Printed by LSC Communications, United States of America

DEDICATION

With much love and respect, I dedicate this book to my spiritual sisters,
Ηγουμένη Χρυσοβαλάντη και Αδελφή Αρσενία της Ιεράς
Μονής του Οσίου Παταπίου Λουτρακίου.

"Εις δόξαν Θεού"

BRIEF CONTENTS

TABLE OF CONTENTS

PREFACE

The reason d'etre of this book is to spark interest in the field of cybercriminology and to stimulate criminological thought and debate on important issues that are currently not receiving the attention they deserve. The hope is to draw attention to the dearth of data and empirical studies in this field and motivate those in criminology, computer science, and criminal justice fields to analyze cybercrimes through the lens of criminology, update curricula to include cybercriminology, and increase research contributions in this field. There is a serious deficit in the national capacity for cybercrime and cybersecurity positions. Because of this, there is a push toward advancing knowledge in the field of cybercrime and cybersecurity and enhancing existing educational programs in these areas. This is evident in current educational grant opportunities, strategic plans of universities throughout the United States (and abroad), and laws promoting the creation of educational programs and jobs in these fields. Given that few things personal and professional have been left untouched by the Internet and technology, making the inclusion of cyber-related material in science, social science, and even humanities curricula is critical.

What is currently lacking is a comprehensive examination of these criminal behaviors through the lens of criminology. This book introduces students to criminological theories, types of cybercrimes, and the nature and extent of cybercrime in the United States and abroad. Particularly, it examines victim and offender behavior in the online environment. This book can be described as a classical criminology textbook with a twist; after the discussion of traditional criminological theories, it covers their applicability to cybercrimes by providing an in-depth analysis of existing literature and empirical studies and their ability in explaining various cybercrimes committed in developed nations and developing countries. In short, this book comprehensively analyzes criminological theories as they apply to cybercrime on the national and international level.

This book is designed to appeal to a wide audience by critically exploring cybercrime, theories of cybercrime, countermeasures, and their implications for a number of different fields—criminology, computer science, criminal justice, law, sociology, psychology, political science, global affairs, security, police studies, and public policy and administration. Anyone interested in learning about cybercrime, cybervictims, cyberoffenders, the causes of cybercrime, and national and international responses to cybercrime, will find food for thought in this work.

INSTRUCTOR RESOURCES

This book is accompanied by instructor resources, such as an instructor's manual, Power-Point presentations, and a test question bank.

ACKNOWLEDGMENTS

I would like to warmly thank Steve Helba at Oxford University Press for his support, direction, and guidance throughout the development and production process of this book and Larissa Albright, also at Oxford, for her assistance on this project. I am especially grateful to Lauren Shapiro, Michelle Miranda, and Tina Tsiokris for graciously taking the time to critically review and comment on the chapters of this book. I would also like to thank the following reviewers for their input: Mark H. Beaudry, University of Massachusetts, Lowell; Timothy Buzzell, Baker University; Mario Caire, The University of Texas at El Paso; Galen A. Grimes, Pennsylvania State University, Greater Allegheny Campus; Raymond Hsieh, California University of Pennsylvania; Stephen C. McCraney Sr., Mississippi College; Brooke Miller, University of North Texas; Jordana Navarro, Tennessee Tech University; Joseph L. Nedelec, University of Cincinnati; Michael G. Overholt, La Roche College; Jeffery M. Owen, University of Central Missouri and Missouri Western State University; Damon Petraglia, University of New Haven; Shalon Simmons, Oklahoma State University Institute of Technology.

PART 1

THE NATURE AND EXTENT OF CYBERCRIME

This part introduces students to cybercrime, different types of cybercrimes, cybercriminology, and key thematic concerns in the field of cybercriminology.

CHAPTER 1

CYBERCRIME AND CYBERCRIMINALS

The Development of Cybercriminology

KEYWORDS

Crime
Criminal
Criminology
Cybercrime
Cybercriminal
Cybercriminology
Cyberdeviance

Cyberpredation
Cyberspace
Cybertheft
Cybertrespass
Cybervandalism
Cybervice
Interpersonal cybercrime

Law
Organized cybercrime
Political cybercrime
Public order cybercrime
Swatting
Wardriving

In fantasy football, the players of this virtual recreational activity create a new league or join an existing league and draft real National Football League (NFL) players (according to a predetermined salary cap for the entire team) to build an imaginary football team (i.e., a fantasy football team). These teams are awarded points as follows: During the NFL season, fantasy football teams compete against each other. For example, two fantasy football teams are paired up each week to compete against each other. Points are awarded to each team based on real points obtained by NFL players on the football field (i.e., real game statistics during the NFL season). If, for example, Team A and Team B are paired off and the NFL players in Team A receive more points than the NFL players in Team B during real games, then fantasy football Team A wins. Fantasy football websites such as DraftKings and FanDuel require an entry fee, and monetary prizes are awarded to teams that win.[1]

In the United States, sports betting is considered an illegal practice (with a few exceptions).[2] Because of this, many have questioned the legality of fantasy football.[3] The questions that follow are (1) Is fantasy football legal? and (2) What makes this and other acts legal or illegal? This chapter seeks to answer these very questions by examining illicit acts online and the categories that these illicit acts fall under. The chapter concludes by exploring how these illicit acts are studied.

CYBERCRIME: THE BASICS

A **crime** is an act which violates existing laws. A **law** is a binding rule, custom, or practice that regulates individuals' actions and provides penalties for noncompliance. An individual who violates the law is known as a **criminal**. When a person uses the Internet, computers and related technology in the commission of a crime, he or she is considered as a **cybercriminal**. Cybercriminals also engage in illicit acts that target websites, computers, and other digital devices. Given society's increased reliance on the Internet, computers and related technology (ICRT), the potential exploitation of these by cybercriminals is inevitable.

Cybercriminals can attack, offend, threaten, humiliate, harass, steal from, and otherwise harm victims and exploit and damage computers and other technological devices. The crimes perpetrated by these actors are referred to as **cybercrimes**. This type of crime occurs on a far greater scale than traditional crime because of its ability to reach and affect individuals around the globe. Furthermore, cybercrime is not restricted by physical, geographical borders; instead, it transcends them.

Cyberspace is the environment within which communications and other online activities through Internet-enabled digital devices take place. This space has transformed the way in which individuals communicate, disclose, exchange, and retrieve information, develop and maintain relationships, and move money. Cyberspace has also enhanced trade by enabling sellers to access customers all over the world and buyers to purchase goods beyond establishments within their own countries.

CYBERCRIME CATEGORIES

Cybercrime can fall under the following six proposed typologies: cybertrespass and cybervandalism; cybertheft; interpersonal cybercrime; cyberdeviance and public order cybercrime; organized cybercrime; and political cybercrime. Each of these is explored individually below.

CYBERTRESPASS AND CYBERVANDALISM

Cybertrespass refers to unauthorized access to computer systems and digital devices utilizing the ICRT. Hacking is a form of cybertrespass. Hackers seek to gain unauthorized access to systems and devices for a variety of reasons (e.g., personal, social, and political reasons). Adrian Lamo hacked into the systems of such companies as WorldCom, Excite@Home, and the *New York Times* with the intention of subsequently publicly exposing the compromise.[4] Lamo is also known for revealing the person who was responsible for leaking U.S. classified information to Wikileaks, a journalistic organization founded by Julian Assange—namely, Bradley Manning (now known as Chelsea Manning).[5] Once hackers gain access to a system or digital device, they can review, steal, modify, download, and/or delete content any time they choose or disrupt access to the system or device by legitimate users.

Even journalists have been charged with and convicted of hacking. In 2005, the British royal family complained to the police that Rupert Murdoch's *News of the World (NoW)*, a British tabloid, had possibly hacked into their phones.[6] The following year, an editor at *NoW*, Clive Goodman, and a private investigator working for *NoW*, Glenn Mulcaire, were arrested for phone hacking and subsequently convicted of this crime in 2007.[7] In 2011, Scotland Yard revealed that the same tabloid had interfered with an investigation of a missing child, Milly Dowler, who, it was later revealed, had been abducted, raped, and murdered by Levi Bellfield.[8] *NoW* journalists hacked into Milly's phone and "deleted [messages] . . . in order to free up space for more messages. As a result, friends and relatives of Milly concluded wrongly that she might still be alive."[9] Public backlash ensued after this revelation and the tabloid was forced to close. A couple of journalists, Greg Miskiw and Neville Thurlbeck, were charged, convicted, and imprisoned for their roles in the phone hacking; others received a suspended sentence.[10] Another journalist, Dan Evans, was charged and convicted for hacking into two hundred voicemail accounts of politicians, celebrities, and sportspeople and for corruption because he paid off prison and police officials for information; ultimately, his sentence was suspended because he served as a prosecution witness for the trial of a senior editor of *NoW*, Andy Coulson.[11] Coulson received an eighteen-month prison sentence for his role in the phone hacking scandal.[12]

Groups have engaged in hacking as well. A well-known hacking group is LulzSec, which declared that it engages in cyberattacks "because . . . [members] find it entertaining."[13] *Lulz* is a term used to describe actions that occur at someone's expense in order to hurt the individual or create mayhem for enjoyment purposes. The arrests of key members of this group was the beginning of a series of events which ultimately led to the group's public declaration in June 2011 that it was disbanding.[14] Despite its alleged dissolution, the following month LulzSec engaged in **cybervandalism** by defacing the website of a British tabloid, the *Sun*, which is owned by Rupert Murdoch, in response to the phone hacking scandal. In this incident, LulzSec gained unauthorized access to the tabloid's website and posted a false story that Rupert Murdoch had died. This group declared responsibility for the incident

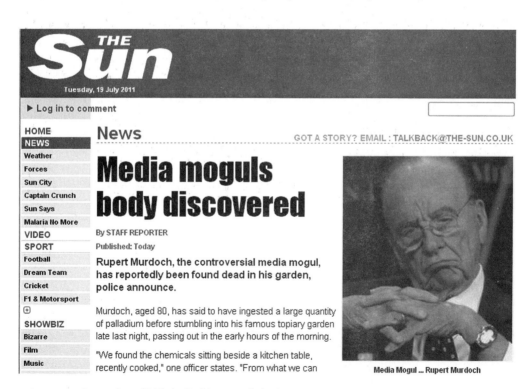

IMAGE 1-1   Screenshot of Website Defacement of *The Sun*.

through Twitter: "WE HAVE JOY WE HAVE FUN, WE HAVE MESSED UP MURDOCH'S SUN."[15] LulzSec also posted "Not so fun to get hacked, Mr. Murdoch, is it? u MAD?"[16]

A perpetrator committing a cybercrime in this category not only attempts to gain unauthorized access into a computer system or related digital device and modify, damage, or delete content within these devices but may also seek to disrupt the target's services. This can occur through a denial of service (DoS) attack, in which a perpetrator utilizes an Internet-enabled computer or other digital device to overwhelm a target's resources in order to prevent legitimate users from accessing and utilizing the services provided by the target. What may also occur is a distributed denial of service (DDoS) attack, which utilizes multiple systems infected with malicious software (i.e., malware) to target a system or website in order to prevent access to it by legitimate users. In 2014, the St. Louis County (Missouri) Police Association website experienced a DDoS attack.[17] Specialized malware is utilized to infect the computers that are the target of the DDoS attacks in order to turn them into zombie computers, which can be remotely controlled by the person who distributed (and possibly created) the malware.

CYBERTHEFT

Cybertheft refers to stealing money or personal, medical, or financial information through use of the ICRT. In 2016, eighty-one million dollars was siphoned from Bangladesh's central bank account at the Federal Reserve Bank of New York.[18] The information obtained from cybertheft is often used for fraudulent purposes. For instance, the Internet has enabled cybercriminals around the world to commit impersonation fraud, which involves pretending to be a particular person or organization in order to commit fraud or another crime. Scam artists in Nigeria have impersonated schools in order to obtain supplies, such as laptops and printer ink.[19] According to the Federal Bureau of Investigation (FBI), to avoid arousing suspicion, the supplies are sent to a U.S. address provided by the scam artists.[20] The person at this U.S. address often believes he or she is working for a legitimate business that enables people to work from home. This individual, once he or she receives the supplies, then forwards them to a Nigerian address. Scam artists have also pretended to be the police, contacting victims from a number that appears to be from a police department.[21] In this scam, victims are informed that someone they know is in jail and that money is needed to bail them out. The money is to be provided via prepaid credit or debit cards. Scam artists have further pretended to be technical support from a computer or telephone company, claiming that they can assist targets with purported computer or Internet access issues.[22]

Impersonation fraud is made possible by identity theft, whereby an individual assumes the identity of a target by unlawfully obtaining and using the target's name, Social Security number (SSN), employer identification number (EIN), bank account number, or other identifying information to commit a crime. This information can be obtained by perpetrators from online websites and forums that include this information or by gaining unauthorized access to the systems of individuals or companies. Numerous companies have reported breaches of their databases and theft of their data. For example, TJMaxx, Marshalls, Designer Shoe Warehouse, Barnes and Noble, Sports Authority, and other major commercial institutions have reported data breaches. The perpetrators of these data breaches, Albert Gonzalez, Christopher Scott, and Damon Patrick Toey, hacked into vulnerable networks utilizing a tactic known as **wardriving** (i.e., driving around areas looking for vulnerable Wi-Fi networks to hack into).[23] Between 2005 and 2007, Gonzalez, Scott, and Toey used this tactic to steal consumers' debit and credit card data from these commercial institutions and then distribute the data to co-conspirators outside of the United States to sell online.[24]

Other commercial institutions have been targeted by cybercriminals as well. In 2013, Neiman Marcus experienced a data breach resulting in the theft of 350,000 customers' debit and credit card data.[25] In 2014, Staples suffered a malware intrusion that resulted in the theft of credit and debit card data of 1.16 million customers.[26] In addition to these companies, hotels suffered data breaches and cybertheft. In 2014 and 2015, hotels that are part of the Trump Hotel Collection and those managed by White Lodging Services Corporation (a hotel franchise management company), such as the Starwood Hotels & Resorts Worldwide, Hilton, the Marriot, and Sheraton Hotels, experienced cyberbreaches that resulted in the theft of customer card data.[27] Even credit bureau agencies have reported breaches of consumer data. In 2015, Experian North America experienced a data breach resulting in the exposure of the "name, address, Social Security number, date of birth, identification number (typically a driver's license, military ID, or passport number) and additional information used in T-Mobile's own credit assessment" of approximately 15 million users who applied for financing from the telecommunications and electronic communications provider T-Mobile USA.[28] The primary issue with these breaches is that not all data is replaceable. Although credit and debit card data can be replaced, other types of stolen personal information cannot be replaced, or at the very least cannot be easily replaced.

In addition to impersonation fraud and identity theft, "click bait" scams take advantage of people's interest in important news stories and celebrities to get individuals to click on links that surreptitiously download malware onto a user's machine.[29] Securities fraud, which involves the manipulation of financial markets or the defrauding of investors through deception, has also been perpetrated online. In 2015, the Securities and Exchange Commission charged more than thirty hackers and traders with stealing private data and illicitly utilizing it in trading to make a profit.[30] In this incident, newswire services were hacked to obtain corporate earnings statements before they were released to the public.

Furthermore, copyright infringement occurs online (i.e., digital piracy). Copyrights, which protect literary and artistic works of users, can be infringed through the illegal streaming, downloading, and distribution of movies, TV shows, music, and other copyrighted works. In the late 1990s, Napster was created, which enabled peer-to-peer music file sharing without the permission and remuneration of copyright holders.[31] As such, Napster and other similar peer-to-peer file-sharing networks (e.g., Morpheus and Kazaa) were, at the time, facilitating digital piracy on their platforms.

INTERPERSONAL CYBERCRIME

Interpersonal cybercrime includes crimes committed via the ICRT against an individual which the perpetrator (a family member, intimate partner, classmate, acquaintance, community member, or stranger) is communicating with or has some form of real or imagined relationship with. An example of an interpersonal cybercrime is cyberbullying, a cybercrime involving children whereby the perpetrator humiliates or verbally attacks a victim (or victims). In 2010, a fifteen-year-old girl, Phoebe Prince, committed suicide after being physically assaulted, bullied offline, and cyberbullied by schoolmates via text and Form-spring, Facebook, and MySpace, among other online sites.[32]

Another form of interpersonal cybercrime is cyberharassment, whereby a perpetrator verbally abuses or otherwise attacks another individual utilizing the ICRT. Neighbors of James Lyons Jr., William and Gail Johnson, engaged in cyberharassment by paying a third party to send the victim (Lyons Jr.) e-mails with false accusations of illicit behavior and the victim's personal information (SSN and date of birth).[33] This third party also posted the victim's home address and other personal information (mobile phone number and e-mail) with items Lyons Jr. was supposedly selling or giving away on websites, resulting in the victim being bombarded with phone calls and e-mails from individuals seeking to obtain the items and, in some cases, individuals coming to the victim's home to receive the ficti-tious items.[34] The Johnsons also made false child abuse allegations against him.

Social media applications, or apps, have been used by individuals to engage in cyber-harassment. A case in point is YikYak, a social media app which enables users to post anonymous comments that individuals within a specific geographic area can review. No followers or friends are needed (nor available through the app) for others to review posts. This app was used in the cyberharassment of a professor, Margaret Crouch, at Eastern Michigan University. Her cyberharassers' posts included "demeaning, . . . crude, [and] sexually explicit language and imagery."[35]

A further example of an interpersonal cybercrime is cyberstalking, whereby a perpetra-tor repeatedly threatens, harasses, or frightens another user online. A tactic used by cyber-stalkers, cyberharassers, and other cybercriminals is a practice known as swatting. **Swatting** occurs when an individual places a hoax call to emergency services that a crime or other critical incident which requires an emergency police response is underway. In 2014, a serial swatter was arrested, a seventeen-year-old boy who used this tactic to harass numerous women who utilized Twitch, an online website that enables users to watch others play games and chat with others on the site.[36] Celebrities such as Tom Cruise, Justin Timberlake, and Ashton Kutcher have also been subjected to these tactics.[37]

Interpersonal cybercriminals engage in **cyberpredation** by preying on people through the use of the ICRT. Cases in point are child sexual predators and those who engage in, distribute, and collect depictions of children under the age of eighteen engaging in sexual activities (i.e., child pornography). A now defunct website called Landslide, which was run by the now imprisoned Thomas and Janice Reedy, served as a portal to child pornography sites that had images of sexual abuse of infants and children.[38] Despite the efforts of law enforcement agencies, child pornography is plentiful online.

BOX 1-1 CELEBRITIES, NUDE PHOTOGRAPHS, AND THE CLOUD

Christopher Chaney gained unauthorized access to the Google and Yahoo e-mail accounts of over fifty celebrities.[39] Chaney used the information about celebrities on blog sites to guess their passwords. Once he gained access to their e-mail accounts, he set up e-mail forwarding, sending copies of messages to his account. He obtained nude images of women, including celebrities (e.g., Scarlett Johansson and Renee Olstead), and posted online these photos and other information he obtained from the hacked e-mail accounts.[40]

Celebrity accounts were also targeted by a hacker group known as hackappcom. In this incident, nude photographs of celebrities such as Jennifer Lawrence were illegally obtained

(continued)

and subsequently "distributed and discussed via anonymous image-board 4chan and Reddit.com," among other online sites.[41] This occurrence was dubbed "the fappening," "a portmanteau of a slang term for masturbation popular on Reddit, 'fap,' and 'the happening.'"[42] Hackappcom gained access to celebrities' iCloud accounts (which store images and data on the Internet instead of digital devices) by guessing usernames and passwords.[43] At the time of the hacking incident, iCloud did not limit the number of times a user could input a username and password combination incorrectly by locking the user out after a predetermined number of failed attempts.[44]

CYBERDEVIANCE AND PUBLIC ORDER CYBERCRIME

Cyberdeviance involves use of the ICRT to engage in conduct which violates social norms and expectations. An example of cyberdeviance is online paraphilias, which are abnormal sexual desires. This paraphilia could be legal (e.g., foot fetish) or illegal (e.g., biastophilia, which involves abnormal sexual desires obtained from violent assaults).

BOX 1-2   VIRTUAL RAPE AS CYBERDEVIANCE

Rape refers to the use of a sex organ, other body part, or foreign object to engage in the unlawful sexual penetration of another person's vagina, anus, or mouth without the person's consent. For a crime to be committed, two elements are required: *actus reus* (guilty act) and *mens rea* (guilty mind). In the case of a rape, *actus reus*

> is constituted by: the sexual penetration, however slight: (a) of the vagina or anus of the victim by the penis of the perpetrator or any other object used by the perpetrator; or (b) the mouth of the victim by the penis of the perpetrator; where such sexual penetration occurs without the consent of the victim. . . . The mens rea is the intention to effect this sexual penetration, and the knowledge that it occurs without the consent of the victim.[45]

Rape is considered a form of sexual deviance because it violates social norms and expectations because of the nonconsent of one party in the sexual act. By way of extension, virtual rape can be considered a form of cyberdeviance.

In virtual reality environments, such as Multi-User Dimensions (MUDs), cases of virtual rape have been reported. Julian Dibbell reported one incident in a MUD, LambdaMOO, in which a player (the perpetrator) utilized a voodoo doll in a virtual reality to "possess" and ultimately control other players.[46] The perpetrator used this doll to force other players to perform sex acts on the perpetrator's character, others, and themselves. According to Dibbell, the perpetrator "had committed a MOO crime, and his punishment, if any, would be meted out via the MOO."[47] Eventually, the perpetrator's character was removed from LambdaMOO by being erased from the virtual environment.[48]

A **public order cybercrime** is an illicit act that offends the public's shared norms, morals, values, and customs and which is committed via the ICRT. A deviant cyberact or a public order cybercrime can be considered a **cybervice** as it includes behavior that is deemed immoral because it violates accepted codes of conduct. What is considered immoral varies between countries; so too does the legality of certain cybervices. Ultimately, what cybervice is considered illegal depends on the act, the location of the person (or persons) who engaged in the act, and the country defining the act as either legal or illegal.

An example of a cybervice is Internet gambling, which involves the transmission of a bet or wager online. Like other cybervices, the legality of Internet gambling varies by country. In 2015, INTERPOL led an international operation targeting illicit online gambling activities in the Philippines, Vietnam, Thailand, and Korea (*Operation Aces*).[49] The legality of Internet gambling also varies between counties and states within countries. Consider, once again, fantasy football. A federal law which prohibits sports betting in the United States is the Unlawful Internet Gambling Enforcement Act of 2006. Under this act, particularly 31 U.S.C. § 5362(1)(E)(ix), fantasy football is not considered a form of sports betting if it "does not include . . . participation in any fantasy or simulation sports game or educational game or contest in which (if the game or contest involves a team or teams) no fantasy or simulation sports team is based on the current membership of an actual team that is a member of an amateur or professional sports organization." In addition, pursuant to 31 U.S.C. § 5362(1)(E)(ix)(II), if the winning outcome of a game or contest, like fantasy football, is based on "knowledge and skill of the participants and . . . determined predominantly by accumulated statistical results of the performance of individuals (athletes in the case of sports events) in multiple real-world sporting or other events," then it is not considered to be a form of sports betting. What is more, "winning outcome[s] . . . [must not be] based . . . on the score, point-spread, or any performance or performances of any single real-world team or any combination of such teams; or . . . solely on any single performance of an individual athlete in any single real-world sporting or other event."[50] Many U.S. states, however, vary in their views of the legality of fantasy football. Indeed, existing law in some states may prohibit this practice, other state laws seem to downright prohibit it (e.g., Iowa, Arkansas, Tennessee, Arizona, and Louisiana), whereas others allow it but call for its regulation (e.g., Nevada).[51]

ORGANIZED CYBERCRIME

Organized cybercrime involves planning and executing illegal business ventures online by either hierarchical groups or decentralized networks that often conduct their operations from more than one state or country. Even traditional organized crime groups have engaged in cybercrime. In the United States, members of the Genovese crime family were arrested and sentenced for their roles in online gambling (i.e., sports betting).[52]

The illicit activities of organized cybercrime groups are not restricted to those online. Indeed, these groups often engage in both offline and online illegal activities. Offline, a common tactic utilized by these groups is skimming of automated teller machines (ATMs). Skimmers are electronic devices that are used to steal the personal information stored on users' credit or debit cards and to record the users' PIN numbers. An example of a skimmer is a card reader placed over the ATM's real card slot in order to steal card information; a camera is also placed in a location on the ATM where the PIN that the user inputs can be viewed. Keyboards that record this information have been placed over the real keyboards on ATMs as well. In fact, in Brazil, ATM skimmers have included both a hidden camera and fake keypads.[53] The data obtained from these skimming devices is then sold online or used to create credit and debit cards that can be purchased online. The organized cybercrime group can then use runners or cashers to purchase goods and ship them to the group, who will then resell the items online.

Organized cybercriminals engage in multiple forms of cybercrime. Consider organized cybercrime groups engaging in online financial fraud. Nicolae Popescu, a member of an organized cybercrime group and one of the FBI's most wanted cybercriminals, was part of an Internet fraud scheme involving the posting of online advertisements for cars and other goods that did not exist.[54] Popescu and co-conspirators negotiated prices for these nonexisting items, provided invoices to customers (that appeared to be legitimate), and accepted payment for these fictitious items by deposit to the perpetrators' bank accounts.[55] Another Internet fraud scheme conducted by Vladimir Tsastsin and his co-conspirators affected over one hundred countries by infecting an estimated four million computers with malware that enabled a click hijacking scheme, which rerouted users with infected machines to designated websites and advertisements.[56] Under this scheme, the perpetrators were paid each time a user visited the

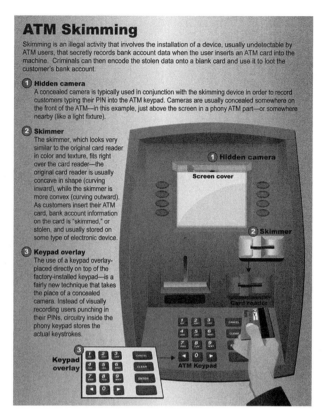

IMAGE 1-2 Information about ATM Skimming.

designated websites or clicked on the advertisements on these websites. In addition to cyber-crime, organized cybercriminals have engaged in the illicit procurement and sale of drugs, humans, firearms, cigarettes, and wildlife (e.g., shahtoosh shawls, which are made from Tibetan antelopes), data, and stolen goods online, among other illegal activities.[57]

POLITICAL CYBERCRIME

Political cybercrime involves cybercrime committed by individuals, groups, or nations in furtherance of a political goal. An example of a political cybercrime was the 2014 hacking incident involving Sony Pictures Entertainment. In this incident, e-mails from employers and the personal data of employees (past and present), freelancers, and celebrities were obtained.[58] The perpetrators threatened to attack U.S. movie theaters that screened *The Interview* and release the stolen personal information about employees, including the content of e-mails.[59] The FBI attributed the attacks to a hacker group believed to be backed by North Korea. The initial response to the threat to attack theaters and release personal information and e-mails was to pull the movie from the theaters. Such actions are particularly problematic because they send the message to cybercriminals that in order to effect change, illicit actions work in gaining concessions from organizations. In the end, Sony released the film through TV and online streaming instead of the theater. The personal information and e-mails of Sony employees were released shortly thereafter. Both the FBI and U.S. president

Barack Obama openly blamed North Korea, and specifically its leader, Kim Jong-un, for the hack on Sony. The North Korean government denied responsibility for the incident; despite this, the United States responded by implementing sanctions against North Korea.[60]

There are several forms of political cybercrimes. Cyberespionage can be classified as a form of political cybercrime when it involves the theft of a trade secret[61] via the ICRT for the benefit of a foreign government. An example of cyberespionage involved an employee of DuPont, Hong Meng. According to the U.S. Attorney's Office of the District of Delaware, "while still employed by DuPont and without informing the company, Meng accepted a position as a faculty member at Peking University, College of Engineering, Department of Nanotechnology, (PKU), in Beijing, China."[62] Meng sent DuPont's "protected chemical process" (i.e., trade secrets) to his Peking University e-mail account and downloaded a copy of this data to a USB, which he later saved to his personal computer.[63] Meng received fourteen months' imprisonment for his trade secret theft.[64] Cyberespionage may also involve the theft of a trade secret for the benefit of an individual or corporation via the ICRT. This type of cyberespionage can be classified as a form of cybertheft.

Another type of political cybercrime is hacktivism, the use of the Internet, computers, and related technology to obtain unauthorized access to a system or website in order to modify, delete, or render it temporarily or permanently unusable in furtherance of a political goal. Several instances of hacktivism have been linked to groups and hackers in Russia. The Eurasian Youth Union, a Russian-based radical group, engaged in DDoS attacks against the homepage of the Ukrainian president Viktor Yushchenko.[65] Russian hackers have also been known to engage in cyberattacks against pro-Chechen websites.[66]

Other instances of hacktivism could not be definitively linked to Russia. In 2007, cyberattacks were conducted against Estonia following the government's announcement that it would move a World War II memorial statue (a Soviet soldier) from the center of Tallinn. In the aftermath of this announcement, a series of DDoS attacks were conducted against Estonian government, financial, and media websites.[67] There were even postings online on how to engage in these attacks. Specifically, Russian blogs and forums provided instructions for users on how to launch DDoS attacks and solicit donations to commit such attacks; they also offered users the option of buying malware that would enable them to control other computers and use them in DDoS attacks.[68] Some did not view the Estonian cyberattacks as hacktivism; instead, these cyberattacks were erroneously viewed as cyberwarfare,[69] which refers to cyberattacks against a nation that amount to an act of force commenced by another nation or those acting on behalf of a nation. Others inaccurately called these cyberattacks acts of cyberterrorism,[70] which involves the use of the ICRT to target critical infrastructure vital to the functioning of society with the intention of causing fear, damage, serious bodily harm, or death in order to effect some form of change in the government or population in furtherance of a goal. Notwithstanding, the Russian government has not accepted responsibility for these attacks.

THE FIELD OF CYBERCRIMINOLOGY

Cybercrime is a complex, multifaceted phenomenon requiring further study through the lens of **criminology**. Criminology is the scientific study of the causes of crime, the scope of crime, the responses to crime by the public, media, social and political institutions, and criminal justice systems and the ways to control, mitigate, and prevent crime. **Cybercriminology** can be viewed as the scientific study of cybercrime through the lens of criminology. It tests the applicability of mainstream criminological theories to cybercrimes committed in developed nations and developing countries. It also seeks to shed light on the nature and extent of cybercrime, assess reactions to cybercrime and the implications of these reactions, and evaluate the efficacy of existing methods used in the control, mitigation, and prevention of cybercrime. What is currently lacking is a *comprehensive* examination of this criminal behavior through the lens of criminology.

This deficit is particularly problematic given that today few areas in individuals' day-to-day lives and few traditional crimes have been left untouched by the ICRT. What is more, such technologies have enabled new crimes to be committed—crimes that would not have been possible without them. The increasing reliance on communications, information, and computer technologies by societies around the globe has greatly expanded vulnerabilities to cybercrime. Moreover, the interconnectivity and interdependency of existing telecommunication networks and electronic communications systems worldwide have made cybercrime possible. Instead of decreasing these vulnerabilities by disconnecting systems, new technologies continue to be developed that increase vulnerabilities to cybercrime by creating more connections between digital devices, enabling the transfer of data in real time anywhere in the world with an Internet connection.

Presently, there is a push toward advancing knowledge in the field of cybercrime and cybersecurity and enhancing existing educational programs in these areas. This is evident in current educational grant opportunities, strategic plans of universities throughout the United States (and abroad), and laws promoting the creation of educational programs and jobs in these fields. Regardless of this push, scholarly studies on cybercrime are sparse and primarily focus on the investigative and technical issues associated with cybercrime. Although these investigative and technical issues are important, they should not be the sole emphasis of curricula and scholarly works. What is needed is the incorporation of criminological works in educational courses and programs on cybercrime and cybersecurity to a far greater extent than is currently practiced, as well as more empirical studies on cybercriminology.

Overall, cybercrimes have not received the attention they deserve by criminological scholars. In fact, this discipline is still in its infancy. The reality is that available criminological literature and empirical studies primarily focus on traditional, offline crimes. This is attributed to lack of knowledge of cybercrimes, the belief that most traditional criminological theories do not apply to cybercrime, and the overall dearth in cybercrime data.[71] This book seeks to fill the void in the available literature by including a comprehensive analysis of criminological theories as they apply to cybercrime on the national and international level. The following chapters delve into the complex subject of cybercriminology, looking in particular at measurements of cybercrime; the impact of cybercrime on cybervictims and the roles of these victims in cybercrime; the reasons offenders engage in cybercrime; cyberwitnesses' roles and reactions to cybercrime; significant theories and perspectives of criminology and how they relate to specific cybercrimes; and the measures needed to control cybercrime.

CASE STUDY

A Japanese woman played MapleStory, a virtual reality game where characters form relationships, engage in social activities together, and even fight enemies in the game.[72] Her character married another character in the game. The player of her character's husband gave her his login credentials. At one point, he divorced her character in the game. To exact revenge, she logged into his MapleStory account and deleted his character. Japanese authorities subsequently arrested her. In the news, this incident has been described as a "virtual murder."[73]

1. What cybercrime was committed?
2. What makes the act she committed illegal?
3. Was this a virtual murder? If so, will this influence how the case will be handled? Why do you think so?

REVIEW QUESTIONS

1. What is cybercrime? How does it differ from traditional crime?
2. What is cybertrespass? What is cybervandalism? Give an example of one cybercrime that falls under each category.
3. What is interpersonal cybercrime? What two cybercrimes fall under this category?
4. What is cybertheft? Name and describe two cybercrimes that fall under this category.
5. What is a public order cybercrime?
6. What is a cybervice? Are cybervices illegal?
7. What is organized cybercrime?
8. What is a political cybercrime? Describe one type of political cybercrime.
9. What is cybercriminology?
10. Why is the study of cybercrime important?

LAWS

Unlawful Internet Gambling Enforcement Act of 2006 (United States)

DEFINITIONS

Crime. An act which violates existing laws.

Criminal. A person who violates the law.

Criminology. The scientific study of the causes of crime, the scope of crime, the responses to crime by the public, media, social and political institutions, and criminal justice systems, and the ways to control, mitigate, and prevent crime.

Cybercrime. An illicit act that targets digital devices or is committed via the Internet, computers, and related technology.

Cybercriminal. A person who utilizes the ICRT to violate the law.

Cybercriminology. The study of cybercrime through the lens of criminology.

Cyberdeviance. Use of the ICRT to engage in conduct that violates social norms and expectations.

Cyberpredation. Preying on children, adults, and the elderly through communications, information, and computer technologies.

Cyberspace. The environment within which communications and other online activities through Internet-enabled digital devices take place.

Cybertheft. Stealing personal information, medical information, financial information, and/or money via the ICRT for personal or other use.

Cybertrespass. Unauthorized access to computer systems and digital devices utilizing the ICRT.

Cybervandalism. The virtual defacement of someone else's property.

Cybervice. Online behavior that is deemed immoral because it violates accepted codes of conduct.

Interpersonal cybercrime. Crime committed via communications, information, and computer technologies against an individual with whom the perpetrator is communicating or has some form of relationship (real or imagined).

Law. The system of rules that regulate the public's actions and provide penalties for noncompliance.

Organized cybercrime. Planning and executing illegal business ventures online by either hierarchical groups or decentralized networks that often conduct their operations from more than one country.

Political cybercrime. A cybercrime committed by individuals, groups, or nations in furtherance of some political goal or agenda.

Public order cybercrime. A crime committed via the ICRT that offends the public's shared norms, morals, values, and customs.

Swatting. An act wherein an individual places a hoax call to emergency services that a crime or other critical incident which requires an emergency police response is underway.

Wardriving. Driving around areas looking for vulnerable Wi-Fi networks to hack into.

ENDNOTES

1. D. Harwell, "All the Reasons You (Probably) Won't Win Money Playing Daily Fantasy Sports," *Washington Post*, October 12, 2015, https://www.washingtonpost.com/news/the-switch /wp/2015/10/12/all-the-reasons-you-probably-wont-win-money-playing-daily-fantasy-sports/.

2. See Chapter 12 for further information.

3. *Economist*, "How Daily Fantasy Sports Leagues Work," http://www.economist.com/blogs /economist-explains/2015/10/economist-explains-11; C. Isidore, "Why Fantasy Football Is Legal," *CNN Money*, October 6, 2015, http://money.cnn.com/2015/10/06/news/companies /fantasy-sports-legal/; M. Edelman, "Is It Legal to Play Fantasy Football for Money?" *Forbes*, September 3, 2013, http://www.forbes.com/sites/marcedelman/2013/09/03/is-it-legal-to-play -fantasy-football-for-money/#4b4ed7f157dc.

4. J. Kahn, "The Homeless Hacker v. the *New York Times*," *Wired*, April 1, 2004, http://www .wired.com/2004/04/hacker-5/.

5. M. Sledge, "Adrian Lamo, Hacker Who Turned Bradley Manning In, Testifies at Trial," *Huffington Post*, June 4, 2013, http://www.huffingtonpost.com/2013/06/04/adrian-lamo-bradley -manning_n_3384679.html.

6. CNN, "UK Phone Hacking Scandal Fast Facts," October 24, 2013, http://www.cnn.com /2013/10/24/world/europe/uk-phone-hacking-scandal-fast-facts/.

7. Ibid.

8. L. Dearden, "Milly Dowler's Family Speak of Torment after Revealing Details of Levi Bellfield's Abduction, Rape, Torture and Murder," *Independent* (London), February 10, 2016, http://www.independent.co.uk/news/uk/crime/milly-dowlers-family-speak-of-torment -after-revealing-details-of-levi-bellfields-abduction-rape-a6864886.html.

9. N. Davies and A. Hill, "Missing Milly Dowler's Voicemail Was Hacked by News of the World," *Guardian* (Manchester), July 5, 2011, http://www.theguardian.com/uk/2011/jul/04/milly -dowler-voicemail-hacked-news-of-world.

10. A. Cowel and K. Bennhold, "Andy Coulson Gets 18 Months in Tabloid Phone Hacking," *New York Times*, July 4, 2014, http://www.nytimes.com/2014/07/05/world/europe/andy-coulson -to-be-sentenced-in-phone-hacking-case.html.

11. M. Evans, "Phone Hacking Journalist Dan Evans Given Suspended Sentence," *Telegraph* (London), July 24, 2014, http://www.telegraph.co.uk/news/uknews/phone-hacking/10988578 /Phone-hacking-journalist-Dan-Evans-given-suspended-sentence.html; BBC News, "Phone

Hacking Reporter Dan Evans Spared Jail," July 24, 2014, http://www.bbc.com/news/uk
-28459720.

12. Cowell and Bennhold, "Andy Coulson Gets 18 Months," *New York Times*, July 4, 2014, http://
www.nytimes.com/2014/07/05/world/europe/andy-coulson-to-be-sentenced-in-phone
-hacking-case.html.

13. J. Vecchi, "Advanced Threat Protection & Visibility: Hacktivists," *Security Week*, April 16,
2013, http://www.securityweek.com/advanced-threat-protection-visibility-hacktivists.

14. R. Gallagher, "Why Hacker Group LulzSec Went on the Attack," *Guardian* (London), July 14,
2011, http://www.theguardian.com/technology/2011/jul/14/why-lulzsec-decided-to-disband.

15. R. Sanchez, "Phone Hacking: The Sun's Website 'Hacked by Lulzsec' with Fake Story about
Rupert Murdoch's Death," *Telegraph* (London), July 19, 2011, http://www.telegraph.co.uk
/news/uknews/phone-hacking/8646558/Phone-Hacking-The-Suns-website-hacked-by
-LulzSec-with-fake-story-about-Rupert-Murdochs-death.html.

16. A. Mehta, "LulzSec Returns with Bang, Hacks News International Websites," *International
Business Times*, July 18, 2011, http://www.ibtimes.com/lulzsec-returns-bang-hacks-news
-international-websites-299953.

17. U.S. Attorney's Office, Eastern District of Missouri, "Area Man Sentenced for Cyber-Attack
of the St. Louis County Police Union Website," December 7, 2015, https://www.justice.gov
/usao-edmo/pr/area-man-sentenced-cyber-attack-st-louis-county-police-union-website.

18. R. Gladstone, "Bangladesh Bank Chief Resigns after Cyber Theft of $81 Million," *New York
Times*, March 15, 2016, http://www.nytimes.com/2016/03/16/world/asia/bangladesh-bank
-chief-resigns-after-cyber-theft-of-81-million.html; J. W. Phippen, "The Mystery of Bangladesh's
Missing Millions," *Atlantic*, March 23, 2016, http://www.theatlantic.com/international
/archive/2016/03/bangladesh-philippines-bank-heist/474423/.

19. FBI, "Understanding School Impersonation Fraud: A Look Inside the Scam," April 29, 2014,
https://www.fbi.gov/news/stories/understanding-school-impersonation-fraud.

20. Ibid.

21. A. Puig, "Scammers Impersonate the Police" (blog), *Federal Trade Commission*, July 17, 2015,
http://www.consumer.ftc.gov/blog/scammers-impersonate-police.

22. Better Business Bureau, "BBB Top Ten Scams of 2014," January 27, 2015, https://www.bbb
.org/council/news-events/consumer-tips/2015/01/bbb-top-ten-scams-of-2014/.

23. T. Lush, "Hacker to Plead Guilty in Major Identity Theft Case," *Washington Post*, August 29,
2009, http://www.washingtonpost.com/wp-dyn/content/article/2009/08/28/AR2009082803779
.html.

24. U.S. Department of Justice, "Retail Hacking Ring Charged for Stealing and Distributing
Credit and Debit Card Numbers from Major U.S. Retailers," August 5, 2008, https://www
.justice.gov/archive/opa/pr/2008/August/08-ag-689.html.

25. K. Zetter, "Neiman Marcus: 1.1 Million Credit Cards Exposed in Three-Month Hack," *Wired*,
January 24, 2014, http://www.wired.com/2014/01/neiman-marcus-hack/.

26. B. Hardekopf, "The Big Data Breaches of 2014," *Forbes*, January 13, 2015, http://www.forbes
.com/sites/moneybuilder/2015/01/13/the-big-data-breaches-of-2014/#5e61dca53a48.

27. Krebs on Security, "Hyatt Card Breach Hit 250 Hotels in 50 Nations" (blog), January 15,
2016, http://krebsonsecurity.com/tag/white-lodging-breach/.

28. T-Mobile, "Overview and FAQs from Experian," last modified October 8, 2015, http://www
.t-mobile.com/landing/experian-data-breach-faq.html.

29. Better Business Bureau, "BBB Top Ten Scams."

30. U.S. Securities and Exchange Commission, "SEC Charges 32 Defendants in Scheme to Trade
on Hacked News Releases: Hackers, Traders Allegedly Reaped More Than $100 Million of Il-
legal Profits," August 11, 2015, http://www.sec.gov/news/pressrelease/2015-163.html.

31. T. Lamont, "Napster: The Day the Music Was Set Free," *Guardian* (London), February 23, 2013,
http://www.theguardian.com/music/2013/feb/24/napster-music-free-file-sharing; Electronic

Frontier Foundation, "RIAA v. The People: Five Years Later," September 30, 2008, https://www.eff.org/wp/riaa-v-people-five-years-later.

32. A. Giacobbe, "Who Failed Phoebe Prince?" *Boston Magazine*, June 2010, http://www.bostonmagazine.com/2010/05/phoebe-prince/; R. Goldman, "Teens Indicted after Allegedly Taunting Girl Who Hanged Herself," *ABC News*, March 29, 2010, http://abcnews.go.com/Technology/TheLaw/teens-charged-bullying-mass-girl-kill/story?id=10231357; E. Eckholm and K. Zezima, "6 Teenagers Are Charged After Classmate's Suicide," *New York Times*, March 29, 2010, http://www.nytimes.com/2010/03/30/us/30bully.html?pagewanted=all&_r=0.

33. S. Ebbert, "Online Vendetta Leads to $4.8M Jury Award for Lawmaker," *Boston Globe*, May 25, 2015, https://www.bostonglobe.com/metro/2015/05/24/cyberharassment-case-awards-million-damages-for-andover-state-representative/GKD2IoqMm9azlg68iyIXMJ/story.html; J. R. Ellement and T. Andersen, "Harassment via Internet a Crime, SJC Rules," *Boston Globe*, December 23, 2014, https://www.bostonglobe.com/metro/2014/12/23/sjc-harassment-using-internet-crime-not-free-speech/HNjQn9RLIoJAZb5i4kNqDI/story.html.

34. Ebbert, "Online Vendetta"; Ellement and Andersen, "Harassment via Internet."

35. J. Mahler, "Who Spewed That Abuse? Anonymous Yik Yak App Isn't Telling," *New York Times*, March 8, 2015, http://www.nytimes.com/2015/03/09/technology/popular-yik-yak-app-confers-anonymity-and-delivers-abuse.html?_r=0.

36. E. Reynolds, "Obnoxious the Troll and the Deadly Art of 'Swatting,'" December 18, 2015, http://www.news.com.au/technology/online/hacking/obnoxious-the-troll-and-the-deadly-art-of-swatting/news-story/d35e6e4799f04b72076de633cc982665.

37. J. Fagone, "The Serial Swatter," *New York Times*, November 24, 2015, http://www.nytimes.com/2015/11/29/magazine/the-serial-swatter.html?_r=0.

38. Y. Jewkes and C. Andrews, "Policing the Filth: The Problems of Investigating Online Child Pornography in England and Wales," *Policing and Society* 15, no. 1 (2005), 48.

39. BBC News, "US Scarlett Johansson Hacker Chaney Given 10 Years," http://www.bbc.com/news/entertainment-arts-20763788.

40. Associated Press, "'Hollywood Hacker' Who Targeted Scarlett Johansson Given 10 Years in Jail," *Guardian* (London), December 17, 2012, http://www.theguardian.com/technology/2012/dec/17/hollywood-hacker-christopher-chaney-10-years-jail.

41. A. Massanari, "#Gamergate and The Fappening: How Reddit's Algorithm, Governance, and Culture Support Toxic Technocultures," *New Media & Society*, (October 9, 2015), 1–2.

42. Ibid., 15.

43. D. Lewis, "iCloud Data Breach: Hacking and Celebrity Photos," *Forbes*, September 2, 2014, http://www.forbes.com/sites/davelewis/2014/09/02/icloud-data-breach-hacking-and-nude-celebrity-photos/.

44. Ibid.

45. *The Prosecutor v. Dragoljub Kunarac, Radomir Kovac and Zoran Vukovic* (Judgment) Case No. IT-96-23-T& IT-96-23/1-T (February 22, 2001), para. 460, http://www.icty.org/x/cases/kunarac/tjug/en/kun-tj010222e.pdf.

46. J. Dibbell, "Rape in Cyberspace, or How an Evil Clown, a Haitian Trickster Spirit, Two Wizards, and a Cast of Dozens Turned a Database into a Society," *Village Voice*, December 23, 1993, http://www.villagevoice.com/news/a-rape-in-cyberspace-6401665; S. Turkle, "Virtuality and Its Discontents: Searching for Community in Cyberspace," *American Prospect* 24, no. 1 (1996): 55.

47. Dibbell, "Rape in Cyberspace," para. 30.

48. S. Turkle, "Virtuality and Its Discontents: Searching for Community in Cyberspace," *American Prospect* 24, no. 1 (1996): 55; S. J. Drucker and G. Gumpert, "Cybercrime and Punishment," *Critical Studies in Media Communication* 17, no. 2 (2000): 154–155.

49. INTERPOL, "Illegal Online Gambling in Asia Targeted in INTERPOL Operation," August 4, 2015, http://www.interpol.int/News-and-media/News/2015/N2015-109.

50. 31 U.S.C. § 5362(1)(E)(ix)(III)(aa)(bb).

51. M. Edelman, "A Short Treatise on Fantasy Sports and the Law: How America Regulates Its New National Pastime," *Harvard Journal of Sports & Entertainment Law* 3, no. 1 (2012): 1–53; M. Edelman, "Navigating the Legal Risks of Daily Fantasy Sports: A Detailed Primer in Federal and State Gambling Law," *University of Illinois Law Review* 1, (2016): 117–150.

52. U.S. Attorney's Office, Northern District of New York, "Arrests Made in Internet Gambling Investigation," April 10, 2013, https://www.fbi.gov/albany/press-releases/2013/arrests-made -in-internet-gambling-investigation; U.S. Attorney's Office, Southern District of New York, "Five Gambino Crime Family Members and Associates Plead Guilty in Manhattan Federal Court," April 26, 2012, https://www.fbi.gov/newyork/press-releases/2012/five-gambino-crime -family-members-and-associates-plead-guilty-in-manhattan-federal-court.

53. J. Graham, ed., *Cyber Fraud: Tactics, Techniques, and Procedures* (Boca Raton, FL: CRC Press, 2009), 163.

54. FBI, "Cyber's Most Wanted," accessed August 4, 2016, https://www.fbi.gov/wanted/cyber.

55. Ibid.

56. U.S. Attorney's Office, Southern District of New York, "Estonian National Pleads Guilty in Manhattan Federal Court to Charges Arising from Massive Cyber Fraud Scheme That Infected Millions of Computers Worldwide," July 8, 2015, https://www.justice.gov/usao-sdny /pr/estonian-national-pleads-guilty-manhattan-federal-court-charges-arising-massive-cyber.

57. Europol, "The Internet Organised Crime Threat Assessment," September 29, 2014, https:// www.europol.europa.eu/content/internet-organised-crime-threat-assesment-iocta; A. J. Nichols and E. C. Heil, "Challenges to Identifying and Prosecuting Sex Trafficking Cases in the Midwest United States," *Feminist Criminology* 10, no. 1 (2015): 7–35; President's Working Group on Unlawful Conduct on the Internet, "The Electronic Frontier: The Challenge of Unlawful Conduct Involving the Use of the Internet," Appendix E, February 2000, http:// www.politechbot.com/docs/unlawfulconduct.html; GAO, "Internet Cigarette Sales: Giving ATF Investigative Authority May Improve Reporting and Enforcement: Report to Congressional Requesters," GAO-02-743, August 2002, http://www.gao.gov/new.items/d02743.pdf; IFAW, "Caught in the Web: Wildlife Trade on the Internet, 9 and 11," 2005, http://www.ifaw .org/sites/default/files/Report%202005%20Caught%20in%20the%20web%20UK.pdf.

58. S. Musil, "Sony Hack Leaked 47,000 Social Security Numbers, Celebrity Data," *CNET*, December 4, 2014, http://www.cnet.com/news/sony-hack-said-to-leak-47000-social-security -numbers-celebrity-data/.

59. E. Perez, J. Sciutto, and J. Diamond, "Obama: Sony 'Made a Mistake,'" *CNN*, December 19, 2014, http://www.cnn.com/2014/12/19/politics/fbi-north-korea-responsible-sony/; D. E. Sanger and M. Fackler, "N.S.A. Breached North Korean Networks Before Sony Attack, Officials Say," *New York Times*, January 18, 2015, http://www.nytimes.com/2015/01/19/world/asia/nsa -tapped-into-north-korean-networks-before-sony-attack-officials-say.html?_r=0.

60. M. Park and D. Ford, "North Korea to U.S.: Show Evidence We Hacked Sony," *CNN*, January 14, 2015, http://www.cnn.com/2015/01/13/asia/north-korea-sony-hack/; Sanger and Fackler, "N.S.A. Breached North Korean Networks."

61. Under 18 U.S.C. § 1839(3), trade secrets are: "all forms and types of financial, business, scientific, technical, economic, or engineering information, including patterns, plans, compilations, program devices, formulas, designs, prototypes, methods, techniques, processes, procedures, programs, or codes, whether tangible or intangible, and whether or how stored, compiled, or memorialized physically, electronically, graphically, photographically, or in writing."

62. U.S. Attorney's Office, District of Delaware, "Former DuPont Chemist Pleads Guilty," June 8, 2010, https://www.fbi.gov/baltimore/press-releases/2010/ba060810a.htm.

63. Ibid.

64. U.S. Attorney's Office, District of Delaware, "Former DuPont Chemist Sentenced to 14 Months in Prison for Stealing DuPont Trade Secrets," October 21, 2010, https://www.fbi.gov /baltimore/press-releases/2010/ba102110a.htm.

65. Graham, *Cyber Fraud*, 123.

66. Ibid.

67. Ibid., 126.

68. Ibid.

69. I. Traynor, "Russia Accused of Unleashing Cyberwar to Disable Estonia," *Guardian* (London), May 16, 2007, http://www.theguardian.com/world/2007/may/17/topstories3.russia; BBC News, "Estonia Hit by 'Moscow Cyber War,'" May 17, 2017, http://news.bbc.co.uk/2/hi/europe /6665145.stm.

70. A. Blomfield, "Russia Accused over Estonian 'Cyber-Terrorism,'" *Telegraph* (London), May 17, 2007, http://www.telegraph.co.uk/news/worldnews/1551850/Russia-accused-over-Estonian -cyber-terrorism.html; BBC News, "The Cyber Raiders Hitting Estonia," May 17, 2007, http:// news.bbc.co.uk/2/hi/europe/6665195.stm.

71. This lack of cybercrime data is explored in greater detail in Chapter 2.

72. B. Leach, "Woman Arrested after Virtual Murder," *Telegraph* (London), October 25, 2008, http://www.telegraph.co.uk/news/newstopics/howaboutthat/3257876/Woman-arrested -after-virtual-murder.html.

73. BBC News, "Woman in Jail over Virtual Murder," October 24, 2008, http://news.bbc.co.uk/2 /hi/asia-pacific/7688091.stm; Leach, "Woman Arrested after Virtual Murder."

CHAPTER 2

MEASURING CYBERCRIME

KEYWORDS

Crime Survey for England
and Wales
Dark figure of crime
Expected utility theory
Federal Crime Data
(United States)
General Social Survey
(Canada)
Hierarchy rule
Identity Theft
Supplement

International Crime
Victim Survey
National Computer
Security Survey
(United States)
National Crime
Victimization Survey
(United States)
National Incident-Based
Reporting System
(United States)

NIST Cybersecurity
Framework
Risk
Self-report survey
Supplemental
Victimization Survey
(United States)
Uniform Crime
Reporting Program
(United States)

Cybercrime is viewed as one of the greatest economic and national security threats facing the United States.[1] Other countries also consider it to be their top security concern.[2] However, an often overlooked point is the manner in which these conclusions are drawn. The absence of comprehensive cybercrime data means that the true nature and extent of these cybercrimes is unknown. This assessment cannot be adequately made, because of the lack of uniform practices for the collection and analysis of cybercrime data.

This chapter examines various crime measurement instruments in the United States and abroad and determines whether they can assess cybercrime, and if so, to what extent. Some of the tools included in this analysis are the Uniform Crime Reporting Program, National Incident-Based Reporting System, National Crime Victimization Survey, National Computer Security Survey, Crime Survey for England and Wales, and the International Crime Victim Survey. Recommendations are made to improve existing measurements of cybercrime on the national and international levels.

UNIFORM CRIME REPORTING PROGRAM

An official source of crime data in the United States is the **Uniform Crime Reporting Program** (hereafter UCR Program). Pursuant to 28 U.S.C. 534(a)(1), the attorney general can "acquire, collect, classify, and preserve identification, criminal identification, crime, and other records." In 1930, the attorney general designated the FBI as the national clearing-house for this crime data.[3] From that point on, the FBI compiled and published UCR Program official statistics from data provided by participating U.S. law enforcement agencies. Since 1958, this information has been made available in the *Crime in the United States (CIUS)* publication.[4]

The UCR Program in its traditional *Summary Reporting System (SRS)* includes data about Part 1 and Part 2 offenses (see Figure 2-1). Part 1 offenses include violent crimes and property crimes. The violent crimes recorded in Part 1 are murder and nonnegligent manslaughter, forcible rape, robbery, and aggravated assault. The property crimes recorded in Part 1 are burglary, larceny-theft, motor vehicle theft, and arson (however, depending on the type of arson, it may be classified as a violent crime).[5] The crimes included in the *SRS* are considered to be serious crimes which are likely to occur and be reported to law enforcement authorities.[6] From the eight offenses listed in Part 1, violent crimes are considered the most severe. According to the FBI, "in descending order of severity, the violent crimes are murder and nonnegligent manslaughter, [forcible] rape, robbery, and aggravated assault, followed by the

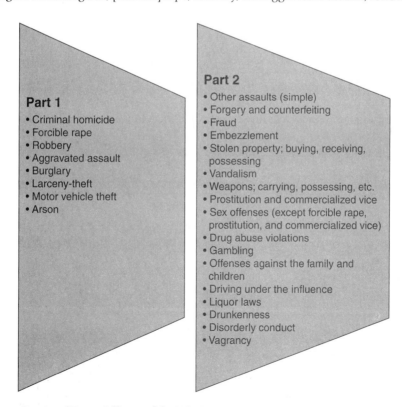

Part 1
- Criminal homicide
- Forcible rape
- Robbery
- Aggravated assault
- Burglary
- Larceny-theft
- Motor vehicle theft
- Arson

Part 2
- Other assaults (simple)
- Forgery and counterfeiting
- Fraud
- Embezzlement
- Stolen property; buying, receiving, possessing
- Vandalism
- Weapons; carrying, possessing, etc.
- Prostitution and commercialized vice
- Sex offenses (except forcible rape, prostitution, and commercialized vice)
- Drug abuse violations
- Gambling
- Offenses against the family and children
- Driving under the influence
- Liquor laws
- Drunkenness
- Disorderly conduct
- Vagrancy

FIGURE 2-1   Part 1 and Part 2 Offenses of the UCR Program.
Source: FBI, "Appendix II – Offenses in Uniform Crime Reporting," accessed August 4, 2016, https://www2.fbi.gov/ucr/cius_04/appendices/appendix_02.html.

property crimes of burglary, larceny-theft, and motor vehicle theft."[7] If multiple offenses are committed in one criminal incident, only the most serious of the offenses is recorded (this is known as the **hierarchy rule**). The only crime that does not follow the hierarchy rule is arson. If multiple offenses are committed in conjunction with arson, all crimes are reported. In 2013, the UCR Program began collecting data on "human trafficking/commercial sex acts"[8] and "human trafficking/involuntary servitude"[9] as crimes included under Part 1 offenses of the *SRS* pursuant to the William Wilberforce Trafficking Victims Protection Reauthorization Act of 2008.[10] Each month, participating law enforcement agencies disclose the number of reported Part 1 offenses, "includ[ing] . . . clearances; types and values of stolen and recovered property; and the age, sex, and race of persons who are arrested."[11] Part 2 offenses include other crimes against persons, public order crimes, alcohol offenses, white-collar crimes, and "other" crimes. For Part 2 offenses, only arrest data is recorded, which includes information about the age, gender, and race of arrestees.[12]

The UCR Program interprets computer crime (i.e., cybercrime) as "common-law offenses of larceny, embezzlement, [and] trespass," among other crimes, committed through the use of the Internet, computers, and related technologies.[13] Because of this viewpoint, new classifications for different types of cybercrime have not been created. In 2014, the **Federal Crime Data** report was created and became part of the "Uniform Crime Reporting (UCR) Program's Federal Crime Data compilation."[14] This report provides information about the number of arrests by FBI field office on human trafficking, hate crime, and criminal computer intrusion; the latter includes crimes that involve "wrongfully gaining access to another person's or institution's computer software, hardware, or networks without authorized permissions or security clearances."[15] In 2014, FBI field offices reported 105 arrests for criminal computer intrusion (see Table 2-1 for arrests by FBI field office). Before this report, only a few federal agencies were providing UCR data; these agencies were part of the U.S. Department of the Interior, namely, the National Park Service, Fish and Wildlife Service, Bureau of Indian Affairs, Bureau of Land Management, and Bureau of Reclamation.[16] As of 2016, local, state, and tribal law enforcement agencies will be reporting these cybercrimes to the UCR Program as hacking/computer invasion.[17]

Table 2-1 FBI Arrests for Criminal Computer Intrusion, 2014

Atlanta	1	Los Angeles	22
Baltimore	4	Miami	10
Charlotte	1	Milwaukee	3
Chicago	4	New York	19
Cincinnati	1	St. Louis	2
Cleveland	1	San Antonio	4
Denver	6	San Diego	3
Detroit	5	San Francisco	12
Houston	1	Washington, D.C.	3
Las Vegas	3		

Source: Table 2-1 includes arrests reported by FBI field offices and was obtained (but partially modified) from: FBI, UCR Program, "Federal Crime Data, 2014," in *Crime in the United States, 2014,* Fall 2015, 6, https://www.fbi.gov/about-us/cjis/ucr/crime-in-the-u.s/2014/crime-in-the-u.s.-2014/additional-reports/federal-crime-data/federal-crime-data.pdf

One of the main issues with UCR data is that it is part of a voluntary reporting program and all law enforcement agencies in the United States do not participate. The latest figure from 2014 shows that "law enforcement agencies active in the UCR Program represented more than 311 million United States inhabitants (97.7 percent of the total population). The coverage amounted to 98.6 percent of the population in Metropolitan Statistical Areas, 91.6 percent of the population in cities outside metropolitan areas, and 92.6 percent of the population in nonmetropolitan counties."[18] Another issue with the UCR Program is that it is common practice for "estimation procedures [to be used by the FBI] to account for missing data" in its *CIUS* publication.[19] Moreover, the UCR Program data only includes the most serious crimes (with the exception of arson) pursuant to the hierarchy rule. Furthermore, all relevant information is not collected in Part 1 of the UCR Program (e.g., data about weapons used is collected only for certain crimes—nonnegligent manslaughter, robbery, and aggravated assault) or for Part 2 offenses, for which only arrest data is collected.[20] Due to the limitations in the UCR Program, an alternative system was sought to supplement it in order to improve the quantity and quality of available crime data.

NATIONAL INCIDENT-BASED REPORTING SYSTEM

In 1970, the **National Incident-Based Reporting System** (NIBRS) was established to provide more detailed information about crimes committed in the United States. Particularly for the NIBRS, "law enforcement agencies collect detailed data regarding individual crime incidents and arrests and submit them in separate reports using prescribed data elements and data values to describe each incident and arrest."[21] Unlike the *CIUS* publication, the NIBRS does not apply estimation procedures for missing crime data by participating and nonparticipating jurisdictions.[22]

Information about Group A and Group B offenses is recorded in the NIBRS (see Figure 2-2). In 2013, the NIBRS began collecting data on "human trafficking/commercial sex acts" and "human trafficking/involuntary servitude" as part of Group A offenses.[23] Group A currently includes twenty-three categories of crime and forty-six criminal offenses. Group B offenses include ten crime categories; incident-specific data is not recorded for the crimes within these categories, only arrest data.[24] Cybercrime is not listed as part of Group A or Group B offenses, but it is recorded in the NIBRS. If a cybercrime has occurred, the officer has "the capability to indicate whether the computer was the object of the crime" and "to indicate whether the offender(s) used computer equipment to perpetrate a crime."[25] This can be done by entering particular codes in the system when recording the cybercrime.[26] Similar recording practices exist in law enforcement databases: if a computer was involved in a crime in some way, the recording officer checks the box which indicates the role of the computer in the crime. Specifically, the recording officer will check a box indicating whether the computer was either the target of the crime or was used in the commission of the crime. This does not adequately depict what specific cybercrime was committed; rather, it only includes the role of the computer in the offense.

UNDERREPORTING OF CYBERCRIME

UCR Program and NIBRS data only include incidents reported to or observed by law enforcement agencies. As such, these data sources do not provide any insight into unreported figures of crime (i.e., the **dark figure of crime**). What currently drives the availability of

Group A

1. Arson
2. Assault Offenses - Aggravated Assault, Simple Assault, Intimidation
3. Bribery
4. Burglary/Breaking and Entering
5. Counterfeiting/Forgery
6. Destruction/Damage/Vandalism of Property
7. Drug/Narcotic Offenses - Drug/Narcotic Violations, Drug Equipment Violations
8. Embezzlement
9. Extortion/Blackmail
10. Fraud Offenses - False Pretenses/Swindle/Confidence Game, Credit Card/Automatic Teller Machine Fraud, Impersonation, Welfare Fraud, Wire Fraud
11. Gambling Offenses - Betting/Wagering, Operating/Promoting/Assisting Gambling, Gambling Equipment Violations, Sports Tampering
12. Homicide Offenses - Murder and Nonnegligent Manslaughter, Negligent Manslaughter, Justifiable Homicide
13. Human Trafficking - Commercial Sex Acts, Involuntary Servitude
14. Kidnapping/Abduction
15. Larceny/Theft Offenses - Pocket-picking, Purse-snatching, Shoplifting, Theft from Building, Theft from Coin-Operated Machine or Device, Theft from Motor Vehicle, Theft of Motor Vehicle Parts or Accessories, All Other Larceny
16. Motor Vehicle Theft
17. Pornography/Obscene Material
18. Prostitution Offenses - Prostitution, Assisting or Promoting Prostitution
19. Robbery
20. Sex Offenses, Forcible - Forcible Rape, Forcible Sodomy, Sexual Assault With An Object, Forcible Fondling
21. Sex Offenses, Nonforcible - Incest, Statutory Rape
22. Stolen Property Offenses (Receiving, etc.)
23. Weapon Law Violations

Group B

1. Bad Checks
2. Curfew/Loitering/Vagrancy Violations
3. Disorderly Conduct
4. Driving Under the Influence
5. Drunkenness
6. Family Offenses, Nonviolent
7. Liquor Law Violations
8. Peeping Tom
9. Trespass of Real Property
10. All Other Offenses

FIGURE 2-2 Group A and Group B Offenses of NIBRS.
Source: FBI, "National Incident-Based Reporting System (NIBRS)," accessed August 4, 2016, https://www2.fbi.gov/ucr/faqs.htm.

information about the number of crimes and cybercrimes is police observation and victim and witness reporting of these offenses. Nevertheless, crime and cybercrime are significantly underreported by both individuals and businesses.[27] For example, research has shown that approximately less than one-third of fraud victims report their victimization to law enforcement authorities in the United States, the United Kingdom, Australia, and Canada.[28] Research has also shown that victims report cyberfraud at an even lower rate than fraud.[29] Victims of cyberfraud, particularly online auctions, underreport this form of

cybercrime because they are embarrassed for being duped by perpetrators and view themselves as partially responsible for their cybervictimization.[30]

Expected utility theory can explain why individuals may choose not to report cybercrime. The theory holds that individuals will engage in an activity if the expected utility (i.e.,
the likely gain) from the activity exceeds the utility from using their time and resources on
other activities.[31] In light of this, individuals will not report cybercrime if they believe that
the benefit of doing so is small (e.g., chance of recovery of funds or items is small or nonex-
istent or the amount of money individuals have taken is small).[32] Research has shown that
individuals do not report cybercrime where the losses are relatively minor and not worth the
time and effort needed to report the incident.[33] Research has also shown that individuals
will most likely not report instances of cybercrime if they do not believe they will receive
restitution for their losses.[34] For these reasons, it is believed that there is a higher likelihood
that a loss will be reported when the expected utility is high than when it is low.[35]

Cybercrime is also underreported because victims do not view law enforcement agencies as experts in this field.[36] More specifically, individuals may not report cybercrimes
because they lack confidence in the ability of the police to deal with cybercrime. Individuals often believe that the police do not have the necessary resources to investigate cybercrime, are unlikely to identify the perpetrators, and, ultimately, are unable to arrest the
person responsible for the illicit act. Moreover, the victim may not know that he or she
has been a target of cybercrime. For example, victims' data may be stolen from a
third-party database, and unless these victims suffer an adverse consequence or are in
some other way alerted to the theft of their data, they will not know a cybercrime was committed against them.

Furthermore, underreporting may be the result of lack of public awareness about
cybercrime and where to report it.[37] With respect to the latter, the UK Home Office reported that this was one of the main reasons why individuals did not report cybercrimes.[38]
The UK National Crime Agency's National Cybercrime Unit was developed to coordinate
national responses to cybercrime.[39] On the National Cybercrime Unit's website, users are
directed to report a cybercrime that is underway to their local police service. If a cybercrime has already been committed, the victims are informed to report the online illicit
activities to Action Fraud.

In the United States, confusion exists as to where to report cybercrimes because users
can report them to a wide variety of public and private agencies and organizations. For
example, some cybervictims may contact local, state, and tribal law enforcement agencies
to report a crime; others may contact federal law enforcement agencies. Apart from directly
reporting cybercrime to law enforcement authorities, cybervictims can report illicit acts
committed against them to the Internet Crime Complaint Center (IC3), which is "a partnership between the FBI and the National White Collar Crime Center."[40] Complaints filed
are analyzed "to identify links and commonalities with other complaints. These groups of
similar complaints are then referred to the appropriate local, state, federal, tribal, or even
international law enforcement agency for potential investigation."[41] The data collected is
then published in an annual report in order to identify cybercrime trends.

Other cybervictims may choose to report certain types of conduct that violate the law,
such as digital piracy, to Internet service providers. In the case of online financial fraud,
such as online debit or credit card fraud, victims report these cybercrimes to the financial
institution that issued the card, which refunds victims' money (with few exceptions).

Because this refund is provided, victims do not feel the need to also report this cybercrime to law enforcement agencies. For other cybercrimes, for example, cyberidentity theft, a police report is considered an essential document needed to prove that a victim's identity was stolen;[42] therefore, notifications of such cybercrimes help stop further incidents and mitigate the impact of these cybercrimes.

If the cybercrime is fraud related, U.S. consumers may contact one or more of the credit bureau agencies (i.e., Equifax, Experian, TransUnion) as well as consumer protection agencies, such as the Federal Trade Commission (FTC), to report the crime. Complaints to the FTC, along with consumer complaints submitted to various other organizations and agencies (see Table 2-2), are housed in the Consumer Sentinel database. A cybervictim may report a crime to one or more of the organizations and agencies listed in Table 2-2. Research has shown that cybervictims tend to report cybercrime to just one organization or agency, if at all.[43] Cybervictims who report the crime to one agency may do so because they believe that this agency will forward their complaint to other relevant agencies. However, in the United States, agencies do not usually contact other relevant agencies when a cybercrime is reported unless there is some benefit and/or they are required by law to do so. Therefore, what is lacking in the United States is a unified policy for reporting

Table 2-2 Organizations to Which Victims May Report Cybercrimes

Alaska Attorney General	Los Angeles County Department of Consumer and Business Affairs	Oregon Department of Justice
California Attorney General	Louisiana Attorney General	Privacy Rights Clearinghouse
Canada Competition Bureau[44]	Maine Attorney General	PrivacyStar
Canadian Anti-Fraud Centre[45]	Massachusetts Attorney General	Publishers Clearing House
Colorado Attorney General	Michigan Attorney General	South Carolina Department of Consumer Affairs
Consumer Financial Protection Bureau	Mississippi Attorney General	Tennessee Division of Consumer Affairs
Council for Better Business Bureaus	MoneyGram International	U.S. Department of Defense
Green Dot Corporation	Montana Department of Justice	U.S. Department of Education
Hawaii Department of Commerce and Consumer Affairs	National Consumers League	U.S. Department of Veterans Affairs
Idaho Attorney General	Nevada Attorney General	Washington Attorney General
Indiana Attorney General	Nevada Department of Business and Industry	Western Union Company
Iowa Attorney General	North Carolina Department of Justice	Xerox Corporation
Lawyers' Committee for Civil Rights	Ohio Attorney General	

Source: Federal Trade Commission, "Consumer Sentinel Network Data Contributors," accessed July 15, 2016, https://www.ftc.gov/enforcement/consumer-sentinel-network/data-contributors.

cybercrime: one that calls for the creation of a single, central system of reporting that will review reported cybercrimes and contact all relevant agencies. This single, central system of reporting is also needed because the number of reported cybercrime incidents may be affected by the number of entities the incidents are reported to.[46]

Like consumers, businesses often do not report certain cybercrimes because losses are covered by insurance and the illicit acts are viewed as too trivial to report to law enforcement agencies.[47] In 2013, a report by the UK Commercial Victimization Survey revealed that only 2 percent of cybercrimes were reported to law enforcement agencies by businesses.[48] Underreporting may also be the result of fear that reporting can have adverse consequences for businesses and their reputation.[49] Companies in particular are reticent to report cybercrimes because they want to avoid the negative publicity for concern it will adversely affect consumer confidence and business reputation. For these reasons, the reported incidents of cybercrime by businesses may not accurately reflect the actual number of such offenses. It is clear that information from cybervictims should additionally be assessed in other ways, through crime measurement tools that do not involve law enforcement agencies.

NATIONAL CRIME VICTIMIZATION SURVEY

In 1972, the Bureau of Justice Statistics implemented the **National Crime Victimization Survey** (NCVS), which became an official data source for U.S. crime statistics. This survey is distributed twice a year to a nationwide representative sample of approximately 90,000 households comprising an estimated 160,000 individuals (twelve years of age or older).[50] The data from this survey provides information on the number of individuals who experienced "violent crimes (rape or sexual assault, robbery, aggravated assault, and simple assault) and . . . personal larceny. . . . For crimes against households (burglary, theft, and motor vehicle theft), each household affected by a crime is counted as a single victimization."[51] The NCVS includes information about the crime, victimization experience, impact of victimization, offender, and whether or not the crime was reported to the police. Accordingly, the NCVS seeks to shed light on the dark figure of crime by providing information on crime that has not been reported to the police.

Several identifiable issues are associated with the NCVS. First, this crime measurement tool does not validate victims' claims of experienced crime. Second, it excludes certain victims, such as victims under the age of twelve.[52] Third, like the UCR Program and NIBRS, victims may overreport or underreport crime. For instance, victims may underreport crime because they are unable to adequately recall details of the crime and the offender. Finally, the NCVS does not cover all forms of crime, and, as such, it does not depict the true scope of crime.

Cybercrime is not measured by the NCVS, with the exception of questions included about certain types of cybercrime in supplemental surveys.[53] In 2006, the Department of Justice funded a study on stalking that served as a supplement to the NCVS, namely, the **Supplemental Victimization Survey** (SVS). The SVS was one of the first measurement tools for cyberstalking. Data on cyberstalking revealed that one in four stalking victims has been cyberstalked.[54] The manner in which cyberstalking most frequently occurred was through e-mails and instant messaging.[55] Notwithstanding this survey, the true nature and extent of cyberstalking is unknown apart from existing studies and reporting by victims. What is known, however, is that cyberstalking, like stalking, is an underreported crime.[56]

OTHER NATIONAL VICTIMIZATION SURVEYS

Outside of the United States, victimization surveys have certain special editions or modules that include questions about a particular type of cybercrime or certain cybercrimes.[57] The **International Crime Victim Survey** (ICVS) includes only one question about cybercrime, which involves fraud encountered by victims during online shopping.[58] Similarly, in the United States, the **Identity Theft Supplement**, appended to the NCVS of 2014, also included questions about online shopping behavior.[59] In Canada, the 2009 **General Social Survey** collected data on various forms of cybervictimization from a sample of 19,422 households.[60] The survey collected cybervictimization data on online child sexual predation (i.e., child luring), Internet bank fraud, and other online fraud (e.g., phishing, nondelivery of items purchased online, and delivery of items of lesser quality than what was advertised).[61] This survey also included self-report data on cyberbullying, which revealed that the majority of the victims did not report their cyberbullying victimization to the police.[62] The 2014 General Social Survey included questions about Canadians' cyberstalking and cyberbullying victimization.[63]

As in the United States, in the United Kingdom, crime is measured through official statistics which include reported crime to the police and victimization surveys. With respect to victimization surveys, the **Crime Survey for England and Wales** (CSEW; formerly known as the British Crime Survey) is distributed to households in order to obtain information about the dark figure of crime. The UK Office of National Statistics also publishes estimates on cybercrime as part of its annual CSEW. The 2015 CSEW "estimated there were 2.5 million incidents of crime falling under the Computer Misuse Act, the most common incident . . . [of which was] the victim's computer or other internet enabled device . . . [being] infected by a virus; it also included incidents where the respondent's email or social media accounts had been hacked."[64] The CSEW includes only a small fraction of questions that relate to cybercrime as part of a survey focusing on crime in general. For this reason, the UK Home Office has encouraged the addition of more cybercrime-related questions in the CSEW in order to provide insight into the dark figure of cybercrime in England and Wales.[65]

SELF-REPORT SURVEY

As with the NCVS, data collected from a **self-report survey** also seeks to understand causes and incident rates of crime. In self-report surveys, individuals are requested to report on their own illicit activity. Self-report surveys ask respondents to reveal participation in criminal activity. Prior studies exist which show that individuals who engage in delinquent and criminal behavior are willing to provide information on their illicit acts provided that their anonymity is maintained and that there are no adverse consequences for doing so.[66] These surveys are normally distributed to individuals in groups with the promise of anonymity to ensure truthful answers from respondents. Unlike the previously discussed crime measurement tools, self-report surveys provide an unofficial account of crime.

Although self-report surveys are an important cybercrime measurement tool, the ability of these surveys to ensure the validity and reliability of data—that is, to provide accurate information and to do so in a consistent manner—has been questioned.[67] What is more, such studies are often conducted on a small and nonrepresentative portion of the wider population, for example, student samples. Indeed, the often cited limitation of research using self-report surveys is the lack of generalizability of findings to the larger population.[68] Overall, self-report surveys do not accurately reflect the actual number of cybercrimes and the types of cybercrimes committed.

NATIONAL COMPUTER SECURITY SURVEY

In 2005, the **National Computer Security Survey** (NCSS) collected data from businesses about the cybercrimes they experienced.[69] The survey was "cosponsored by the Bureau of Justice Statistics and the National Cyber Security Division (NCSD) of the U.S. Department of Homeland Security."[70] The data from this survey was collected by the RAND (Research and Development) Corporation. The objective of the NCSS was to shed light on the nature and extent of cybercrimes committed against businesses and the impact of these crimes. The survey also asked whether these incidents were reported to the police, and in the event that they were not, the reasons they were not reported. The results of the NCSS revealed that the majority of the businesses surveyed did not report cybercrime to the police.[71] This survey also revealed that the primary reasons companies do not report cybercrime to the police are the potential negative publicity and loss of consumer confidence.[72]

Of the 8,079 businesses that responded to the NCSS, approximately 7,800 reported using computers.[73] The survey examined the nature and extent of the following cybercrimes:[74] cybercrimes where the computer is the target of the illicit act (i.e., malware, denial of service attacks, and sabotage); cybertheft (i.e., cyberfraud, embezzlement, and theft of personal data, financial data, and intellectual property); and "other" cybersecurity incidents (e.g., port scanning and spoofing). Two-thirds of the businesses (5,081) reported experiencing at least one cybersecurity incident in 2005; an estimated three-fifths of these respondents reported experiencing more than one cybersecurity incident.[75] Although more than half of the respondents reported having been targeted by computer viruses, the majority were able to prevent infection from this malicious software.[76]

The manner in which cybercrime was reported in this survey raises some concerns. *Computer virus* was the term used to describe computer viruses, computer worms, and Trojan horses. However, these are not similar forms of malware.[77] Also, other forms of malware, such as spyware, were placed in the "other" cybersecurity incidents category.[78] In addition to cybertheft, other forms of cyberfraud, such as phishing and even identity theft, were placed in the "other" cybersecurity incidents category.[79] The overlap in the cybercrime categories of this survey makes it difficult to determine the nature and extent of reported cybercrimes. Another limitation of this survey is that while the NCSS did provide insight into underreported cybercrimes by businesses, the survey has not been repeated, nor have similar surveys been implemented in the United States on an annual basis.

BOX 2-1 RISK AND CYBERCRIME

It is difficult to determine whether cybercrime "constitutes a major threat or a minor threat that is only perceived as great because of the manner in which it is magnified and amplified by the media."[80] Actually, the **risk** of cybercrime is hard to assess objectively absent data. Some cybercrime risks are attributed to subjective assessments, that is, individuals' perception of risk. These perceptions are based on quick and intuitive assessments of cybercrime. By contrast, objective risk assessments of cybercrime are based on measurements. These assessments

(continued)

(*continued*)

are essential in managing risks. Consider organizations in which risk management identifies and evaluates three key areas of concern with respect to cybercrime:

1. *Assets.* An asset is something of importance or value and can include people (e.g., employees, customers, visitors, contractors, vendors), property (e.g., real property, equipment, systems, supplies, furnishings), proprietary information (e.g., digital files, paper files, forms), and business reputation.
2. *Potential threats.* Examples of threats to financial institutions include competitors, insiders, skilled hackers (outsider, lone agent), nations, hacktivists, organized criminals, and terrorists.
3. *Existing vulnerabilities.* Some vulnerabilities include abuse or misuse of systems and information by internal employees or contractors, malware infections, and exploits of unpatched/misconfigured systems and devices.

Ultimately, risks to an organization or other target can be calculated by the magnitude of the harm of the threat should it materialize (*criticality*), the likelihood of the harm materializing (*probability*), and the vulnerability of an individual or organization (depending on what is being assessed) to the threat.

OTHER BUSINESS SURVEYS

Cybercrime data is also available through business surveys and reports on certain cybercrimes. Information about, for example, cybertrespass, cybervandalism, and cybertheft is often obtained through media accounts, which selectively focus on cybercrimes, and business surveys.[81] Businesses and private organizations have created independent cybercrime surveys. These surveys should be examined to ensure that representative samples are used. Reports from industry may be biased, especially in light of the data, which is primarily provided by companies selling antivirus and antispyware software (e.g., Symantec and McAfee). Indeed, for certain cybercrimes, data regarding the prevalence of certain illicit acts, such as malware and phishing, is primarily available from security software vendors.[82] A conflict of interest may exist in such situations and with respect to other companies that sell cybersecurity products. Reporting procedures at companies also influence cybercrime data; these procedures may vary by organization. The reality is that cross-comparisons cannot be made, due to the variation that exists in the definitions of cybercrime and the criteria these surveys use to measure cybercrime.

BOX 2-2 NIST CYBERSECURITY FRAMEWORK

In 2013, Executive Order 13636 directed the National Institute of Standards and Technology (NIST) to develop cybersecurity guidelines, standards, and practices for designated U.S. critical infrastructure sectors (e.g., energy, financial, communications, and information technology sectors, to name a few).[83] Pursuant to this directive, in 2014, the **NIST Cybersecurity Framework** was created to help public and private critical infrastructure sectors improve their cybersecurity posture. This framework identified the following five essential cybersecurity functions:[84]

Identify. Create (wherever needed) and foster a risk management culture within the organization. Some critical activities here include identifying assets, risks, risk priorities, information security policies, legal and regulatory requirements regarding cybersecurity, and the cybersecurity roles of the workforce.

Protect. Develop safeguards to protect people, property, and systems and the availability, integrity, and confidentiality of information. Key activities in this function are implementing effective access control; identifying and creating effective cybersecurity responsibilities of employees; developing cybersecurity awareness and training programs; creating and implementing the measures needed to protect the confidentiality, integrity, and availability of information; developing policies, processes, and procedures designed to protect systems and assets; and prescribing maintenance procedures for systems and assets. Ultimately, this function

(*continued*)

is dedicated to developing and implementing appropriate measures to ensure the delivery of services and the protection of assets.

Detect. Identify, create, and implement the appropriate measures needed to detect cybersecurity threats. Core activities in this function include identifying processes involved in monitoring systems and assets; evaluating the processes involved in detecting anomalous activity; identifying the ways in which detection processes and procedures are maintained and tested; and developing effective detection processes and procedures (if needed). In the end, this function evaluates the measures that were in place at the time of the incident and the manner in which these measures will be maintained and tested.

Respond. Develop and implement appropriate actions to deal with detected cybersecurity threats. The central activities here are identifying the process of responding to cybersecurity incidents; identifying who is involved in investigating the cybersecurity incident; identifying the measures available and those that need to be taken to mitigate or eliminate the detected cybersecurity event; evaluating existing measures used to respond to and mitigate cybersecurity incidents; and creating effective response measures to prevent or at the very least mitigate the impact of such incidents in the future (wherever needed). Overall, the purpose of this function is to identify, develop, and implement the appropriate actions to take in response to cybersecurity threats.

Recover. Create and implement the measures needed to restore services and operations to the preincident state. The main activities in this function include identifying the processes involved in recovering from a cybersecurity event; evaluating recovery strategies; and identifying lessons learned. This function seeks to identify, develop, and implement the appropriate actions to maintain plans for resilience and restore any capabilities or services that were impaired due to the cybersecurity incident.

INTERNATIONAL MEASUREMENTS OF CYBERCRIME

Currently, no international measurement tool exists that validly and reliably measures cybercrime against individuals and businesses.[85] The United Nations Office on Drugs and Crime's *Comprehensive Study on Cybercrime* (hereafter UNODC report) revealed that the most common cybercrimes reported by police in various countries included the following:[86]

- Illegal data interference or system damage
- Illegal access to a computer system
- Illegal access, interception or acquisition of computer data
- Computer-related copyright and trademark offenses
- Sending or controlling sending of spam
- Computer-related fraud and forgery
- Computer-related acts involving racism and xenophobia
- Computer-related acts in support of terrorism offenses
- Breach of privacy or data protection measures
- Computer-related identity offenses
- Computer-related solicitation or 'grooming' of children
- Computer-related acts causing personal harm
- Computer-related production, distribution or possession of child pornography

The UNODC report showed that approximately one-third of cybercrimes across the reporting regions were cyberfraud related (i.e., computer-related fraud and forgery).[87] One-third of cybercrimes reported, and in some regions half of cybercrimes reported, related to computer content (computer-related copyright and trademark offenses, computer-related acts in support of terrorism offenses, and computer-related production, distribution, or possession of child pornography).[88] Child pornography crimes were identified as being more common in

Europe and the Americas.[89] Computer-related acts causing personal harm were reported as being more common in Africa, the Americas, Asia, and Oceania.[90] One-third of the cybercrimes reported in some countries related to illicit activity against the confidentiality, integrity, and availability of systems (e.g., illegal access to a computer, illegal data interference or system damage, and illegal access, interception, or acquisition of computer data); in other countries, however, these acts made up only approximately 10 percent of the cybercrimes.[91] Furthermore, cybercrime victimization rates were found to be higher in developing countries.[92] However, this rate of victimization depends on the cybercrime. For instance, online credit card fraud was more prevalent in highly developed countries.[93]

The manner in which cybercrime was reported and the categories of cybercrimes in the UNODC report were different from those included in crime measurement tools inside and outside of the United States. Accordingly, cross-national comparisons cannot be made, due to the variation that exists in the definitions of cybercrime and the criteria used to measure cybercrime. Essentially, "cross-national comparisons may only be made where national legislation—and corresponding categories used for statistical purposes—are equivalent."[94] Crime victim surveys both nationally and internationally also do not include standardized questions that relate to cybercrime.[95] The questions, if included at all, are limited and varied. Ultimately, standardized reporting and recording mechanisms should exist. What is also needed is the development of a classification system that adequately reflects cybercrime.[96] Recording systems tend to lump all forms of cybercrime within one category. Because of this flaw, an accurate picture of cybercrime may not be provided.

To improve cybercrime statistics, flags are required in existing databases to indicate that a cybercrime is reported. This feature is mandatory for law enforcement recording crimes in the United States. However, this is not the case in other countries. In the United Kingdom, in order to obtain information about cybercrimes which are not reported to Action Fraud, the UK Home Office created a reporting feature for cybercrime. Using this feature, police are able to record cybercrime in their databases using a "cyberflag"; this flag, however, is used on a voluntary basis.[97] To understand the true nature and extent of cybercrime, cybercrime recording should be mandated, and new crime measurement tools should be developed or existing tools should be adequately updated to record all forms of cybercrimes.

Data collection and analysis is essential for crime control and reduction initiatives as it provides insight into crime patterns and the nature and extent of crime. This information can also be used to inform the public of risks and the ways in which it can protect itself from these risks. The same holds true for crime perpetrated using Internet-enabled digital technologies.

CASE STUDY

Pete is tasked with reviewing crime measurement tools both inside and outside of the United States. Particularly, his assignment involves examining these crime measurement tools and determining whether they measure cybercrime.

Step into the role of Pete. Choose a crime measurement tool.

1. Can it measure cybercrime? Can it measure different forms of cybercrimes? If it can measure different forms of cybercrimes, which ones? Would you make any modifications to it? Why or why not?

2. If it cannot measure cybercrime or cannot measure different forms of cybercrimes, could you modify the tool so it can record various types of cybercrimes? What would you change? Please explain your response.

REVIEW QUESTIONS

1. What are the official crime measurement tools in the United States? What data do they record?
2. What are the limitations of the official crime measurement tools in the United States?
3. Why are cybercrimes underreported by individuals?
4. Why are cybercrimes underreported by businesses?
5. What measures can be implemented to deal with the underreporting of cybercrime?
6. What is the dark figure of crime?
7. What crime measurement tools shed light on the dark figure of crime in the United States?
8. Name and describe two crime measurement tools used outside of the United States. Do they record cybercrime? If so, which types of cybercrimes?
9. Are there any international crime measurement tools which can validly and reliably measure cybercrime? Why do you think so?
10. Can cross-national comparisons of cybercrimes be made? Why or why not?

LAWS

Computer Misuse Act of 1990 (United Kingdom)
Executive Order 13636 of 2013 (United States)
William Wilberforce Trafficking Victims Protection Reauthorization Act of 2008 (United States)

DEFINITIONS

Crime Survey for England and Wales. An official crime measurement tool in England and Wales which collects information about victimization.

Dark figure of crime. The dark figure of crime refers to crime that has not been reported to the police.

Expected utility theory. A person will engage in an activity if the likely gain (i.e., expected utility) from that activity exceeds the utility the person would receive from utilizing time and resources on other activities.

Federal Crime Data. A report that is now part of the UCR Program and includes information about the number of arrests on human trafficking, hate crime, and criminal computer intrusion reported by FBI field offices.

General Social Survey. An official crime measurement tool in Canada which collects information about victimization.

Hierarchy rule. This rule requires that only the most serious crime of multiple offenses be recorded in the UCR Program.

Identity Theft Supplement. A supplementary survey on identity theft to the National Crime Victimization Survey.

International Crime Victim Survey. This survey collects victimization data from several countries and victims' views on their own security.

National Computer Security Survey. This survey collected information from U.S. businesses about cybercrimes they were subjected to.

National Crime Victimization Survey. An official crime measurement tool in the United States which collects information about victimization.

National Incident-Based Reporting System. An official crime measurement tool which includes more detailed information about crimes committed within the United States than the UCR Program.

NIST Cybersecurity Framework. This framework provides guidance on how organizations can enhance their cybersecurity posture.

Risk. The probability of harm or damage or threat of harm or damage from a security threat due to vulnerabilities.

Self-report survey. A survey asking respondents to report on their own participation in criminal activity.

Supplemental Victimization Survey. A supplementary survey on stalking to the National Crime Victimization Survey.

Uniform Crime Reporting Program. An official crime measurement tool in the United States which collects, compiles, and distributes official crime statistics provided by participating U.S. law enforcement agencies.

ENDNOTES

1. Executive Office of the President of the United States, The Comprehensive National Cybersecurity Initiative, 2010, http://www.whitehouse.gov/issues/foreign-policy/cybersecurity /national-initiative; Dilanian, K., "Cyber-Crime Tops Threats to U.S., Intelligence Chief Says," *Los Angeles Times*, March 12, 2013, http://articles.latimes.com/2013/mar/12/news/la-pn -cybercrime-threat-20130312; Ackerman, E., "Secretary of Homeland Security: Cybercrime As Big a Threat As Al Qaeda," *Forbes*, June 3, 2012, http://www.forbes.com/sites/eliseackerman /2012/06/03/secretary-of-homeland-security-cybercrime-as-big-a-threat-as-al-qaeda/.

2. For example, the United Kingdom; see BBC News, "Cyber-Attacks and Terrorism Head Threats Facing UK," October 18, 2010, http://www.bbc.co.uk/news/uk-11562969.

3. FBI, Uniform Crime Reporting (UCR) Program, *Data Quality Guidelines*, April 19, 2016, https://www.fbi.gov/about-us/cjis/ucr/data_quality_guidelines.

4. FBI, UCR Data Online, "UCR Offense Definitions," last modified January 23, 2009, http:// www.ucrdatatool.gov/offenses.cfm.

5. Arson was added to the UCR Program in 1979.

6. FBI, "Appendix II—Offenses in Uniform Crime Reporting," in *Crime in the United States, 2004*, Fall 2005, https://www2.fbi.gov/ucr/cius_04/appendices/appendix_02.html.

7. FBI, UCR Program, "Property Crimes," in *Crime in the United States, 2014*, Fall 2015, https:// www.fbi.gov/about-us/cjis/ucr/crime-in-the-u.s/2014/crime-in-the-u.s.-2014/offenses -known-to-law-enforcement/property-crime.

8. Human trafficking/commercial sex acts is defined as "inducing a person by force, fraud, or coercion to participate in commercial sex acts, or in which the person induced to perform such act(s) has not attained 18 years of age." FBI, "UCR Program Adds Human Trafficking Offenses to Data Collection, Includes More Specific Prostitution Offenses," *CJIS (Criminal Justice Information Services) Link* (newsletter), May 7, 2013, https://www.fbi.gov/services/cjis /cjis-link/ucr-program-adds-human-trafficking-offenses-to-data-collection-includes-more -specific-prostitution-offenses.

9. Human trafficking/involuntary servitude is defined as "the obtaining of a person through recruitment, harboring, transportation, or provision, and subjecting such persons by force, fraud, or coercion into involuntary servitude, peonage, debt bondage, or slavery (not to include commercial sex acts)." FBI, "UCR Program Adds Human Trafficking."

10. FBI, UCR Program, "About the UCR Program," in *Crime in the United States, 2014*, Fall 2015, https://www.fbi.gov/about-us/cjis/ucr/crime-in-the-u.s/2014/crime-in-the-u.s.-2014 /resource-pages/about-ucr; FBI, UCR Program, "UCR Program Adds Human Trafficking."

11. FBI, National Incident-Based Reporting System, *Volume 1: Data Collection Guidelines*, August 2000, 5, https://www2.fbi.gov/ucr/nibrs/manuals/v1all.pdf.
12. FBI, UCR Program, "Offense Definitions," in *Crime in the United States, 2009,* September 2010, https://www2.fbi.gov/ucr/cius2009/about/offense_definitions.html; FBI, "About Crime in the U.S. (CIUS)," September 2015, https://www.fbi.gov/about-us/cjis/ucr/crime-in-the-u.s/2014/crime-in-the-u.s.-2014/cius-home.
13. FBI, National Incident-Based Reporting System, *Volume 1,* 19.
14. FBI, UCR Program, "Federal Crime Data, 2014," in *Crime in the United States, 2014,* Fall 2015, 1, https://www.fbi.gov/about-us/cjis/ucr/crime-in-the-u.s/2014/crime-in-the-u.s.-2014/additional-reports/federal-crime-data/federal-crime-data.pdf.
15. Ibid., 2.
16. Ibid.
17. Ibid.
18. FBI, UCR Program, "About the UCR Program."
19. FBI, "The Expansion of NIBRS," Fall 2015, https://www.fbi.gov/about-us/cjis/ucr/nibrs/2014.
20. N. James and L. R. Council, *How Crime in the United States Is Measured* (CRS Report for Congress RL34309, January 3, 2008), 19–20, https://www.fas.org/sgp/crs/misc/RL34309.pdf.
21. FBI, National Incident-Based Reporting System, *Volume 1,* 5.
22. FBI, "The Expansion of NIBRS."
23. FBI, UCR Program, "UCR Program Adds Human Trafficking."
24. FBI, National Incident-Based Reporting System, "The Basics," accessed July 14, 2016, https://www2.fbi.gov/ucr/faqs.htm.
25. FBI, National Incident-Based Reporting System, *Volume 1,* 19.
26. Here, the recording officer enters a "07 = Computer Hardware/Software into Data Element 15 [Property Description]" when the computer was the target of the crime and "C = Computer Equipment into Data Element 8 [Offenders Suspected of Using]" when a computer was used in the commission of a crime. FBI, National Incident-Based Reporting System, *Volume 1,* 20.
27. K. Finklea and C. A. Theohary, *Cybercrime: Conceptual Issues for Congress and U.S. Law Enforcement* (CRS Report R4254, January 15, 2015), 20, http://fas.org/sgp/crs/misc/R42547.pdf.
28. A. Schoepfer and N. L. Piquero, "Studying the Correlates of Fraud Victimization and Reporting," *Journal of Criminal Justice* 37, no. 2 (2009): 209–215; R. Smith, "Consumer Scams in Australia: An Overview," *Trends and Issues in Crime and Criminal Justice,* no. 331 (2007): 1–6; R. G. Smith, "Coordinating Individual and Organizational Responses to Fraud," *Crime Law and Social Change* 49, no. 5 (2008): 379–396; K. Mason and M. Benson, "The Effect of Social Support on Fraud Victims' Reporting Behaviour: A Research Note," *Justice Quarterly* 13, no. 3 (1996): 511–524; R. Titus, F. Heinzelman, and J. Boyle, "Victimisation of Persons by Fraud," *Crime and Delinquency* 41, no. 1 (1995): 54–72; C. Cross, "No Laughing Matter: Blaming the Victim of Online Fraud," *International Review of Victimology* 21, no. 2 (2015): 187–204; S. M. Smyth and R. Carleton, *Measuring the Extent of Cyber-Fraud in Canada: A Discussion Paper on Potential Methods and Data* (Public Safety Canada, Report No. 020, 2011), http://publications.gc.ca/collections/collection_2011/sp-ps/PS14-4-2011-eng.pdf.
29. Smith, "Consumer Scams," 1–6; R. G. Smith and T. Akman, "Raising Public Awareness of Consumer Fraud in Australia," *Trends and Issues in Crime and Criminal Justice,* no. 349 (2008): 1–6; Cross, "No Laughing Matter," 187–204.
30. S. McQuade, *Understanding and Managing Cybercrime* (Boston: Pearson, 2006); K. Choi, *Risk Factors in Computer-Crime Victimization* (El Paso, TX: LFB Scholarly, 2010); C. Conradt, "Online Auction Fraud and Criminological Theories: The Adrian Ghighina Case," *International Journal of Cyber Criminology* 6, no. 1 (2012): 912–923.
31. G. S. Becker, "Crime and Punishment: An Economic Approach," *Journal of Political Economy* 76, no. 2 (1968): 176.

32. D. G. Gregg and J. E. Scott, "The Role of Reputation Systems in Reducing On-Line Auction Fraud," *International Journal of Electronic Commerce* 10, no. 3 (2006): 100.

33. W. G. Skogan, "Reporting Crime to the Police: The Status of World Research," *Journal of Research in Crime and Delinquency* 21, no. 2 (1984): 113–137; T. C. Hart and C. Rennison, *Reporting Crime to the Police, 1992–2000* (Washington, DC: U.S. Bureau of Justice Statistics, 2003), 1–8.

34. A. Schoepfer and N. L. Piquero, "Studying the Correlates of Fraud Victimization and Reporting," *Journal of Criminal Justice* 37, no. 2 (2009): 209–215; K. Holtfreter, N. L. Piquero, and A. R. Piquero, "And Justice for All? Investigators' Perceptions of Punishment for Fraud Perpetrators," *Crime, Law and Social Change* 49, no. 5 (2008): 397–412.

35. M. Tcherni, A. Davies, G. Lopes, and A. Lizotte, "The Dark Figure of Online Property Crime: Is Cyberspace Hiding a Crime Wave?" *Justice Quarterly* 33, no. 5 (2016): 890–911.

36. D. S. Wall, *Cybercrime* (Cambridge: Polity, 2007), cited in S. Fafinski, W. H. Dutton, and H. Margetts, *Mapping and Measuring Cybercrime* (Oxford Internet Institute, OII Forum Discussion Paper No. 18, 2010), 12, http://www.oii.ox.ac.uk/webcasts/?id=157.

37. M.-H. Maras, "Combating Cybercrime: Dealing with Barriers to International Investigations and Enforcement in Cyberspace," *Criminal Justice and Law Enforcement Annual: Global Perspectives* 7, no. 2 (2015): 175–201.

38. M. McGuire and S. Dowling, *Cyber Crime: A Review of the Evidence* (UK Home Office Research Report 75: Summary of Key Findings and Implications, 2013), 4, https://www.gov.uk/government/uploads/system/uploads/attachment_data/file/246749/horr75-summary.pdf; S. Fafinski and N. Minassian, *UK Cybercrime Report 2009* (Nottingham, UK: Garlik, 2009), 23, https://www.garlik.com/file/cybercrime_report_attachement; A. Schoepfer and N. L. Piquero, "Studying the Correlates of Fraud Victimization and Reporting," *Journal of Criminal Justice* 37, no. 2 (2009): 209–215.

39. National Crime Agency, "National Cyber Crime Unit," accessed July 14, 2016, http://www.nationalcrimeagency.gov.uk/about-us/what-we-do/national-cyber-crime-unit.

40. FBI, *FBI/National White Collar Crime Center (NW3C) Release*, March 30, 2009, https://www.fbi.gov/news/pressrel/press-releases/fbi-national-white-collar-crime-center-nw3c-release.

41. FBI, "IC3: The Front Door for Reporting Internet Crime," *News Blog*, October 6, 2014, https://www.fbi.gov/news/news_blog/ic3-the-front-door-for-reporting-internet-crime.

42. See Chapter 11 for further information about this.

43. Finklea and Theohary, *Cybercrime*.

44. This network includes consumer complaints on anticompetitive activities (e.g., deceptive marketing practices) reported to the Canadian Competition Bureau.

45. This network also includes consumer complaints on identity theft and telecommunications and electronic communications fraud reported to the Canadian Anti-Fraud Centre (originally known as PhoneBusters).

46. Finklea and Theohary, *Cybercrime*.

47. Fafinski and Minassian, *UK Cybercrime Report 2009*, 23.

48. UK Home Office, "Crime against Businesses: Headline Findings from the 2012 Commercial Victimisation Survey," news release, January 2013, https://www.gov.uk/government/uploads/system/uploads/attachment_data/file/147935/crime-business-prem-2012-pdf.pdf; McGuire and Dowling, *Cyber Crime*, 4.

49. M.-H. Maras, "Combating Cybercrime: Dealing With Barriers to International Investigations and Enforcement in Cyberspace," *Criminal Justice and Law Enforcement Annual: Global Perspectives* 7, no. 2 (2015), 175–201.

50. U.S. Bureau of Justice Statistics, "Data Collection," National Crime Victimization Survey, 1973–2014, accessed August 4, 2016, http://www.bjs.gov/index.cfm?ty=dcdetail&iid=245#Methodology.

51. U.S. Bureau of Justice Statistics, "Methodology," National Crime Victimization Survey, last modified August 8, 2016, http://www.bjs.gov/developer/ncvs/methodology.cfm.

52. L. R. Shapiro and M.-H. Maras, *Multidisciplinary Investigation of Child Maltreatment* (Burlington, MA: Jones and Bartlett, 2015), 375.

53. B. Mazowita and M. Vézina, *Police-Reported Cybercrime in Canada, 2012*, Statistics Canada, last modified November 30, 2015, http://www.statcan.gc.ca/pub/85-002-x/2014001/article/14093-eng.htm.

54. K. Baum, S. Catalano, M. Rand, and K. Rose, *Stalking Victimization in the United States* (Bureau of Justice Statistics Special Report NCJ 224527, 2009), 1.

55. Ibid.

56. N. Parsons-Pollard and L. J. Moriarty, "Cyberstalking: Utilizing What We Know," *Victims and Offenders: International Journal of Evidence-Based Research, Policy, and Practice* 4, no. 4 (2009): 435–441; B. Fischer, F. Cullen, and M. Turner, "Being Pursued: Stalking Victimization in a National Study of College Women," *Criminology & Public Policy* 1, no. 2 (2002): 257–308.

57. United Nations Office on Drugs and Crime, *Comprehensive Study on Cybercrime*, February 2013, 263–264, http://www.unodc.org/documents/organized-crime/UNODC_CCPCJ_EG.4_2013/CYBERCRIME_STUDY_210213.pdf.

58. International Crime Victim Survey, "Questionnaire 2008," accessed August 4, 2016, http://wp.unil.ch/icvs/questionnaires/questionnaire-2008/.

59. See, for example, the 2014 Identity Theft Supplement to the National Crime Victimization Survey, Bureau of Justice Statistics, 2015, http://www.bjs.gov/index.cfm?ty=dcdetail&iid=245.

60. S. Perreault, "Self-Reported Internet Victimization in Canada, 2009," Statistics Canada, last modified June 5, 2013, http://www.statcan.gc.ca/pub/85-002-x/2011001/article/11530-eng.htm.

61. Ibid.

62. Ibid.

63. Statistics Canada, "The General Social Survey: An Overview," last modified November 30, 2015, http://www.statcan.gc.ca/pub/89f0115x/89f0115x2013001-eng.htm.

64. UK Office of National Statistics, "Improving Crime Statistics in England and Wales," October 15, 2015, http://www.ons.gov.uk/ons/rel/crime-stats/crime-statistics/year-ending-june-2015/sty-fraud.html.

65. McGuire and Dowling, *Cyber Crime*, 7.

66. A. Porterfield, "Delinquency and Outcome in Court and College," *American Journal of Sociology, 49* (1943): 199–208; J. S. Wallerstein and C. J. Wylie, "Our Law-abiding Law-breakers," *Probation, 25* (1947): 107–112; cited in T. P. Thornberry and M. D. Krohn, "The Self-Report Method for Measuring Delinquency and Crime," *Criminal Justice* (2000): 34–35.

67. J. Junger-Tas and I. H. Marshall, "The Self-Report Methodology in Crime Research," *Crime and Justice* 25 (1999): 291–367.

68. See, for example, O. Tade and B. Akinleye, "'We are Promoters not Pirates': A Qualitative Analysis of Artistes and Pirates on Music Piracy in Nigeria," *International Journal of Cyber Criminology* 6, no. 2 (2012): 1026.

69. A pilot study was conducted prior to this using the Computer Security Survey in 2002, http://www.bjs.gov/index.cfm?ty=pbdetail&iid=770.

70. U.S. Bureau of Justice Statistics, "Data Collection: National Computer Security Survey," accessed August 4, 2016, http://www.bjs.gov/index.cfm?ty=dcdetail&iid=260.

71. Ibid.

72. R. R. Rantala, "Cybercrime against Businesses, 2005," Bureau of Justice Statistics, Special Report, NCJ 221943 (September 2008), 8, http://www.bjs.gov/content/pub/pdf/cb05.pdf.

73. Ibid., 3.

74. U.S. Bureau of Justice Statistics, "Cybercrime," http://www.bjs.gov/index.cfm?ty=tp&tid=41; Rantala, "Cybercrime against Businesses."

75. Rantala, "Cybercrime against Businesses."

76. Ibid.

77. See Chapter 11 for differences between computer viruses, computer worms, and Trojan horses.

78. Rantala, "Cybercrime against Businesses."

79. Ibid.

80. L. A. Hughes and G. J. DeLone, "Viruses, Worms, and Trojan Horses: Serious Crimes, Nuisance, or Both?" *Social Science Computer Review* 25, no. 1 (2007): 82.

81. Ibid., 79.

82. Wall, *Cybercrime.*

83. The United States has sixteen designated critical infrastructures. U.S. Department of Homeland Security, "Critical Infrastructure Sectors," https://www.dhs.gov/critical-infrastructure-sectors.

84. National Institute of Standards and Technology, *Cybersecurity Framework*, February 12, 2014, 8–9, 20–35, http://www.nist.gov/cyberframework/upload/cybersecurity-framework-021214.pdf.

85. A. Galetsas, *Statistical Information on Network Security: European Commission Information Society and Media Directorate-General* (Brussels: European Commission, 2007); D. S. Wall, "Cybercrime, Media and Insecurity: The Shaping of Public Perceptions of Cybercrime," *International Review of Law, Computers and Technology* 22, no. 1 (2008): 45–63.

86. United Nations Office on Drugs and Crime, *Comprehensive Study on Cybercrime*, 26.

87. Ibid.

88. Ibid.

89. Ibid.

90. Ibid.

91. Ibid.

92. Ibid., 28.

93. Ibid., 29.

94. Ibid., 259.

95. Ibid., 263.

96. Ibid., 262.

97. McGuire and Dowling, *Cyber Crime.*

CHAPTER 3

CYBERVICTIMIZATION

KEYWORDS

Active personal
  guardianship
Avoidance personal
  guardianship
Contradictory act
Criminogenic
Cybervictimology
High-exposure offender
High-exposure victim
Lifestyle exposure theory
Low-exposure offender

Low-exposure victim
Medium-exposure victim
Modus operandi
  exposure
Offender exposure
Passive physical
  guardianship
Physical guardianship
Precautionary act
Primary cybervictimization
Routine activity theory

Secondary
  cybervictimization
Secondary victimization
Situational exposure
Social guardianship
Tertiary cybervictimization
Victim contribution
Victim precipitation theory
Victim proneness
Victim provocation
Victimology

Social media can provide information to criminals that enables them to commit crimes online and offline. For example, posting information about an upcoming vacation and posting information about new items obtained places the user at risk of victimization from burglars. In the United Kingdom, an actress, Helen Flanagan, was the victim of a burglary after she tweeted that her boyfriend, a famous soccer player named Scott Sinclair, was away and she was home alone. Three armed assailants entered her home and attempted to rob her, but before they had the opportunity to do so, she hid in a utility room, while her home was burglarized.[1] In the United States, a family's home was burglarized after the daughter posted about the family's vacation to Las Vegas on Facebook.[2] Similarly, celebrity homes were burglarized in 2008 and 2009 by individuals monitoring social media to determine the whereabouts of targeted celebrities. This information was used by the burglars, later identified as Rachel Lee, Alexis Neiers, Courtney Ames, Diana Tamayo, Nick Prugo, and Ray Lopez Jr. (dubbed the Bling Ring by the media),[3] to burglarize the homes of Orlando Bloom, Miranda Kerr, Megan Fox, Brian Austin Green, Rachel Bilson, Paris Hilton,

Lindsay Lohan, Ashley Tisdale, and Audrina Patridge.[4] The items stolen were money and goods that could be carried out, such as jewelry and clothes, and other personal items, such as photographs.[5] The stolen items (apart from those the members kept) were later fenced by Jonathan Ajar, an associate of the burglars.[6] This incident illustrates the important role of victims' online behavior in their victimization. This chapter explores this role of the victim, looking in particular at theories (victim precipitation, lifestyle exposure, and routine activity theory) and research on cybervictimization. Before this examination, patterns in cybervictimization and the profiles of cybervictims are explored.

BEING A CYBERVICTIM AND ALL THAT IT ENTAILS

Victimology refers to the comprehensive scientific study of cybervictims, including the victims' physical characteristics; behavior before, during, and after the crime; medical, psychological, and criminal history; home life; family; work life; colleagues; social life; friends and acquaintances; and experiences in the aftermath of the crime. The victim is studied to determine why he or she was chosen by the offender. Ultimately, victimology explores how a victim knowingly or unknowingly in some way contributes to the victimization (i.e., an incident whereby a person, community, or organization experiences harm or damage). Likewise, **cybervictimology** refers to the scientific study of online victimization, the impact of the cybercrime on the cybervictims, and the types of victims that experience cybercrime.

A cybervictim can be a person, a public or private organization, or society at large. There are three types of cybervictims: primary, secondary, and tertiary (see Figure 3-1). With **primary cybervictimization**, the victim is the target of the cybercrime. The harm suffered by the victim is a direct result of the crime. An example of primary cybervictimization would be the losses suffered by a user whose digital device is hacked or organization whose data is breached by a cybercriminal. With **secondary cybervictimization**, the victim is the indirect target of the crime. For example, when the database of an organization is breached, a victim's data stored in the database may be stolen. In this scenario, the primary cybervictim is the organization and the secondary cybervictim is the individual. Finally, **tertiary cybervictimization** refers to the impact of cybercrime on society. For example, in the event that digital piracy (i.e., the illicit online theft of proprietary goods) occurs, the public will eventually pay higher costs for the stolen online goods in order to offset companies' losses from this cybercrime.

Cybercrime can adversely affect people, organizations, and society as a whole. Cybervictims' experiences with cybercrime depend on the cybercrime and their ability to deal

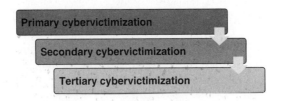

FIGURE 3-1   Types of Cybervictimization.

with its consequences. The effects of cybercrime can be direct or indirect. The *direct costs* of cybercrime are the immediate or proximal impacts of the illicit act. The person or organization may experience financial, professional, psychological, and social harm. *Financial harm* may include loss of money, theft of data and intangible goods, costs incurred from any damage to property, loss of wages, loss of productivity (if the victim is an organization), and the costs incurred from the victim's participation in the criminal justice system. Many countries have suffered significant financial harm from cybercrime. In 2014, the country that suffered the greatest financial harm from cybercrime was the United States (see Table 3-1 for other countries that suffered significant economic harm from cybercrime that year).

Cybercrime can cause *professional harm* to the victim, including loss of reputation or job due to the incident. It can also inflict *psychological harm* on a victim. Those who suffer psychological effects from a cybercrime may need assistance and intervention, which again causes a victim financial harm. Consider the following interpersonal cybercrimes: cyberbullying, a cybercrime involving children whereby the perpetrator humiliates or verbally attacks the victim; and cyberstalking, a cybercrime whereby a perpetrator repeatedly

Table 3-1 Economic Harm from Cybercrime, 2014

United States	$672,080,323
Canada	$11,838,789
Australia	$11,149,880
Hong Kong	$8,683,462
United Kingdom	$8,641,506
Chile	$6,585,354
South Africa	$6,581,690
India	$5,888,264
Spain	$4,651,181
China	$3,673,131
Germany	$3,147,174
Nigeria	$2,999,357
United Arab Emirates	$2,865,701
Saudi Arabia	$2,157,234
Mexico	$2,034,155
Mongolia	$2,005,774
Republic of Korea	$1,965,255
Japan	$1,941,273
Norway	$1,695,877
Netherlands	$1,659,926

Source: Internet Crime Complaint Center, *2014 Internet Crime Report*, accessed August 3, 2016, 23, https://pdf.ic3.gov/2014_IC3Report.pdf.

threatens, harasses, or frightens another user online. The psychological impact of cyber-bullying and cyberstalking includes low self-esteem, shame, guilt, anxiety, hopelessness, depression, powerlessness, and fear of the cybercrime.[7] What is more, victims of interpersonal cybercrime, such as cyberstalking, have reported experiencing "abrupt changes in sleep and eating patterns, nightmares, hypervigilance [a condition associated with post-traumatic stress disorder, or PTSD], anxiety, helplessness, and fear for safety."[8] Fear of cybercrime is frequently reported for other cybercrimes as well, including cyberidentity theft, which involves the unlawful obtainment of names, Social Security numbers (SSNs), bank account numbers, or other identifying data of a user via the Internet, computers, and related technology in order to commit another criminal activity. The fear of cybercrime can have larger social and economic consequences. Indeed, a 2009 study revealed that as individuals' perception of the risk of cyberidentity theft increased, their online purchases decreased.[9] This finding has been supported by other studies showing that people who view the risk of cyberidentity theft as great tend to spend less time online and make fewer online purchases.[10]

Victims have reported experiencing fear of the offender in other interpersonal cybercrimes as well, for example, cyberharassment. Verbally abusing or attacking an individual online is known as cyberharassment. Victims of this crime have reported feeling fear of the unknown (i.e., "not knowing when . . . [the cybercrime] will happen next"); fear that the harassing behavior online will not cease; and fear of bodily harm.[11] Individuals' fear of cybervictimization can make them afraid to engage in online activity. The victim may be reticent to browse the Internet or otherwise engage in online activities for fear of revictimization. This fear of cybervictimization can thus inflict *social harm* on a person by adversely affecting the person's quality of life. A 1997 study revealed that victims of e-mail harassment experience "disruptions in their daily routines" and adverse emotional reactions to the crimes.[12]

In addition to direct costs, cybercrime results in *indirect costs*, which are secondary costs of an illicit act beyond that directly experienced by the victim. For instance, the government sustains financial costs when it investigates and prosecutes cybercrime. In the case of cyberidentity theft, the companies involved in this cybercrime also incur costs (i.e., in the form of time and money spent investigating the incident and compensating the victims for losses). Overall, the recorded losses from cybercrime are substantial, and these represent only a fraction of the actual losses, because of the substantial underreporting of this type of crime (see Chapter 2).

THE PROFILE OF A CYBERVICTIM

Attempts have been made to profile cybervictims and identify common demographic factors associated with cybercrime, particularly gender, age, race, marital or relationship status, and education, income, and employment status.

> *Gender.* Some research has shown that the gender of a user is not associated with cybervictimization.[13] This contradicts other studies showing that this factor increases the likelihood of cybervictimization.[14] Indeed, research on the role of gender in cybervictimization is mixed. Some studies have found that gender is not a statistically significant predictor of cyberbullying.[15] Others have revealed that girls are at greater risk of cyberbullying than boys.[16] Similarly, studies on cyberstalking have found gender (i.e., female) to be a predictor of this cybercrime.[17] Likewise, data collected

by the Working to Halt Online Abuse (WHOA) between 2000 and 2011 revealed that victims of cyberharassment are primarily female.[18] Cyberfraud and cyberidentity theft cases have shown that gender is a predictor of these cybercrimes. More specifically, males are more likely than females to experience cyberidentity theft.[19] Males are also more likely to fall victim to Internet scams.[20]

Age. Studies on the role of age in cybervictimization have also yielded conflicting results. In a 2010 study, consumer age was found not to be a good predictor of cybervictimization with respect to cyberidentity theft,[21] whereas a 2013 study showed that youth are less likely to experience cyberidentity theft.[22] Data collected by the Internet Crime and Complaint Center (IC3) also revealed that those most likely to fall victim to Internet scams in 2014 were individuals between 40 and 59 years of age; the next age group most likely to be victimized by online scammers were individuals between the ages of 20 and 39.[23] This data from the IC3 also revealed that the role of age in cybervictimization from cyberfraud varied depending on the type of online fraud committed. Age was also found to be a good predictor of victimization by malware infection (where youth were more likely to have their digital devices infected by malware).[24] The results of studies on the role of age in cybervictimization from interpersonal cybercrime have varied. Individuals between the ages of 18 and 30 years were more likely to be victims of cyberharassment.[25] In addition, children younger than 10 years old were more likely to be targets of online child sexual predators. Specifically, the Internet Watch Foundation found that 81 percent of the child victims in this study were ten years of age or under.[26] In contrast, the UK Child Exploitation and Online Protection Centre found that the child victims most targeted for online sexual exploitation by predators were thirteen and fourteen years old.[27]

Race. Studies have shown that Caucasians are less likely to be victims of malware infection than other races (African American, Asian, and Native American).[28] In other studies on interpersonal cybercrimes, Caucasians were found to be more likely than other races to become victims of these forms of cybercrimes. For instance, studies by the UK Child Exploitation and Online Protection Centre and the Internet Watch Foundation found that the child victims most targeted for online sexual exploitation are Caucasians.[29] In addition, Caucasians were most likely to be victims of cyberharassment.[30] Other studies, however, have found that race does not play a role in cybervictimization.[31]

Marital or Relationship Status. The results of a study reported in 2011 indicated that marital or relationship status of a user (i.e., single, married, divorced, life partner, separated, widowed, or in a nonmarital romantic relationship) is not associated with cybervictimization.[32] This contradicts other studies that have shown that this factor increases the likelihood of cybervictimization.[33] For example, for certain interpersonal cybercrimes, like cyberstalking, the relationship status (i.e., nonsingle) of the victim has been shown to be a predictor of cyberstalking,[34] whereas other studies have shown that individuals who are single are more likely to be victims of cyberharassment.[35]

Education, Income, and Employment Status. Research has shown that the level of education of a user is not a good predictor of cybervictimization with respect to cyberidentity theft and digital piracy.[36] Other studies have shown that those with a higher-education level (i.e., those with more than sixteen years of schooling) are more likely to be victims of cybercrime.[37] Research has also shown that income and employment status are good predictors of cybervictimization. Those with higher incomes are more likely to experience cyberidentity theft.[38] In addition, individuals with full-time or part-time employment are less likely to be cyberharassed than unemployed individuals.[39] In contrast, other studies have found that those individuals who are without income or are unemployed are more likely to experience cybervictimization.[40]

Overall, the findings for each predictor of cybercrime are mixed. Additionally, the above-mentioned studies have the following limitations: they are often conducted on populations that do not represent the general public, such as student populations (which may or may not be representative of the larger student population), and they rely on selective official and self-reporting data, which do not accurately reflect the types of individuals that fall victim to cybercrimes and the actual number of cybercrimes that occur annually (see Chapter 2). Barring these limitations, the results of the research discussed earlier illustrate a very important point: that anyone can be a victim of cybercrime. The reality is that one profile does not fit all cybervictims, not even for similar cybercrimes.

BOX 3-1   THE PROFILE OF A CYBERCRIMINAL

Attempts have also been made to profile cyberoffenders and identify common demographic factors associated with cybercrime, particularly gender, age, sexual orientation, employment status, intelligence, education, race, marital or relationship status, and criminal history. Studies on interpersonal cybercrime, such as cyberstalking, have revealed that "cyberstalkers are not a homogeneous group."[41] Research on other forms of interpersonal cybercrime have shown mixed results. On the one hand, studies have revealed that girls are more likely to be cyberbullies than boys.[42] Also, females have been shown to be more involved in cyberbullying than in traditional bullying.[43] On the other hand, other studies have found a greater involvement in cyberbullying by boys.[44] Still others have revealed little to no statistically significant gender differences in cyberbullying.[45] In addition to these studies, research has revealed gender differences in the methods used to engage in cyberbullying. Specifically, researchers have found that boys are more likely to post images and videos online as a form of cyberbullying, and girls are more likely to engage in cyberbullying via instant messaging, chat rooms, and e-mails.[46] Studies have further shown age differences in cyberbullying. One study found no gender differences in cyberbullying, but did find age differences: older students were found to engage in cyberbullying to a greater extent than younger students.[47] Furthermore, studies have shown no statistically significant differences in cyberbullying between heterosexual and nonheterosexual young adults.[48]

Research on another form of interpersonal cybercrime revealed significant gender differences exist in those who engage in online child sex offending, with those engaging in online sex offending being primarily male.[49] Indeed, studies have shown that few females engage in online child sex offending.[50] Also, other studies have revealed that a small but significant number of child sex offenders are women and children (including those who have themselves been abused).[51] Moreover, research has shown that online child pornography offenders were more likely to be younger,[52] employed,[53] of greater intelligence,[54] and more educated[55] than contact sex offenders.[56] Other studies have shown no statistically significant differences in the education level and employment status of online sex offenders and non-online offenders.[57] In regard to race, online child pornographers were found more likely to be Caucasian than contact sex offenders.[58] Studies have also revealed that those who engage in online child pornography offenses (but not contact sex offenses) are more likely to be in a relationship or married at the time they commit an offense.[59] Studies have further revealed that Internet child pornographers do not often have a prior criminal record.[60] This conflicts with parallel studies on these Internet sex offenders that have shown they have some criminal convictions.[61] Notwithstanding, one must keep in mind that these studies are based only on known offenders. This does not take into account the "dark figure" of online sex offending, those that have not yet come to the attention of authorities through victim, offender, or third-party reporting. The underreporting of crimes by this population makes the scope of the crime perpetrated by individuals of this age and gender difficult to assess.[62] In the end, like a cybervictim, there is no single, universal profile of a cybercriminal.

VICTIMIZATION THEORIES

Theories of victimology exist that seek to explain why certain individuals become targets of cybercriminals, and ultimately, victims of crime. Three of these theories are explored in the next sections, namely, victim precipitation, lifestyle exposure theory, and routine activity theory.

VICTIM PRECIPITATION THEORY

Victim precipitation theory holds that the victim is in some way responsible for the victimization (i.e., provoking or somehow precipitating the event). This theory seeks to explain victimization through an analysis of the situational contingencies and dynamics that exist in interpersonal interactions. It has three facets: victim proneness, victim contribution, and victim provocation.[63] **Victim proneness** refers to the characteristics of a victim that make the individual more likely than others to become a victim of a crime. **Victim contribution** refers to the activities of a victim which make the individual susceptible to crime. Finally, **victim provocation** views the victim as the cause of his or her victimization. Here, even innocent interactions between the victim and criminal may precipitate victimization. Indeed, certain personality traits and behaviors that the victim exhibits may be seen as provocative by a criminal. These precipitating behaviors are subjective and what triggers one criminal may not trigger another. This facet of victim precipitation (i.e., victim provocation) has been studied extensively for crimes; a notable example is the landmark study of victim provocation in homicides by Marvin Wolfgang.[64] Wolfgang found that certain victims precipitated their own death by, for example, initiating the violence in some way (i.e., brandishing a weapon he or she had on their person or striking the offender first).

BOX 3-2   RELATIONSHIP OF CYBERVICTIMS AND CYBEROFFENDERS

With respect to a cybervictim, a cybercriminal can be a spouse, boyfriend, girlfriend, friend, family member, acquaintance, colleague, employer, or stranger. The relationship of the cybervictim and the cyberoffender has been studied in an effort to understand cybercrime. Cases in point are online child sexual predation, cyberbullying, and cyberstalking. Research has shown that those engaging in online child sexual predation tend to target children that they do not have a relationship with (i.e., nonfamilial children); this is in stark contrast to contact sex offenders, who tend to victimize intrafamilial children.[65] Research on the relationship between the victim and the offender in cyberbullying has shown mixed results. In an effort to explain cyberbullying, Pyzalski developed typologies of the relationships between cybervictims and cyberbullies. In this study, six types of relationships were identified:[66]

1. *Cyberaggression against peers*. Here, the cybervictim and the cyberoffender are members of the same group.
2. *Cyberaggression against the vulnerable*. The cyberbully targets weak cybervicitms.

3. *Random cyberaggression*. The cyberbully targets an unknown cybervictim.
4. *Cyberaggression against groups*. The cyberbully targets cybervictims belonging to a particular group (e.g., based on race, ethnicity, or religion).
5. *Cyberaggression against celebrities*. The cyberbully targets individuals who are famous.
6. *Cyberaggression against school staff*. The cyberbully targets teachers or other staff at schools.

Research has shown that a significant number of cybervictims have been cyberbullied by known peers.[67] A 2015 study by Whittaker and Kowalski showed that individuals tend to view cyberbullying against peers as indicative of a greater malicious intent by the perpetrators than when such cyberbullying is directed at random users or celebrities.[68] What is particularly interesting is that the behavior in the cases examined was similar; what changed was the cybervictim. By contrast, cyberstalking was found to be more likely to be perpetrated by acquaintances or strangers than by former intimate partners.[69] Nonetheless, the reality is that cybervictims may or may not know their perpetrators.

Benjamin Mendelson created victim typologies to explain the relationship between the victim and the offender and the degree of victim culpability. He classified victims as follows:[70]

1. Victim bears no responsibility for crime
2. Victim is inadvertently harmed and puts himself or herself in a situation where he or she could be harmed
3. Victim bears shared responsibility with offender for crime
4. Victim provokes the offense
5. Victim is victimized while committing a crime
6. Victim is not a victim but only imagines he or she is victimized

Hans von Hentig believed that all victims in some way contribute to their victimization. In *The Criminal and His Victim: Studies on the Sociobiology of Crime* (1948), von Hentig created thirteen victim types based on the characteristics of victims:[71] young; female; old; mentally defective and deranged; immigrants (due to lack of familiarity with a given culture); minorities; dull normals (i.e., simple-minded, naive); depressed; acquisitive (i.e., greedy); wanton (i.e., promiscuous); lonesome or heartbroken; tormentor (i.e., becomes a victim while committing a crime); and the blocked, exempted, or fighting (i.e., victims of the crime of blackmail, confidence scams, or extortion).

Stephen Schafer proposed seven victim typologies based on the degree to which victims were responsible (if at all) for the illicit act committed against them: four types of victims bore no responsibility for the crime committed against them (*unrelated victim; biologically weak victim; socially weak victim;* and *political victim*); one type of victim bore some responsibility for the crime (*precipitative victim*); one type of victim shared responsibility for the crime (*provocative victim*); and the last type of victim was responsible for the crime (*self-victim*).[72]

These typologies shed light on the factors that make victims susceptible to crime. By way of extension, the vulnerabilities of a cybervictim to a cybercriminal can be determined by the cybervictim's personality traits and behavior. For example, research has shown that perpetrators of cybercrime are likely to become victims of cybercrime themselves.[73] Information about the vulnerability of victims can be used to inform crime prevention efforts both offline and online. These theories ultimately propose that a victim can avoid being a target of crime by adjusting his or her own behavior and altering and controlling interactions with likely offenders.[74]

Victim precipitation theories have been lambasted by victims and victim advocates as promoting victim-blaming attitudes.[75] Such attitudes have long been held about rape victims, who have been told that their behavior in some way provokes the crime committed against them.[76] Victim-blaming attitudes are also prevalent with cybercrimes. For instance, victims of cyberfraud are viewed as greedy and gullible and responsible for the illicit act committed against them.[77] Victim-blaming attitudes may result in **secondary victimization**, which occurs when the victim experiences victimization from the negative attitudes and behaviors of others after the crime or cybercrime. Secondary victimization may occur as a result of the victim's experience with the criminal justice system. For example, agents of the criminal justice system may trivialize or otherwise negatively respond to a victim's cybercrime complaint.

LIFESTYLE EXPOSURE THEORY

Lifestyle exposure theory holds that the lifestyle of a person determines whether or not he or she becomes a victim. This theory focuses on the factors contributing to individuals' victimization. It explains victimization as a consequence of the personal characteristics and associations of victims and offenders. Particularly, this theory explores behaviors, habits, and circumstances that expose victims to harm.[78] In cyberspace, cybervictims' online activities and habits leave them vulnerable to cybercriminals. These activities can expose them to a cybercriminal.

The exposure of a victim to crime is determined by the victim's lifestyle or harmful factors that exist in the victim's everyday life.[79] Three categories of victim exposure were created based on the degree to which a victim's personal or professional life leaves the victim susceptible to crime: low exposure, medium exposure, and high exposure.[80] An individual whose personal and professional life does not expose the individual to crime is known as a **low-exposure victim**. The amount of data about the person dictates the level of exposure. The more information about individuals' personal and professional lives that is available to others, the greater their exposure to cybercrime. An individual whose personal and professional life can expose him or her to crime is known as a **medium-exposure victim**. An individual whose personal and professional life continually exposes the individual to crime is known as a **high-exposure victim**. A cybervictim's exposure to cyberoffenders increases with the amount of time the victim spends online and the types of online activities the victim engages in (e.g., instant messaging, sending and receiving e-mails, and posting information, photos, and videos on social media websites). The exposure of cybervictims to offenders online was found to have a statistically significant effect on online victimization.[81] Other studies have found it to be a weak predictor of certain cybercrimes, like cyberstalking.[82]

The vulnerability of the cybervictim to a cybercriminal is determined by the cybervictim-cyberoffender interaction or the lifestyle and activities of the cybervictim. Individuals who participate in deviant lifestyles and activities are at risk for victimization[83] and cybervictimization.[84] For instance, users who access pornography websites and view pornography are at great risk of cybervictimization from malware.[85] By contrast, studies have shown that victims of online fraud are often targeted not because of deviant lifestyles but during the course of daily routine nondeviant behaviors.[86] Patterns in routine daily activities can predict the likelihood of exposure to **criminogenic** situations. These online daily routine behaviors may not be considered deviant but may be deemed "risky." For example, users' overreliance on a wide variety of applications and technology to engage in various daily activities, including communications, banking, health, and even leisure activities, can put them at risk of theft of their data and tracking of their movements. Indeed, research has shown that individuals who readily publish their personal data online are at greater risk of cybervictimization by identity thieves.[87]

Individuals who engage in risky behavior online can also place third parties (even friends and associates) at risk of cybervictimization. Consider the terms of service agreements for apps that users download. These terms often request access to a user's address book, which may include the private information (name, e-mail address, and phone number) of third parties. By consenting to the terms of service agreements (which alerts users about access to their address book), the user is placing his or her contacts at risk for use of their information in ways that the contacts had neither intended nor desired. For instance, apps such as Path have been exposed for sharing users' contact information from their address book.[88] Path is not the only app that collects and shares user information. Snapchat collected the names and numbers of all contacts from users' address books even though it told users that only the person's e-mail, phone number, and Facebook ID would be collected to enable users to contact friends.[89]

Online activities such as visiting unknown websites, clicking on pop-up messages, visiting file-sharing websites, downloading freeware, and opening e-mails from unknown senders were found to increase individuals' risk of cybervictimization.[90] Interacting with unknown users online was also found to increase the risk of cybervictimization.[91] The use of social media sites and instant messaging was found to be associated with cybervictimization as well.[92] Additionally, empirical studies have shown that a range of online activities (e.g., instant messaging, use of chat rooms, and social media posts) and a strong Internet presence are associated with cyberharassment.[93] Moreover, the following online routines are associated with an increased risk of cyberfraud and other forms of cyber-victimization: time spent online, Internet browsing, Internet shopping, online banking, sending e-mails, instant messaging, and downloading content (e.g., music and films).[94] Other studies have revealed that some types of offline and online activities are riskier than others. Offline, a user's access to the Internet through public and university computers increases the risk of cybervictimization.[95] Online, one of the riskiest activities associated with cyberbuylling is, contrary to popular belief, instant messaging, and not the use of social media sites.[96]

The level of risk posed by an environment depends on the number and types of offenders that operate within it. Cyberspace is unique in that it removes traditional obstacles for offenders that limited access to victims. Given the universal reach of the Internet (as long as an Internet connection exists), offenders can access victims anywhere in the world. **Offender exposure** refers to the level of exposure of perpetrators to law enforcement detection and apprehension. Offender exposure depends on the perpetrator's behavior and activities. It is determined by situational exposure and modus operandi (i.e., method of operation) exposure. **Situational exposure** refers to the vulnerability to detection and apprehension because of personality traits of the criminal and the environment within which the criminal operates.[97] **Modus operandi exposure** (or MO exposure) refers to the likelihood of detection and capture of an offender through the offender's MO. This form of exposure is determined from the use of precautionary and contradictory acts. A **precautionary act** is an action of an offender that is designed to evade detection and capture by authorities.[98] These acts seek to conceal the identity and whereabouts of the offender and confuse or hinder the investigation of the crime in some way.[99] A **contradictory act** refers to offender behaviors that increase the likelihood of his or her detection and apprehension by authorities before, during, and after a crime.[100] The modus operandi of a criminal will dictate whether the offender has high or low exposure. A **low-exposure offender** is a skilled cybercriminal and engages in meticulous planning and preparation before, during, and after a crime.[101] An individual that is a **high-exposure offender** has few skills and lacks the necessary foresight and planning before, during, and after the crime; as such, he or she is more likely to be detected by authorities.[102]

ROUTINE ACTIVITY THEORY

Routine activity theory (RAT) suggests that the solution to crime is not fixing offenders but rather fixing "places" and "situations" so that opportunities for crime are blocked. Specifically, RAT holds that for crime to be committed, two elements must be present—a motivated offender (i.e., a person willing to engage in a crime if the opportunity exists to do so)[103] and a suitable target—and one element must be absent, that is, capable guardians (anything or anyone that serves to frustrate the attempts of the offender to commit the crime). The convergence of these three factors in time and space invites crime to occur.

Empirical studies have been conducted to test the applicability of RAT to specific crimes. RAT has been used to explain vandalism,[104] fraud,[105] burglary,[106] and larceny,[107] among other crimes. Academics have discussed the applicability of RAT to cybercrime.[108] The literature has examined RAT's application to interpersonal cybercrimes (e.g., cyberstalking, cyberharassment, and cyberbullying) and cyberfraud, cybertrespass, and cybervandalism (e.g., hacking, phishing, and malware).[109] The time and space requirement seems prima facie to limit the application of RAT to cybercrime. As Yar has argued, "routine activity theory holds that the 'organization of time and space is central' for criminological explanation . . . ,[110] yet the cyber-spatial environment is chronically spatio-temporally disorganized."[111] Despite this limitation, Eck and Clarke claimed that RAT applies to crimes where the victim and offender do not exist in the same time and space.[112] Particularly, the Internet makes possible "the asynchronous intersection in time and space of the victim and the offender; . . . [this] convergence is contingent on (a) the network providing a conduit for interaction between victim and offender, with cyberspace acting as a proxy for physical space, and (b) an eventual overlap in time or a completed transaction across time."[113] Ultimately, the real-time convergence of offenders and targets in time and space is unnecessary to create opportunities for offending in cyberspace.[114]

Motivated offenders commit cybercrime because of the plethora of suitable targets from anywhere in the world with an Internet connection and the absence of online guardians. In RAT, the motivated offender is considered a given; what is analyzed, therefore, is the suitable target and the absence of a capable guardian. A target's suitability is determined by four criteria, value, inertia, visibility, and accessibility, which can be summed up by the acronym VIVA (see Figure 3-2).

> *Value.* Online targets can be people, organizations, tangible and intangible items (e.g., pirated works such as films and music), and information. The value of the target is subjective and determined by the offender, depending on his or her wants, needs, and desires.
>
> *Inertia.* If an object is high in inertia, it is difficult to move. Offenders tend to avoid items that are high in inertia (e.g., stealing a refrigerator from a home). Instead, they seek to obtain items that are easily moved and obtained (e.g., jewelry and mobile digital devices). The same holds true if the target is a person. The offender will seek to victimize someone the offender can easily overpower. Even data and other online items retain some inertial properties. For instance, inertial resistance could exist for vast quantities of data. The ability of a cybercriminal to steal (i.e., download) this quantity of data depends on the storage capacity of the offender's digital devices.

Visibility. Here, offenders usually target an object or person that is visible (e.g., money flashed at a bar or a handbag or money left in a vehicle). In cyberspace, this can refer to a user's online presence and public activities on websites. For example, online activities such as engaging in chat room discussions increases users' visibility.[115] Individuals' online presence through social media profiles also increases their visibility to offenders.[116] Research has shown that individuals' Internet access and use exposes them to phishing[117] and online fraud.[118] Overall, the sharing of personal details about relationship status, home life, personal beliefs, and real-time information about daily activities and routines places users at risk of victimization and cybervictimization.

Accessibility. Offenders usually target an accessible object or person (e.g., easy access into a home due to lax or no home security). Online this criteria refers to the extent to which a perpetrator can access a user and a user's personal information. For instance, the availability of information about a user's home address, date of birth, marital status, and names of relatives increases the user's risk of cyberidentity theft.[119] This data can be used for fraudulent purposes.[120] By and large, the accessibility of a user can be determined by his or her routine online activities and the activities of others (i.e., failure to properly secure a database that holds the user's data) that expose the target to cybercriminals.

Of the above-mentioned criteria, Neuman and Clarke held that online target accessibility and visibility increase the likelihood of cybervictimization.[121] Another acronym, CRAVED, which was developed by Clarke, has been used to determine online target suitability (see Figure 3-2).[122] CRAVED stands for concealable, removable, available, valuable, enjoyable,

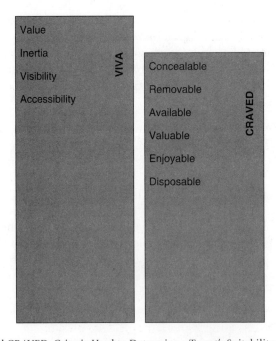

FIGURE 3-2   VIVA and CRAVED: Criteria Used to Determine a Target's Suitability.

FIGURE 3-3   Problem Analysis Triangle.

FIGURE 3-4   Crime Analysis and Controllers Triangles.

and disposable.[123] CRAVED can be applied to cybercrime; for instance, data, such as users' names and credit and debit card data, fit the criteria of CRAVED.[124]

Although there are three components at the heart of RAT—a motivated offender, suitable target, and capable guardian—the reason a crime occurs is because the capable guardian is absent during the commission of the crime. This leaves two components: the motivated offender and a suitable target. To understand why crime occurs when a motivated offender and suitable target are present, the location (or place) that the crime occurs must be examined. The motivated offender, suitable target, and place of the crime are depicted in the problem analysis triangle shown in Figure 3-3, which was created to help criminal justice professionals visualize, analyze, and understand crime and by extension cybercrime problems. The three sides of the triangle in Figure 3-3 represent the offender, the place, and the target/victim. A more contemporary version of the problem (or crime) analysis triangle also includes an outer triangle of "controllers" for each of the three factors (see Figure 3-4).

Figure 3-4 illustrates how the crime analysis triangle analyzes both the elements of crime (offender, place, and target/victim) and potential responses and interventions for each of the elements of the crime (as depicted on the larger triangle).

Offender. For the *offender*, the controller is the handler. The handler is someone who knows the offender and can influence and exercise some control over the offender.

Handlers can be parents, spouses, siblings, friends, teachers, and probation and parole officers. For example, for cyberbullies, the handler may be a parent or other guardian. Extending Felson's argument about crime, to be an effective controller of cybercrime, online guardians "must be knowledgeable about their immediate surroundings and the context in which they could potentially perform as guardians."[125] In the case of cybercrimes involving children, parents or other guardians may not be well versed in navigating the Internet safely nor communicating safe Internet practices and the dangers of the Internet to children.

Place. For the location or *place*, the controller is the manager. The manager is responsible for controlling behavior in a specific location. Examples of managers are a professor in a college classroom or a flight attendant on an airplane. Online, Internet service providers are managers; so too are administrators of chat rooms. Administrators of websites and other online forums, as well as ordinary users, can serve as guardians monitoring information posted and communications and informally sanctioning those who engage in offensive or any other type of behavior that violates the rules of acceptable behavior on the websites or forums.[126]

Target/victim. For the *target/victim*, the controller is the capable guardian (as it is in the original formulation of RAT). Guardians include family members, friends, neighbors, co-workers, public police, and private security. It could also include surveillance systems like closed-circuit television (CCTV).

The space where motivated cybercriminals and suitable targets converge is the Internet.[127] In this space, frequent online activity in multiple forums has been found to increase cybervictimization, especially when capable guardians are absent.[128] Online, two types of guardianship have been identified: physical and social.[129] **Physical guardianship** refers to the measures taken to protect a user and his or her digital devices and frustrate the attempts of cybercriminals to commit crime. Physical guardianship includes measures such as antivirus and antispyware programs, firewalls, intrusion detection systems, content-filtering and blocking software, profile trackers (which enable users to know who is monitoring their profiles and accessing their data), using privacy settings on social media accounts, preventing strangers from accessing these accounts, and limiting or deleting online personal information.[130] The efficacy of these measures varies; for example, the efficacy of antivirus and antispyware programs depends on certain factors, such as the quality of software and whether or not it is frequently updated.

Research on the impact of online physical guardianship has shown conflicting results. Certain studies have shown that physical guardianship does not impact cybercrime.[131] Particularly, studies have shown that the absence or presence of online physical guardianship is not linked to cybervictimization.[132] By contrast, Grabosky and Smith found that cybervictimization is the result of the absence of physical guardianship.[133] This, however, depends on the cybercrime. The lack of physical guardianship has been found to increase the risk of malware victimization.[134] Conversely, physical guardianship does not protect against all forms of interpersonal cybercrimes. For instance, some studies have revealed that physical guardianship does not affect cyberharassment and cyberbullying victimization.[135] Nonetheless, the impact is dependent on the type of physical guardianship. In fact, filtering software has been found to affect cyberbullying (decreasing the likelihood of cybervictimization when present).[136] In addition to certain interpersonal cybercrimes, the impact of physical guardianship on other cybercrimes has mixed results. One study revealed that physical guardianship does not reduce the risk of cyberidentity theft victimization.[137] The ability of physical guardianship to minimize the risk of cybervictimization depends on the measure used. For example, filtering systems for e-mails are not very effective, especially with respect to spam and phishing. In fact, spam and phishing may still be received in a user's inbox despite the existence of filtering software for these types of e-mails.

Social guardianship refers to the presence of third parties that could discourage crime because of their presence.[138] Lack of social guardianship online increases cybercrime risk and increases users' suitability as a target, because they are accessible to the offender and are considered easy targets as they lack a guardian.[139] Social guardianship helps protect against interpersonal cybercrimes (e.g., cyberbullying). An example of such guardianship is parents monitoring children's online activities or restricting children's access to the Internet and the time they spend online.[140] Often there is little oversight of children's use of the Internet and digital devices when they communicate with others online.[141] Unsupervised use of the Internet by children may expose them to Internet predators and cyberbullies. Research has shown that predators often ask children about whether or not their parents review their communications or have access to the computer the child is using to determine whether or not they are likely to be caught.[142] Indeed, routines and lifestyles of children that lack parental or other guardian supervision increase the risk of children to cybervictimization.[143] Lack of social guardianship has also been linked to peer deviancy. A 2011 study by Reyns, Henson, and Fisher measured the lack of social guardianship by the likelihood that a user's friend would utilize the information that he or she posted online to cyberharass, cyberstalk, or otherwise victimize the person.[144] Deviant peers, those most likely to engage in the illicit conduct, were less likely to serve as capable guardians for the user.

Williams further distinguished between **passive physical guardianship** (e.g., antivirus and antispyware software), **active personal guardianship** (e.g., frequently changing passwords), and **avoidance personal guardianship** (e.g., avoiding online banking and online shopping).[145] Research has shown that *passive physical guardianship* reduces the likelihood of cyberidentity theft.[146] Research has also shown that certain guardianship routines that involve *active personal guardianship* can reduce cyberidentity theft and hinder motivated offenders.[147] Active personal guardianship can involve changing the privacy settings of social media accounts. Social media sites can be public or private depending on the user's preferences. For example, Facebook enables users to set their own privacy settings and block or limit the visibility of their posts, images, messages, and videos, and the accessibility of these by others. Accordingly, users can block or restrict access to their profiles as a form of active personal guardianship. Studies have shown that those who engage in active personal guardianship have likely experienced cybervictimization in the past.[148] The final form of guardianship, *avoidance personal guardianship*, is effective in limiting the target's visibility and accessibility to cybercriminals; however, it is not a viable long-term solution, due to ever increasing incentives to engage in online activity (e.g., discounts on items, promotional sales only available online) and the existing push to increase rather than decrease online activities (e.g., adding more and more financial services online, such as check depositing).

Ultimately, of the three theories discussed, RAT can be used to inform cybercrime prevention strategies. The criteria used by cybercriminals to determine target suitability can also be employed by criminal justice professionals to inform the measures taken to prevent or at the very least reduce instances of cybercrime. Suitable targets can be reduced by educating the public on how to navigate the Internet safely and the ways to enhance the cybersecurity of their computers and digital devices (see Chapters 10 and 11 on ways to do this). The eventual goal of the application of RAT is to make cybercrime appear less attractive to motivated cybercriminals. This can occur by increasing the risks associated with committing cybercrime and decreasing the benefits associated with committing the crime (see Chapter 4 for further information). In the end, to prevent cybercrime, RAT holds that at least one of the core elements—a motivated offender, an available target or the absence of a capable guardian—must be changed. The most effective strategy, however, will change all three.

CASE STUDY

Nils Christie highlighted the distinction of victims in the criminal justice system in his work *The Ideal Victim*. He differentiated between ideal and nonideal victims. According to Christie, an ideal victim is "a person or category of individuals who—when hit by a crime—most readily are given the complete and legitimate status of being a victim."[149] He proposed six attributes of an ideal victim:[150]

1. The victim is weak with respect to the offender (e.g., an infant or elderly person)
2. The victim is carrying out a virtuous task or at the very least engaging in legitimate activities
3. The victim could not be blamed for the crime
4. The offender is dangerous and frightening
5. The offender is a stranger
6. The "victim has the right combination of power, influence, or sympathy to successfully elicit victim status without threatening (and thus risking opposition from) strong countervailing vested interests."[151]

According to Christie, who would be an ideal victim? Why do you think so? Can this term be applied to victims of cybercrime? Why or why not?

REVIEW QUESTIONS

1. Why study cybervictims?
2. What are the three types of cybervictimization? Please describe each of them.
3. What are the effects of cybercrime on victims?
4. Is there a profile for a cybervictim? Why do you think so?
5. Which cybervictims are blamed for their victimization? Why?
6. Is there a profile of a cyberoffender? Why do you think so?
7. Can victim precipitation theory explain cybercrime?
8. Can lifestyle exposure theory explain cybercrime?
9. Name the two types of capable guardians. How do they apply to cybervictims?
10. Can routine activity theory explain cybercrime?

DEFINITIONS

Active personal guardianship. A user takes certain actions to avoid cybervictimization.

Avoidance personal guardianship. A user avoids certain actions in an attempt to prevent cybervictimization.

Contradictory act. An offender behavior that increases the likelihood of his or her detection and apprehension by authorities before, during, and after a crime.

Criminogenic. A state or situation that causes or tends to cause crime.

Cybervictimology. The scientific study of online victimization, the impact of the cybercrime on the cybervictim, and the types of victims that experience cybercrime.

High-exposure offender. An offender who has few skills and lacks the necessary foresight and planning before, during, and after the crime; as such, he or she is more likely to be detected by authorities.

High-exposure victim. A person whose personal and professional life continually expose him or her to crime.

Lifestyle exposure theory. A theory positing that the lifestyle of a person determines whether or not he or she becomes a victim.

Low-exposure offender. A skilled cybercriminal who engages in meticulous planning and preparation before, during, and after a crime.

Low-exposure victim. A person whose personal and professional life does not expose him or her to crime.

Medium-exposure victim. A person whose personal and professional life can expose him or her to crime.

Modus operandi exposure. Modus operandi exposure refers to the likelihood of detection and capture of an offender through the offender's MO.

Offender exposure. The level of exposure of perpetrators to law enforcement detection and apprehension.

Passive physical guardianship. Protective measures which largely go unnoticed by users and automatically shape users' behaviors.

Physical guardianship. The measures taken to protect a user and the user's digital devices and frustrate the attempts of cybercriminals to commit crime.

Precautionary act. An action of an offender designed to evade detection and capture by authorities.

Primary cybervictimization. The cybervictim is the target of the cybercrime.

Routine activity theory. Routine activity theory holds that for crime to be committed two elements must be present—a motivated offender and a suitable target—and one element, a capable guardian, must be absent. The convergence of these three factors in time and space invites crime to occur.

Secondary cybervictimization. The cybervictim is the indirect target of the cybercrime.

Secondary victimization. Secondary victimization occurs when the victim experiences victimization from the negative attitudes and behaviors of others after the cybercrime.

Situational exposure. The vulnerability to detection and apprehension stemming from personality traits of the criminal and the environment within which the criminal operates.

Social guardianship. The presence of third parties that could discourage crime because of their presence.

Tertiary cybervictimization. The impact of cybercrime on society.

Victim contribution. The activities of victims that make them susceptible to crime.

Victim precipitation theory. Victim precipitation theory holds that the victim is in some way responsible for his or her victimization (i.e., provoking or somehow precipitating the event). This theory seeks to explain victimization through an analysis of the situational contingencies and dynamics that exist in interpersonal interactions.

Victim proneness. The characteristics of an individual that make the individual more likely than others to become a victim of a crime.

Victim provocation. Victim provocation views the victim as the cause of his or her victimization.

Victimology. The scientific study of cybervictims, including the victims' physical characteristics; behavior before, during, and after the crime; medical, psychological, and criminal history; home life; family; work life; colleagues; social life; friends and acquaintances; and experiences in the aftermath of the crime.

ENDNOTES

1. M. Evans, "Celebrity Tweeters Leaving Themselves Open to Burglary," *Telegraph*, July 2, 2013, http://www.telegraph.co.uk/technology/twitter/10155422/Celebrity-tweeters-leaving-themselves-open-to-burglary.html.
2. ABC News, "Burglars Use Social Media to Find Next Victims," December 23, 2014, http://abc7news.com/travel/burglars-use-social-media-to-find-next-victims/448107/.
3. A. Salkin, "Going for the Bling: Hollywood Burglars," *New York Times*, November 13, 2009, http://www.nytimes.com/2009/11/15/fashion/15bling.html?_r=0.
4. A. Ghebremedhin, E. Mcniff, and J. Dubreuil, "Exclusive: Inside Hollywood's 'Bling Ring,'" *ABC News*, March 4, 2010, http://abcnews.go.com/2020/TheLaw/bling-ring-celebrity-hollywood-burglaries-cops/story?id=9999401.
5. P. Harris, "'Bling Ring' on Trial for Hollywood Celebrity Burglaries," *Guardian*, January 16, 2010, http://www.theguardian.com/lifeandstyle/2010/jan/17/bling-ring-los-angeles-hollywood.
6. Salkin, "Going for the Bling."
7. J. Raskauskas and A. D. Stoltz, "Involvement in Traditional and Electronic Bullying among Adolescents," *Developmental Psychology* 43, no. 3 (2007): 564–575, cited in A. Williford, L. C. Elledge, A. J. Boulton, K. J. DePaolis, T. D. Little, and C. Salmivalli, "Effects of the KiVa Antibullying Program on Cyberbullying and Cybervictimization Frequency Among Finnish Youth," *Journal of Clinical Child & Adolescent Psychology* 42, no. 6 (2013): 821; S. Hinduja and J. W. Patchin, "Offline Consequences of Online Victimization: School Violence and Delinquency," *Journal of School Violence* 6, no. 3 (2007): 89–112; R. S. Tokunaga, "Following You Home from School: A Critical Review and Synthesis of Research on Cyberbullying Victimization," *Computers in Human Behavior* 26, no. 3 (2010): 277–287; A. G. Dempsey, M. L. Sulkowski, R. Nichols, and E. A. Storch, "Differences between Peer Victimization in Cyber and Physical Settings and Associated Psychosocial Adjustment in Early Adolescence," *Psychology in Schools* 46, no. 10 (2009): 962–972; J. N. Navarro and J. L. Jasinski, "Going Cyber: Using Routine Activities Theory to Predict Cyberbullying Experiences," *Sociological Spectrum* 32, no. 1 (2012): 81–94; C. D. Marcum, G. E. Higgins, and M. L. Ricketts, "Juveniles and Cyber Stalking in the United States: An Analysis of Theoretical Predictors of Patterns of Online Perpetration," *International Journal of Cyber Criminology* 8, no. 1 (2014): 47–56.
8. M. L. Pittaro, "Cyber Stalking: An Analysis of Online Harassment and Intimidation," *International Journal of Cyber Criminology* 1, no. 2 (2007): 180–197.
9. M. D. Reisig, T. C. Pratt, and K. Holtfreter, "Risk of Internet Theft Victimization: Examining the Effects of Social Vulnerability and Financial Impulsivity," *Criminal Justice and Behavior* 36, no. 4 (2009): 369–384.
10. L. D. Roberts, D. Indermaur, and C. Spiranovic, "Fear of Cyber-Identity Theft and Related Fraudulent Activity," *Psychiatry, Psychology and Law* 20, no. 3 (2013): 324–325.
11. N. Parsons-Pollard and L. J. Moriarty, "Cyberstalking: Utilizing What We Do Know," *Victims & Offenders* 4, no. 4 (2009): 437.
12. M. Pathè and P. E. Mullen, "The Impact of Stalkers on Their Victims," *British Journal of Psychiatry* 170, no. 1 (1997): 12–17, cited in Parsons-Pollard and Moriarty, "Cyberstalking," 438.

13. T. F. Ngo and R. Paternoster, "Cybercrime Victimization: An Examination of Individual and Situational-Level Factors," *International Journal of Cyber Criminology* 5, no. 1 (2011): 788.
14. Ibid.
15. T. Beran and Q. Li, "Cyber-Harassment: A Study of a New Method for an Old Behavior." *Journal of Educational Computing Research* 32, no. 3 (2005): 265–277; J. W. Patchin and S. Hinduja, "Bullies Move beyond the Schoolyard: A Preliminary Look at Cyberbullying," *Youth Violence and Juvenile Justice* 4, no. 2 (2006): 148–169.
16. R. M. Kowalski and S. P. Limber "Electronic Bullying among Middle School Students," *Journal of Adolescent Health* 4, no. 6 (2007): S22–S30; J. Wolak, K. Mitchell, and D. Finkelhor, *Online Victimization of Youth: Five Years Later,* National Center for Missing and Exploited Children, 2006, http://www.missingkids.com/en_US/publications/NC167.pdf; J. N. Navarro and J. L. Jasinski, "Why Girls? Using Routine Activities Theory to Predict Cyberbullying Experiences between Girls and Boys," *Women & Criminal Justice* 23, no. 4 (2013): 286–303; Navarro and Jasinski, "Going Cyber," 81–94.
17. B. Reyns, B. Henson, and B. S. Fisher, "Being Pursued Online: Applying Cyberlifestyle-Routine Activities Theory to Cyberstalking Victimization," *Criminal Justice and Behavior* 38, no. 11 (2011): 1149–1169.
18. Working to Halt Online Abuse, "Online Harassment/Cyberstalking Statistics: Cumulative Statistics for the Years 2000–2011," accessed August 3, 2016, http://www.haltabuse.org/resources/stats/; L. J. Moriarty and K. Freiberger, "Cyberstalking: Utilizing Newspaper Accounts to Establish Victimization Patterns," *Victims & Offenders* 3, no. 2-3 (2008): 131–141.
19. B. W. Reyns, "Online Routines and Identity Theft Victimization: Further Expanding Routine Activity Theory beyond Direct-Contact Offenses," *Journal of Research in Crime and Delinquency* 50, no. 2 (2013): 216–238.
20. Internet Crime Complaint Center, *2014 Internet Crime Report,* accessed August 3, 2016, 9, https://pdf.ic3.gov/2014_IC3Report.pdf.
21. T. C. Pratt, K. Holtfreter, and M. D. Reisig, "Routine Online Activity and Internet Fraud Targeting: Extending the Generality of Routine Activity Theory," *Journal of Research in Crime and Delinquency* 47, no. 3 (2000): 267–296.
22. Reyns, "Online Routines and Identity Theft," 216–238.
23. Internet Crime Complaint Center, *2014 Internet Crime Report* (2015), 9.
24. Ngo and Paternoster, "Cybercrime Victimization," 782.
25. Working to Halt Online Abuse, "Online Harassment/Cyberstalking Statistics."
26. Internet Watch Foundation, *Internet Watch Foundation Annual & Charity Report 2013*, accessed August 3, 2016, 6, https://www.iwf.org.uk/assets/media/annual-reports/annual_report_2013.pdf.pdf.
27. UK Child Exploitation and Online Protection Centre, *Threat Assessment of Child Sexual Exploitation and Abuse*, June 2013, 11, http://ceop.police.uk/Documents/ceopdocs/CEOP_TACSEA2013_240613%20FINAL.pdf.
28. Ngo and Paternoster, "Cybercrime Victimization," 788.
29. UK Child Exploitation and Online Protection Centre, *Threat Assessment of Child Sexual Exploitation and Abuse,* 11; Internet Watch Foundation, *Internet Watch Foundation Annual & Charity Report 2013.*
30. Working to Halt Online Abuse, "Online Harassment/Cyberstalking Statistics."
31. A. Hinduja and J. W. Patchin, "Cyberbullying: An Exploratory Analysis of Factors Related to Offending and Victimization," *Deviant Behavior* 29, no. 2 (2008): 129–156.
32. Ngo and Paternoster, "Cybercrime Victimization," 788.
33. Ibid.
34. Reyns et al., "Being Pursued Online," 1149–1169.
35. Working to Halt Online Abuse, "Online Harassment/Cyberstalking Statistics."

36. Pratt et al., "Routine Online Activity," 267–296; A. C. Kiger, "Infringing Nations: Predicting Software Piracy Rates, BitTorrent Tracker Hosting, and P2P File Sharing Client Downloads between Countries," *International Journal of Cyber Criminology* 7, no. 1 (2013): 66.
37. P. N. Ndubueze, E. U. M. Igbo, and U. O. Okoye, "Cyber Crime Victimization among Internet Active Nigerians: An Analysis of Socio-Demographic Correlates," *International Journal of Criminal Justice Sciences* 8, no. 2 (2013): 229.
38. Reyns, "Online Routines and Identity Theft," 216–238.
39. Ngo and Paternoster, "Cybercrime Victimization," 788.
40. Ndubueze et al., "Cyber Crime Victimization among Internet active Nigerians," 230.
41. L. McFarlane and P. Bocij, "An Exploration of Predatory Behaviour in Cyberspace: Towards a Typology of Cyberstalkers," *First Monday* 8, no. 9 (2003), http://ojphi.org/ojs/index.php/fm/article/view/1076/996; L. P. Sheridan and T. Grant, "Is Cyberstalking Different?" *Psychology, Crime & Law*, 13, no. 6 (2007): 627–640.
42. I. Rivers and N. Noret, "'I h8 u': Findings from a Five-Year Study of Text and Email Bullying," *British Educational Research Journal* 36, no. 4 (2010): 643–671; Kowalski and Limber, "Electronic Bullying among Middle School Students," S22–S30.
43. P. K. Smith "Cyberbullying and Cyber Aggression," in *Handbook of School Violence and School Safety: International Research and Practice*, ed. S. R. Jimerson, A. B. Nickerson, M. J. Mayer, and M. J. Furlong (New York: Routledge, 2012), 93–103.
44. Q. Li, "Cyberbullying in Schools: A Research of Gender Differences," *School Psychology International* 27, no. 2 (2006): 157–170; K. A. Fanti, A. G. Demetriou, and V. V. Hawa, "A Longitudinal Study of Cyberbullying: Examining Risk and Protective Factors," *European Journal of Developmental Psychology* 9, no. 2 (2012): 168–181; E. Calvete, I. Orue, A. Estevez, L. Villardon, and P. Padilla, "Cyberbullying in Adolescents: Modalities and Aggressors' Profile," *Computers in Human Behavior* 26, no. 5 (2010): 1128–1135; P. K. Smith, G. Steffen, and R. Sittichai, "The Nature of Cyberbullying and an International Network," in *Severability through the New Media: Findings from an International Network*, ed. P. K. Smith and G. Steffen (New York: Psychology Press, 2013), 6.
45. Li, "Cyberbullying in Schools," 157–170; R. Slonje, P. K. Smith, and A. Frisen, "Processes of Cyberbullying, and Feelings of Remorse by Bullies: A Pilot Study," *European Journal of Developmental Psychology* 9, no. 2 (2012); S. Livingston, L. Haddon, A. Gorzig, and K. Olafsson, *Risks and Safety on the Internet: The Perspective of European Children*, London School of Economics, EU Kids Online, 2011, http://www.lse.ac.uk/media%40lse/research/EUKidsOnline/EU%20Kids%20II%20(2009-11)/EUKidsOnlineIIReports/D4FullFindings.pdf; P. K. Smith, J. Mahdavi, M. Carvalho, S. Fisher, S. Russell, and N. Tippett, "Cyberbullying: The Nature and Impact in Secondary School Pupils," *Journal of Child Psychology and Psychiatry* 49, no. 4 (2008): 376–385; P. K. Smith, G. Steffen, and R. Sittichai, "The Nature of Cyberbullying and an International Network," *Severability through the New Media: Findings from an International Network*, ed. P. K. Smith and G. Steffen (New York: Psychology Press, 2013), 6.
46. E. Menesini, A. Nocentini, and P. Calussi, "The Measurement of Cyberbullying: Dimensional Structure and Relative Item Severity and Discrimination," *Cyberpsychology & Behavior* 4, no. 5 (2011): 267–274.
47. Slonje et al., "Cyberbullying."
48. K. Wensley and M. Campbell, "Heterosexual and Nonheterosexual Young University Students' Involvement in Traditional and Cyber Forms of Bullying," *Cyberpsychology, Behavior, and Social Networking* 15, no. 12 (2012): 649–654.
49. L. Webb, J. Craisatti, and S. Keen, "Characteristics of Internet Child Pornography Offenders: A Comparison with Child Molesters," *Sexual Abuse: A Journal of Research and Treatment* 19, no. 4 (2007): 449–465; K. M. Babchisin, R. K. Hanson, and C. A. Hermann, "The Characteristics of Online Sex Offenders: A Meta-Analysis of Online Sex Offenders," *Sexual Abuse: A Journal of Research and Treatment*, 23, no. 1 (2010): 92–123; E. Quayle and R. Sinclair, "An Introduction

to the Problem," in *Understanding and Preventing Online Sexual Exploitation of Children*, ed. E. Quayle and K. M. Ribisl (New York: Routledge, 2012), 7.

50. A. Bates and C. Metcalf, "Psychometric Comparison of Internet and Non-Internet Sex Offenders from a Community Treatment Sample," *Journal of Sexual Aggression* 13, no. 1 (2007): 11–20; A. Burke, S. Sowerbutts, B. Blundell, and M. Sherry, "Child Pornography and the Internet: Policing and Treatment Issues," *Psychiatry, Psychology and Law* 9, no. 1 (2002): 79–84; K. Sheldon and D. Howitt, *Sex Offenders and the Internet* (Chichester, UK: Wiley, 2007); Quayle and Sinclair, "An Introduction to the Problem," 11.

51. Burke et al., "Child Pornography and the Internet," 79–84.

52. S. Tomak, F. S. Weschsler, M. Ghahramanlou-Holloway, T. Virden, and M. E. Nademin, "An Empirical Study of the Personality Characteristics of Internet Sex Offenders," *Journal of Sexual Aggression* 15, no. 2 (2009): 139–148; Bates and Metcalf, "Psychometric Comparison of Internet and Non-Internet Sex Offenders," 11–20; Sheldon and Howitt, *Sex Offenders and the Internet*; Quayle and Sinclair, "An Introduction to the Problem," 11.

53. B. Blundell, M. Sherry, A. Burke, and S. Sowerbutts, "Child Pornography and the Internet: Accessibility and Policing," *Australian Police Journal*, no. 1 (2002): 59–65; M. C. Calder, "The Internet: Potential, Problems, and Pathways to Hands-On Sexual Offending," in *Child Sexual Abuse and the Internet: Tackling the New Frontier*, ed. M. C. Calder (Lyme Regis: Russell House, 2004); M. F. Schwartz and S. Southern, "Compulsive Cybersex," in *Cybersex: The Darkside of the Force*, ed. A. Cooper (New York: Brunner/Mazel, 2000); J. Wolak, K. Micthell, and D. Finkelhor, *Internet Sex Crimes Against Minors: The Response from Law Enforcement* (Alexandria, VA: Crimes Against Children Research Center, 2003); J. Wolak, D. Finkelhor, and K. J. Mitchell, *Child Pornography Possessors Arrested in Internet-Related Crimes: Findings from the National Juvenile Online Victimization Study* (Alexandria, VA: National Center for Missing and Exploited Children, 2005).

54. Babchisin et al., "The Characteristics of Online Sex Offenders," 92–123; Quayle and Sinclair, "An Introduction to the Problem," 7.

55. Babchisin et al., "The Characteristics of Online Sex Offenders," 92–123; Quayle and Sinclair, "An Introduction to the Problem," 7; Webb et al., "Characteristics of Internet Child Pornography Offenders," 449–465; Tomak et al., "An Empirical Study of the Personality Characteristics of Internet Sex Offenders," 139–148.

56. Burke et al., "Child Pornography and the Internet," 79–84.

57. Wolak et al., *Child Pornography Possessors Arrested.*

58. Sheldon and Howitt, *Sex Offenders and the Internet*, 11.

59. A. W. Eke, M. C. Seto, and J. Williams, "Examining the Criminal History Future Offending of Child Pornography Offenders: An Extended Prospective Follow-Up Study," *Law and Human Behavior* 35, no. 6 (2011): 466–478; Wolak et al., *Child Pornography Possessors Arrested*; Babchisin et al., "The Characteristics of Online Sex Offenders," 92–123; M. C. Seto, *Internet Sex Offenders* (American Psychological Association, Washington, DC, 2013), 144.

60. Seto, *Internet Sex Offenders*, 144.

61. Y. Jewkes, "Online Pornography, Pedophilia and the Sexualized Child: Mediated Myths and Moral Panics," in *Understanding and Preventing Online Sexual Exploitation of Children*, ed. E. Quayle and K. M. Ribisl (New York: Routledge, 2012), 124.

62. M. Taylor and E. Quayle, *Child Pornography: An Internet Crime* (Hove, UK: Brunner-Routledge, 2003); Jewkes, "Online Pornography, Pedophilia and the Sexualized Child," 124.

63. M. E. Wolfgang and S. I. Singer, "Victim Categories of Crime," *Journal of Criminal Law and Criminology* 69, no. 3 (1978): 389.

64. M. E. Wolfgang, "Victim-Precipitated Criminal Homicide," *Journal of Criminal Law, Criminology and Police Science* 48, no. 1 (1957), 1–11.

65. K. Sheldon and D. Howitt, "The Role of Cognitive Distortions in Pedophilic Offending: Internet and Contact Offenders Compared," *Psychology, Crime and Law* 13, no. 5 (2007): 469–486.

66. J. Pyzalski, "From Cyberbullying to Electronic Aggression: Typology of the Phenomenon," *Emotional and Behavioural Difficulties* 17, no. 3-4 (2012): 305–317.

67. Kowalski and Limber, "Electronic Bullying among Middle School Students," S22–S30; J. Juvonen and E. F. Gross, "Extending the School Grounds? Bullying Experiences in Cyberspace," *Journal of School Health* 78, no. 9 (2008): 496–505; R. Slonje and P. K. Smith, "Cyberbullying: Another Main Type of Bullying?" *Scandinavian Journal of Psychology* 49, no. 2 (2008): 147–154; E. Whittaker and R. M. Kowalski, "Cyberbullying via Social Media," *Journal of School Violence* 14, no. 1 (2015): 11–29.

68. Whittaker and Kowalski, "Cyberbullying via Social Media," 11–29.

69. P. Bocij, *Cyberstalking: Harassment in the Internet Age and How to Protect Your Family* (Westport, CT: Praeger, 2004); Sheridan and Grant, "Is Cyberstalking Different?" 627–640; Marcum et al., "Juveniles and Cyber Stalking," 49–50.

70. B. Mendelsohn, "Rape in Criminology," *Giustizia Penale* (1940).

71. H. von Hentig, *The Criminal and His Victim: Studies on the Sociobiology of Crime* (New Haven, CT: Yale University Press, 1948); B. E. Turvey, *Criminal Profiling: An Introduction to Behavioral Evidence Analysis*, 3rd ed. (Burlington, MA: Elsevier, 2008), 381–383.

72. S. Schafer, *Victimology: The Victim and His Criminal* (New York: Random House, 1968).

73. J. M. Ostrov, "Forms of Peer Aggression and Victimization during Early Childhood: A Short-Term Longitudinal Study," *Journal of Abnormal Child Psychology* 36, no. 3 (2008): 311–322; A. Williford, L. C. Elledge, A. J. Boulton, K. J. DePaolis, T. D. Little, and C. Salmivalli, "Effects of the KiVa Antibullying Program on Cyberbullying and Cybervictimization Frequency among Finnish Youth," *Journal of Clinical Child & Adolescent Psychology* 42, no. 6 (2013): 820–833.

74. P. Wilcox, "Theories of Victimisation," in *Encyclopedia of Victimology and Crime Prevention*, ed. B. Fisher and S. Lab (Thousand Oaks, CA: Sage, 2010), 977–985.

75. B. Galaway and J. Hudson, *Perspectives on Crime Victims* (St. Louis, MO: Mosby, 1981).

76. S. Estrich, *Real Rape* (Cambridge, MA: Harvard University Press, 1987).

77. C. Cross, "No Laughing Matter: Blaming the Victim of Online Fraud," *International Review of Victimology* 21, no. 2 (2015): 187–204.

78. A. W. Burgess, C. Regehr, and A. R. Roberts, *Victimology: Theories and Applications* (Burlington, MA: Jones and Bartlett, 2010), 283.

79. Turvey, *Criminal Profiling*, 378.

80. Ibid., 383.

81. C. D. Marcum, *Adolescent Online Victimization: A Test of Routine Activities Theory* (El Paso, TX: LFB Scholarly, 2009).

82. Reyns et al., "Being Pursued Online,"1149–1169.

83. C. J. Scheck and B. S. Fisher, "Specifying the Influence of Family and Peers on Violent Victimization: Extending Routine Activities and Lifestyle Theories," *Journal of Interpersonal Violence* 19, no. 9 (2004): 1021–1041; Burgess et al., *Victimology*, 47; B. Henson, P. Wilcox, B. W. Reyns, and F. T. Cullen, "Gender, Adolescent Lifestyles, and Violent Victimization: Implications for Routine Activity Theory," *Victims and Offenders* 5, no. 4 (2010): 1–26; J. L. Lauritsen, J. H. Laub, and R. J. Sampson, "Conventional and Delinquent Activities: Implications for the Prevention of Violent Victimization among Adolescents," *Violence and Victims* 7, no. 2 (1992): 91–108; J. L. Lauritsen, R. J. Sampson, and J. H. Laub, "The Link between Offending and Victimization among Adolescents," *Criminology* 29, no. 2 (1991): 265–292; G. F. Jensen and D. Brownfield, "Gender, Lifestyles, and Victimization: Beyond Routine Activity," *Violence and Victims* 1, no. 2 (1986): 85–99.

84. K. Choi, "Computer Crime Victimization and Integrated Theory: An Empirical Assessment," *International Journal of Cyber Criminology* 2, no. 1 (2008): 308–333.

85. P. Szor, *The Art of Computer Virus Research and Defense* (New York: Addison-Wesley, 2005).

86. K. Holtfreter, M. Reisig, and T. Pratt, "Low Self Control, Routine Activities, and Fraud Victimization," *Criminology* 46, no. 1 (2008): 189–220; Pratt et al., "Routine Online Activity," 267–296.

87. B. W. Reyns and B. Henson, "The Thief with a Thousand Faces and the Victim with None: Identifying Determinants for Online Identity Theft Victimization with Routine Activity Theory," *International Journal of Offender Therapy and Comparative Criminology* 60, no. 10 (2016): 1119–1139.

88. JVG, "Your Address Book Is Mine: Many Iphone Apps Take Your Data," *Venture Beat*, February 14, 2012, http://venturebeat.com/2012/02/14/iphone-address-book/.

89. K. Burnhma, "5 Ways Snapchat Violated Your Privacy Security," *Information Week*, May 9, 2014, http://www.informationweek.com/software/social/5-ways-snapchat-violated-your -privacy-security/d/d-id/1251175.

90. Choi, "Computer Crime Victimization and Integrated Theory," 308–333; S. D. Moitra, "Developing Policies for Cybercrime," *European Journal of Crime, Criminal Law and Criminal Justice* 13, no. 3 (2005): 435–464; M. Yar, "The Novelty of 'Cybercrime:' An Assessment in Light of Routine Activity Theory," *European Journal of Criminology* 2, no. 4 (2005): 407–427; Reyns and Henson, "The Thief with a Thousand Faces and the Victim with None"; Marcum, "Identifying Potential Factors of Adolescent Online Victimization," 346–367; Ngo and Paternoster, "Cybercrime Victimization," 777.

91. M. L. Ybarra, K. J. Mitchell, D. Finkelhor, and J. Wolak, "Internet Prevention Messages: Targeting the Right Online Behaviors," *Archives of Pediatrics & Adolescent Medicine* 161, no. 2 (2007): 138–145.

92. Reyns et al., "Being Pursued Online," 1149–1169.

93. J. van Wilsem, "Worlds Tied Together? Online and Non-Domestic Routine Activities and Their Impact on Digital and Traditional Threat Victimization," *European Journal of Criminology* 8, no. 2 (2011): 115–127; Marcum, "Identifying Potential Factors of Adolescent Online Victimization"; C. D. Marcum, G. E. Higgins, and M. L. Ricketts, "Potential Factors of Online Victimization of Youth: An Examination of Adolescent Online Behaviors Utilizing Routine Activity Theory," *Deviant Behavior* 31, no. 5 (2010): 381–410.

94. Pratt et al., "Routine Online Activity," 267–296; Reyns, "Online Routines and Identity Theft," 216–238; J. van Wilsem, "'Bought It, But Never Got It:' Assessing Risk Factors for Online Consumer Fraud Victimization," *European Sociological Review* 29, no. 2 (2013): 168–178.

95. M. L. Williams, "Guardians Upon High: An Application of Routine Activities Theory to Online Identity Theft in Europe at the Country and Individual Level," *British Journal of Criminology* (published online, April 27, 2015).

96. T. Beran and Q. Li, "Cyber-Harassment: A Study of a New Method for an Old Behavior," *Journal of Educational Computing Research* 32, no. 3 (2005): 265–277; Patchin and Hinduja, "Bullies Move beyond the Schoolyard," 148–169; J. Raskauskas and A. D. Stoltz, "Involvement in Traditional and Electronic Bullying among Adolescents," *Developmental Psychology* 43, no. 3 (2007): 564–575; Smith et al., "Cyberbullying," 376–385; Wolak et al., "Online Victimization of Youth"; Navarro and Jasinski, "Going Cyber," 81–94.

97. Turvey, *Criminal Profiling*, 385–386.

98. Ibid., 169.

99. Ibid.

100. Ibid., 221.

101. Ibid., 386.

102. Ibid.

103. R. L. Akers and C. S. Sellers, *Criminological Theories: Introduction, Evaluation, and Application*, 4th ed. (Los Angeles: Roxbury, 2004).

104. R. Tewksbury and E. E. Mustaine, "Routine Activities and Vandalism: A Theoretical and Empirical Study," *Journal of Crime and Justice* 23, no. 1 (2000): 81–110.

105. Holtfreter et al., "Low Self Control, Routine Activities, and Fraud Victimization," 189–220.

106. L. E. Cohen and M. Felson, "Social Change and Crime Rate Trends: A Routine Activity Approach," *American Sociological Review* 44, no. 4 (1979): 588–608.

107. T. Coupe and L. Blake, "Daylight and Darkness Targeting Strategies and the Risks of Being Seen at Residential Burglaries," *Criminology* 44, no. 2 (2006): 431–464.

108. P. Grabosky, "Virtual Criminality: Old Wine in New Bottles?" *Social and Legal Studies* 10, no. 2 (2001): 243–249; G. Newman and R. Clarke, *Superhighway Robbery: Preventing Ecommerce Crime* (Cullompton, UK: Willan, 2003); Yar, "The Novelty of Cybercrime," 407–427.

109. R. G. Morris and A. G. Blackburn, "Cracking the Code: An Empirical Exploration of Social Learning Theory and Computer Crime," *Journal of Crime and Justice* 32, no. 1 (2009): 1–34.; Ngo and Paternoster, "Cybercrime Victimization," 773–793; J. Nhan, P. Kinkade, and R. Burns, "Finding a Pot of Gold at the End of an Internet Rainbow: Further Examination of Fraudulent Email Solicitation," *International Journal of Cyber Criminology* 3, no. 1 (2009): 452–475; Choi, "Computer Crime Victimization and Integrated Theory," 308–333; van Wilsem, "Worlds Tied Together?" 115–127; van Wilsem, "'Bought It, But Never Got It,'" 168–178; Williams, "Guardians Upon High," 1–28.

110. M. Felson, *Crime and Everyday Life*, 2nd ed. (Thousand Oaks, CA: Pine Forge Press, 1998), 148.

111. Reyns et al., "Being Pursued Online," 1151.

112. Eck and Clarke, "Classifying Common Police Problems," 34.

113. Reyns et al., "Being Pursued Online," 1149–1169, esp. 1152; Eck and Clarke, "Classifying Common Police Problems," 7–39.

114. Eck and Clarke, "Classifying Common Police Problems," 7–39; Reyns et al., "Being Pursued Online," 1150.

115. A. Hinduja and J. W. Patchin, "Cyberbullying: An Exploratory Analysis of Factors Related to Offending and Victimization," *Deviant Behavior* 29, no. 2 (2008): 129–156; Choi, "Computer Crime Victimization and Integrated Theory," 308–333; Marcum, "Identifying Potential Factors of Adolescent Online Victimization," 346–367; A. Hutchings and H. Hayes, "Routine Activity Theory and Phishing Victimization: Who Gets Caught in the 'Net'?" *Current Issues in Criminal Justice* 20, no. 3 (2009): 433–451; Reyns et al., "Being Pursued Online," 1149–1169; Pratt et al., "Routine Online Activity," 267–297.

116. M. Yar, "E-Crime 2.0: The Criminological Landscape of New Social Media," *Information & Communications Technology Law* 21, no. 3 (2012): 207–219; M. L. Ybarra and K. J. Mitchell, "How Risky are Social Networking Sites? A Comparison of Places Online Where Youth Sexual Solicitation and Harassment Occurs," *Pediatrics* 121, no. 2 (2008): e350–e357.

117. Hutchings and Hayes, "Routine Activity Theory and Phishing Victimization," 433–451.

118. Pratt et al., "Routine Online Activity," 267–297; Holtfreter et al., "Low Self-Control, Routine Activities, and Fraud Victimization," 189–220.

119. Smith, "Identity Theft and Fraud," in Jewkes and Yar, *Handbook of Internet Crime*, 277.

120. Yar, "E-Crime 2.0," 207–219.

121. Newman and Clarke, *Superhighway Robbery*.

122. R. V. Clarke, *Hot Products: Understanding, Anticipating and Reducing Demand for Stolen Goods* (London: Home Office, 1999).

123. Clarke, *Hot Products*, 1.

124. Pratt et al., "Routine Online Activity," 274; Newman and Clarke, *Superhighway Robbery*.

125. Z. I. Vakhitova and D. M. Reynald, "Australian Internet Users and Guardianship against Cyber Abuse," *International Journal of Cyber Criminology* 8, no. 2 (2014): 158.

126. Yar, "The Novelty of Cybercrime," 423.

127. Reyns, "Online Routines and Identity Theft," 221.

128. Reyns, "Online Routines and Identity Theft," 221; van Wilsem, "Worlds Tied Together?" 115–127; van Wilsem, "'Bought It, But Never Got It,'" 168–178.

129. E. E. Mustaine and R. Tewksbury, "Predicting Risks of Larceny Theft Victimization: A Routine Activity Analysis Using Refined Lifestyles Measures," *Criminology* 36, no. 4 (1998): 829–858;

E. E. Mustaine and R. Tewksbury, "A Routine Activity Theory Explanation for Women's Stalking Victimizations," *Violence Against Women* 5, no. 1 (1999): 43–62; R. Tewksbury and E. E. Mustaine, "College Students' Lifestyles and Self-Protective Behaviors: Further Considerations of the Guardianship Concept in Routine Activity Theory," *Criminal Justice and Behavior* 30, no. 3 (2003): 302–327; van Wilsem, "Worlds Tied Together?" 115–127; van Wilsem, "'Bought It, But Never Got It,'" 168–178.

130. Choi, "Computer Crime Victimization and Integrated Theory," 308–333; D. Denning, *Information Warfare and Security* (New York: Addison-Wesley, 1999), 353–369; Vakhitova and Reynald, "Australian Internet Users and Guardianship against Cyber Abuse," 159; Hutchings and Hayes, "Routine Activity Theory and Phishing Victimization," 433–451; Marcum, "Identifying Potential Factors of Adolescent Online Victimization," 346–367; Navarro and Jasinski, "Going Cyber," 81–94.

131. Marcum, "Identifying Potential Factors of Adolescent Online Victimization," 346–367; Ngo and Paternoster, "Cybercrime Victimization," 777.

132. Ngo and Paternoster, "Cybercrime Victimization," 773–793; Reyns et al., "Being Pursued Online," 1149–1169.

133. P. Grabosky and R. Smith, "Telecommunication Fraud in the Digital Age: The Convergence of Technologies," in *Crime and the Internet*, ed. D. Wall (London: Routledge, 2001).

134. Choi, "Computer Crime Victimization and Integrated Theory," 308–333.

135. P. Storm and R. Storm, "Cyberbullying by Adolescents: A Preliminary Assessment," *The Educational Forum* 70, no. 1 (2005): 21–36; Wolak et al., "Online Victimization of Youth."

136. Navarro and Jasinski, "Going Cyber," 81–94.

137. Williams, "Guardians Upon High," 1–28.

138. M. Felson, "Those Who Discourage Crime," in *Crime and Place*, ed. J. E. Eck and D. Weisburd (Monsey, NY: Criminal Justice Press, 1995), 53–66.

139. S. E. Wolfe, C. D. Marcum, G. E. Higgins, and M. L. Ricketts, "Routine Cell Phone Activity and Exposure to Sext Messages: Extending the Generality of Routine Activity Theory and Exploring the Etiology of a Risky Teenage Behavior," *Crime & Delinquency* (published online, July 15, 2014), 9.

140. Vakhitova and Reynald, "Australian Internet Users and Guardianship against Cyber Abuse," 159.

141. A. Lenhart, *Teens and Sexting: How and Why Minor Teens are Sending Sexually Suggestive Nude or Nearly Nude Images via Text Messages* (Washington, DC: Pew Internet & American Life Project, 2009), http://www.pewinternet.org/2009/12/15/teens-and-sexting/?beta=true&utm_expid=53098246-2.Lly4CFSVQG2lphsg-KopIg.1&utm_referrer=https%3A%2F%2Fwww.google.com; K. Martinez-Prather and F. M. Vandiver, "Sexting among Teenagers in the United States: A Retrospective Analysis of Identifying Motivating Factors, Potential Targets, and the Role of a Capable Guardian," *International Journal of Cyber Criminology* 8, no. 1 (2014): 26.

142. S. Webster, J. Davidson, and P. Gottschalk, "Understanding Online Grooming: Findings from the EOGP Study," in S. Webster, J. Davidson, and A. Bifulco, *Online Offending Behavior and Child Victimization: New Findings and Policy* (New York: Palgrave-Macmillan, 2015), 60.

143. Wolfe et al., "Routine Cell Phone Activity and Exposure to Sext Messages."

144. Reyns et al., "Being Pursued Online," 1149–1169.

145. Williams, "Guardians Upon High," 1–28.

146. ENISA, *National Cyber Security Strategies: Setting the Course for National Efforts to Strengthen Security in Cyberspace* (European Union Agency for Network and Information Security, 2012); ENISA, *National Cyber Security Strategies: Practical Guide on Development and Execution* (European Union Agency for Network and Information Security, 2012); Home Office (UK),

New Campaign Urges People to be "Cyber Streetwise," January 13, 2014, https://www.gov.uk /government/news/new-campaign-urges-people-to-be-cyber-streetwise; Williams, "Guardians Upon High," 1–28.

147. Reyns and Henson, "The Thief with a Thousand Faces and the Victim with None."

148. Williams, "Guardians Upon High," 1–28.

149. N. Christie, "The Ideal Victim," in *From Crime Policy to Victim Policy*, ed. E. Fattah (Basingstoke, UK: Macmillan, 1986), 18.

150. Christie, "The Ideal Victim," in Fattah, *From Crime Policy to Victim Policy*, 18–19.

151. J. Dignan, *Understanding Victims and Restorative Justice* (Berkshire, UK: Open University Press, 2005), 17.

PART 2

CYBERCRIME CAUSATION AND REDUCTION

In this part, each chapter is devoted to discussing significant theories and perspectives of criminology and how they relate to specific cybercrimes.

CHAPTER 4

CYBERCRIME, RATIONAL CHOICE, AND EMOTIONS
Punishment and Reduction of Cyberoffending

KEYWORDS

Absolute deterrence
Attribution
Capital punishment
Chain of custody
Classical school of
    criminology
Club good
Cyberdeterrence
Deserts-based theory
Displacement
Economic theory of crime

Encryption
General deterrence
Incapacitation
Instrumental rationality
Letters rogatory
Mutual legal assistance
    treaties
Private good
Procedural rationality
Punishment
Rational choice theory

Rehabilitation
Restorative justice
Restrictive deterrence
Retribution
Rules of evidence
Situational crime
    prevention
Specific deterrence
Target hardening
Utilitarianism

The Gozi virus infected over one million computers and resulted in millions of dollars in damages worldwide. The virus was distributed through a PDF document via e-mail.[1] When the user opened the PDF, the malicious software was designed to surreptitiously download onto the user's machine and steal bank account numbers, usernames, and passwords.[2] Hackers subsequently used this information to steal money from the victim's bank accounts. The investigation and prosecution of the cybercriminals responsible for the creation and distribution of the Gozi virus involved a multitude of countries, including Germany, the United States, the United Kingdom, Finland, Romania, the Netherlands, Switzerland, Latvia, and Moldova.[3]

Cases such as this one illustrate the reality of cybercrime: it transcends borders and often involves more than one jurisdiction. This chapter explores the investigation of cybercrimes that span multiple countries, looking in particular at jurisdiction issues, cybercrime laws, and the enforcement of cybercrime laws. The chapter further examines the various types of punishments for cybercriminals, as well as the measures in place and those needed to reduce cybercrime. Preceding this examination, the chapter considers theories explaining cybercrime as a rational choice and the role of emotions in motivating cyberoffending.

THE REASONING CYBERCRIMINAL

Some theorists hold that criminals engage in crime in response to opportunities that are presented to them and their ability to take part in them.[4] Thus, individuals engage in crime because *they want to* and *they can*. By way of extension, cybercrime here is viewed as an outcome of rational thought and opportunity. The view of crime as a rational choice is originally attributed to the **classical school of criminology**. The emphasis of the classical school is on the criminal—a person capable of calculating what he or she wants to do. The classical school of criminology includes the work of Cesare Beccaria and Jeremy Bentham. Beccaria viewed individuals as self-determining, hedonistic, intelligent, and rational beings.[5] First, people had free will to engage in actions of their choice (*self-determining*). Here, human beings are viewed as free to choose from a wide variety of behaviors the attractiveness of which depend on the person. Free will is what enables a human being to make a deliberate choice to engage in an act from various available courses of action. Second, individuals' main purpose in life is to achieve pleasure or happiness and avoid pain (*hedonism*). A similar argument was presented by Bentham: "Nature has placed mankind under the governance of two sovereign masters, pain and pleasure. It is for them alone to point out what . . . [humans] ought to do, as well as to determine what . . . [humans] shall do."[6] Choice is, therefore, driven by behaviors that seek to maximize pleasure and minimize pain. Third, Beccaria viewed human beings as capable of creative thought (*intelligent*). Finally, he viewed people as capable of logical thought (*rational*).

Beccaria believed that rational, hedonistic individuals make choices based on a pain-pleasure analysis,[7] also known as, a cost-benefit analysis. This concept is attributed to the ancient Greek philosopher Epicurus, who performed such an analysis to determine the amount of pain and pleasure resulting from an act. Bentham employed mathematical modeling in his analysis of criminal behavior, arguing that criminals were rational actors engaging in a cost-benefit analysis before committing a crime.[8] This first presupposes that the criminal is a rational actor who engages in a cost-benefit analysis in order to determine if he or she will commit a crime (**rational choice theory**).[9] This weighing (which may occur in a split second) considers the benefits and costs of a crime. If the benefits outweigh the costs, the criminal commits the crime. Rational choice theory is derived from the **economic theory of crime** proposed by Gary Becker. Becker equated crime to an outcome of expected utility theory (i.e., an individual's preferences among choices with uncertain outcomes).[10] According to Becker, a person will commit a crime if the expected utility (gain) of the illicit act exceeds the utility received by refraining from the conduct or engaging in other actions.[11] The utility value of an action (which is subjective and depends on an individual's perspective) influences an individual's decision to commit a crime.

Rational choice theory has been supported by studies on offline crime, such as theft, sexual assault, and terrorism.[12] What about online illicit behavior? Cybercriminals are believed to engage in the same cost-benefit analysis. Hackers' behaviors, for example, can be explained by expected utility theory. Specifically, a hacker will choose to engage in an action that provides the highest expected utility at a low cost; such a choice is made after consideration of the risks.[13] Indeed, cybercriminals consider the costs and benefits of committing a cybercrime before taking action. The costs associated with cybercrime are failure, detection by authorities, arrest by authorities, and ultimately prosecution and punishment. The benefits of cybercrime depend on the cybercriminal and include monetary rewards, thrill, enjoyment, and revenge.[14] For instance, hackers may even engage in the act to gain a reputation and be treated like a celebrity.[15] In Russia, "successful Russian hackers are often viewed with pride and respect for their ability to live well by tricking wealthy foreigners."[16] The value of an act is determined by an individual's perception of the gain from that act.[17] This decision to commit a cybercrime is also shaped by the value of the act, perceived need of the perpetrator, and the immediacy of the perceived need. Cybercriminals will take advantage of the opportunities that are present to satisfy their needs and further their goals. In the end, cybercriminals seek to maximize the benefits of the illicit acts while minimizing the failure and effort needed to successfully engage in their illicit activities. Accordingly, when faced with these benefits and costs, a cybercriminal would most likely engage in cybercrime if the benefits of committing the illicit act outweigh its costs.

Cybercrime is thus a product of strategic choice, whereby cybercriminals plan their illicit acts and make logical choices in order for their illegal actions to be successful. The choice to engage in cybercrime is made no matter how rudimentary the process was to reach that conclusion. This process shows the rationality of a cybercriminal. This process is also limited by the constraints of available information. What often occurs is not what Frank Zagare termed **procedural rationality**, whereby the actor makes a "clear, cool-headed ends-means calculation after considering all possible courses of action and carefully weighing the pros and cons of each of them."[18] Instead, the cybercriminal often compares options based on their availability (e.g., by the ease with which they come to mind) and chooses the one that will produce the highest utility (**instrumental rationality**). Ultimately, a rational cybercriminal is one that pursues identifiable goals, connects the actions he or she takes pursuant to these goals, and decides whether to take the actions based on costs and benefits of these acts and their probability for success.

SEDUCTIONS AND REPULSIONS OF CYBERCRIME

Opponents of rational choice theory have three main arguments. First, they claim that certain individuals do not have a choice when engaging in illicit acts, while others argue that when a person chooses to commit a crime, it is not based on a rational calculation.[19] Second, they do not believe that rational choice theory explains irrational behavior. The reality is that this theory cannot explain all forms of criminal behavior, especially illicit acts committed by irrational offenders (e.g., those under the influence of alcohol and drugs). Third, opponents believe that rational choice theory disregards emotions in the decision-making process.[20]

Consider this third reason in depth. Theorists such as Jack Katz are concerned that rational choice theory disregards the role of emotions in an offender's decision to commit a crime, and overemphasizes rationality in criminal activity.[21] For Katz, emotions should be considered in crime causation models.[22] He has further argued that individuals would not engage in crime if they rationally considered the benefits and costs of the crime. The belief here is that lures and pressures are what push individuals to commit crimes, which according to Katz do not factor into cost-benefit calculation.[23] Specifically, benefits, such as thrills and excitement, and costs, such as shame, anxiety, and guilt, do not factor in rational decision-making. In reality, human behavior is governed not only by rational decision-making but by emotions as well. Indeed, emotions influence thinking and behavior and thus play a role in rational decision-making.

Despite the fact that "the economic model of crime does not fit the opportunistic and reckless nature of much crime and irrationality of offenders,"[24] this theory can be used to explain certain forms of cybercrime. Rational actors are propelled by pain and pleasure evaluations—pleasure involves emotional rewards as opposed to tangible and intangible rewards. Indeed, the emotion one gets from committing a particular activity may be considered a benefit (*seduction of cybercrime*).[25] An infamous hacker (now security consultant), Kevin Mitnick, reported, "When I was a hacker my motivation was curiosity, pursuit of knowledge and seduction of adventure."[26] The Bling Ring (mentioned in Chapter 3) also engaged in burglaries primarily for the thrill of it (and not for profit).[27] What is more, writers of computer viruses have reported the thrill of their work appearing in the news and antivirus companies' websites as a motive for engaging in this illicit behavior.[28] The emotions one gets when either attempting to or engaging in a criminal activity could also be considered a cost (*repulsion of cybercrime*). For example, a person may feel guilty or ashamed for his or her actions. Research has shown that feelings of guilt have been reported by digital pirates (i.e., those who engage in the illegal online trade in books, software, videos, and music); despite these feelings, they decided to engage in acts of digital piracy because the rewards of the activity far outweighed its costs.[29]

If emotions are considered during an individual's decision-making process, these will either reduce or increase the likelihood that a crime will be committed. This will depend on the emotion exhibited and its influence on the individual. Accordingly, emotions and rational thought are not mutually exclusive; an individual influenced by emotion is still capable of rational thought.[30] Neuroscience research has supported this by revealing that emotions subtly influence rational thought.[31] Research has also shown that emotions have served as a metric by which individuals judge the desirability or attractiveness of a particular act.[32]

PUNISHING CYBERCRIMINALS

Cybercriminals' actions offend the moral order; as such, cybercriminals are required to pay for this disruption. This payment is rendered pursuant to punishment. **Punishment** can be defined as "the legal process whereby violators of criminal law are condemned and sanctioned in accordance with specified legal categories and procedures."[33] Accordingly, punishment is the penalty imposed on an individual (e.g., a cybercriminal) by the criminal justice system for an offense committed (e.g., a cybercrime). Punishment can be imprisonment, fines, and/or community service. If punishment was represented by a deity, that deity would be Janus. Janus was a Roman deity who was believed to have two faces, one that looked into the past and the other into the future. Like Janus, punishment can be backward looking (past oriented) and forward looking (future oriented). These directions are represented by the retributive perspective and the utilitarian perspective.

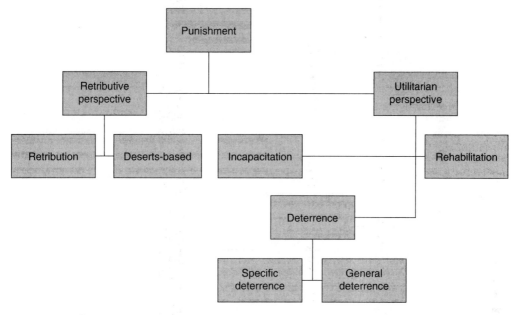

FIGURE 4-1   Perspectives on Punishment.

RETRIBUTIVE PERSPECTIVE

Retrospective forms of punishment are applied after the offending behavior has occurred and are thus provided to the offenders to deal with past illicit activities. **Retribution** (a retrospective punishment) seeks to inflict harm or deprivation on the offender for the harm or deprivation inflicted on the victim. Aristotle was the first to argue that punishment was a warranted repercussion for an offense committed. Similarly, Immanuel Kant believed that people who engage in wrongdoing deserve to be punished; in this manner, society is paying them back (i.e., exacting retribution) for their wrongdoing.[34] Punishment, therefore, occurs because a criminal deserves it. As a result, justice is achieved through punishment of the offense. The criminal justice system aims at punishing the offender, and in so doing, "righting" the "wrongs" committed against the state. For these reasons, the end sought by retributivists is not another goal (e.g., to prevent a future crime) but punishment itself.

Cybercriminals Getting Their "Just Deserts"

Historically, retribution was justified on the principle of *lex talionis:* the punishment of the offender should be equal to the harm caused to the victim.[35] Put simply, the punishment should fit the crime. Issues of proportionality arise in the retributive philosophy of punishment in **deserts-based theory**. According to this theory, "punishment is justified as the only appropriate response to crime: those who commit offenses deserve punishment, it is claimed, and the amount of punishment should be proportionate to the degree of wrongdoing."[36] Deserts-based punishment also views "the offender as a moral agent, . . . having the capacity to evaluate and . . . respond to an official evaluation of [his or her] conduct. This evaluation is communicated by imposing a proportionate sentence, and not any greater sentence that punishes the offender in order to achieve a preventive goal."[37] In view of that, a sentence given is aimed at proportionately punishing an offender for wrongdoing and communicating denunciation for the offense.

UTILITARIAN PERSPECTIVE

The other perspective of punishment—utilitarian—is of course forward looking. This perspective is derived from utilitarian philosophy. **Utilitarianism**, a form of consequentialism, holds that justice is best served by taking action that brings about the best possible outcomes and looks only at the consequences of actions (the end result). For utilitarians, punishment is a means to an end. The end seeks to protect society in some way by incapacitating an offender (this prevents the person from reoffending); reforming the offender (to prevent the person from wanting to engage in future criminal conduct); deterring the punished offender; and deterring others from engaging in future criminal activity. Utilitarian thinking holds that the goal of punishment is to prevent something (i.e., criminal conduct) in the future. The aim of such punishment, therefore, should not be retrospective; that is, the purpose of punishment is not to undo past harm.[38] Instead, it should seek to prevent future harm, which can be accomplished through incapacitation, rehabilitation, and deterrence.[39] Ultimately, utilitarians seek to create a better society, with punishments ranging from temporary solutions (incapacitation) to long-term solutions (rehabilitation, deterrence).

Incapacitation and Rehabilitation

Incapacitation incarcerates an offender to prevent them from reoffending against the public for a finite period. The behavior of the offender is not targeted by any services in the form of rehabilitation. Given that incarceration protects the public from the offender during his or her term of imprisonment, what happens if this offender is released? Incapacitation without any rehabilitation program serves only as a temporary solution if the criminals are released back into society after their sentence is completed. Consider a career cybercriminal. If this individual serves a sentence after which he or she is subsequently released back into the community, what prevents the individual from reoffending? To prevent cybercriminals from conducting future cybercrimes, rehabilitation is required.

Punishment such as **rehabilitation** is designed to reform the criminal. This form of punishment, therefore, fits the criminal and not the illicit act. Rehabilitation focuses on changing the mindset and behavior of an offender in an effort to prevent the person from reoffending. When applied to a cybercriminal, rehabilitation seeks to change those aspects of the cybercriminal's traits, views, and lifestyle that predisposed the offender to cybercrime and to provide the offender with the necessary knowledge, abilities, and skills to desist from engaging in cybercrime. Rehabilitative programs that target cybercriminals show them that their actions are immoral and violate legal and social norms (see Chapter 5). Accordingly, what is imposed on an individual is designed to change the perception and behaviors of the person concerning the offense. After fulfilling the requirements of his or her rehabilitative punishment, the offender does not engage further in offending because he or she has been reformed and now views that behavior as "wrong." This should not be confused with desistance from crime, which is merely the process of abstaining from future criminal behavior. Rehabilitation programs for cybercriminals should be used in conjunction with and not in lieu of incapacitation.

BOX 4-1 PUNISHING CYBERTHEFT OF VIRTUAL GOODS

In the "Zarnecki Incursion" episode of *The Big Bang Theory* (season 4, episode 19, aired March 31, 2011), one of the main characters, Dr. Sheldon Cooper, contacts the police for a cybertheft that has occurred. His roommate, Dr. Leonard Hofstadter, enters the apartment and finds Sheldon with a police officer:

POLICEMAN: Here. Breathe into this bag.

LEONARD: What's going on?

SHELDON: They stole everything, Leonard, everything.

POLICEMAN: Are you the roommate?

LEONARD: Yeah, Leonard Hofstadter. What happened?

POLICEMAN: Your friend here called 911 to report a robbery.

LEONARD: Oh, my God, what did they get?

SHELDON: What didn't they get? They got my enchanted weapons, my vicious gladiator armor, my wand of untainted power, and all my gold.

LEONARD: You called the police because someone hacked your *World of Warcraft* account?

SHELDON: What choice did I have? The mighty Sheldor, level 85 blood elf, hero of the Eastern kingdoms, has been picked clean, like a carcass in the desert sun. Plus, the FBI hung up on me.

POLICEMAN: Into the bag.

SHELDON: They took my battle ostrich.

LEONARD: Oh, no, not Glenn?

SHELDON: Yes, Glenn! The only bird I ever loved.

POLICEMAN: Good luck, fellas.

LEONARD: Thank you, officer.

SHELDON: Wait a minute! You're not going to do anything?

POLICEMAN: Mr. Cooper, there's nothing . . .

SHELDON: Doctor Cooper.

POLICEMAN: Seriously?

LEONARD: Not the kind with access to drugs.

POLICEMAN: Fine. Dr. Cooper. I'm sorry for your loss, but the Pasadena Police Department doesn't have jurisdiction in Pandora.

SHELDON: That's from *Avatar*, *World of Warcraft* takes place in Azeroth. Goodness gracious, how are you allowed to carry a gun?

As in the above scenario, the theft of virtual goods may occur through hacking. This type of theft can also occur through deceit. A person may be tricked into leaving items unattended by offering to trade with the victim in the virtual world. The perpetrator takes the items left by the victim and does not trade anything in return. Those with virtual goods may also be subjected to phishing scams designed by perpetrators seeking to gain access to a player's account. The phishing e-mail sent to the player informs the player that he or she had their account suspended due to unusual activity and must click on the link in the

e-mail to restore access to their account. The link is designed to surreptitiously record any data the issuer inputs or downloads malware onto the user's digital device. In all but the instances of theft by deceit (where the user violates end-user license agreements), the perpetrator has not committed cybertheft but unauthorized access to an account or digital device. In reality, cases such as these involve cybertheft of property (albeit intangible property); however, this is not what perpetrators are charged with when they commit this cybercrime. These cases often center on unauthorized access charges and only if the theft occurs in this manner. For example, in the United States, two players pled guilty to using a remote access tool to gain unauthorized access to other players' accounts and stealing their virtual items and gold. These items and gold were collected by the perpetrators' avatars.[40] Their intention was to sell the items and gold for money at an in-game auction house, but they were kicked out of the auction house before they were able to do so.

The aforementioned script from *The Big Bang Theory* also illustrates an important concern: Who do you call when theft of virtual property occurs? And what can be done in such instances? Often the handling of virtual goods theft is left to the gaming companies and is pursued if end-user license agreements have been violated. End-user license agreements set the rules of the game, delineating what is considered appropriate conduct in the game. Victims of virtual goods theft have contacted the FBI. The FBI tends to pursue cases that span more than one jurisdiction; however, this is not always the case. The reality is that there are few cases that have been pursued by the FBI involving virtual goods theft; this is due in large part to lack of understanding or unwillingness to deal with this form of cybercrime and lack of clarity as to how to proceed with these cases in the criminal justice system. The lack of clarity on how to handle these cases results in limited prosecutions of perpetrators for their crimes, sending the message that this is a high reward and low risk cybercrime.

Some countries have provided this clarity. Virtual goods theft has not been equated to property theft, with one exception. In the Netherlands, an individual was physically assaulted and threatened with serious bodily harm at knifepoint with the intention of getting the person to hand over virtual items from a game called *RuneScape* to the perpetrators.[41] The issue at hand in this case was not the assault, but whether or not the perpetrators stole property. The lawyers for the perpetrators argued that the virtual items were not property because they were intangible and of no commercial value.[42] The Dutch court disagreed, holding that virtual items have intrinsic value due to the time and energy a user invests in acquiring these items and extrinsic value because these items are of great economic value on the market and can be purchased for money.[43] Virtual goods are also considered property because the game grants users rights over the items.[44]

Companies of virtual reality games usually own the content created by users.[45] This ownership is communicated to

(continued)

players through the end-user license agreements that the players must agree to in order to play the games. Despite these agreements, users believe that ownership of such items exists; this may well explain why certain virtual goods are sold for outrageous prices (e.g., a virtual resort was purchased for $635,000).[46] LindenLab, which created *Second Life* (a virtual reality game), sought to differentiate itself from other gaming companies by recognizing virtual property rights of users, that is, "recogniz[ing] participants' full intellectual property protection for the digital content they created or otherwise owned in Second Life."[47] *RuneScape* also provided its users with ownership of content. Nonetheless, this is not the norm, and in many countries theft of virtual goods is not treated like theft of property.

Deterrence

Deterrence is a form of punishment that seeks to discourage future offending. Bentham described the process of deterrence as follows:

> Pain and pleasure are the great springs of human action. When a man perceives or supposes pain to be the consequence of an act, he is acted upon in such manner as tends, with a certain force, to withdraw him, as it were, from the commission of that act. If the apparent magnitude . . . of that pain be greater than the apparent magnitude . . . of the pleasure . . . he expects to be the consequence of that act, he will be absolutely prevented from performing it.[48]

This illustrates two important goals of this form of punishment: to "control action"[49] and to attain "general prevention."[50]

Beccaria argued that the principal aim of deterrence is "nothing other than to prevent the offender from doing fresh harm to his fellows and to deter others from doing likewise."[51] Here, Beccaria is referring to two types of deterrence: specific and general deterrence. **Specific deterrence** seeks to dissuade a perpetrator of a crime from reoffending in the future. By contrast, **general deterrence** is a form of punishment of criminals that seeks to send a message to the public that perpetrators will be punished for their crimes, in an effort to dissuade them from engaging in illicit activity. Other forms of deterrence have also been proposed: for example, absolute and restrictive deterrence. **Absolute deterrence** refers to the ability of the threat of punishment to prevent an individual from engaging in crime, whereas **restrictive deterrence** is targeted at those who have offended in the past. This type of deterrence is designed to minimize the likelihood of reoffending.[52]

Cyberdeterrence seeks to discourage engagement in cybercrime. Online warning messages about illegal activity are a form of cyberdeterrence.[53] For cyberdeterrence to work, three elements are required: severity, swiftness, and certainty of punishment. The first element, *severity of punishment*, requires that the penalty for committing cybercrime be sufficient enough to dissuade someone from committing that activity. The severity of punishment refers to the magnitude of the penalty that could be given to the perpetrator if convicted of the crime. U.S. laws have increased penalties for cybercrimes. For example, the Uniting and Strengthening America by Providing Appropriate Tools Required to Intercept and Obstruct Terrorism (USA Patriot) Act of 2001 and Cyber Security Enhancement Act of 2002, which is part of the Homeland Security Act of 2002, provided severe penalties for certain cybercrimes, such as twenty years and even life imprisonment, depending on the cybercrime and its consequences. Additionally, the Foreign Economic Espionage Penalty Enhancement Act of 2012 increased the penalty for those engaging in economic espionage (cyber or otherwise) for the benefit of a foreign government. In other countries—for instance, Pakistan—certain cybercriminals who cause death as a result of their actions can be given **capital punishment** (i.e., the deliberate killing of the offender by the state for a criminal offense the offender has been convicted of in a court of law) under the Prevention of Electronic Crimes Ordinance of 2007.

Not all cybercrimes, however, carry a severe penalty. Matjaz Skorjanc, the creator of malware which infected 12.7 million computers and caused significant damage worldwide, received only a 58-month sentence in Slovenia, a 4,000-euro fine, and a court order to surrender an apartment and car he bought with the criminal proceeds.[54] Cases like these are by no means unique. Notwithstanding, the severity of punishment is subjective; as such, it depends on the view and beliefs of the perpetrator.

The second element of cyberdeterrence, *swiftness of punishment*, requires that punishment be meted out shortly after the cybercrime is committed and that this punishment be visible to the public. Swiftness in punishment helps the cybercriminal connect the illicit act to the punishment received. The longer the period between the cybercrime and the punishment the cybercriminal receives, the weaker this connection will be.

Although severity and swiftness in punishment are important elements in cyberdeterrence, the most important element is the last one, *certainty of punishment*. The certainty of punishment refers to the likelihood of being arrested and given a penalty for an illicit act. In the case of digital piracy, individuals who perceive the risk of being identified by law enforcement agencies as high reduce the frequency with which they engage in the conduct.[55] In the case of hacking, hackers usually view the probability of getting caught as low.[56] Kshetri explains that hackers believe that there is a low risk of detection because law enforcement agencies do not have the necessary knowledge, skills, and abilities to detect and investigate them; targets are reluctant to report incidents to law enforcement due to embarrassment or lack of confidence in the ability of the police to help; and the offenders' knowledge, skills, and abilities enable them to evade detection and capture by authorities.[57] The same holds true for those who engage in identity theft. Identity thieves view the risk of being prosecuted for this crime as low: "Identity thieves claimed that they had developed a portfolio of skills that allowed them to appropriate funds and to avoid unwanted attention successfully. By relying on their skills—including enhanced social skills, intuition, and technical knowledge—they believed they could stay one step ahead of the law."[58] Likewise, those engaging in online fraud believe that while the benefits associated with engaging in this crime are high, the risks associated with it are low.[59]

Attribution is needed for this last element of cyberdeterrence.[60] Attribution refers to the process of identifying a perpetrator of a cybercrime and/or the location from which a cybercrime was committed. While cybertrails can be followed to determine the system from which an attack occurred, the person behind the attack cannot be determined with absolute certainty. Nonetheless, attribution may not deter a cybercriminal. For example, rather than being deterred, a hacker who is rational and understands the attribution process from both legal and technical standpoints may take actions that are designed to evade detection.[61]

The certainty element requires that cybercriminals be punished each time they commit an illicit online activity. This way, cybercriminals know that if they commit a cybercrime, they will inevitably be punished. Unfortunately, this is not currently the situation. Many cases of cybercrime go unpunished due to lack of attribution, financial and human resources, and cooperation among nations. Offenders who commit certain fraud crimes, such as spammers, phishers, and identity thieves, and certain personal crimes, like cyberbullying, cyberharassment, and cyberstalking, largely go unpunished for their crimes. This trend is by no means unique to these cybercrimes and actually can be seen with all forms of cybercrimes (with a few exceptions). For instance, those responsible for malware creation and distribution often go unpunished.[62]

BOX 4-2 IN THE EVENT OF A CYBERCRIME, WHOM ARE YOU GOING TO CALL?

In the United States, law enforcement agencies tend to focus on cybercrimes that are amenable to the methods used to police offline crimes. Also, the illicit activities that serve as the focus for police are those in which the computer and other digital devices are incidental to the crime. This excludes cybercrimes, which are only possible because of the Internet, computers, and related technology. Accordingly, a victim may be able to file a police report for cybercrime, and at worst, the victim may be turned away or told that the crime is beyond the jurisdiction of the police. To assist users in contacting the right agency, the Computer Crime and Intellectual Property Section of the Department of Justice includes information on which federal agencies to contact to report particular cybercrimes (see Table 4-1)

Table 4-1 Federal Agencies to Contact to Report Particular Cybercrimes

Cybercrime	Federal Agency to Report To
Child exploitation and Internet fraud matters that have a mail nexus	• U.S. Postal Inspection Service • Internet Crime Complaint Center
Child pornography or exploitation	• FBI local office • Internet Crime Complaint Center • U.S. Immigration and Customs Enforcement (if imported)
Counterfeiting of currency	• U.S. Secret Service
Digital piracy	• FBI local office • U.S. Immigration and Customs Enforcement (ICE) • Internet Crime Complaint Center
Hacking	• FBI local office • U.S. Secret Service • Internet Crime Complaint Center
Internet bomb threats	• FBI local office • ATF local office
Internet fraud and SPAM	• FBI local office • U.S. Secret Service • Federal Trade Commission • Securities and Exchange Commission (if securities fraud or investment-related SPAM e-mails) • Internet Crime Complaint Center
Internet harassment	• FBI local office
Password trafficking	• FBI local office • U.S. Secret Service • Internet Crime Complaint Center
Theft of trade secrets/Economic espionage	• FBI local office
Trademark counterfeiting	• FBI local office • U.S. Immigration and Customs Enforcement • Internet Crime Complaint Center
Trafficking in explosive or incendiary devices or firearms over the Internet	• FBI local office • ATF local office

Source: Computer Crime and Intellectual Property Section, Department of Justice, "Reporting Computer, Internet-Related, or Intellectual Property Crime," December 14, 2015, http://www.justice.gov/criminal-ccips/reporting-computer-internet-related-or-intellectual-property-crime.

(continued)

Other countries have law enforcement agencies that investigate cybercrime, such as the UK Serious Organised Crime Agency, the Royal Canadian Mounted Police, and the Australian Federal Police. Internationally, there are several law enforcement agencies that investigate cybercrime. INTERPOL, an international law enforcement agency that investigates international crimes and has powers of arrest, works with national law enforcement to detect and arrest cybercriminals. The United Nations Office on Drugs and Crime also assists countries with cybercrime investigations. Furthermore, the G8, which is made up of the United Kingdom, France, Germany, Italy, the United States, Canada, Japan, and Russia, created the G8 Subgroup on High-Tech Crime to help the G8 countries prevent cybercrime, and investigate and prosecute cybercriminals.[63]

REDUCING CYBERCRIME

The punishment of cybercriminals can work toward reducing cybercrime. Yet, in order for this to occur, the harmonization of cybercrime laws and the effective enforcement of these laws are required.

CYBERCRIME LAWS

Nationally, the United States has a primary cybercrime law, the Computer Fraud and Abuse Act of 1986, which has been amended over the years. Other laws are also in place dealing with crimes that are not traditionally perpetrated online (e.g., harassment and identity theft). Regional and multilateral cybercrime and cybersecurity conventions and agreements have been implemented as well, including the African Union[64] Convention on the Confidence and Security in Cyberspace of 2014; the Arab League's[65] Arab Convention on Combating Information Technology Offences of 2010; the Shanghai Cooperation Organization[66] Agreement on Cooperation in the Field of Information Security of 2009; the Commonwealth of Independent States[67] Agreement on Cooperation in Combating Offences related to Computer Information of 2001; and the Convention on Cybercrime of 2001 that applies only to its signatories, which include members of the Council of Europe and some countries outside of the Council of Europe (e.g., Canada and Japan).[68] The Convention on Cybercrime is also limited to certain types of cybercrimes: child pornography; crimes against the confidentiality, integrity, and availability of data and systems; fraud and forgery; and intellectual property theft.[69]

CYBERCRIME ENFORCEMENT

Countries sometimes work together when international crimes occur. This collaboration depends on *dual criminality*; that is, an act must be considered illegal in both countries in order for cooperation to occur. Accordingly, if the perpetrator lives in a country that does not have a cybercrime law, he or she cannot be punished for engaging in such an act. Moreover, international cybercrime investigations frequently suffer from lack of cooperation of other countries due to insufficient funds to deal with requests to cooperate and lack of qualified personnel to help in the investigations.

Cases such as the Gozi virus illustrate not only the importance of cooperation and collaboration between nations but also the need to harmonize existing cybercrime laws and cyberspace policies. This does not mean that universal policies are sought. Such an exercise is met with cultural, social, legal, and economic obstacles that make implementing these policies extremely difficult.[70] Indeed, many countries do not have the financial resources to enforce policies, and nations differ significantly in their cultures and views on social issues, which influence policy. Moreover, countries have different legal traditions, making acceptance of one policy by all unattainable. What is being argued is that a unified and structured response to cybercrime is possible and could be achieved through harmonization of cybercrime laws between countries and effective enforcement of these laws.

Harmonization of cybercrime laws can lead to elimination of cybercrime safe havens. Because of the universal reach of cybercrime, countries can effectively investigate and prosecute cybercrimes only if all countries involved in the illicit act have adequate cybercrime laws. The I LOVE YOU computer virus illustrated the need for domestic cybercrime laws in cases that traverse borders. In this case, Onel de Guzman, a resident of the Philippines, created and released this virus, causing billions of dollars in damages in the United States, Asia, and Europe.[71] De Guzman was not prosecuted for his crime because at the time what he did was not considered a crime in his country. While his actions were considered illegal in other countries, he could not be prosecuted in the Philippines nor extradited to another country for prosecution, because his country did not have a cybercrime law in effect that prohibited his behavior.

Harmonization of cybercrime laws makes the prosecution of cybercriminals possible. It is also needed for enforcement of **mutual legal assistance treaties**, which are agreements between countries that dictate the type of assistance to be provided by each nation in criminal investigations (e.g., with respect to evidence and resources) and requests for extradition of cybercriminals.[72] Variation in national cybercrime legislation, absence of mutual legal assistance treaties, and resistance to cooperation between nations has made the investigation and prosecution of cybercriminals particularly challenging.

Apart from harmonization of laws, what nations require is consistent enforcement of these laws. Enforcement of cybercrime laws can serve as a deterrent to crime. While there are laws and treaties that enable certain countries to work together, this is not enough, especially in light of enforcement issues. The reality is that there is a need for better enforcement of existing regulations targeting cybercriminals.

Regardless of the existence of these laws and treaties, international cooperation in cybercrime investigations is further complicated by divergence in countries' membership in bilateral, regional, and multilateral cybercrime and cybersecurity agreements and conventions. Even countries that have these agreements and conventions are not without problems. For instance, there is no time requirement when cooperative requests are made. Response times for information-sharing can take months, not days; this unnecessarily impedes cybercrime investigations and prosecution of cybercriminals. Notwithstanding, urgent channels for responding to mutual legal assistance requests exist in certain countries. Another issue that adversely affects response times in cybercrime investigations is cybercrime's relative importance with respect to other crimes (e.g., murder), which varies by country. Moreover, even between different types of cybercrimes, priority is assigned (e.g., online child pornography is accorded greater importance than fraud). Delays in requests for information also exist because the data sought may have to be translated. This may not only delay the investigation but also requires an investment in financial resources. Many countries may not be able to afford these expenses, especially developing countries that are inundated with other transnational security issues that take precedence, such as water and food insecurity.[73]

To obtain cybercrime evidence, formal and informal information-sharing procedures can be used. For formal procedures, **letters rogatory** can be used. Judges from the United

States can request evidence through these letters, which are drafted by the U.S. Attorney's Office and include information about the case, a description of the evidence needed and why it is needed, and a promise for reciprocity in future cases.[74] Another way to obtain evidence from a foreign country is through a mutual legal assistance treaty, which defines the parameters of cooperation between countries in specific criminal matters and dictates the formal procedure to be followed when making requests of parties to the treaty.

The informal information-sharing process involves police-to-police cooperation. Although informal channels are faster for retrieving information than formal channels, the evidence obtained may be inadmissible in a court of law because a **chain of custody** is not maintained. The chain of custody provides detailed information about who obtained the evidence, when and where the evidence was obtained, how it was obtained, and anyone who accessed the evidence and for what reasons it was accessed.[75] This evidence may also be inadmissible because **rules of evidence** differ between countries (even in countries with similar legal traditions). Because of this, formal channels, while slower, are preferred.

A final barrier to enforcement of cybercrime laws is lack of national capacity. Some countries do not have the necessary human, technical, and financial resources to conduct cybercrime investigations. This deficit in national capacity, observed in countries around the globe, was revealed in a 2013 United Nations Office on Drugs and Crime (UNODC) report.[76] The report revealed that countries were unable to keep up with the ever-increasing requests for digital evidence.[77] Because of increasing costs of cybercrime investigations, often only large-scale cybercrime activities are pursued. These actions result in many cybercrimes going unpunished, sending the message that this is a high reward, low risk crime. Furthermore, the UNODC report revealed that countries suffer from a critical shortage in criminal justice professionals that can handle cybercrime cases.[78] Countries suffering from this lack of human, technical, and financial capacity to conduct investigations on their own can receive assistance from UNODC and INTERPOL. This, however, is a short-term solution to the capacity deficit.

Given the global nature of cybercrime, it is imperative that all nations build capacities to detect, investigate, and respond independently to online illicit activities. How do we build this capacity? Conferences and training in *digital forensics*, "a branch of forensic science that focuses on criminal procedure law and evidence as applied to computers and related devices,"[79] is one way to do so. However, digital forensics should not be a specialized unit in law enforcement agencies. Nonspecialized law enforcement personnel, who receive basic training to serve as police officers, should be provided with basic computer knowledge and trained in digital forensics in police academies. Such basic training is crucial because very few crimes have been left untouched by computers and related technology. Therefore, it is reasonable to assume that nonspecialized law enforcement officers will at some point be faced with cybercrime. Initiatives should thus be created to improve cybercrime-related training for nonspecialized law enforcement officers.

SITUATIONAL CRIME PREVENTION

Another way to reduce cybercrime is through **situational crime prevention** (SCP). SCP differs from other criminological theories which seek to explain criminal behavior. This theory does not focus on the offender; instead, it focuses on the environment within which the criminal operates. Accordingly, instead of trying to change aspects of the offender, what is primarily sought is a change in the environment (a form of *situational engineering*). SCP thus focuses on ways to reduce the opportunities for offending. Opportunities for cybercrime can be reduced by increasing the risks of failure for cybercrime, increasing the effort involved to block or prevent cybercriminals from committing illicit activity online, reducing the rewards of cybercrime, and removing temptations, provocations, and excuses for cybercrime. The ultimate goal of SCP is to increase the chances of a cybercriminal being caught and make it more difficult for a cybercriminal to commit a crime.

SCP can also serve as a deterrent to cybercrime through denial of opportunity and denial of capability. Each of these is designed to reduce cybercrime. The first, *denial of opportunity*, denies potential cybervictims access to the cybercriminal through protective measures and hardening of personal digital systems and devices or prevents cybercriminals from accessing the cybervictim through efforts to obstruct their illicit activities. For example, to protect themselves from malware, users should have up-to-date antivirus and antispyware programs on their systems. The second deterrent, *denial of capability*, seeks to limit a cybercriminal's ability to engage in a cyberattack. Consider, for example, hackers' exploits of software vulnerabilities. In the United States, the U.S. Computer Emergency Readiness Team (US-CERT) recommended disabling Java after identifying yet another exploit making users vulnerable to cybercriminals.[80] The attack involved using malware that would download to a user's machine if the user accessed a compromised website. Because of repeated exploits of vulnerabilities identified in Java and Adobe Flash Player, users have been advised to disable these programs. In 2015, to protect users, Mozilla Firefox blocked all versions of Adobe Flash Player from automatically running within its browser and began warning users of the risk posed from updating Flash Player.[81]

SCP is one of the applications of routine activity theory (discussed in Chapter 3). In this application, suitable targets are hardened to discourage offenders by making it more difficult and less profitable or otherwise rewarding to commit a crime.[82] **Target hardening** may cause offenders to change their tactics and targets but not necessarily to desist from the illicit activity. Indeed, targets that are difficult to reach or attack may lead cybercriminals to delay or defer the attack. For instance, users who have strong passwords for digital devices and use **encryption** (which physically blocks third-party access to data by making it unreadable) may prevent unwanted and unauthorized access to digital devices and data. Efforts to harden certain targets can lead to **displacement**, wherein cybercrimes intended for one target are directed at another that does not have the same protections in place. In the end, target hardening efforts should make it more difficult for cybercriminals to achieve their objectives and thus increase the perceived costs of engaging in cybercrime. If the effort required to succeed in a task is raised high enough, the cybercriminals might give up on that task or take longer to execute their operations. As an effective constraint on cybercrime, SCP should focus on ways to frustrate cybercriminals by making it more difficult and risky to commit cybercrime and by reducing its rewards. Costs of an outcome depend on environmental constraints. Because of this, the constraints can be manipulated to reduce cybercriminals' opportunity to engage in illicit activity.

SCP enables victims to do something about cybercrime by providing them with some form of power and control over their security. Ultimately, it is a victim-centered approach, as opposed to other criminological theories that are centered on the offender (e.g., see the theories in Chapter 5). In shifting the emphasis to the victim, cybercrime now becomes the responsibility of the user. Indeed, SCP is, in large part, the responsibility of individuals, especially with respect to interpersonal cybercrimes, cybertrespass, cybervandalism, and cyberidentity theft. However, the issue here is that SCP facilitates the commodification of cybersecurity.

Cybersecurity, therefore, becomes a **private good** or a **club good** not available to all. It can be considered a private good if it is exclusive (i.e., excludes some individuals from obtaining the good) "and rival [(i.e., the benefits of the good diminishes by the number of users)] because the defense or protection of an individual or a state typically excludes others, and because others cannot employ the same resources for their own protection."[83] As a club good, cybersecurity is only available to members of the club, who pay for the good or receive it for free as a result of club membership. These private and club goods exclude the portion of the population that cannot afford them.

Cybersecurity is thus a privilege for those who can purchase it. Accordingly, this reinforces the socioeconomic division in society and facilitates social exclusion by making protection against cybercrime a commodity available only to those who can afford it. Purchased cybersecurity measures help to prevent cyberattacks from certain digital devices but leave other devices without such protections vulnerable to cyberattacks. Although there are free antivirus and antispyware programs, they do not have all the features of those products users pay for (this of course depends on the product). Individuals and companies are required to purchase the necessary software to protect their systems from internal and external threats. This commodification of cybersecurity, however, is extremely problematic. As one researcher has argued, "all citizens within a political community should be entitled (simply on account of their membership) to certain basic levels of protection (or, to put it another way, to a 'fair' share of scarce security resources) . . . the market cannot rule in this sphere;"[84] at the very least, it should not entirely rule in this sphere. Furthermore, this commodification of cybersecurity is problematic given the fact that certain cybercrimes take advantage of vulnerable systems and utilize them to conduct cyberattacks on other protected systems.

CASE STUDY

Restorative justice seeks to repair the harm done by the offender to the victim and the community. Basically, it attempts "to make good the harm done and in so doing to shift attention from the culpability of the offender to the harms suffered."[85] The basic notion behind restorative justice is to move away from state punishment and attempt to restore the harm done to the victims by the offender through various practices and techniques. For example, one of these practices is victim-offender meetings, in which a mediator facilitates discussion between the victim and the offender. This discussion occurs in an attempt to have the victim and offender work together to devise a plan to alleviate the harm caused by the offense.[86]

Restorative punishment focuses on healing or repairing the harm between an offender and the victim, and possibly an offender and the community. Here, in order for justice to occur, some researchers have claimed that the healing of victims, offenders, and communities injured by crime is required.[87] Others have concurred: "Crime injures victims, communities, and offenders: therefore, the criminal justice system should repair those injuries."[88] Overall, if the aim of punishment is restorative, then the outcome to be achieved is restoration of relationships—those that involve the key stakeholders (offenders, victims, community)—and reparation for the harm done.

Restorative justice has been used to deal with a wide range of antisocial and criminal behaviors, including bullying. The restorative justice process includes important players in the bullying process: the offender (or offenders), the victim, the parents of the offender (or offenders), the parents of the victim, a district attorney, the police officer (or officers) who investigated the incident, school administrators, teachers, and bystanders and witnesses to bullying (the latter two have an essential role to play, especially when the goal is to change the culture that makes bullying possible). A common outcome of the restorative justice process in bullying cases is for all parties to sign an agreement that outlines the consequences for the perpetrators of the act, the role of the parents to prevent future incidents, and the work that the school and the participating criminal justice agencies must do to prevent such behaviors in the future (e.g., implement education programs; see Chapter 10).

Restorative justice may have applications to antisocial behavior online and cybercrimes, such as cyberbullying. Cyberbullying requires a different version of the restorative justice process, one that can occur online (in the event that the cyberbullies are in different geographic locations). What would a restorative justice process for cyberbullying look like? What would the program entail?

REVIEW QUESTIONS

1. What are the central tenets of the classical school of criminology?
2. What is the economic theory of crime?
3. Is cybercrime a rational choice?
4. What role do emotions play in cybercrime?
5. What is punishment? Describe the different types of punishment.
6. Are cybercriminals susceptible to deterrence? Why do you think so?
7. In what ways can cybercrime be reduced?
8. What are the obstacles to international cybercrime investigations?
9. How can a country build its national capacity to conduct cybercrime investigations?
10. How can situational crime prevention be applied to cybercrime?

LAWS

Agreement on Cooperation in Combating Offences related to Computer Information of 2001 (Commonwealth of Independent States)
Agreement on Cooperation in the Field of Information Security of 2009 (Shanghai Cooperation Organization)
Arab Convention on Combating Information Technology Offences of 2010 (Arab League)
Computer Fraud and Abuse Act of 1986 (United States)
Convention on Cybercrime of 2001 (Council of Europe)
Convention on the Confidence and Security in Cyberspace of 2014 (African Union)
Cyber Security Enhancement Act of 2002 (United States)
Foreign Economic Espionage Penalty Enhancement Act of 2012 (United States)
Homeland Security Act of 2002 (United States)
Prevention of Electronic Crimes Ordinance of 2007 (Pakistan)
Uniting and Strengthening America by Providing Appropriate Tools Required to Intercept and Obstruct Terrorism Act of 2001 (USA Patriot Act of 2001) (United States)

DEFINITIONS

Absolute deterrence. The ability of the threat of punishment to prevent an individual from engaging in crime.
Attribution. The process of identifying a perpetrator of a cybercrime or the location from which a cybercrime was committed.

Capital punishment. The deliberate killing of an offender by the state for a criminal offense for which the accused has been convicted of in a court of law.

Chain of custody. A chain of detailed information about who obtained the evidence in a case, when and where the evidence was obtained, how it was obtained, and anyone who accessed the evidence and the reasons it was accessed.

Classical school of criminology. The classical school of criminology viewed crime as an outcome of a criminal's free choice.

Club good. A good available only to the members of a club, who pay for the good or receive it for free as a result of club membership.

Cyberdeterrence. An action to discourage engagement in cybercrime.

Deserts-based theory. A theory holding that those who commit offenses deserve punishment, and the amount of punishment should be proportionate to the degree of wrongdoing.

Displacement. A situation in which efforts to harden certain targets leads to a crime being redirected at another target that does not have the same protections in place.

Economic theory of crime. A theory proposing that a person will commit a crime if the expected utility (gain) of the illicit act exceeds the utility received by refraining from the conduct or engaging in other actions.

Encryption. The physical blocking of third-party access to data by rendering it unusable by scrambling the data and making it unreadable.

General deterrence. A form of punishment that seeks to send a message to the public that perpetrators will be punished for their crimes, in an effort to dissuade them from engaging in illicit activity.

Incapacitation. The incarceration of an offender to prevent the person from reoffending against the public for a finite period.

Instrumental rationality. The process by which a person compares options based on their availability (e.g., by the ease with which they come to mind) and chooses the one that will produce the highest utility.

Letters rogatory. Letters drafted by the U.S. Attorney's Office and used to request evidence from other countries. These letters include information about the case, a description of the evidence needed and why it is needed, and a promise for reciprocity in future cases.

Mutual legal assistance treaties. Agreements between countries that dictate the type of assistance provided by each nation in criminal investigations and extradition requests for criminals.

Private good. A good not available to all users and whose consumption diminishes its benefits.

Procedural rationality. The process whereby a person engages in an act only after considering all possible actions and carefully weighing the benefits and costs of these actions.

Punishment. The penalty imposed on an individual by the criminal justice system for an offense committed.

Rational choice theory. A theory holding that the criminal is a rational actor who engages in a cost-benefit analysis to determine whether to commit a crime. If the benefits outweigh the costs, the criminal commits the crime.

Rehabilitation. A course of action aimed at changing the mindset and behavior of an offender in an effort to prevent the offender from reoffending.

Restorative justice. A process of restoration aimed at repairing the harm between an offender and victim, and possibly an offender and the community.

Restrictive deterrence. A form of deterrence targeted at those who have offended in the past, designed to minimize the likelihood of reoffending.

Retribution. The act of inflicting harm or deprivation on the offender for the harm or deprivation inflicted on the victim.

Rules of evidence. Rules specifying the criteria used to determine evidence admissible in court.

Situational crime prevention. Crime prevention strategies focusing on ways to reduce the opportunities for offending.

Specific deterrence. A form of deterrence that seeks to dissuade a perpetrator of a crime from reoffending in the future.

Target hardening. Instituting measures designed to deter potential offenders by causing them to change their tactics and targets but not necessarily desist from the illicit activity.

Utilitarianism. A form of consequentialism holding that justice is best served by taking action that brings about the best possible outcomes.

ENDNOTES

1. B. Van Voris and P. Hurtado, "Three Charged for Cybervirus That Targeted Bank Accounts," *Bloomberg News*, January 23, 2013, http://www.bloomberg.com/news/articles/2013-01-23/three-charged-with-using-computer-virus-to-steal-records-1-.

2. U.S. Department of Justice, U.S. Attorney's Office, Southern District of New York, "Three Alleged International Cyber Criminals Responsible for Creating and Distributing Virus That Infected Over One Million Computers and Caused Tens of Millions of Dollars in Losses Charged in Manhattan Federal Court" (press release), January 23, 2013, http://www.justice.gov/usao-sdny/pr/three-alleged-international-cyber-criminals-responsible-creating-and-distributing-virus.

3. G. Smith, "'Gozi' Virus Creators Charged by FBI with Stealing Millions from Online Bank Customers," *Huffington Post*, January 23, 2013, http://www.huffingtonpost.com/2013/ 01/23/gozi-virus-fbi_n_2535282.html.

4. D. B. Cornish and R. V. Clarke, eds., *The Reasoning Criminal: Rational Choice Perspectives in Offending* (New York: Springer, 1986).

5. C. Beccaria, *An Essay on Crimes and Punishments*, by Marquis Beccaria of Milan, a new edition corrected (Albany, NY: W.C. Little & Co., 1872).

6. J. Bentham, *An Introduction to the Principles of Morals and Legislation* (Oxford: Clarendon, 1907), http://www.econlib.org/library/Bentham/bnthPML1.html.

7. Beccaria C. (1872). *An Essay on Crimes and Punishments*, by Marquis Beccaria of Milan. A New Edition Corrected. Albany, New York: W.C. Little & Co.

8. B. E. Harcourt, "Beccaria's 'On Crimes and Punishments:' A Mirror on the History of the Foundations of Modern Criminal Law" (Coase-Sandor Working Paper Series in Law and Economics, Coase-Sandor Institute for Law and Economics, University of Chicago Law School, 2013), 10.

9. Cornish and Clarke, *The Reasoning Criminal*; R. V. Clarke and M. Felson, "Introduction: Criminology, Routine Activity and Rational Choice," vol. 5 of *Routine Activity and Rational Choice*, *Advances in Criminological Theory*, ed. R. V. Clarke and M. Felson (New Brunswick, NJ: Transaction Publishers, 1993); D. B. Cornish and R. V. Clarke, "Crime as Rational Choice," in *Criminological Theories: Bridging the Past to the Future*, ed. S. Cote (London: Sage, 2002), 291.

10. G. S. Becker, "Crime and Punishment: An Economic Approach," *Journal of Political Economy* 76, no. 2 (1968): 176.

11. Ibid.

12. D. S. Nagin and R. Paternoster, "Enduring Individual Differences and Rational Choice Theories of Crime," *Law & Society Review* 27, no. 3 (1993): 467–496; R. Bachman, R. Paternoster, and S. Ward, "The Rationality of Sexual Offending: Testing a Deterrence/Rational Choice Conception of Sexual Assault," *Law and Society Review* 26, no. 2 (1992): 343–372; R. V. Clarke and G. R. Newman, *Outsmarting the Terrorists* (London: Praeger Security International, 2006).

13. R. Young, L. Zhang, and V. R. Prybutok, "Hacking into the Mind of Hackers," *Information Systems Management*, 24, no. 4 (2007): 281–287.

14. R. Chiesa, S. Ducci, and S. Ciappi, *Profiling Hackers: The Science of Criminal Profiling as Applied to the World of Hacking* (Boca Raton, FL: Auerbach, 2008); P. T. Leeson and C. J. Coyne, "The

Economics of Computer Hacking," *Journal of Law, Economics and Policy* 1, no. 2 (2006): 511–532; M. Yar, *Cybercrime and Society.* (Thousand Oaks, CA: Sage, 2006); S. C. McQuade, *Understanding and Managing Cybercrime* (Boston: Pearson, 2006); D. S. Wall, *Cybercrime: The Transformation of Crime in the Information Age* (Cambridge, UK: Polity, 2007).

15. O. Skorodumova, "Hackers as Information Space Phenomenon," *Social Sciences* 35, no. 4 (2004): 105–113.

16. J. Graham, ed., *Cyber Fraud: Tactics, Techniques, and Procedures* (Boca Raton, FL: CRC Press, 2009), 94; Skorodumova, "Hackers," 105–113.

17. L. E. Cohen and M. Felson, "Social Change and Crime Rate Trends: A Routine Activity Approach," *American Sociological Review* 44, no. 4 (1979): 588–608; Clarke and Felson, *Routine Activity and Rational Choice.*

18. S. Verba, "Assumptions of Rationality and Non-Rationality in Models of the International System," in *The International System: Theoretical Essays*, ed. K. Knorr and S. Verba (Princeton, NJ: Princeton University Press, 1961), 95, cited in F. C. Zagare, "Rationality and Deterrence," *World Politics* 42, no. 2 (1990): 239.

19. W. de Haan and J. Vos, "A Crying Shame: The Over-Rationalized Conception of Man in the Rational Choice Perspective," *Theoretical Criminology* 7, no. 1 (2003): 31; W. de Haan and I. Loader, "On the Emotions of Crime, Punishment and Social Control," *Theoretical Criminology* 6, no. 3 (2002): 243–253.

20. E. Collins, "Emotional Energy as the Common Denominator of Rational Action," *Rationality and Society* 5, no. 2 (1993): 203–230.

21. J. Katz, *Seductions of Crime: Moral and Sensual Attractions in Doing Evil* (New York: Basic Books, 1998).

22. Ibid.

23. Ibid., 216.

24. De Haan and Vos, *A Crying Shame*, 31; de Haan and Loader, "On the Emotions of Crime, Punishment and Social Control," 243–253.

25. J. M. Bouffard, L. Exum, and R. Paternoster, "Whither the Beast? The Role of Emotions in Rational Choice Theory of Crime," in *Of Crime and Criminality: The Use of the Theory in Everyday Life* (Thousand Oaks, CA: Pine Forge, 2000).

26. M. Dunn, "Once the World's Most Wanted Hacker, Kevin Mitnick Now Helps Companies Combat Attack," news.com.au, May 7, 2015, http://www.news.com.au/technology/online/hacking/once-the-worlds-most-wanted-hacker-kevin-mitnick-now-helps-companies-combat-attacks/news-story/9baa7bcbc668a0f067706c100b5b0bbe.

27. P. Harris, "'Bling Ring' on Trial for Hollywood Celebrity Burglaries," *Guardian*, January 16, 2010, http://www.theguardian.com/lifeandstyle/2010/jan/17/bling-ring-los-angeles-hollywood.

28. C. Thompson, "The Virus Underground," *New York Times*, February 8, 2004, http://www.nytimes.com/2004/02/08/magazine/the-virus-underground.html.

29. J. R. Schultz, "Warez Everyone Going: An Exploratory Look at Online Piracy" (honors thesis, California State University, Long Beach, CA, 2005), http://web.csulb.edu/colleges/cba/honors/thesis/documents/Joshua_Schultz_Thesis.pdf.

30. M. L. Benson and T. L. Sams, "Emotions Choice and Crime," in *The Oxford Handbook of Criminological Theory*, ed. F. T. Cullen and P. Wilcox (Oxford: Oxford University Press, 2013), 500.

31. Benson and Sams, "Emotions Choice and Crime," 506.

32. Collins, "Emotional Energy," 203–230.

33. D. Garland, *Punishment and Modern Society* (Oxford: Oxford University Press, 1990), 17.

34. I. Kant, *Justice and Punishment*, trans. W. Hastie, in *Philosophical Perspectives on Punishment*, ed. G. Ezorsky (Albany: State University of New York Press, 1972), 103–104.

35. Kant, *Justice and Punishment*, 104.

36. A. Ashworth, "Sentencing," in *The Oxford Handbook of Criminology*, 3rd ed., ed. M. MaGuire, R. Morgan, and R. Reiner (Oxford: Oxford University Press, 2002), 1076.
37. A. Ashworth, *Sentencing and Criminal Justice*, 4th ed. (Cambridge: Cambridge University Press, 2005), 84.
38. Beccaria, Chapter 7.
39. J. Kaplan, *Criminal Law* (Boston: Little, Brown, 1996), cited in *Psychology and the Legal System*, ed. L. S. Wrightsman, E. Greene, M. T. Nietzel, and W. H. Fortune (Belmont, CA: Wadsworth/Thompson Learning, 2002), 476.
40. M. Tomsen, "When Videogame Companies Help Prosecute Their Players," *Forbes*, May 30, 2015, http://www.forbes.com/sites/michaelthomsen/2015/05/30/when-videogame-companies-help-prosecute-their-players/.
41. E. Feldmann, "Netherlands Teen Sentenced for Stealing Virtual Goods," *PC World*, October 23, 2008, http://www.pcworld.com/article/152673/virtual_theft.html.
42. Associated Press, "Teen Steals Virtual Items, Gets Real Punishment," *CBS News*, January 31, 2012, http://www.cbsnews.com/news/teen-steals-virtual-items-gets-real-punishment/.
43. O. Herzfeld, "What Is the Legal Status of Virtual Goods?" *Forbes*, December 4, 2012, http://www.forbes.com/sites/oliverherzfeld/2012/12/04/what-is-the-legal-status-of-virtual-goods/; Associated Press, "Online Game Theft Earns Real-World Conviction," *NBC News*, January 31, 2012, http://www.nbcnews.com/id/46207779/ns/technology_and_science-games/t/online-game-theft-earns-real-world-conviction/#.VljHr79XGb0.
44. Supreme Court of the Netherlands, Judgment LJN no. BQ9251, January 31, 2012.
45. A. V. Arias, "Comment: Life, Liberty, and the Pursuit of Swords and Armor: Regulating the Theft of Virtual Goods," *Emory Law Journal* 57, no. 5 (2008), 1301.
46. Herzfeld, "What Is the Legal Status of Virtual Goods?"
47. *Bragg v. Linden Research, Inc.*, 487 F. Supp. 2d 593, 595-96 (E.D. Pa. 2007).
48. J. Bentham, *The Works of Jeremy Bentham, published under the Superintendence of his Executor, John Bowring* (Edinburgh: William Tait, 1843), 396.
49. J. H. Burns and H. L. A. Hart, eds., *Jeremy Bentham: An Introduction to the Principles of Morals and Legislation* (London: Athlone, 1970), 158.
50. Bentham, *The Works of Jeremy Bentham*, Chapter 3.
51. R. Bellamy, *Beccaria: "On Crimes and Punishments" and Other Writings*, trans. R. Davies (Cambridge: Cambridge University Press, 1995), 31.
52. J. Gibbs, *Crime, Punishment, and Deterrence* (New York: Elsevier Scientific, 1975); B. A. Jacobs, "Deterrence and Deterrability," *Criminology* 48, no. 2 (2010): 417–441.
53. D. Maimon, M. Alper, B. Sobesto, and A. Cukier, "Restrictive Deterrent Effects of a Warning Banner in an Attacked Computer System," *Criminology* 52, no. 1 (2014): 33–59.
54. BBC News, "Mariposa Botnet 'Mastermind' Jailed in Slovenia," December 24, 2013, http://www.bbc.com/news/technology-25506016.
55. Schultz, "Warez Everyone Going."
56. Young, Zhang, and Prybutok, "Hacking into the Mind of Hackers," 281–287.
57. N. Kshetri, "The Simple Economics of Cybercrimes," *IEEE Security and Privacy* 4, no. 1 (2006): 33–39.
58. H. Copes and L. M. Vieraitis, "Bounded Rationality of Identity Thieves: Using Offender-Based Research to Inform Policy," *Criminology & Public Policy* 8, no. 2 (2009): 237–262.
59. C. Conradt, "Online Auction Fraud and Criminological Theories: The Adrian Ghighina Case," *International Journal of Cyber Criminology* 6, no. 1 (2012): 912–923.
60. R. K. Knake, *Untangling Attribution: Moving to Accountability in Cyberspace*, July 15, 2010, http://science.house.gov/sites/republicans.science.house.gov/files/documents/hearings/071510_Knake.pdf
61. C. Guiton, "Criminals and Cyber Attacks: The Missing Link between Attribution and Deterrence," *International Journal of Cyber Criminology* 6, no. 2 (2012): 1030–1043.

62. L. A. Hughes and G. J. DeLone, "Viruses, Worms, and Trojan Horses: Serious Crimes, Nuisance, or Both?" *Social Science Computer Review* 25, no. 1 (2007): 78–98.

63. Meeting of G8 Justice and Home Affairs Ministers, *Best Practices for Network Security, Incident Response and Reporting to Law Enforcement*, May 11, 2004, http://www.justice.gov/sites/default/files/ag/legacy/2004/05/11/ G8_Best_Practices_Network_Security.pdf.

64. The African Union was created in 1999 and is composed of the following countries, which cooperate in social, economic, and political matters: People's Democratic Republic of Algeria, Republic of Angola, Republic of Benin, Republic of Botswana, Burkina Faso, Republic of Burundi, Republic of Cameroon, Republic of Cabo Verde, Central African Republic, The Republic of Chad, Union of the Comoros, Republic of the Congo, Democratic Republic of the Congo, Republic of Djibouti, Arab Republic of Egypt, Republic of Equatorial Guinea, State of Eritrea, Federal Democratic Republic of Ethiopia, Gabonese Republic, Republic of Ghana, Republic of Guinea, Republic of Guinea-Bissau, Republic of Cote d'Ivoire, Republic of Kenya, Kingdom of Lesotho, Republic of Liberia, Libya, Republic of Madagascar, Republic of Malawi, Republic of Mali, Republic of Mauritania, Republic of Mauritius, Republic of Mozambique, Republic of Namibia, Republic of Niger, Federal Republic of Nigeria, Republic of Rwanda, Republic Arab Saharawi Democratic, Democratic Republic of Sao Tome and Principe, Republic of Senegal, Republic of Seychelles, Republic of Sierra Leone, Somali Republic, Republic of South Africa, Republic of South Sudan, Republic of the Sudan, Kingdom of Swaziland, United Republic of Tanzania, Republic of the Gambia, Togolese Republic, Tunisian Republic, Republic of Uganda, Republic of Zambia, and Republic of Zimbabwe.

65. The Arab League was founded in 1945 and is composed of the following countries, which cooperate in cultural, economic, financial, health, and security affairs: Algeria, Bahrain, Comoros, Djibouti, Egypt, Iraq, Jordan, Kuwait, Lebanon, Libya, Mauritania, Morocco, Oman, Palestine, Qatar, Saudi Arabia, Somalia, Sudan, Syria, Tunisia, United Arab Emirates, and Yemen.

66. The Shanghai Cooperation Organization is composed of China, Russia, Kazakhstan, Kyrgyzstan, Tajikistan, and Uzbekistan and cooperates in security matters that affect these countries.

67. The Commonwealth of Independent States was created in 1991 and is composed of the following countries, which cooperate in financial, trade, and security affairs: Azerbaijan, Armenia, Belarus, Georgia, Kazakhstan, Kyrgyzstan, Moldova, Russia, Tajikistan, Turkmenistan, Uzbekistan, and Ukraine.

68. See signatories of Council of Europe, Convention on Cybercrime, CETS No. 185, 2001, http://www.coe.int/en/web/conventions/full-list/-/conventions/treaty/185/signatures?p_auth=2RXVhgbE.

69. Ibid.

70. A. Whitmore, N. Choi, and A. Arzrumtsyan, "One Size Fits All? On the Feasibility of International Internet Governance," *Journal of Information Technology & Politics* 6, no. 1 (2009): 7–9.

71. Maras, *Computer Forensics*, 10–11.

72. M.-H. Maras, *Transnational Security* (Boca Raton, FL: CRC Press, 2014), 141–142.

73. N. Kshetri, "Diffusion and Effects of Cyber-Crime in Developing Economies," *Third World Quarterly* 31, no. 7 (2010): 1063.

74. A. E. Bell, "Investigating International Cybercrimes," *Police Chief* 74, no. 3 (2007), http://www.policechiefmagazine.org/magazine/index.cfm?fuseaction=display_arch&article_id=1135&issue_id=32007.

75. M.-H. Maras and M. D. Miranda, "Forensic Science," In *Encyclopedia of Law and Economics*, ed. J. Backhaus, Springer, September 20, 2014, http://link.springer.com/referenceworkentry/10.1007%2F978-1-4614-7883-6_11-1.

76. United Nations Office on Drugs and Crime (UNODC), *Comprehensive Study on Cybercrime*, February 2013, http://www.unodc.org/documents/organized-crime/UNODC_CCPCJ_EG.4_2013/CYBERCRIME_STUDY_210213.pdf

77. Ibid., 163.

78. Ibid., 172, 177–178, and 229.

79. Maras, *Computer Forensics*, 29.

80. G. Gross, "US-CERT: Disable Java in Browsers Because of Exploit," *Computerworld*, January 11, 2013, http://www.computerworld.com/article/2494068/malware-vulnerabilities/us-cert --disable-java-in-browsers-because-of-exploit.html.

81. G. Keizer, "Mozilla Blocks All Flash in Firefox after Third Zero-Day," *Computerworld*, July 14, 2015, http://www.computerworld.com/article/2947898/security/mozilla-blocks-all-flash-in-firefox-after-third-zero-day.html.

82. R. V. Clarke, "Situational Crime Prevention," in vol. 19 of Crime and Justice, *Building a Safer Society: Strategic Approaches to Crime Prevention* (Chicago, IL: University of Chicago Press, 1995), 91–150.

83. E. Krahmann, "Security: Collective Good or Commodity?" *European Journal of International Relations* 14, no. 3 (2008): 387.

84. I. Loader, "Private Security and the Demand for Protection in Contemporary Britain," *Policing and Society* 7, no. 3 (1997): 377–394; L. Zedner, "Too Much Security?" *International Journal of the Sociology of Law* 31, no. 3 (2003): 177.

85. L. Zedner, *Criminal Justice* (Oxford: Oxford University Press, 2004), 101.

86. R. A. Strickland, *Restorative Justice* (New York: Peter Lang, 2004), 9–10.

87. D. Van Ness and K. H. Strong, *Restoring Justice* (Cincinnati, OH: Anderson, 1997), 8–9.

88. N. A. Carlson, K. M. Hess, and C. M. Orthman, *Corrections in the 21st Century* (Belmont, CA: West/Wadsworth, 1999), 31, cited in Wrightsman et al., *Psychology and the Legal System*, 478.

CHAPTER 5

CYBERCRIME AND THE PROPENSITY TO OFFEND

KEYWORDS

Antisocial personality
  disorder
Arousal theory
Asperger's syndrome
Atavism
Attachment theory
Autism spectrum disorder
Biological theories
Compulsive-impulsive
  disorder
Criminal anthropology
Criminal profiling
Cyberslacking
Dependency

Ego
Electra complex
Id
Information technology
  insiders
Intelligence
Internet addiction
Internet gaming disorder
Mental disorder
Narcissistic injury
Narcissistic personality
  disorder
Oedipus complex
Personality theories

Phrenology
Physiognomy
Positivism
Psychoanalytical theories
Psychological theories
Relapse
Salience
Scientific method
Superego
Testosterone
Tolerance
Trait theories
Withdrawal

In 2015, the Georgia Bureau of Investigation conducted *Operation Secret Guardian*, which led to the arrest of persons engaged in the possession, production, and distribution of child pornography via the Internet.[1] In such efforts to reduce cybercrimes, it is important that investigators learn what motivates cybercriminals. Biological and psychological theories can provide such insight by examining offenders' physiology, anatomy, mental processes, and behavior. These approaches study illicit behavior using the **scientific method**. The scientific method is a systematic process of inquiry that involves the development, testing, and modification of hypotheses based on observation and experimentation. This chapter examines the ability of biological and psychological theories to explain certain forms of cybercrimes. Special emphasis is placed on the concept of Internet addiction and what measures have been implemented to deal with it.

THE POSITIVIST SCHOOL AND TRAIT THEORIES

Positivism moved beyond explanations of actions as an outcome of free choice, choosing instead to explain criminal behavior as a result of internal and external forces. These forces were believed to be responsible for criminal behavior—either completely or by serving as an undue influence. Accordingly, positivists view crime as largely outside of an individual's control. Therefore, instead of focusing on situational disposition, positivists focus on the disposition of an individual to commit a criminal offense using casual mechanisms to explain criminality.

Positivists seek to explain criminal behavior through the lens of biology, psychology, and sociology.[2] This chapter examines the biological and psychological explanations of crime and cybercrime in which the primary unit of analysis for study is the individual. These theories, known as **trait theories**, explain crime and cybercrime as a product of predisposition or underlying motivation.

CYBERCRIMINALS: BORN THAT WAY

Biological theories of criminality seek to explain the behavior of offenders and biological predispositions to offending. The identified biological traits of an offender are not viewed as causing crime; instead, these traits are viewed as predisposing individuals to commit crime. Biological theories of criminality have largely focused on the physiological characteristics, brain abnormalities, and chemical compositions (specifically, the hormones) of criminals.

Physiological Characteristics

Physiognomy is the study of facial characteristics to reveal an individual's personality traits. Even though the validity of physiognomy has largely been disputed and is considered a pseudoscience, facial features can reveal certain genetic disorders (e.g., Down syndrome). Aristotle was the first to discuss physiognomy, laying the groundwork for its later application in the medical and social science community.

The first person to apply physiognomy in the medical community was the German physician Franz Joseph Gall. In 1796, Gall developed the discipline of **phrenology**, which maps the physiological characteristics of individuals to the brain. Gall posited that certain actions of the brain had localized functions that were associated with criminality. Criminality could thus be explained by studying these localized functions.

Physiognomy was later applied to the social sciences. Indeed, early biological theories explain illicit behavior through **criminal anthropology**, which examines the relationship between criminality and the physical characteristics of the offender. Cesare Lombroso was the first social scientist to explain illegal behavior through criminal anthropology. In his book *Criminal Man,* originally published in 1876, Lombroso claimed that criminals' brains were less developed than those of noncriminals. Based solely on his examination of incarcerated individuals (predominantly the poor and uneducated, who could not afford legal defense and had little or no access to good nutrition and medical care), he also asserted that criminals had certain distinct facial features. Particularly, he argued that a person was born criminal if the person had at least five of eighteen physical characteristics:[3]

1. Deviation in head size and shape from the type common to the race and region from which the criminal came
2. Asymmetry of the face

3. Excessive dimensions of the jaw and cheekbones
4. Eye defects and peculiarities
5. Ears of unusual size, or occasionally very small, or standing out from the head as do those of chimpanzees
6. Nose twisted, upturned, or flattened in thieves, or aquiline or beaklike in murderers, or with a tip rising like a peak from swollen nostrils
7. Lips fleshy, swollen, and protruding
8. Pouches in the cheek like those of some animals
9. Peculiarities of the palate, such as a large central ridge, a series of cavities and protuberances such as are found in some reptiles, or cleft palate
10. Abnormal dentition
11. Chin receding, or excessively long or short and flat, as in apes
12. Abundance, variety, and precocity of wrinkles
13. Anomalies of the hair, marked by characteristics of the hair of the opposite sex
14. Defects of the thorax, such as too many or too few ribs, or supernumerary nipples
15. Inversion of sex characteristics in the pelvic organs
16. Excessive length of arms
17. Supernumerary fingers and toes
18. Imbalance of the hemispheres of the brain (asymmetry of cranium)

In his research, Lombroso also identified nonphysical characteristics (e.g., tattoos) associated with criminals.[4]

Lombroso used the term **atavism** to describe individuals resembling ancestral human beings. In addition to atavism, Lombroso identified *insane criminals* as those who were moral degenerates and suffered from mental disorders. An insane criminal becomes criminal due to chemical imbalances in the brain. He further developed a general category of criminals known as *criminaloids*. These individuals have no special characteristics identifying them as a criminal; however, the psychological and emotional composition of these individuals supposedly predisposes them to crime in certain instances. Lombroso further classified these criminals as *habitual criminals*, who engage in criminality because of contact with other criminals.

Building on Lombroso's work, others linked criminality with human physiques. In the 1940s, William Herbert Sheldon studied human physiques and found that certain *somatotypes* (i.e., body types) were associated with particular personality traits:[5]

1. *Ectomorph.* This individual had a thin and wiry frame and was identified as an introvert, emotionally restrained, and socially anxious.
2. *Endomorph.* This individual was round and overweight and was identified as sociable, friendly, relaxed, and having a need for affection.
3. *Mesomorph.* This individual had a muscular frame and was identified as being adventurous, assertive, aggressive, and having a need for power.

Mesomorphs were found to be more likely to engage in crime than the other body types due to their intimidating physical appearance.[6]

Biological theories have been both supported and refuted by studies. For example, Earnest Hooton compared incarcerated and nonincarcerated individuals between 1927 and 1939, concluding that criminals were physiologically inferior to noncriminals.[7] By contrast, Charles Goring, working earlier in the 1900s, did not find any significant difference between criminal and noncriminal physical characteristics.[8] In the end, the consensus in the scientific community is that there is no correlation between the way a person looks and the person's propensity to crime (i.e., a criminal does not have a particular look). Even though the theories of Gall, Lombroso, Sheldon, and other early positivists have been largely discredited, they paved the way for the use of the scientific method in the study of criminality.

Few researchers have focused on the biological makeup of cybercriminals as a way to explain criminality. Most of the work that has been done has focused exclusively on the brain functions and chemical imbalances of cybercriminals and has focused predominantly on Internet sex offenders.[9]

Brain Abnormalities

Brain injuries have been associated with deviant behaviors, but particularly with abnormal sexual desires and acts.[10] For instance, brain traumas sustained to the frontal and temporal lobes have been found to be associated with abnormal sexual desires among men.[11] Overall, research has shown links between neuropsychological abnormalities and neurodevelopmental trauma and pedophilia.[12] Other studies have examined the white matter of the brain, which affects brain functioning, in pedophiles (see Image 5-1). Abnormalities and alterations in white matter have been found to be associated with illicit

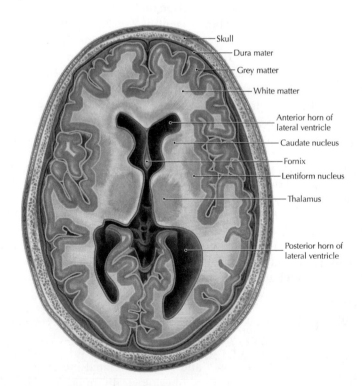

IMAGE 5-1   Depiction of White Matter of the Brain.

behavior (e.g., child sexual predation, online and offline).[13] Accordingly, there is evidence, albeit rather limited, that there are brain dysfunctions in certain sex offenders.

Hormones

High levels of certain hormones have been associated with aggressive crimes such as sex offending. A case in point is **testosterone**, which is a hormone associated with sexual fantasies and desires (i.e., libido). Studies have shown that testosterone influences sex drive and aggression.[14] Studies on the testosterone levels of sex offenders are mixed. Sex offenders have been found by some researchers to have extremely high levels of testosterone;[15] other studies have not found high levels.[16]

Research on abnormal hormone levels informs the use of drugs to regulate hormones (e.g., to lower testosterone levels) as a way to reduce sexual violence. Chemical castration through cyproterone acetate, diethylstilbestrol, and medroxyprogesterone acetate has been used in Canada, Europe, and the United States to lower recidivism rates of child sex offenders.[17] However, studies of the efficacy of hormone treatment in preventing child sex crimes and in reducing recidivism have resulted in mixed findings; that is, some researchers report success and others do not.[18]

Ultimately, biological trait theories seek to determine whether traits of individuals can be extrapolated to create a profile of an offender (i.e., **criminal profiling**). Despite popular belief, there is no single, specific profile of a cybercriminal, not even for similar cybercrimes; hackers, for example, do not fit the profile propagated by popular movies, such as *War Games* (1983), that depict hackers as males in their teens that live with their parents.[19] Instead, what criminal profiling seeks to do is develop "a general psychological description of the most likely type of suspect, including personality and behavioral characteristics suggested by a thorough analysis of the crimes committed."[20] As such, these profiles move beyond biological traits, by examining psychological traits of existing offenders or identifying psychological traits of potential offenders.

THE INTELLIGENCE OF CYBERCRIMINALS AND THE PSYCHOLOGY OF CYBERCRIME: THE NEW POSITIVISTS

Whereas early positivists focused on biological explanations of crime, new positivists seek to explain cybercrime through the lens of psychology. Like biological studies, psychological studies on cybercriminals are limited in scope. These psychological studies have focused on hackers, malware writers and distributors, digital pirates, cyberstalkers, cyberbullies, and Internet child sex offenders. The studies have applied existing **psychological theories** to explain these cybercrimes, looking in particular at intelligence, mental disorders, personality theories, psychoanalytical theories, and attachment theory.

INTELLIGENCE

The genetic makeup, chemical composition, and brain functions of cybercriminals have been found to influence their intelligence.[21] Intellectual deficiencies have been associated with an individual's inability to control sexual impulses and to understand that child sexual predation is wrong.[22] Apart from intellectual deficiencies, studies have shown that average and above-average intelligence has been linked to crime and cybercrime.[23] For instance, several studies of online child pornographers have revealed that they were well educated and had above-average intelligence.[24] Furthermore, Internet child sex offenders were found to be of greater intelligence than offline child sex offenders.[25]

Intelligence is associated with an individual's reasoning, analytical thinking, and logic skills. As such, intelligence is often linked to a cybercriminal's ability to engage in cybercrime, albeit sometimes erroneously. For example, hackers are viewed as individuals with higher intelligence because of the level of technical knowledge, ability, and skill needed to engage in computer programming. Today, however, even computer users with average levels of intelligence can engage in hacking because of the availability of programs (e.g., existing scripts, malware toolkits). By contrast, computer virus writers require a high level of technical acumen to code. Studies on computer virus writers have supported this claim, as these individuals have been found to have above-average intelligence.[26]

MENTAL DISORDERS

A **mental disorder** is a chemical imbalance, illness, disease, or disability of the mind that impairs a person's normal psychological functioning. The World Health Organization defines a mental disorder as "the existence of a clinically recognizable set of symptoms or behaviors associated in most cases with distress and with interference with personal functions."[27] Mental disorders are classified in the *Diagnostic and Statistical Manual of Mental Disorders* of the American Psychiatric Association. Mental disorders are also classified in the International Classification of Diseases of the World Health Organization.

Some psychological theorists and researchers hold that individuals engage in cybercrime because they suffer from some form of mental disorder. One study of cyberstalkers found that one type of cyberstalker—a *delusional cyberstalker*—suffers from a mental disorder.[28] Such individuals delusively believe they are in a romantic relationship with the victim. Other perpetrators of interpersonal cybercrimes—namely, online child pornographers—have also been found to suffer from mental disorders. Specifically, studies have found a correlation between access to online child pornography and depression and mental disorders, such as schizophrenia.[29] Certain cybercriminals have also been diagnosed with personality disorders, such as antisocial personality disorder and narcissistic personality disorder.[30]

Individuals diagnosed with **antisocial personality disorder** are aggressive, manipulative, and lack remorse for illicit and immoral activity. A study on Internet child pornographers found that these offenders engage in behaviors to advance their own interests, often at the expense of others (i.e., manipulative-exploitative personality traits).[31] These individuals were also found to manipulate and exploit various facets of the Internet to access child pornography. A predisposition for this personality disorder is reputed to be parental neglect. Kevin Mitnick, an infamous hacker, reported that he was neglected by his mother, who had to work two jobs to support the family, leaving him isolated.[32] **Narcissistic personality disorder** is characterized by exaggerated feelings of self-importance, an excessive need for admiration, selfishness, and lack of empathy. Sigmund Freud posited that narcissism may lead to abnormal sexual desires and engagement in abnormal sexual activity.[33]

Studies have also suggested a link between hacking and Asperger's syndrome.[34] **Asperger's syndrome** is characterized by repetitive behaviors and social deficits and difficulties in communication.[35] It is considered a mild form of **autism spectrum disorder,** and those diagnosed with it are viewed as highly functional individuals. Individuals with Asperger's syndrome have above average intelligence.[36] They are not cognitively impaired but have difficulty interacting with people because their repetitive behaviors make them appear awkward; furthermore, they have poor social skills and interpersonal relationships and lack social acumen, particularly as they cannot ascertain people's emotional reactions or determine others' emotions from facial cues.[37] The level of severity of symptoms varies.

Certain well-known hackers have been diagnosed with Asperger's syndrome. Owen Thor Walker, a teenager from New Zealand, was arrested in 2007 for writing and distributing malware that was responsible for infecting millions of computers around the world and causing millions of dollars in damages to the computers.[38] Walker pled guilty and the charges against him were dismissed after he paid a fine and forfeited the cash he received for engaging in the illicit acts.[39] Gary McKinnon, a resident of the United Kingdom, hacked into U.S. Department of Defense computers to obtain proof of the existence of aliens. His actions took the DOD systems offline for several hours and cost $800,000 in damages.[40] The United States sought to extradite McKinnon to the United States pursuant to the U.S./UK Extradition Treaty, but the UK Home Secretary prevented it in light of McKinnon's Asperger's diagnosis and because he suffered from depression.[41] Overall, more empirical research in this area is needed before a correlation can be made between hacking and Asperger's syndrome.

PERSONALITY THEORIES

Personality influences behavior. As such, **personality theories** have been used to explain cybercrime by attributing cybercrime to elements of an offender's personality. Research has actually shown that there is no general cybercriminal personality, or at least, not one that can be used to explain all forms of cybercrimes and cybercriminals' motivations. Nevertheless, there are certain personality traits that have been linked to various cybercrimes. One such trait is impulsiveness.[42] Results from research on the links between impulsivity and cybercrime are inconsistent.[43] A 2001 study revealed that online hebophiles (i.e., adult males who are attracted to adolescent girls and boys) tend to be impulsive and have a desire for power.[44] However, other studies have found that Internet child sex offenders, unlike other interpersonal cybercriminals, such as cyberbullies, are not impulsive.[45]

Another personality trait that has been linked to cybercrime is aggressiveness. Not surprisingly, findings from research on the link between aggressiveness and certain cybercrimes are also mixed. A 2008 study revealed that online sexual predators tend not to be violent or aggressive.[46] In contrast, cyberbullies have been found to be aggressive and unable to control their anger.[47] The results for hackers have been very inconsistent, some studies having found that hackers have high levels of aggression and others showing the opposite.[48]

Another personality trait associated with cybercrime is empathy. A person with a low level or complete lack of empathy is unable to recognize the consequences of his or her actions on others. Research has shown that cyberbullies do not empathize with their victims, or at the very least, show low empathic understanding of their victims.[49] Exposure to media violence has been associated with cyberbullying.[50] Research has shown that exposure to media violence desensitizes viewers; consequently, violent criminal offenders tend to feel little sympathy for their victims.[51] Child predators also do not empathize with victims, enabling offenders to disregard the child's distress and feel no remorse or guilt for harm to the victim inflicted by the sexual abuse.[52] Studies have shown that while Internet sex offenders tend to have low empathy for their victims, they have greater empathy for their victims than do contact child sex offenders.[53] Compared with most nonoffenders, child sexual offenders have also been found to be amoral and dishonest.[54] A 2007 study found that Internet child sex offenders have emotional difficulties and difficulties in interpersonal relationships.[55] Offenders who collect Internet child pornography have been found to suffer from emotional dysfunctions and problems with intimacy.[56] For other online child pornographers, "accessing images on the Internet may function as a way of avoiding or dealing with difficult emotional states."[57] Contrary to this view, some studies have shown that online sex offenders do not have emotional difficulties, nor problems with interpersonal relationships.[58]

Typologies of online groomers (i.e., individuals who utilize the Internet, computers, and related technology to manipulate children, gain their trust, and, ultimately, convince them to engage in sexual activities) situate them within a psychopathological framework based on both personality and mental functioning. The *intimacy seeker* has difficulty with offline relationships, is sexually attracted to children, and relates to children due to social and emotional immaturity.[59] Intimacy seekers feel more accepted online and thus seek relationships that start online.[60] The *adaptable groomer* shows psychopathic traits and has a low degree of empathy, is morally indiscriminant, and is deceptive and manipulative.[61] The adaptable groomer adapts his or her behavior to the individual child based on how the child is represented online.[62] The *hypersexualized groomer* requests sexual activity from children online. Once contact is made with the victim, the groomer quickly escalates the conversation to introduce sexual content and demands sexual acts from the victim. The hypersexualized groomer depersonalizes contact with victims and dehumanizes them.[63] The groomer may choose sex acts with children as one of many abnormal sexual activities, but may not even prefer children over adults.[64]

Apart from Internet sex offenders, the interpersonal relationships and social skills of hackers and malware writers have been examined. Overall, the research findings on the interpersonal relations of hackers and malware writers have been mixed. Earlier studies revealed that hackers abstain from interpersonal relationships and view the computer as a friend and extension of themselves.[65] In particular, the computer becomes a substitute for real-world interpersonal relationships and interactions.[66] Hackers find it easier to relate to computers and technology than to people.[67] Additionally, computer virus writers have been found to have poor social skills, leading to difficulties in relationships in their personal and professional environments.[68] The same holds true for hackers. Other studies have supported this popular belief, revealing that hackers are loners and have weaker relationships with family than those who did not engage in this conduct.[69] Other studies, however, have found that hackers are not always loners, and they may have healthy interpersonal relationships (e.g., romantic relationships) and active sex lives.[70]

Hans Jurgen Eysenck's personality theory holds that criminal behavior is the product of the neuropsychological makeup of an individual and environmental conditions. The theory, which focuses on genetics, personality traits, and environmental factors, examines how these factors and the interactions of these factors influence an individual's likelihood of engaging in criminal activity.[71] Eysenck believed that an essential aspect of an individual's personality is temperament, which has three dimensions: extraversion/introversion (E); psychoticism and socialization (P); and neuroticism and stability (N). Eysenck's research revealed that individuals with high levels of these personality traits (E, P, and N) were more likely than those with average or low levels of these traits to engage in criminal activity.

Studies have supported the link of one of these personality traits—extraversion—with criminality.[72] In fact, studies have shown that extraversion is a predictor of cybercrime and cyberdeviance.[73] This contradicts other findings showing that low levels of extraversion (i.e., introversion) are linked to criminality.[74] For example, a 2006 study of individuals who write computer viruses found that introversion is a significant predictor of this cybercrime.[75] Introversion was also found to be a predictor of computer technology insiders (or information technology insiders). An **information technology insider** is a current or former employee of an organization who intentionally seeks to gain unauthorized access to adversely affect the confidentiality, integrity, and availability of the organization's computer information system. Information technology insiders with the personality trait of introversion have been found to be "less likely to deal with stress in an overt, constructive manner, and less likely to seek direct assistance" and to have low self-esteem, low feelings of loyalty, and weak social skills.[76] They also tend to be computer dependent, lack empathy, feel entitled, and have personal and social frustration problems (e.g., with coworkers, a boss, or at home with a spouse, significant others, children, and/or other family members).[77]

PSYCHOANALYTICAL THEORIES

Psychoanalytical theories view crime as the outcome of abnormal or dysfunctional mental processes.[78] They explain cybercrime as a manifestation of the psychic conflict that exists between the **id** (i.e., the unconscious mental processes that seek immediate gratification of needs), the **ego** (i.e., the individual's conscious, which recognizes the need to delay gratification in order to achieve long-term goals and creates strategies that enable the maximization of pleasure and minimization of pain from an activity), and the **superego** (i.e., the individual's unconscious and conscious mental processes that serve as a moral guide between right and wrong). Psychoanalytical theorists view predisposition to cybercrime as a result of a poorly developed superego; such individuals may seek immediate gratification of needs without thoughts about the consequences of their actions.

Psychoanalytical theories have been used to explain online child sexual predation. It has been suggested that sexual predators are "fixated at a primitive stage of psychosexual development."[79] Freud claimed that the most important crisis a child experiences in development is during the phallic stage; the child seeks maximum gratification of the id through genital stimulation and experiences an overwhelming but unattainable sexual desire for the parent of the opposite sex.[80] These sexual desires are repressed (pushed into the subconscious) because the child feels threatened by the same-sex parent and fears that he or she will be punished by that parent. This conflict experienced by a boy is known as the **Oedipus complex**, whereas the conflict experienced by a girl is known as the **Electra complex**.[81] Ultimately, the child resolves the conflict through identification with the same-sex parent and coming to understand that sexual desires for the opposite-sex parent are forbidden.

Paraphilias (i.e., mental conditions characterized by unusual sexual desires and legal or illegal sexual activities) may arise from fixation in the phallic stage due to unresolved sexual issues in a person's childhood. Specifically, lack of effective resolution of the Oedipus complex for boys and the Electra complex for girls has been associated with online and offline sexually deviant behavior.[82] Psychoanalysts also attribute paraphilia to traumatic events individuals experience early in life that eventually cause them to engage in abnormal sexual activity as a coping mechanism.[83] A third explanation for paraphilia is disruption in maternal attachment,[84] a topic discussed in the next section.

ATTACHMENT THEORY

John Bowlby proposed that a healthy personality is developed in infants and children when they are in a warm and close relationship with their mother or other primary caregiver.[85] These relationships help infants and children to form secure attachments to their mother and other caregivers. Bowlby identified three forms of attachment: secure attachment, anxious avoidant attachment, and anxious resistant attachment. *Secure attachment* is the healthiest form of attachment; the child is confident that his or her caregiver is responsible and available when needed. *Anxious avoidant* is a type of attachment that results from the rejection of the child by the caregiver. Because of this rejection, the child is not confident that the caregiver will be present and available when needed. *Anxious resistant* attachment refers to the feelings of anxiety and uncertainty children experience, leaving them fearful of their environment and overdependent on their caregivers.

Attachment theory utilizes a lifespan development approach in explaining illicit behavior as a product of experiences with caregivers earlier in life.[86] Failure to develop secure attachments in childhood can lead to **narcissistic injury**, ultimately resulting in a damaged self-image and inhibiting proper development of a person's morality and identity. Narcissistic injury has been associated with violent behavior (i.e., *narcissistic rage*). This narcissistic rage occurs as a result of feelings of humiliation and rejection that the person feels and is directed at the person's damaged self, and then projected onto the victim.

Insecure attachments between the caregiver and the child may be responsible for criminal behavior in adulthood. Indeed, criminality has been linked to adults who had anxious avoidant and anxious resistant insecure attachments with their caregivers as infants and children. As a result of insecure childhood attachments, these individuals tend to have poor relationships with others, low self-esteem, and high rates of mental disorders.[87] Adults who had insecure child-parent relationships (i.e., anxious avoidance or anxious resistant attachments) also tend to suffer from emotional disorders such as anxiety and depression.[88] Sex offenders have been found to exhibit insecure attachment, particularly avoidance attachment,[89] whereas individuals with paraphilia may exhibit lack of empathy, low self-esteem, poor social skills, and insecure/inadequate attachment to parents.[90]

Parental neglect, conflicts, and other dysfunctions of the family unit have been associated with cybercrime.[91] A 2002 study supported this claim by showing that hackers have reported conflict in the family and a dysfunctional family environment during their youth.[92] Nonetheless, the reality is that while several hackers have come from dysfunctional families, this is not an adequate predictor of a person's engagement in this activity.[93]

BOX 5-1 HUMAN-ROBOT INTERACTIONS AND EMOTIONAL ATTACHMENT

Sherry Turkle, author of *Alone Together: Why We Expect More from Technology and Less from Each Other,* conducted an experiment on "human" robot interactions with children who had low views of self-worth and self-importance and who lacked sufficient parental attention to foster improvement in these areas.[94] One of the robots in her experiment (Cog) was programmed to react to what it sees, touches, and hears; the other (Kismet) was programmed to simulate emotional responses.[95] Both Cog and Kismet exhibited traits that would likely lead children to become attached to the robots. Children interacted with them and reported their experiences. One child reported, "I could never get tired of Cog. . . . It is not like a toy because you cannot teach a toy; it is like something that is part of you, you know, something you love, kind of like another person, like a baby. I want to be its friend, and the best part of being his friend would be to help it learn. . . . In some ways Cog would be better than a person-friend because a robot would never try to hurt your feelings."[96] Another child's interactions with Kismet were observed and recorded. During a discussion with the robot, the child informed Kismet that "some of the girls in her school are mean."[97] She subsequently stated that Kismet was "nicer than they are."[98] Overall, the children reported developing an emotional attachment to Cog and Kismet because the robots provided them with the attention and emotional responses they were missing from their parents.[99]

The beliefs that an abnormal cybercriminal personality exists and that psychological factors are the primary motivators of cybercrime have been questioned by scholars. A review of available literature shows some links between cybercriminals and mental disorders, but there is little evidence to support the notion that cybercriminals are dysfunctional or pathological or that prior pathology causes individuals to engage in cybercrime.

Individuals who subscribe to psychological perspectives of cybercrime fail to realize that behavior is a product of not only individual (or internal) factors but also situational (or external) factors. The situational factors are the product of one's environment. In reality, like all behaviors (aberrant or otherwise), cybercrime is too complex a phenomenon to be attributed to a single factor, or even to similar factors, for all types of cybercriminals and their respective behaviors.

INTERNET ADDICTION AND CYBERCRIME

Arousal theory holds that individuals who are aroused or excited by an activity will continue to engage in the act to receive the same stimulation. It has been argued that arousal theory may well explain certain cybercrimes, particularly when offenders experience psychological thrills from engaging in illicit acts.[100] Cases in point are hacking and cyberstalking.[101] Individuals have also reported receiving pleasure from online gaming and other online activities.[102] The arousal experienced from these activities is a predictor of addiction.

Another predictor of addiction is a user's inability to control his or her behavior. Research has shown that certain individuals are unable to effectively regulate their computer and Internet use.[103] Research has also shown that hackers are computer dependent.[104] This computer **dependency** can amount to an abnormal attachment to the computer and the Internet if these are overused or used to deal with the user's stress, anxiety, depression, or loneliness.[105] This abnormal attachment has been linked to Internet addiction. **Internet addiction** refers to the compulsive overuse of the Internet in a manner that has a detrimental impact on individuals and their personal and professional lives and results in negative emotions (e.g., irritability) when the activity is reduced.

Internet addiction is characterized by the salience of the activity. The **salience** of an activity refers to the degree to which the behavior dominates an individual's thinking, feelings, and behavior. In Internet addiction, this behavior is all-consuming and often happens in lieu of other important personal and professional activities. Addicted individuals do not understand the need to disconnect from the Internet and engage in other activities.[106] The activities online often take precedent over offline relationships, contact, and communication with others, leading to conflict in the person's life. Internet addicts may also experience conflict because they know their behaviors are wrong but continue to engage in them anyway.

Individuals can build a **tolerance** to an activity when they frequently engage in it. These addicts build a tolerance toward the behavior, requiring engagement in that activity with greater frequency to achieve the same results. For instance, online child pornography is a progressive addiction; those who view it become desensitized to it, requiring more extreme versions of it to receive the same stimulus (i.e., the previous level of gratification).[107] Much the same, Internet addiction is also characterized by the need for increasingly greater consumption. The addicted person may exhibit adverse symptoms when he or she is not engaged in the behavior (**withdrawal**).[108] Particularly, these addicts experience physiological and psychological symptoms (e.g., anxiety, aggressiveness, irritability, restlessness, and obsessively thinking about the Internet) when they refrain from engaging in the activity.[109] A hacker in a 1999 study reported that he would become "depressed when away from a networked computer for too long," considered himself "addicted" to hacking, and if he were ever in a position where he knew his computer activity was over for the rest of his life, he would "suffer withdrawal."[110] Studies have shown that individuals have experienced withdrawal symptoms, mood swings, and anxiety when disengaging from online activity. Some have even suffered serious physical symptoms (e.g., dehydration) and even death. Finally, addicted individuals may **relapse** into similar or more extreme engagements in these behaviors.

Those with Internet addictions have reported experiencing significant social and psychological harm.[111] The impact on adolescents, who are most vulnerable to Internet addiction,[112] can include truancy and dropping out of school.[113] Studies have shown that Internet dependency is linked to poor academic performance.[114] They have shown that individuals who are heavy users of the Internet and spend a significant amount of time online often perform poorly academically.[115] Others have reported physiological harm, such as back strain, eye strain, and disruptions in sleep patterns due to excessive use of the Internet.[116] In South Korea, Internet addiction is considered a significant public health risk and has resulted in the deaths of individuals from cardiopulmonary-related issues.[117] Online gaming addiction, which is considered as a subtype of Internet addiction,[118] is also considered a significant public health risk in South Korea. Deaths have been reported among those addicted to online gaming. For example, a 24-year-old man died after playing an online game for 84 hours without a break and, in so doing, failing to attend to his most basic needs, such as food, sleep, and even breaks to use the restroom.[119] Another example involved a 28-year-old man who died from heart failure after playing an online game, *Starcraft*, at an Internet café for over 50 hours without a break.[120] These deaths, while rare, are nonetheless disconcerting. Ultimately, individuals with an Internet addiction are unable to control their use of the Internet and digital devices in a way that does not affect their personal and professional activities or health and well-being. As such, the individual persists in this activity despite its adverse personal consequences.

MEASURING INTERNET ADDICTION

Internet addiction is viewed by some as a misnomer. These individuals argue that people cannot be addicted to the entire Internet but can, however, be addicted to particular online activities.[121] This has led some researchers to use the term *problematic Internet use* instead.[122] Moreover, in addition to also being described as pathological Internet use, Internet addiction has been described as compulsive Internet use, excessive Internet use, and Internet addiction disorder.[123]

Several instruments have been created to measure Internet addiction. These instruments seek to establish the criteria that can be used to determine whether an individual has an addiction. The criteria for instruments that measure other disorders have been used to create Internet addiction instruments such as the Young Internet Addiction Test, the Problematic Internet Use Questionnaire, and the Chen Internet Addiction Scale. Of these three instruments, the most widely used is the Young Internet Addiction Test (IAT). The IAT has been validated in the United States, the United Kingdom, Finland, and South Korea.[124] It assesses an individual's ability to control Internet use, the extent to which a user is preoccupied with the Internet, the extent of lying, hiding, or other ways of minimizing use of the Internet, and the negative impact associated with the use of the Internet.[125] The IAT, like the other two instruments, is based on the criteria used to determine impulse control disorders.

Internet addiction is viewed as a **compulsive-impulsive disorder**, which is characterized by online behavior that interferes with an individual's life. It involves excessive computer or digital device use that results in loss or neglect of basic needs (food, water, and hygiene), withdrawal symptoms when the user is not engaging in the activity (stress, anxiety, and anger), tolerance to the activity, need or desire for additional time online to achieve the same gratification, and negative consequences, such as isolation from and conflict with others, that may be due to the activity and lying about engaging in it. In South Korea, the criteria used to determine Internet addiction are comparable to those used to assess compulsive-impulsive disorders. Specifically, four factors have been used to assess Internet addiction: excessive Internet use, withdrawal when disengaging from Internet activity, tolerance, and negative impact from Internet use.[126]

Pursuant to the IAT, a person is diagnosed with Internet addiction if five or more of eight criteria in the instrument are positively identified by the individual:[127]

1. Preoccupation with the Internet
2. Greater consumption needed to achieve satisfaction
3. Unsuccessful attempts to reduce or withdraw from activity
4. Symptoms when activity is reduced or stopped
5. Longer online activity than originally intended
6. Adverse impact on professional or personal life
7. Concealment of the extent of involvement in the activity from family, therapist, and others
8. Use of the Internet to escape from problems or to relieve a dysphoric mood (e.g., anxiety, depression, guilt).

Beard and Wolf modified the IAT diagnostic criteria for Internet addiction.[128] According to the modified version, the presence of the first five criteria of the IAT in addition to one of the last three criteria (which assess coping functions and interactions of individuals) are required for a diagnosis.

Most of the diagnostic criteria for pathological gambling were adopted in formulating the IAT.[129] Pathological gambling is a form of compulsive-impulsive disorder. Similarly, others have adopted criteria for pathological gambling to diagnose Internet addiction, employing such terminology as excessive Internet use,[130] pathological Internet use,[131] and problematic Internet use[132] to explain it.

BOX 5-2 PERSONALITY TRAITS AND INTERNET ADDICTION

Certain personality traits have been identified in those diagnosed with Internet addiction.[133] Studies have shown that it is associated with low self-esteem.[134] Low self-esteem and loneliness may indeed play a role in the development of Internet addiction; however, they may also be the result of Internet addiction. Internet addiction has also been linked to high sensation-seeking behavior, which is a subtrait of impulsivity.[135] Nevertheless, some researchers have not found a link between impulsivity and Internet addiction.[136] Moreover, sensation seeking has been found not to be a precursor to pathological gambling; this contradicts pathological studies that show such a link, especially since the diagnostic criteria for Internet addiction were based on these studies.[137]

A 2001 study by Richard A. Davis found that problematic thought processes lead to pathological behaviors.[138] Davis distinguished between pathological specific Internet use (i.e., use of the Internet for a specific purpose) and pathological generalized Internet use (i.e., Internet use for a multitude of purposes); of the two, pathological generalized Internet use led to "a greater severity of problematic Internet behavior."[139] Other studies revealed that the length of time one spends online has been correlated with Internet addiction.[140] On its own, however, length of time spent online is not an adequate predictor of Internet addiction.[141] Those who utilize the Internet as a form of process gratification have been found to be more likely to develop an Internet addiction or pathological Internet use.[142] Interactive online activities (i.e., chat rooms, online games, bulletin boards, and gambling) have also been associated with increased pathological Internet use.[143]

Scott E. Caplan developed the Generalized Problematic Internet Use Scale (GPIUS) to measure the cognitions and behaviors of an individual that are associated with Davis' generalized pathological Internet use construct.[144] Utilizing the term "problematic Internet use" (or PIU) instead of "pathological Internet use," Caplan's study revealed that PIU cognitions and behaviors (e.g., guilt about using the Internet and using the Internet to escape from problems) intensify over time leading to negative outcomes for the individual (e.g., social isolation and withdrawal).[145] Particularly, PIU has been associated with adverse personal impacts (e.g., divorce and neglect of child care) and adverse professional impacts (e.g., loss of employment).[146] This construct has also been linked to behavioral addictions.[147] A behavioral addiction can be passive (e.g., viewing Internet web pages, videos, images, and posts) or active (e.g., playing computer games, posting comments on social media, and engaging in discussions in chat rooms).[148] Some researchers have argued that PIU and other behavioral addictions do not have a measurable physiological impact on the individual.[149] Others have found that behavioral addictions stimulate the same reward pathways as abuse of substances.[150]

While some researchers have linked Internet addiction to pathological gambling,[151] others have equated it with substance abuse.[152] The criteria for pathological gambling diagnoses are similar to those used to diagnose substance abuse. In fact, individuals who are addicted to the Internet also exhibit symptoms that meet the diagnostic criteria for substance abuse and other addictions.[153] The fourth edition of the *Diagnostic and Statistical Manual of Mental Disorders (DSM–IV)* lists the criteria for determining whether someone has a substance abuse disorder. These criteria have been utilized in instruments that measure Internet addiction, more specifically, the Internet Addiction Disorder Diagnostic Criteria and the Internet-Related Addictive Behavior Inventory.

Along with Internet addiction, PIU has been linked to substance abuse addictions.[154] Even cybercriminals have likened their experiences with Internet and computer addiction with substance abuse. In the *Hacker's Manifesto*, the writer uses language similar to that of an addict: "I made a discovery today. I found a computer. Wait a second, this is cool. . . . And then it happened. . . . A door opened to a world. . . . Rushing through the phone line like heroin through an addict's veins, an electronic pulse is sent out, a refuge from the day-to-day incompetencies is sought . . . a board is found. 'This is it . . . this is where I belong.' . . . I am a hacker."[155]

Chemical and behavior addictions involve exposure to a stimulus followed by repetitions of the behavior to obtain the same gratification as obtained with the initial stimulus; the continuous repetition of this act leads to addiction.[156] Behavioral addictions such as sex addiction are omitted from the *Diagnostic and Statistical Manual of Mental Disorders (DSM–V)*. Internet addiction is also not included in the *DSM–V*. This omission is due to the current lack of sufficient medical evidence to support its classification as a mental disorder. Despite this omission, **Internet gaming disorder** is listed in the *DSM–V* as requiring further study (under the section titled "Conditions for Further Study"). Interestingly, under this section, Internet gaming disorder is defined as a "persistent and recurrent use of the Internet to engage in games, often with other players, leading to clinically significant impairment or distress as indicated by five (or more) [criteria] in a 12-month period."[157] Currently, the majority of the studies on this disorder have been conducted on young men in Asia. According to the American Psychiatric Association, this disorder was included in this section because further research is required "to determine whether the condition should be added to the manual as a disorder."[158]

The arguments against the existence of Internet addiction hinge on general lack of physiological data to support its existence and impact on users. Physiological measures to support these reports (e.g., taking of a users' blood pressure and pulse) are lacking (albeit not entirely). Addictions activate areas of the brain associated with pleasure, and when these areas are activated, various neurochemicals are produced; however, with the passage of time, users may develop a need for increased stimulation (derived from a chosen activity) to feel pleasure from the activity. As such, the user engages in a particular behavior more frequently than before to obtain pleasure and avoid any potential withdrawal symptoms. Neuroimaging has been used to display areas in which cerebral activity occurs and any changes made in these activities when a person engages in the addictive behavior.[159] Neuroimaging studies of individuals with Internet addiction have revealed that those addicted have cerebral activity abnormalities similar to those of persons with behavioral addictions and substance abuse addictions.[160] Researchers have also reported a link between cerebral structural changes and Internet addiction. These changes are associated with dysfunctional cognitive control and goal-oriented behaviors in the use of the Internet.[161] Furthermore, studies examining the effects of Internet addiction on the brain have revealed structural and functional abnormalities of those with Internet addiction.[162] On the whole, neurobiological studies on Internet addiction are limited.

Massively multiplayer online role-playing games (MMORPGs) are believed to increase risks of Internet addiction. These games often have no end, and new quests and adventures are continuously being added to the game. Users have reported feeling a rush triggered by a release of endorphins (i.e., chemicals in the brain that stimulate pleasure when released) when they play. A 2009 study showed that those who excessively played video games activated the same areas in the brain as those who engaged in substance abuse.[163] According to one study, the "right orbito-frontal cortex, right nucleus accumbens, bilateral anterior cingulate and medial frontal cortex, right dorsolateral prefrontal cortex, and right caudate nucleus" of those addicted to the Internet were activated, in contrast to the control group.[164] Activation of these regions was associated with the urge to engage in online gaming and recollections of their experiences while gaming.[165] These activations occurred when participants were exposed to images related to online gaming. The results illustrated that "neural substrates of cue-induced gaming urge/craving in online gaming addiction was similar to that of the cue-induced craving in substance dependence. Thus, . . . the gaming urge/craving in online gaming addiction and craving in substance dependence might share the same neurobiological mechanism."[166]

The main concern with Internet addiction and PIU is the possibility of comorbidity with other psychiatric disorders. "When two disorders or illnesses occur in the same person, simultaneously or sequentially, they are described as comorbid. Comorbidity also implies interactions between the illnesses that affect the course and prognosis of both."[167] The presence of comorbidity with other mental disorders means that the behaviors and

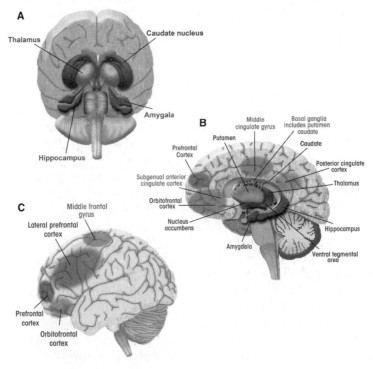

IMAGE 5-2 Areas of the Brain.

symptoms of Internet addiction or PIU may be attributed to the other disorders. For example, PIU has been linked to psychopathology, such as obsessive-compulsive disorder and social phobias.[168] Studies have shown that those who suffer from social phobias are also at risk for Internet addiction.[169] They have also shown "high comorbidity of Internet addiction with psychiatric disorders, such as affective disorders, anxiety disorders (including generalized anxiety disorder, social anxiety disorder), and attention deficit hyperactivity disorder (ADHD)."[170] A review of studies published between 2000 and 2009 revealed that the majority of those who engaged in PIU in the studies were diagnosed with anxiety disorders.[171] Other studies have revealed that the majority of individuals diagnosed with Internet addiction are also diagnosed with depression.[172] Research conducted in the United States and South Korea reported that those with Internet addiction also had been diagnosed with avoidant personality disorder, borderline personality disorder, and obsessive-compulsive personality disorder.[173] Overall, the findings suggest that there is a tendency for several addictions to be present in the individual.[174]

Some argue that Internet addiction is merely a secondary manifestation of a preexisting or underlying psychopathology.[175] This psychopathology does not cause Internet addiction but is a necessary element to its subjective development. Exposure to the Internet may serve as a stressor or trigger to this disposition.[176] Those with PIU have been found to have a mental disorder, such as bipolar or anxiety disorder (e.g., PTSD and social phobias).[177] The reality is that depression may predispose an individual to PIU or serve as a catalyst for it.[178] The directional relationship between these two disorders has yet to be established.[179] Internet addiction and PIU must be further studied before they can be conclusively defined as a disorder. In particular, researchers should examine biological factors, genetics, familial disposition, as well as an individual's response to treatment in order to understand whether there is a causal or correlational relationship between mental disorders and Internet addiction.

TREATMENT

At least one researcher has posited that criminal behavior can be viewed as an addiction, and as such, should be treated.[180] Individuals with addiction have received treatment in the form of medication. In fact, due to comorbidity with other mental disorders, pharmacological agents have been used to treat Internet addiction.[181] Individuals with Internet addiction have also been hospitalized and placed in programs in treatment centers.[182] The treatments for criminal behavior can be similar to those given for substance addictions. In fact, certain cybercriminals, such as hackers, have been viewed and treated by the criminal justice system as addicts. Consequently, the punishment given to these hackers has been rehabilitation. Rehabilitation does not view crime as a moral choice, but rather as an illness or pathology that needs to be cured in some way. Indeed, this was the view held by Cesare Lombroso, who viewed the criminal as subnormal or abnormal, as being of diseased mind or morals.[183] Because the criminal is viewed as having a diseased mind or morals, he or she must be isolated and treated.

Attorneys for well-known hacker Kevin Mitnick successfully argued in court that he had a computer addiction and deserved rehabilitation, ultimately leading to his serving his sentence in a halfway house for those with compulsive disorders.[184] The program was unsuccessful and he reoffended. Like Mitnick, Paul Bedworth, a resident of the United

Kingdom, also utilized an Internet addiction defense in court. His attorney specifically stated, "Paul Bedworth was obsessed, addicted, he just had to go on. He was so taken over by a compulsive need to be online that having those specific intents was the last thing on his mind. In fact his obsession or addiction was such that he was incapable of forming these specific intents."[185] He was the first person to be prosecuted under the UK Computer Misuse Act of 1990. In the end, the jury in the case of *Regina v. Bedworth* (1993) "acquitted Bedworth of hacking offenses, accepting his defense that an addiction to hacking precluded him from having the requisite intent needed to be convicted."[186] The Internet addiction defense has been used in other cases as well. Michael Ian Campbell made an online threat against Columbine High School.[187] His defense was that he was addicted to the Internet and thus was not criminally responsible for his acts.[188] Ultimately, he pled guilty and received 4 months' imprisonment and was ordered to attend counseling.[189]

In addition to criminal cases, Internet addiction has been used in civil courts and wrongful termination disputes. A woman in the United Kingdom contested that she was unfairly fired after her excessive use of the Internet during work hours.[190] The wasting of employer's time by surfing the web and engaging in online activities (irrelevant to employment) during work hours is known as **cyberslacking**. The woman claimed, albeit unsuccessfully, that she was addicted to the Internet and should not have been fired. Had this decision been favorable toward her, she could have asked for compensation pursuant to the UK Disability Discrimination Act of 1995. Similar wrongful termination cases have been heard in the United States. In *Pacenza v. IBM Corporation* (2009), James Pacenza unsuccessfully claimed that he was wrongfully terminated under the Americans with Disabilities Act of 1990 because of his Internet addiction disability.[191] In the United States, Internet addiction is not viewed as a disability under the Americans with Disabilities Act. Nevertheless, as this form of addiction gains acceptance among the psychiatric community (through more research supporting the existence of the disorder), this view may ultimately change.

CASE STUDY

Bob is a self-proclaimed hacker. When he gains unauthorized access to a system, he seeks to damage it, steal from it, and/or render it inoperable for some duration. He grew up in a dysfunctional family, is highly intelligent, lacks empathy for his targets, has poor social skills, and has problems with interpersonal relationships.

What theory or theories included in this chapter can explain Bob's behavior? Please analyze his case using this theory (or these theories).

REVIEW QUESTIONS

1. What is positivism? Can it explain cybercrime?
2. Are cybercriminals born that way?
3. Which biological theories can explain Internet sex offending?
4. Is intelligence linked to cybercrime? Why or why not?
5. Is cybercrime attributed to mental disorders? Why or why not?
6. Can personality theories explain cybercrime? Please explain your response.
7. What are the central tenets of psychoanalytical theories? Can these theories be used to explain cybercrime?

8. Can attachment theory explain cybercrime? Please explain your response.
9. What is Internet addiction? How can it be diagnosed?
10. How can Internet addiction be treated? Are the current types of treatment effective?

LAWS

Americans with Disabilities Act of 1990 (United States)
Computer Misuse Act of 1990 (United Kingdom)
Disability Discrimination Act of 1995 (United Kingdom)

DEFINITIONS

Antisocial personality disorder. Individuals diagnosed with antisocial personality disorder are aggressive, manipulative, and lack remorse for illicit and immoral activity.
Arousal theory. Arousal theory holds that individuals who are aroused or excited by an activity will continue to engage in the act to receive the same stimulation from that activity.
Asperger's syndrome. A mild form of autism spectrum disorder, and those diagnosed with it are viewed as highly functional individuals.
Atavism. A term used to describe individuals resembling ancestral human beings.
Attachment theory. Attachment theory utilizes a life span development approach in explaining illicit behavior as a product of experiences with caregivers earlier in life.
Autism spectrum disorder. A disorder characterized by repetitive behaviors and social deficits and difficulties in communication.
Biological theories. Biological theories of criminality seek to explain the behavior of offenders and biological predispositions to offending.
Compulsive-impulsive disorder. A disorder characterized by habitual and impetuous behavior that interferes with an individual's life.
Criminal anthropology. The study of the relationship between criminality and the physical characteristics of the offender.
Criminal profiling. The process of inferring traits about a person who has committed a crime.
Cyberslacking. The wasting of employer's time by surfing the web and engaging in online activities (irrelevant to employment) during work hours.
Dependency. Dependency manifests itself in the form of an intense desire for a substance or behavior, and inability or extreme difficulty in controlling its potential withdrawal symptoms when the substance is not consumed or the behavior is stopped.
Ego. The individual's conscious, which recognizes the need to delay gratification in order to achieve long-term goals and creates strategies that enable the maximization of pleasure and minimization of pain from an activity.
Electra complex. The conflict girls experience from an overwhelming sexual desire for the parent of the opposite sex, which is repressed because the girls feel threatened by the same-sex parent and fear that they will be punished by that parent.
Id. The unconscious mental processes that seek immediate gratification of needs.
Information technology insider. A current or former employee of an organization who intentionally seeks to exceed authorized access or gain unauthorized access to adversely affect the confidentiality, integrity, and availability of the organization's computer information system.
Intelligence. Intelligence refers to intellectual functioning and is associated with an individual's reasoning, analytical thinking, and logic skills.
Internet addiction. Internet addiction refers to the compulsive overuse of the Internet in a manner that has a detrimental impact on individuals and their personal and professional lives and results in negative emotions when the activity is reduced.

Internet gaming disorder. Under the *DSM-V*, Internet gaming disorder is defined as a "persistent and recurrent use of the Internet to engage in games, often with other players, leading to clinically significant impairment or distress as indicated by five (or more) [criteria] in a 12-month period."

Mental disorder. A chemical imbalance, illness, disease, or disability of the mind that impairs the normal psychological functioning of a person.

Narcissistic personality disorder. Individuals diagnosed with this personality disorder are grandiose, lack empathy and are selfish.

Narcissistic injury. Narcissistic injury refers to a narcissist's perceived threat to his or her ego and self-esteem (i.e., a damaged self-image), which can result in violent behavior.

Oedipus complex. The conflict boys experience from an overwhelming sexual desire for the parent of the opposite sex, which is repressed because the boys feel threatened by the same-sex parent and fear that they will be punished by that parent.

Personality theories. Personality theories attribute crime to elements of an offender's personality.

Phrenology. Phrenology holds that physiological characteristics of individuals can be mapped to the brain.

Physiognomy. The study of facial characteristics to reveal an individual's personality traits.

Positivism. Positivism explains criminal behavior as a result of internal and external forces.

Psychoanalytical theories. Psychoanalytical theories view crime as the outcome of abnormal or dysfunctional mental processes.

Psychological theories. Psychological theories scientifically study the behavior of offenders and attribute illicit behavior to individual factors.

Physiognomy. The study of facial characteristics to reveal an individual's personality traits.

Relapse. The recurrence of symptoms of a disease (e.g., Internet addiction) after a period of improvement.

Salience. The degree to which a behavior (e.g., Internet use) dominates an individual's thinking, feelings, and behavior.

Scientific method. A systematic study of inquiry that involves the development, testing, and modification of hypotheses based on observation and experimentation.

Superego. The individual's unconscious and conscious mental processes that serve as a moral guide between right and wrong.

Testosterone. A hormone associated with sexual fantasies and sexual desires.

Trait theories. Trait theories explain crime and cybercrime as a product of predisposition or underlying motivation.

Tolerance. Individuals build a tolerance to a behavior, requiring engagement in that activity with greater frequency to achieve the same results.

Withdrawal. Withdrawal refers to the adverse symptoms individuals exhibit when they are not engaged in an addicted behavior.

ENDNOTES

1. Georgia Bureau of Investigation, "Update—'Operation Secret Guardian' Targets People Trading Child Pornography," October 15, 2015, https://gbi.georgia.gov/press-releases/2015-10-16/update-%E2%80%9Coperation-secret-guardian%E2%80%9D-targets-people-trading-child.
2. The latter is discussed in detail in the next chapters.
3. C. Lombroso, *The Criminal Man*, trans. M. Gibson and N. H. Rafter (Durham, NC: Duke University Press, 2006), cited in G. B. Vold and T. Bernard, *Theoretical Criminology* (New York: Oxford University Press, 1986), 50–51.

4. Lombroso, *The Criminal Man*. For further information about tattoos and criminology, see M. D. Miranda, *Forensic Analysis of Tattoos and Tattoo Inks* (Boca Raton, FL: CRC Press, 2015), 25–29.

5. W. H. Sheldon, *The Varieties of Human Physique: An Introduction to Constitutional Psychology* (New York: Harper, 1940); W. H. Sheldon and S. S. Simons, *The Varieties of Temperament: A Psychology of Constitutional Differences* (New York: Harper, 1942).

6. Sheldon and Simons, *The Varieties of Temperament*.

7. E. Hooton, *The American Criminal: An Anthropological Study*, vol. 1, *The Native White Criminal of Native Parentage* (Cambridge, MA: Harvard University Press, 1939); E. Hooton, *Crime and the Man* (Cambridge, MA: Harvard University Press, 1939).

8. C. Goring, *The English Convict: A Statistical Study* (London: His Majesty's Stationery Office, 1913).

9. See, for example, W. Webster, J. Davidson, and A. Bifulco, eds., *Online Offending Behavior and Child Victimization: New Findings and Policy* (New York: Palgrave-Macmillan, 2015).

10. J. R. Absher, B. A. Vogt, D. G. Clark, D. L. Flowers, D. G. Gorman, and J. W. Keyes, "Hypersexuality and Hemiballism due to Subthalamic Infraction," *Neuropsychiatry, Neuropsychology, and Behavioral Neurology* 13, no. 3 (2000): 220–229.

11. Ibid.; R. Langevin, "Sexual Anomalies and the Brain," in *Handbook of Sexual Assault: Issues, Theories, and Treatment of the Offender*, ed. W. L. Marshall, D. R. Laws, and H. E. Barbaree (New York: Plenum Press, 1990), 103–113. .

12. N. D. Zalser, "Sexual Dysfunction," in *Neuropsychiatry of Traumatic Brain Injury*, ed. J. M. Silver, S. C. Yudofsy, and R. E. Hales (Washington DC: American Psychiatric Press, 1994), 274–312; R. Blanchard, J. M. Cantor, and L. K. Robichaud, "Biological Factors in the Development of Sexual Deviance and Aggression in Males," in *The Juvenile Sex Offender*, 2nd ed., ed. H. E. Barbaree and W. L. Marshall (New York: Guilford, 2006), 77–104.

13. J. M. Cantor, N. Kabani, B. K. Christensen, R. B. Zipursky, H. W. Barbaree, R. Dickey, P. E. Klassen, D. Mikulis, M. E. Kuban, B. A. Blak, M. K. Hanratty, and R. Blanchard, "Cerebral White Matter Deficiencies in Pedophilia Men," *Journal of Psychiatric Research*, 42, no. 3 (2008): 167–183; J. Davidson and S. Webster, "The Theoretical Context of Online Child Sexual Abuse," in Webster et al., *Online Offending Behavior*, 29.

14. L. Ellis, "Evidence of Neuroandrogenic Etiology of Sex Roles from a Combined Analysis of Human, Nonhuman Primate and Nonprimate Mammalian Studies," *Personality and Individual Differences* 7, no. 4 (1986): 519–552; I. C. McManus and M. P. Bryden, "Geschwind's Theory of Cerebal Lateralization: Developing a Formal, Causal Model," *Psychological Bulletin* 11, no. 2 (1991): 237–253.

15. K. Jordan, P. Fromberger, G. Stolpmann, and J. L. Müller, "The Role of Testosterone in Sexuality and Paraphilia—A Neurobiological Approach. Part II: Testosterone and Paraphilia," *The Journal of Sexual Medicine* 8, no. 11 (2011): 3008-3029; F. S. Berlin and G. S. Coyle, "Sexual Deviation Syndromes," *Johns Hopkins Medical Journal* 149, no. 3 (1981): 119–125; J. H. Brooks and J. R. Reddon, "Serum Testosterone in Violent and Nonviolent Young Offenders," *Journal of Clinical Psychology* 52, no. 4 (1996): 475–483.

16. S. Stoléru, "The Brain, Androgens, and Pedophilia," in *Hormones and Social Behaviour*, ed. D. W. Pfaff, C. Kordon, P. Chanson, and Y. Christen (Berlin Heidelberg: Springer, 2008), 163–175; P. S. Gurnani and M. Dwyer, "Serum Testosterone Levels in Sex Offenders," *Journal of Offender Counseling Services Rehabilitation* 11, no. 1 (1986): 39–45.

17. Cantor et al., "Cerebral White Matter Deficiencies," 167–183; Davidson and Webster, "The Theoretical Context of Online Child Sexual Abuse," in Webster et al., *Online Offending Behavior*, 29–30.

18. D. A. Kingston, M. C. Seto, A. G. Ahmed, P. Fedoroff, P. Firestone, and J. M. Bradford, "The Role of Central and Peripheral Hormones in Sexual and Violent Recidivism in Sex Offenders," *Journal of the American Academy of Psychiatry and the Law* 40, no. 4 (2012): 476–485.

19. See Chapter 3 for further information on the lack of a single profile for cybercriminals and Chapter 9 for further information on the role of gender in hacking.

20. E. Greene and K. Heilbrun, *Wrightsman's Psychology and the Legal System* (Victoria, Australia: Wadsworth/ Cengage Learning, 2011), 142.

21. J. Lickiewicz, "Cyber Crime Psychology—Proposal of an Offender Psychological Profile," *Problems of Forensic Sciences* 87 (2011): 239–252.

22. L. Miller, "Traumatic Brain Injury and Aggression," in *The Psychobiology of Aggression: Engines, Measurement, Control*, ed. M. Hillbrand and N. J. Pallone (New York: Haworth, 1994), 91–103; L. Miller "Sexual Offenses against Children: Patterns and Motives," *Aggression and Violent Behavior* 18, no. 5 (2013): 506–519.

23. S. Z. Levine, "Using Intelligence to Predict Subsequent Contacts with the Criminal Justice System for Sex Offences," *Personality and Individual Differences* 44, no. 2 (2008): 453–463; M. Lopez-Leon and R. Rosner, "Intellectual Quotient of Juveniles Evaluated in a Forensic Psychiatry Clinic after Committing a Violent Crime," *Journal of Forensic Sciences* 55, no. 1 (2010): 229–231.

24. A. Burke, S. Sowerbutts, B. Blundell, and M. Sherry, "Child Pornography and the Internet: Policing and Treatment Issues," *Psychiatry, Psychology and Law* 9, no. 1 (2002): 79–84; L. Webb, J. Craissati, and S. Keen, "Characteristics of Internet Child Pornography Offenders: A Comparison with Child Molesters," *Sexual Abuse: a Journal of Research and Treatment* 19, no. 4 (2007): 449–65; J. Wolak, D. Finkelhor, and K. Mitchell, *Child-Pornography Possessors Arrested in Internet-Related Crimes: Findings from the National Juvenile Online Victimization Study* (Alexandria, VA: National Center for Missing and Exploited Children, 2005); A. Frei, N. Erenay, V. Dittmann, and M. Graf, "Paedophilia on the Internet—A Study of 33 Convicted Offenders in the Canton of Lucerne," *Swiss Medical Weekly* 135, no. 33-34 (2005): 488–494; M. D. O'Brien and S. D. Webster, "The Construction and Preliminary Validation of the Internet Behaviours and Attitudes Questionnaire (IBAQ)," *Sex Abuse* 19, no. 3 (2007): 237–256; D. L. Riegel, "Effects on Boy-Attracted Pedosexual Males of Viewing Boy Erotica," *Archives of Sexual Behavior* 33, no. 4 (2004): 321–323; K. C. Siegfried, R. W. Lovely, and M. K. Rogers, "Self-Reported Online Child Pornography Behaviour: A Psychological Analysis," *International Journal of Cyber Criminology* 2, no. 1 (2008): 286–297.

25. K. Sheldon and D. Howitt, *Sex Offenders and the Internet* (Chichester, UK: Wiley, 2007); Burke et al., 79–84; O'Brien and Webster, "The Construction and Preliminary Validation of the Internet Behaviours and Attitudes Questionnaire," 237–256.

26. S. Gordon, "The Generic Virus Writer," paper presented at the 4th International Virus Bulletin Conference, Jersey, September 8–9, 1994, http://vxheaven.org/lib/asg03.html#GENERIC.

27. World Health Organization, "Proposed declassification of disease categories related to sexual orientation in the International Statistical Classification of Diseases and Related Health Problems (ICD-11)," *Bulletin of the World Health Organization* 92, no. 9 (2014): 673.

28. A. Mishra and D. Mishra, "Cyber Stalking: A Challenge for Web Security," in *Cyber Warfare and Cyber Terrorism*, ed. L. J. Janczewski and A. M. Colarik (Hershey, PA: Information Science Reference, 2008): 216–225.

29. N. W. Galbreath, F. S. Berlin, and D. Sawyer, "Paraphilias and the Internet," in *Sex and the Internet: A Guidebook for Clinicians*, ed. A. Cooper (New York: Brunner-Routledge, 2002), 187–205; S. Laulik, J. Allam, and L. Sheridan, "An Investigation into Maladaptive Personality Functioning in Internet Sex Offenders," *Psychology, Crime and Law* 13, no. 5 (2007): 523–535.

30. M. L. Pittaro, "Cyberstalking: An Analysis of Online Harassment and Intimidation," *International Journal of Cyber Criminology* 1, no. 2 (2007): 180–197.

31. Siegfried et al., "Self-Reported Online Child Pornography Behaviour," 286–297.

32. K. Mitnick, *Ghost in the Wires: My Adventures as the World's Most Wanted Hacker* (New York: Little, Brown, 2011).

33. T. E. Kasper, M. B. Short, and A. C. Milam, "Narcissism and Internet Pornography Use," *Journal of Sex and Marital Therapy* 41, no. 5 (2015): 481–486.

34. A. Hunter, "High-Tech Rascality: Asperger's Syndrome, Hackers, Geeks, and Personality Types in the ICT Industry," *New Zealand Sociology* 24, no. 2 (2009): 39–61.

35. National Institute of Neurological Disorders and Stroke, *Asperger Syndrome Fact Sheet*, last modified February 1, 2016, http://www.ninds.nih.gov/disorders/asperger/detail_asperger.htm.

36. BBC News, "What Is Autism?" April 19, 2014, http://www.bbc.co.uk/science/0/21700034.

37. National Institute of Neurological Disorders and Stroke, *Asperger Syndrome*; D. Sue, D. W. Sue, and S. Sue, *Essentials of Understanding Abnormal Behavior* (Boston: Houghton Mifflin, 2005).

38. M. Hodgson, "Teenager Guilty of Million-Dollar Hacking Campaign," *Guardian*, March 31, 2008, http://www.theguardian.com/technology/2008/apr/01/hitechcrime.hacking; P. Chapman, "Police May Offer 18-Year-Old Computer Hacker a Job," *Telegraph*, July 15, 2008, http://www.telegraph.co.uk/news/worldnews/ australiaandthepacific/newzealand/2403953/Police -may-offer-18-year-old-computer-hacker-a-job.html.

39. *Telegraph*, "Teenage Hacker Linked to Crime Gang Hired by New Zealand Telecoms Company," March 25, 2009, http://www.telegraph.co.uk/technology/5047287/Teenage-hacker -linked-to-crime-gang-hired-by-New-Zealand-telecoms-company.html.

40. BBC News, "Hacker Gary McKinnon Will Not Face UK Charges," December 14, 2012, http:// www.bbc.com/news/uk-20730627.

41. BBC News, "Gary McKinnon Extradition to US Blocked by Theresa May," October 16, 2012, http://www.bbc.com/news/uk-19957138.

42. M. H. Meier, W. S. Slutske, S. Arndt, and R. J. Cadoret, "Impulsive and Callous Traits Are More Strongly Associated with Delinquent Behavior in Higher Risk Neighborhoods among Boys and Girls," *Journal of Abnormal Psychology* 117, no. 2 (2008): 377–385.

43. L. Broidy, E. Cauffman, D. L. Espelage, P. Mazerolle, and A. Piquero, "Sex Differences in Empathy and Its Relation to Juvenile Offending," *Violence and Victims* 18, no. 5 (2003): 503–516; D. Jolliffe, and D. P. Farrington, "Empathy and Offending: A Systematic Review and Meta-analysis." *Aggression and Violent Behaviour* 9, no. 5 (2004): 441–476; Meier et al., "Impulsive and Callous Traits," 377–385.

44. K. Lanning, "Child Molesters and Cyber Paedophiles: A Behavioural Perspective," in *Practical Aspects of Rape Investigation: A Multidisciplinary Approach*, 3rd ed., ed. R. Hazelwood and A. W. Burgess (Boca Raton, FL: CRC Press, 2001), 199–220.

45. J. Wolak, D. Finkelhor, K. Mitchell, and M. Ybarra, "Online 'Predators' and Their Victims: Myths, Realities, and Implications for Prevention and Treatment," *American Psychologist* 63, no. 2 (2008): 111–128; C. S. Bhat, "Cyber Bullying: Overview and Strategies For School Counsellors, Guidance Officers, and All School Personnel," *Australian Journal of Guidance and Counselling* 18, no.1 (2008): 53–66.

46. Wolak et al. "Online 'Predators' and Their Victims," 111–128.

47. Bhat, "Cyber Bullying," 53–66.

48. C. Platt, "Hackers: Threat or Menace?" *Wired*, November 1, 1994, www.wired.com/wired /archive/2.11/hack. cong.html.

49. P. K. Smith and D. Thompson, eds., *Practical Approaches to Bullying* (London: David Fulton, 1991); R. P. Ang, and D. H. Goh, "Cyberbullying among Adolescents: The Role of Affective and Cognitive Empathy, and Gender," *Child Psychiatry and Human Development* 41, no. 4 (2010): 387–397; L. Lazuras, J. Pyżalski, V. Barkoukis, and H. Tsorbatzoudis, "Empathy and Moral Disengagement in Adolescent Cyberbullying: Implications for Educational Intervention and Pedagogical Practice," *Studia Edukacyjne*, NR 23/2012, 62; Bhat, "Cyber Bullying," 53–66; G. Steffgen, A. König, J. Pfetsch, and A. Melzer, "Are Cyberbullies Less Empathic? Adolescents' Cyberbullying Behaviour and Empathic Responsiveness," *Cyberpsychology, Behavior and Social Networking* 14, no. 11 (2011): 643–648.

50. E. Calvete, I. Orue, A. Estevez, L. Villardon, and P. Padilla, "Cyberbullying in Adolescents: Modalities and Aggressors' Profile," *Computers in Human Behavior* 26, no. 5 (2010): 1128–1135; E. Kuntsche, W. Pickett, M. Overpeck, W. Craig, W. Boyce, and M. Gaspar de Matos, "Television Viewing and Forms of Bullying among Adolescents from Eight Countries," *Journal of Adolescent Health* 39, no. 6 (2006): 908–915; F. J. Zimmerman, G. M. Glew, D. A. Christakis, and W. Katon, "Early Cognitive Stimulation, Emotional Support and Television Watching as Predictors of Bullying among Grade-School Children," *Archives of Pediatric Adolescent Medicine* 159, no. 4 (2005): 384–388; K. A. Fantia, A. G. Demetriou, and V. V. Hawa, "A Longitudinal Study of Cyberbullying: Examining Risk and Protective Factors," *European Journal of Developmental Psychology* 9, no. 2 (2012): 168–181.

51. K. A. Fanti, E. Vanman, C. C. Henrich, and M. N. Avraamides, "Desensitization to Media Violence over a Short Period of Time," *Aggressive Behavior* 35, no. 2 (2009): 179–187.

52. K. J. Elsegood and S. C. Duff, "Theory of Mind in Men Who Have Sexually Offended against Children: A U.K. Comparison Study between Child Sex Offenders and Nonoffender Controls," *Sexual Abuse: A Journal of Research and Treatment* 22, no. 1 (2010): 112–131; J. Thakker, T. Ward, and S. Navathe, "The Cognitive Distortions and Implicit Theories of Child Sexual Abusers," in *Aggressive Offenders' Cognition: Theory, Research, and Practice*, ed. T. A. Gannon, T. Ward, A. R. Beech, and D. Fisher (Hoboken, NJ: John Wiley & Sons, 2007), 11.

53. K. M. Babchishin, R. K. Hanson, and C. A. Hermann, "The characteristics of online sex offenders: a meta-analysis." *Sex Abuse* 23, no. 1 (2011): 92–123.

54. Siegfried et al., "Self-Reported Online Child Pornography Behaviour," 286–297.

55. S. Laulik, J. Allam, and L. Sheridan, "An Investigation into Maladaptive Personality Functioning in Internet Sex Offenders," *Psychology, Crime and Law* 13, no. 5 (2007): 523–535.

56. T. Ward and R. Siegert, "Toward a Comprehensive Theory of Child Sexual Abuse: A Theory of Knitting Perspective," *Psychology, Crime and Law* 8, no. 4 (2002): 319–351.

57. E. Quayle, M. Vaughan, and M. Taylor, "Sex Offenders, Internet Child Abuse Images and Emotional Avoidance: The Importance of Values," *Aggression and Violent Behavior* 11, no. 1 (2006): 1–11.

58. G. K. Wall, E. Pearce, and J. McGuire, "Are Internet Offenders Emotionally Avoidant?" *Psychology, Crime and Law* 17, no. 5 (2011): 381–401; Burke et al., 79–84.

59. Whittle et al., "A Review of Online Grooming," 62–70; V. Caretti, A. Schimmenti, and A. Bifulco, "Psychopathology of Online Grooming," in Webster et al., *Online Offending Behavior*, 95–96.

60. Whittle et al., "A Review of Online Grooming," 62–70; Caretti et al., "Psychopathology of Online Grooming," in Webster et al., *Online Offending Behavior*, 96.

61. Caretti et al., "Psychopathology of Online Grooming," in Webster et al., *Online Offending Behavior*, 97.

62. Ibid.

63. Ibid.

64. R. M. Holmes and S. T. Holmes, *Profiling Violent Crimes: An Investigative Tool*, 2nd ed. (Thousand Oaks, CA: Sage, 1996).

65. J. W. Chesebro and D. G. Bonsall, *Computer-Mediated Communication: Human Relationships in a Computerized World* (Tuscaloosa: University of Alabama Press, 1989); S. Turkle, *The Second Self: Computers and the Human Spirit* (New York: Simon and Schuster, 1984).

66. Turkle, *The Second Self*.

67. C. Murphy, "Inside the Mind of the Hacker," *Accountancy Ireland* 36, no. 3 (June 2004): 12.

68. M. Rogers, "A Social Learning Theory and Moral Disengagement Analysis of Criminal Computer Behaviour: An Exploratory Study," University of Manitoba, Manitoba, 2001; E. Shaw "The Role of Behavioral Research and Profiling in Malicious Cyber Insider Investigation," *Digital Investigation* 3, no. 1 (2006): 20–31; P. Bocij, *The Dark Side of the Internet: Protecting Yourself and Your Family from Online Criminals* (Westport, CT: Praeger, 2006).

69. R. Chiesa, S. Ducci, and S. Ciappi, *Profiling Hackers: The Science of Criminal Profiling as Applied to the World of Hacking* (Boca Raton, FL: CRC Press, 2009).

70. J. J. Woo, Y. Kim, and J. Dominick, "Hackers: Militants or Merry Pranksters? A Content Analysis of Defaced Web Pages," *Media Psychology* 6, no. 1 (2004): 63–82.

71. H. J. Eysenck, *Crime and Personality*, 3rd ed. (London: Routledge, 1977); J. H. "Eysenck, Personality Theory and the Problem of Criminality," in *Criminological Perspectives: A Reader*, ed. J. Muncie, E. McLaughlin, and M. Langan (London: Sage, 1996), 81–98; S. B. G. Eysenck and H. J. Eysenck, "Crime and Personality: An Empirical Study of the Three-Factor Theory," *British Journal of Criminology* 10 (1970): 225–239; S. B. G. Eysenck and H. J. Eysenck, "Personality Differences between Prisoners and Controls," *Psychological Reports* 40 (1977): 1023–1028.

72. M. K. Rogers, K. Seigfried, and K. Tidke, "Self-Reported Computer Criminal Behavior: A Psychological Analysis," *Digital Investigation* 3 (2006): S116–S120.

73. Ibid.

74. M. K. Rogers, N. Smoak, and J. Liu, "Self-Reported Criminal Computer Behavior: A Big-5, Moral Choice and Manipulative Exploitive Behavior Analysis," *Deviant Behavior* 2 (2006): 1–24.

75. Rogers, Seigfried, and Tidke, "Self-Reported Computer Criminal Behavior," S116– S120.

76. E. Shaw, K. G. Ruby, and J. M. Post, "The Insider Threat to Information Systems: The Psychology of the Dangerous Insider," *Security Awareness Bulletin*, No. 2-98, http://www.pol-psych .com/sab.pdf, cited in B. E. Turvey, *Criminal Profiling: An Introduction to Behavioral Evidence Analysis*, 3rd ed. (Burlington, MA: Elsevier, 2008), 676.

77. Shaw, "The Role of Behavioral Research and Profiling," 20–31; E. D. Shaw, J. Post, and K. Ruby, "Inside the Mind of the Insider," *Security Management* 43, no. 12 (1999): 34–44; E. D. Shaw, J. Post, and K. Ruby, "Managing the Threat from Within: The Personnel Security Audit," *Information Security*, July (2000): 62–72; Turvey, *Criminal Profiling*, 676.

78. S. Freud, "The Ego and the Id," in *The Standard Edition of the Complete Psychological Works of Sigmund Freud, Volume 19 (1923–1925): The Ego and the Id and Other Works* (London: The Hogarth Press, 1923): 1–66.

79. Caretti et al., "Psychopathology of Online Grooming," in Webster et al., *Online Offending Behavior*, 96.

80. S. Freud, *Introductory Lectures on Psychoanalysis*, 9th ed. (1922; London: Allen and Unwin, 1952).

81. Ibid.

82. Davidson and Webster, "The Theoretical Context of Online Child Sexual Abuse," in Webster et al., *Online Offending Behavior*, 31.

83. K. Beckham and A. Prohaska, "Deviant Men, Prostitution, and the Internet: A Qualitative Analysis of Men Who Killed Prostitutes Whom They Met Online," *International Journal of Criminal Justice Sciences* 7, no. 2 (2012): 639.

84. Ibid.

85. J. Bowlby, *Attachment and Loss: Vol. 1, Attachment* (New York: Basic Books, 1969).

86. J. Bowlby, "Attachment, Communication, and the Therapeutic Process," in *A Secure Base: Parent-Child Attachment and Healthy Human Development* (London: Basic Books, 1988), 137–157.

87. A. Bifulco and G. Thomas, *Understanding Adult Attachment and Family Relationships: Research, Assessment and Intervention* (London: Routledge, 2012).

88. A. Bifulco and T. Pham, "Young Victims Online," in Webster et al., *Online Offending Behavior*, 150.

89. T. Ward, S. M. Hudson, W. L. Marshall, and R. Siegert, "Attachment Style and Intimacy Deficits and Sex Offenders: A Theoretical Framework," *Sexual Abuse: A Journal of Research and Treatment* 7, no. 4 (1995): 317–335.

90. D. Fisher and K. Howells, "Social Relationships in Sexual Offenders," *Sexual and Marital Therapy* 8, no. 2 (1993): 123–136.

91. D. Verton, *The Hacker Diaries: Confessions of Teenage Hackers* (Berkeley, CA: McGraw-Hill, 2002).

92. Ibid., xvii–xviii, 37, 86, 102, 105, 142, 145, 170, 188.
93. J. Littman, *The Fugitive Game: Online with Kevin Mitnick* (Toronto: Little Brown, 1995); J. Littman, *The Watchman: The Twisted Life and Crimes of Serial Hacker Kevin Poulsen* (Toronto: Little Brown, 1997); K. Hafner and J. Markoff, *Cyberpunks: Outlaws and Hackers on the Computer Frontier* (Toronto: Simon and Schuster, 1995).
94. S. Turkle, *Alone Together: Why We Expect More from Technology and Less from Each Other* (New York: Basic Books, 2011).
95. Ibid., 83–84.
96. Ibid., 93.
97. Ibid., 95.
98. Ibid.
99. Ibid., 101.
100. S. C. McQuade, *Understanding and Managing Cybercrime* (Boston, MA: Allyn and Bacon, 2006).
101. Ibid.
102. A. Weinstein and M. Lejoyeux, "Internet Addiction or Excessive Internet Use," *American Journal of Drug and Alcohol Abuse* 36, no. 5 (2010): 277–283.
103. R. LaRose, C. A. Lin, and M. S. Eastin, "Unregulated Internet Usage: Addiction, Habit, or Deficient Self-Regulation?" *Media Psychology* 5, no. 3 (2003): 225–253; K. S. Young, "Internet Addiction: A New Clinical Phenomenon and Its Consequences," *American Behavioral Scientist* 48, no. 4 (2004): 402–415.
104. A. Chandler, "The Changing Definition and Image of Hackers in Popular Discourse," *International Journal of Sociology and Law* 24, no. 2 (1996): 229–251; P. Taylor, *Hackers: Crime in Digital Sublime* (New York: Routledge, 2000); J. Lickiewicz, "Psychological Characteristics of Persons Committing Computer Crimes," *Problems of Forensic Sciences* 61, no. LXI (2005): 30–41.
105. LaRose et al., "Unregulated Internet Usage," 230.
106. Young, "Internet Addiction," 402–415.
107. B. Schell, M. Martin, P. Hung, and L. Rueda, "Cyber Child Pornography: A Review Paper of the Social and Legal Issues and Remedies—A Proposed Technological Solution," *Aggression and Violent Behavior* 12, no. 1 (2007), 45–63; A. W. Burgess, C. Regehr and A. R. Roberts, *Victimology: Theories and Applications* (Burlington, MA: Jones and Bartlett, 2010), 374.
108. LaRose et al., "Unregulated Internet Usage," 230.
109. Young, "Internet Addiction: A New Clinical Phenomenon," 402–415.
110. P. Taylor, *Hackers: Crime in the Digital Sublime* (London: Routledge, 1999).
111. Young, "Internet Addiction, A New Clinical Phenomenon," 402–415; S. Yılmaz, S. Hergüner, A. Bilgiç and U. Işık, "Internet Addiction Is Related to Attention Deficit but Not Hyperactivity in a Sample of High School Students," *International Journal of Psychiatry in Clinical Practice* 19, no. 1 (2015): 18.
112. R. Kaltiala-Heino, T. Lintonen, and A. Rimpela, "Internet Addiction? Potentially Problematic Use of the Internet in a Population of 12–18-Year-Old Adolescents," *Addiction Research & Theory* 12, no. 1 (2004): 89–96.
113. Y. H. Choi, "Advancement of IT and Seriousness of Youth Internet Addiction," 2007 International Symposium on the Counseling and Treatment of Youth Internet Addiction, National Youth Commission, Seoul, Korea, 20.
114. L. C. Soule, L. W. Shell, and B. A. Kleen, "Exploring Internet Addiction: Demographic Characteristics and Stereotypes of Heavy Internet Users," *Journal of Computer Information Systems* 44, no. 1 (2003): 64–73; M. O'Reilly, "Internet Addiction: A New Disorder Enters the Medical Lexicon," *Canadian Medical Association Journal* 154, no. 12 (1966): 1882–1883.
115. F. Cao and L. Su, "Internet Addiction among Chinese Adolescents: Prevalence and Psychological Features," *Child: Care, Health & Development* 33, no. 3 (2006): 275–281; Soule et al., "Exploring Internet Addiction," 64–73; O'Reilly, "Internet Addiction," 1882–1883.

116. K. S. Young, "Internet Addiction: The Emergence of a New Clinical Disorder," *Cyberpsychology & Behavior* 1, no. 3 (2009): 237–244.

117. Choi, "Advancement of IT and Seriousness of Youth Internet Addiction," 20; D. H. Ahn, "Korean Policy on Treatment and Rehabilitation for Adolescents' Internet Addiction," 2007 International Symposium on the Counseling and Treatment of Youth Internet Addiction, National Youth Commission, Seoul, Korea, 49.

118. Weinstein and Lejoyeux, "Internet Addiction," 277.

119. K. Socia and K. J. McCarthy, "Association, Online," in *Encyclopedia of Cybercrime*, ed. S. C. McQuade (Westport, CT: Greenwood Press, 2009).

120. BBC News, "South Korean Dies After Games Session," August 10, 2005, http://news.bbc .co.uk/2/hi/technology/4137782.stm.

121. V. Starcevic, "Is Internet Addiction a Useful Concept?" *Australian and New Zealand Journal of Psychiatry* 47, no. 1 (2013): 16–19; M. Pawlikowski, I. W. Nader, C. Burger, S. Stieger, and M. Brand, "Pathological Internet Use—It Is a Multidimensional and Not a Unidimensional Construct," *Addiction Research and Theory* 22, no. 2 (2014): 167.

122. Pawlikowski et al., "Pathological Internet Use," 167.

123. N. A. Shapira, M. C. Lessig, T. D. Goldsmith, S. T. Szabo, M. Lazoritz, M. S. Gold, and D. J. Stein, "Problematic Internet Use: Proposed Classification and Diagnostic Criteria," *Depression and Anxiety* 17, no. 4 (2003): 207–216; L. Widyanto and M. Griffiths, "Internet Addiction: A Critical Review," *International Journal of Mental Health and Addiction* 4, no. 1 (2006): 31–51.

124. L. Widyanto and M. McMurran, "The Psychometric Properties of the Internet Addiction Test," *Cyberpsychology & Behavior* 7, no. 4 (2004): 443–450; S. Bernardi and S. Pallanti, "Internet Addiction: A Descriptive Clinical Study Focusing on Comorbidities and Dissociative Symptoms," *Comprehensive Psychiatry* 50, no. 6 (2009): 510–516; J. Korkeila, S. Kaarlas, M. Jaaskelainen, T. Vahlberg and T. Taiminen, "Attached to the Web—Harmful Use of the Internet and Its Correlates," *European Psychiatry* 25, no. 4 (2010): 236–241; D. Han, Y. Lee, C. Na, J. Ahn, U. Chung, M. Daniels, C. Haws, and P. Renshaw, "The Effect of Methylphenidate on Internet Video Game Play in Children with Attention-Deficit/Hyperactivity Disorder," *Comprehensive Psychiatry* 50, no. 3 (2009): 251–256; Weinstein and Lejoyeux, "Internet Addiction," 277–283.

125. K. S. Young, "Treatment Outcomes with Internet Addicts," *Cyberpsychology & Behavior* 10, no. 5 (2007): 671–679.

126. Young, "Internet Addiction: A New Clinical Phenomenon," 402–415; M. H. Hur, "Current Trends of Internet Addiction Disorder Research: A Review of 2000–2008 Korean Academic Journal Articles," *Asia Pacific Journal of Social Work and Development* 22, no. 3 (2012): 195.

127. K. W. Beard and E. M. Wolf, "Modification in the Proposed Diagnostic Criteria for Internet Addiction," *Cyberpsychology & Behavior* 4, no. 3 (2001): 379; J. Orford, *Excessive Appetites: A Psychological View of the Addictions*, 2nd ed. (Chichester, UK: John Wiley, 2001); N. L. Warden, J. G. Phillips, and J. R. P. Ogloff, "Internet Addiction," *Psychiatry, Psychology and Law* 11, no. 2 (2004): 284.

128. Beard and Wolf, "Modification in Criteria for Internet Addiction," 377–383.

129. Young, "Internet Addiction: A New Clinical Disorder," 237–244.

130. M. D. Griffiths, "Internet Addiction—Time To Be Taken Seriously?" *Addiction Research & Theory* 8, no. 5 (2000): 413–418.

131. R. A. Davis, "A Cognitive–Behavioral Model of Pathological Internet Use," *Computers in Human Behavior* 17, no. 2 (2001): 187–195.

132. Beard and Wolf, "Modification in Criteria for Internet Addiction," 377–383.

133. C-N. Lin, M-L. Shih, B-H. Liao, and Y-F. Zhang, Y-F., "Research on the Relationship among Children's Personality Traits, Learning Attitudes and Internet Addiction," *Journal of Statistics and Management Systems* 12, no. 6 (2009): 1153.

134. L. Armstrong, J. G. Phillips, and L. L. Saling, "Potential Determinants of Heavier Internet Usage," *International Journal of Human-Computer Studies* 53, no. 4 (2000): 537–550; G. Dong,

Q. Lu, H. Zhou, and X. Zhao, "Precursor or Sequela: Pathological Disorders in People with Internet Addiction Disorder," *PLoS One* 6, no. 2 (2011): 1.

135. H. J. Shaffer, "Understanding the Means and Objects of Addiction: Technology, the Internet, and Gambling," *Journal of Gambling Studies* 12, no. 4 (1996): 461–469; E. C. Hirschman, "The Consciousness of Addiction: Toward a General Theory of Compulsive Consumption," *Journal of Consumer Research* 19, no. 2 (1992): 155–179.

136. Armstrong et al., "Potential Determinants of Heavier Internet Usage," 537–550.

137. A. P. Blaszczynski, A. C. Wilson, and N. McConaghy, "Sensation Seeking and Pathological Gambling," *British Journal of Addiction* 18, no. 1 (1986):113–117.

138. Davis, "A Cognitive–Behavioral Model of Pathological Internet Use," 187–195.

139. Ibid., cited in J. Czincz and R. Hechanova, "Internet Addiction: Debating the Diagnosis," *Journal of Technology in Human Services* 27, no. 4 (2009): 263.

140. Young, "Internet Addiction: A New Clinical Disorder," 237–244; Griffiths, "Internet Addiction—Time To Be Taken Seriously?" 413–418.

141. Griffiths, "Internet Addiction—Time To Be Taken Seriously?" 413–418.

142. LaRose et al., "Unregulated Internet Usage," 225–253.

143. S. M. Li and T. M. Chung, "Internet Function and Internet Addictive Behavior," *Computers in Human Behavior* 22, no. 6 (2006): 1067–1071; J. Morahan-Martin and P. Schumacher, "Incidence and Correlates of Pathological Internet Use among College Students," *Computers in Human Behavior* 16, no. 1 (2000): 13–29; S. C. Yang and C. J. Tung, "Comparison of Internet Addicts and Non-addicts in Taiwanese High School," *Computers in Human Behavior* 23, no. 1 (2007): 79–96; Young, "Internet Addiction: A New Clinical Disorder," 237–244.

144. S. E. Caplan, "Problematic Internet Use and Psychosocial Well-Being: Development of a Theory-Based Cognitive-Behavioral Measurement Instrument," *Computers in Human Behavior* 18, no. 5 (2002): 553–575.

145. Ibid.

146. J. Levy and R. Strombeck, "Health Benefits and Risks of the Internet," *Journal of Medical Systems* 26, no. 6 (2002): 495–510.

147. F. Cao, L. Su, T. Liu, and X. Gao, "The Relationship between Impulsivity and Internet Addiction in a Sample of Chinese Adolescents," *European Psychiatry* 22, no. 7 (2007): 466–471; Warden et al., "Internet Addiction," 280–295.

148. Widyanto and McMurran, "The Psychometric Properties of the Internet Addiction Test," 443–450.

149. Shapira et al., "Problematic Internet Use," 207–216.

150. J. Schmitz, "The Interface between Impulse-Control Disorders and Addictions: Are Pleasure Pathway Responses Shared Neurobiological Substrates?" *Sexual Addiction & Compulsivity* 12, no. 2-3 (2005): 149–168.

151. K. Young, "Psychology of Computer Use: Addictive Use of the Internet: A Case that Breaks the Stereotype," *Psychological Reports* 79, no. 3 (1996): 899–902; O. Egger and M. Rauterberg, "Internet Behavior and Addiction," 1966, www.idemployee.id.tue.nl/g.w.m.rauterberg/ibq /report.pdf; Morahan-Martin and Schumacher, "Incidence and Correlates of Pathological Internet Use," 13–29; M. Griffiths, "Internet Addiction: Does It Really Exist?" in *Psychology and the Internet: Intrapersonal, Interpersonal and Transpersonal Implications*, ed. J. Gackenbach (San Diego, CA: Academic Press, 1998), 61–75; M. Orzack, "Computer Addiction: Is It Real or Virtual?" *Harvard Mental Health Letter* 15, no. 7 (1999): 8; D. N. Greenfield, "Psychological Characteristics of Compulsive Internet Use: A Preliminary Analysis," *CyberPsychology and Behavior* 2, no. 5 (2000): 403–412; R. L. Gilbert, N. A. Murphy, and T. McNally, "Addiction to the 3-Dimensional Internet: Estimated Prevalence and Relationship to Real World Addictions," *Addiction Research & Theory* 19, no. 4 (2011): 380–390.

152. V. Brenner, "Psychology of Computer Use: XLVII. Parameters of Internet Use, Abuse and Addiction: The First 90 Days of the Internet Usage Survey," *Psychological Reports* 80, no. 3 (1997): 879–882; K. J. Anderson, "Internet Use among College Students: An Exploratory Study," *Journal of American College Health* 50, no. 1 (2001): 21–26.

153. D. W. Black, G. Belsare, and S. Schlosser, "Clinical Features, Psychiatric Comorbidity, and Health-Related Quality of Life in Persons Reporting Compulsive Computer Use Behavior," *Journal of Clinical Psychiatry* 60, no. 12 (1999): 839–844; N. A. Shapira, T. D. Goldsmith, P. E. Keck Jr., U. M. Khosla, and S. L. McElroy, "Psychiatric Features of Individuals with Problematic Internet Use," *Journal of Affective Disorders* 57, no. 1–3 (2000): 267–272; M. Shaw and D. W. Black, "Internet Addiction: Definition, Assessment, Epidemiology and Clinical Management," *CNS Drugs* 22, no. 5 (2008): 353–365.

154. Young, "Internet Addiction: A New Clinical Disorder," 237–244; Verton, *The Hacker Diaries*, 35, 39, 41, 51; Anderson, "Internet Use among College Students," 21–26; Brenner, "Psychology of Computer Use," 879–882.

155. The Mentor, *The Hacker Manifesto*, 1986, https://www.usc.edu/~douglast/202/lecture23/manifesto.html.

156. Griffiths, "Internet Addiction—Time To Be Taken Seriously?" 413–418; Orford, *Excessive Appetites*; Warden et al., "Internet Addiction," 281.

157. American Psychiatric Association, *Diagnostic and Statistical Manual of Mental Disorders*, 5th ed. (Arlington, VA: American Psychiatric Association, 2013).

158. American Psychiatric Association, "Internet Gaming Disorder," May 2013, http://www.dsm5.org/Documents/Internet%20Gaming%20Disorder%20Fact%20Sheet.pdf.

159. K. Yuan, W. Qin, Y. Liu, and J. Tian, "Internet Addiction: Neuroimaging Findings," *Communicative and Integrative Biology* 4, no. 6 (2011): 637.

160. B. Fischl and A. M. Dale, "Measuring the Thickness of the Human Cerebral Cortex from Magnetic Resonance Images," *Proceedings of the National Academy of Sciences of the United States of America* 97, no. 20 (2000): 11050–11055; J. J. Levitt, M. Kubicki, P. G. Nestor, H. Ersner-Hershfield, C. F. Westin, J. L. Alvarado, R. Kikinis, F. A. Jolesz, R. W. McCarley, and M. E. Shenton, "A Diffusion Tensor Imaging Study of the Anterior Limb of the Internal Capsule in Schizophrenia," *Psychiatry Research* 184, no. 3 (2010): 143–150; J. Liu, X. P. Gao, I. Osunde X. Li, S. K. Zhou, H. R. Zheng, and L. J. Li, "Increased Regional Homogeneity in Internet Addiction Disorder: A Resting State Functional Magnetic Resonance Imaging Study," *Chinese Medical Journal* 123, no. 14 (2010): 1904–1908; Y. Zhou, F. Lin, Y. Du, L. Qin, Z. Zhao, Z., J. R. Xu, and Y. Du, "Gray Matter Abnormalities in Internet Addiction: A Voxel Based Morphometry Study," *European Journal of Radiology* 79, no. 1 (2011): 95; G. Dong, Q. Lu, H. Zhou, and X. Zhao, "Impulse Inhibition in People with Internet Addiction Disorder: Electrophysiological Evidence from a Go/Nogo Study," *Neuroscience Letters* 485, no. 2 (2010): 138–142; B. Fischl, M. I. Sereno, and A. M. Dale, "Cortical Surface-Based Analysis. II: Inflation, Flattening and a Surface-Based Coordinate System," *Neuroimage*, 9, no. 2 (1999): 195–207; C. H. Ko, G. Liu, S. Hsiao, J. Yen, M. Yang, W. C. Lin, C. F. Yen, and C. S. Chen, "Brain Activities Associated with Gaming Urge of Online Gaming Addiction," *Journal of Psychiatric Research* 43, no. 7 (2009): 739–747; G. Schoenbaum, A. A. Chiba, and M. Gallagher, "Orbitofrontal Cortex and Basolateral Amygdala Encode Expected Outcomes during Learning," *Nature Neuroscience* 1, no. 2 (1998): 155–159; G. Schoenbaum, M. R. Roesch, and T. A. Stalnaker, "Orbitofrontal Cortex, Decision-Making and Drug Addiction," *Trends in Neurosciences* 29, no. 2 (2006): 116–124; C. H. Ko, S. Hsiao, G. Liu, J. Yen, M. Yang, and C. F. Yen, "The Characteristics of Decision Making, Potential to Take Risks and Personality of College Students With Internet Addiction," *Psychiatry Research* 175, no. 1–2 (2010): 121–125; L. Tremblay and W. Schultz, "Relative Reward Preference in Primate Orbitofrontal Cortex," *Nature* 398, no. 6729 (1999): 704–708.

161. Yuan et al., "Internet Addiction," 638.

162. Ibid.

163. D. H. Han, Y. S. Lee, C. Na, J. Y. Ahn, U. S. Chung, M. A. Daniels, C. A. Haws, and P. F. Renshaw, "The Effect of Methylphenidate on Internet Video Game Play in Children with Attention-Deficit/Hyperactivity Disorder," *Comprehensive Psychiatry* 50, no. 3 (2009): 251–256.

164. Weinstein and Lejoyeux, "Internet Addiction," 279.

165. Ibid.

166. Ibid.

167. National Institute on Drug Abuse, *Comorbidity: Addiction and Other Mental Illnesses*, last updated September 2010, https://www.drugabuse.gov/publications/research-reports /comorbidity-addiction-other-mental-illnesses/what-comorbidity.

168. D. W. Black, G. Belsare, and S. Schlosser, "Clinical Features, Psychiatric Comorbidity, and Health-Related Quality of Life in Persons Reporting Compulsive Computer Use Behavior," *Journal of Clinical Psychiatry* 60, no. 12 (1999): 839–844; J. Ha, H. Yoo, I. Cho, B. Chin, D. Shin, and J. Kim, "Psychiatric Comorbidity Assessed in Korean Children and Adolescents Who Screen Positive for Internet Addiction," *Journal of Clinical Psychiatry* 67, no. 5 (2006): 821–826; J. Y. Yen C. H. Ko, C. F. Yen, H. Y. Wu, and M. J. Yang, "The Comorbid Psychiatric Symptoms of Internet Addiction: Attention Deficit and Hyperactivity Disorder (ADHD), Depression, Social Phobia, and Hostility," *Journal of Adolescent Health* 41, no. 1 (2007): 93–98.

169. C. Ko, J. Yen, C. Chen, C. Chen, and C. Yen, "Psychiatric Comorbidity of Internet Addiction in College Students: An Interview Study," *CNS Spectrums* 13, no. 2 (2008): 147–153; R.-M. Shepherd and R. Edelmann, "Reasons for Internet Use and Social Anxiety," *Personality and Individual Differences* 39, no. 5 (2005): 949–958.

170. Weinstein and Lejoyeux, "Internet Addiction," 277–283; Ko et al., "Psychiatric Comorbidity of Internet Addiction in College Students," 147–153.

171. Weinstein and Lejoyeux, "Internet Addiction," 277–283.

172. J. H. Ha, S. Y. Kim, S. C. Bae, S. Bae, H. Kim, M. Sim, I. K. Lyoo, and S. C. Cho, "Depression and Internet Addiction in Adolescents," *Psychopathology* 40, no. 6 (2007): 424–430; K. Kim, E. Ryu, M. Y. Chon, E. J. Yeun, S. Y. Choi, J. S. Seo, and B. W. Nam, "Internet Addiction in Korean Adolescents and its Relation to Depression and Suicidal Ideation: A Questionnaire Survey," *International Journal of Nursing Studies* 43, no. 2 (2006): 185–192; Weinstein and Lejoyeux, "Internet Addiction," 277–283; S. J. Kim, D.-H. Park, S-H. Ryu, J. Yu, and J. H. Ha, "Usefulness of Young's Internet Addiction Test for Clinical Populations," *Nordic Journal of Psychiatry* 67, no. 6 (2013): 393; Ko et al., "Psychiatric Comorbidity of Internet Addiction in College Students," 147–153; Ha et al., "Psychiatric Comorbidity Assessed in Korean Children," 821–826.

173. S. Bernardi and S. Pallanti, "Internet Addiction: A Descriptive Clinical Study Focusing on Co-morbidities and Dissociative Symptoms," *Comprehensive Psychiatry* 50, no. 6 (2009): 510–516; Weinstein and Lejoyeux, "Internet Addiction," 277–283; Kim et al., "Usefulness of Young's Internet Addiction Test," 393.

174. S. A. Haylett, G. M. Stephenson, and R. M. H. Lefever, "Covariation in Addictive Behaviors: A Study of Addictive Orientations Using the Shorter PROMIS Questionnaire," *Addictive Behaviors* 29, no. 1 (2004): 61–71.

175. R. A. Davis, "A Cognitive-Behavioral Model of Pathological Internet Use," *Computers in Human Behavior* 17, no. 2 (2001): 187–195.

176. Ibid.

177. Shapira et al., "Psychiatric Features of Individuals with Problematic Internet Use," 267–272.

178. R. Kraut, V. Lundmark M. Patterson, S. Kiesler, T. Mukopadhyay, and W. Scherlis, "Internet Paradox: A Social Technology That Reduces Social Involvement and Psychological

Well-Being?" *American Psychologist* 53, no. 9 (1998): 1017–1031; Young, "Internet Addiction: A New Clinical Disorder," 237–244.

179. Warden et al., "Internet Addiction," 281, 289.
180. D. Howitt, *Introduction to Forensic and Criminal Psychology*, 3rd ed. (Harlow, UK: Pearson, 2009).
181. Weinstein and Lejoyeux, "Internet Addiction," 277–283.
182. Ahn, "Korean Policy on Treatment and Rehabilitation," 49.
183. Lombroso, *The Criminal Man*; Vold and Bernard, *Theoretical Criminology*.
184. J. Christensen, "The Trials of Kevin Mitnick," *CNN*, March 18, 1999, http://www.cnn.com/SPECIALS/1999/mitnick.background/.
185. S. Watts, "Teenage Hacker 'Enslaved by Habit,'" *Independent*, March 4, 1993, http://www.independent.co.uk/news/uk/teenage-hacker-enslaved-by-habit-1495697.html.
186. "Computer Hackers 'Broke into NASA,'" *Herald* (Scotland), May 21, 1993, http://www.heraldscotland.com/news/12628147.Computer_hackers__apos_broke_into_Nasa_apos_/.
187. M. Janofsky, "Youth Pleads an Addiction to the Internet in Threat Case," *New York Times*, January 13, 2000, http://www.nytimes.com/2000/01/13/us/youth-pleads-an-addiction-to-the-internet-in-threat-case.html.
188. Ibid.
189. Ibid.
190. R. Verkaik, "Woman Fired for Internet Over-Use, *Independent*, August 22, 1999, http://www.independent.co.uk/news/woman-fired-for-internet-over-use-1114544.html.
191. No. 04 Civ. 5831 (PGG) 21 American Disabilities Case (BNA) 1260 (S.D.N.Y. 2009).

CHAPTER 6

CYBERCRIME, CULTURE, AND INEQUALITY

KEYWORDS

Anomie
Anomie theory
Broken windows theory
Chicago School of
   Criminology
Collective efficacy
Concentric zone theory
Delinquent subculture
   theory

Differential opportunity
   theory
General strain theory
Hacker ethic
Human ecology
Institutional anomie theory
Phreakers
Reaction formation
Relative deprivation

Relative deprivation
   theory
Social capital
Social disorganization
Social disorganization
   theory
Strain
Subcultural theories
Subculture

In 2015, the operator of the second-largest music piracy website (RockDizFile.com), Rocky Ouprasith, was sentenced to thirty-six months' imprisonment.[1] In addition to hosting the illegal music, he also encouraged and solicited others to upload pirated works to his website. What theory can be used to explain his behavior? What about those who upload and download pirated works? Why do they engage in this criminal behavior? This chapter seeks to answer these questions by examining social disorganization, anomie, institutional anomie, relative deprivation, strain, and cultural deviance theories. Before this examination, the central tenets of the Chicago School of Criminology are explored.

CHICAGO SCHOOL OF CRIMINOLOGY

The **Chicago School of Criminology** includes the first major body of works which sought to explain the causes, control, and dynamics of crime spatially by examining neighborhood, community, urban, and environmental factors. The central tenet of this criminological work is that criminal offending is not randomly distributed across space. Instead, crime is viewed as being more likely to occur in particular areas in cities than it is in rural areas. The spaces in which crime occurs are also characterized by a slew of social problems, such as poverty and unemployment. This conclusion was based on the Chicago School scholars' examination of the expansion of the Chicago population, the implications of the social groupings that occurred in specific areas, and the places where certain social problems were concentrated. Through their spatial mapping of social problems, these researchers sought to explain why certain areas persist in having high crime rates and attendant social problems despite high turnover rates within the population. More specifically, the Chicago School of Criminology addressed the question: What is it about the structure and culture of neighborhoods that reproduces these social problems through generations over long periods of time?

One of the main theorists of the Chicago School was Robert E. Park, who studied crime through the lens of **human ecology** by examining the relationship between individuals and the environment.[2] One of the forces governing these relationships was competition. Park argued that competition between individuals for land and other resources ultimately led to the compartmentalization of urban spaces into zones populated by individuals who share similar social characteristics because they have been subjected to similar ecological pressures. Another theorist of the Chicago School, Ernest Burgess, proposed a zonal theory for the development of a city, the **concentric zone theory**.[3] This theory conceptualized the city as consisting of five primary concentric zones (see Figure 6-1). The *inner zone*, a non-residential area of the city, included major government buildings, financial institutions, and retail and commercial establishments. The second zone, the *zone in transition*, was the area where the poor resided and interacted. This zone included the city's factories and oldest residential buildings. Individuals who resided in this area were those who could only afford the cheapest residences, and, as such, new immigrants tended to populate these areas. Once these individuals became more economically established, they moved out of this zone. The zone in transition was characterized by high crime rates and **social disorganization**, a condition in a community whereby its structure and culture do not reflect the values and best interests of its residents. Social disorganization was attributed to community heterogeneity and the mobility of its residents.[4] As the name implies, the *zone of the working man*, the third zone, was where the working class resided. This area of the city was primarily populated by the children of immigrants (second-generation families who moved out of the zone in transition). The offspring of these families sought to move out of this zone as well. In the fourth zone, the *residential zone*, the middle-class resided. The last zone, the *commuter zone*, was the suburbs, where both the middle class and the wealthy resided. Hence, in the last three zones, residents lived in accordance with their affluence and social status. Park and Burgess thus sought to explain criminality through the characteristics of the location where crime occurred. Their work viewed the city as an ecosystem wherein the behavior of residents was influenced by social structures and the neighborhood environment.

SOCIAL DISORGANIZATION THEORY

Building upon ideas and work by Park and Burgess, Clifford Shaw and Henry McKay, who were also part of the Chicago School, developed a criminological theory known as **social disorganization theory**.[5] Social disorganization theory holds that crime occurs in locations

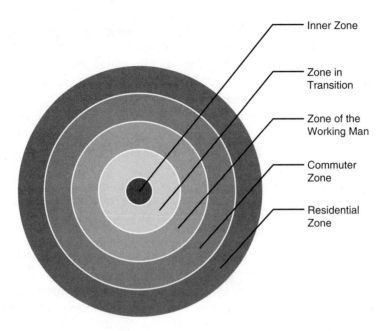

FIGURE 6-1 Primary Concentric Zones of the City.

where a community is no longer able to regulate the conduct of its members according to accepted conventional norms, values, and beliefs (i.e., unable to maintain social control) and instead realizes the unconventional values of its residents.[6] These neighborhoods are characterized not only by lack of existing self-regulatory mechanisms but also by weak social integration. These areas have high rates of accepted delinquent and criminal norms, which compete with existing conventional norms. These neighborhoods also produce deviant and criminal traditions that are transmitted to successive generations through beliefs and actions. Socially disorganized communities are incubators of deviance and crime due to lack of effective control mechanisms and the cultural transmission of deviant and criminal values. Therefore, what needs to be dealt with is not the pathology of the individual, but rather the disorganization of the communities.

Studying official data, existing life history, and ecological location, Shaw and McKay showed that while crime was distributed throughout the city, it was most prevalent in the zones closest to the business district.[7] The neighborhoods with the highest crime rates were those closest to the industrial and commercial buildings, with few residential buildings, and with the highest number of condemned buildings. Indeed, Shaw and McKay found that crime was highest in the zone in transition and declined with distance from this zone.[8] Those within the high crime rate zones were also of low economic status, suffering from poverty and material deprivation. These areas were characterized by high rates of delinquency and a greater acceptance of nonconventional norms, values, and beliefs by its residents. These nonconventional values and traditions can become embedded within a community and exist alongside conventional values and traditions.

Cyberspace has been viewed as producing social disorganization because the main factors conducive to crime and deviance that exist in socially disorganized communities are also present in cyberspace.[9] Cyberspace, like the *zone in transition*, is characterized by transiency and heterogeneity (i.e., anyone can freely, quickly, and continuously "move" through cyberspace).[10] Additionally, the quick turnover that exists in online spaces (e.g., chat rooms) "contributes to the frequency and the nature of deviance [and crime] within . . . [them] by creating a perpetual state of social disorganization."[11] These spaces also play a pivotal role in the cultural transmission of delinquent and criminal values. In fact, online communities of cybercriminals (e.g., hackers and digital pirates) are notorious for transmitting deviant and criminal traditions to other (potential) cybercriminals.

Social Capital and Collective Efficacy

Social order (or social organization) is present when social bonds exist within a community. These communities are characterized by social cohesion whereby residents show consensus on the goals and behaviors that should be pursued by its members. In contrast, socially disorganized and high-crime communities are characterized by lack of **social capital**. Social capital refers to the extent to which an individual has developed relations with others and societal institutions over his or her life.[12] These relations and the investment of the individual in them reduces the likelihood of offending. Social capital exists "when relations among persons facilitate action, 'making possible the achievements of certain ends that in its absence would not be possible.'"[13] Strong social capital fosters trust among residents and produces collective action.[14] **Collective efficacy** refers to the ability of residents and the community to control illicit behavior. More specifically, collective efficacy is made possible through the actions of community residents to maintain order (e.g., reporting illicit behavior to law enforcement agencies) within its public areas. These actions are designed to foster trust and build relationships with other community members. Conversely, low levels of collective efficacy have been found to be associated with crime.

The body of work on social capital and collective efficacy seeks to shed light on why crime persists in a socially disorganized neighborhood by examining the neighborhood's culture. "Neighborhood" (i.e., community) culture and the absence of social capital and collective efficacy online have been associated with crime in cyberspace.[15] Social capital is related to users' perceptions of the trustworthiness of other people online, of online information, and of the websites the users visit.[16] Social capital is also related to users' online activities, as their perceptions of online collective efficacy affect their participation in collective action online.[17] When social capital and collective efficacy are present in online forums, users are likely to trust content, understand expectations and norms of behavior, and enforce existing norms through online communication and relations with other participants.[18] Moreover, when these components are present in online forums, users are also more likely to participate in formal and informal crime and deviancy reduction activities (e.g., reporting misconduct and violations of the policies of websites to the appropriate authorities). When social capital and collective efficacy are absent, these online forums are characterized by dysfunctional behaviors and lack of formal and informal sanctioning of criminal and deviant behavior, and those utilizing the websites distrust the content and other participants.[19]

BOX 6-1 COGNITIVE MAPS IN CYBERSPACE

Cognitive maps are mental representations of the attributes in one's environment. They are created by navigating offline and virtual spaces. Montello identified two distinct processes involved in navigation: locomotion and wayfinding.[20] *Locomotion* refers to movement within an environment.[21] *Wayfinding* refers to identifying a desired destination and planning a route that a person will follow to reach that destination.[22] In criminology, Gerald Suttles introduced the concept of cognitive maps.[23] Patricia and Paul Braninghan discussed how individuals create cognitive maps of their residential areas; these maps differentiate known and well-known residential areas.[24] Individuals map the environment in which they live not only for mobility reasons but also for security and safety reasons. The reputation of an area plays a role in creating cognitive maps based not only on personal experiences but also on information retrieved from media sources and gossip. Research has shown that some areas acquire certain negative reputations that have adverse consequences for residents.[25]

Just as in the offline world, in the online world certain areas have acquired particular reputations. Pornography websites, for example, are viewed as being infected with malware, and chat rooms are known to be frequented by cyberpredators. Ultimately, cognitive maps enable people to find ways to negotiate the environment within which they live, work, and play, the places they go, and the places to avoid and the time of the day to avoid them. These cognitive maps have a direct effect on individuals' spatial behavior offline and online.

CYBERSPACE: APPLYING THE BROKEN WINDOWS THEORY In 1982, James Q. Wilson and George Kelling developed the **broken windows theory** to explain the "signaling effect" of socially disorganized neighborhoods.[26] This theory holds that persistent disorder and incivility within a community is associated with future occurrences of serious crimes in that area. The prevalence of disorder and incivility in a community sends the message to residents and nonresidents that the area is unsafe. This conclusion leads to the weakening of social control mechanisms within the neighborhood, thereby diminishing further the ability of the community to maintain order in public spaces. The existing disorder and incivility thus invite increased criminality by sending the message to perpetrators that "anything goes" in the area. Accordingly, disorder and incivility are viewed as causing the following chain of events: the presence of disorder and incivility leads to fear among residents; this fear causes a breakdown in social capital and collective efficacy; and the breakdown of social capital and collective efficacy ultimately leads to more serious crime in the area (see Figure 6-2).

The most notable application of the broken widows theory was by New York City Police Department police commissioner William Bratton in the 1990s. Commissioner Bratton implemented a quality of life initiative on crime (later termed the *zero-tolerance initiative*) in which police officers were tasked with dealing with low-level, public order crimes (i.e., illicit acts that offend the public's shared norms, morals, values, and customs) and antisocial behaviors, such as prostitution, panhandling, drunk and disorderly conduct, graffiti, and turnstile jumping at train stations. In carrying out the initiative, the police "fixed" the "broken windows" in the communities in which they worked.[27] During this initiative, reported crime rates decreased.[28]

Law enforcement agencies should deal with low-level cybercrimes in a similar fashion. The level of importance accorded to specific cybercrimes by these law enforcement agencies determines whether or not they are viewed as a low-level or high-level cybercrime. Currently, low-level cybercrimes (e.g., online scams and the defacement of a website) are often ignored by law enforcement agencies due to lack of human and financial resources

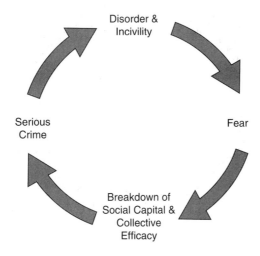

FIGURE 6-2 Broken Windows Theory: Chain of Events.

and the priority that is given to other crimes and cybercrimes.[29] According to the broken windows theory, failure to attend to these low-level cybercrimes invites increased cyber-criminality. Law enforcement agencies should thus follow Bratton's innovation for taking a more proactive approach by targeting low-level cybercrimes to ultimately reduce high-level cybercrimes (e.g., distributed denial of service attacks). The public also has a central role to play here with respect to reporting crimes to law enforcement agencies. One of the main advantages of this theory is that adhering to it can effect change in cybercrime more quickly than responses designed to deal with social disorganization, which seek to deal with structural issues in society (e.g., poverty and inequality).

ANOMIE THEORY

Anomie refers to a state of society characterized by "normlessness,"[30] a disruption in the normal conditions of society. This state of society is characterized by a breakdown of norms and the inability of society to control individuals within it. Émile Durkheim viewed crime as a product of social forces and social stressors.[31] For Durkheim, anomie arose from changes or disruptions in society. Crime resulted from the state of anomie that occurred during times of social and technological change.[32]

Robert Merton utilized Durkheim's anomie concept in his **anomie theory**.[33] However, unlike Durkheim, Merton did not believe that anomie was caused by sudden changes or disruptions in society. Instead, he viewed anomie as the outcome of society's provision of similar goals to all individuals within society but unequal means to achieve them. Deviancy and crime were thus viewed as the product of individuals' inability to achieve these goals using the means available to them. More specifically, building upon Durkheim's anomie concept, Merton proposed that crime is a product of the disparities that exist between cultural aspirations (the achievement of the American Dream, that is, the achievement of wealth, occupation, status, and education) and the opportunities available to individuals to achieve these. In anomic societies, individuals become fixated on the same goals (viewed as markers of success), which cannot be achieved by all equally in a legal fashion.

The primary reason for this inability to achieve these goals is that not all members of society have the resources needed to achieve them. When these goals cannot be achieved using legal means, illegal means are utilized. When an anomic culture exists, an individual will choose the easily available and efficient option, regardless of the morality and legality of that option. Merton proposed five responses or adaptations to anomie (see Figure 6-3).

Conformity. In cyberspace, Internet users who utilize the Internet in socially acceptable ways can be viewed as conformists. With this mode of adaptation, individuals who utilize the Internet as a tool for financial gain can be classified as conformists if they accept the goals of society (e.g., pursuit of wealth) and the available means to achieve them (e.g., setting up a website to sell goods), even though these goals predominantly remain unrealized.

Innovation. Individuals who are characterized as innovators accept the goals of society but reject the available means to achieve them; instead, they opt to use different and typically illegal means to achieve them. Individuals who utilize the Internet as a tool for financial gain can be classified as innovators[34] if, unable to obtain wealth through legitimate means, they rely on an alternative, illicit means to achieve wealth.

Ritualism. Ritualists reject the goals of society but still engage in the legitimate means that can be used to achieve such goals. Douglas Coupland's fictional novel *Microserfs* depicts computer programmers who are consumed with work but not to achieve material wealth.[35] These individuals, the microserfs, can thus be classified as ritualists because they are in low-paying jobs to which they are dedicated but do not engage in the work to achieve societal goals (i.e., material wealth), nor are they able to realize these goals despite following prescribed societal means.

Retreatism. Retreatists reject the goals of society and the legitimate means to achieve them. Individuals utilizing this mode of adaptation stop becoming productive members of society. An example of a retreatist is someone with an Internet addiction, such as an online gaming addiction, where the goal that matters is playing the game. Gaming takes precedent over all other activities and becomes all-consuming.

Rebellion. Like retreatists, rebels reject the goals of society and the legitimate means to achieve them. However, unlike retreatists, these individuals create new goals and new means to achieve them. Rebels are motivated by other goals, such as thrills, and reject the goals and means to achieve financial success.[36] Individuals who fall into this category are those who engage in hacktivism (i.e., individuals who utilize the Internet and digital devices to gain unauthorized access to a system or target the system in any other way to impair its functionality in furtherance of a political goal). A well-known hacktivist group is the Electrohippies (or Ehippies). This group targeted the websites of major international organizations that were viewed as promoting policies favoring corporations.[37]

FIGURE 6-3 Merton's Proposed Adaptations to Anomie.

Research has shown that lack of legitimate opportunities in society leads individuals to pursue illegitimate opportunities. More specifically, individuals with cybersecurity skills in Eastern Europe and Russia who could not find legitimate employment within their own country have sought to work for organized crime groups to support themselves and their families.[38] Ultimately, the response or method of adaptation one pursues depends on the person's view of the goals and the means available to achieve these goals. Other than the above-mentioned modes of adaptations, the options for individuals faced with blocked opportunities are to reduce their aspirations or for society to increase available opportunities and provide individuals with the means to achieve societal goals, neither of which is realistic.

INSTITUTIONAL ANOMIE THEORY

As in Merton's anomie theory, the American Dream plays a pivotal role in **institutional anomie theory**.[39] The American Dream is the commitment of the individual to attain material success.[40] The pursuit of the American Dream may occur by any means necessary if the chosen means is the most efficient way to achieve it. Also, similarly to Merton, Stephen F. Messner and Richard Rosenfeld argue that the culture in the United States places too great an emphasis on the American Dream.[41] Merton's solution for an anomic society is to create additional economic opportunities. However, Messner and Rosenfeld believe that increased economic opportunities might actually make the anomic situation worse by reinforcing society's preoccupation with material wealth and thus, ultimately, creating greater anomie.[42]

Building upon Merton's work focusing on the aspects of social structures that provide opportunities for achieving the American Dream, Messner and Rosenfeld created an institutional anomie theory that considers the role of societal institutions (e.g., family, school, and religious institutions) in individuals' cultural perception of goals and the achievement of them.[43] Messner and Rosenfeld sought to explain why one structural institution, the economy, dominated other societal institutions, such as the family.

The American Dream sustains the imbalance between the economy and other societal institutions. This imbalance prevents other institutions from controlling members of society and insulating them from criminogenic pressures that stem from the pursuit of the American Dream. This imbalance even exists outside of the United States. In fact, institutional anomie is present in countries with cultures that promote materialism above all else and those that suffer from a high level of political corruption and failing social institutions. A case in point is Nigeria, a country that was made infamous by the members of its population known as Yahoo boys, who engage in Internet fraud targeting victims all over the world. According to Tade and Aliyu, "Yahoo-boyism is a glaring reflection of institutional anomie in Nigerian society. . . . Institutional corruption among government officials . . . [and the preaching of the supremacy of materialism by social institutions] contribut[e] to the emergence and sustenance of yahoo-boys . . . in Nigerian . . . institutions."[44] The existing cultural pressures to obtain material wealth, coupled with the inability of noneconomic social institutions to control and insulate members of society from these pressures, thus promotes crime and cybercrime.

RELATIVE DEPRIVATION THEORY

Some theorists and researchers hold that poverty causes individuals to engage in crime and cybercrime. However, the evidence on the socioeconomic status of criminals and cybercriminals varies.[45] Indeed, some individuals have engaged in crime and cybercrime because they are poor.[46] While poverty might explain why certain individuals engage in crimes and cybercrimes, this is not true for all criminals and cybercriminals.

Material wealth, therefore, does not account for all forms of crime and cybercrime. If it did, then crime and cybercrime would be committed only by individuals who were poor. Existing research does not support this notion. Accordingly, actual material deprivation per se is not an accurate predictor of crime and cybercrime. Instead, a good predictor is **relative deprivation**,[47] which refers to the discrepancy that exists between what an individual expects in life and what the individual actually gets. According to **relative deprivation theory**, an individual may perceive himself or herself as being disadvantaged with respect to others in a reference group believed to be in similar situations and having similar attributes.[48] The key word here is *perceived*, because these individuals may not actually be disadvantaged. They may feel that they are entitled to have the same number and types of assets as others in their reference group and seek to obtain them at any cost.

Relative deprivation is associated with the idiom "Keeping up with the Joneses." This phrase is attributed to a comic strip first published in 1913, titled "Keeping Up with the Joneses," by cartoonist Arthur R. ("Pop") Momand (see Image 6-1). The comic strip depicted a family that lived well beyond their means in order to keep up with their well-to-do neighbors, the Joneses, who actually never made an appearance in the comic strip. The comic strip was thus a parody of the preoccupation of Americans with material goods and the notion that these goods are indicators of individuals' social standing. An example of a material good that is designed to symbolize status is a luxury good. Luxury goods are exclusive goods and are not available to all due to their high costs. Cases in points are clothing, apparel, and jewelry from brands such as Chanel, Louis Vuitton, Christian Dior, Hermes, and Gucci. According to McAdams "consumers . . . use goods . . . to symbolize their status, whether truthfully or fraudulently."[49] Status can be fraudulently depicted by, for example, the possession of counterfeit luxury goods that bear close resemblance to the original goods. The demand for such items has led to their proliferation online. Indeed, counterfeit luxury goods, such as handbags, jewelry, and clothes, among other items, are widely available on auction and other websites. In 2015, Evan Patterson and his co-conspirator were arrested for selling numerous counterfeit luxury goods (e.g., Armani, Burberry, Cartier,

What Did Pa Mean?

IMAGE 6-1 Keeping Up with the Joneses Comic Strip.

Fendi, Nike, Ralph Lauren, Rolex, and Versace) obtained from unauthorized suppliers located in China on seventeen different websites.[50] Cases such as these abound.[51]

GENERAL STRAIN THEORY

Apart from material and relative deprivation, individuals commit cybercrime because of **strain** they experience (e.g., denial of civil liberties, discrimination, family conflict, physical and psychological abuse).[52] This strain need not be experienced by the individual or group engaging in the cybercrime. Individuals will engage in cybercrime if others with whom they identify are experiencing strain as a direct response to harm done to others. For example, a hacktivist known as Jester engaged in a cyberattack against Wikileaks because it posted classified information from U.S. diplomatic cables on its website.[53]

Robert Agnew proposed the **general strain theory**, which focuses on the various types of strains a user experiences.[54] This theory explains criminality from strained experiences at individual (e.g., biological and psychological traits), interpersonal (e.g., dysfunction or dissatisfaction with a group), and structural (e.g., socioeconomic classes and opportunities within society) levels.[55] General strain theory holds that individuals seek societal goals but society limits the ability of certain individuals to achieve them. Individuals measure their self-worth based on the achievement of these goals and blame structural conditions to overcome the guilt or remorse they feel with repeated anticipated failure to access opportunities.

General strain theory seeks to explain the impact of an individual's environment on his or her behavior. Agnew proposed three types of strain experienced from the:[56]

1. failure of a person to achieve goals that the individual positively valued;
2. removal or threat of removal of stimuli positively valued by the person; and
3. introduction or threat of introduction of stimuli negatively valued by the person.

First, the individual experiences strain when he or she fails to achieve goals or experiences treatment that he or she perceives as unjust.[57] Second, individuals may experience strain from the removal of positive social forces, such as jobs and relationships. Third, individuals may experience strain from negative life events. The negative events directly influence crime or indirectly influence it by increasing negative emotions. Individuals who experience strain and negative emotions from that strain are viewed as being more likely to engage in illicit behavior. Indeed, negative life events can provoke adverse emotional reactions (e.g., anger and frustration) as the individual tries to cope with the events.[58]

Individuals use various coping strategies to adapt to strain that may or may not be criminal. These coping strategies can be cognitive, emotional, and behavioral.[59] Cognitive coping strategies minimize the negative outcomes of the strain, maximize positive outcomes of the strain, or accept responsibility for the strain (e.g., "it's not important," "it's not that bad," or "I deserve it").[60] Emotional coping strategies include activities to alleviate or relieve negative emotions (e.g., substance abuse and exercise). Behavioral coping strategies seek to eliminate or reduce the sources of strain by actively seeking positive stimuli or avoiding negative stimuli (e.g., negotiation, truancy, and assault). In light of this, programs should be adopted that enable individuals to deal constructively with strain and the negative emotions they experience as a result of the strain. Overall, Agnew viewed crime as a sporadic phenomenon.[61] If the strain an individual experiences is removed, then he or she will desist from the illicit activity.

Studies conducted on the links between cybercrime and strain have shown mixed results. Research on cyberbullying has revealed that youths who report experiencing strains and negative emotions from these strains (anger and frustration) are more likely to engage in this type of cybercrime.[62] General strain theory has also been applied to digital piracy, such as music piracy. Music is perceived as essential to youths' social status and fitting in with peers. Music piracy is believed to result from the strains a youth experiences from his or her inability to purchase or otherwise obtain music for personal use.[63] As children do not have an income or a credit card, they have to rely on their parents or guardian for money to purchase music. Even when such money is provided in the form of allowances or gifts, the cost of music may prohibit children from buying it (with a few exceptions; for example, music downloaded online). Nonetheless, even those who have funds to purchase items have still sought to obtain them illegally and without cost.[64] Parents may additionally limit what music children hear and what games they play. For example, music may be prohibited due to its explicit lyrics; even video games may be prohibited if they are rated for use by older children and adults only. This prohibition of the items to youths means that parents must purchase the items for them, and only if the parent so desires. The desire to obtain music and the inability to obtain it using legitimate means causes strain. This strain may encourage an individual to seek illicit means to obtain the desired music.[65]

Indeed, the negative stimulus youths experience and the frustration and anger from this prohibition may be relieved through digital piracy. While certain studies have shown that strains are strong predictors of digital piracy,[66] others have shown that strain is not a salient predictor of digital piracy.[67] The reality is that strain theory cannot adequately explain why individuals turn to cybercrime for a specific and limited time when strains continue to be present. Moreover, this theory fails to explain why individuals who experience similar strain to that of the cybercriminal do not also engage in cybercrime.

CULTURAL DEVIANCE THEORIES

Subcultural criminology rejects the depiction of offenders in individualistic terms. A **subculture** is a "group . . . that share[s] many elements of the dominant culture but maintain[s] their own distinctive customs, values, norms and lifestyles."[68] Subcultures emerge when individuals that become part of this subculture are neglected or isolated from society. These subcultures form as a way for individuals to adjust to the strains they experience as a result of blocked opportunities. Those who are unable to achieve the goals of society tend to form groups to engage in delinquent or criminal behavior, which become the norm for the group. A subculture is thus a subdivision of mainstream culture with its own beliefs, norms, and values. Often, subcultures license and reward behavior at odds with mainstream social norms and laws. A subculture, therefore, adheres to and reinforces its own code.[69] This code also includes sharing information and mentoring new members (newbies); this behavior is frequently observed in hacking subcultures.[70]

Subcultural theories explain why these subcultures exist, what type of subculture is created, and why these subcultures persist. These theories hold that crime is the product of conformity to the cultural norms and values of a lower class subculture. This subculture is characterized by unique cultural norms and values that differ from those of mainstream society. Two types of cultural deviance theories are explored in the next section, the theory of delinquent subcultures and the theory of differential opportunity.

DELINQUENT SUBCULTURE THEORY

Unlike Merton, Albert Cohen saw crime and deviance as "nonutilitarian, malicious, and negativistic."[71] Another point of departure was Cohen's view that working class youth disproportionately experience strain.[72] His research, which examines juvenile subcultures, revealed that the most common type of subculture was a gang and those most likely to become part of subcultures were lower class (i.e., working class) boys. He posited that these groups persist because members of these subcultures pass on definitions of criminal behaviors from member to member.

Cohen's **delinquent subculture theory** proposes that delinquent subcultures that emerge have beliefs, values, and norms different from those of mainstream society. Mainstream culture embodies middle class values. Individuals within society are held accountable to a set of standards known as the *middle class measuring rod*, which includes standards for academic performance, language proficiency, and behavior. The inability of male youths of the working class to meet these standards leads to strain. Delinquent subculture theory argues that juveniles faced with strain will adapt to the situation in one of three ways:[73]

> *College boys.* College boys adapt to their environment and engage in actions within their limited means and capabilities. They seek to adopt a lifestyle that is traditional and in line with that of mainstream society. More specifically, they embrace middle class values and engage in acts to achieve them. When faced with strain, these individuals do not give up but work even harder to achieve middle class status. The college boys are similar to Merton's conformist. This mode of adaptation is not commonly chosen, due to individuals' limited resources and its low rate of success. These individuals spend time in the subculture group for support.
>
> *Corner boys.* The corner boy adaptation is the most common among juveniles. Corner boys are similar to Merton's retreatists. They retreat into a subculture wherein status can be achieved in the group without the need of the individual to conform or comply with middle class values. The purpose of the subculture is not delinquent; however, individuals within the group may become involved in delinquent activities (e.g., truancy and substance abuse), as this is the most available means to them.
>
> *Delinquent boys.* Cohen argued that youths initially internalize middle class values and pursue them.[74] When they realize that opportunities are blocked, they experience frustration. Because of this frustration, they resort to **reaction formation**, whereby they create a culture that rewards values that oppose those of the middle class. Reaction formation is characteristic of delinquent boys, who adopt a culture that includes values in direct opposition to those of mainstream society. Delinquent boys form a group that often engages in illicit acts randomly and impulsively. Academics have associated delinquent boys with Merton's rebels and innovators.[75]

Cohen's adaptations to strain differs from that of Merton. Merton believed that individuals adapted to strain individually, whereas Cohen believed they adapted collectively. In Ghana, the Sakawa boys reported that they respond to the strains experienced in their countries by engaging in Internet fraud.[76]

DIFFERENTIAL OPPORTUNITY THEORY

Echoing Merton, Richard Cloward and Lloyd Ohlin argue that individuals of the lower class become part of a subculture because of blocked opportunities.[77] A main point of departure between Merton and Cloward and Ohlin's work is the types of opportunities blocked. Unlike Merton, Cloward and Ohlin, in their **differential opportunity theory**, propose that the social structure provides unequal access to both legitimate and illegitimate means to success. In their view, the social structure makes legitimate and illegitimate opportunities for success possible. The legitimate opportunities are made available primarily to the middle class. Individuals in the working class are denied access to legitimate opportunities. Because of this denial, illegitimate opportunities for achieving success are considered acceptable by them, but not all illicit means are available to them (e.g., professional thief or drug kingpin). According to Cloward and Ohlin, the environment of blocked legitimate and illegitimate opportunities enables delinquent subcultures to thrive.[78] This has been observed with credit card fraud committed by cybercriminals in Ghana. Legitimate opportunities to gain wealth in Ghana (a societal goal) are limited; likewise, opportunities to engage in, for example, online credit card fraud are limited to those in particular positions, such as those employed as hotel clerks, because of their access to credit cards.[79]

In their study of delinquents, Cloward and Ohlin identified three types of gang subcultures.[80]

> *Criminal gang.* A criminal gang operates like a criminal organization. It is stable within a community and is highly organized. Within this subculture, older criminals teach younger members criminal skills and serve as their role models. Here, illegitimate and legitimate behavior are integrated in daily life along with legitimate and illegitimate businesses. This criminal subculture is motivated by utilitarian gain (i.e., wealth and profit). This gang is the most likely to persist.
>
> *Conflict or violent gang.* Unlike criminal gangs, a criminal organization is not present with this gang. The subculture is unstable and lacks an overall purpose and long-term plans. The gang does not pursue wealth; individuals within this gang engage in violence for the sake of violence. A conflict subculture resists the goals and institutions of mainstream society and is known for creating alternative methods to obtain status within the subculture. These individuals reject mainstream goals and the means to achieve them because they were blocked from both legitimate and illegitimate opportunities.
>
> *Retreatist gang.* A retreatist gang also lacks the presence and influence of a criminal organization and is unsuccessful in both legitimate and illegitimate endeavors (*double failures*). A retreatist subculture rejects the goals of society and the means to achieve them and engages in self-destructive behavior (e.g., persistent drug use). Individuals in this gang could not attain status in mainstream society, nor in criminal or conflict gangs.

The success of a gang subculture depends on its level of integration within the community.

In the United States, gangs commit cybercrime and actively recruit those with the necessary knowledge, skills, and abilities to conduct these illicit acts or promote the education of existing gang members in fields that will provide them with the knowledge, skills, and abilities to commit cybercrime.[81] Research has supported this finding by showing links between gangs and cybercrimes. The level of involvement of a gang member in cybercrime depends on the member's computer knowledge, skills, and abilities.[82]

Sela-Shayovitz identified three different groups of gang members based on their computer skills and engagement in cybercrime.[83]

1. *Surfing and abstaining.* These individuals have low-level computer skills and do not commit cybercrime. They engage in offline delinquent and criminal acts.[84]
2. *Surfing and causing harm.* These individuals have mid-level computer skills and commit some types of cybercrimes, particularly digital piracy, malware distribution, and gambling.[85]

3. *Surfing and hacking.* These individuals have high-level computer skills and frequently engage in hacking.[86]

Despite existing research showing links between gangs and cybercrime, gang members currently use the Internet primarily for "Internet banging" to gain notoriety,[87] interacting with others,[88] and boasting about their accomplishments.[89]

Subcultures in the Virtual Environment

Subcultures exist online (e.g., digital piracy subcultures).[90] Cybercriminals associate with individuals who hold similar views and beliefs about their behavior. An example of a cybercriminal subculture is the Yahoo boys of Nigeria mentioned earlier in this chapter.[91] Another example is hacking subcultures.[92] In these subcultures, associations and interactions with members occur both offline (e.g., at DEF CON conventions) and online.[93] Online, research has shown that these associations and interactions occur primarily in online chat rooms and bulletin boards.[94] The behavior of individuals in this subculture "takes place in a distinctive socio-cultural context and 'communal' structure."[95] The hacker subculture is viewed as different from that of mainstream society. In fact, these hacking subcultures resist conventional and mainstream society and its norms, values, and beliefs.[96] A well-known example of an antiestablishment hacker subculture is **phreakers**, who exploited vulnerabilities of telephone switching networks, enabling them to make free long-distance phone calls, and shared this know-how with others.

Hackers are not judged according to conventional norms and goals of society (e.g., wealth). The hacking subculture is based entirely on rules of behavior that revolve around the use of the Internet and digital devices. Steven Levy has identified a **hacker ethic** (i.e., common norms, values, and beliefs of the hacking community):[97]

1. Access to computers—and anything which might teach you something about the way the world works—should be unlimited and total
2. All information should be free
3. Mistrust authority—promote decentralization
4. Hackers should be judged by their hacking, not bogus criteria such as degrees, age, race, or position
5. You can create art and beauty on a computer
6. Computers can change your life for the better

A hacker's ultimate goal is: hacking. The acts he or she engages in are in pursuit of that goal. Status is obtained within the subculture based on identifiable expertise and how well the hacker achieves the goal. Status is thus based on achievements that are valued and admired by the subculture. The norms, values, and beliefs adopted by a hacker ultimately depend on the type of hacker and the hacker's objective (i.e., whether or not the individual has harmful intent to alter, delete, damage, destroy, or disrupt systems and data).[98]

BOX 6-2 GROUP PSYCHOLOGY, BELONGINGNESS, AND CYBERCRIME

Crime and deviance can be explained through group membership and influences of the group. Cybercriminals tend to separate those in the in-group (i.e., members of the group and those who support the group and hold the same attitudes, values, and objectives of the group) and the out-group (i.e., everyone who does not fit within the in-group description). Individuals within groups can collectively engage in illicit behavior. When all members are engaged in this conduct, it tends to weaken moral controls of members and results in their not taking responsibility for their conduct.[99]

Group psychology may well explain cybercrime. Individuals' need for friendship and belonging motivates them to join groups. For certain individuals, these groups can become substitute families, and in cases where groups have identifiable leaders, a substitute parent. These groups can also provide an individual with a sense of purpose. For example, a key attraction to online gaming communities is the ability to enhance one's social life by interacting with other players, making friends, and being part of a social group.[100] Additionally, groups within hacker communities provide them with social identity and a sense of belonging.[101] These groups can also be used to fill their need for love and belongingness, a primary need identified by Abraham Maslow as motivating behavior,[102] which may be missing offline. The relationships these individuals form online thus help them fulfill this essential need.[103] The same holds true for online sex offender communities, where offenders have reported strong attachments to their online associations with other child pornographers and participating in these communities to fulfill their need for belonging.[104]

CASE STUDY

Eleven-year-old Marika's classmates go to the movies every weekend. Marika's family is unable to give her an allowance, so she cannot attend the movies with her friends. She feels rejected by them, particularly when they are talking about the latest film. Marika rarely gets invited to go with them to see the latest film because her friends know she will say no. They have not even been asking her to lunch on Monday because they do not want her around while they chat about the movie they just saw. Marika wants to be part of her peer group, so she browses the Internet and finds an illegal website that provides free online access to pirated versions of the latest movies currently playing in the theaters. She accesses the website and watches several of the movies that her classmates discussed over the past few weeks. The next day, she chats with her classmates about the movies, but does not mention that she watched them from an illegal website.

What theory or theories included in this chapter can explain Marika's behavior? Please analyze her case using this theory (or these theories).

REVIEW QUESTIONS

1. Can social disorganization explain cybercrime?
2. How does the presence and/or absence of social capital and collective efficacy influence online behavior?
3. Explain broken windows theory. How does it apply to cybercrime?
4. Can anomie theory explain cybercrime?
5. What is institutional anomie theory? Can it be used to explain certain forms of cybercrime? Why or why not?
6. What is relative deprivation? Can it explain cybercrime?
7. What does it mean to "Keep up with the Joneses"? Can it explain cybercrime? Why do you think so?

8. Which type (or types) of cybercrime can strain theory explain? Please explain why the theory applies to the cybercrime (or cybercrimes).
9. Can delinquent subculture theory explain cybercrime? Please explain your response.
10. What is the differential opportunity theory? Can it explain cybercrime? Please explain your response.

DEFINITIONS

Anomie. A state of society characterized by "normlessness," a disruption in the normal conditions of society.

Anomie theory. A theory positing that crime is a product of the disparities that exist between cultural aspirations and the opportunities available to individuals to achieve these.

Broken windows theory. A theory holding that persistent disorder and incivility within a community is associated with future occurrences of serious crimes within that area.

Chicago School of Criminology. The Chicago School of Criminology sought to explain the causes, control, and dynamics of crime spatially by examining neighborhood, community, urban, and environmental factors.

Collective efficacy. The ability of residents and the community to control illicit behavior.

Concentric zone theory. A zonal theory for the development of a city used to explain social structures in an urban environment.

Delinquent subculture theory. A theory proposing that delinquent subcultures have different beliefs, values, and norms from those of mainstream society.

Differential opportunity theory. A theory proposing that the social structure provides unequal access to both legitimate and illegitimate means to success.

General strain theory. General strain theory holds that individuals seek goals desired by society but society limits the ability of certain individuals to achieve them.

Hacker ethic. The common norms, values, and beliefs of the hacking community.

Human ecology. The study of the relationship between individuals and the environment.

Institutional anomie theory. A theory holding that the American Dream sustains an imbalance between the economy and other societal institutions, which prevents the latter institutions from controlling members of society and insulating them from criminogenic pressures that stem from the pursuit of the American Dream.

Phreakers. A hacking subculture that exploited vulnerabilities of telephone switching networks, enabling them to make free long-distance phone calls.

Reaction formation. The process whereby an individual engages in conduct in opposition to mainstream society as a result of status frustration.

Relative deprivation. The discrepancy existing between what an individual expects in life and what the individual actually gets.

Relative deprivation theory. A theory arguing that individuals may perceive themselves as being disadvantaged with respect to others in a group of reference believed to be in similar situations and having similar attributes.

Social capital. The extent to which individuals have developed relations with others and societal institutions.

Social disorganization. A condition in a community whereby its structure and culture are not reflective of the values and best interests of its residents.

Social disorganization theory. A theory proposing that crime occurs in locations where communities are no longer able to regulate the conduct of their members according to accepted conventional norms, values, and beliefs and instead realize the unconventional values of its residents.

Strain. Societal pressures, such as denial of civil liberties, discrimination, family conflict, and physical and psychological abuse, which block individuals from opportunities and meeting their needs.

Subculture. A group that primarily shares norms, values, customs, and beliefs different from that of mainstream society.

Subcultural theories. Theories explaining why subcultures exist, what type of subcultures are created, and why these subcultures persist.

ENDNOTES

1. Department of Justice, Office of Public Affairs, "Operator of Second-Largest Music Piracy Cyberlocker in United States Sentenced to 36 Months in Prison for Criminal Copyright Infringement," November 17, 2015, http://www.justice.gov/opa/pr/operator-second-largest -music-piracy-cyberlocker-united-states-sentenced-36-months -prison.

2. R. E. Park, "Human Ecology," *American Journal of Sociology* 42, no. 1 (1936): 1–15.

3. E. W. Burgess, "The Growth of the City: An Introduction to a Research Project," in *The City*, ed. R. E. Park, E. W. Burgess and R. D. McKenzie (Chicago: University of Chicago Press, 1925).

4. R. R. Kornhauser, *Social Sources of Delinquency: An Appraisal of Analytic Models* (Chicago: University of Chicago Press, 1978).

5. C. R. Shaw and H. D. McKay, *Juvenile Delinquency and Urban Areas* (Chicago: University of Chicago Press, 1942).

6. R. J. Sampson and W. B. Groves, "Community Structure and Crime: Testing Social-Disorganization Theory," *American Journal of Sociology* 94, no. 4 (1989): 774–802.

7. C. R. Shaw and H. D. McKay, *Juvenile Delinquency and Urban Areas* (Chicago: University of Chicago Press, 1942).

8. Ibid.

9. R. D. Evans, "Examining the Informal Sanctioning of Deviance in a Chat Room Culture," *Deviant Behavior* 22, no. 3 (2001): 195.

10. Ibid., 200.

11. Ibid., 208.

12. J. S. Coleman, "Social Capital in the Creation of Human Capital," *American Journal of Sociology* 94, Supplement: Organizations and Institutions: Sociological and Economic Approaches to the Analysis of Social Structure (1988): S95–S120; R. D. Putnam, *Making Democracy Work: Civic Traditions in Modern Italy* (Princeton, NJ: Princeton University Press, 1993); R. D. Putnam, *Bowling Alone: The Collapse and Revival of American Community* (New York: Simon & Schuster, 2000).

13. J. S. Coleman, "Social Capital in the Creation of Human Capital," *American Journal of Sociology* 94, Supplement: Organizations and Institutions: Sociological and Economic Approaches to the Analysis of Social Structure (1988): S95–S120.

14. Ibid.

15. For example, B. W. Drushel, "HIV/AIDS, Social Capital, and Online Social Networks," *Journal of Homosexuality* 60, no. 8 (2013): 1230–1249; T. Kobayashi, K. Ikeda, and K. Miyata, "Social Capital Online: Collective Use of the Internet and Reciprocity as Lubricants of Democracy," *Information, Communication & Society* 9, no. 5 (2006): 582–611; M. Sheng and R. Hartono, "An Exploratory Study of Knowledge Creation and Sharing in Online Community: A Social Capital Perspective," *Total Quality Management & Business Excellence* 26, no. 1-2 (2015): 93–107.

16. D. V. Shah, N. Kwak, and R. L. Holbert, "'Connecting' And 'Disconnecting' With Civic Life: Patterns of Internet Use and the Production of Social Capital," *Political Communication* 18, no. 2 (2001): 141–162.

17. A. Velasquez and R. LaRose, "Youth Collective Activism Through Social Media: The Role of Collective Efficacy," *New Media & Society* 17, no. 6 (2015): 899–918.

18. L. Chi, W. K. Chan, G. Seow, and K. Tam, "Transplanting Social Capital to the Online World: Insights From Two Experimental Studies," *Journal of Organizational Computing and Electronic Commerce* 19, no. 3 (2009): 216.

19. Ibid., 214–215.

20. D. R. Montello, "Navigation," in *The Cambridge Handbook of Visuospatial Thinking*, ed. P. Shah and A. Miyake (Cambridge: Cambridge University Press, 2005), 258.

21. Ibid., 258–259.

22. Ibid., 259.

23. G. Suttles, *The Social Order of the Slum: Ethnicity and Territory in the Inner City* (Chicago: University of Chicago University Press, 1968).

24. P. J. Brantingham and P. L. Brantingham, "Notes on the Geometry of Crime," in *Environmental Criminology*, ed. P. J. Brantingham and P. L. Brantingham (Beverly Hills, CA: Sage, 1981); see also C. J. Smith and G. E. Patterson, "Cognitive Mapping and the Subjective Geography of Crime," in *Crime: A Spatial Perspective*, ed. D. E. Georges-Abeyie and K. D. Harries (New York: Columbia University Press, 1980).

25. S. Damer, "Wine Alley: The Sociology of a Dreadful Enclosure," *Sociological Review* 22, no. 2 (1974): 221–248.

26. J. Q. Wilson and G. Kelling, "Broken Windows: The Police and Neighborhood Safety," *Atlantic*, March 1982, http://www.theatlantic.com/magazine/archive/1982/03/broken-windows/304465/.

27. M. Tonry and H. Bildsten, "Antisocial Behavior," in *The Oxford Handbook of Crime and Public Policy*, ed. M. Tonry (Oxford: Oxford University Press, 2009), 587; J. E. Greene, "Zero Tolerance and Policing," in *The Oxford Handbook of Police and Policing*, ed. M. D. Reisig and R. J. Kane (Oxford: Oxford University Press, 2014).

28. G. L. Kelling and W. J. Bratton, "Declining Crime Rates: Insiders' Views of the New York City Story," *Journal of Criminal Law and Criminology* 88, no. 4 (1998): 1217–1232; Nonetheless, some instances of fabrication of statistics by police officers were revealed during this period. Indeed, "the push to bring down crime rates had the unintended consequence of encouraging unscrupulous officers to fabricate statistics." A. Nagy and J. Podlony, *William Bratton and the NYPD Crime: Control through Middle Management Reform*, Yale School of Management, Yale case 07-015, February 12, 2008, 1. http://som.yale.edu/sites/default/files/files/Case_Bratton_2nd_ed_Final_and_Complete.pdf.

29. See Chapter 4 of this book for a detailed explanation as to why this occurs.

30. The term *anomie* was coined by Émile Durkheim. E. Durkheim, *The Division of Labor in Society*, trans. G. Simpson (New York: Free Press, 1947).

31. E. Durkheim, *The Division of Labor in Society*, trans. G. Simpson (New York: Free Press, 1947).

32. M. Abrahamson, "Sudden Wealth, Gratification, and Attainment: Durkheim's Anomie of Affluence Reconsidered," *American Sociological Review* 45, no. 1 (1980): 49–57.

33. E. Merton, "Social Structure and Anomie," *American Sociological Review* 3, no. 5 (1938): 672–682.

34. M. L. Rustad, "Private Enforcement of the Cybercrime on the Electronic Frontier," *Southern California Interdisciplinary Law Journal* 11, no. 1 (2001): 72–73.

35. D. Coupland, *Microserfs* (New York: Harper Perennial, 2008).

36. Rustad, "Private Enforcement of the Cybercrime on the Electronic Frontier," 78.

37. D. M. Boje, "Carnivalesque Resistance to Global Spectacle: A Critical Postmodern Theory of Public Administration," *Administrative Theory and Praxis 23*, no. 3 (2001): 431–458.

38. J. Blau, "Russia—A Happy Haven For Hackers," *Computer Weekly*, May 26, 2004, http://www.computerweekly.com/feature/Russia-a-happy-haven-for-hackers; P. Warren, "Hunt For Russia's Web Criminals," *Guardian*, November 14, 2007, http://www.theguardian.com/technology/2007/nov/15/news.crime; J. D. Serio and A. Gorkin, "Changing Lenses: Striving For Sharper Focus on the Nature of the 'Russian Mafia' and its Impact on the Computer Realm," *International Review of Law, Computers and Technology* 17, no. 2 (2003): 191–202.

39. R. Rosenfeld and S. F. Messner, "Crime and the American Dream: An Institutional Analysis," in *The Legacy of Anomie Theory*, ed. F. Adler and W. S. Laufer (New Brunswick, NJ: Transaction, 1995).

40. Material success is the only important goal. Even individuals' actions with respect to obtaining an education are driven by material success.

41. S. F. Messner and R. Rosenfeld, *Crime and the American Dream* (Belmont, CA: Wadsworth, 1994).

42. Ibid., 99–101, 108.

43. S. F. Messner and R. Rosenfeld, *Crime and the American Dream* (Belmont, CA: Wadsworth, 1994).

44. O. Tade and I. Aliyu, "Social Organization of Internet Fraud Among University Undergraduates in Nigeria," *International Journal of Cyber Criminology* 5, no. 2 (2011): 873.

45. See, for example, C. Jencks, *Rethinking Social Policy: Race, Poverty, and the Underclass* (Cambridge, MA: Harvard University Press, 1992); B. R. E. Wright, A. Caspi, T. E. Moffitt, and P. A. Silva, "Reconsidering the Relationship Between SES and Delinquency: Causation but not Correlation," *Criminology* 37, no. 1 (1999): 175–194; J. D. Hawkins, T. Herrenkohl, D. P. Farrington, D. Brewer, R. Catalano, and T. W. Harachi, "A Review of Predictors of Youth Violence," in *Serious and Violent Juvenile Offenders: Risk Factors and Successful Interventions*, ed. R. Loeber and D. P. Harrington (Thousand Oaks, CA: Sage, 1998); F. B. Okeshola and A. K. Adeta, "The Nature, Causes and Consequences of Cyber Crime in Tertiary Institutions in Zaria-Kaduna State, Nigeria," *American International Journal of Contemporary Research* 3, no. 9 (2013): 98–114; T. T. Moores, "An Analysis of the Impact of Economic Wealth and National Culture on the Rise and Fall of Software Piracy Rates," *Journal of Business Ethics* 81, no. 1 (2008): 39–51; A. R. Andrés, "Software Piracy and Income Inequality," *Applied Economics Letters* 13, no. 2 (2006): 101–105; A. C. Kirgerl, "Infringing Nations: Predicting Software Piracy Rates, BitTorrent Tracker Hosting, and P2P File Sharing Client Downloads Between Countries," *International Journal of Cyber Criminology* 7, no. 1 (2013): 62–80.

46. See, for example, K. C. Land, P. L. McCall, and L. E. Cohen, "Structural Covariates of Homicide Rates: Are There any Invariances Across Time and Social Space?" *American Journal of Sociology* 95, no. 4 (1990): 922–963; R. G. Shelden, S. K. Tracy, and W. B. Brown, *Youth Gangs in American Society*, 2nd ed. (Belmont, CA: Wadsworth, 2001); J. Bishop, "Who are the Pirates? The Politics of Piracy, Poverty and Greed in a Globalized Music Market," *Popular Music and Society* 27, no. 1 (2004): 104; W. D. Gunter, G. E. Higgins, R. E. Gealt, and W. DeCamp, "Pirating Youth: Examining the Correlates of Digital Music Piracy Among Adolescents," *International Journal of Cyber Criminology* 4, no. 1-2 (2010): 657–671; Okeshola and Adeta, "The Nature, Causes and Consequences of Cyber Crime in Tertiary Institutions in Zaria-Kaduna State, Nigeria," 98–114.

47. See, for example, J. R. Blau and P. M. Blau, "The Cost of Inequality: Metropolitan Structure and Violent Crime," *American Sociological Review* 47, no. 1 (1982): 114–129; M. Yip and C. Webber, "Hacktivism: A Theoretical and Empirical Exploration of China's Cyber Warriors," *ACM Web Science Conference 2011* (Koblenz, Germany, June 14 – 17, 2011).

48. J. Davis, "A Formal Interpretation of the Theory of Relative Deprivation," *Sociometry* 22, no. 4 (1959): 280–296; W. G. Runciman, *Relative Deprivation and Social Justice* (Berkeley, CA: University of California Press, 1966); R. K. Merton and A. S. Rossi, "Contributions to the Theory of Reference Group Behavior," in *Social Theory and Social Structure*, ed. R. K. Merton (New York: Free Press, 1968).

49. R. H. McAdams, "Relative Preferences," *Yale Law Journal* 102, no. 1 (1992), 38.

50. See, for example, U.S. Immigration and Customs Enforcement, "North Texas Man Admits Role in Counterfeit Goods Trafficking Conspiracy," October 13, 2015, https://www.ice.gov/news/releases/north-texas-man-admits-role-counterfeit-goods-trafficking-conspiracy.

51. See, for example, Department of Justice, U.S. Attorney's Office, Northern District of Iowa, "New York Man Pleads Guilty to Selling Counterfeit Merchandise," September 29, 2015, http://www.justice.gov/usao-ndia/pr/new-york-man-pleads-guilty-selling-counterfeit-merchandise; J. Swartz and E. Weise, "Online Buyer, Beware: Dangerous Fake Goods Thrive on Web," *USA Today*, April 30, 2014, http://www.usatoday.com/story/tech/2014/04/30/counterfeit-sites-dark-web-series/6374451/.

52. R. Agnew and H. R. White, "An Empirical Test of General Strain Theory," *Criminology* 30, no. 4 (1992): 475-499; R. Paternoster and P. Mazerolle, "General Strain Theory and Delinquency: A Replication and Extension," *Journal of Research in Crime and Delinquency* 31, no. 3 (1994): 235–263; N. L. Piquero and M. D. Sealock, "Generalizing General Strain Theory: An Examination of an Offending Population," *Justice Quarterly* 17, no. 3 (2000): 449–484; R. Agnew, *Pressured into Crime: An Overview of General Strain Theory* (Los Angeles: Roxbury, 2006).

53. R. A. Greene and N. Hughes, "'Hacktivist for Good' Claims WikiLeaks Takedown," *CNN*, November 29, 2010, http://www.cnn.com/2010/US/11/29/wikileaks.hacker/.

54. R. Agnew, "A Revised Strain Theory of Delinquency," *Social Forces* 64, no. 1 (1985): 151–167; R. Agnew, "Foundation for a General Strain Theory of Crime and Delinquency," *Criminology* 30, no. 1 (1992): 47–87.

55. Agnew, "Foundation for a General Strain Theory of Crime and Delinquency."

56. Ibid.

57. R. Agnew, "Building on the Foundation of General Strain Theory: Specifying the Types of Strain Most Likely to Lead to Crime and Delinquency," *Journal of Research in Crime and Delinquency* 38, no. 4 (2001): 319–361.

58. Agnew, "A Revised Strain Theory of Delinquency."

59. Agnew, "Foundation for a General Strain Theory of Crime and Delinquency"; Agnew, *Pressured into Crime: An Overview of General Strain Theory*; R. Agnew, "General Strain Theory: Current Status and Directions for Further Research," in *Taking Stock: The Status of Criminological Theory, Advances in Criminological Theory*, ed. F. T. Cullen, J. P. Wright, and K. R. Belvins (New Brunswick, NJ: Transaction, 2006).

60. R. Agnew, "Controlling Delinquency: Recommendations from General Strain Theory," in *Crime and Public Policy: Putting Theory to Work*, ed. H. D. Barlow (Boulder, CO: Westview, 1995), 46.

61. R. Agnew, "The Contribution of Social Psychological Strain Theory to the Explanation of Crime and Delinquency," in *The Legacy of Anomie Theory*, ed. F. Adler and W. S. Laufer (New Brunswick, NJ: Transaction, 1995).

62. J. W. Patchin and S. Hinduja, "Traditional and Nontraditional Bullying Among Youth: A Test of General Strain Theory," *Youth and Society* 43, no. 2 (2011): 727–751.

63. S. Hinduja, "General Strain, Self-Control, and Music Piracy," *International Journal of Cyber Criminology* 6, no. 1 (2012), 951–967.

64. M. L. Benson, "Denying the Guilty Mind: Accounting for Involvement in a White Collar Crime," *Criminology* 23 no. 4 (1985): 583–608; M. L. Benson and E. Moore, "Are White-Collar and Common Offenders the Same? An Empirical and Theoretical Critique of a Recently Proposed General Theory of Crime," *Journal of Research in Crime and Delinquency* 29, no. 3 (1992): 251–272; J. W. Coleman, *The Criminal Elite: The Sociology of White-Collar Crime* (New York: St. Martin's Press, 1989); and S. M. Rosoff, H. M. Pontell, and R. Tillman, *Profit Without Honor: White-Collar Crime and the Looting of America* (Upper Saddle River, NJ: Prentice Hall, 2002), cited in S. Hinduja, "General Strain, Self-Control, and Music Piracy," 954.

65. Hinduja, "General Strain, Self-Control, and Music Piracy," 954–955.

66. D. A. Hohn, L. R. Muftic, and K. Wolf, "Swashbuckling Students: An Exploratory Study of Internet Piracy," *Security Journal* 19, no. 2 (2006), 110–127.

67. R. G. Morris and G. E. Higgins, "Neutralizing Potential and Self-Reported Digital Piracy: A Multitheoretical Exploration Among College Undergraduates," *Criminal Justice Review* 34, no. 2 (2009): 189; Hinduja, "General Strain, Self-Control, and Music Piracy," 951–967.

68. W. E. Thompson and J. V. Hickey, *Society in Focus: An Introduction to Sociology* (New York: Harper Collins, 1994), 81.

69. K. Hafner and J. Markoff, *Cyberpunks: Outlaws and Hackers on the Computer Frontier* (Toronto: Simon and Schuster, 1995).

70. C. Fitch, *Crime and Punishment: The Psychology of Hacking in the New Millennium* (Bethesda, MD: SANS Institute, 2004); P. A. Taylor, "Hackers: Cyberpunks or Microserfs?" *Information, Communication & Society* 1, no. 4 (1998): 401–419.

71. A. K. Cohen, *Delinquent Boys: The Culture of the Gang* (Glencoe, IL: Free Press, 1955), 25.

72. Cohen, *Delinquent Boys: The Culture of the Gang.*

73. Ibid.

74. Ibid.

75. S. G. Tibbetts, *Criminological Theory: The Essentials* (Thousand Oaks, CA: Sage, 2011), 117.

76. E. L. Davison, "Charges Without Borders: Consumer Credit Card Fraud in Ghana," in *Crimes of the Internet*, ed. F. Schmalleger and M. Pittaro (Upper Saddle River, NJ: Pearson/Prentice Hall, 2009); J. Warner, "Understanding Cyber-Crime in Ghana: A View From Below," *International Journal of Cyber Criminology* 5, no. 1 (2011), 736–749.

77. R. A. Cloward and L. E. Ohlin, *Delinquency and Opportunity: A Theory of Delinquent Gangs* (Glencoe, IL: Free Press, 1960).

78. Ibid.

79. E. L. Davison, "Charges Without Borders: Consumer Credit Card Fraud in Ghana," in *Crimes of the Internet*, ed. F. Schmalleger and M. Pittaro (Upper Saddle River, NJ: Pearson/Prentice Hall, 2009).

80. R. A. Cloward and L. E. Ohlin, *Delinquency and Opportunity: A Theory of Delinquent Gangs* (Glencoe, IL: Free Press, 1960).

81. National Gang Intelligence Center, *2013 National Gang Report*, accessed August 3, 2016, 39, https://www.fbi.gov/stats-services/publications/national-gang-report-2013.

82. D. C. Pyrooz, S. H. Decker, and R. K. Moule Jr., "Criminal and Routine Activities in Online Settings: Gangs, Offenders, and the Internet," *Justice Quarterly* 32, no. 3 (2015): 471–499.

83. R. Sela-Shayovitz, "Gangs and the Web: Gang Members' Online Behavior," *Journal of Contemporary Criminal Justice* 28, no. 4 (2012): 397.

84. Ibid.

85. Ibid.

86. Ibid., 398.

87. D. U. Patton, R. D. Eschmann, and D. A. Butler, "Internet Banging: New Trends in Social Media, Gang Violence, Masculinity and Hip Hop," *Computers in Human Behavior* 29, no. 5 (2013): A54–A59.

88. S. H. Decker and D. C. Pyrooz, *Moving the Gang: Logging Off, Moving On*, paper commissioned by Google Ideas, November 2011, http://artisresearch.com/articles/Decker_Pyrooz_Leaving_the_gang.pdf.

89. J. A. King, C. E. Walpole, and K. Lamon, "Surf and Turf Wars Online: Growing Implications of Internet Gang Violence," *Journal of Adolescent Health* 41, no. 6 (2007): 66–68.

90. J. Cooper and D. M. Harrison, "The Social Organization of Audio Piracy on the Internet," *Media, Culture and Society* 23, no. 1 (2001), 71–89.

91. A. Adeniran, "The Internet and Emergence of Yahooboys Sub-culture in Nigeria," *International Journal of Cyber Criminology* 2, no. 2 (2008), 368–381.

92. J. Muncie, *Youth and Crime: A Critical Introduction* (London: Sage, 1999), 178–183; P. Taylor, *Hackers: Crime in the Digital Sublime* (London: Routledge, 1999), x, 26.

93. C. Fitch, *Crime and Punishment: The Psychology of Hacking in the New Millennium* (Bethesda, MD: SANS Institute, 2004), 8–9; M. Yar, "Computer Hacking: Just Another Case of Juvenile Delinquency?" *Howard Journal of Criminal Justice* 44, no. 4 (2005): 396.

94. Yar, "Computer Hacking: Just Another Case of Juvenile Delinquency?" 396.

95. Ibid.; Taylor, *Hackers: Crime in the Digital Sublime, x*, 26.

96. Taylor, *Hackers: Crime in the Digital Sublime*, 24–26.

97. S. Levy, *Hackers: Heroes of the Computer Revolution* (New York: Dell, 1984).

98. The typologies of hackers are explored in Chapter 8 of this book.

99. A. Bandura, C. Barbaranelli, G. V. Caprara, and C. Pastorelli, "Mechanisms of Moral Disengagement in the Exercise of Moral Agency," *Journal of Personality and Social Psychology* 71, no. 2 (1996): 365.

100. S. Caplan, D. Williams, and N. Yee, "Problematic Internet Use and Psychosocial Well-Being Among MMO Players," *Computers in Human Behavior* 25, no. 6 (2009): 1312–1319; M. Pawlikowski, I. W. Nader, C. Burger, A. Stieger, and M. Brand, "Pathological Internet Use—It is a Multidimensional and Not a Unidimensional Construct," *Addiction Research & Theory* 22, no. 2 (2014): 172.

101. M. Rogers, *A New Hacker Taxonomy* (University of Manitoba, Canada, 2000), http://homes.cerias.purdue.edu/~mkr/hacker.doc; R. Chiesa, S. Ducci, and S. Ciappi, *Profiling Hackers: The Science of Criminal Profiling as Applied to the World of Hacking* (Boca Raton, FL: CRC Press, 2009).

102. A. H. Maslow, "A Theory of Human Motivation," *Psychological Review* 50, no. 4 (1943): 370–396.

103. A. Bifulco and T. Pham, "Young Victims Online," in *Online Offending Behavior and Child Victimization: New Findings and Policy*, ed. S. Webster, J. Davidson, and A. Bifulco (New York: Palgrave-Macmillan, 2015), 158.

104. E. Quayle and M. Taylor, "Child Pornography and the Internet: Perpetuating a Cycle of Abuse," *Deviant Behavior* 23, no. 4 (2002): 365–395.

CHAPTER 7

CONFORMITY, LEARNING, AND SOURCES OF SOCIAL CONTROL

KEYWORDS

Age-graded theory
Anonymity
Cognitive distortions
Cognitive reconstruction
Containment theory
Control balance theory
Cyberaggression
Dehumanization
Deindividuation
Developmental and
     life-course criminology
Differential association
     theory

Differential reinforcement
Disinhibition
External controls
General theory of crime
Groupthink
Imitation
Internal controls
Investment fraud
Latent trait perspective
Life-course perspective
Modeling
Moral disengagement
Negative punishment

Negative reinforcement
Neutralization theory
Operant behavior
Operant conditioning
Positive punishment
Positive reinforcement
Pump and dump
Self-control
Social control theory
Social learning theory
Social process theories
Socialization
White-collar cybercrime

In 2013, Rebecca Ann Sedwick committed suicide. She was twelve years old at the time of her death. An investigation revealed that she had been subjected to relentless cyberbullying by children close to her age. These cyberbullies repeatedly goaded her to commit suicide. Some of the messages Rebecca received from social media apps and forums included "Go kill yourself"; "Why don't you go kill yourself?"; "You should die"; "Drink bleach and die"; "Why aren't you dead?"; "Wait a minute, why are you still alive?"; and "Can you die please?"[1] Two perpetrators, a twelve-year-old and a fourteen-year-old, were primarily responsible for cyberbullying Rebecca; however, more than a dozen others participated in the cyberbullying as well.[2]

What social processes can explain the behavior of cyberbullies? How do these cyberbullies justify their behavior? This chapter seeks to answer these questions by examining social process theories, social learning theories, and developmental and life-course criminology. Special attention is paid to the ways in which cyberoffenders learn cybercriminality and the neutralization techniques they use.

143

CONTROLLING CYBERCRIMINALITY

Social process theories view individuals as being predisposed to criminality and seek to explain the forces that keep individuals from engaging in criminal activity. More specifically, these theories seek to explain why individuals conform even though they are subjected to temptations, pressures, and inducements. Thus, conformity can be explained through existing social control in an individual's life. When these controlling social forces are weakened or absent, individuals commit crime. One of the earliest social control theorists, Edward Alsworth Ross, believed that an individual's belief system (e.g., sense of justice or resentment for laws and the criminal justice system) controlled the individual's behavior.[3] There are two types of social controls: internal and external. **Internal controls** are the traits and characteristics of potential offenders that keep them from offending. **External controls** are the organizations and individuals responsible for keeping a potential offender from committing illicit activity.

Social control theorists also explain criminality as a product of **socialization,** the process whereby an individual learns specific behaviors that are considered acceptable in society. This socialization can result in law-abiding or criminal behavior. The socialization process influences the development of internal controls over an individual's behavior. Ivan Nye argued that the socialization process is essential to the development of an individual's conscience.[4]

The social control theorist Walter Reckless held that an individual's behavior was the product of inner pushes (e.g., discontent, anxiety, and agitation) and outer pulls (e.g., criminal associations).[5] He proposed the **containment theory,** which holds that individuals have an inner and outer containment structure that shields them from the pushes and pulls to commit crime. *Inner containment* is composed of traits within a person that shield the person from criminal pressures, such as conscientiousness, dependability, maturity, and diligence. *Outer containment* refers to aspects of one's social environment that protects a person from destructive outside influences. Reckless' theory prompted the development of subsequent social control theories.

Travis Hirschi's **social control theory** (or social bond theory) explains individuals' obedience to following laws and refrainment from committing crimes. This theory holds that human nature draws individuals to commit crimes,[6] but social bonds prevent them from doing so. These social bonds are created through socialization. The groups and institutions that contribute to an individual's socialization process include family, peers, professional groups, and religious institutions. The bonds individuals form with other people and institutions shape their behavior; individuals refrain from behavior that violates social norms when these social bonds are present. When these bonds are broken, or at the very least weakened, individuals may engage in deviant or criminal acts. Four social bonds have been identified as being associated with socialization and conformity: attachment, involvement, commitment, and belief.[7] These bonds are explored below.

> *Attachment.* Attachment refers to the links of individuals with others. Strong and healthy attachments with others are associated with law-abiding behavior. Attachment to family, schools, and peers was found to influence crime and delinquent behavior.[8] The first key social institution identified in Hirschi's work is the family. The family

shapes individuals' future social and political attitudes. Juveniles with strong attachments to their parents are less likely to commit crime because of the adverse impact it would have on their relationship with their parents.

Another key institution identified in social control theory is the school. Individuals with strong attachments to school are less likely to commit crime. This attachment is linked with academic performance, the students' views of the institution, and the relationship of the student with his or her teachers and peers. Schools affect students' self-image, values, beliefs, and attitudes. In schools, students can develop a positive or negative self-image. Schools are also instrumental in peer relations. An unfortunate observable outcome of these relationships is the development of hierarchical groups in schools that emphasize popularity for entry within these groups while excluding those who are viewed as unpopular. Such discriminatory and exclusionary environments foster antisocial behaviors, leading to interpersonal crimes and cybercrimes committed by and against youths (e.g., cyberbullying).[9] Research has shown that individuals with positive social support and school environments are less likely to engage in or be a victim of cyberbullying.[10] A final key attachment identified by Hirschi is that with peers, who influence an individual's interests. Of these three forms of attachment, the individual's bonds with parents and the school are considered to have greater influence than the individual's bonds with peers from childhood to middle adolescence.[11]

Commitment. Commitment refers to the time, energy, and resources devoted to conforming behavior (e.g., obtaining an education). Put simply, it refers to the extent to which an individual is invested in conventional goals and activities.[12] The level of commitment is associated with deviancy and criminal behavior. Crime and deviance are viewed as unappealing to individuals with strong commitments to society.[13] Individuals invested in society are less likely to offend due to the risk of losing their investment. A 2007 study on hackers found that the stronger this social bond was, the less likely the individual was to engage in illegal hacking.[14]

Involvement. Involvement explains conformity through an individual's active participation in conventional activities. Hirschi posited that youths' involvement in school and recreational activities shields them from illicit behavior that may result from idle and unmonitored time.[15] The amount of time spent on these activities has an impact on crime. The greater the involvement in conventional activities, the less likely the individual is to engage in deviant or criminal behaviors. Ultimately, people who are engrossed in conventional activities are viewed as having no time to also engage in online illicit activities, such as cyberbullying or hacking.

Belief. Belief refers to the extent to which an individual adheres to conventional norms, values, and attitudes. An individual will obey rules of society if the individual agrees with them. If the individual's beliefs conflict with those of mainstream society, the person is more likely to offend. Individuals who share beliefs similar to those of mainstream society and agents of the criminal justice system tend to respect the law. People who believe that the law is unfair and agents of the criminal justice system respond in an unequal and discriminatory manner are less likely to obey the law. Hirschi believed that juvenile delinquents rejected conventional norms, values, and attitudes.[16] Cybercriminals, such as hackers, have been known to reject certain conventional beliefs.[17]

Overall, social control theory holds that if these social bonds are strong enough, people will refrain from committing crime. More specifically, the greater an individual's attachment to others, commitment to and involvement in conventional activities, and belief in conventional norms and values of society, the less likely the individual is to engage in illicit behavior.

One of the main criticisms of social control theory is that it cannot explain illicit activity committed by individuals with strong social bonds. For example, the Yahoo boys (or yahoo-yahoo boys) in Nigeria are invested in conventional activities such as pursuing an education. In fact, a large portion of this group is made up of students.[18] Despite their investment in education, these individuals are well known all over the world for conducting online scams. What is more, their engagement in cybercrime often has an adverse impact on their academic performance, with the exception of those who are able to both engage in cybercrime and commit to their studies, as well as those who bribe their professors to obtain good grades.[19] In addition, social control theory has been criticized for its inability to explain white-collar crime, "a crime committed by a person of respectability and high social status in the course of his occupation."[20] A white-collar crime (and by way of extension, **white-collar cybercrime**) is financially motivated and perpetrated by individuals preoccupied with conventional activities. A case in point is **investment fraud**, in which a person intentionally engages in behavior designed to deceive or defraud investors, in violation of the Securities Act of 1933, the Securities Exchange Act of 1934, and the Investment Advisors Act of 1940. An example of an online investment fraud is the **pump and dump** scheme, wherein individuals engage in fraudulent tactics designed to increase the prices of stock, only to sell the stock once it reaches a desired level in order to make a profit. A recent pump and dump incident involved the artificial inflation of the stock prices of penny stocks; the cybercriminals responsible for this cybercrime gained approximately $3 million from the stocks they sold.[21] Despite their involvement in conventional activities, white-collar cybercriminals still engage in illicit behavior.

LEARNING CYBERCRIMINALITY

Albert Bandura's **social learning theory** explains criminality as a learned behavior. Research supports the application of social learning theory to crime.[22] Social learning theory has also been used to explain certain types of cybercrime (e.g., digital piracy and hacking).[23] A central tenet of this theory is that behavior is the product of learning through social interactions. The process by which behavior is learned is similar whether the act is licit or illicit. Individuals can be socialized to commit crime through groups, whereby criminal behavior is learned from members of the group. A youth can learn deviant behaviors from those in his or her social sphere, such as family, peers, classmates, and others with whom the individual associates. The most powerful agents of socialization are the family (particularly parents) and peers. Individuals are thus socialized into rule breaking as a result of contact and association with others engaging in crime.[24] Research has supported this claim by showing that individuals who learned cybercrime from actors within their social sphere were more likely to engage in such behavior.[25]

Additionally, this theory identifies communication and socialization as essential to learning patterns of behavior and the attitudes, values, and beliefs supporting this behavior. Individuals tend to alter behavior and interests to fit those of the group. For instance, social learning of interpersonal cybercrimes can occur among peers where such behaviors are considered acceptable and encouraged.[26] An individual's attitudes, values, and beliefs are strongly influenced by group membership and dynamics. The person's attitudes and beliefs may be influenced by **groupthink** (i.e., the subordination of one's self and taking on the identity of the group). Through this process, the individual's own thoughts and beliefs are replaced by those of the group. Individuals not only adopt similar attitudes, values, and beliefs and learn patterns of behavior but also learn the rationalizations and justifications associated with engaging in these activities, as well as the knowledge and skills needed to engage in these activities.[27] Online illicit behavior is also learned through similar social interactions, whereby individuals learn behaviors, rationalizations accompanying those behaviors, and the skills and techniques needed to engage in those behaviors from others. The learning can occur in a wide variety of forums. For example, hackers participate in annual conferences (e.g., DEF CON) and weekly meetings of hacker organizations (e.g., the 2600 organization) in order to exchange knowledge, tools, and techniques on hacking.[28]

Legal and illegal behavior can thus be explained by interactions with others that shape behavior. Attitudes, values, and beliefs are shared during these interactions. These attitudes, values, and beliefs are either in support or in opposition of illicit behavior. Whether or not an individual who is predisposed to crime engages in illicit activity also depends on the priority of learning and how early the illicit behavior was learned. The earlier the illicit activity is learned, the more likely the individual will persist in engaging in this behavior.[29] Frequency, the amount of time an individual spends with other criminals which encourages the illicit behavior, and duration, the extent to which an individual is exposed to the criminal activity, also influence criminality.

IMAGE 7-1   Screenshot of Website for 2600 Magazine: The Hacker Quarterly.

Social learning factors have been identified that determine the type of criminal behavior one engages in, its frequency, the targets of the behavior, and the situations in which the behavior is displayed. These factors have been used to explain why individuals commit crimes and cybercrimes, and continue to associate with others engaging in or supporting these illicit activities. Specifically, research has shown that those most likely to commit crime:[30]

1. are differentially associated with criminals or individuals who support either verbally or through their actions the violation of social and legal norms;
2. have criminal behaviors differentially reinforced;
3. are primarily exposed to role models who are more likely to engage in illicit behavior; and
4. learn definitions favorable toward criminality.

First, differential association has been used to explain crime and cybercrime. Edwin Sutherland's **differential association theory** holds that individuals learn criminal or deviant behavior through associations with others and learn the norms, values, and beliefs that validate this illicit or deviant behavior.[31] The central tenets of his theory include (a) illicit behavior is learned; (b) criminal behavior is learned through social interactions; (c) the crux of this learning occurs within social groups; and (d) the criminal behavior learning process includes the techniques for committing the illicit activity and the beliefs, motives, rationalizations, and justifications for committing the illegal activity (see Figure 7-1).[32] Individuals of the hacking subculture interact and learn from one another.[33] These subcultures provide members with rationalizations and justifications for hacking and introduce them to the language used and activities hackers engage in.[34] Individuals (especially youths) are subjected to social inducements to behave badly, especially from peers. If individuals associate with criminals and engage in criminal behavior that is reinforced by these associations, they will continue to invest their time and energy in these illegal activities; consequently, they will have less time and energy for engaging in noncriminal activities and associating with law-abiding citizens.

Research has supported differential association theory. Groups have been found to influence an individual's decision to engage in or refrain from crime,[35] especially association with delinquent peers, which was linked to an individual's engagement in delinquent acts.[36] What is more, virtual peers and virtual peer groups have been found to influence deviant behavior.[37] With respect to cybercrime, differential association is thought to be a significant predictor of attempts to gain unauthorized access and manipulate files by attaching malware to them.[38] Additionally, studies have identified links between differential association and digital piracy, in general, and music piracy, in particular.[39] Individuals' perception of digital piracy is related to the attitude of peers on this matter. Indeed, favorable attitudes toward digital piracy are linked to affiliations with deviant peers.[40] Individuals' association with deviant peers has been shown to increase likelihood to engage in this cybercrime.[41]

A second social learning factor determining criminal behavior is **differential reinforcement,** the process whereby the desired behavior is reinforced by internal or external sources.[42] The desired behavior is more likely to occur if it is frequently and extensively reinforced. Differential reinforcement can be explained as a balancing of rewards (reinforcements) and punishments. The types of reinforcements and punishments are positive and negative.[43]

Edwin Sutherland's Nine Basic Propositions of Differential Association Theory

⇒ Criminal behavior is learned.

⇒ Criminal behavior is learned in interaction with other persons in a process of communication.

⇒ The principal part of the learning of criminal behavior occurs within intimate personal groups.

⇒ When criminal behavior is learned, the learning includes
    (a) techniques of committing the crime, which are sometimes very complicated, sometimes simple;
    (b) the specific direction of motives, drives, rationalizations, and attitudes

⇒ The specific direction of motives and drives is learned from definitions of the legal codes as favorable or unfavorable.

⇒ A person becomes delinquent because of an excess of definitions favorable to violation of law over definitions unfavorable to violation of the law.

⇒ Differential associations may vary in frequency, duration, priority, and intensity.

⇒ The process of learning criminal behavior by association with criminal and anti-criminal patterns involves all of the mechanisms that are involved in any other learning.

⇒ While criminal behavior is an expression of general needs and values, it is not explained by those needs and values, since non-criminal behavior is an expression of the same needs and values

FIGURE 7-1 Edwin Sutherland's Nine Basic Propositions of Differential Association Theory.

When the desired behavior is rewarded, it is reinforced; as such, the behavior is more likely to be repeated and become more frequent. With **positive reinforcement**, the positive stimulus is added following the behavior. The positive stimulus involves the introduction of something desirable to increase the likelihood of desired behavior. Criminal behavior results from positive reinforcement of illicit behavior. Positive reinforcement also increases the likelihood that a cybercriminal will repeat the illicit behavior. Studies have supported this for crime and cybercrime (e.g., Internet child pornography, digital piracy, and hacking).[44] This positive reinforcement is often in the form of peer recognition. For example, peer recognition among hackers and virus writers was cited as a reason for engaging in these cybercrimes.[45] Cybercriminals that receive illicit gains from their actions or other types of rewards or reinforcements are less likely to cease their illicit behavior. Internet child pornographers receive positive reinforcement from other like-minded individuals online.[46] The reinforcement Internet child pornographers receive from other like-minded individuals online is encouragement, support, and a sense of belongingness.[47]

In contrast, **negative reinforcement** is the removal of a negative stimulus following the desirable behavior. Here, something undesirable is removed to increase the likelihood of the desired behavior. For instance, a child pornographer might be granted access to an exclusive online child sex offender forum that the pornographer was previously blocked from after the pornographer provides that forum with a new image of child pornography (one that is not in circulation). In this example, the unpleasant consequence is that viewers are denied access to a desired online child sex offender forum. The desired behavior is for the people requesting access to submit a new image of child pornography (i.e., one that is not in circulation). Hence, offenders who provide the forum with a new child pornographic image will have the "block" to the forum removed.

When the undesirable behavior results in punishment, the frequency of this behavior decreases. **Positive punishment** is the adding of a negative stimulus following the undesirable behavior, that is, introducing something undesirable to reduce the likelihood of the unwanted behavior. **Negative punishment** involves removing a positive stimulus following the undesirable behavior. Removing something desirable after bad behavior reduces the likelihood of that behavior in the future. Punishment, such as being ignored, ostracized, or banned from a community, will lead to desistance from that behavior. However, the reality is that cybercriminals are not socially ostracized when they engage in illicit behavior; instead, they find solace and camaraderie among like-minded individuals and groups online (e.g., hackers and Internet child sex offenders).

Reinforcements and punishments are thus used to control **operant behavior,** that is, a person's responses to rewards and punishments.[48] An individual's behavior is conditioned by environmental responses and consequences of one's actions. This process of social learning is known as **operant conditioning**, "behavior . . . acquired or conditioned by the effects, outcome, or consequences it has on the person's environment."[49] Accordingly, these individuals can be conditioned to behave in a particular way through rewards and punishments designed to reinforce desired conduct and punish undesirable conduct. This conditioning, however, may occur even if the individual does not make a cognizant connection between the individual's actions and the consequences the individual experiences.

The third social learning factor used to explain crime and cybercrime is learning through observation. Individuals learn to commit crime from observing others, offline and online. Albert Bandura posited that behavior is learned through imitation and modeling.[56] **Imitation** occurs when an individual directly observes a behavior and

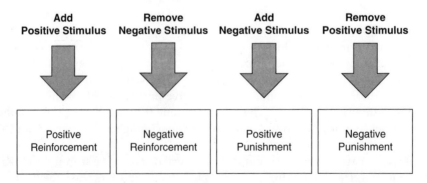

FIGURE 7-2 Depicts Positive and Negative Reinforcement and Punishment.

BOX 7-1 INTERNET ADDICTION AS A LEARNED BEHAVIOR

Internet use is integrated into individuals' personal and professional lives, making the temptations, opportunities, pressures, and inducements for Internet addiction pervasive. This makes the behavior harder to control. Internet use is a learned behavior. As such, Internet addiction can be explained through operant conditioning.[50] If the individual engages in this behavior to deal with or in some way alleviate anxiety, stress, or feelings of depression and derives pleasure or is rewarded in other ways for that activity, it can become an addictive behavior. In fact, these uses of the Internet are associated with Internet addiction.[51] An individual will continue to engage in these activities if the behavior is positively or negatively reinforced in some way.[52] Individuals use the Internet "to compensate [for] their real life deficits" in communication and relationships.[53] Research has shown that "the user receives reinforcement [online]

in terms of (dysfunctional) coping with negative feelings or problems in everyday life. At the same time, the Internet use expectancies are positively reinforced, because the Internet acted as anticipated (e.g., reducing feelings of emotional or social loneliness)."[54] For individuals who use the Internet as a coping mechanism for anxiety, stress, or depression, the Internet also serves as a place for them to escape difficult situations and emotions. According to researchers Brand, Young, and Laier, "the more general psychopathological tendencies (e.g., depression, social anxiety) are supposed to be negatively reinforced. This may be due to the fact that . . . specific Internet applications (e.g., Internet pornography) can be used to distract from problems in the real life or to avoid negative feelings, such as loneliness or social isolation."[55] Ultimately, positive and negative reinforcement increases the likelihood that individuals will continue to use the Internet to experience the same impact with future use.

subsequently emulates it. Criminals and cybercriminals learn how to commit illicit activities through imitation.[57] For example, imitation plays a significant role in the use and creation of malware.[58] Behavior **modeling** refers to learning a behavior by observation and then imitating the observed behavior at a later time. For instance, individuals in online gangs learn from those that have higher-level skills in computing through imitation and modeling.[59] Reinforcement of the imitated/modeled behavior is key. This reinforcement is vicarious: On the one hand, if a person sees someone rewarded for a behavior, he or she is more likely to imitate/model that behavior. On the other hand, if a person sees someone punished for a behavior, he or she is less likely to imitate/model that behavior.

Finally, an individual will commit illicit activities if the individual learns an excess of definitions favorable to violations of the law over definitions unfavorable to these violations. If an individual has developed definitions unfavorable to the illicit act in question, he or she will be less likely to engage in the action. Definitions unfavorable to the engagement in crime are moral objections to it. Conversely, positive definitions of a crime justify the act. Having several definitions favorable to cybercrime has been found to be a significant predictor of such behavior.[60] For instance, definitions favorable to pirating software play a role in individuals' decisions to engage in this cybercrime.[61]

Research on the role of social learning variables in explaining cybercriminality is mixed;[62] not all of these variables have been found to play a prominent role in cybercrime. Studies have indicated that specific components of social learning theory, such as differential association, definitions favorable to crime and deviance, imitation, and differential reinforcement, play more of a pivotal role in crime and deviance than others. For instance, with respect to digital piracy, differential association and definitions favorable to crime and deviancy have been found to be main factors in one's engagement in software piracy.[63] Both differential association and favorable definitions of cybercrime have also been found to be significant predictors of gaining unauthorized access by guessing passwords.[64] Other components of social learning theory (imitation and differential reinforcement) have been found not to have a significant role in software piracy.[65]

Because individuals learn cybercriminal behaviors, these theories hold that crime and cybercrime can be controlled through rehabilitation. Here, criminals can be rehabilitated to learn law-abiding behavior. Individuals with bad behavior can be rehabilitated by re-educating and resocializing them. What is more, given the primary role of deviant and criminal peer associations in learning deviance and criminal behaviors, contacts should be increased with those who do not condone these behaviors. This is one way individuals may learn definitions unfavorable to deviance and crime offline and online. Ultimately, a cybercriminal should be exposed to people with attitudes and beliefs different from those held by the individuals in his or her deviant or criminal group.

NEUTRALIZING CYBEROFFENSES

In his book *Delinquency and Drift*, David Matza argued that individuals live their lives along a continuum between two extremes: absolute freedom and total constraints.[66] Individuals are believed to move from one extreme to another; this process is known as *drift*.[67] Individuals drift between law-abiding and illicit behavior. Even though social bonds exist, individuals learn how to override them when social control is weak in order to engage in illegal activities. When social control is strong, individuals drift back to lawful behavior.

Gresham Sykes and David Matza rejected the notion of subcultures, which maintain attitudes, beliefs, and values that are separate and different from mainstream society.[68] Instead, criminals and noncriminals were viewed as holding attitudes, beliefs, and values similar to those of mainstream society.[69] As such, a key assumption of **neutralization theory** is that individuals share conventional attitudes, beliefs, and values even though they may violate them with their behavior. Neutralization theory thus seeks to explain why individuals engage in both law-abiding and criminal behavior, at times simultaneously.

According to neutralization theory, individuals learn techniques to temporarily free themselves from conventional restraints on behavior by excusing or justifying illicit conduct. The cognitive techniques that enable users to drift in and out of deviance and crime are known as *neutralization techniques*, which enable individuals to temporarily neutralize their attitudes, beliefs, and values in order to engage in illicit behavior. While these techniques enable individuals to break societal rules should they choose, they do not compel them to do so. Neutralization theory sheds light on individuals' persistence in crime when neutralizations are accepted and their desistance from crime when neutralizations are rejected.

To overcome feelings of remorse or guilt for behavior that is contrary to conventional norms, values, and beliefs of society, individuals use five neutralization techniques identified by Sykes and Matza.[70]

1. *Denial of responsibility.* Individuals who utilize this technique know that their behavior is wrong but do not take responsibility for their actions.[71] For example, individuals may justify digital piracy on the grounds that the work sought was unavailable for purchase. A further example involves computer virus writers. Even though these cybercriminals understand the difference between right and wrong, they deny responsibility for their actions by claiming that the release of the malware was accidental.[72]

2. *Denial of the victim.* With this neutralization technique, individuals deny that there is a victim of their deviant or criminal act. Victims are also believed to be responsible for the crime committed against them and to have brought the deviant or criminal act upon themselves. Hackers view that their behavior, while illegal, is not wrong in light of the circumstances (i.e., the end sought).[73] Hackers utilize this neutralization technique when they blame system administrators for failing to adequately protect systems and computer programmers for writing code with flaws that are not patched in a timely manner.[74] Lax security and poor programming are to blame, but not the hackers themselves. Any loss or damage to the system is thus deemed the fault of the owner for failing to take adequate precautions.

3. *Denial of injury.* The individual who uses this neutralization technique claims that a crime was not committed, as harm was not done or the target could afford any losses suffered. Individuals often justify digital piracy on the grounds that no harm was done to the owners.[75] Some may even argue that their actions benefit the owner of the copyrighted work by making the item available to others and increasing its visibility.[76] Likewise, hackers may maintain gaining unauthorized access to a system does not cause harm; what causes harm is any alteration to or deletion of content in the system.[77] Nonetheless, even when they steal or damage a system, they deny that real damage was caused, due to redundancy features in place.[78]

4. *Condemnation of condemners.* With this neutralization technique, individuals divert attention from their actions to the motives of those who are criticizing their conduct.[79] Here, individuals view their condemners as "hypocrites, deviants in disguise, or impelled by personal spite."[80] For instance, those who engage in digital piracy view those in the movie and music industry as hypocrites who have been stealing from consumers for years with high prices for products.[81]

5. *Appeal to higher loyalties.* Individuals use this technique to justify an illicit act on the grounds that it was conducted in defense of attitudes, beliefs, and values that are viewed as more important than those of society. According to Sykes and Matza, "deviation from certain norms may occur not because the norms are rejected but because other norms, held to be more pressing or involving a higher loyalty, are accorded precedence."[82] This neutralization technique enables individuals to engage in criminal behavior that they consider personally and socially acceptable. Hackers may justify their actions as serving a higher, altruistic purpose (e.g., fighting for civil liberties, such as freedom of information).[83] Hackers effectively neutralize their behavior, showing little, if any, remorse or guilt for their illicit actions.[84]

James Coleman proposed two neutralization techniques, *claim of normalcy* (i.e., everyone else is doing it) and *claim of entitlement*.[85] With claim of normalcy, individuals argue that most people engage in similar illicit behavior. This technique has been adopted by digital pirates who view digital piracy as a prevalent and normal behavior.[86] With the claim of entitlement, the individual justifies his or her actions by claiming that he or she deserves the rewards obtained from that conduct.

Other neutralization techniques include *denial of negative intent* (i.e., the person was just kidding) and *claim of relative acceptability* (i.e., the person draws attention to the acts of others that are more serious in comparison with the act in question).[87] The *metaphor of the ledger* is another neutralization technique used by individuals to rationalize illicit conduct and the guilt or remorse associated with it. An individual utilizing this technique argues that the law-abiding behavior the individual engaged in that contributes to society outweighs the illicit action the individual engaged in.[88] Finally, the *defense of necessity* is a neutralization technique used to justify actions as essential to the survival and livelihood of the individual.[89] Individuals who use this neutralization technique blame structural conditions for their situation and actions.

Research has shown that some, but not all, neutralization techniques have been employed by cybercriminals. For instance, an investigation by Tugeman-Goldschmidt did not find support for adoption of the denial of responsibility neutralization technique by hackers.[90] With respect to digital piracy, the neutralization techniques employed by cybercriminals varied.[91] In one study, the most commonly used neutralization techniques were denial of victim, denial of injury, and claim of normalcy.[92] In another study, along with denial of injury and denial of victim, a commonly used neutralization technique was appeal to higher loyalties.[93] Yet another study found that some neutralization techniques were inversely related to digital piracy, particularly denial of responsibility, condemnation of condemners, and the metaphor of the ledger.[94] The neutralization techniques of appeal to higher loyalties, claim of normalcy, and defense of necessity, were found to be significant predictors of different forms of digital piracy.[95] Individuals who engage in music piracy were found to employ the neutralization techniques of defense of necessity, appeal to higher loyalties, and claim of normalcy.[96] For movie piracy, the most utilized technique was claim of normalcy.[97] By contrast, for software piracy, appeal to higher loyalties, condemnation of condemners, and defense of necessity were the most common neutralization techniques.[98]

MORAL DISENGAGEMENT

Individuals refrain from behavior which violates their own moral beliefs and provokes negative feelings, such as guilt and self-censure.[99] They have self-regulatory mechanisms to prevent them from engaging in behaviors that violate their moral beliefs and

---

BOX 7-2   ON BECOMING A CYBERCRIMINAL

Howard Becker conducted a study on marijuana users.[100] At first blush, his study would seem irrelevant to a discussion on cybercrime. However, there are parallels that can be drawn between Becker's work on becoming a marijuana smoker and the process whereby an individual becomes a cybercriminal. Becker studied marijuana smokers to better understand and explain the process whereby individuals become marijuana smokers. His research revealed that the motive for engaging in the act and the continued engagement in that behavior evolve through the engagement in that behavior in the presence of others. Utilizing the central tenets of his theory and applying it to cybercrime, the following can be observed:

1. An individual will learn the technique of using Internet-enabled technologies to commit cybercrime.
2. The individual will learn to identify the effect of the act on himself or herself.

3. The individual will learn to identify the effect as a positive one.
4. The individual will subsequently learn how to commit the cybercrime on his or her own.
5. The individual will learn how to neutralize the impact of social control on his or her behavior.

While this theory has yet to be tested on cybercriminals in empirical studies, certain tenets have been supported by the available literature and studies on cybercrime. For example, online child pornographers may learn from others in forums on how to use the Internet to locate child pornography.[101] Moreover, the stigma associated with this act can be neutralized by the individual through identification with other like-minded individuals who can support or reinforce the behavior. Generally, studies have supported the notion that cybercrime is a learned behavior and that cybercriminals learn to neutralize their behavior to avoid censure and negative emotions.[102]

standards.[103] These mechanisms include self-control over one's behavior (*self-monitoring*) and evaluation of one's actions based on moral standards, situational contexts, and self-reactions. The mechanisms engage or disengage internal controls, preventing or enabling the illicit or immoral conduct.[104] As Bandura argued, "moral standards do not function as fixed internal regulators of conduct. Self-regulatory mechanisms do not operate unless they are activated, and there are many psychological processes by which control reactions can be disengaged from inhumane conduct.[105] Selective activation and disengagement of moral self-sanctions permit different types of conduct despite the same moral standards."[106] Criminals can bypass these self-regulatory mechanisms through moral disengagement.

Moral disengagement is the process whereby individuals construct rationalizations for behavior in order to overcome any internal inhibitions. These rationalizations are used to justify actions that violate existing moral and ethical norms by arguing that these norms do not apply to the person in the person's current situation in order to avoid guilt or shame for the person's actions.[107] Moral disengagement thus involves cognitive processes that seek to justify illicit conduct in order to avoid or reduce the negative emotions associated with that act. Hackers utilize moral disengagement tactics to avoid experiencing negative emotions from their illicit acts.[108] Similarly, individuals engaged in digital piracy "choose to morally disengage from the non-ethical nature of the act in an attempt to avoid feeling guilty about illegally downloading and also to avoid any blame being attributed to them personally."[109] Moral disengagement has been found to play a prominent role in other forms of offending and cyberoffending. Studies have shown that moral disengagement influences involvement in gangs.[110] Other studies revealed that cyberbullies use moral disengagement tactics.[111] Nonetheless, the literature on moral disengagement and cybercrime is mixed. For instance, while some studies have revealed associations between cyberbullying and moral disengagement,[112] others have not found any statistically significant associations.[113]

Moral disengagement can occur through the following mechanisms: cognitive reconstruction, displacing or diffusing responsibility, distorting the impact of a behavior, or attributing blame to or dehumanizing the victim.[114]

Cognitive reconstruction. **Cognitive reconstruction** occurs when an illegal, immoral, or reprehensible act is reconstructed as a righteous and legitimate act in light of the circumstances. Therefore, cognitive reconstruction seeks to alter the view of a negative, immoral, or illegal behavior by framing it in a positive light. Cognitive reconstruction can occur through the use of euphemistic language and labels for an activity, moral justifications for conduct, and engagement in advantageous comparisons to explain behavior. First, *euphemistic language and labels* for an activity enable an individual to view that behavior as acceptable through positive language. This positive language is used to conceal the negative impact of the activity. For instance, those who engage in music piracy argue that their actions benefit musicians by creating a wide fan base.[115] Rationalization for hacking occurs when hackers believe their actions contribute to existing knowledge about hacking.[116] Some hackers also believe that their actions benefit society.[117] Hackers also sometimes "believe the act of hacking helps companies improve their systems. Through such euphemistic language, hacking is made personally acceptable within the mind of a hacker and socially acceptable within the hacking community in general."[118] Second, *moral justifications for conduct* are provided, which view behavior as justified and appropriate in light of the circumstances. Finally, *advantageous comparisons to explain behavior* are employed to justify the particular behavior as being better than worse behavior exhibited by others. Indeed, the seriousness of an act can be downplayed by comparing it to more serious crimes.

Displacing or diffusing responsibility. Individuals seek to displace and diffuse responsibility for their actions in an effort to minimize their role in the immoral, deviant, or criminal behavior. One way that such responsibility is displaced or diffused is by emphasizing the role of peers, leaders, or the group as a whole in decision-making.[119] In this manner, an individual believes that he or she is not the agent of his or her action, thereby reducing self-censure.[120] What is also emphasized is that the actions of the individual arise from social pressures.[121] Individuals also justify their actions as a result of their socioeconomic status and other personal and societal pressures. In their view, an individual who steals because he or she has no alternative cannot be considered guilty. These justifications seek to prevent self-censure by absolving individuals of responsibility for their actions.

Distorting the impact of a behavior. Individuals distort consequences of their behavior by minimizing, ignoring, or denying its adverse impact, viewing it in a positive light instead. Self-censure is prevented by minimizing the harm or damage their behavior causes. Research has shown that hackers minimize the consequences of their actions.[122] This moral disengagement mechanism has also been associated with **cyberaggression**,[123] "any type of harassment or bullying, including teasing, telling lies, making fun of, making rude or mean comments, spreading rumors, or making threatening or aggressive comments," that occurs online.[124] Such actions and the harm they cause are minimized by, for example, teenagers with phrases like "It is just high school," as if this behavior is to be expected and should be expected. When the consequences of one's actions are minimized, distorted, or ignored, self-censorship of illicit behavior cannot occur.

This moral disengagement mechanism is further employed by Internet child sex offenders and child pornographers, who ignore the negative impact of their illicit activities through **cognitive distortions**, which include "offense-supportive attitudes, cognitive processing during an offense sequence, as well as post hoc neutralizations or excuses for offending."[125] Cognitive distortions are used by offenders to justify their conduct and assist them in maintaining their positive self-image. For instance, Internet child sex offenders may justify their actions by stating that children want to have sex, sex with children is natural, it helps children become sexually expressive, and it helps children learn sexual behavior.[126] These cognitive distortions enable offline and online child sex offenders to rationalize, justify, minimize, or deny illicit behavior.[127] Child sex offenders have a sense of entitlement to engage in sex acts with whom they desire, be it adult or child.[128] They also view sexual activity with children as normal.[129] Online child pornographers minimize the consequences of their actions and deny any further injury is done to the victim because the videos and images already exist online.[130] As such, the viewing of this material is not perceived as causing any further harm to the child or children depicted in the images and videos or to society.[131] Overall, cognitive distortions have been found to play a key role in the processes whereby an individual engages in predatory crimes against children.[132]

Attributing blame to victim. Individuals justify their behavior by claiming they were provoked by the victim and thus the victim brought the action on himself or herself (*blaming the victim*). This is similar to the *denial of victim* neutralization technique. The blame for the act is transferred to the victim. Individuals view their actions as defensive tactics in response to provocation by the victim. Here, the perpetrators view themselves as the victims. Accordingly, they blame the real victims for the harm or damage they sustain. Cybercriminals such as hackers often blame their victims.[133] Particularly, "when confronted about illegal hacking activities, hackers blame the victim for the consequences of the illegal hacking activity and effectively shift the appropriate feelings of guilt and shame to an external entity, the victim."[134]

Dehumanizing victim. Another moral disengagement mechanism used is the **dehumanization** of the victim.[135] Dehumanization is the psychological process of making the target seem less human. With dehumanization, the victim is stripped of human attributes. This dehumanization occurs to reduce the negative feelings associated with committing the illicit act. This process also enables offenders to view victims as unhuman or subhuman and undeserving of empathy. Research has supported the notion that perpetrators of interpersonal crimes and cybercrimes against women treat women as objects and not humans.[136] With respect to interpersonal cybercrimes, female victims who have experienced cyberharassment reported "receiving highly sexual comments and visual pornography that dehumanize women."[137] Research has also shown that online child sex offenders, in general, and online child pornographers, in particular, dehumanize their victims.[138]

The widespread utilization of neutralization techniques and moral disengagement mechanisms by cybercriminals highlights the need to counter the excuses and justifications individuals use to rationalize, explain, and legitimate illicit behavior.

DISINHIBITION, DEINDIVIDUATION, AND ANONYMITY

Research has shown that **disinhibition** facilitates cybercrime.[139] Behavioral disinhibition occurs when established social norms and codes of conduct are violated. Online, individuals experience what is known as a disinhibition effect, which has been posited to have three dimensions.[140]

1. *Dissociative anonymity.* Individuals are under the impression that whatever they say online and the actions they engage in cannot be linked to them directly. Accordingly, people do not hold themselves accountable for their online speech and behavior.

2. *Deindividuation.* The Internet enables a process known as **deindividuation,** a psychological state whereby a person's "inner restraints are lost when individuals are not seen or paid attention to as individuals."[141] Deindividuation is linked to the process of depersonalization, wherein a user has a diminished self-awareness, self-identity, and low self-control.[142] Self-awareness and self-identity assist individuals in understanding their relationships and interactions with others. A loss of self-awareness and self-identity may occur if an individual feels the need to conform to others' beliefs even though those beliefs conflict with the individual's personal beliefs and moral views. Deindividuation has been found to foster immoral and illegal behavior.[143]

3. *Dissociative imagination*. Individuals disassociate their online personas and their behavior from that of their real-world persona and behavior. They also believe that the same rules, norms, and beliefs do not apply in the online world.

A further disinhibiting and deindividuating characteristic of the Internet is invisibility,[144] the ability of a person to use the Internet without other users' knowledge of his or her activities. Individuals experience invisibility online because others cannot see them, and, depending on the forum and methods used by the individuals, others may not be aware of their presence.

Individuals can also hide their identities due to the **anonymity** that the Internet affords them. Research has shown that anonymity facilitates cybercrime.[145] For instance, anonymity and the arousal obtained from engaging in online child sex offending serve as catalysts for this cybercrime because these can inhibit existing internal controls that would prevent this type of sexual activity.[146] Indeed, disinhibition and deindividuation, along with the anonymity afforded by the Internet, trigger behaviors that are suppressed in the offline world by social constraints.[147] Anonymity emboldens individuals to behave in ways that they would not engage in offline due to social control.

A case in point is cyberbullying. Research has shown that the presence of online disinhibition and anonymity are associated with cyberbullying.[148] The presence of these two factors may well explain why certain individuals engage in cyberbullying but not bullying. Particularly, one study revealed that while the majority of cyberbullies also bully victims offline, some cyberbullies do not bully others offline due to the absence of online disinhibition.[149] A cyberbully does not come face to face with his or her victim. This distance from the victim is believed to enable perpetrators to engage in cyberbullying without feeling guilty about their behavior.[150] For cyberstalkers, appealing aspects of the Internet are the opportunities for deception[151] and "depersonalization of the victims and reduced risk of retaliation."[152]

Other researchers have found that lack of physical proximity of cyberbullies to the victim enables them to fully dissociate themselves from moral responsibility for the immoral act they commit. Here, a form of deindividuation occurs. According to Zimbardo's deindividuation theory, "if people were unable to identify another person, this would lead to less internalized controls such as shame or guilt. To draw parallels from this theory to the phenomenon of cyberbullying, often the cyberbully cannot see or hear the one they are targeting and in some instances they may not even know whom they are targeting, i.e., they do not identify their victim. This could therefore lead to fewer feelings of shame, guilt or remorse compared to a face-to-face interaction."[153] This process emboldens perpetrators to engage in conduct online that they might not engage in during face-to-face communications

IMAGE 7-2 Screenshot of Messages from Rebecca Ann Sedwick's Cyberbullies.

with the target. This was observed in the case of Rebecca Ann Sedwick (discussed in the beginning of the chapter). A mob mentality fueled the cyberbullies in her case; in addition to Rebecca's primary cyberbullies, more than a dozen other children added to the array of texts and messages egging her on to kill herself.

The absence of social constraints can embolden individuals to take advantage of the Internet and engage in cybercrime. This may well explain why cyberaggression is more prevalent in forums where users are anonymous and on websites where anonymous comments can be made.[154] Anonymity is also associated with lack of fear of sanctions for bad behavior. When present, formal and informal sanctions can reduce the likelihood of offending behavior. When informal sanctions are absent, this increases the likelihood of offending behavior. An example of an informal sanction is social censure, which is largely absent in online interactions. Social censure for cyberbullying is often absent due to lack of face-to-face interactions with the target and social controls online.[155] In view of that, individuals who engage in antisocial and criminal behaviors online benefit from the anonymity the Internet affords them by avoiding real-world repercussions for their immoral, deviant, or criminal acts.

DEVELOPMENTAL AND LIFE-COURSE CYBERCRIMINOLOGY

Developmental and life-course criminology recognizes that while offenders' predisposition to crime and deviance remains stable throughout a person's lifetime, the manifestations of crime and deviancy during that period may change. Two main perspectives in developmental and life-course criminology are the latent trait and the life-course perspective.

LATENT TRAIT PERSPECTIVE

The **latent trait perspective** views human behavior as directed by a master trait which an individual has at birth or develops during childhood. This trait is viewed as constant throughout one's life. The latent trait perspective proposes certain biological and psychological traits that predispose individuals to criminal activity, such as personality disorders, defective

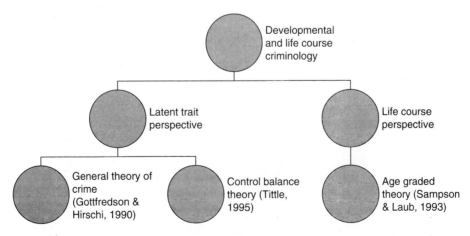

FIGURE 7-3 Main Developmental and Life-Course Criminology Perspectives and Theories.

intelligence, chemical imbalances, and genetic abnormalities.[156] Individuals with these traits are predisposed to criminality and criminal careers. Those with these traits who offend during childhood are likely to offend in adulthood. While the traits remain relatively stable throughout an individual's lifetime, the environment within which the person operates changes and the opportunities that an individual is faced with also change over time. These fluctuations in environmental influences and opportunities explain desistance from crime.

A widely studied trait in criminology is control. The **control balance theory**, proposed by Charles Tittle, focuses on the relationship between the perceived control of others by an individual and the control the individual purports to be experiencing.[157] When the perceived control of others is equal to the control the individual is experiencing, *control balance* exists, which makes conformity possible. The complete control of others by the individual is known as a *control surplus*. The complete control of the individual by others is known as a *control deficit*. Both control surpluses and control deficits are forms of control imbalance, which has been liked to criminality. According to Tittle, individuals with a control deficit or a control surplus are more likely to engage in illicit behavior in an effort to acquire, preserve, or intensify control over others.[158] Numerous other studies have supported control deficits and control surpluses as predictors of illicit behavior.[159] According to control balance theory, even if a predisposition exists to offend and the motivation is present, in order for deviancy or crime to occur, the opportunity to offend must be present and existing constraints must be overcome (these could be in the form of social bonds or fear of punishment).[160]

Another control trait that has been studied is **self-control**. Lanier and Henry argued that a trait which differentiates criminals and noncriminals is the ability of noncriminals to suppress or resist the urge to engage in an illicit act for immediate gratification and excitement.[161] This trait is known as self-control. Those who lack or have low self-control are impulsive and seek immediate gratification of desires and needs without consideration for future consequences.[162] There are four types of self-control: inability to control unwanted thoughts; inability to resist temptation (i.e., lack of impulse control); inability to control mood and emotions; and inability to control performance.

Individuals with this personality trait (i.e., low self-control) seek immediate and efficient resolution of a conflict or the achievement of a goal through an illicit act. Low self-control is characterized by poor impulse control when faced with opportunities to offend.[163] Self-control has thus been used to explain a person's propensity to commit crime. Particularly, self-control influences the likelihood that someone will engage in illicit behavior and the frequency and extent to which he or she will engage in that behavior. Those with no or low self-control are more likely to engage in illicit behavior than those with high self-control. High self-control "effectively reduces the possibility of crime—that is, those possessing it will be substantially less likely at all periods of life to engage in criminal acts."[164] Those with high self-control are prone to conform and thus can also resist temptations and incentives to commit crimes. Nevertheless, studies have shown that this ability to resist tends to weaken with repeated temptations.[165]

A General Theory of Cybercrime

In 1990, Michael Gottfredson and Travis Hirschi proposed a **general theory of crime**. Particularly, the theory holds that low self-control accounts for all forms of criminality.[166] Structural factors in society are considered irrelevant; what matters is the proper development of self-control. Low self-control is thought to be relatively stable throughout one's life, however.[167]

Gottfredson and Hirschi's theory posits that crime is the product of low self-control developed during an individual's childhood.[168] It also holds that parental relationships are an essential socialization source for children.[169] The quality of parental relationships influences the child's behavior, in general, and the development of self-control, in particular. Low self-control or lack of self-control is considered the result of poor and ineffective parenting and monitoring of the child's behavior, inadequate or inappropriate disciplining of the child, and lack of a bond with parents.[170]

Just as low self-control has been linked to criminal behavior in general,[171] research has also shown that low self-control is associated with cybercrime.[172] For instance, low self-control has been found to be a predictor of hacking. Indeed, in one study of the hacking community, some hackers reported feeling a rush so powerful that they were unable to control their behavior.[173] Low self-control has further been linked to interpersonal cybercrimes.[174] Moreover, studies have revealed that low self-control is a significant predictor of one's engagement in digital piracy.[175] Those with low self-control seek to satisfy their needs in the quickest way possible. The ease with which such digital works can be downloaded, as well as individuals' low self-control, may well explain why these individuals engage in digital piracy.[176] In fact, studies have shown that low self-control is a significant predictor of various forms of digital piracy, particularly movie piracy,[177] music piracy,[178] and software piracy.[179] By contrast, some studies have shown only a moderate correlation between low self-control and digital piracy.[180] Furthermore, other studies have shown that low self-control is not a statistically significant predictor of digital piracy.[181] This finding conflicts with previous studies showing that low self-control is a statistically significant predictor of digital piracy.[182] In reality, not all persons who engage in crime and cybercrime exhibit low self-control. As such, the possibility of a general theory of crime, and the potential for a general theory of cybercrime that applies to all criminals and cybercriminals and all forms of crime and cybercrime is refuted.

LIFE-COURSE PERSPECTIVE

Criminal career studies examine the onset, continuity, and eventual desistance from crime. Sheldon Glueck and Eleanor Glueck's research in the 1930s was the first to examine criminal careers, looking in particular at the biological, psychological, and sociological characteristics of those engaged in persistent offending.[183] The Gluecks found that family dynamics influence criminality; that is, dysfunctional family dynamics play a role in criminal activity. In the 1980s, Robert Sampson and John Laub reanalyzed the data from the Gluecks' study on juvenile delinquents,[184] and they similarly observed that dysfunctional family dynamics play a key role in persistent offending. Other studies have revealed that antisocial behaviors in childhood are a good predictor of problems during adult development. Specifically, children who exhibit antisocial behavior are likely to engage in deviancy or criminal behavior later on in life.[185] Nevertheless, research has also shown that individuals have engaged in illicit activities without any prior history of offending.[186] What is more, research has shown that certain offenders, such as child sex offenders, began offending at later stages in their lives.[187] Furthermore, studies on offline crime have shown that children and young adults are less likely to continue to engage in offending throughout their life.[188] Similar findings have been reported for cybercrime. For example, computer virus writers tend to age out of their criminal career.[189]

Contrary to the developmental perspective, the **life-course perspective** "conceptualize[s] crime as an emergent process reducible neither to the individual nor the environment."[190] According to this perspective, a criminal career results from criminogenic influences one experiences throughout his or her lifetime. The life-course perspective examines criminal careers throughout the individual's life, including how these careers began and how they ended.

One of the main theories of the life-course perspective is Sampson and Laub's **age-graded theory**,[191] which explains variation in criminality as the result of changes in criminal involvement across the individual's life span. According to this theory, involvement in conventional activities and engagement in criminal offending changes over time.[192] As in social control theory, social bonds are considered essential in preventing individuals from offending. And similarly to Hirschi in *Causes of Delinquency* (1969), Sampson and Laub posited that broken or weakened social bonds may result in deviant or criminal behavior. Likewise, they found that individuals with broken attachments to family and school and those with delinquent peers were likely to engage in delinquent behavior.[193] Where Hirschi and Sampson and Laub differed is in the stage in one's life at which the social bonds exist and influence behaviors. Hirschi's social control theory was criticized for attributing crime to early life experiences only. While individual traits and experiences one has during childhood are important, these factors alone cannot explain criminal careers. Therefore, unlike Hirschi, Sampson and Laub believed that the experiences one has during adulthood influence criminality. These social bonds can explain fluctuations in engagement in criminality over one's life span.[194] Specifically, the social bonds an adult develops in life may well explain variations in crime in adulthood and desistance from deviant or criminal acts.[195] The social bonds in adulthood are thus associated with law-abiding behavior and offending behavior; the latter behavior is associated with broken social bonds in adulthood.

Sampson and Laub examined and mapped criminal trajectories (i.e., the path or courses of action a person takes in life, such as employment, marriage, parenthood, and illicit behavior).[196] They proposed several developmental stages (childhood, adolescence, and adulthood) that include patterns of criminal behavior associated with age.[197] In addition to these stages, their age-graded theory proposes turning points (i.e., life events which influence and change the development of a criminal career) and transitions (i.e., particular events that occur within trajectories) in individuals' lives associated with legitimate and illegitimate behavior.[198] Therefore, to explain criminal careers, the age-graded theory examines trajectories, turning points, and major transitions in an individual's life. Ultimately, the theory holds that while "individual traits and childhood experiences are important for understanding behavioral stability, experiences in adolescence and adulthood can redirect criminal trajectories in either a more positive or more negative manner."[199]

Laub and Sampson identified two life-course events that reduce criminality later on in an individual's life: marriage and stable, legitimate employment.[200] These prosocial ties were found to serve as a deterrent to crime. For example, stable careers in one's life were found to inhibit the individual's engagement in crime.[201] These careers create strong social ties between the individual and society, thus decreasing the likelihood that he or she will commit crime.[202] By way of extension, negative life events (e.g., divorce) were associated with crime. For instance, studies have shown that individuals predisposed to child sex offending are more likely to engage in this behavior offline or online if they experience negative life events (e.g., separation or divorce) in interpersonal relationships or rejection or blockages in adult relationships.[203]

In view of that, Sampson and Laub argued that the informal prosocial relationships of individuals within society prevent individuals from offending.[204] These relationships change across one's life span. With respect to crime (and by way of extension, cybercrime), changes in illicit behavior are associated with changes in personal relationships (e.g., family and friends) and professional relationships (e.g., colleagues and employers). The personal and professional bonds of individuals thus explain variation in criminality (and cybercriminality) and adult development throughout the person's life course.

CASE STUDY

The Gamer was a 2009 film based on life in 2024, when the gaming industry has invented technology which enables the full control of a human being. These human beings, the characters in a game called *Society*, are controlled by gamers. These "characters" are used to engage in a wide variety of extreme, antisocial, and criminal behaviors (e.g., extreme pornography and rape). Another game, *Slayers*, uses real inmates on death row and those who are serving a life sentence. These individuals become characters in the game and are controlled by players of the game. The task of the characters in *Slayers* is to fight and kill other characters in matches. If a person wins thirty matches, he or she is set free. To win the match, he or she must kill an opponent. The movement of the characters in *Slayers* is controlled by the players (i.e., the gamers). The decision to kill is made by the characters. No communication is allowed between the character and the gamer. Even though the gamers are playing a game, the characters are real human beings. In these games, real human beings are being forced to engage in a wide variety of immoral and illicit behaviors.

1. What theory or theories can explain gamers' participation in these games?
2. How would the gamers justify their conduct?
3. What role, if any, do others play in gamers' participation in these games?
4. What tactics can be used to stop gamers from playing these games?

REVIEW QUESTIONS

1. What are social bonds? How can they be used to explain conformity?
2. Can social control theory explain cybercrime? Why or why not?
3. What is social learning theory? Can it explain cybercrime? Why do you think so?
4. Can differential association theory explain cybercrime? Why or why not?
5. In what ways can cybercriminality be reinforced? Please explain your response through positive and negative reinforcement.
6. How do cybercriminals neutralize offenses?
7. Choose a cybercrime. What methods would the cybercriminal use to morally disengage from this behavior?
8. What is disinhibition and deindividuation? Do these facilitate cybercrime? If so, in what ways?
9. Can low self-control explain cybercrime? Why or why not?
10. What is the age-graded theory? Can it explain cybercrime? Why do you think so?

LAWS

Investment Advisors Act of 1940 (United States)
Securities Act of 1933 (United States)
Securities Exchange Act of 1934 (United States)

DEFINITIONS

Age-graded theory. A theory that explains variation in criminality as the result of changes in criminal involvement across the individual's life span.

Anonymity. Anonymity enables individuals to engage in activities without revealing their identities.

Cognitive distortions. Cognitive distortions are used by offenders to justify their conduct and assists them in maintaining their positive self-image.

Cognitive reconstruction. Cognitive reconstruction occurs when an illegal, immoral, or reprehensible act is reconstrued as a righteous and legitimate act in light of the circumstances.

Containment theory. A theory holding that individuals have an inner containment structure and an outer containment structure that shield them from the pushes and pulls to commit crime.

Control balance theory. A theory focusing on the relationship between the perceived control of others by an individual and the control the individual purports to be experiencing.

Cyberagression. A term used to describe bullying, harassment, ridiculing, and offensive, threatening, and aggressive communications online.

Dehumanization. The psychological process of making the target seem less human.

Deindividuation. A psychological state linked to the process of depersonalization, wherein a user has diminished self-awareness and self-identity and low self-control.

Developmental and life-course criminology. An approach to criminology recognizing that while offenders' predisposition to crime and deviance remains stable throughout a person's lifetime, the manifestations of crime and deviancy during that period may change.

Differential association theory. A theory holding that individuals learn criminal or deviant behavior through associations with others and learn the norms, values, and beliefs that validate this illicit or deviant behavior.

Differential reinforcement. The process whereby the desired behavior is reinforced from internal or external sources.

Disinhibition. The loss or reduction of restraints on behavior that violates established social norms and codes of conduct.

External controls. The organizations and individuals responsible for keeping a potential offender from committing illicit activity.

General theory of crime. A theory positing that low self-control accounts for all forms of criminality.

Groupthink. The subordination of one's self and taking on the identity of the group.

Imitation. Imitation occurs when an individual directly observes a behavior and subsequently emulates it.

Internal controls. The traits and characteristics of potential offenders that keep them from offending.

Investment fraud. A fraud in which a person intentionally or willfully engages in behavior designed to deceive or defraud investors.

Latent trait perspective. A perspective viewing human behavior as directed by a master trait that an individual has at birth or develops during childhood.

Life-course perspective. A perspective holding that a criminal career results from criminogenic influences one experiences throughout his or her lifetime.

Modeling. The learning of a behavior by observing and then mimicking that behavior at a later time.

Moral disengagement. The process whereby individuals construct rationalizations for behavior in order to overcome any internal inhibitions.

Negative punishment. The removal of a positive stimulus following undesirable behavior.

Negative reinforcement. The removal of a negative stimulus following desirable behavior.

Neutralization theory. A theory holding that individuals share conventional attitudes, beliefs, and values even though they may violate them with their behavior and utilize techniques to temporarily neutralize their attitudes, beliefs, and values in order to engage in illicit behavior.

Operant behavior. A person's responses to rewards and punishments.

Operant conditioning. An individual's behavior is conditioned by environmental responses and consequences of one's actions.

Positive punishment. The adding of a negative stimulus following undesirable behavior.

Positive reinforcement. The adding of a positive stimulus following desired behavior.

Pump and dump. A fraud in which individuals engage in tactics designed to increase the price of stock, only to sell the stock once it reaches a desired level in order to make a profit.

Self-control. The ability of an individual to suppress or resist the urge to engage in an act for immediate gratification and excitement.

Social control theory. A theory holding that human nature draws individuals to commit crimes but social bonds prevent them from doing so.

Social learning theory. A theory positing that behavior is the product of learning through social interactions.

Social process theories. Theories maintaining that people are predisposed to criminality and seeking to explain the forces that keep individuals from engaging in criminal activity.

Socialization. The process whereby an individual learns specific behaviors that are considered acceptable in society.

White-collar cybercrime. A financially motivated cybercrime committed by a professional person.

ENDNOTES

1. L. Alvarez, "Girl's Suicide Points to Rise in Apps Used by Cyberbullies," *New York Times*, September 13, 2013, http://www.nytimes.com/2013/09/14/us/suicide-of-girl-after-bullying-raises-worries-on-web-sites.html?_r=0; S. Almasy, K. Segal, and J. Couwels, "Sheriff: Taunting Post Leads to Arrests in Rebecca Sedwick Bullying Death," *CNN*, October 16, 2013, http://www.cnn.com/2013/10/15/justice/rebecca-sedwick-bullying-death-arrests/.
2. B. Leibowitz, "Rebecca Ann Sedwick Update: Fla. Police Confirm Suicide of Girl, 12, After Cyber-Bullying, Probe Possible Charges," *CBS News*, September 12, 2013, http://www.cbsnews.com/news/rebecca-ann-sedwick-update-fla-police-confirm-suicide-of-girl-12-after-cyber-bullying-probe-possible-charges/.
3. E. A. Ross, *Social Control: A Survey of the Foundations of Order* (New York: Macmillan, 1901).
4. I. Nye, *Family Relationships and Delinquent Behavior* (New York: Wiley, 1958).
5. W. Reckless, *The Crime Problem* (New York: Appleton-Century-Crofts, 1961).
6. T. Hirschi, *Causes of Delinquency* (Berkeley: University of California Press, 1969).
7. Ibid.
8. Ibid.
9. S. Shariff and R. Gouin, "Cyber-Dilemmas: Gendered Hierarchies of Power in a Virtual School Environment," Paper Presented at the International Conference on Cyber-Safety, Oxford Internet Institute, Oxford University, UK, accessed August 4, 2016, http://www.oii.ox.ac.uk/research/cybersafety/extensions/pdfs/papers/shaheen_shariff.pdf.
10. J. Wang, R. J. Iannotti, and T. R. Nansel, "School-Bullying Among Adolescents in the United States: Physical, Verbal, Relational, and Cyber," *Journal of Adolescent Health* 45, no. 4 (2009): 368–375; K. R. Williams and N. G. Guerra, "Prevalence and Predictors of Internet Bullying," *Journal of Adolescence Health* 41, no. 6 (2007): 14–21.
11. T. Hirschi, *Causes of Delinquency* (Berkeley: University of California Press, 1969).
12. Ibid.

13. Ibid.

14. R. Young and L. Zhang, "Illegal Computer Hacking: An Assessment of Factors that Encourage and Deter the Behavior," *Journal of Information Privacy and Security 3*, no. 4 (2007): 33–52.

15. T. Hirschi, *Causes of Delinquency* (Berkeley: University of California Press, 1969).

16. Ibid.

17. P. Taylor, *Hackers: Crime in the Digital Sublime* (London: Routledge, 1999); K. Hafner and J. Markoff, *Cyberpunks: Outlaws and Hackers on the Computer Frontier* (Toronto: Simon and Schuster, 1995).

18. U. A. Ojedokun and M. C. Eraye, "Socioeconomic Lifestyles of the Yahoo-Boys: A Study of Perceptions of University Students in Nigeria," *International Journal of Cyber Criminology* 6, no. 2 (2012): 1002.

19. Ibid., 1011.

20. E. H. Sutherland, *Principles of Criminology*, 3rd ed. (Philadelphia, PA: Lippincott, 1939).

21. P. Muncaster, "FBI Pump-and-Dump Arrests Linked to JPMorgan Breach," *Infosecurity*, July 23, 2015, http://www.infosecurity-magazine.com/news/fbi-pumpanddump-arrests-linked/.

22. R. L. Akers, *Social Learning and Social Structure: A General Theory of Crime and Deviance* (Boston: Northeastern University Press, 1998); R. L. Akers, M. D. Krohn, L. Lanza-Kaduce, and M. Radosevich, "Social Learning and Deviant Behavior: A Specific Test of a General Theory," *American Sociological Review* 44, no. 4 (1979): 636–655, cited in R. G. Morris and G. E. Higgins, "Neutralizing Potential and Self-Reported Digital Piracy: A Multitheoretical Exploration Among College Undergraduates," *Criminal Justice Review* 34, no. 2 (2009): 173–195.

23. R. L. Akers, *Social Learning and Social Structure: A General Theory of Crime and Deviance* (Edison, NJ: Transaction, 2009); G. E. Higgins, B. D. Fell, and A. L. Wilson, "Low Self-Control and Social Learning in Understanding Students' Intentions to Pirate Movies in the United States," *Social Science Computer Review* 25, no. 3 (2007): 339–357; S. Hinduja and J. Ingram, "Self-Control and Ethical Beliefs on the Social Learning of Intellectual Property Theft," *Western Criminology Review* 9, no. 2 (2008): 52–72; S. Hinduja and J. Ingram, "Social Learning Theory and Music Piracy: The Differential Role of Online and Offline Peer Influences," *Criminal Justice Studies* 22, no. 4 (2009): 405–420; B. F. Skinner and A. M. Fream, "A Social Learning Theory Analysis of Computer Crime Among College Students," *Journal of Research in Crime and Delinquency* 34, no. 4 (1997): 495–518; G. E. Higgins, B. D. Fell, and A. L. Wilson, "Digital Piracy: Assessing the Contributions of an Integrated Self-Control Theory and Social Learning Theory Using Structural Equation Modeling," *Criminal Justice Studies* 19, no. 1 (2006): 3–22; S. Hinduja, "General Strain, Self-Control, and Music Piracy," *International Journal of Cyber Criminology* 6, no. 1 (2012): 951–967.

24. R. L. Akers, *Deviant Behavior: A Social Learning Approach*, 3rd ed. (Belmont, CA: Wadsworth, 1985).

25. R. L. Akers, *Social Learning and Social Structure: A General Theory of Crime and Deviance* (Edison, NJ: Transaction, 2009); G. E. Higgins, B. D. Fell, and A. L. Wilson, "Low Self-Control and Social Learning in Understanding Students' Intentions to Pirate Movies in the United States," *Social Science Computer Review* 25, no. 3 (2007): 339–357; B. F. Skinner and A. M. Fream, "A Social Learning Theory Analysis of Computer Crime Among College Students," *Journal of Research in Crime and Delinquency* 34, no. 4 (1997): 495–518; S. Hinduja and J. Ingram, "Self-Control and Ethical Beliefs on the Social Learning of Intellectual Property Theft," *Western Criminology Review* 9, no. 2 (2008): 52–72; M. Warr, *Companions in Crime: The Social Aspects of Criminal Conduct* (Cambridge: Cambridge University Press, 2002); R. C. Hollinger, "Crime by Computer: Correlates of Software Piracy and Unauthorized Account Access," *Security Journal* 4, no. 1 (1993), 2–12.

26. C. D. Marcum, G. E. Higgins, and M. L. Ricketts, "Sexting Behaviors Among Adolescents in Rural North Carolina: A Theoretical Examination of Low Self-Control and Deviant Peer Association," *International Journal of Cyber Criminology* 8, no. 2 (2009): 71.

27. C. Fitch, *Crime and Punishment: The Psychology of Hacking in the New Millennium* (Bethesda, MD: SANS Institute, 2004); Taylor, *Hackers: Crime in the Digital Sublime.*

28. S. Furnell, *Cybercrime: Vandalizing the Information Society* (Boston: Addison-Wesley, 2002), 70–77; M. Yar, "Computer Hacking: Just Another Case of Juvenile Delinquency?" *Howard Journal of Criminal Justice* 44, no. 4 (2005): 387–399.

29. Akers, *Social Learning and Social Structure: A General Theory of Crime and Deviance*; A. Bandura, *Social Learning Theory* (Englewood Cliffs, NJ: Prentice Hall, 1977).

30. Akers, *Deviant Behavior: A Social Learning Approach.*

31. E. H. Sutherland and D. R. Cressey, *Principles of Criminology*, 9th ed. (Philadelphia, PA: Lippincott, 1974).

32. E. H. Sutherland, *Principles of Criminology*, 3rd ed. (Philadelphia, PA: Lippincott, 1939).

33. Furnell, *Cybercrime: Vandalizing the Information Society*; B. Clough and P. Mungo, *Approaching Zero: Data Crime and the Computer Underworld* (London: Faber and Faber, 1992); B. Sterling, *The Hacker Crackdown: Law and Disorder on the Electronic Frontier* (Harmondsworth, UK: Penguin, 1994); M. Slatalla and J. Quitner, *Masters of Deception: The Gang That Ruled Cyberspace* (London: Harper Collins, 1996).

34. M. Rogers, *A New Hacker Taxonomy* (University of Manitoba, Canada, 2000), http://homes .cerias.purdue.edu/~mkr/hacker.doc.

35. C. Gibson and J. Wright, "Low Self-Control and Coworker Delinquency: A Research Note," *Journal of Criminal Justice* 29, no. 6 (2001): 483–492; G. E. Higgins and D. A. Makin, "Does Social Learning Theory Condition the Effects of Low Self-Control on College Students' Software Piracy?" *Journal of Economic Crime Management* 2, no. 2 (2004): 1–22; G. E. Higgins and D. A. Makin, "Self-Control, Deviant Peers, and Software Piracy," *Psychological Reports* 95, no. 3 (2004): 921–931; D. Longshore, E. Chang, S.-C. Hsieh, and N. Messina, "Self-Control and Social Bonds: A Combined Control Perspective on Deviance," *Crime & Delinquency* 50, no. 4 (2004): 542–564.

36. T. P. Thornberry, A. J. Lizotte, M. D. Krohn, M. Farnworth, and S. J. Jang, "Delinquent Peers, Beliefs, and Delinquent Behavior: A Longitudinal Test of Interactional Theory," *Criminology* 32, no. 1 (1994): 47–84; R. L. Akers and G. Lee, "A Longitudinal Test of Social Learning Theory: Adolescent Smoking," *Journal of Drug Issues* 26, no. 2 (1996): 317–343; R. Agnew, "The Interactive Effects of Peer Variables on Delinquency," *Criminology* 29, no. 1 (1991): 47–72; T. Brezina and A. R. Piquero, "Exploring the Relationship Between Social and Nonsocial Reinforcement," in *Social Learning Theory and the Explanation of Crime: A Guide for the New Century, Advances in Criminological Theory*, vol. 11, ed. R. L. Akers and G. F. Jensen (New Brunswick, NJ: Transaction, 2003), 265–288.

37. Warr, *Companions in Crime: The Social Aspects of Criminal Conduct*; Skinner and Fream, "A Social Learning Theory Analysis of Computer Crime Among College Students."

38. R. G. Morris and A. G. Blackburn, "Cracking the Code: An Empirical Exploration of Social Learning Theory and Computer Crime," *Journal of Crime and Justice* 32, no. 1 (2009): 19–20.

39. G. E. Higgins, C. D. Marcum, T. L. Freiburger and M L. Ricketts, "Examining the Role of Peer Influence and Self-Control on Downloading Behavior," *Deviant Behavior* 33, no. 5 (2012): 412–423; Higgins, Fell, and Wilson, "Digital Piracy: Assessing the Contributions of an Integrated Self-Control Theory and Social Learning Theory Using Structural Equation Modeling"; G. E. Higgins and D. A. Makin, "Self-Control, Deviant Peers, and Software Piracy," *Psychological Reports* 95, no. 3 (2004): 921–931; Hinduja and Ingram, "Self-Control and Ethical Beliefs on the Social Learning of Intellectual Property Theft."

40. J. Malin and B. J. Fowers, "Adolescent Self-Control and Music and Movie Piracy," *Computers in Human Behavior* 25, no. 3 (2009): 718–722.

41. Higgins, Marcum, Freiburger and Ricketts, "Examining the Role of Peer Influence and Self-Control on Downloading Behavior."

42. R. L. Akers, "Rational Choice, Deterrence, and Social Learning Theory in Criminology: The Path Not Taken," *Journal of Criminal Law and Criminology* 81, no. 3 (1990): 655.

43. B. F. Skinner identified two types of reinforcement (positive and negative) and one form of punishment. B. F. Skinner, *Science and Human Behavior* (New York: Free Press, 1953). Two forms of punishment, positive and negative, were identified in works of other scholars. For example, A. C. Catania, ed., *Contemporary Research in Operant Behavior* (Glenview, IL: Scott, Foresman, 1968); H. Rachlin, *Introduction to Modern Behaviorism* (San Francisco: Freeman, 1970); H. Rachlin, *Behavior and Learning* (San Francisco: Freeman, 1976); and W. H. Redd, A. L. Porterfield, and B. L. Anderson, *Behavior Modification* (New York: Random House, 1979).

44. S. C. McQuade, *Understanding and Managing Cybercrime* (Boston: Allyn and Bacon, 2006); Hinduja and Ingram, "Self-Control and Ethical Beliefs on the Social Learning of Intellectual Property Theft."

45. R. Jordan and P. Taylor, "A Sociology of Hackers," *Sociological Review* 46, no. 4 (1998): 757–780; P. Bocij, *The Dark Side of the Internet: Protecting Yourself and Your Family from Online Criminals* (Westport, CT: Praeger, 2006); S. Goode and S. Cruise, "What Motivates Software Crackers?" *Journal of Business Ethics* 65, no. 2 (2006): 173–201.

46. M. Taylor and E. Quayle, *Child Pornography: An Internet Crime* (Brighton, UK: Routledge, 2003); E. Quayle and M. Taylor, "Child Seduction and Self-Representation on the Internet," *Cyberpsychology & Behavior* 4, no. 5 (2001): 597–604; E. Quayle and M. Taylor, "Pedophiles, Pornography and the Internet: Assessment Issues," *British Journal of Social Work* 32, no. 7 (2002): 863–875; E. Quayle and M. Taylor, "Model of Problematic Internet Use in People with a Sexual Interest in Children," *Cyberpsychology & Behavior* 6, no. 1 (2003): 93–106.

47. Ibid.

48. Skinner, *Science and Human Behavior*; B. F. Skinner, *Beyond Freedom and Dignity* (New York: Knopf, 1971).

49. Akers, *Deviant Behavior: A Social Learning Approach*, 42, cited in Akers, "Rational Choice, Deterrence, and Social Learning Theory in Criminology: The Path Not Taken," 670.

50. R. LaRose, C. A. Lin, and M. S. Eastin, "Unregulated Internet Usage: Addiction, Habit, or Deficient Self-Regulation?" *Media Psychology* 5, no. 3 (2003): 230.

51. M. Pawlikowski, I. W. Nader, C. Burger, S. Stieger, and M. Brand, "Pathological Internet Use—It is a Multidimensional and not a Unidimensional Construct," *Addiction Research and Theory* 22, no. 2 (2014): 172.

52. J. Kim and P. M. Haridakis, "The Role of Internet User Characteristics and Motives in Explaining Three Dimensions of Internet Addiction," *Journal of Computer-Mediated Communication* 14, no. 4 (2009): 988–1015.

53. K. Chak and L. Leung, "Shyness and Locus of Control as Predictors of Internet Addiction and Internet Use," *Cyberpsychology & Behavior* 7, no. 4 (2004): 559–570; S. Ebeling-Witte, M. L. Frank, and D. Lester, "Shyness, Internet Use, and Personality," *Cyberpsychology & Behavior* 10, no. 5 (2007): 713–716.

54. M. Brand, K. S. Young, and C. Laier, "Prefrontal Control and Internet Addiction: A Theoretical Model and Review of Neuropsychological and Neuroimaging Findings," *Frontiers in Human Neuroscience* 8, no. 375 (2014), 3.

55. Ibid.

56. A. Bandura, *Social Foundations of Thought and Action: A Social Cognitive Theory* (Englewood Cliffs, NJ: Prentice Hall, 1986).

57. McQuade, *Understanding and Managing Cybercrime*; S. Hinduja, "Trends and Patterns Among Software Pirates," *Ethics and Information Technology* 5, no. 1 (2003): 49–61.

58. Morris and Blackburn, "Cracking the Code: An Empirical Exploration of Social Learning Theory and Computer Crime," 20.

59. Yar, "Computer Hacking: Just Another Case of Juvenile Delinquency?" 396.

60. Skinner and Fream, "A Social Learning Theory Analysis of Computer Crime Among College Students."

61. G. Higgins and C. D. Marcum, *"Digital Piracy: An Integrated Theoretical Approach* (Durham, NC: Carolina Academic Press, 2011).

62. Skinner and Fream, "A Social Learning Theory Analysis of Computer Crime Among College Students."

63. Ibid.

64. Morris and Blackburn, "Cracking the Code: An Empirical Exploration of Social Learning Theory and Computer Crime," 19.

65. Morris and Higgins, "Neutralizing Potential and Self-Reported Digital Piracy: A Multitheoretical Exploration Among College Undergraduates," 178.

66. D. Matza, *Delinquency and Drift* (New York: John Wiley & Sons, 1964).

67. Ibid.

68. G. Sykes and D. Matza, "Techniques of Neutralization: A Theory of Delinquency," *American Sociological Review* 22, no. 6 (1957): 664–670.

69. Ibid.

70. Ibid., 667–669.

71. Ibid., 667.

72. S. Gordon, "The Generic Virus Writer," Fourth International Virus Bulletin Conference (Jersey, UK, September 8–9, 1994), http://vxheaven.org/lib/asg03.html; S. Gordon, "The Generic virus writer II," Sixth International Virus Bulletin Conference (Brighton, UK, September 19–20, 1996), http://vxheaven.org/lib/asg04.html.

73. R. Young, L. Zhang, and V. R. Prybutok, "Hacking Into the Mind of Hackers," *Information Systems Management* 24, no. 4 (2007): 285.

74. Ibid.

75. J. S. Ulsperger, D. H. Hodges, and J. Paul, "Pirates on the Plank: Neutralization Theory and the Criminal Downloading of Music Among Generation Y in the Era of Late Modernity," *Journal of Criminal Justice and Popular Culture* 17, no. 1 (2010): 137–138.

76. Ibid., 138–139.

77. Young, Zhang, and Prybutok, "Hacking Into the Mind of Hackers," 285.

78. D. E. Denning, "Concerning Hackers Who Break into Computer Systems," Paper Presented at the Thirteenth National Computer Security Conference (Washington, DC, October 1–4, 1990), http://cyber.eserver.org/hackers.txt.

79. Sykes and Matza, "Techniques of Neutralization: A Theory of Delinquency," 668.

80. Ibid.

81. Ulsperger, Hodges, and Paul, "Pirates on the Plank: Neutralization Theory and the Criminal Downloading of Music Among Generation Y in the Era of Late Modernity," 142.

82. Sykes and Matza, "Techniques of Neutralization: A Theory of Delinquency," 669.

83. R. Chiesa, S. Ducci, and S. Ciappi, *Profiling Hackers: the Science of Criminal Profiling as Applied to the World of Hacking* (Boca Raton, FL: CRC Press, 2009).

84. P. Craig, *Software Piracy Exposed* (Rockland, MA: Syngress, 2005); S. Goode and S. Cruise, "What Motivates Software Crackers?" *Journal of Business Ethics* 65, no. 2 (2006): 173–201.

85. J. W. Coleman, *The Criminal Elite: The Sociology of White Collar Crime* (New York: St. Martin's, 1985).

86. Ulsperger, Hodges, and Paul, "Pirates on the Plank: Neutralization Theory and the Criminal Downloading of Music Among Generation Y in the Era of Late Modernity," 141; S. Hinduja, "Neutralization Theory and Online Software Piracy: An Empirical Analysis," *Ethics and Information Technology* 9, no. 3 (2007): 187–204; J. R. Ingram and S. Hinduja, "Neutralizing Music Piracy: An Empirical Examination," *Deviant Behavior* 29, no. 4 (2008): 334–366; T. Wingrove, A. Korpas, and V. Weisz, "Why Were Millions of People Not Obeying the Law? Motivational Influences on Non-Compliance with the Law in the Case of Music Piracy," *Psychology, Crime & Law* 17, no. 3 (2011): 261–276.

87. M. Lanier and S. Henry, *Essential Criminology* (New York: Free Press, 1998); S. Lyman, "Accounts: Roots and Foundations," in *Encyclopedia of Criminology and Deviant Behavior,* ed. C. D. Bryant (Philadelphia: Brunner–Routledge, 2000); I. Fritsche, "Account Strategies for the Violation of Social Norms: Integration and Extension of Sociological and Psychological Typologies," *Journal for the Theory of Social Behavior* 32, no. 4 (2002): 371–394; W. Minor, "Techniques of Neutralization: A Reconceptualization and Empirical Examination," *Journal of Research in Crime and Delinquency* 18, no. 2 (1981): 295–318; E. D. Nelson and R. D. Lambert, "Sticks, Stones and Semantics: The Ivory Tower Bully's Vocabulary of Motives," *Qualitative Sociology* 24, no. 1 (2001): 83–106.

88. C. B. Klockars, *The Professional Fence* (New York: Free Press, 1974).

89. W. Minor, "Techniques of Neutralization: A Reconceptualization and Empirical Examination."

90. O. Turgeman-Goldschmidt, "The Rhetoric of Hackers' Neutralisations," in *Crimes of the Internet,* ed. F. Schmalleger and M. Pittaro (Upper Saddle River, NJ: Pearson, 2009).

91. Hinduja, "Neutralization Theory and Online Software Piracy: An Empirical Analysis"; Hinduja and Ingram, "Self-Control and Ethical Beliefs on the Social Learning of Intellectual Property Theft"; G. E. Higgins, S. E. Wolfe, and C. D. Marcum, "Digital Piracy and Neutralization: A Trajectory Analysis from Short-Term Longitudinal Data," *International Journal of Cyber Criminology* 2, no. 2 (2008): 324–336; R. Moore and E. McMullan, "Neutralizations and Rationalizations of Digital Piracy: A Qualitative Analysis of University Students," *International Journal of Cyber Criminology* 3, no. 1 (2009): 441–451; Morris and Higgins, "Neutralizing Potential and Self-Reported Digital Piracy: A Multitheoretical Exploration Among College Undergraduates"; Hinduja, "General Strain, Self-Control, and Music Piracy."

92. Ibid.

93. Ingram and Hinduja, "Neutralizing Music Piracy: An Empirical Examination," 334.

94. J. L. Smallridge and J. R. Roberts, "Crime-Specific Neutralizations: An Empirical Examination of Four Types of Digital Piracy," *International Journal of Cyber Criminology* 7, no. 2 (2013): 137.

95. Ibid.

96. Ibid., 133.

97. Ibid.

98. M. Siponen and A. Vance, "Neutralization: New Insights Into the Problem of Employee Information Systems Security Policy Violation," *Management Information Systems Quarterly* 34, no. 3 (2010): 487–502; Smallridge and Roberts, "Crime-Specific Neutralizations: An Empirical Examination of Four Types of Digital Piracy," 134.

99. A. Bandura, "Selective Moral Disengagement in the Exercise of Moral Agency," *Journal of Moral Education* 31, no. 2 (2002), 102.

100. H. S. Becker, "Becoming a Marihuana User," *American Journal of Sociology* 59, no. 3 (1953): 235–242.

101. E. Quayle and R. Sinclair, "An Introduction to the Problem," in *Understanding and Preventing Online Sexual Exploitation of Children,* ed. E. Quayle and K. M. Ribisl (New York: Routledge, 2012), 3–22.

102. For example, Moore and McMullan, "Neutralizations and Rationalizations of Digital Piracy: A Qualitative Analysis of University Students"; Ingram and Hinduja, "Neutralizing Music Piracy: An Empirical Examination," 334–366; Turgeman-Goldschmidt, "The Rhetoric of Hackers' Neutralisations"; R. G. Smith, P. N. Grabosky, and G. F. Urbas, *Cyber Criminals on Trial* (Cambridge: Cambridge University Press, 2004).

103. A. Bandura, "Selective Moral Disengagement in the Exercise of Moral Agency," *Journal of Moral Education* 31, no. 2 (2002), 102.

104. S. Hymel and R. A. Bonanno, "Moral Disengagement Processes in Bullying," *Theory into Practice* 53, no. 4 (2014), 278–285.

105. A. Bandura, *Social Foundations of Thought and Action: A Social Cognitive Theory* (Englewood Cliffs, NJ: Prentice Hall, 1986).

106. A. Bandura, "The Role of Selective Moral Disengagement in Terrorism and Counterterrorism," in *Understanding Terrorism: Psychological Roots, Consequences and Interventions,* ed. F M. Mogahaddam and A. J. Marsella (Washington, DC: American Psychological Association Press, 2004), 121–122.

107. A. Bandura, C. Barbaranelli, G. V. Caprara, and C. Pastorelli, "Mechanisms of Moral Disengagement in the Exercise of Moral Agency," *Journal of Personality and Social Psychology* 71, no. 2 (1996): 364–374.

108. Young, Zhang, and Prybutok, "Hacking Into the Mind of Hackers," 285.

109. S. Bonner and E. O'Higgins, "Music Piracy: Ethical Perspectives," *Management Decision* 48, no. 9 (2010): 1341–1354; A. Garbharran and A. Thatcher, "Modeling Social Cognitive Theory to Explain Software Piracy Intention," in *Human Interface and the Management of Information: Interacting with Information,* ed. M. J. Smith and G. Salvendy, Symposium on Human Interface: HCI International, Part 1 (Berlin: Springer-Verlag, 2011), 301–310.

110. T. P. Thornberry, M. Krohn, A. J. Lizotte, and C. A. Smith, *Gangs and Delinquency in Developmental Perspective* (Cambridge, UK: Cambridge University Press, 2003); F. A. Esbensen, D. Peterson, T. J. Taylor, and A. Freng, *Youth Violence: Sex and Race Differences in Offending, Victimization, and Gang Membership* (Temple, PA: Temple University Press, 2010); D. L. Haynie and D. W. Osgood, "Reconsidering Peers and Delinquency: How Do Peers Matter?" *Social Forces* 84, no. 2 (2005): 1109–1130.

111. K. Busseya, S. Fitzpatricka, and A. Ramana, "The Role of Moral Disengagement and Self-Efficacy in Cyberbullying," *Journal of School Violence* 14, no. 1 (2015): 30–46; S. Hymel and R. A. Bonanno, "Moral Disengagement Processes in Bullying," *Theory Into Practice* 53, no. 4 (2014): 278–285.

112. S. Bauman, "Cyberbullying in a Rural Intermediate School: An Exploratory Study," *Journal of Early Adolescence* 30, no. 6 (2010): 803–833; C. D. Pornari and J. Wood, "Peer and Cyber Aggression in Secondary School Students: The Role of Moral Disengagement, Hostile Attribution Bias, and Outcome Expectancies," *Aggressive Behavior* 36, no. 2 (2010): 81–94.

113. S. Bauman and H. Pero, "Bullying and Cyberbullying Among Deaf Students and their Hearing Peers: An Exploratory Study," *Journal of Deaf Studies and Deaf Education* 16, no. 2 (2011): 236–253; S. Perren and E. Gutzwiller-Helfenfinger, "Cyberbullying and Traditional Bullying in Adolescence: Differential Roles of Moral Disengagement, Moral Emotions, and Moral Values," *European Journal of Developmental Psychology* 9, no. 2 (2012): 205.

114. A. Bandura, C. Barbaranelli, G. V. Caprara, and C. Pastorelli, "Mechanisms of Moral Disengagement in the Exercise of Moral Agency," *Journal of Personality and Social Psychology,* 71, no. 2 (1996): 364–374.

115. Moore and McMullan, "Neutralizations and Rationalizations of Digital Piracy: A Qualitative Analysis of University Students."

116. For example, *The Legion of Doom* and *2600: The Hacker Quarterly.*

117. Turgeman-Goldschmidt, "The Rhetoric of Hackers' Neutralisations," 391; R. G. Smith, P. N. Grabosky, and G. F. Urbas, *Cyber Criminals on Trial* (Cambridge: Cambridge University Press, 2004), 112.

118. Young, Zhang, and Prybutok, "Hacking Into the Mind of Hackers," 285.

119. A. Bandura, "Selective Activation and Disengagement of Moral Control," *Journal of Social Issues* 46, no. 1 (1990): 27–46; Bandura, Barbaranelli, Caprara, and Pastorelli, "Mechanisms of Moral Disengagement in the Exercise of Moral Agency."

120. Bandura, "Selective Moral Disengagement in the Exercise of Moral Agency," 106.

121. Bandura, "Selective Activation and Disengagement of Moral Control"; Bandura, Barbaranelli, Caprara, and Pastorelli, "Mechanisms of Moral Disengagement in the Exercise of Moral Agency."

122. C. S. Fötinger and W. Ziegler, *Understanding a Hacker's Mind—A Psychological Insight into the Hijacking of Identities* (Danube University, Krems, Austria: RSA Security, 2004).

123. Pornari and Wood, "Peer and Cyber Aggression in Secondary School Students: The Role of Moral Disengagement, Hostile Attribution Bias, and Outcome Expectancies."

124. C. David-Ferdon and M. F. Hertz, *Electronic Media and Youth Violence: A CDC Issue Brief for Researchers* (Atlanta, GA: Centers for Disease Control, 2009), 3, http://www.cdc.gov /ViolencePrevention/pdf/EA-brief-a.pdf.

125. S. Maruna and R. E. Mann, "A Fundamental Attribution Error? Rethinking Cognitive Distortions," *Legal and Criminological Psychology* 11, no. 2 (2006): 155.

126. G. G. Abel, D. K. Gore, C. L. Holland, N. Camp, J. V. Becker, and B. A. Rathner, "The Measurement of the Cognitive Distortions of Child Molesters," *Annals of Sex Research* 2, no. 2 (1989): 135–153; L. R. Shapiro and M.-H. Maras, *Multidisciplinary Investigation of Child Maltreatment* (Burlington, MA: Jones and Bartlett, 2015).

127. D. Howitt and K. Sheldon, "The Role of Cognitive Distortions in Paedophilic Offending: Internet and Contact Offenders Compared," *Psychology, Crime and Law* 13, no. 5 (2007): 469–486.

128. A. W. Burgess and C. Hartman, "Child Abuse Aspects of Child Pornography," *Psychiatric Annals* 17, no. 4 (1987): 248–253; E. Quayle and M. Taylor, "Child Pornography and the Internet: Perpetuating a Cycle of Abuse," *Deviant Behavior* 23, no. 4 (2002): 365–395; K. Sheldon and D. Howitt, *Sex Offenders and the Internet* (Chichester, UK: Wiley, 2007); M. Taylor and E. Quayle, *Child Pornography: An Internet Crime* (Hove, UK: Brunner-Routledge, 2003); T. Ward and R. Siegert, "Toward a Comprehensive Theory of Child Sexual Abuse: A Theory of Knitting Perspective," *Psychology, Crime and Law* 8, no. 4 (2002): 319–351.

129. Ibid.

130. Ibid.

131. Ibid.

132. D. Finkelhor, *Child Sexual Abuse: New Theory and Research* (New York: Free Press, 1984); D. Finkelhor, *A Source Book on Child Sexual Abuse* (London: Sage, 1986); G. C. Hall and R. Hirschman, "Towards a Theory of Sexual Aggression: A Quadripartite Model," *Journal of Consulting and Clinical Psychology* 59, no. 5 (1991): 662–669; T. Ward, "A Critique of Hall and Hirschman's Quadripartite Model of Child Sexual Abuse," *Psychology, Crime and Law* 7, no. 1–4 (2001): 363–374; Ward and Siegert, "Toward a Comprehensive Theory of Child Sexual Abuse: A Theory of Knitting Perspective"; V. Caretti, A. Schimmenti, and A. Bifulco, "Psychopathology of Online Grooming" in *Online Offending Behavior and Child Victimization: New Findings and Policy,* ed. S. Webster, J. Davidson, and A. Bifulco (New York: Palgrave-Macmillan, 2015), 103.

133. Young, Zhang, and Prybutok, "Hacking Into the Mind of Hackers," 281–287.

134. J. McDevitt, J. Balboni, L. Garcia, and J. Gu, "Consequences for Victims: A Comparison of Bias- and Non-Bias-Motivated Assaults," *American Behavioral Scientist* 45, no. 4 (2001): 697–713; Young, Zhang, and Prybutok, "Hacking Into the Mind of Hackers," 285.

135. Bandura, "Selective Moral Disengagement in the Exercise of Moral Agency," 108–109.

136. M. Farley, E. Schuckman, J. M. Golding, K. Houser, L. Jarrett, P. Qualliotine, and M. Decker, *Comparing Sex Buyers with Men Who Don't Buy Sex,* July 15, 2011, 12, http://www .prostitutionresearch.com/pdfs/Farleyetal2011ComparingSexBuyers.pdf; L. Bennetts, "The Growing Demand for Prostitution," *Newsweek,* July 18, 2011, http://www.newsweek.com/ growing-demand-prostitution-68493; Q. Li, "A Cross-Cultural Comparison of Adolescents' Experience Related to Cyberbullying," *Educational Research* 50, no. 3 (2008): 226.

137. S. Brail, "Take Back the Net!" *On the Issues* (Winter 1994), 40–42; C. Soukup, "The Gendered Interactional Patterns of Computer-Mediated Chatrooms: A Critical Ethnographic Study," *Information Society* 15, no. 3 (1999): 171; Li, "A Cross-Cultural Comparison of Adolescents' Experience Related to Cyberbullying," 226.

138. R. Pierce, "Child Pornography: A Hidden Dimension of Child Abuse," *Child Abuse and Neglect* 8, no. 4 (1984): 483–493; H. Wood, "Internet Pornography and Paedophilia," *Psychoanalytic Psychotherapy* 27, no. 4 (2013): 319–338.

139. Hinduja, "Neutralization Theory and Online Software Piracy: An Empirical Analysis."

140. J. Suler, "The Online Disinhibition Effect," *Cyberpsychology & Behavior* 7, no. 3 (2004): 321–326.

141. C. Demetriou and A. Silke, "A Criminological Internet 'Sting': Experimental Evidence of Illegal and Deviant Visits to a Website Trap," *British Journal of Criminology* 43, no. 1 (2003): 213–222, cited in J. Bishop, "The Effect of De-Individuation of the Internet Troller on Criminal Procedure Implementation: An Interview with a Hater," *International Journal of Cyber Criminology* 7, no. 1 (2013): 29.

142. C. H. Chao and Y. H. Tao, "Human Flesh Search: A Supplemental Review," *Cyberpsychology, Behavior, and Social Networking* 15, no. 7 (2012): 350–356.

143. S. Milgram, "Behavioral Study of Obedience," *Journal of Abnormal and Social Psychology* 67, no. 4 (1963): 371–378.

144. S. Webster, J. Davidson, and A. Bifulco, eds., *Online Offending Behavior and Child Victimization: New Findings and Policy* (New York: Palgrave-Macmillan, 2015), 37.

145. Hinduja, "Neutralization Theory and Online Software Piracy: An Empirical Analysis."

146. P. J. Carnes, "The Anatomy of Arousal: Three Internet Portals," *Sexual and Relationship Therapy* 18, no. 3 (2003): 309–328; A. Cooper, D. L. Delmonico, E. Griffin-Shelley, and R. M. Mathy, "Online Sexual Activity: An Examination of Potentially Problematic Behaviors," *Sexual Addiction & Compulsivity* 11, no. 3 (2004): 129–14; E. Quayle and M. Taylor, "Model of Problematic Internet Use in People With Sexual Interest in Children," *CyberPsychology & Behavior* 6, no. 1 (2003): 93–106.

147. A. Barak, "Sexual Harassment on the Internet," *Social Science Computer Review* 23, no. 1 (2005): 77–92.

148. N. E. Willard, *Cyberbullying and Cyberthreats: Responding to the Challenge of Online Social Aggression, Threats, and Distress* (Champaign, IL: Research Press, 2007).

149. K. Twyman, C. Saylor, L. A. Taylor, and C. Comeaux, "Comparing Children and Adolescents Engaged in Cyberbullying to Matched Peers," *Cyberpsychology, Behavior, and Social Networking* 13, no. 2 (2010): 195–199.

150. R. Slonje and P. K. Smith, "Cyberbullying: Another Main Type of Bullying?" *Scandinavian Journal of Psychology* 49, no. 2 (2008): 147–154.

151. J. R. Meloy, "The Psychology of Stalking," in *The Psychology of Stalking: Clinical and Forensic Perspectives*, ed. J. R. Meloy (San Diego, CA: Academic Press, 1998), 1–23.

152. P. Bocij and L. McFarlane, "Cyberstalking: The Technology of Hate," *Police Journal* 76, no. 1 (2003): 204–221; L. P. Sheridan and T. Grant, "Is Cyberstalking Different?" *Psychology, Crime & Law* 13, no. 6 (2007): 629.

153. P. G. Zimbardo, "The Human Choice: Individuation, Reason, and Order vs. Deindividuation, Impulse, and Chaos," in *Nebraska Symposium on Motivation*, ed. W. J. Arnold and D. Levine (Lincoln: University of Nebraska Press, 1969), cited in R. Slonje, P. K. Smith, and A. Frisen, "Processes of Cyberbullying, and Feelings of Remorse by Bullies: A Pilot Study," *European Journal of Developmental Psychology* 9, no. 2 (2012): 84.

154. E. Whittaker and R. M. Kowalski, "Cyberbullying via Social Media," *Journal of School Violence* 14, no. 1 (2015): 11–29.

155. K. Bussey, S. Fitzpatrick, and A. Raman, "The Role of Moral Disengagement and Self-Efficacy in Cyberbullying," *Journal of School Violence* 14, no. 1 (2015): 30–46.

156. L. Ellis, "Neurohormonal Basis of Varying Tendencies to Learn Delinquent and Criminal Behavior," in *Behavioral Approaches to Crime and Delinquency*, ed. E. Morris and C. Braukmann (New York" Plenum, 1988), 599–618.

157. C. R. Tittle, *Control Balance: Toward a General Theory of Deviance* (Boulder, CO: Westview Press, 1995).

158. Ibid.

159. S. W. Baron, D. R. Forde, and F. M. Kay, "Self-Control, Risky Lifestyles, and Situation: The Role of Opportunity and Context in the General Theory," *Journal of Criminal Justice* 35, no. 2

(2007): 119–136; T. R. Curry, "Integrating Motivating and Constraining Forces in Deviance Causation: A Test of Causal Chain Hypotheses in Control Balance Theory," *Deviant Behavior* 26, no. 6 (2005): 571–599; T. R. Curry and A. R. Piquero, "Control Ratios and Defiant Acts of Deviance: Assessing Additive and Conditional Effects with Constraints and Impulsivity," *Sociological Perspectives* 46, no. 3 (2003): 397–415.

160. Tittle, *Control Balance: Toward a General Theory of Deviance.*
161. Lanier and Henry, *Essential Criminology.*
162. M. R. Gottfredson and T. Hirschi, *A General Theory of Crime* (Palo Alto, CA: Stanford University Press, 1990), 90.
163. Higgins, Fell, and Wilson, "Digital Piracy: Assessing the Contributions of an Integrated Self-Control Theory and Social Learning Theory Using Structural Equation Modeling."
164. Gottfredson and Hirschi, *A General Theory of Crime*, 80.
165. R. Benabon and J. Tirole, "Willpower and Personal Rules," *Journal of Political Economy* 112, no. 4 (2004): 848–885; L. A. Fennell, "Willpower and Legal Policy," *Annual Review of Law and Social Science* 5, (2009): 91–113; N. Shover, A. Hochstetler, and T. Alalehto, "Choosing White-Collar Crime," in *The Oxford Handbook of Criminological Theory*, ed. F. T. Cullen and P. Wilcox (Oxford, UK: Oxford University Press, 2013), 487.
166. Gottfredson and Hirschi, *A General Theory of Crime.*
167. B. J. Arneklev, J. K. Cochran, and R. R. Gainey, "Testing Gottfredson and Hirschi's 'Low Self-Control' Stability Hypothesis: An Exploratory Study," *American Journal of Criminal Justice* 23, no. 1 (1998): 107–127; M. G. Turner and A. R. Piquero, "The Stability of Self-Control," *Journal of Criminal Justice* 30, no. 6 (2002): 457–471.
168. Gottfredson and Hirschi, *A General Theory of Crime*, 90.
169. Ibid.
170. Gottfredson and Hirschi, *A General Theory of Crime*; J. J. Gibbs, D. Giever, and J. S. Martin, "Parental Management and Self-Control: An Empirical Test of Gottfredson and Hirschi's General Theory," *Journal of Research in Crime & Delinquency* 35, no. 1 (1998): 40–70; J. J. Gibbs, D. Giever, and G. E. Higgins, "A Test of Gottfredson and Hirschi's General Theory Using Structural Equation Modeling," *Criminal Justice and Behavior* 30, no. 4 (2003): 441–458.
171. Gottfredson and Hirschi, *A General Theory of Crime*; S. W. Baron, "Self-Control, Social Consequences, and Criminal Behavior: Street Youth and the General Theory of Crime," *Journal of Research in Crime & Delinquency* 40, no. 4 (2003): 403–425; B. T. Conner, J. A. Stein, and D. Longshore, "Examining Self-Control as a Multidimensional Predictor of Crime and Drug Use in Adolescents with Criminal Histories," *Journal of Behavioral Health Services and Research* 36, no. 2 (2008): 137–149; K. Holtfreter, M. D. Reisig, N. L. Piquero, and A. R. Piquero, "Low Self-Control and Fraud: Offending, Victimization and their Overlap," *Criminal Justice and Behavior* 37, no. 2 (2010): 188–203; A. R. Piquero, T. E. Moffitt, and B. E. Wright, "Self-Control and Criminal Career Dimensions," *Journal of Contemporary Criminal Justice* 23, no. 1 (2007): 72–89.
172. G. E. Higgins, "Can Low Self-Control Help Understand the Software Piracy Problem?" *Deviant Behavior* 26, no. 1 (2005): 1–24; G. E. Higgins, "Gender Differences in Software Piracy: The Mediating Roles of Self-Control Theory and Social Learning Theory," *Journal of Economic Crime Management* 4, (2006): 1–22; G. E. Higgins, "Digital Piracy: An Examination of Low Self-control and Motivation Using Short-Term Longitudinal Data," *CyberPsychology & Behavior* 10, no. 4 (2007): 523–529; G. E. Higgins, S. E. Wolfe, and M. L. Ricketts, "Digital Piracy: A Latent Class Analysis," *Social Science Computer Review* 27, no. 1 (2009): 24–40.
173. Taylor, *Hackers: Crime in the Digital Sublime*, 46–50, 56–58.
174. Marcum, Higgins, and Ricketts, "Sexting Behaviors Among Adolescents in Rural North Carolina: A Theoretical Examination of Low Self-Control and Deviant Peer Association," 72.
175. Higgins, Fell, and Wilson, "Low Self-Control and Social Learning in Understanding Students' Intentions to Pirate Movies in the United States"; Malin and Fowers, "Adolescent Self-Control and Music and Movie Piracy"; R. LaRose, Y. J. Lai, R. Lange, B. Love, and Y. Wu,

"Sharing or Piracy? An Exploration of Downloading Behaviour," *Journal of Computer-Mediated Communication* 11, no. 1 (2005): 1–21; Higgins, Fell, and Wilson, "Digital Piracy: Assessing the Contributions of an Integrated Self-Control Theory and Social Learning Theory Using Structural Equation Modeling"; G. E. Higgins and D. A. Makin, "Does Social Learning Theory Condition the Effects of Low Self-Control on College Students' Software Piracy?" *Journal of Economic Crime Management* 2, (2004): 1–22.

176. Hinduja, "General Strain, Self-Control, and Music Piracy," 956.

177. Higgins, Fell, and Wilson, "Low Self-Control and Social Learning in Understanding Students' Intentions to Pirate Movies in the United States"; Higgins, Fell, and Wilson, "Digital Piracy: Assessing the Contributions of an Integrated Self-Control Theory and Social Learning Theory Using Structural Equation Modeling."

178. G. E. Higgins, S. E. Wolfe, and C. D. Marcum, "Music Piracy and Neutralization: A Preliminary Trajectory Analysis From Short-Term Longitudinal Data," *International Journal of Cyber Criminology* 2, no. 2 (2008): 324–36; Hinduja and Ingram, "Self-Control and Ethical Beliefs on the Social Learning of Intellectual Property Theft"; Higgins, Fell, and Wilson, "Low Self-Control and Social Learning in Understanding Students' Intentions to Pirate Movies in the United States"; G. E. Higgins and A. L. Wilson, "Low Self-Control, Moral Beliefs, and Social Learning Theory in University Students' Intentions to Pirate Software," *Security Journal* 19, no. 2 (2006): 75–92; Hinduja, "General Strain, Self-Control, and Music Piracy."

179. Higgins and Wilson, "Low Self-Control, Moral Beliefs, and Social Learning Theory in University Students' Intentions to Pirate Software"; B. Moon, J. D. McCluskey, and C. P. McCluskey, "A General Theory of Crime and Computer Crime: An Empirical Test," *Journal of Criminal Justice* 38, no. 4 (2010): 767–772.

180. Higgins and Wilson, "Low Self-Control, Moral Beliefs, and Social Learning Theory in University Students' Intentions to Pirate Software"; Higgins, Wolfe, and Marcum, "Digital Piracy and Neutralization: A Trajectory Analysis from Short-Term Longitudinal Data"; G. E. Higgins, S. E. Wolfe, and C. D. Marcum, "Digital Piracy: An Examination of Three Measurements of Self-Control," *Deviant Behavior* 29, no. 5 (2008): 440–460; Hinduja, "General Strain, Self-Control, and Music Piracy."

181. Morris and Higgins, "Neutralizing Potential and Self-Reported Digital Piracy: A Multitheoretical Exploration Among College Undergraduates," 188.

182. Higgins, Fell, and Wilson, "Digital Piracy: Assessing the Contributions of an Integrated Self-Control Theory and Social Learning Theory Using Structural Equation Modeling"; Higgins and Makin, "Does Social Learning Theory Condition the Effects of Low Self-Control on College Students' Software Piracy?"; Higgins and Makin, "Self-Control, Deviant Peers, and Software Piracy."

183. D. Glueck and E. Glueck, *500 Criminal Careers* (New York: Knopf, 1930); D. Glueck and E. Glueck, *One Thousand Juvenile Delinquents* (Cambridge, MA: Harvard University Press, 1934).

184. J. Laub and R. J. Sampson, "Unraveling Families and Delinquency: A Reanalysis of the Gluecks' Data," *Criminology* 26, no. 3 (1988): 355–380.

185. R. J. Sampson and J. H. Laub, "Crime and Deviance Over the Life Course: This Salience of Adult Social Bonds," *American Sociological Review* 55, no. 5 (1990): 609–627.

186. E. P. Eggleston and J. H. Laub, "The Onset of Adult Offending: A Neglected Dimension of the Criminal Career," *Journal of Criminal Justice* 30, no. 6 (2002): 603–622.

187. P. Lussier, S. Tzoumakis, J. Cale, and J. Amirault, "Criminal Trajectories of Adults Sex Offenders and the Age Effect: Examining the Dynamic Aspect of Offending in Adulthood," *International Criminal Justice Review* 20, no. 2 (2010): 147–168; V. Caretti, A. Schimmenti, and A. Bifulco, "Psychopathology of Online Grooming," 101.

188. For example, D. P. Farrington, "Age, Period, Cohort and Offending," in *Policy and Theory in Criminal Justice: Contributions in Honour of Leslie T. Wilkins*, ed. D. M. Gottfredson and R. V. Clarke (Aldershot, UK: Avebury, 1990), 51–75.

189. S. Gordon, "The Generic Virus Writer," Fourth International Virus Bulletin Conference (Jersey, UK, September 8–9, 1994), http://vxheaven.org/lib/asg03.html; S. Gordon, "The Generic virus writer II," Sixth International Virus Bulletin Conference (Brighton, UK, September 19–20, 1996), http://vxheaven.org/lib/asg04.html.

190. R. J. Sampson and J. H. Laub, "A Life-Course View of the Development of Crime," *Annals of the American Academy of Political and Social Science* 602, no. 1 (2005): 12.

191. R. J. Sampson and J. H. Laub, "Desistance from Crime Over the Life Course," in *Handbook of the Life Course*, ed. J. T. Mortimer and M. Shanahan (New York: Kluwer Academic/Plenum, 2003), 295–310.

192. G. Geis, "On the Absence of Self-Control as the Basis for a General Theory of Crime: A Critique," *Theoretical Criminology* 4, no. 1 (2000): 35–53; R. Loeber and M. LeBlanc, "Toward a Developmental Criminology," in *Crime and Justice*, ed. M. Tonry and N. Morris (Chicago: University of Chicago Press, 1995), 375–437; Caretti, Schimmenti, and Bifulco, "Psychopathology of Online Grooming," 101.

193. Sampson and Laub, "Crime and Deviance Over the Life Course: This Salience of Adult Social Bonds."

194. Ibid.

195. R. J. Sampson and J. H. Laub, "Life-Course Desisters? Trajectories of Crime Among Delinquent Boys Followed to Age 70," *Criminology* 41, no. 3 (2003): 301-339; J. H. Laub and R. J. Sampson, *Shared Beginnings, Divergent Lives: Delinquent Boys to Age 70* (Cambridge, MA: Harvard University Press, 2003); R. J. Sampson and J. H. Laub, "Desistance From Crime Over the Life Course," in *Handbook of the Life Course*, ed. J. T. Mortimer and M. Shanahan (New York: Kluwer Academic/Plenum, 2003), 295–310.

196. R. J. Sampson and J. H. Laub, *Crime in the Making: Pathways and Turning Points Through Life* (Cambridge, MA: Harvard University Press, 1993).

197. Ibid.

198. Ibid.

199. Sampson and Laub, "A Life-Course View of the Development of Crime," 16.

200. J. H. Laub and R. J. Sampson, "Understanding Desistance from Crime," *Crime and Justice* 28, no. 1 (2001): 1–69.

201. Sampson and Laub, *Crime in the Making: Pathways and Turning Points Through Life*; Sampson and Laub, "Life-Course Desisters? Trajectories of Crime Among Delinquent Boys Followed to age 70"; Sampson and Laub, "Desistance From Crime Over the Life Course."

202. Laub and Sampson, *Shared Beginnings, Divergent Lives: Delinquent Boys to Age 70*.

203. J. Wolak, D. Finkelhor, and K. J. Mitchell, *Child Pornography Possessors Arrested in Internet-Related Crimes: Findings From the National Juvenile Online Victimization Study* (Alexandria, Virginia: National Center for Mission and Exploited Children, 2005); Ward and Siegert, "Toward a Comprehensive Theory of Child Sexual Abuse: A Theory of Knitting Perspective"; J. A. McCarthy, "Internet Sexual Activity: A Comparison Between Contact and Noncontact Child Pornography Offenders," *Journal of Sexual Aggression* 16, no. 2 (2010): 181–195; L. Webb, J. Craissati, and S. Keen, "Characteristics of Internet Child Pornography Offenders: A Comparison With Child Molesters," *Sexual Abuse: A Journal of Research and Treatment* 19, no. 4 (2007): 449–465; Caretti, Schimmenti, and Bifulco, "Psychopathology of Online Grooming," 103.

204. Sampson and Laub, *Crime in the Making: Pathways and Turning Points Through Life*.

CHAPTER 8

CONSTRUCTING AND REACTING TO CYBERCRIME
Labeling and Moral Panics

KEYWORDS

Black hat hacker
Defiance theory
Deviancy amplification
Disintegrative shaming
Elite hacker
Grey hat hacker
Labeling theory

Looking glass self
Media agenda-setting
   theory
Media framing theory
Moral entrepreneurs
Moral panic
Phenomenology

Primary deviance
Reintegrative shaming
Script kiddie
Secondary deviance
Self-fulfilling prophecy
Symbolic interactionism
White hat hacker

Crime is socially constructed, as it is the community that labels certain behaviors as "deviant" or "normal." Behaviors are deemed to be "normal" by the public if they are consistent with societal norms and laws. Moreover, those who engage in behaviors considered immoral or illegal are labeled as "deviants," "delinquents," or "criminals."

Early criminological literature did not cover social constructions of crime, that is, the factors that determine which behaviors are considered criminal by societies. To remedy this deficit in criminological literature, theories were developed which sought to explain how crime is socially constructed through labels and reactions to crime. This chapter covers the social constructions of cybercrime, looking in particular at labeling theory and moral panics. Motivating questions for this analysis include: What are the practical implications of saying that cybercrime is socially constructed? How useful are notions of labeling and moral panics in the analysis of public reactions to certain cybercrimes?

LABELING CYBERCRIMINALS

Labeling theory examines deviant and criminal taxonomies and how they shape individual identities and influence behavior.[1] This theory particularly explores how these taxonomies and the social reactions to those who are assigned to these taxonomies influence deviant and criminal behavior. The classification is believed to encourage users to alter their behavior to avoid being labeled as a deviant or a criminal. However, labeling is also criminogenic, that is, it tends to lead to crime. Individuals who are labeled according to these taxonomies ultimately have two choices: to reject or accept the labels.[2] If the individual rejects the label, the individual will seek to counter the label through words and actions that are contrary to behaviors associated with the label. If the individual accepts the label, the individual may exhibit the behaviors attributed to this label. The result of accepting the label may result in a **self-fulfilling prophecy**, which refers to "a false definition of the situation evoking a new behavior which makes the originally false conception come true."[3]

Labeling theory predicts not only that a deviant or criminal behavior will occur as a result of the label and responses to the label but also that the deviant or criminal behavior will increase as a result of the label. If individuals accept the deviant or criminal label, the deviant or criminal behavior associated with the label will increase (**deviancy amplification**). In fact, as societal responses toward the labeled individuals become increasingly severe, their isolation from society grows concomitantly. This isolation results in the labeled individuals identifying with others similarly labeled and cultivating an environment of deviancy and criminality targeted at the society which isolated them.

Edwin Lemert distinguished between two types of deviance: primary and secondary. **Primary deviance** involves deviant acts committed that are not attributed to a deviant label. Here, the offender neither views himself or herself as a deviant nor lives life according to this identity.[4] **Secondary deviance** includes acts committed because of the deviant label and societal responses to the deviant act. At this stage, the offender may be stigmatized by stereotypes and labels.[5] The most common reaction to societal responses to the deviant act is acceptance of the deviant label by the individual. Once this label is accepted, the person lives his or her life according to the identity associated with the label. The person has now transitioned from primary to secondary deviance. An individual's label as a deviant (or criminal) is thus a contributing factor to the individual's future deviancy (or criminality).

Literature on social psychology has supported the central tenets of labeling theory by showing that the feedback individuals receive from others about their behavior shapes their self-identity and behavior. If individuals accept the label, they adapt expectations of behaviors that the labelers have ascribed to them. This process is known as the **looking glass self**. According to Charles Horton Cooley, an individual's self-perception and behaviors are influenced by the perceptions of others and how individuals believe others perceive them and expect them to behave.[6] Howard Becker observed that individuals who have been labeled are stripped of their own identity and the label society assigns them eventually becomes their identity.[7] George Herbert Mead proposed two aspects of the self which interact—the *me* and the *I*.[8] The *me* is related to social control[9] and includes "the organized set of attitudes of others which one himself (or herself) assumes."[10] The *I* aspect of the self is associated with self-expression free from control[11] and consists of "the impulses of the self and constitutes the response to the attitudes of others."[12] Social control exists when the dominant aspect of the self which is expressed becomes the *me*.[13]

A student of Mead's, Herbert Blumer, coined the term **symbolic interactionism**, which explains human behavior as facilitated by symbols whose meanings are derived from and interpretations are modified by social interactions with others.[14] According to symbolic interactionism, the feedback individuals receive from others about their behavior (e.g., verbal communication and gestures) can influence future behavior. Likewise, Jack Katz described crime through the lens of **phenomenology**, highlighting that criminals provide symbolic meanings to their own actions, as well as the actions of others.[15] A prominent phenomenologist, Carl Rogers, referred to the self or self-concept as an "organized, consistent, conceptual gestalt composed of perceptions and characteristics of the 'I' or 'me' and the perceptions of the relationships of the 'I' or 'me' to others and to various aspects of life, together with values attached to these perceptions."[16] An individual's interactions with his or her environment thus gradually becomes incorporated into the individual's self. As such, an individual's self-concept (or perceived self) influences the person's perceptions and behavior.

The cybercrime of hacking exemplifies the consequences of labeling. In an attempt to differentiate individuals with harmful intent to alter, delete, damage, destroy, or disrupt systems and data from individuals with benign intentions, researchers have developed the terms *black hat, white hat,* and *grey hat.* A **black hat hacker** is used to describe those individuals who gain unauthorized access to a system for malicious reasons with the intention of causing harm (e.g., damaging systems or stealing data). These individuals seek to find vulnerabilities in systems to exploit. A **white hat hacker** is viewed as an ethical hacker; such individuals use their technical knowledge, skills, and abilities within the constraints of the law. An ethical hacker is one that gains authorized access to a system to determine weaknesses and inform the owner, operator, or employer responsible for the system about these vulnerabilities, potentially along with suggestions on how to deal with them. An example of a white hat hacker is a cybersecurity consultant that has been hired by a company to compromise their system in order to identify system susceptibility to hacking. Once identified, these vulnerabilities are communicated to the hiring organizations so they can patch the vulnerabilities to prevent further exploitation in the future. A **grey hat hacker** is one who does not fit in the black hat or white hat hacker label, falling instead somewhere in between. This person may gain unauthorized access to a system to determine its vulnerabilities, which he or she will then communicate to the organization— sometimes for a fee—so it can patch the exploits. While this type of hacker does not have harmful intent, he or she did commit a crime by engaging in the act.

BOX 8-1   SOCIAL CONTROL, LABELING THEORY, AND SYMBOLIC INTERACTIONISM

Walter Reckless was a social control theorist who was influenced by labeling theory and symbolic interactionism. He proposed containment theory, which holds that personal traits and one's social environment influence criminal behavior. Reckless argued that if society responds to individuals in a positive manner, they in turn will develop a positive self-image and respond to society in a positive manner.[17] Conversely, he believed that if society responds to people in a negative manner, they will develop negative self-images and respond to society in a negative manner, rejecting its norms, values, and beliefs.

Hackers have also been classified according to their technical knowledge, skills, and abilities as elite hackers and script kiddies. An **elite hacker** is innovative and has the technical acumen needed to exploit and manipulate systems, whereas **script kiddies** can only engage in hacking when they utilize the tools provided by elite hackers.[18] Script kiddies have also been labeled "point-and-clickers," who neither study nor understand computer programs and associated tools used to engage in hacking and other illicit activities.[19] Overall, the term *hacker* is used among the hacking community to describe individuals with highly technical acumen and abilities in computer programming.[20] Steven Levy identified three generations of hackers: (1) those involved with the early development of computer programming, (2) those involved with the development of the earliest personal computers (PCs), and (3) those involved with the beginning of computer game architecture.[21] However, the term *hacker* no longer reflects these individuals outside of the hacker community.[22] Today, the term is applied to those individuals who seek illicit access to other people's computer systems or digital devices.

Once deviant or criminal labels have been applied, it is often difficult for members of society to see these individuals as anything other than what the labels ascribe to them, even if the labels have been applied erroneously. Ultimately, labels may dominate an individual's behavior. For instance, those imprisoned and subsequently released are viewed as "ex-cons" or "ex-convicts." The label "ex-convict" has far-reaching implications beyond incarceration, even disqualifying individuals from certain types of work (e.g., higher-paying jobs and positions of trust) and leaving them access to primarily low-paying jobs. Consequently, to these individuals, illicit activity becomes a better choice than law-abiding behavior, as the latter severely limits the individual's access to wealth and power. However, the ex-convict label does not often result in negative consequences for hackers, many of whom enjoy a positive self-image and no adverse employment impact.[23]

Many criminals who are labeled may be stigmatized as well. For example, individuals who commit sex offenses in the United States and other countries are stigmatized and experience public condemnation to a greater extent than those who commit other crimes.[24] The stigma associated with a deviant or criminal behavior is believed to cause deviancy amplification. If the deviant or criminal status of the individual is continually accentuated, and the individual is continually rebuked in public, then the individual will be less likely than those who were never caught and labeled to engage in conforming behavior. Instead, these individuals are likely to internalize the deviant or criminal label and the associated identity imposed on them by the labelers (e.g., the criminal justice system, the media, and the public) and become the criminals predicted by their labels as part of the self-fulfilling prophecy. Ultimately, labeling individuals as criminals is believed to perpetuate crime instead of controlling or reducing it; however, studies have shown that this is not always the case.[25]

SHAMING, CENSORSHIP, AND DEFIANCE

John Braithwaite proposed **reintegrative shaming** as an alternative to labeling theory. According to Braithwaite, shaming is central to social control; this includes "all processes of expressing disapproval which have the intention or effect of invoking remorse in the person being shamed and/or condemnation by others who become aware of the shaming."[26] Shaming can be reintegrative or disintegrative. Reintegrative shaming has a positive effect on recidivism and does not stigmatize. Although the purpose of this form of shaming is to elicit societal disapproval of the offender's action, it is also designed "to reintegrate the offender back into the community of law-abiding or respectable citizens through words or gestures of forgiveness or ceremonies to decertify the offender as deviant."[27] Reintegrative shaming can thus serve as a way to repair the harm done by the offender to society. By contrast, **disintegrative shaming** has a negative effect on recidivism and creates outcasts by stigmatizing those it targets.[28] This type of shaming ultimately results in the offender's further entrenchment in crime.

It is believed that naming and shaming individuals helps draw attention to an issue and enlists the public to pressure government to punish those named and shamed. Public shaming is not a new phenomenon; however, the Internet has changed the nature and extent of shaming and its impact on those shamed. Content posted online is permanent. Such permanency did not exist before the Internet, apart from an original print work, audio, or video piece or a copy of it. In essence, a person who engages in real or perceived wrongdoing may be shamed indefinitely online, and the shaming comments made against the individual can remain indefinitely online. This form of shaming is not a positive form of shaming; it is a form of negative, disintegrative shaming.

Self-censorship occurs when individuals are adversely labeled for exercising their free speech and suffer adverse consequences when exercising free speech (e.g., lose their job). Self-censorship was observed in the case of Catherine Deveny, an Australian comedian. At one point, Deveny tweeted that she hoped that the daughter of the late Steve Irwin (known as the Crocodile Hunter), Bindi Irwin, who was 11 years old at the time, got laid (the exact tweet was "I do so hope Bindi Irwin gets laid").[29] Deveny was subsequently fired from her job as a columnist at the newspaper the *Age*. A question that follows is: Is firing an appropriate response to ignorant and offensive comments and behaviors online? The answer to this question depends on the person's stance on the comments and behaviors and the person's views of online shaming.

Actually, real social issues cannot be adequately dealt with through online shaming. Online shaming serves as a way to permanently silence some individuals on online platforms, instead of engaging in an open and free discussion of social issues. The purpose of online shaming is to target those who do not behave the way the shamers want them to behave. Online shamers have used "flaming, harshly criticizing or insulting another person on a public posting or a private e-mail" in order to "informally control . . . behavior in cyberspace."[30] They have also used fear tactics and direct and indirect threats to get people to stop engaging in the behavior they view as undesirable. The behavior that results in the shaming may or may not violate the law, but it does contradict the shamer's views of accepted norms of behavior. Public shaming has been used by individuals to promote their own self-serving interests and personal ideologies. Eventually, shaming may result in behavior that is considered acceptable by those responsible for the shaming. As a result for the person shamed, his or her *I* is replaced with the *me*.

Online, lynch mobs of shamers have formed. Like traditional lynch mobs, these individuals have taken it upon themselves to ensure that "justice" is served. Their interpretation of how to achieve justice and the means to achieve it varies according to their social and political views on the issue at hand and the appropriate ways to deal with it. An American dentist, Walter Palmer, found himself in the center of a controversy when it was revealed that he was the hunter responsible for killing Cecil the Lion of the Hwange National Park in Zimbabwe. Palmer was not found to have engaged in any wrongdoing and no charges were brought against him. However, he did experience what is known as *trial by Internet*. In the matter of public opinion, he was guilty and should be punished. Indeed, following the revealing of his role in Cecil's death, he was labeled a "terrorist"[31] and received numerous death threats (as did his family), and his Yelp page was flooded with stinging "reviews" and calls to boycott his practice.[32]

The online comments of an animal rights organization, People for the Ethical Treatment of Animals (PETA), exemplified the lynch mob mentality which was present in Palmer's case. PETA stated that for his actions he "need[ed] to be extradited, charged, and, preferably, hanged."[33] PETA also led the charge urging social media shaming of Palmer: "Let's have some social media shaming for an American dentist Walter Palmer paid $55,000 to SHOOT & KILL African lion #CecilTheLion."[34] Ironically, PETA has also been on the receiving side of shaming. It has been accused of animal cruelty for euthanizing the majority of "the dogs in its shelters . . . [because] it could not place [them] into loving homes."[35] Even celebrities, who are frequent targets of such shaming and have expressed indignation toward the shaming

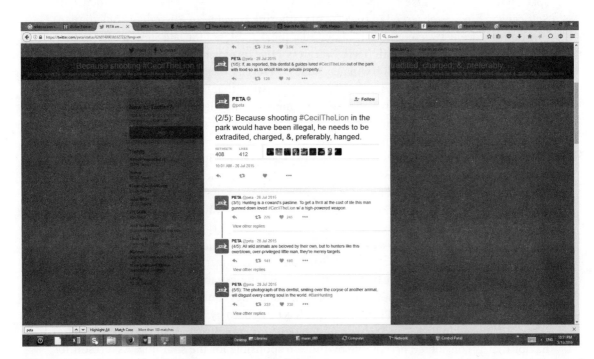

IMAGE 8-1 Screenshot of PETA's Tweets About Walter Palmer.

they unjustly receive online (e.g., for the way that they look), participated in the online shaming of the dentist.[36] Piers Morgan went so far as to claim, "I'd love to go hunting for killer dentist Dr Walter Palmer, so I can stuff & mount him for MY office wall."[37]

In a *trial by Internet*, the verdict and impact are permanent and inescapable. No matter what the individual does from that point forward, the shame remains due to the permanent record of the shaming online. Shaming comments, while opinion, are often taken as fact by individuals who read them. This shaming, which targets people's real or perceived undesirable beliefs or behaviors, can have significant life consequences (e.g., it can lead to the firing of individuals and prevent them from obtaining future employment). The Internet has drastically changed the shaming landscape, resulting in often irreversible adverse consequences to people. A proposed solution to online shaming is to "shame the shamers." The reality of this is that this exacerbates the problem and gives legitimacy to this tactic. It provides individuals with a justification to use the tactic; the key is to remove justifications for engaging in this tactic. The only way to do this is not to engage in online shaming at all.

Lawrence Sherman developed **defiance theory** because he believed the original conception of labeling theory did not "account for the many examples of sanctions reducing crime."[38] For him, defiance refers to the "increase in the prevalence, incidence, or seriousness of future offending against a sanctioning community caused by a proud, shameless reaction to the administration of a criminal sanction."[39] If individuals feel they are being treated unfairly by the criminal justice system, or are actually treated unfairly by the criminal justice system, they are likely to be defiant and act defiantly. In these situations, they do not accord legitimacy to the sanctions against them, and thus such sanctions are unable to affect recidivism. In fact, the sanctions have the opposite effect, and instead of reducing recidivism, they exacerbate it. This response has also been observed with cybercrimes, including digital piracy.[40] Disturbingly, individuals who refuse to acknowledge the shame associated with the sanction may instead view it in a positive light and engage in additional illicit behavior to exact revenge on those who are responsible for attempting to punish them. Sanctions can thus have a boomerang effect whereby individuals may defy the sanctions and create a self-fulfilling prophecy.

BOX 8-2 THE RIGHT TO BE FORGOTTEN

In *Google Spain v. AEPD and Mario Costeja González*,[41] González sought to have a debt collection announcement from 1998 in the newspaper *La Vanguardia* removed from Google search results. He wanted the information removed online because it was no longer relevant and he had long since paid his debt. He filed a complaint with the Spanish Data Protection Agency seeking to have the newspaper remove it from its website and to have this information not appear in Google search results. The Spanish Data Protection Agency dismissed the complaint against the newspaper, but not the complaint against Google. The European Court of Justice examined, among other things, whether Internet users have the right to request that information about them be removed from search results, and if so, in what circumstances. Ultimately, the court ruled that companies which gather personal information must remove access to it when such removal is requested by the user, as long as the information sought to be removed is no longer relevant and there are no countervailing or superseding interests in keeping it available.[42] This ruling created what has come to be known as "the right to be forgotten."

CYBERCRIMINALS AS "THE OTHERS"

As Howard Becker noted, "social groups create deviance by making the rules whose infraction constitutes deviance, and by applying those rules to particular people and labeling them as outsiders."[43] Hackers, malware writers, and those who launch DDoS attacks, among other cybercriminals, are viewed as outsiders.[44] These outsiders, labeled *others*, constitute a category used to describe a deviant or criminal population (e.g., pornographers, cyberpredators). Who is labeled as *others* varies depending on the period, country, and the labeler. The *others* category is believed to apply to a distinct group of deviants or criminals. Despite claims to the contrary, the category of *others* is not clearly defined. As such, individuals who are part of the *us* group (i.e., law-abiding citizens) may find themselves part of the *others* (or *them*) group once boundaries of the group are redefined. These categories or labels can also create a moral panic in society.

MORAL PANICS

A **moral panic** is defined as "a condition, episode, person or group of persons . . . [which] emerges . . . as a threat to societal values and interests."[45] A moral panic involves an attempt by the *us* group to explain perceived threats to the social order. An essential element of a moral panic is the reaction of the public and governmental and social institutions to issues or events which seem to threaten order within the society. Moral panics are not myths; they center around real events or behavior. The threat inducing a moral panic may be a unique occurrence or it may be a situation that has existed for quite some time.[46] Another characteristic of a moral panic is that "sometimes the object of the panic is quite novel and at other times it is something which has been in existence long enough, but suddenly appears in the limelight."[47] A moral panic can relate to a real threat (e.g., child predators) or a perceived threat (e.g., "pharm" parties by teenagers, at which they bring drugs from their parents' cabinets and place them in a bowl for other teenagers to consume without knowing what drugs they are taking).[48]

Negative social constructions of cybercriminals are propagated by the media, criminal justice agents, private organizations, and governments. Typically what is observed with a moral panic is that the phenomenon triggering it is distorted and exaggerated; therefore, a moral panic is a real or perceived threat that has been overblown.[49] Accordingly, a moral panic, as applied to cybercrime, is a hyperbole of a cyberdeviant or cybercriminal act. This overstatement on the cyberdeviance or cybercrime in question concerns those involved in the illicit activity and the impact of this activity on society. This overemphasis on the threat leads to a hyperbolic concern by the public with the purported threat to order. The outcome of this excessive concern is an overreaction to the threat by politicians, policymakers, lawmakers, and agents of the criminal justice system.

Stanley Cohen identified several actors that play key roles in a moral panic: folk devils, criminal justice agents, the media, politicians, moral entrepreneurs, and the public (see Figure 8-1).

Folk devils.[50] Cohen used the term *folk devils* to describe the *others*—the individuals who trigger a moral panic.[51] These individuals embody the deviant or criminal behavior that violates societal norms and threatens existing social order. Over the years,

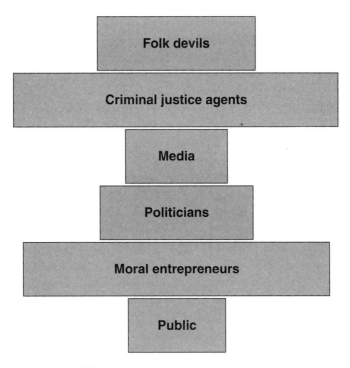

FIGURE 8-1 Key Actors in Moral Panics.

various forms of crime and cybercrime have become the object of public anxieties that have induced moral panics, particularly terrorism, school shootings, child kidnappings, children who kill other children, and pedophilia and child pornography (offline and online).[52] Indeed, Internet child pornography has been at the center of many moral panics.[53] Moral panics have also arisen with respect to social media, missing children, drug use, and youth subcultures (e.g., ravers and punks).[54]

Criminal justice agents. Cohen held that an essential element of the moral panic process is a response by authorities.[55] These individuals are required to identify, arrest, and punish the *others*. Depending on who the *others* are, criminal justice agencies may call for greater power to deal with *them*. Moral panics are characterized by overreactions by criminal justice agents. This was observed in the case of Rebecca Ann Sedwick (discussed in Chapter 7). The sheriff, Grady Judd, arrested Rebecca's cyberbullies, who were charged with felonies for aggravated stalking pursuant to Florida Statute Annotated § 784.048.[56] The sheriff also informed the media that the 14-year-old cyberbully "posted a comment on Facebook, saying: 'I bullied Rebecca (and) she killed herself' and 'IDGAF'—code for 'I don't give a fuck.'"[57] This was communicated to the media and consequently to the wider public to anger people and garner their support for his pursuit of the cyberbullies. Felony charges against cyberbullies are not the norm; usually, such individuals are charged, if at all, with misdemeanor offenses.[58]

Similar tactics were utilized by criminal justice agents in other cyberbullying cases, including that of Megan Meier, a 13-year-old girl from Missouri who committed suicide in 2006. Her neighbor Lori Drew created a fake MySpace profile online of a boy named Josh Evans. Posing as Josh, Drew contacted Megan and formed an online relationship with Megan to find out what she was saying about Drew's daughter, Sarah. One day, Megan received the following message: "Everybody in O'Fallon knows how you are. You are a bad person and everybody hates you. Have a shitty rest of your life. The world would be a better place without you."[59] She committed suicide by hanging herself shortly thereafter. Criminal justice agents could not bring charges of cyberbullying against Lori Drew because Missouri did not have a law in place at the time that criminalized her conduct. Because of this, criminal justice agents brought charges against her pursuant to the Computer Fraud and Abuse Act of 1986, for violating MySpace's Terms of Service.[60] The argument of the government in this case was that Drew's violation of MySpace's Terms of Service made her access to the site "unauthorized" under the act.[61] However, the charges against her were dismissed by the Ninth U.S. Circuit Court of Appeals because prosecution for Terms of Service violations constitutes an unjustified overreach in the application of this law as "millions of unsuspecting individuals would find that they are engaging in criminal conduct."[62]

An overreaction was also observed in the case of Aaron Schwartz, who was charged with several felony offenses pursuant to the Computer Fraud and Abuse Act of 1986.[63] This case involved the mass download of academic journal articles from the JSTOR database. Aaron was authorized to access the JSTOR database through the Massachusetts Institute of Technology. The issue at hand in his case was not unauthorized access per se; it was the mass download of articles from the database and the manner in which this occurred. Specifically, he used a program, keepgrabbing.py, to bypass restrictions that prevented users from mass downloading content.[64] The issue, therefore, was the bypassing of these restrictions. The federal prosecution received significant backlash, which became more pronounced after Aaron committed suicide over the charges (even culminating in petitions to the White House to have the prosecutors fired), for seeking what was viewed as disproportionate punishment for the crimes committed.[65]

The Media. The media communicates information about threats to the public. In fact, the public relies on the media for their primary source of information concerning social and political issues. Because of this, the media plays an important role in shaping the public's perception of the risk of crime and cybercrime.[66] Indeed, the manner in which the news is reported affects individuals' perceptions and interpretations of the risks presented to them.

The media focuses on crimes selectively based on information that is newsworthy. Public interest helps determine the newsworthiness of an event. Stanley Cohen and Jock Young identified two models of media reporting: the market model and the manipulative model.[67] Under the market model, facts are reported objectively and the news is determined by public interest. In the manipulative model, newsworthiness is determined by the news media source and not the public. Cohen and Young argued that the ability of news media sources to operate under the manipulative model is apparent, enabling them to shape and distort the image of whatever phenomenon they are reporting.[68] Others argue that news organizations operate under the organizational model, which utilizes components of both the market model and the manipulative model.[69]

The original purpose of the media was to inform the masses in an unbiased way and to educate them in order to facilitate the public's knowledge about various issues—allowing them to have informed opinions and participate in their own governance. The reality is, however, that the media has strayed from its original purpose. In fact, in today's world, and with the increasing reliance on social media, efficiency of the news (i.e., being the first to report on an issue deemed newsworthy) takes precedence over efficacy (i.e., a good outcome, which involves the reporting of the news after an in-depth investigation of an issue). Efficiency means that news sources are primarily concerned with getting the information out, often sacrificing the fact checking and the fact finding in the process of releasing information. Several news sources also tailor their reports to maximize ratings through sensationalized reports and headlines, at the expense of objective and unbiased information. In fact, Gallup polls have shown that the majority of citizens in the United States, Britain, Greece, Hungary, France, Germany, and Austria, among other countries, view the media as biased and doubt "the quality and integrity of their media."[70]

Bernard Cohen stated that the media "may not be successful much of the time in telling people what to think, but it is stunningly successful in telling its readers what to think *about*;"[71] this has come to be known as the **media agenda-setting theory**. According to this theory, individuals exposed to the same media will consider the same issues that the media focuses on as important.[72] **Media framing theory** focuses on the manner in which the media organizes and presents the news.[73] This framing of the news not only influences and colors individuals' perception of the issues covered but also informs them of what issues they should focus on. The bottom line is that the media influences public opinion. The media framing theory and the media agenda-setting theory highlight that the manner in which an issue is reported influences the way in which individuals process and assess issues and the ways in which they respond to them.[74]

Anecdotal evidence has been utilized in media reports to show trends and patterns of criminal or deviant behavior. These incidents of deviant and criminal behavior are presented as being just those that have been brought to the attention of authorities and the media, often hinting at the existence of more of these incidents. Indeed, phrases like "tip of the iceberg" are utilized to describe the cases that have come to the attention of authorities or the media: "Cyber Attack on CENTCOM: Just the Tip of the Iceberg?"[75]; "Game Hacking Tip of the Iceberg as Threat of Cybercrimes Looms Ever Larger;"[76] "The Tip of the Iceberg? Why Massive Russian Cyber Attack Should Be a Wake-Up Call;"[77] "Data Breach That Exposed Millions Is Just 'Tip of the Iceberg,' UB expert says;"[78] and "Hundreds of Kids Cybercrime Victims, and It's Tip of Iceberg—PSNI Has Warned."[79] Such statements are nearly impossible to disprove.

The manner of reporting tends to amplify particular threats, causing widespread fear of risks that do not pose significant threats. Indeed, media attention to certain

issues is disproportionate to the actual threat these risks pose to society. The disproportionate attention of the media to certain risks may spur moral panics. In fact,
intense media focus on certain cybercrimes is found to trigger moral panics sur-
rounding these illicit acts.[80]

The media is saturated with reports of particular forms of deviancy and crime.
This overemphasis on certain risks makes the public think that these are common
and likely to occur. This was observed in a 2016 Gallup poll in which the top critical
issues identified by Americans "as . . . leading threat[s] to U.S. vital interests in the
next 10 years" were those that have saturated the news, "international terrorism,
cyberterrorism and nuclear weapons negotiations with Iran."[81] This overemphasis
and saturation of media reports with a particular risk piques the interest of the
public, who in turn tune in or purchase news media reports (e.g., newspapers or
online subscriptions) to keep abreast of information concerning the deviant or
criminal behavior. As Young pointed out, "the media . . . can create social problems,
they can present them dramatically and overwhelmingly, and, most important,
they can do it suddenly. The media can very quickly and effectively fan public in-
dignation and engineer what one might call 'a moral panic' about a certain type of
deviancy."[82] The media is thus the most influential actor of the moral panic because
it distorts the deviant or criminal behavior in question, overemphasizes it by inflat-
ing its seriousness, and makes it appear more insidious than it is.

Politicians. Politicians want to be seen as taking the moral high ground, taking retributive
stances on policies and laws targeting the *others*. As such, they often align themselves
with criminal justice agencies and the media. This alignment occurs in an effort to
curry public opinion. The statements made by politicians are designed to appeal to
the public's emotions and obtain the public's support by causing anger and outrage
over an issue. This phenomenon was observed in the case of Apple's confrontation
with the FBI over whether the government should be allowed to force Apple to create
new software to bypass its encryption.

Encryption has existed for quite some time; so too has concern over the use of encryption by criminals. In the 1990s, concerns were raised that encryption could be used
by terrorists and foreign entities to hide plotting for attacks.[83] These concerns have been
raised since then intermittently. Discussions about encryption were revived following
the 2015 mass shooting by terrorists in San Bernardino, California. On December 2,
2015, a married couple, Syed Rizwan Farook and Tashfeen Malik, who had pledged
their allegiance to the Islamic State of Iraq and Syria (ISIS; aka the Islamic State), a
religious insurgent terrorist group operating in Iraq and Syria, entered into a social services center and opened fire, killing fourteen individuals and injuring seventeen.[84]

Today, encryption concerns have led to the call for sweeping changes in encryption in the name of combating terrorism. The U.S. government has asked Apple to
modify iOS software for smartphones and tablets to enable government agencies to
hack into phones pursuant to an investigation.[85] This request involves Apple modifying its iOS software to undo the current features that protect the device against unauthorized intrusions.[86] As Apple pointed out to its customers in an open letter, "the

FBI wants us to make a new version of the iPhone operating system, circumventing several important security features, and install it on an iPhone recovered during the investigation. . . . The government suggests this tool could only be used once, on one phone. But that's simply not true. Once created, the technique could be used over and over again, on any number of devices."[87] To rally the public against Apple's refusal to modify its software, Senator Tom Cotton of Arkansas stated, "Apple chose to protect a dead Isis terrorist's privacy over the security of the American people."[88] These statements are designed to provoke anger toward Apple for purportedly protecting an ISIS terrorist. Furthermore, what is particularly problematic about such statements is that security and human rights are framed as being mutually exclusive, even though they are mutually dependent—you cannot have one without the other. Furthermore, these statements are purposely designed to distract from the real issues at the heart of the conflict: that these changes will affect all users of these devices, not just the terrorist, contrary to the claims of government officials.

Moral entrepreneurs. Moral panics are sustained by moral entrepreneurs (or moral crusaders), who are concerned with promoting what they consider to be good character and behavior. These moral entrepreneurs play a key role in defining and drawing attention to deviant and criminal behavior of their choosing. They leverage the media to draw the public's attention to an issue and rally support to pressure authorities to exercise social control and implement regulation over those engaging in the immoral behavior.[89] As such, moral entrepreneurs can be *rule creators* through their efforts to pass policies and laws and *rule enforcers* by way of implementation of these policies and laws.[90] A prime example of a moral entrepreneur is a copyright organization, which protects literary or artistic works and works toward creating rules with respect to copyright protection and enforcing them.[91]

The Public. The role of the public is to consume the media message and support relevant actors in their recommendations on how to solve problems associated with the *others*. A moral panic can only be sustained if the public is angered and directs its rage toward the *others* and supports policies, laws, and other practices promoted by criminal justice agents, the media, politicians, and moral entrepreneurs to deal with the real or perceived threat that brought on the moral panic.

The public has an exaggerated fear of crime and cybercrime. When the public is exposed to atypical stories, moral panics may arise due to the fear that such incidents may provoke. Individuals utilize cognitive heuristics to process information. These heuristics enable them to process information quickly and intuitively but often at the expense of sound, rational judgments.[92] Individuals utilize heuristics to assess risks. These heuristics can explain why individuals overreact to high-impact but low-probability risks. Individuals tend to overreact to unusual or involuntary risks and overestimate their likelihood of occurring.[93] The creation of laws, media coverage of threats, and the frequency of these threats and their coverage also lead individuals to believe that a threat is more severe and more likely to occur than it really is.[94] This concentration of the threat leads to the belief that what is covered is a great risk to the security and stability of a nation. This overemphasis and the narratives of the media and politicians that present particular *others* as an omnipresent enemy propagate fear, ultimately leading to calls for government action.[95] Emotions such as fear can thus explain the overreactions seen in moral panics.[96]

The Literature on Moral Panics

Several works have examined moral panics. *Deviancy amplification,* a term coined by Leslie Wilkins,[97] may unintentionally increase deviancy due to widespread and repeated media coverage of crime and cybercrime, particularly sensationalized news,[98] and the response of governments and criminal justice agents to cybercrime (with respect to legislation and its enforcement).[99] As such, overreactions by the media, criminal justice agencies, and the government toward criminals and cybercriminals may also increase the likelihood of crime and cybercrime in the near future. Like Young, Stanley Cohen discussed deviancy amplification during a moral panic as a product of the reactions by the media, the public, and other relevant actors to relatively minor disturbances—in Cohen's case, disturbances conducted by certain youth cultures, the Mod and Rockers, in England.[100] He concluded that these reactions resulted in the development and enforcement of policies and laws aimed at this group and the purported threat they posed.

A study by Stuart Hall et al. examined the muggings in Britain between 1972 and 1973 and the moral panic that ensued.[101] This study discussed the *signification spirals* which occurred during the moral panics: sensationalized media reports draw attention to an issue and an individual or group; the individuals that are the target of this attention become isolated from society; and this ultimately leads to a greater identification of these individuals with one another, which, in turn, fosters and cultivates deviance and criminality.

Erich Goode and Nachman Ben-Yehuda contributed to the literature of moral panics by identifying and highlighting the structural characteristics of a moral panic. They identified five key attributes of moral panics:[102]

1. *Concern.* Moral panics are characterized by increasing public anxiety over identifiable *others*. Here, a concern exists over the behavior of those causing the moral panic and the purported impact of this behavior.
2. *Hostility.* Intense negative emotions (e.g., enmity and disgust) are displayed toward an identified group of *others* which society views as a threat. Cybercriminals have been labeled "morally bankrupt," "evil," and "monsters" by the media, criminal justice agents, and politicians to provoke negative emotions in the public and rally interest and support for endeavors seeking to target the cybercriminals.[103]
3. *Consensus.* Consensus exists that the group of *others* serves as a threat to society from the view of powerful individuals who have the ability to shape policies, laws, and measures against the targets. Those in the target group of the moral panic are persecuted.
4. *Disproportionality.* The concern of the public is misplaced because it is disproportionate to the danger posed by the identifiable *others*. The reactions to a threat are more severe than the threat itself.[104] Indeed, moral panics result in an overreaction of society to a particular threat. Those deemed to be the target of moral panics may as a result receive sentences that are out of proportion with the punishment originally attributed to

them. For example, crimes that are usually considered to be misdemeanor offenses are now charged as felonies. This reaction was observed in the case of Rebecca Ann Sedwick's cyberbullies (discussed earlier in this chapter) who were charged with felony offenses. This was also observed in the case of Lori Drew (also discussed earlier in this chapter). In another instance, a law was passed in Missouri after Megan Meier committed suicide after being cyberbullied, which made it a felony to "knowingly communicate . . . with another person who is, or who purports to be, seventeen years of age or younger and in so doing and without good cause recklessly frightens, intimidates, or causes emotional distress to such other person."[105] Under this law, Missouri Revised Statutes § 565.090.2, "harassment is a class A misdemeanor unless," for instance, it is "committed by a person twenty-one years of age or older against a person seventeen years of age or younger"; then it will be considered as "a class D felony."

5. *Volatility.* Moral panics appear suddenly but dissipate quickly. Indeed, despite the quick dissolution, changes to policies, laws, and measures regarding the *others* occasionally remain. The concern that arises and is directed toward the threat at the core of the moral panic does not ultimately last; this occurs even when the threat is a long-standing issue. However, despite the fact that it is a transient phenomenon, it could have long-standing consequences.

Cohen observed that "sometimes the panic passes over and is forgotten, except in folk-lore and collective memory; at other times it has more serious and long-lasting repercussions and might produce such changes as those in legal and social policy or even in the way society conceives itself."[106] A moral panic about Internet pornography in the 1990s led to the passage of laws preventing children's access to it. One such law was the Communications of Decency Act of 1996. Sections of this law made it illegal for Internet pornography to be accessible to children. The Supreme Court ultimately struck down these provisions in *Reno v. American Civil Liberties Union* (1997).[107] The Child Online Protection Act of 1998 was subsequently created to prevent children's exposure to Internet pornography. This law, like the one before it, was struck down by the U.S. Supreme Court as unconstitutional.[108] A further attempt to regulate Internet pornography, the Children's Internet Protection Act of 2000, required federally funded libraries to install filtering software to block access to the Internet. This law was not struck down by the Court.[109] Generally, legislation influences the trajectory of a moral panic, especially when it is implemented after an event that draws significant attention and causes public outrage. The results and effects of a moral panic can usually be seen in policies that are misguided and misdirected at a particular issue to effect changes in the actions of *others*.

Goode and Ben-Yehuda noted that moral panics serve as a distraction; that is, government actors, the wealthy, and other elite members of society create moral panics to direct attention away from real issues, such as social problems (e.g., unemployment and income inequality).[110] For example, the promotion of identity theft as a problem by social institutions (such as law enforcement agencies, governments, and banks) created panic that distracted the public from focusing on the more essential problems, like the protection and use of people's personal data by the government and sale of this data by businesses.[111] It further distracted the public from the fact that most personal data is stored in remote databases beyond their reach and control.

The Internet Gaming Moral Panic

Internet gaming has all of the essential elements of a moral panic: a threat to social order; hyperbolic concern over this threat; and overreaction by the media, politicians, legislators, and criminal justice agents. A case of moral panic over Internet gaming arose in South Korea and saturated local and international news media. This case involved a parental couple that neglected their child, while they played a game, Prius, in which they were raising an Internet fairy child; this neglect ultimately led to the death of the child. It was reported that the inexperienced parents "applied the parenting skills they learned from raising this Anima to raising this baby: feed it, game for ten hours, come back, feed it. . . . And the baby lacked the interface to communicate with them what it needs; it didn't have display buttons on it that said, more this! They didn't know how to read the needs of their baby because they could only read an online environment."[112] This single incident of parental neglect of a child by parents playing online games, coupled with a few cases of online gamers dying due to neglecting their basic bodily needs, spurred creation of a law in South Korea, the Shutdown Law of 2011 (also known as the Cinderella law; Article 25 of the Juvenile Protection Act of 2011), which limited youths' access to online games in an effort to stem what was viewed as a widespread Internet gaming addiction that was believed to develop during childhood.[113]

The Cinderella law ultimately led to prohibiting youth from playing games in PC bangs (hip South Korean Internet cafés) between midnight and 6 a.m.[114] Individuals under the age of sixteen were automatically kicked out of online games at midnight. To ensure that the law was followed, individuals playing Internet games had to register their online gaming accounts by submitting their social insurance number (similar to a U.S. Social Security number). Nonetheless, children were able to bypass the restrictions set by the Cinderella law by using their parents' social insurance number.

Parents also complained about the law's overreach into the area of parental rights, arguing that parents should decide whether to grant permission to children to play after midnight.[115] As a result of these complaints, another law was passed which enabled parents to

IMAGE 8-2 PC Bang.

regulate access to online games for children under the age of 18;[116] the restrictions for children's online gaming are now set and controlled by parents. China has also implemented far-reaching measures, such as the Online Game Anti-Addiction System, which requires "online game service developers to monitor users' playtime" in an effort to prevent Internet gaming addiction.[117] With the Online Game Anti-Addiction System, users are limited to three hours of gaming time.[118] Despite these efforts, users have found ways to bypass the restrictions imposed on them by the system.[119]

CASE STUDY

Justine Sacco, a former communications executive at IAC, posted the following tweet before boarding a plane to South Africa: "Going to Africa. Hope I don't get AIDS. Just kidding. I'm white!"[120] She stated that she "thought there was no way that anyone could possibly think . . . [what she said] was literal."[121] Her offensive tweet became a trending topic, and those responding to her post made comments such as "We are about to watch this @ JustineSacco bitch get fired. In REAL time. Before she even KNOWS she's getting fired."[122] Sacco was fired from her position shortly thereafter for the offensive tweet. In firing her, her employees issued the following statement: "There is no excuse for the hateful statements that have been made and we condemn them unequivocally. . . . We hope, however, that time and action, and the forgiving human spirit, will not result in the wholesale condemnation of an individual who we have otherwise known to be a decent person at core."[123] Others have also been fired for tweets and other posts on social media platforms. For instance, Lindsey Stone was fired from her job as a care worker at Living Independently Forever, Inc. (LIFE) after an image of her "giving the finger next to a sign at the Arlington National Cemetery" was shared via Facebook.[124] She claimed that she never intended to disrespect those who served their country and was reacting to the sign.[125]

1. Should Justine Sacco have been fired from her job? Why or why not?
2. Should Lindsey Stone have been fired from her job? Why or why not?
3. Are there any other ways to deal with Justine's and Lindsey's case? Why do you think so?
4. How does Braithwaite's reintegrative and disintegrative shaming apply to these cases?

REVIEW QUESTIONS

1. Can labeling theory explain cybercrime? Why or why not?
2. What labels have been used to describe hackers?
3. What is primary deviance? What is secondary deviance? Can they be applied to cybercrime? If so, in what ways?
4. What is deviancy amplification? How does this relate to cybercrime?
5. What type of shaming occurs online? Why do you think so?
6. Can defiance theory explain certain types of cybercrime? If so, which one or which ones? Why?
7. What is a moral panic? Do moral panics relate to real threats? Why do you think so?
8. Which actors play a key role in a moral panic? Discuss the role of each actor in a moral panic over a particular cybercrime.

9. Who is a moral entrepreneur? Provide an example as it relates to cybercrime.
10. What are the five key attributes of moral panics? Explain each attribute, utilizing a cyber-crime as the cause of the moral panic.

LAWS

Child Online Protection Act of 1998 (United States)
Children's Internet Protection Act of 2000 (United States)
Communications of Decency Act of 1996 (United States)
Computer Fraud and Abuse Act of 1986 (United States)
Juvenile Protection Act of 2011 (South Korea)

DEFINITIONS

Black hat hacker. A person who gains unauthorized access to a system for malicious reasons with the intention of causing harm.

Defiance theory. A theory holding that individuals may react to sanctions by defying them if the sanctions are viewed as unjust, which ultimately leads to an increase rather than decrease in crime.

Deviancy amplification. A theory positing that labels of deviancy ascribed to individuals by society increase rather than decrease deviant or criminal behavior.

Disintegrative shaming. A form of shaming that creates outcasts by stigmatizing offenders, resulting in their further entrenchment in crime.

Elite hacker. An innovative hacker who has the technical acumen needed to exploit and manipulate systems.

Grey hat hacker. A hacker who does not fit the black hat or white hat hacker label, falling instead somewhere in between.

Labeling theory. A theory examining the formation of deviant and criminal taxonomies and how these classifications and social reactions to them influence deviant and criminal behavior.

Looking glass self. A process whereby an individual adopts expectations of behavior that others assign to him or her.

Media agenda-setting theory. A theory holding that individuals believe that the issues which the media focuses on are the most important.

Media framing theory. A theory positing that the manner in which the media organizes and presents the news influences and colors individuals' perception of issues and informs them about what issues people should focus on.

Moral entrepreneurs. Individuals seeking to influence a target to adapt a behavior and to enforce rules concerning that behavior.

Moral panic. A hyperbolic concern and emotional reactions to incidents viewed as threats to the social order because of overblown and exaggerated media reports and reactions to them by politicians, policymakers, lawmakers, and agents of the criminal justice system.

Phenomenology. A school of thought that seeks to shed light on the meanings of individuals' actions by focusing on how individuals understand, process, interpret, and respond to objects and events (i.e., phenomena).

Primary deviance. Involves deviant acts committed by individuals who do not view themselves as deviants nor live life according to this identity.

Reintegrative shaming. A form of shaming designed to both elicit societal disapproval for offenders' actions and repair the harm done by offenders to society.

Script kiddies. Individuals who engage in hacking by utilizing the tools provided by elite hackers; these individuals do not understand nor study computer programming and the tools they use to engage in hacking and other illicit activities.

Secondary deviance. Involves acts committed by individuals because of the deviant label ascribed to them, which they internalize and then act out accordingly in future criminal activity.

Self-fulfilling prophecy. A positive or negative belief that ultimately materializes because it is believed to be true.

Symbolic interactionism. A sociological perspective maintaining that behavior and communication is facilitated by symbols whose meanings are derived from and interpretations are modified by social interactions with other people.

White hat hacker. A hacker who uses his or her technical knowledge, skills, and abilities within the constraints of the law.

ENDNOTES

1. H. Becker, *Outsiders: Studies in the Sociology of Deviance* (New York: Free Press, 1963).
2. J. Young, *The Drugtakers: The Social Meaning of Drug Use* (London: MacGibbon and Kee, 1971).
3. R. K. Merton, *Social Theory and Social Structure*, 2nd ed. (New York: Free Press, 1968), 477.
4. E. M. Lemert, *Social Pathology* (New York: McGraw-Hill, 1951), 75.
5. Ibid., 75–76.
6. C. H. Cooley, *Social Organization: A Study of the Larger Mind* (New York: Charles Scribner's Sons, 1909).
7. Becker, *Outsiders*.
8. G. H. Mead, *Mind, Self and Society from a Standpoint of a Social Behaviorist* (Chicago, IL: University of Chicago, 1934).
9. G. H. Mead, *On Social Psychology: Selected Papers* (Chicago: University of Chicago Press, 1964), 239.
10. R. L. Matsueda, "Criminological Implications of the Thought of George Herbert Mead," in M. Deflem, ed., *Sociological Theory and Criminological Research: Views from Europe and the United States* (Oxford: Elsevier, 2006), 82; M.-H. Maras, "The Social Consequences of a Mass Surveillance Measure: What Happens When We Become the 'Others'?" *International Journal of Law, Crime and Justice* 40, no. 2 (2012): 74.
11. Mead, *On Social Psychology,* 239.
12. Mead, *Mind, Self and Society,*175; Maras, "The Social Consequences of a Mass Surveillance Measure," 74.
13. Mead, *Mind, Self and Society*, 209–213.
14. H. Blumer, *Symbolic Interactionism: Perspective and Method* (Englewood Cliffs, NJ: Prentice-Hall, 1969).
15. J. Katz, *Seductions of Crime: Moral and Sensual Attractions in Doing Evil* (New York: Basic Books, 1988).
16. C. R. Rogers, "A Theory of Therapy, Personality and Interpersonal Relationships, as Developed in the Client-Centered Framework," in S. Koch (ed.), *Psychology: A Study of Science* (New York: McGraw-Hill, 1959), 200.
17. W. Reckless, *The Crime Problem* (New York: Appleton-Century-Crofts, 1961).
18. E. Mollick, "Tapping into the Underground," *Sloan Management Review* 46, no. 4 (2005): 21–24.

19. R. Chiesa, S. Ducci, and S. Ciappi, *Profiling Hackers: The Science of Criminal Profiling as Applied to the World of Hacking* (Boca Raton, FL: Auerbach Publications, 2008), 53.

20. M. Milone, "Hacktivism: Securing the National Infrastructure," *Knowledge, Technology, & Policy* 16, no. 1 (2003): 77.

21. S. Levy, *Hackers: Heroes of the Computer Revolution* (New York: Bantam Doubleday Dell, 1984).

22. P. A. Taylor, "Hackers: Cyberpunks or Microserfs?" *Information, Communication & Society* 1, no. 4 (1998): 402.

23. O. Turgeman-Goldschmidt, "Meanings That Hackers Assign to Their Being a Hacker," *International Journal of Cyber Criminology* 2, no. 2 (2008): 393.

24. R. N. Lancaster, *Sex Panic and the Punitive State* (Berkeley: University of California Press, 2011); J. T. Pickett, C. Mancini, and D. P. Mears, "Vulnerable Victims, Monstrous Offenders, and Unmanageable Risk: Explaining Public Opinion on the Social Control of Sex Crime Criminology," *Criminology* 51, no. 3 (2013): 729–759.

25. For example, O. Turgeman-Goldschmidt, "Meanings That Hackers Assign," 382–396; B. Wible, "A Site Where Hackers are Welcome: Using Hack-In Contests to Shape Preferences and Deter Computer Crime," *Yale Law Journal* 112, no. 6 (2003): 1577–1623.

26. J. Braithwaite, *Crime, Shame, and Reintegration* (Cambridge: Cambridge University Press, 1989), 9.

27. Ibid., 100–101.

28. Ibid., 155.

29. S. L. Brown, "The Age Dumps Catherine Deveny following Bindi Irwin, Rove Logies Twitter," *ABC Melbourne*, May, 5, 2010, http://www.abc.net.au/local/stories/2010/05/05/2890384.htm.

30. S. J. Drucker and G. Gumpert, "Cybercrime and Punishment," *Critical Studies in Media Communication* 17, no. 2 (2000): 151.

31. D. Bailey, "Minnesota Dentist Who Killed Zimbabwe's Cecil the Lion Draws Threats," *Reuters*, July 29, 2015. Protests. http://www.reuters.com/article/us-zimbabwe-wildlife-lion-usa-idUS KCN0Q32HE20150730.

32. H. Regan, "Cecil the Lion, Walter Palmer and the Psychology of Online Shaming," *Time*, July 30, 2015, http://time.com/3978216/online-shaming-social-media-walter-palmer-cecil-lion/.

33. J. Worland, "PETA Wants Lion-Hunting Dentist Killed," *Time*, July 29, 2015. http://time .com/3976578/peta-cecil-lion/; M. E. Miller, "PETA Calls for Walter Palmer to Be 'Hanged' for Killing Cecil the Lion," *Washington Post*, July 30, 2015, https://www.washingtonpost.com/ news/morning-mix/wp/2015/07/30/peta-calls-for-walter-palmer-to-be-hanged-for-killing -cecil-the-lion/.

34. E. Izadi and A. Ohlheiser, "As Anger Escalates over Lion's Death, Zimbabwean Men Appear in Court," *Washington Post*, July 29, 2015, https://www.washingtonpost.com/news/speaking- of-science/wp/2015/07/28/american-dentist-says-he-regrets-killing-cecil-the-lion -believed-zimbabwe-hunt-was-legal/.

35. A. Greenwood, "PETA Euthanized a Lot of Animals at its Shelter in 2014, and No-Kill Advocates are Not Happy About It," *Huffington Post*, March 24, 2015, http://www.huffingtonpost .com/2015/02/05/pets-shelter-euthanization-rate_n_6612490.html; M. Winerip, "PETA Finds Itself on Receiving End of Others' Anger," *New York Times*, July 6, 2013, http://www.nytimes .com/2013/07/07/us/peta-finds-itself-on-receiving-end-of-others-anger.html; A. Greenwood, "PETA Won't Answer Some Very Basic Questions about Why It Kills So Many Shelter Animals," *Huffington Post*, September 27, 2015, http://www.huffingtonpost.com/entry/peta -euthanasia-shelter-animals_us_55fc17d7e4b00310edf6a608.

36. O. Bahou, "22 Women Who Expertly Shut Down Their Body Shamers," *Cosmopolitan*, April 14, 2015, http://www.cosmopolitan.com/lifestyle/news/a39027/women-shut-down-body-shamers/.

37. Izadi and Ohlheiser, "As Anger Escalates over Lion's Death."

38. L. W. Sherman, "Defiance, Deterrence, and Irrelevance: A Theory of the Criminal Sanction," *Journal of Research in Crime and Delinquency* 30, no. 4 (1993): 457.

39. Ibid., 459.

40. R. Andrews, "Copyright Infringement and the Internet: An Economic Analysis of Law," *Boston University Journal of Science and Technology Law* 11 (2005): 279–280.

41. *Google Spain SL, Google Inc. v. Agencia Española de Protección de Datos, Mario Costeja González*, ECJ Case C-131/12, May 13, 2014.

42. Ibid.

43. Becker, *Outsiders*.

44. H. Nissenbaum, "Hackers and the Contested Ontology of Cyberspace," *New Media & Society* 6, no. 2 (2004): 211; J. Thomas, "The Moral Ambiguity of Social Control in Cyberspace: A Retro-Assessment of the 'Golden Age' of Hacking," *New Media & Society* 7, no. 5 (2005): 599–624.

45. S. Cohen, *Folk Devils and Moral Panics* (London: MacGibbon and Kee, 1972), 9.

46. R. H. Potter and L. A. Potter, "The Internet, Cyberporn, and Sexual Exploitation of Children: Media Moral Panics and Urban Myths for Middle-Class Parents?" *Sexuality and Culture* 5, no. 3 (2001): 31–48.

47. Cohen, *Folk Devils and Moral Panics*.

48. P. Jenkins, *Moral Panic: Changing Concepts of the Child Molester in Modern America* (New Haven, CT: Yale University Press, 2004); J. Shafer, "Down on the Pharm, Again: Debunking 'Pharm Parties' for the Third Time," *Slate*, March 25, 2008, http://www.slate.com/articles/news_and_politics/press_box/2008/03/down_on_the_pharm_again.html.

49. I. Marsh and G. Melville, "Moral Panics and the British Media—A Look at Some Contemporary "Folk Devils," *Internet Journal of Criminology* (2011), http://www.internetjournalofcriminology.com/marsh_melville_moral_panics_and_the_british_media_march_2011.pdf.

50. Cohen, *Folk Devils and Moral Panics*.

51. Ibid.

52. D. Killingbeck, "The Role of Television News in the Construction of School Violence as a 'Moral Panic,'" *Journal of Criminal Justice and Popular Culture* 8, no. 3 (2001): 186–202; T. Monahan, "The Surveillance Curriculum: Risk Management and Social Control in the Neoliberal School," in *Surveillance and Security: Technological Politics and Power in Everyday Life*, ed. T. Monahan (New York: Routledge, 2006), 116; F. Furedi, *Culture of Fear: Risk-Taking and the Morality of Low Expectation* (London: Cassell, 1997), 24, 109–110; P. Jenkins, *Beyond Tolerance: Child Pornography on the Internet* (New York: New York University Press, 2001); P. Jenkins, *Images of Terror* (New York: Aldine de Gruyter, 2003); A. Cavanagh, "Taxonomies of Anxiety: Risk, Panics, Paedophilia and the Internet," *Electronic Journal of Sociology* 10, no. 1 (2007): 1–16; Y. Jewkes, *Media and Crime*, 2nd ed. (London: Sage, 2010); Y. Jewkes, "Online Pornography, Pedophilia and the Sexualized Child: Mediated Myths and Moral Panics," in *Understanding and Preventing Online Sexual Exploitation of Children*, ed. E. Quayle and K. M. Ribisl (New York: Routledge, 2012), 116–132; T. Lawson and C. Comber, "Censorship, the Internet and Schools: A New Moral Panic," *The Curriculum Journal* 11, no. 2 (2000), 274.

53. Y. Jewkes, "Online Pornography, Pedophilia and the Sexualized Child," 116–132; A. Littlewood, "Cyberporn and Moral Panic: An Evaluation of Press Reactions to Pornography on the Internet," *Library and Information Research* 27, no. 86 (2003): 8–18; Jenkins, *Beyond Tolerance*; Jenkins, *Images of Terror*; Cavanagh, "Taxonomies of Anxiety," 1–16; Jewkes, *Media and Crime*.

54. J. Cassell and M. Cramer, "High Tech or High Risk: Moral Panics about Girls Online," in *Mac-Arthur Foundation Series on Digital Media and Learning: Digital Youth, Innovation, and the Unexpected*, ed. T. McPherson (Cambridge, MA: MIT Press, 2007), 53–75; D. Rothe and S. L. Muzzatti, "Enemies Everywhere: Terrorism, Moral Panic, and US Civil Society," *Critical Criminology* 12, no. 3 (2004), 328; Jewkes, *Media and Crime*, 67; J. Young, "Moral Panic," *British Journal of Criminology* 49, no. 1 (2009): 4–16; J. Best, *Threatened Children: Rhetoric and Concern about Child Victims* (Chicago: University of Chicago Press, 1990).

55. Cohen, *Folk Devils and Moral Panics*.

56. *Chicago Tribune*, "Bullying Is Cruel, but a Crime? Questionable Charges Against Two Girls in Florida," October 19, 2013, http://articles.chicagotribune.com/2013-10-19/opinion/ct-edit-bully-20131019_1_rebecca-ann-sedwick-hate-crime-law-law-professor. Florida does not have a cyberbullying law but has a cyberstalking law, which could be used to prosecute cyberbullies if a true threat was communicated (see Chapter 10 for more information on true threats).

57. S. Almasy, K. Segal, and J. Couwels, "Sheriff: Taunting Post Leads to Arrests in Rebecca Sedwick Bullying Death," *CNN*, October 16, 2013, http://www.cnn.com/2013/10/15/justice/rebecca-sedwick-bullying-death-arrests/.

58. See Chapter 10 for information on cyberbullying laws and prosecutions of cyberbullies.

59. S. Pokin, "Megan's Story" [originally posted in the *St. Charles (MO) Journal*, November 13, 2007], http://www.meganmeierfoundation.org/megans-story.html.

60. *U.S. v. Drew*, 259 F.R.D. 449 (C.D. Cal. 2009).

61. V. Ranieri, "United States v. Drew: Conviction in Lori Drew MySpace Case Thrown Out," *JOLT Digest*, September 4, 2009, http://jolt.law.harvard.edu/digest/jurisdiction/9th-circuit/united-states-v-drew-3.

62. D. Kravets, "Court Rebukes DOJ, Says Hacking Required to Be Prosecuted as Hacker," *Wired*, April 10, 2012, http://www.wired.com/2012/04/computer-fraud-and-abuse-act/.

63. N. Cohen, "A Data Crusader, a Defendant and Now, a Cause," *New York Times*, January 13, 2013, http://www.nytimes.com/2013/01/14/technology/aaron-swartz-a-data-crusader-and-now-a-cause.html?_r=0.

64. D. Kravets, "Feds Charge Activist with 13 Felonies for Rogue Downloading of Academic Articles," *Wired*, September 18, 2012, http://www.wired.com/2012/09/aaron-swartz-felony/.

65. G. Greenwald, "Carmen Ortiz and Stephen Heymann: Accountability for Prosecutorial Abuse," *Guardian*, January 16, 2013, http://www.theguardian.com/commentisfree/2013/jan/16/ortiz-heymann-swartz-accountability-abuse; Z. Carter, R. Grim, and R. J. Reilly, "Carmen Ortiz, U.S. Attorney, Under Fire over Suicide of Internet Pioneer Aaron Swartz," *Huffington Post*, January 14, 2013, http://www.huffingtonpost.com/2013/01/14/aaron-swartz-carmen-ortiz_n_2472146.html.

66. V. J. Callanan, *Feeding the Fear of Crime: Crime-Related Media and Support for Three Strikes* (New York: LFB Scholarly Publishing, 2005), 61.

67. S. Cohen and J. Young, *The Manufacture of News*, 2nd ed. (New York: Sage, 1981).

68. Cohen and Young, *The Manufacture of News*.

69. R. Surette, *Media, Crime, and Criminal Justice: Images and Realities* (Pacific Grove, CA: Brooks/Cole, 1992).

70. L. Morales, "Many Americans Remain Distrusting of News Media," *Gallup*, October 1, 2009, http://www.gallup.com/poll/123365/americans-remain-distrusting-news-media.aspx; J. Ray, "Majority of Britons Distrusted Media Before Hacking Scandal," *Gallup*, July 27, 2011, http://www.gallup.com/poll/148679/Majority-Britons-Distrusted-Media-Hacking-Scandal

.aspx?g_source=hacking&g_medium=search&g_campaign=tiles; L. Morales, "Snapshot: Britons Less Trusting of Media," *Gallup*, December 7, 2012, http://www.gallup.com/poll/159110 /snapshot-britons-less-trusting-media.aspx?g_source=hacking&g_medium=search&g _campaign=tiles; L. Morales, "Majority in U.S. Continues to Distrust the Media, Perceive Bias," Gallup, September 22, 2011, http://www.gallup.com/poll/149624/Majority-Continue -Distrust-Media-Perceive-Bias.aspx?g_source=distrust%20media&g_medium=search&g _campaign=tiles; L. Morales, "U.S. Distrust in Media Hits New High," *Gallup*, September 21, 2012, http://www.gallup.com/poll/157589/distrust-media-hits-new-high.aspx?g_source=distrust %20 media&g_medium=search&g_campaign=tiles.

71. B. C. Cohen, *The Press and Foreign Policy* (Princeton, NJ: Princeton University Press, 1963).

72. M. McCombs and D. L. Shaw, "The Agenda-Setting Function of the Mass Media," *Public Opinion Quarterly* 36, no. 2 (1972): 176–185; M. E. McCombs and D. L. Shaw, "The Evolution of Agenda-Setting Research: Twenty-Five Years in the Marketplace of Ideas," *Journal of Communication* 43, no. 2 (1993): 58–67.

73. D. A. Scheufle and D. Tewksbury, "Framing, Agenda Setting and Priming: The Evolution of Three Media Effects Models," *Journal of Communication* 57, no. 1 (2007): 9–20.

74. H. Vandebosch, R. Simulioniene, M. Marczak, A. Vermeulen, and L. Bonettie, "The Role of the Media," in *Cyberbullying through the New Media: Findings from an International Network*, ed. P. K. Smith and G. Steffgen (New York: Psychology Press, 2013), 99–119; C. H. De Vreese, "News Framing: Theory and Typology," *Information Design Journal + Document Design* 13, no. 1 (2005): 51–62; McCombs and Shaw, "The Agenda-Setting Function of Mass Media," 176–187; Scheufle and Tewksbury, "Framing, Agenda Setting and Priming," 9–20.

75. D. Kennedy, "Cyber Attack on CENTCOM: Just the Tip of the Iceberg?" *Fox News*, January 12, 2015, http://www.foxnews.com/on-air/on-the-record/2015/01/13/cyber-attack-centcom-just-tip -iceberg.

76. Associated Press, "Game Hacking Tip of the Iceberg as Threat of Cybercrimes Looms Ever Larger," *Fox Business*, September 4, 2014, http://www.foxbusiness.com/features/2014/09/04/ game-hacking-tip-iceberg-as-threat-cybercrimes-looms-ever-larger.html.

77. P. Muncaster, "The Tip of the Iceberg? Why Massive Russian Cyber Attack Should Be a Wake-Up Call," *Infosecurity*, August 7, 2014, http://www.infosecurity-magazine.com/magazine -features/massive-russian-cyber-attack/.

78. R. Stern, "Data Breach That Exposed Millions Is Just 'Tip of the Iceberg,' UB Expert Says," *University of Buffalo News Center*, June 5, 2015, http://www.buffalo.edu/news/releases/2015/06/013.html.

79. D. McAleese, "Hundreds of Kids Cyber Crime Victims, and It's Tip of Iceberg—PSNI Has Warned," *Belfast Telegraph*, May 13, 2014, http://www.belfasttelegraph.co.uk/news/northern -ireland/hundreds-of-kids-cyber-crime-victims-and-its-tip-of-iceberg-psni-has -warned-30267519.html.

80. M. Levi, "Between Risk and the Reality Falls the Shadow: Evidence and Urban Legends in Computer Fraud," in *Crime and the Internet*, ed. D. Wall (London: Routledge, 2001), 44–58.

81. J. McCarthy, "Americans Cite Cyberterrorism among Top Three Threats to U.S.," Gallup, February 10, 2016, http://www.gallup.com/poll/189161/americans-cite-cyberterrorism-among-top-three-threats.aspx?g_source=cyber terrorism%20fear&g_medium=search&g_campaign=tiles.

82. J. Young, *The Role of the Police as Amplifiers of Deviance: Negotiators of Drug Control as Seen in Notting Hill*, in *Images of Deviance*, ed. S. Cohen (Harmondsworth, UK: Penguin, 1971), 37.

83. J. Markoff, "Judge Rules against U.S. in Encryption Case," *New York Times*, December 19, 1996, http://www.nytimes.com/1996/12/19/business/judge-rules-against-us-in-encryption-case.html.

84. A. Nagourney, I. Lovett, and R. Pérez-Peña, "San Bernardino Shooting Kills at Least 14; Two Suspects Are Dead," *New York Times*, December 2, 2015, http://www.nytimes.com/2015/12/03/us/san-bernardino-shooting.html.

85. H. S. Edwards, "Apple Leans on 227-Year-Old Law in Encryption Fight," *Time*, February 17, 2016, http://time.com/4227236/apple-fbi-san-bernardino-encryption/.

86. A. Selyukh and C. Domonoske, "Apple, The FBI and iPhone Encryption: A Look at What's at Stake," *NPR*, February 19, 2016, http://www.npr.org/sections/thetwo-way/2016/02/17/467096705/apple-the-fbi-and-iphone-encryption-a-look-at-whats-at-stake.

87. Apple, "A Message to Our Customers," February 16, 2016, http://www.apple.com/customer-letter/.

88. P. Engle, "GOP Senator Unloads: 'Apple Chose to Protect a Dead ISIS Terrorist's Privacy over the Security of the American People,'" *Business Insider*, February 17, 2016, http://www.businessinsider.com/tom-cotton-apple-san-bernardino-shooter-phone-lock-2016-2.

89. Becker, *Outsiders*.

90. Ibid.

91. J. P. Fishman, "Copyright Infringement and the Separated Powers of Moral Entrepreneurship," *American Criminal Law Review* 51, no. 22 (2014): 359–401.

92. M.-H. Maras, "Risk Perception, Fear and Its Consequences Following the 2004 Madrid and 2005 London Bombings," in *The Political Psychology of Terrorism Fears*, eds. S. J. Sinclair and D. Antonius (Oxford: Oxford University Press, 2013), 227.

93. P. Slovic, "Perception of Risk," *Science* 236 (April 1987): 280–285; C. R. Sunstein, *Laws of Fear: Beyond the Precautionary Principle* (Cambridge: Cambridge University Press, 1987), 35; Furedi, *Culture of Fear*, 51.

94. A. Tversky and D. Kahneman, "Availability: A Heuristic for Judging Frequency and Probability," in *Judgment Under Uncertainty: Heuristics and Biases*, ed. D. Kahneman, P. Slovic, and A. Tversky (Cambridge: Cambridge University Press, 1982); T. Kuran and C. R. Sunstein, "Availability Cascades and Risk Regulation," *Stanford Law Review* 51, no. 4 (1999): 683–768; P. Slovic, B. Fischhoff, and S. Lichtenstein, "Rating the Risks," in *The Perception of Risk*, ed. P. Slovic (London: Earthscan, 2000).

95. R. E. Kasperson, O. Renn, P. Slovic, H. S. Brown, J. Emel, R. Goble, J. X. Kasperson, and S. Ratick, "The Social Amplification of Risk: A Conceptual Framework," in *The Perception of Risk* (London: Earthscan, 2000), 241–242; J. S. Lerner and D. Keltner, "Fear, Anger and Risk," *Journal of Personality of Social Psychology* 81, no. 1 (2001): 146–159.

96. R. Jervis, "Introduction: Approach and Assumptions," in *Psychology and Deterrence*, ed. R. Jervis, R. N. Lebow, and J. G. Stein (Baltimore, MD: Johns Hopkins University Press, 1989), 1–12; Cohen, *Folk Devils and Moral Panics*; S. Hall, C. Critcher, T. Jefferson, J. Clarke, and B. Roberts, *Policing the Crisis: Mugging, the State, and Law and Order* (London: Macmillan, 1978); E. Goode and N. Ben-Yehuda, *Moral Panics: The Social Construction of Deviance*, 2nd ed. (Chichester, UK: John Wiley & Sons, 2009).

97. L. T. Wilkins, *Social Policy, Action, and Research: Studies in Social Deviance* (London: Tavistock, 1967).

98. J. Young, *The Drugtakers: The Social Meaning of Drug Use* (London: MacGibbon and Kee, 1971).

99. Wilkins, *Social Policy, Action, and Research*.

100. S. Cohen, *The Creation of the Mods and Rockers* (London: MacGibbon and Kee, 1972).

101. Hall et al., *Policing the Crisis*.

102. Goode and Ben-Yehuda, *Moral Panics*, 37–43.

103. J. Thomas, "The Moral Ambiguity of Social Control in Cyberspace: A Retro-Assessment of the 'Golden Age' of Hacking," *New Media & Society* 7, no. 5 (2005): 599–624.
104. Cohen, *Folk Devils and Moral Panics*, 28.
105. Missouri Revised Statutes § 565.090.1(4).
106. Cohen, *Folk Devils and Moral Panics*.
107. *Reno v. American Civil Liberties Union*, 521 U.S. 844 (1997).
108. *Ashcroft v. American Civil Liberties Union*, 535 U.S. 564 (2002).
109. *United States v. American Library Association*, 539 U.S. 194 (2003).
110. Goode and Ben-Yehuda, *Moral Panics*.
111. S. A. Cole and H. N. Pontell, "Don't Be Low Hanging Fruit: Identity Theft as Moral Panic," in Monahan, *Surveillance and Security*, 142–143.
112. S. A. Elder, "A Korean Couple Let a Baby Die While They Played a Video Game," *Newsweek*, July 27, 2014, http://www.newsweek.com/2014/08/15/korean-couple-let-baby-die-while-they-played-video-game-261483.html.
113. M. Tran, "Girl Starved to Death while Parents Raised Virtual Child in Online Game," *Guardian*, March 5, 2010, http://www.theguardian.com/world/2010/mar/05/korean-girl-starvedonline-game; Associated Press, "South Korean MPs Consider Measures to Tackle Online Gaming Addiction," *Guardian*, December 11, 2013, http://www.theguardian.com/world/2013/dec/11/south-korea-online-gaming-addiction.
114. Associated Press, "South Korean MPs Consider Measures to Tackle Online Gaming Addiction," *Guardian*, December 11, 2013, http://www.theguardian.com/world/2013/dec/11/south-korea-online-gaming-addiction; D. Lee, "The Real Scars of Korean Gaming," *BBC News*, June 5, 2015, http://www.bbc.com/news/technology-32996009.
115. Lee, "The Real Scars of Korean Gaming."
116. Ibid.
117. J. D. Zhan and H. C. Chan, "Government Regulation of Online Game Addiction," *Communications of the Association for Information Systems* 30, no. 13 (2012): 193.
118. Ibid.
119. *China Daily*, "Regulation to Fight Gaming Addiction," July 30, 2011, http://www.china.org.cn/china/2011-07/30/content_23104750.htm.
120. E. Pilkington, "Justine Sacco, PR Executive Fired over Racist Tweet, 'Ashamed.'" *Guardian*, December 22, 2013, http://www.theguardian.com/world/2013/dec/22/pr-exec-fired-racist-tweet-aids-africa-apology.
121. E. Kim, "13 People Who Got Fired over a Single Tweet," *Business Insider*, May 10, 2015, http://www.businessinsider.com/fired-over-a-tweet-2015-5#this-pr-consultant-became-one-of-the-most-hated-people-on-earth-overnight-2.
122. J. Ronson, "How One Stupid Tweet Blew Up Justine Sacco's Life," *New York Times*, February 12, 2015, http://www.nytimes.com/2015/02/15/magazine/how-one-stupid-tweet-ruined-justine-saccos-life.html.
123. K. Dimitrova, S. Rahmanzadeh, and J. Lipman, "Justine Sacco, Fired after Tweet on AIDS in Africa, Issues Apology," *ABC News*, December 22, 2013, http://abcnews.go.com/International/justine-sacco-fired-tweet-aids-africa-issues-apology/story?id=21301833.
124. H. Regan, "Cecil the Lion, Walter Palmer and the Psychology of Online Shaming," *Time*, July 30, 2015, http://time.com/3978216/online-shaming-social-media-walter-palmer-cecil-lion/.
125. CBS, "Facebook Photo of Plymouth Woman at Tomb of the Unknowns Sparks Outrage," November 20, 2012, http://boston.cbslocal.com/2012/11/20/facebook-photo-of-plymouth-woman-at-tomb-of-the-unknowns-sparks-outrage/.

CHAPTER 9

CONFLICT CYBERCRIMINOLOGY
Cybercrime, Power, and Gender

KEYWORDS

Biological determinism
Bourgeoisie
Conflict theories
Conservative feminism
Cyberdystopianism
Cyberfeminism
Cyberutopianism
Feminism
Feminist criminology

Hegemonic masculinity
Ladette culture
Left realism
Liberal feminism
Lumpenproletariat
Marxist criminology
Marxist feminism
Patriarchy
Peacemaking criminology

Primitive rebellion
   hypothesis
Proletariat
Radical criminology
Radical feminism
Social justice warrior
Socialist feminism

A person's participation in online discourse may both empower and endanger the person. On the one hand, accessing the Internet provides the user with innumerable opportunities to share knowledge and communicate with others. On the other hand, some users seek to exploit the benefits of the Internet for criminal purposes. Hence, the dual use of cyberspace results in conflict between what could be wondrous advantages and severe disadvantages for society. This chapter explores this phenomenon by examining the sources of the conflict, how the conflict evolves, and how it can be eradicated according to **conflict theories**, looking in particular at Marxist criminology, left realism, peacemaking criminology, and feminist criminology.

MARXIST CRIMINOLOGY

"If you suffer your people to be ill-educated, and their manners to be corrupted from their infancy, and then punish them for those crimes to which their first education disposed them, what else is to be concluded from this, but that you first make thieves and then punish them."[1] —Thomas More, 1516

Plutarch highlighted the inequalities in wealth and power in the population that generated conflicts within society. Capitalism is at the heart of this conflict because it creates inequalities in society. Conflict theories are based on the writings of Karl Marx and Friedrich Engels. Marx and Engels focused on conflict resulting from class structures competing for economic interests,[2] an unavoidable outcome of capitalism.[3] Marx and Engels proposed two classes in a capitalist society: the **proletariat** (the have-nots) and the **bourgeoisie** (the haves).[4] The *proletariat* is the working class, those who do not have power or wealth. The *bourgeoisie* is the upper class, those who have power and wealth. These two groups come into conflict because the conditions of society concomitantly empower the bourgeoisie while disenfranchising the proletariat.

Engels applied the principle of social conflict to the family.[5] He observed that the severe economic inequality of the proletariat in a capitalist society resulted in the weakening of the family institution. Because of the impoverished conditions to which they were exposed, all members of the proletariat family were required to work, leaving children to fend for themselves.[6] Proletarians were forced to engage in mindless, menial, tedious, and repetitive work, often under dangerous conditions and for extensive hours per week for low pay.[7] Women, who also needed to work, were paid significantly less for their jobs than men.[8] Like Engels, Willem Bonger believed that capitalism undercut family stability and the education of its members.[9]

Influenced by Marxist thought, **radical criminology** holds that capitalist societies precipitate crime by enabling those with power to use laws and enforcement of them to control less powerful groups and suppress any threats to those in power. In such a society, law is considered a tool of repression of the bourgeoisie designed to subjugate and control the proletariat. Those without power and wealth are subjected to laws aimed at punishing their behavior, forcing them to come into contact with the criminal justice system.[10] The law and the criminal justice system of capitalist societies are thus viewed as biased and benefiting the bourgeoisie. In cyberspace, this is observed in policies designed to protect elites. For example, Twitter originally implemented a filter for abusive and harassing tweets *only* for verified users, that is, those "users in music, acting, fashion, government, politics, religion, journalism, media, sports, business and other key interest areas."[11] Although the threatening and abusive messages remained on the platform, this filter prevented verified users from seeing threatening messages and having these messages pop up on their mention list. Until 2015, unverified users were unable to benefit from this service.[12]

Radical criminology and other criminological works based on Marxist thought (i.e., **Marxist criminology**) also view the enforcement of law as disproportionately affecting those less powerful in society, resulting in the elite receiving no sentence or less severe sentences than those without power for comparable crimes. Cases in point are celebrities who have received minimal sentences for serious crimes. For example, the actor who played Pee-wee Herman, Paul Reubens, was found in possession of digital images of child pornography. For his crimes, he received a $100 fine and 3 years' probation; he was also required to register as a sex offender for the duration of his probation.[13] Nevertheless, such reduced sentences are not enjoyed by all those in power. For instance, a former mayor of Seven Fields, Pennsylvania, Edward Bayne, was sentenced to 7 years' imprisonment for possession of digital images of child pornography obtained from online file-sharing networks in exchange for a guilty plea.[14]

Bonger viewed capitalism as criminogenic because it created conditions of competition that pitted individuals against each other for the attainment of scarce resources.[15] The capitalist system, which is a predatory system, promoted material consumption, yet few people were able to obtain material goods. According to Richard Quinney, "Crime is inevitable under capitalist conditions . . . a response to the material conditions of life. Permanent unemployment and the acceptance of that condition—can result in a form of life where criminality is an appropriate and consistent response."[16] As such, individuals in this position commit crime primarily to survive. What is observed is the **primitive rebellion hypothesis**: "Crime in capitalist societies is often a rational response to the circumstances in which people find themselves."[17] Crime is thus viewed as the outcome of the struggle against the existing prevailing conditions a person may face.[18] Individuals engaging in illicit acts view severe economic inequality and their respective impoverished position as a justification to engage in crime. Those with certain innate social sentiments, particularly egoism (whereby an individual selfishly pursues his or her own self-interests at the expense of others), are viewed as being prone to crime.[19] A capitalist society weakens altruistic sentiment (i.e., an individual's concern for the well-being of other members of society).[20] A socialist system (grounded in beliefs of common ownership and mutual consumption of goods) is believed to strengthen altruistic sentiment.

In line with traditional Marxist criminology, radical criminologists argue that in order to reduce conflict in society—an inevitable consequence of the capitalist regime—existing social structures in society must be dismantled and the capitalist regime should be replaced with a communist or socialist regime. The solution to the crime problem thus lies in the abolition of a capitalist regime and its replacement with another regime. Both Marx and Engels believed that the illicit acts committed in capitalist societies could be resolved only through revolution against the ruling class.[21] According to Marx and Engels, the resolution to the conflict between these two groups is the overthrow of the capitalist regime and its replacement with a communist (classless) regime.[22] The solution, therefore, is to "centralise all instruments of production in the hands of the state."[23] However, doing so creates another ruling class (i.e., the state) that monopolizes property and results in a "brutal class struggle."[24] Other radical criminologists proposed the replacement of a capitalist regime with a socialist regime. William Chambliss and Robert Seidman viewed socialist societies as having less crime than capitalist societies because of lack of intense class struggle characteristic of a capitalist society.[25] The reality is, however, that this assumption has not been empirically supported and depends on the crime in question.

Marxist thought and radical criminology ultimately hold that conflict can be resolved by redistributing wealth in society. This redistribution of wealth is also viewed as a way to reduce crime. Consider the TV show *Mr. Robot*, in which the main character, Elliot Alderson, joins a group of hacktivists[26] targeting E-Corp (which Alderson calls Evil Corp), a corporation which owns 70 percent of the global credit industry.[27] This group, fsociety, is seeking to hack into Evil Corp's servers and damage them; by doing this, "every record of every credit card, loan and mortgage would be wiped clean . . . [creating] the single biggest

IMAGE 9-1   Mask Worn by Members of *fsociety* in Mr. Robot.

incident of wealth redistribution in history."[28] Upon accomplishing this task, fsociety released a prerecorded message to TV viewers:

> Evil Corp, we have delivered on our promise as expected. The people of the world who have been enslaved by you have been freed. Your financial data has been destroyed. Any attempts to salvage it will be utterly futile. Face it: you have been owned. We at fsociety will smile as we watch you and your dark souls die. That means any money you owe these pigs has been forgiven by us, your friends at fsociety. The market's opening bell this morning will be the final death knell of Evil Corp. We hope as a new society rises from the ashes that you will forge a better world. A world that values the free people, a world where greed is not encouraged, a world that belongs to us again, a world changed forever. And while you do that, remember to repeat these words: "We are fsociety, we are finally free, we are finally awake!"[29]

This anticapitalist and antiestablishment sentiment is prevalent in the hacking literature. Existing literature also reveals that hacking is viewed as the product of "conflict and contestation between various social groups."[30] An example of groups that are sources of conflict for hackers is antipiracy organizations. These organizations are viewed as leveraging the Internet to promote their own personal interests at the expense of others by censoring individuals and preventing the spread of information. As stated in McKenzie Wark's *Hacker's Manifesto,*

> Information, like land or capital, becomes a form of property monopolised by a class of vectoralists, so named because they control the vectors along which information is abstracted, just as capitalists control the material means with which goods are produced, and pastoralists the land with which food is produced. Information circulated within working class culture as [sic] a social property belonging to all. But when information in turn becomes a form of private property, workers are dispossessed of it, and must buy their own culture back from its owners, the vectoralist class. The whole of time, time itself, becomes a commodified experience.[31]

The *Hacker's Manifesto*, influenced by Marxist thought, criticizes intellectual property (i.e., ownership rights to intangible property, such as information) as criminogenic. Nevertheless, intellectual property and freedom of information are not always at odds with each other.[32] Indeed, certain open source platforms and websites, such as Wikipedia, enable the free flow of information.

LEFT REALISM

Left realism was developed in response to the deficiencies identified in radical criminology. Left realists argue that too great an emphasis is placed on the powerful elites, largely ignoring the street crimes committed against the lower class. The people most likely to be victims and perpetrators of crimes are those in marginalized communities. John Lea and Jock Young argued that lower class individuals largely engage in street crimes.[33] According to them, these crimes are linked to social problems, such as material and relative deprivation.[34]

Left realism draws attention to the impact of street crimes and those it targets, the lower class. Left realism rejects the notion that street criminals are revolutionaries who resist capitalist regimes and instead view them as **lumpenproletariats**,[35] unproductive members of society who are considered predators and parasites because they live off of the work of others (i.e., the lower class). The people of the lower class are victims of both street criminals of their own class and noncriminals of the capitalist system.

For left realists, the solution is not abolition of the capitalist regime. Instead, this school of thought advocates for less radical reform. Specifically, it promotes practical policies designed to deal with the issues that give rise to crime and emphasizes prosocial justice through affordable housing, job opportunities, and community policing.[36] In cyberspace, "the need for community policing against cybercrime arises not because of the antagonistic relationship between law enforcement and computer users, but rather from an understanding that . . . [community policing] can be applied to take advantage of the strengths of third-party actors to prevent cybercrime."[37] Community policing can occur online in the form of public-private partnerships between Internet service providers and law enforcement agencies, in proactively enforcing Terms of Service on websites, and in reporting behavior by participants that violates the law.[38]

PEACEMAKING CRIMINOLOGY

Peacemaking criminology differs from radical criminology, which focuses on ways to stop criminal activity through radical societal reform, by paying particular attention to ways to create peace between individuals in society and the criminal justice system.[39] Peacemaking criminologists hold that societies' overemphasis on punishment increases rather than decreases criminal activity. This form of criminological thought advocates for the end of repressive policies; in its place it calls for social change through creation of new practices and implementation of existing policies that serve as viable alternatives to repressive policies. According to this school of thought, the solution to the crime problem is conflict resolution and the diversion of offenders from the criminal justice system.

Peacemaking criminologists are advocates for restorative justice. As discussed in Chapter 4, restorative justice seeks to repair the harm caused by an offender's illicit act against a victim and the community. In restorative justice programs, all participants (victim, offender, and community) come together to discuss the crime and its impact. The outcome of the restorative justice process usually includes some kind of reparation to the victim and consequences for the offender. The restorative justice process has been used to deal with a wide variety of offenses, including trespass, theft, fraud, identity theft, and interpersonal crime (e.g., bullying). This process can also be used when these crimes occur online and the offender is known, and both the victim and offender are willing to engage in the restorative justice process.[40]

BOX 9-1 CAPITAL PUNISHMENT FOR CYBERCRIMINALS: A JUSTIFIED RESPONSE?

The most violent and repressive policy of the state is capital punishment. For certain cybercrimes that result in death, capital punishment has been deemed an appropriate punishment (e.g., Pakistan's Prevention of Electronic Crimes Ordinance of 2007). The main justification for capital punishment is retribution. From a retributivist's view, a cybercriminal deserves to die because he or she has killed another. For Kant and other retributivists, therefore, the only appropriate penalty for killing another human being is death.[41] Retributivists thus justify capital punishment on the grounds that the punishment, the death penalty, fits the crime, namely, the murder of a person or persons. Nonetheless, the reality is that the punishment given, capital punishment, does not exactly fit the crime committed. Supporting this claim, Albert Camus argued,

> But what is capital punishment if not the most premeditated of murders, to which no criminal act, no matter how calculated, can be compared? If there were to be a real equivalence, the death penalty would have to be pronounced upon a criminal who had forewarned his victim of the very moment he would put him to a horrible death, and who, from that time on, had kept him confined at his own discretion for a period of months. It is not in private life that one meets such monsters.[42]

What is more, it is obvious that the exact punishment cannot be given when mass killings have occurred; indeed, a person who has killed more than one person cannot be killed more than once.

From a utilitarian perspective, the provision of capital punishment to a cybercriminal is considered a good result. Indeed, utilitarians, like John Stuart Mill, believed the death penalty serves the greater good.[43] Nevertheless, the utilitarian aim of rehabilitation is not achieved with capital punishment, as offenders are provided no chance of rehabilitation. Additionally,

the benefits of rehabilitation cannot be experienced by society because the offender is executed.

Capital punishment, however, is justified on the grounds of incapacitation. In fact, capital punishment is considered the ultimate form of incapacitation because those subjected to this punishment cannot ever harm society again. Therefore, incapacitation as a justification for capital punishment finds support insofar that the death penalty serves as a permanent solution to the recidivism of the offender; that is, he or she cannot commit any future harm if dead. This claim, however, is problematic. It automatically assumes that the offender will reoffend if released back into society. The reality is that it is impossible to accurately predict whether or not a particular offender will be a future threat to society ("future dangerousness") with any reasonable certainty. Specifically, predictions of future dangerousness by mental health professionals are intuitive, primarily subjective, and notoriously inaccurate.[44] In fact, the American Psychiatric Association has stated that "psychiatric predictions of long-term future dangerousness—even under the best of conditions and on the basis of complete medical data—are of fundamentally low reliability."[45] Despite the lack of research to support assessments on future dangerousness, this factor is still used to justify capital punishment on the grounds of incapacitation of an offender.

Utilitarians also view the death penalty as a legitimate form of punishment because it is believed to deter illicit behavior. Consider, once again, the cost-benefit analysis of an illicit activity. Part of the cost-benefit calculation of cybercriminals is the risk of punishment, even death. If capital punishment was a deterrent, then the cybercriminal would weigh the punishment of receiving the death penalty for certain cybercrimes that result in the loss of life and decide not to commit the offense for fear of receiving the death penalty. Despite claims to the contrary, the death penalty does not serve as a general or specific deterrent of cybercrime; at least, this assumption has not been empirically supported. Even with traditional crimes such as

(continued)

(continued)

murder, general and specific deterrence is not achieved. On the one hand, general deterrence of murder is not achieved through the use of the death penalty. Empirical studies have supported this.[46] On the whole, research on homicide rates and the death penalty do not show that "capital punishment . . . deters murder to a marginally greater extent than does the threat and application of the supposedly lesser punishment of life imprisonment."[47] On the other hand, specific deterrence also cannot be met through capital punishment, because the cyberoffender does not have a chance to reoffend after his or her execution. Peacemaking criminologists reject the violent treatment of offenders, especially capital punishment. Capital punishment and other repressive policies are viewed as perpetuating violence and other forms of criminal behavior.

FEMINIST CRIMINOLOGY

Feminism refers to the various feminist ideologies and movements associated with women's rights and equality with men.

Conservative feminism. Conservative feminism views the causes of gender inequality as relating to evolutionary differences between men and women.[48] Men and women are viewed as biologically unequal with respect to reproductive capacities and hormonal differences. Women and men adapted their behavior according to these biological traits. This perspective does not offer any recommendation or strategy for change due to its view of these differences as a result of biological predispositions.

Liberal feminism. Liberal feminism advocates for equal economic, social, and political rights and treatment of men and women.[49] According to this view, gender inequality exists due to the fact that women are blocked from opportunities in various social spheres which are available to men. Liberal feminism focuses on prohibiting gender discrimination and securing equal rights for men and women. Liberal feminists believe that gender equality can only be achieved through women's sexual liberation.[50] Often this view has led individuals to erroneously equate liberal feminism with pro-porn (this is not necessarily the case). Liberal feminists recommend education and legislation against sex discrimination as a catalyst for changing existing unequal rights and treatment of women.

Radical feminism. Radical feminism views gender inequality as a result of women's biology, particularly the low value placed on so-called feminine qualities and men's desire to dominate and control women.[51] Here, men view themselves as superior

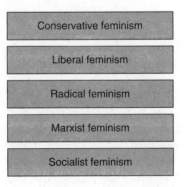

FIGURE 9-1 Types of Feminism.

and being entitled to control women. Radical feminism views gender inequality as the primary oppressor of women of all racial, ethnic, and social classes. In contrast to some liberal feminists, radical feminists believe that pornography subjugates and subordinates women and is ultimately harmful to them.[52]

Marxist feminism. Marxist feminism views gender inequality as the outcome of job inequalities between men and women, the poorly paid jobs predominantly occupied by women, and the trivialization of women's domestic work in the form of housework.[53] Marxist feminism holds that social inequalities are the harbingers of other forms of inequality, such as gender inequality. If a capitalist society is replaced with a communist or socialist regime, the social class inequality and other forms of inequality, such as gender inequality, will be alleviated.

Socialist feminism. Socialist feminism synthesizes central themes of radical feminism and Marxist feminism. Here, gender and class relations between men and women are viewed as central to gender equality. Capitalism and **patriarchy** (i.e., a society in which males hold the power and control females) are viewed as equal and interdependent contributors to gender inequality and women's oppression by men.[54] Women are doubly oppressed through gender and class inequality. Gender inequality is the result of the unequal treatment of individuals within society based on their gender. Class inequality refers to the economic position of women within a capitalist society, which is seen through the unequal pay between men and women in comparable positions in democratic societies.

Irrespective of which perspective one subscribes to, feminists' ultimate goal is to ensure that men and women have equal rights and equal power.

Feminist criminology seeks to explain the causes of female criminality and the differences between male and female offenders. Some gendered perspectives of crime view illicit activities as a consequence of social and economic inequality between men and women.[55] By contrast, other perspectives link emancipation of women to crime committed by female offenders by arguing that female crime results from increasing gender equality, which has provided women with opportunities to engage in legitimate and illegitimate activities that were previously only available to men. Criminologists subscribing to this perspective thus view female offending as an inevitable consequence of the women's liberation movement.[56] The effect of the women's liberation movement on female offending has been studied extensively by Freda Adler and Rita Simon. Adler, in *Sisters in Crime*, claimed that "the movement for full equality has a darker side which has been slighted even by the scientific community. . . . In the same way that women are demanding equal opportunity in the fields of legitimate endeavor, a similar number of determined women are forcing their way into the world of major crimes."[57] Likewise, Simon, in *Women in Crime*, attributed increases in female offending with respect to property crimes, such as theft and embezzlement, to the increase in women in the workforce; similar results, however, were not found for violent crimes.[58] Others opposed the positions of Adler and Simon[59] because their hypotheses "assumed [that] improving girls' and women's economic conditions would lead to an increase in female crime when almost all the existing criminological literature stresses the role played by discrimination and poverty (and unemployment or underemployment) in the creation of crime."[60]

BOX 9-2 FROM THE PERSPECTIVE OF TRAIT THEORIES: THE CRIMINAL WOMAN

In *The Female Offender*, Cesare Lombroso and William Ferrero examined female criminals, whom they viewed as abnormal—an aberration of society.[61] In their work, they stated, "rarely is a woman wicked, but when she is she surpasses the man."[62] They particularly noted a "point of superiority in the female born criminal over the male lies in the refined, . . . cruelty with which she accomplishes her crime. To kill her enemy does not satisfy her, she needs to see him suffer and know the full taste of death."[63]

Utilizing evolutionary theories, Cesare Lombroso and William Ferrero argued that women were "underdeveloped men" and were evolutionarily inferior to men. They based this conclusion on their observation that the average female brain and body is smaller than the male brain and body. Like Lombroso's work on male offenders,[64] the work by Cesare Lombroso and William Ferrero distinguished between different types of female criminals. Unlike "born female offenders," who are viewed as "more perverse than those of their male prototypes"[65] and "completely and intensely depraved," the occasional female offender exhibits a milder form of "perversity and vice" and does not desire "the higher virtues of the sex, such as chastity and maternal love."[66] Overall, female offenders lacked the maternal instinct and had an excessive desire for cruelty, vengeance, and greed.[67] The work of Cesare Lombroso and William Ferrero has been refuted. However, other theories about female offending have been based on **biological determinism**, which holds that human behavior is attributed to the biological makeup of an individual (e.g., genes and physiology).

Differences in psychological and sociological factors between men and women can also explain gender variations in crime.[68] Research has shown that male partners or potential love interests have initiated women into criminal activity.[69] Moreover, the threat of losing established relationships has been found to serve as a trigger for female crime.[70] In addition to these factors, research has shown the following consistent causal factors for male and female offending: learning, differential association, social control, anomie, strain, and self-control.[71] For instance, social learning theory and differential association theory have been used to explain male and female offending:[72] both men and women learn illicit behavior through socialization; however, men "have more opportunities to learn and perform antisocial behavior due to the lower control exerted over them by conventional contexts and to their higher contact with unconventional groups."[73] Indeed, men and women differ in their access to criminal opportunities. There is a glass ceiling of the underworld for women;[74] existing "institutional sexism in the underworld severely limits female involvement in crime groups, ranging from syndicates to loosely structured groups. . ."[75] As in the upperworld, females in the underworld are disadvantaged in terms of selection and recruitment, in the range of career paths and access to them, and in opportunities for tutelage, skill development, and rewards."[76]

Other studies have shown that a combination of the above-mentioned causal factors may well explain gender differences in crime. For example, Thomas Bernard and Karen Haylslett explained gender differences in male and female juvenile offending by combining elements of self-control theory and attachment theory.[77] They attributed variations in male and female juvenile offending to disruptions in childhood attachments with parents or primary caregivers, which ultimately lead to low self-control. Low self-control and disruptions in attachment are disproportionately experienced by boys due to existing cultural differences in the treatment of boys and girls (e.g., gender roles and the manner in which men and women are socialized).

Women's roles and socialization play a role in female offending. According to Hirschi and Gottfredson, the traditional roles of men and women, in which women stay home and take care of the children and men work and provide for the family, can explain low levels of female criminality.[78] Women's attachments and commitments to the conventional roles and norms of women explain low rates of female offending. From a young age, women are socialized to believe that the roles for them are wives and mothers.[79] The interpersonal skills they are taught (e.g., sensitivity, empathy toward others, and prioritizing relationships over themselves) are meant to prepare them for these roles. Gendered norms exist whereby women are taught and encouraged to value social relationships.[80] In line with this reasoning, traditionally, women have been rewarded for creating and maintaining relationships and observing family obligations.[81]

Patriarchal societies shape gender differences in crime. A patriarchal society advocates independence for men and dependence for women. In this society, control is exerted over women; this control is viewed as necessary because women are seen as the weaker species (i.e., lacking the physical strength of men) and in need of protection. Moreover, women are more heavily monitored than men by the family unit in this society; this control is believed to constrain women's involvement in crime.[82] Patriarchal societies value so-called masculine traits of individualism, competitiveness, and aggressiveness and minimize the value of so-called feminist traits such as nurturing, caregiving, noncompetitiveness, and cooperation.[83] Generally, women are viewed as being submissive and are socialized to adopt these so-called feminine traits.[84] Women are also taught to avoid aggression, whereas men are taught to utilize aggression as a form of control and to exercise authority over others and to be competitive and providers for their household.[85] In contrast to these traditional roles, in today's society a **ladette culture** is present, in which women have adopted behaviors traditionally attributed to men.[86]

R. W. Connell used the term **hegemonic masculinity** to describe the actions that promote a dominant position of men in society and the subordination of women.[87] Hegemonic masculinity also subordinates the masculinities that do not fit with the norms of hegemonic males. It emphasizes the ways to be a "real man" in society by being tough, aggressive, and competitive and exerting power and control over others. Certain male cybercriminals are driven by their desire for power, for example, male hackers.[88] In addition to power, developing one's technological skills, technical prowess, and superior coding skills in hacking has become synonymous with a hegemonic masculine identity.[89] Furthermore, the male hacker views himself as a "rebel enemy of establishment and conformity."[90] This struggle between the male hacker and those in power "constitutes a significant portion of formative masculinity."[91] If the male hacker is able to "resist and overcome . . . boundaries and authority," he becomes independent and creates hegemonic masculinity.[92]

VARIATIONS IN CYBERCRIMINALITY: MIND THE GENDER GAP

Internet relay chats (IRCs), multi-user dimensions (MUDs; virtual reality environments), and MUDs, object-oriented (MOOs; virtual reality environments where users can build spaces and create objects), and other virtual environments are gendered spaces.[93] Historically, these virtual environments were predominantly male, as few women participated in them. Fast-forward to the present, and one finds greater involvement of women within these and other virtual environments.

Women have infiltrated other previously male-dominant positions in cyberculture, such as cybersecurity. Parisa Tabriz, for instance, is a hacker who works for Google as an information security engineer and self-identifies as Security Princess.[94] Women have also infiltrated cyberspace subcultures, particularly the hacker subculture. One of the first known women to become part of a hacking group was Susan Headley (also known as Susan Thunder). Research shows that hacking is an overwhelmingly male activity.[95] Nonetheless, there are female hackers besides Susan Headley. Kim Vanvaeck ("Gigabyte") has been linked to hundreds of computer viruses but has yet to be convicted.[96] Another well-known female hacker is Jude Milhon (known as St. Jude), who developed a hacking group known as Cypherpunks.[97] A woman known only by the moniker Natasha Grigori created antichildporn.org, an organization of hackers who identify child pornographers online and report them to law enforcement authorities.[98] Women are also part of hacktivist groups. Carmin Karasic, associated with the hacktivist group Electronic Civil Disobedience, helped write a program that the group uses (FloodNet) to bombard and overwhelm their target's resources with online access requests.[99] The penetration of these subcultures by women has not been easy, as many hacking forums and websites have a locker room culture, which is characterized by misogyny and sexism.[100]

Female cyberpredators also exist, of course. Gemma Baker was sentenced to thirty-three months' imprisonment for sexual assault, creating fake online social media accounts on Facebook, and using these accounts to defraud women into thinking they were in a romantic relationship with her.[101] Courtney Reschke was sentenced to twenty years for using Facebook to contact several of her children's male friends who were fifteen years old and luring them over to her home to have sex with her.[102] In addition to social media websites, cyberpredators use online gaming consoles to identify and contact their targets. Rachel Ann Hicks received twelve years in prison and five years of probation for traveling to a different state and having sexual relations with a minor, a thirteen-year-old boy she met and formed a relationship with online through Xbox Live.[103] Female cyberpredators have also posted online advertisements to meet and ultimately form relationships with their victims or with other like-minded individuals. For example, Theresa Goddard, a woman from British Columbia, Canada, using the online handle "pervstepmom" posted an online advertisement where she described herself as "a 'perverted single female' looking to find a man with children whom she could molest."[104] She was subsequently contacted by someone claiming to be a fifty-one-year-old man with two children (a nine-year-old boy and a ten-year-old girl) similarly seeking an incest family.[105] The person who contacted her was an undercover police officer. Goddard discussed her plans of molesting his children. She was arrested after she traveled to Virginia and met the undercover police officer.[106]

The reality is that women engage in a wide variety of cybercrimes; in view of that, gender is not an adequate predictor of cybercrime. Nevertheless, a gender gap exists with respect to opportunities for cyberoffending (e.g., computer usage and membership in cyberclubs).[107] What is more, consistent with other findings,[108] girls and women report less involvement in cybercrime than do boys and men.[109] Ultimately, more research is required on the role of gender in cyberoffending in order to understand why men are more likely than women to engage in certain cybercrimes.[110]

CYBERFEMINISM

Cyberfeminism refers to the principles and practices of feminists concerning the Internet, computers, and related technology. Cyberfeminism primarily examines the role of gender in cyberspace and the treatment of women online. There are two general schools of thought in cyberfeminism. One school views cyberspace as a liberating environment for women (**cyberutopianism**); the other views cyberspace as another forum within which women can be oppressed (**cyberdystopianism**).

Cyberutopianism views the Internet as a utopia where individuals are freed from social constructs. The belief is that gender inequality will become less pronounced as the Internet and Internet-enabled digital devices become more accessible to women.[111] According to this view, cyberspace "blur[s] the boundaries between human and machine . . . mak[ing] the categories of female and male obsolete."[112] The Internet provides a level of invisibility to users that enables them to mask their gender, race, and other characteristics should they desire to do so. This anonymity is also present in IRCs, MUDs, MOOs, and online games, such as massively multiplayer online games (MMOGs) and massively multiplayer online role-playing games (MMORPGs). For example, participants in IRCs can choose nicknames to mask their true identities. Research has shown that "women tended to mask their gender with their pseudonym choice while males did not."[113] Gender swapping can occur online, whereby individuals create a new persona "to express multiple and often unexplored aspects of the self, to play with their identity and to try out new ones."[114] Judy Wajcman's research has revealed that "many more men adopt a female persona than vice versa."[115] Players of virtual realities and games choose the name, gender, and characteristics of their players and ultimately can build an online persona of their choice. Accordingly, cyberspace serves as an environment that frees women from stereotypical gender norms, enabling them to present themselves in any way they choose without conventional restraints. The invisibility and anonymity afforded by the Internet lead cyberfeminists to view cyberspace as creating a level playing field for men and women.[116]

The reality is, however, that the Internet is still gendered, raced, and classed. This is the perspective of *cyberdystopianism*, which views cyberspace as reproducing power hierarchies that exist offline.[117] Cyberspace is also viewed as intensifying gender differences instead of neutralizing them.[118] Cyberspace is thus a new discriminatory space; the prevalence of harassment, threats, verbal abuse, and ridicule of self-identified women in virtual environments attests to this. Consider Caroline Criado-Perez's very public campaign to have a woman featured again on a British banknote following the replacement of Elizabeth Fry with Winston Churchill on the 5 Great British Pound (GBP) banknote.[119] Her campaign was successful and Jane Austen was placed on the back of a 10 GBP banknote.[120] While victorious in her campaign, she received numerous abusive, harassing, and threatening comments online, including threats of sexual violence and serious bodily harm via Twitter for her actions. Unfortunately, despite claims to the contrary, cyberspace does not provide a safe and bias-free environment for women, at least not on social media platforms and other platforms that are open to all users. The same could be said about other users who have been discriminated against based on race, ethnicity, sexual orientation, and even religion.

#GAMERGATE

Zoe Quinn developed an interactive story about the depression of a young adult called *Depression Quest*. In August 2014, her ex-boyfriend, Eron Gjoni, posted a blog about her attacking her character and credibility. He falsely accused her of cheating on him to further her career in the gaming industry.[121] One such accusation involved a relationship with an individual, Nathan Grayson, who worked at a Gawker property gaming site known as Kotaku (a site that posts gaming news). Gjoni alleged that Quinn's relationship with Grayson led to a favorable review of her game on Kotaku (an allegation which has been proven false).[122] This blog post triggered a cyberharassment campaign against Quinn. In addition to the barrage of hateful, harassing, abusive, and threatening e-mails she received and similar messages about her which were posted on social media platforms and other websites, several of her online accounts were hacked (e.g., Tumblr, Skype, and Dropbox accounts) and she was "doxed" (i.e., her personal information, including phone number and home address were posted online).

Another target of the cyberharassment campaign was Anita Sarkeesian, who analyzed female characters in video games through a feminist lens in a YouTube series titled *Tropes vs. Women in Video Games*, on her website Feminist Frequency.[123] For her feminist critiques of video games and characters, she was cyberharassed and bombarded with hateful and vitriolic comments and threats of bodily harm online and offline. Quinn and Sarkeesian were not the sole targets of the campaign. Others who expressed opinions unfavorable or contradictory to the views of the cyberharassers, even those who poked fun at the controversy, such as Brianna Wu, a female video game developer and co-founder of the game development studio Giant Spacekat, were also targeted.[124] This cyberharassment campaign was given a hashtag by actor Adam Baldwin: #GamerGate.[125]

#GamerGate also criticized those it viewed as social justice warriors. A **social justice warrior**, a term recently added to Oxford dictionaries, is an informal, derogatory way to describe "a person who expresses or promotes socially progressive views."[126] This label is used for people viewed as disingenuous and only engaging in social justice activities or discussing social justice issues to elevate their own position. Purportedly, #GamerGate was a form of protest against political correctness. Individuals also allegedly started the campaign to demand ethics in gaming journalism. Their reactions, however, were not even remotely associated with protesting political correctness and ethics in gaming journalism. These individuals engaged in a cyberharassment campaign primarily against women on Twitter and other online platforms such as Reddit, 4chan, and 8chan. Doxing occurred on these forums; so too did threats of serious bodily harm, such as rape and murder, against

IMAGE 9-2 Screenshot of #GamerGate Tweets.

targets. Quinn noted that before #Gamergate was given its name, "it was nothing but [individuals] trying to get me to kill myself, trying to get others to hurt me, going after my family. There is no mention of ethics in journalism at all outside making the same accusation everyone makes of successful women; that clearly she got to where she is because she had sex with someone."[127] By posting nude photographs and personal data of targets and harassing, abusive, and threatening comments, the actual purpose of #GamerGate was to frighten, defame, debase, and demean targets, attack their credibility, and have others doubt the targets' integrity.

Some individuals who are part of leaderless movements have used the movements as a cover to push their own personal, self-serving interests.[128] This similarly occurred in #GamerGate. Voices of those who might have posted with the hashtag GamerGate to express concerns for ethics in online gaming journalism were drowned out by misogynists, sexists, and others consumed with rage and a mob mentality targeting anyone who opposes them.[129] Ultimately, #GamerGate pitted those for the campaign and in support of its actions (the *us* group) against everyone else that criticized or did not support the campaign in any way (the *them* group). Those in the *us* group engaged in social censorship to silence anyone who opposed them. The gaming industry has largely condemned #GamerGate.[130]

CASE STUDY

Social media platforms should foster free speech by creating an environment in which individuals can speak without fear. Environments free from abuse, harassment, and threats empower individuals to freely express themselves. As such, these social media websites prohibit certain types of conduct on their platforms, such as abuse, harassment, and threats.

It is important to remember that social media platforms are private and not public platforms, which means that these private platforms can regulate conduct as they see fit. When individuals utilize these platforms, they agree to the platform's Terms of Service agreement. These Terms of Service set out the appropriate rules of behavior. It is these rules that individuals are supposed to follow when they utilize these platforms.

Milo Yiannopoulos is a writer for the online tabloid *Breitbart*. He has been characterized as a "professional troll," a person who makes a living posting noxious and sexist comments on Twitter.[131] After a feminist writer complained that she was harassed on Twitter, Yiannopoulos tweeted, "You deserve to be harassed you social justice loser."[132] In another post he stated, "Is it any wonder successful gay men hate feminists, when women, in tax terms as elsewhere, are so . . . well, parasitical?"[133] Yiannopoulos is known for his role in #Gamergate. He wrote an online piece declaring that the gaming industry was "under siege by an 'army of sociopathic feminist programmers and campaigners' who are 'lying, bullying and manipulating their way around the Internet for profit and attention.'"[134] Yiannopoulos is also known for identifying individuals for his followers to target, a phenomenon known as dogpiling.[135] After he posts a Tweet about a target, the target's Twitter account is bombarded with abusive and harassing tweets. Twitter had originally given Yiannopoulos verified status. Verified status is assigned by Twitter at its discretion to "users in music, acting, fashion, government, politics, religion, journalism, media, sports, business and other key interest areas."[136] Verified status is used to assert that the person is who they say they are. This status helps differentiate legitimate accounts from accounts that impersonate users. In 2016, Twitter deverified Yiannopoulos.[137] His account remained active on Twitter until July 2016 (when he was banned), but during that time it was no longer an account with verified status.

The decision of Twitter to deverify Yiannopoulos' account has been praised by some and criticized by Yiannopoulos and others on the grounds of censoring free speech.

1. How would a cyberfeminist describe Twitter?
2. What do you think of Twitter's decision to deverify Yiannopoulos?
3. Was there a better way for Twitter to respond to this person?
4. How should Twitter handle similar individuals on its platforms?

REVIEW QUESTIONS

1. Can conflict theory explain cybercrime?
2. What is Marxist criminology? Can it explain cyberspace policies?
3. How can the conflict experienced by hackers be resolved?
4. What would a peacekeeping criminologist view as an ideal punishment for a cybercriminal?
5. Would a peacekeeping criminologist support the death penalty for a cybercriminal? Why or why not?
6. What is hegemonic masculinity? Can it explain hacking?
7. Are online forums, games, and virtual realities gendered spaces? Why do you think so?
8. What is the cybercrime gender gap?
9. What is cyberfeminism? Describe its two schools of thought.
10. What is #GamerGate? Whom did it target?

LAWS

Prevention of Electronic Crimes Ordinance of 2007 (Pakistan)

DEFINITIONS

Biological determinism. Biological determinism holds that human behavior is attributed to the biological makeup of an individual.

Bourgeoisie. A term used to describe the upper class, which has power and wealth.

Conflict theories. Theories exploring the struggles between individuals and groups with power differentials.

Conservative feminism. A type of feminism that views gender inequality as the outcome of evolutionary differences between men and women.

Cyberdystopianism. A school of thought of cyberfeminism that views cyberspace as a forum within which women can be oppressed.

Cyberfeminism. The ideas, principles, and practices of feminists concerning the Internet, computers, and related technology.

Cyberutopianism. A school of thought of cyberfeminism that views cyberspace as a liberating environment for females.

Feminism. The ideas, principles, and movements relating to women's rights and equality with men.

Feminist criminology. A form of criminology that seeks to explain the causes of female criminality and the differences between male and female offenders.

Hegemonic masculinity. A term used to describe the actions that promote a dominant position of men in society and the subordination of women.

Ladette culture. A subculture wherein women adopt behaviors that are traditionally attributed to men.

Left realism. Left realism holds that crime is linked to social problems and is committed primarily by and against marginalized communities.

Liberal feminism. A type of feminism that promotes women's economic, social, and political rights and equal treatment between men and women.

Lumpenproletariat. A term used to describe unproductive members of society who are considered predators and parasites because they live off of the work of others.

Marxist criminology. Criminology based on Marxist thought, which holds that conflict in a capitalist society is inevitable because of the conditions of a capitalist society that empower those in the upper class and in positions of power and disenfranchise others.

Marxist feminism. A type of feminism that views gender inequality as the product of inequalities in employment between men and women, poorly paid jobs predominantly occupied by women, and the trivialization of women's domestic work.

Patriarchy. A male-dominated society in which males hold the power and females are controlled.

Peacemaking criminology. A form of criminology that advocates for the end of repressive policies and focuses on ways to stop criminal activity through radical societal reform in order to create peace between individuals in society and the criminal justice system.

Primitive rebellion hypothesis. Crime is the rational outcome of the struggle against the existing prevailing conditions a working class individual is faced with in a capitalist society.

Proletariat. A term used to describe the working class, which does not have power or wealth.

Radical criminology. Radical criminology holds that capitalist societies precipitate crime by enabling those with power to use laws to control less powerful groups in society and suppress any threats to those in power.

Radical feminism. A type of feminism that views males' entitlement and perceived superiority as the reasons for gender inequality, which oppresses women.

Social justice warrior. A term used to describe someone who is viewed as disingenuous and only engaging in social justice activities or discussing social justice issues to elevate that person's own position.

Socialist feminism. A type of feminism that views capitalism and patriarchy as equal and interdependent contributors to gender inequality and women's oppression by men.

ENDNOTES

1. T. More, *Utopia* (1516; London: Bibliolis Books, 2010), 24.

2. Unlike Marx, Max Weber focused on conflict produced from a multitude of societal sources, of which class was one but not the most prominent one. For him, class structures were viewed as acceptable.

3. The work was originally written in 1848. K. Marx and F. Engels, *Communist Manifesto*, trans. S. Moore (1848; New York: International Publishers, 2014).

4. Marx and Engels, *Communist Manifesto*.

5. This work was first published in 1845. F. Engels, *The Condition of the Working Class in England in 1844* (Harmondsworth, UK: Penguin, 1987).

6. Engels, *The Condition of the Working Class in England in 1844*, 142–144.

7. Ibid.

8. Ibid., 144–145.

9. W. A Bonger, *Criminality and Economic Conditions*, trans. H. P. Horton (Boston, MA: Little, Brown, 1916).

10. Ibid.

11. Twitter, "FAQs About Verified Accounts," https://support.twitter.com/articles/119135#.

12. "With this new filtering system, tweets sent directly to an individual which are from recently registered accounts and use language similar to previously flagged messages will not automatically show up in the mention column of the user. The featured tweets will still exist on the service, and won't be deleted, but the user being targeted will not see the harassment." A. Hern, "Twitter Announces Crackdown on Abuse with New Filter and Tighter Rules," *Guardian*, April 21, 2015, http://www.theguardian.com/technology/2015/apr/21/twitter-filter-notifications-for-all-accounts-abuse.

13. Associated Press, "Jeffrey Jones, Paul Reubens Charged in Porn Investigation," *USA Today*, November 16, 2002, http://usatoday30.usatoday.com/life/2002-11-15-pee-wee_x.htm; BBC News, "Actor's 'Porn' Claim Rejected," February 13, 2003, http://news.bbc.co.uk/2/hi/entertainment/2756621.stm.

14. T. Ove, "Ex-Mayor of Seven Fields Sentenced to Prison for Child Pornography," *Pittsburgh Post-Gazette*, February 24, 2016, http://www.post-gazette.com/local/north/2016/02/24/Ex-mayor-of-Seven-Fields-sentenced-to-prison-for-child-pornography-pittsburgh-bayne/stories/201602240160.

15. Bonger, *Criminality and Economic Conditions*.

16. R. Quinney, *Class, State, and Crime: On the Theory and Practice of Criminal Justice* (New York: David McKay, 1977), 58.

17. R. M. Bohm and B. Vogel, *A Primer on Crime and Delinquency Theory*, 3rd ed. (Belmont, CA: Wadsworth, 2011), 125.

18. K. Marx and F. Engels, *The German Ideology* (London: Lawrence and Wishart, 1965), 365–367.

19. Bonger, *Criminality and Economic Conditions*.

20. Ibid.

21. Marx and Engels, *Communist Manifesto*.

22. Ibid.

23. Ibid.

24. M. Wark, *Hacker Manifesto*, accessed August 4, 2016, para. 12, http://subsol.c3.hu/subsol_2/contributors0/warktext.html.

25. W. Chambliss and R. Seidman, *Law, Order and Power* (Reading, MA: Addison-Wesley, 1971).

26. Hacktivists use the Internet, computers, and related technologies to gain access or exceed authorized access to a system in order to modify, delete, or render temporarily or permanently unusable a system or website in furtherance of a political goal.

27. J. S. Murphy, "How Mr. Robot Killed the Centerpiece of Prestige Television: Capitalism," *Vanity Fair*, September 2, 2015, http://www.vanityfair.com/hollywood/2015/09/mr-robot -capitalism.

28. A. Eyerly, "TV Preview Wealth Disparity, Hackers and Cyber Threats in 'Mr. Robot,'" *Los Angeles Times*, May 29, 2015, http://www.latimes.com/entertainment/tv/la-ca-st-tvpreview-robot -20150531-story.html.

29. *Mr. Robot*, Episode 10 ("eps1.9zer0-daY.avi"), September 2, 2015.

30. P. Taylor, *Hackers: Crime in the Digital Sublime* (London: Routledge, 1999); M. L. Rustad, "Private Enforcement of the Cybercrime on the Electronic Frontier," *Southern California Interdisciplinary Law Journal* 11, no. 1 (2001): 71.

31. Wark, *Hacker Manifesto*, para 14.

32. Ibid.

33. J. Lea and J. Young, *What Is To Be Done About Law and Order?* (Harmondsworth, UK: Penguin, 1984).

34. Ibid.

35. Marx and Engels, *Communist Manifesto*.

36. Community Oriented Policing Services, "Community Policing Defined," U.S. Department of Justice, rev. 2014, http://ric-zai-inc.com/Publications/cops-p157-pub.pdf.

37. B. R. Jones, "Virtual Neighborhood Watch: Open Source Software and Community Policing Against Cybercrime," *Journal of Criminal Law & Criminology* 97, no. 2 (2007): 617.

38. L. Chi, W. K. Chan, G. Seow, and K. Tam, "Transplanting Social Capital to the Online World: Insights From Two Experimental Studies," *Journal of Organizational Computing and Electronic Commerce 19*, no. 3 (2009): 214–215.

39. H. E. Pepinsky and R. Quinney, eds., *Criminology as Peacemaking* (Bloomington: Indiana University Press, 1991).

40. See the case study in Chapter 4.

41. I. Kant, *Justice and Punishment*, trans. W. Hastie, in *Philosophical Perspectives on Punishment*, ed. G. Ezorsky (Albany: State University of New York Press, 1972), 106.

42. A. Camus, *Reflections on the Guillotine*, trans. R. Howard (Michigan City, IN: Fridtjof-Karla, 1959), 25.

43. J. S. Mill, *In Favor of Capital Punishment*, Speech Given Before Parliament on April 21, 1868, Opposing a Bill (proposed by Mr. Gilpin) that Banned Capital Punishment, http://ethics .sandiego.edu/books/Mill/Punishment/.

44. J. R. Aker, R. M. Bohm, and C. S. Lanier, eds., *America's Experiment with Capital Punishment: Reflections of the Past, Present, and Future of the Ultimate Penalty Sanctions* (Durham, NC: Carolina Academic Press, 1998), 187.

45. American Psychiatric Association, *Brief Amicus Curiae: Barefoot v. Estelle* (No. 82-6080, October 1982), 4.

46. For example, R. Hood and C. Hoyle, *The Death Penalty: A Worldwide Perspective*, 4th ed. (Oxford: Oxford University Press, 2008); J. J. Donohue and J. Wolfers, "Uses and Abuses of Empirical Evidence in the Death Penalty Debate," *Stanford Law Review* 58, no. 3 (2005): 791–846; L. Katz, S. D. Levitt, and E. Shustorovich, "Prison Conditions, Capital Punishment, and Deterrence," *American Law and Economics Review* 5, no. 2 (2003): 318–343.

47. Hood and Hoyle, *The Death Penalty: A Worldwide Perspective*, 230.

48. K. O'Sullivan, "Review: Feminism and Political Philosophy," *Feminist Studies* 8, no. 1 (1982): 179–194; J. Stacey, "The New Conservative Feminism," *Feminist Studies* 9, no. 3 (1983): 559–583.

49. R. Tong, *Feminist Thought: A Comprehensive Introduction* (Boulder, CO: Westview, 1989); L. Kensinger, "(In)Quest of Liberal Feminism," *Hypatia* 12, no. 4 (1997): 178–197.

50. K. Hall, "Cyberfeminism," in *Computer-Mediated Communication: Linguistic, Social, and Cross-cultural Perspectives*, ed. S. Herring (Amsterdam: John Benjamins, 1996), 148–149; A. M. Jaggar, *Feminist Politics and Human Nature* (Totowa, NJ: Rowman & Littlefield, 1983); S. Wendell, "(Qualified) Defense of Liberal Feminism," *Hypatia* 2, no. 2 (1987): 82.

51. M. Daly, *Gyn/Ecology: The Metaethics of Radical Feminism* (Boston: Beacon Press, 1978); C. Gilligan, *In a Different Voice* (Cambridge, MA: Harvard University Press, 1982); C. A. MacKinnon, *Toward a Feminist Theory of the State* (Cambridge, MA: Harvard University Press, 1989); C. A. MacKinnon, *Feminism Unmodified* (Cambridge, MA: Harvard University Press, 1987); M. O'Brien, *The Politics of Reproduction* (New York: Routledge & Kegan Paul, 1981).

52. A. M. Jaggar, *Feminist Politics and Human Nature* (Totowa, NJ: Rowman & Littlefield, 1983).

53. J. W. Messerschmidt, "'Doing Gender:' The Impact and Future of a Salient Sociological Concept," *Gender and Society* 23, no. 1 (2009): 85–88; D. E. Smith, "A Sociology for Women," in J. A. Sherman and E. T. Beck, eds., *The Prism of Sex: Essays in the Sociology of Knowledge* (Madison, WI: University of Wisconsin Press, 1979); S. Gorelick, "Contradictions of Feminist Methodology," *Gender and Society* 5, no. 4 (1991): 459–477.

54. J. W. Messerschmidt, *Capitalism, Patriarchy, and Crime* (Totowa, NJ: Rowman & Littlefield, 1986); J. W. Messerschmidt, *Masculinities and Crime: Critique and Reconceptualization of Theory* (Lanham, MD: Rowman & Littlefield, 1993), 55.

55. S. Box and C. Hale, "Liberation and Female Criminality in England and Wales," *British Journal of Criminology* 23, no. 1 (1983): 35–49; S. Box and C. Hale, "Liberation/Emancipation, Economic Marginalization, or Less Chivalry: The Relevance of Three Theoretical Arguments to Female Crime Patterns in England and Wales, 1951–1980," *Criminology* 22, no. 4 (1984): 473–497; K. Heimer, "Changes in the Gender Gap in Crime and Women's Economic Marginalization," *Criminal Justice* 1 (2000): 427–483; K. Heimer, S. M. Wittrock, and H. Unal, "Gender, Crime and the Economic Marginalization of Women," in *Gender and Crime: Patterns of Victimization and Offending*, ed. K. Heimer and C. Kruttschitt (New York: New York University Press, 2005), 115–136; G. Hunnicutt and L. M. Broidy, "Liberation and Economic Marginalization: A Reformulation and Test of (Formerly?) Competing Models," *Journal of Research in Crime and Delinquency* 41, no. 2 (2014): 130–155.

56. F. Adler, *Sisters in Crime: The Rise of the New Female Criminal* (New York: McGraw-Hill, 1975); R. J. Simon, *Women and Crime* (Lexington, MA: Lexington Books, 1975).

57. Adler, *Sisters in Crime: The Rise of the New Female Criminal*, 3.

58. Simon, *Women and Crime*, 46–47.

59. L. Crites, *The Female Offender* (Lexington, MA: Lexington Books, 1976); L. H. Bowker, *Women and Crime in America* (New York: Macmillan, 1981); M. Chesney-Lind, "Girls' Crime and Woman's Place: Toward a Feminist Model of Female Delinquency," *Crime and Delinquency* 35, no. 1 (1989): 5–29; K. Daly, "Women's Pathways to Felony Court: Feminist Theories of Lawbreaking and Problems of Representation," *Southern California Review of Law and Women's Studies* 2, no. 1 (1992): 11–52.

60. M. Chesney-Lind and R. G. Shelden, *Girls, Delinquency and Juvenile Justice* (Pacific Grove, CA: Brooks/Cole, 1992), 77; D. Steffensmeier and E. Allan, "Gender and Crime: Toward a Gendered Theory of Female Offending," *Annual Review of Sociology* 22, (1996): 469–470.

61. C. Lombroso and W. Ferrero, *The Female Offender* (New York: Appleton and Company, 1898), 104.

62. Ibid., 147.

63. Ibid., 148.

64. C. Lombroso, *The Criminal Man*, trans. M. Gibson and N. H. Rafter (Durham, NC: Duke University Press, 2006).

65. Lombroso and Ferrero, *The Female Offender*, 147.

66. Ibid., 192.

67. Ibid., 147–148, 155, and 162.

68. J. Graham and B. Bowling, *Young People and Crime* (London: Home Office, 1995).

69. M. E. Gilfus, "From Victims to Survivors to Offenders: Women's Routes of Entry and Immersion Into Street Crime," *Women & Criminal Justice* 4, no. 1 (1992): 63–90; D. Steffensmeier, "Organizational Properties and Sex-Segregation in the Underworld: Building a Sociological Theory of Sex Differences in Crime," *Social Forces* 61, no. 4 (1983): 1010–1032; D. Steffensmeier and R. Terry, "Institutional Sexism in the Underworld: A View From the Inside," *Sociological Inquiry* 56, no. 3 (1986): 304–323; D. Steffensmeier and E. Allan, "Gender and Crime: Toward a Gendered Theory of Female Offending," *Annual Review of Sociology* 22 (1996): 467.

70. Steffensmeier and Allan, "Gender and Crime: Toward a Gendered Theory of Female Offending," 467.

71. For example, J. Hagan, *Structural Criminology* (New Brunswick, NJ: Rutgers University Press, 1989); D. A. Smith and R. Paternoster, "The Gender Gap in Theories of Deviance: Issues and Evidence," *Journal of Research in Crime and Delinquency* 24, no. 2 (1987): 140–172.

72. P. C. Giordano and S. M. Rockwell, "Differential Association Theory and Female Crime," in *Of Crime and Criminality: The Use of Theory in Everyday Life,* ed. S. Simpson (Thousand Oaks, CA: Pine Forge, 2000), 3–24; K. Heimer and S. De Costner, "The Gendering of Violent Delinquency," *Criminology* 37, no. 2 (1999): 277–318.

73. V. M. Trillo and L. M. Redondo, "The Role of Gender Identity in Adolescents' Antisocial Behavior," *Psicothema* 25, no. 4 (2013): 507.

74. D. Steffensmeier and J. T. Ulmer, *Confessions of a Dying Thief: Understanding Criminal Careers and Criminal Enterprise* (New Brunswick, NJ: Transaction Aldine, 2005).

75. D. Steffensmeier, "Organizational Properties and Sex-Segregation in the Underworld: Building a Sociological Theory of Sex Differences in Crime," *Social Forces* 61, no. 4 (1983): 1010–1032.

76. Steffensmeier and Allan, "Gender and Crime: Toward a Gendered Theory of Female Offending," 478.

77. K. L. Hayslett-Mccall and T. J. Bernard, "Attachment, Masculinity, and Self-Control: A Theory of Male Crime Rates," *Theoretical Criminology* 6, no. 1 (2002): 5–33.

78. T. Hirschi, *Causes of Delinquency* (Berkeley, California: University of California Press, 1969); M. R. Gottfredson and T. Hirschi, *A General Theory of Crime* (Palo Alto, CA: Stanford University Press, 1990).

79. A. M. Beutel and M. M. Marini, "Gender and Values," *American Sociological Review* 60, no. 3 (1995): 436–448; L. R. Brody, "Gender Differences in Emotional Development: A Review of

Theories and Research," *Journal of Personality* 53, no. 2 (1985): 102–149; A. Rossi, "Gender and Parenthood," *American Sociological Review* 49, no. 1 (1984): 1–19.

80. A. H. Eagley, *Sex Differences in Social Behavior: A Social-Role Interpretation* (Hillsdale, NJ: Lawrence Erlbaum, 1987), 16; K. A. Fox, M. R. Nobles, and B. S. Fisher, "A Multi-Theoretical Framework to Assess Gendered Stalking Victimization: The Utility of Self-Control, Social Learning, and Control Balance Theories," *Justice Quarterly* 33, no. 2 (2014): 339.

81. Steffensmeier and Allan, "Gender and Crime: Toward a Gendered Theory of Female Offending," 476.

82. P. Giordano, S. Cernkovich, and M. Pugh, "Friendships and Delinquency," *American Journal of Sociology* 91, no. 5 (1986): 1170–1202.

83. S. Grana, *Women and (In)Justice: The Criminal and Civil Effects of the Common Law on Women's Lives* (Boston, MA: Allyn & Bacon, 2002); J. W. Messerschmidt, *Masculinities and Crime: Critique and Reconceptualization of Theory* (Lanham, MD: Rowman & Littlefield, 1993).

84. Giordano, Cernkovich, and Pugh, "Friendships and Delinquency," 1170–1202.

85. A. Campbell and S. Muncer, "Sex Differences in Aggression: Social Representation and Social Roles," *British Journal of Social Psychology* 33, no. 2 (1994): 233–240.

86. C. Jackson and P. Tinkler, "'Ladettes' and 'Modern Girls': 'Troublesome' Young Femininities," *Sociological Review* 55, no. 2 (2007): 260.

87. R. Connell, *Gender and Power: Society, the Person and Sexual Politics* (Palo Alto, CA: Stanford University Press, 1987).

88. B. Sterling, *The Hacker Crackdown: Law and Disorder on the Electronic Frontier* (London: Viking, 1992), 19; O. Turgeman-Goldschmidt, "Hackers' Accounts: Hacking as a Social Entertainment," *Social Science Computer Review* 23, no. 1 (2005): 14.

89. S. Turkle, "Hackers: Loving the Machine for Itself," in *Social Issues in Computing: Putting Computing in Its Place,* ed. C. Huff and T. Finholt (New York, McGraw-Hill, 1994), 652; D. Thomas, *Hacker Culture* (Minneapolis: University of Minnesota Press, 2002), xvi; A. Massanari, "#Gamergate and The Fappening: How Reddit's Algorithm, Governance, and Culture Support Toxic Technocultures," *New Media & Society* (2005): 1–18.

90. Turkle, "Hackers: Loving the Machine for Itself," 664.

91. D. Thomas, *Hacker Culture* (Minneapolis: University of Minnesota Press, 2002), xvi.

92. Ibid., 75.

93. S. Turkle, *Life on the Screen: Identity in the Age of the Internet* (New York: Simon & Schuster, 1995), 210–232.

94. J. Ensor, "Google's Top Secret Weapon—A Hacker They Call Their Security Princess," *Telegraph,* October 2014, http://www.telegraph.co.uk/technology/google/11140639/Googles -top-secret-weapon-a-hacker-they-call-their-Security-Princess.html.

95. R. C. Hollinger, "Crime by Computer: Correlates of Software Piracy and Unauthorized Account Access," *Security Journal* 4, no. 1 (1993): 2–12; R. Jordan and P. Taylor, "A Sociology of Hackers," *Sociological Review* 46, no. 4 (1998): 757–780; B. F. Skinner and A. M. Fream, "A Social Learning Theory Analysis of Computer Crime Among College Students," *Journal of Research in Crime and Delinquency* 34, no. 4 (1997): 495–518; P. Taylor, *Hackers: Crime in the Digital Sublime* (London: Routledge, 1999), 32.

96. B. Acohido and J. Swartz, "Malicious-Software Spreaders Get Sneakier, More Prevalent," *USA Today,* April 23, 2006, http://usatoday30.usatoday.com/tech/news/computersecurity/infotheft /2006-04-23-bot-herders_x.htm.

97. S. Dodson, "Judith Milhon," *Guardian,* August 7, 2003, http://www.theguardian.com/tech nology/2003/aug/08/guardianobituaries.obituaries.

98. K. Hafner and J. Markoff, *Cyberpunk: Outlaws and Hackers on the Computer Frontier* (New York: Simon & Schuster, 1995).

99. A. Harmon, "'Hacktivists' of All Persuasions Take Their Struggle to the Web," *New York Times*, October 31, 1998, http://www.nytimes.com/1998/10/31/world/hacktivists-of-all-persuasions-take-their-struggle-to-the-web.html? pagewanted=all.

100. P. Taylor, *Hackers: Crime in the Digital Sublime* (London: Routledge, 1999), 36–40.

101. BBC News (2012), "Staines Woman Dressed as Boy Jailed for Sex Assaults," http://www.bbc.com/news/uk-england-surrey-17256641; J. Lewis, "Gemma Barker Victim: How Girl Dressed as Boy Fooled Everyone." *International Business Times*, March 7, 2012, http://www.ibtimes.co.uk/gemma-barker-victim-explains-girl-dressed-boy-310399.

102. R. Jauregui, "Courtney Sue Reschke, Idaho Woman, Sentenced to 20 Years in Prison for Sex with Minor," *Huffington Post*, July 1, 2013, http://www.huffingtonpost.com/2013/07/01/courtney-sue-reschke-sex-with-minor_n_3529703.html.

103. NBC Los Angeles, "Mother of Three Accused of Having Sex With 13-year-old Boy," January 8, 2011, http://www.nbclosangeles.com/news/local/lake-forest-woman-accused-of-having-sex-with-13-year-old-boy-113113824.html; K. Dize, "California Woman to Serve 12-Year Sentence for Rape of Bel Air Boy, 13," *Baltimore Sun*, August 4, 2011, http://www.baltimoresun.com/explore/harford/news/crime/ph-ag-sex-offender-sentence-0805-20110804-story.html.

104. Huffington Post, "Theresa Goddard, Surrey B.C. Woman, Faces Child Sex Charges in U.S.," last updated July 13, 2013, http://www.huffingtonpost.ca/2013/07/12/theresa-goddard-child-sex-arrest_n_3588573.html.

105. Ibid.

106. M. Zapotosky, "Woman Charged Federally in Child Sex Case," *Washington Post*, June 28, 2013, https://www.washingtonpost.com/local/woman-charged-federally-in-child-sex-case/2013/06/28/0fdb25aa-e021-11e2-b2d4-ea6d8f477a01_story.html.

107. B. Moon, J. D. McCluskey, C. P. McCluskey, and S. Lee, "Gender, General Theory of Crime and Computer Crime: An Empirical Test," *International Journal of Offender Therapy and Comparative Criminology* 57, no. 4 (2013): 475.

108. For example, R. C. Hollinger, "Crime by Computer: Correlates of Software Piracy and Unauthorized Account Access," *Security Journal* 4, no. 1 (1993): 2–12; B. Moon, J. D. McCluskey, and C. P. McCluskey, "A General Theory of Crime and Computer Crime: An Empirical Test," *Journal of Criminal Justice* 38, no. 4 (2010): 767–772; J. N. Navarro and J. L. Jasinski, "Why Girls? Using Routine Activities to Predict Cyber Bullying Experiences Between Girls and Boys," *Women and Criminal Justice* 23, no. 4 (2013): 286–303.

109. Moon, McCluskey, McCluskey, and Lee, "Gender, General Theory of Crime and Computer Crime: An Empirical Test," 474.

110. X. Li, "The Criminal Phenomenon on the Internet: Hallmarks of Criminals and Victims Revisited Through Typical Cases Prosecuted," *University of Ottawa Law & Technology Journal* 5, no. 1-2 (2008): 127–140.

111. D. Haraway, *Simians, Cyborgs and Women: The Reinvention of Nature* (New York: Routledge, 1991); S. Plant, *Zeros + Ones: Digital Women + The New Technoculture* (London: Fourth Estate, 1997); A. Munster, "Is There Postlife After Postfeminism? Tropes of Technics and Life in Cyberfeminism," *Australian Feminist Studies* 14, no. 29 (1999): 119–131.

112. Haraway, *Simians, Cyborgs and Women: The Reinvention of Nature*, cited in K. Hall, "Cyberfeminism," in *Computer-mediated Communication: Linguistic, Social, and Cross-cultural Perspectives*, ed. S. Herring (Amsterdam: John Benjamins, 1996), 147.

113. J. M. Jaffe, Y.-E. Lee, L. Huang, and H. Oshagan, "Gender, Pseudonyms, and CMC: Masking Identities and Baring Souls," Paper Submitted for Presentation to the Forty-Fifth Annual Conference of the International Communication Association (Albuquerque, New Mexico, 1995), http://smg.media.mit.edu/library/jaffe1995.html.

114. Turkle, *Life on the Screen: Identity in the Age of the Internet*, 12.

115. J. Wajcman, "Reflections on Gender and Technology Studies: In What State is the Art?" *Social Studies of Science* 30, no. 3 (2000): 459.

116. S. Luckman, "(En)gendering the Digital Body: Feminism and the Internet," *Hecate* 25, no. 2 (1999): 41.

117. J. Daniels, "Rethinking Cyberfeminism(s): Race, Gender, and Embodiment," *Women's Studies Quarterly* 37, no. 1/2 (2009): 101–124.

118. Hall, "Cyberfeminism," 167.

119. This replacement left no women on British banknotes. S. Hattenstone, "Caroline Criado-Perez: "Twitter has Enabled People to Behave in a Way They Wouldn't Face to Face," *Guardian*, August 4, 2013, http://www.theguardian.com/lifeandstyle/2013/aug/04/caroline-criado-perez-twitter-rape-threats.

120. Z. Williams, "The Jane Austen Banknote Victory Shows Young Women are Packing a Punch," *Guardian*, July 24, 2013, http://www.theguardian.com/commentisfree/2013/jul/24/jane-austen-banknote-victory-young-women.

121. Z. Jason, "Game of Fear," *Boston Magazine*, May 2015, http://www.bostonmagazine.com/news/article/2015/04/28/gamergate/.

122. T. Wofford, "Is GamerGate About Media Ethics or Harassing Women? Harassment, The Data Shows," *Newsweek*, October 25, 2014, http://www.newsweek.com/gamergate-about-media-ethics-or-harassing-women-harassment-data-show-279736.

123. S. T. Collins, "Anita Sarkeesian on GamerGate: "We Have a Problem and We're Going to Fix This," *Rolling Stone*, October 17, 2014, http://www.rollingstone.com/culture/features/anita-sarkeesian-gamergate-interview-20141017.

124. CBS News, "Video Game Designer Drops Out of Convention Over Death Threats," February 26, 2015, http://www.cbsnews.com/news/video-game-designer-drops-out-of-convention-over-death-threats/.

125. A. Elise, "What is the GamerGate Scandal? Female Game Developer Flees Home Amid Online Threats," *International Business Times*, October 13, 2014, http://www.ibtimes.com/what-gamergate-scandal-female-game-developer-flees-home-amid-online-threats-1704046.

126. Oxford Dictionaries, "Social Justice Warrior," http://www.oxforddictionaries.com/us/definition/american_english/ social-justice-warrior.

127. E. Alexander, "Zoe Quinn on GamerGate: 'It's Not About Ethical Journalism; It's Glorified Revenge Porn By My Angry Ex,'" *Independent*, October 30, 2014, http://www.independent.co.uk/news/people/zoe-quinn-on-gamergate-it-s-not-about-ethical-journalism-it-s-glorified-revenge-porn-by-my-angry-ex-9829176.html.

128. E. G. Coleman, *Coding Freedom: The Ethics and Aesthetics of Hacking* (Princeton, NJ: Princeton University Press, 2013).

129. Wofford, "Is GamerGate About Media Ethics or Harassing Women? Harassment, The Data Shows"; C. Dewey, "The Only Guide to Gamergate You Will Ever Need to Read," *Washington Post*, October 14, 2014, https://www.washingtonpost.com/news/the-intersect/wp/2014/10/14/the-only-guide-to-gamergate-you-will-ever-need-to-read/; A. Abad-Santos, "74,140 Reasons

that #GamerGate Isn't About the Ethics of Journalism," *Vox*, October 27, 2014, http://www.vox.com/xpress/2014/10/27/7070983/why-gamergate-isnt-about-the-ethics-of-journalism-in-35188-tweets.

130. D. Lee, "Zoe Quinn: GamerGate Must be Condemned," *BBC News*, October 29, 2014, http://www.bbc.com/news/technology-29821050; H. Tsukayama, "Gamergate 'Personal Attacks and Threats Have to Stop', Say E3 Organisers," *Independent*, October 16, 2014, http://www.independent.co.uk/life-style/gadgets-and-tech/gaming/gamergate-personal-attacks-and-threats-have-to-stop-say-e3-organisers-9798264.html.

131. J. Thompson, "Thank You Twitter: By Unverifying Milo Yiannopoulos, You Are Standing Up for Women Online," *Huffington Post UK*, January 9, 2016, http://www.huffingtonpost.co.uk/jessie-thompson/milo-yiannopoulos-unverified-twitter-blue-tick_b_8944126.html.

132. J. Edwards, "Twitter 'Unverified' the Right-Wing Writer Milo Yiannopoulos and Nobody is Behaving in a Reasonable or Sober Manner About It," *Business Insider*, January 10, 2016, http://www.businessinsider.com/milo-yiannopoulos-nero-unverified-by-twitter-2016-1?r=UK&IR=T.

133. S. A. O'Brien, "Twitter Crackdown on Hate Speech Backfires," *CNN Money*, January 10, 2016, http://money.cnn.com/2016/01/10/technology/twitter-hate-speech-crackdown-milo-yiannopoulos/

134. D. Ng, "Gamergate Advocate Milo Yiannopoulos Blames Feminists for SXSW Debacle," *Los Angeles Times*, October 29, 2015, http://www.latimes.com/entertainment/la-et-milo-yiannopoulos-gamergate-feminists-20151028-story.html.

135. J. Brustein, "Twitter Slaps Down Gamergate Gadfly. Kind of," *Bloomberg*, January 11, 2016, http://www.bloomberg.com/news/articles/2016-01-11/twitter-slaps-down-gamergate-gadfly-kind-of-.

136. Twitter, "FAQs About Verified Accounts," accessed August 17, 2016, https://support.twitter.com/articles/119135#.

137. A. Mamiit, "Twitter Removes Verified Status of Controversial British Writer Milo Yiannopoulos," *Tech Times*, January 12, 2016, http://www.techtimes.com/articles/123377/20160112/twitter-removes-verified-status-of-controversial-british-writer-milo-yiannopoulos.htm.

PART 3

CYBERCRIME TYPOLOGIES

In this last part, each chapter covers specific classifications of cybercrimes, along with the measures implemented to control and combat them.

CHAPTER 10

INTERPERSONAL CYBERCRIME

KEYWORDS

Child Exploitation Tracking System

Child pornography

Child sex tourism

Child Victim Identification Program

Cyberbullying

Cyberharassment

Cyberstalking

Cybertipline

Extreme pornography

Financial Coalition Against Child Pornography

Honeypot

International Centre for Missing and Exploited Children

Internet troll

INTERPOL Child Abuse Image Database

INTERPOL International Child Sexual Exploitation Image Database

National Center for Missing and Exploited Children

Online child grooming

Pedophile

PhotoDNA

Revenge porn

Sex offender registry

Sexting

Sextortion

Unprotected speech

Virtual Global Taskforce

In 2015, Curt Schilling, a former U.S. major league baseball player, initially posted the following tweet on Twitter to his daughter: "Congrats to Gabby Schilling who will pitch for the Salve Regina Seahawks next year." What followed was a barrage of harassing, indecent, and distasteful tweets from strangers about his daughter. The posts from these individuals became more vulgar and aggressive with each new tweet, even describing rape and gang rape of his daughter. The individuals posting these messages are Internet trolls. In response to the Internet trolls, Schilling conducted his own investigation to find out the identities of the people who engaged in this type of conduct. He published the names of certain trolls—at least those who were responsible for the most offensive tweets. One **Internet troll**, who called himself TheSportsGuru, was identified by Schilling as Adam Nagel, a DJ at a student radio station at Brookville Community College.[1] This troll tweeted, among other tweets, "teach me your knuckle ball technique so I can shove my fist in your daughter."[2] Brookville Community College suspended Nagel from school after his identity

IMAGE 10-1 Screenshot of Tweets by Internet Trolls to Curt Schilling's Daughter.

was revealed. Another Internet troll, Hollywood, later identified as Sean MacDonald, was the vice president of a fraternity (Theta Xi) at Montclair State University and worked part-time at Yankee Stadium.[3] After being exposed, he was fired from his job.

Cases such as this one are by no means unique. Social media and other sites on the Internet serve as the primary forums for verbal abuse and threats, bullying, harassment, and stalking, which often go unpunished. On these same sites and others not easily accessible to the public, child sexual predators are searching for children to groom and victimize. These sites further serve as platforms for creating, uploading, and distributing child pornography. These illicit activities make up what is known as interpersonal cybercrime, that is, a crime that is committed online against an individual with which the perpetrator is communicating or has some form of relationship (real or imagined). Interpersonal cybercrime can involve family members, intimate partners, or community members (e.g., classmates, acquaintances, or even strangers). This chapter explores interpersonal cybercrime and online antisocial behavior, namely, Internet trolling, cyberstalking, cyberharassment, cyberbullying, sextortion, and sexual predators' use of the Internet to stalk, lure, and victimize their targets. It also covers the manufacture, possession, and distribution of child pornography and sexting.

INTERNET TROLLS

Internet trolls post highly offensive and inflammatory remarks online to provoke an emotional reaction and response from other users. These posts can be unrelated to the topic being discussed and may simply be posted to promote disharmony online. These trolls benefit from the anonymity afforded to them by the Internet. There have been cases, however, where trolls have been exposed. A well-known case involved a notorious Internet troll on the Reddit website, Michael Brutsch (also known as violentacrez). Brutsch was known for, among other things, establishing or moderating sections known as "subreddits" on the website (e.g., r/chokeabitch, r/incest, r/rapebait, and r/jailbait, to name a few).[4] One of these subreddits, jailbait, included images of underage girls in bikinis and skirts. Moderators of this subreddit, including Brutsch, would monitor the subreddit and delete any image of girls over the age of sixteen or seventeen. After a CNN news report, backlash over the subreddit ensued, and it was eventually banned from Reddit.[5] Brutsch was also well-known for taking pictures of women's breasts and buttocks without their knowledge ("creepshots") and posting them on Reddit.[6] After Gawker exposed his identity, he was fired from his job.

Trolls have been known to post highly offensive and inflammatory remarks on memorial pages, celebrity websites, and social media accounts, as well as to online forums utilized by everyday users. Those discussed in the media but not of celebrity status or a political figure have also been targeted by Internet trolls. Consider the parents of Madeleine McCann, a three-year-old child who disappeared in 2007. Madeleine was abducted from her family's hotel while they were on vacation in Portugal. At the time of her abduction, the parents, British citizens, had left Madeleine with her younger sibling twins unattended while they went to a restaurant to eat dinner. Following Madeleine's disappearance, her parents were subjected to vitriolic comments and death threats. Indeed, Internet trolls posted messages and images on social media sites, message boards, and other online forums calling for the couple to be murdered, hanged, and to suffer a variety of other brutal attacks.[7]

IMAGE 10-2 Screenshot of Posts of Internet Trolls about Madeleine McCann's Parents.

Some countries have criminalized this conduct. For instance, in Singapore, the Protection from Harassment Act of 2014 was passed, which could be used to prosecute Internet trolls.[8] Likewise, the United Kingdom criminalized this conduct pursuant to the Malicious Communications Act of 1988. The United States, however, does not criminalize this conduct unless what is being communicated amounts to cyberbullying, cyberharassment, or cyberstalking or is considered a form of **unprotected speech**. With respect to the latter, only if Internet trolls communicate true threats and other forms of unprotected speech can they be prosecuted for committing crimes. Unprotected speech is that which is excluded from First Amendment protection. According to the First Amendment to the U.S. Constitution, "Congress shall make no law respecting an establishment of religion, or prohibiting the free exercise thereof; or abridging the freedom of speech, or of the press; or the right of the people peaceably to assemble, and to petition the Government for a redress of grievances." Forms of unprotected speech include false statement of facts,[9] fighting words,[10] incitement to violence,[11] obscene speech,[12] words protected by intellectual property law,[13] and true threats.[14] The last form of unprotected speech, true threats, is further considered in the next section, cyberstalking.

CYBERSTALKING

Cyberstalking refers to use of the Internet, computers, and related technology to repeatedly threaten, harass, or frighten another individual. In one such incident in the United Kingdom, Ruth Jeffery was cyberstalked for approximately three and a half years through e-mail and social media by her boyfriend, Shane Webber. Webber hacked into her e-mail and social media accounts, impersonated her, and sent nude and sexually explicit images and messages to the victim's friends and family; for his illicit acts, Webber received four months of jail time.[15] Cyberstalking often involves adults; however, this is not always the case. Cyberstalking has been perpetrated by children against other children. For example, a twelve-year-old girl gained unauthorized access to the Facebook account of her victim (also a twelve-year-old girl) and posted, along with another girl (eleven years old), sexually explicit images on the victim's Facebook page and posted and sent messages with solicitations for sex to the victim's Facebook friends.[16] For these acts, the perpetrators received probation and community service. After the perpetrators completed the terms of their sentence, the charges against them were dismissed.[17] This dismissal of charges is common among juvenile offenders.

Social media has also been used by individuals to stalk their favorite celebrities. In 2015, a person using the online names Alex Mercer and Ralph Alexander, posted an image of a shotgun along with a message that he should have killed Rihanna, a famous singer.[18] Before this post, he had posted an image of himself taken outside of Rihanna's former Los Angeles home, along with the message "Should of killed @rihanna a minute back I would be good right now. Sorcery is a weapon I use guns, bout to get a gun license, can't use my hands." Unfortunately, existing cyberstalking laws do not address general Internet postings about a particular user that amount to stalking and third party stalking.

CRIMINALIZING AND RESPONDING TO CYBERSTALKING

There are two primary U.S. federal laws that can be used to prosecute cyberstalking cases, one of which is 18 U.S.C. § 875(c). This law has been used mostly against those communicating threats via telephone. The courts have ruled that the law applies to electronic communications as well.[19] Accordingly, this law criminalizes the use of a communication device, phone, e-mail, or the Internet to threaten someone. It is applicable only when an actual threat—a true threat—is communicated. Repeated annoyances or threats (absent an actual threat) are not covered. A decision that provided some guidance on how true threats should be interpreted is that in the case of *Elonis v. United States.*[20] In that case, Anthony Elonis was charged with and convicted of communicating "true threats" on Facebook targeting his ex-wife, local law enforcement, the FBI, and elementary schools.[21] He was convicted on objective intent, that is, whether a reasonable person would view his communication as a true threat. The Supreme Court overturned his conviction, holding that a true threat should be interpreted by the subjective intent of the perpetrator, that is, whether the perpetrator *intended* the communication to be interpreted as a threat. Another law that criminalizes cyberstalking is 18 U.S.C. § 2261A. Anyone with the intent to kill, injure, harass, or intimidate who uses electronic communications to engage in conduct that causes reasonable fear or death or serious bodily harm or substantial emotional distress to the victim can be charged pursuant to this law. In addition to these federal statutes, states have also implemented cyberstalking laws or amended existing laws to include cyberstalking (see Table 10-1 for states that have laws criminalizing cyberstalking).

There are no international cyberstalking laws. Although a multilateral agreement on cybercrime exists—the Council of Europe's Cybercrime Convention—this law does not include cyberstalking. If the countries involved in a cyberstalking case have national

Table 10-1 States With Cyberstalking Laws

Alaska	Maine	Oklahoma
Arizona	Massachusetts	Oregon
Arkansas	Michigan	Pennsylvania
California	Minnesota	Rhode Island
Colorado	Mississippi	South Carolina
Connecticut	Missouri	South Dakota
Florida	Montana	Tennessee
Georgia	Nebraska	Utah
Idaho	Nevada	Vermont
Illinois	New Jersey	Virginia
Kansas	New York	Washington
Kentucky	North Carolina	Wyoming
Louisiana	Ohio	

Source: National Conference of State Legislatures, "State Cyberstalking and Cyberharassment Laws," accessed May 7, 2016, http://www.ncsl.org/research/telecommunications-and-information-technology/cyberstalking-and-cyberharassment-laws.aspx

laws, then dual criminality exists, which enables law enforcement agencies and other criminal justice agents of the countries to cooperate in the investigation. In reality, despite the existence of dual criminality, these criminal justice agents may not cooperate with each other. Even domestic criminal justice agencies may not be willing to pursue cyberstalkers by devoting existing (but often limited) human and financial resources that could be used for other crimes and cybercrimes. This happened in Leandra Ramm's case. Leandra, an American opera singer, was relentlessly cyberstalked for several years by Colin Mak Yew Loong, who lived in Singapore.[22] Loong first contacted her in 2005, claiming to be a music festival director who could further her career.[23] She initially responded to him but stopped replying to his messages when she realized that he was not who he said he was. When she stopped responding to his e-mails, he bombarded her with calls and more e-mails. He also created hate groups on Facebook and Twitter and a blog lambasting her, all of which were detrimental to her career. When she contacted several law enforcement agencies about the cyberstalking, they informed her that they could not help her.[24] Undeterred by the refusal of law enforcement agencies to pursue her case, she devoted all of her time and financial resources to hire individuals and create a team that could assist her in getting her case tried in the United States. Because of her unrelenting efforts, the perpetrator was tried and convicted in a U.S. court in December 2013, receiving three years' imprisonment.

Presently, law enforcement authorities are not trained to deal with cyberstalking—or any cyber issue for that matter—if they work outside of specialized cyber units. A misperception that there is an easy fix to cyberstalking also exists: the victim should simply delete online accounts and the cyberstalking will cease. This is not a viable solution today. In fact, the majority of citizens rely on electronic communications not only for personal communications but also for professional communications. Like cyberstalking, cyberharassment receives the same treatment by law enforcement authorities—it is not considered a priority cybercrime, and prosecutions are infrequently pursued.

CYBERHARASSMENT

Cyberharassment refers to use of the Internet and digital devices to intentionally alarm, annoy, attack, or verbally abuse another individual. A well-known case of cyberharassment involved Tyler Clementi, a student at Rutgers University. Tyler's roommate, Dharun Ravi, surreptitiously videotaped him being intimate with another man. Ravi called one of his friends, Molly Wei, to watch the recordings. The recording and what he saw was also discussed by Ravi on social media. For example, one of Ravi's posts stated, "Roommate asked for the room till midnight. I went into Molly's room and turned on my webcam. I saw him making out with a dude. Yay."[25] Ravi also invited others to join and watch another preplanned recording. Tyler became aware of the recording via Ravi's social media posts. On September 22, 2010, Tyler committed suicide by jumping off the George Washington Bridge.[26] Ravi was charged and convicted for his illicit behavior, though not for cyberharassment, because a cyberharassment law was not in place in New Jersey at the time of the incident. For his crimes (e.g., bias intimidation and invasion of privacy), Ravi received twenty months in jail, three years' probation, and three hundred hours of community service and had to pay $10,000 to a fund for bias crime victims.[27] After serving twenty days of his jail time, Ravi was released in 2012.[28]

CRIMINALIZING AND RESPONDING TO CYBERHARASSMENT

Federal law prohibits cyberharassment. The law used to charge those who engage in cyberharassment is 47 U.S.C. § 223. Anyone that uses a communication device to annoy, abuse, harass, or threaten another person can be charged pursuant to this statute. A limitation with this law is that it only applies to direct communications between the victim and offender (e.g., via e-mail). The law does not apply in situations where the perpetrator posts offensive comments on a public bulletin board or chatroom, or enlists or encourages others to harass the victim in these forums. Because it applies only to direct communications (e.g., e-mails and phone calls) between the offender and the victim, it cannot be used to prosecute indirect harassing comments about the victim posted on social media sites and other forums. Moreover, under 47 U.S.C. § 223(a)(1)(c), this law requires that the perpetrator remain anonymous during the incident. Another federal law, 18 U.S.C. § 875(c), is inapplicable to cyberharassment absent the communication of some form of threat.

In addition to federal law, states have criminalized cyberharassment. For instance, under New Jersey Revised Statute § 2C:33-4.1 (2014), cyberharassment occurs

> if, while making a communication in an online capacity via any electronic device or through a social networking site and with the purpose to harass another, the person: . . . threatens to inflict injury or physical harm to any person or the property of any person; . . . knowingly sends, posts, comments, requests, suggests, or proposes any lewd, indecent, or obscene material to or about a person with the intent to emotionally harm a reasonable person or place a reasonable person in fear of physical or emotional harm to his person; . . . [or] threatens to commit any crime against the person or the person's property.

Likewise, other states have developed new statutes or integrated cyberharassment into existing laws (see Table 10-2).

Apart from laws, social media and other websites prohibit cyberharassment and cyberstalking in their Terms of Service agreement. For instance, Twitter considers "targeted abuse or harassment" a violation of Twitter Rules.[29] Twitter also prohibits direct and indirect threats of violence against others or the promotion of violence.[30] Facebook similarly prohibits harassing and threatening content.[31] Flickr also prohibits such conduct. According to Flickr Community Guidelines, the website "is not a venue for . . . [individuals] to harass, abuse, impersonate, or intimidate others."

In addition to these policies, social media and other websites have measures in place to enable users to report violations of Terms of Service. They have features that make it easier for victims of verbal threats or abuse to report these incidents to law enforcement.[32] Twitter enables users to report this type of behavior to the site. Upon doing so, users can request to have the report sent to their e-mail (by clicking the "Email report" button). The report sent to their e-mail includes information about the incident, information about the parties involved in the incident, the threatening tweet and URL, the timestamp of the threatening tweet, the timestamp of the report, and a link to the website's law enforcement guidelines. The user further has the option to "mute" or "block" the party responsible for the verbal threats or abuse. If a user is "muted," the party who muted the user cannot see tweets by the party whom they muted. However, the party who muted the user responsible for the threats can still receive notifications if the muted party mentions them in a tweet or sends them a direct message. If a user "blocks" another party, the user will not be able to

Table 10-2 States That Criminalize Cyberharassment

Alabama	Maryland	Ohio
Arizona	Massachusetts	Oklahoma
Arkansas	Michigan	Oregon
California	Minnesota	Pennsylvania
Colorado	Mississippi	Rhode Island
Connecticut	Missouri	South Carolina
Delaware	Montana	South Dakota
Florida	Nebraska	Tennessee
Hawaii	New Hampshire	Utah
Illinois	New Jersey	Vermont
Indiana	New Mexico	Virginia
Iowa	New York	Washington
Kansas	North Carolina	

Source: National Conference of State Legislatures, "State Cyberstalking and Cyberharassment Laws," accessed May 7, 2016, http://www.ncsl.org /research/telecommunications-and-information-technology/cyberstalking -and-cyberharassment-laws.aspx.

see the tweets of the blocked party nor be able to receive any notifications. Moreover, the blocked party will not be able to follow the user who blocked him or her nor view any of that user's tweets. Reporting and blocking features are also available on other social media sites, including Facebook and Instagram.

If someone is a victim of cyberharassment or cyberstalking, the first thing he or she should do is tell the harasser or stalker to stop. The message should be simple: "Do not contact me again in any way in the future." It is important not to engage in any conversation with the harasser or stalker and not to retaliate. The victim should also save all communications, keeping the original conversations (whenever possible) and using the printscreen function on the computer (or equivalent on a digital device) to capture other information that might be subsequently deleted by the offender. The Internet service provider (ISP) responsible for the content should then be contacted. The general policy is that if a complaint is found to be valid, the offending user will either receive a warning or the offender's account will be deleted.[33] An ISP can refuse to take down content, even if it violates the Terms of Service. The issue is that ISPs often do not enforce their Terms of Service. Ultimately, it is the user's responsibility to contact the ISP to report the offending behavior. In the end, when faced with cyberstalking or cyberharassment the victim must decide what to do in response to the cybercrime: Does the victim want to contact the police? Does the victim want to sue the offender? The answers to these questions will dictate what the victim will do next.

REVENGE PORN AS CYBERHARASSMENT

Revenge porn is a term used to describe the use of sexually explicit photos or videos of the victim without the victim's consent to cause the victim distress, humiliation, or harm in some way. Websites have been developed where users can post revenge porn. The websites primarily target women. In many cases, ex-boyfriends or ex-husbands have used these revenge porn websites against their ex-girlfriends or ex-wives. These individuals post sexually explicit photographs or videos of a former girlfriend or spouse, along with the victim's personal information and degrading, demeaning, or defamatory comments. In California, the operator of a revenge porn website named Hunter Moore was charged and convicted for maintaining the website and for hiring someone (who was also charged and convicted) to obtain naked photos of women without their permission by hacking into their e-mail accounts.[34] The founder of another revenge porn website (UGotPosted.com), Kevin Bollaert, was sentenced to eighteen years' imprisonment for running a website that enabled and even encouraged angry ex-boyfriends and ex-husbands to post nude or sexually explicit photographs and videos of women, along with the women's personal information (e.g., name, address, social media profile).[35] Bollaert also created another website, ChangeMyReputation.com, where women had to pay $250 if they wanted their images, videos, and personal information removed from UGotPosted.com.[36]

A New York revenge porn case illustrated the need to update existing laws. The case involved Ian Barber, who in 2013 sent nude photographs of his girlfriend to her sister and employer. Barber was charged with, among other crimes, aggravated harassment in the second degree (see Article § 240.30, New York Penal Law).[37] Because Barber communicated with the victim's sister and employer, not the victim, he could not be convicted of aggravated harassment in the second degree (recall that the federal cyberharassment law also requires direct communication between the victim and the offender). In an effort to close loopholes in the law, in 2014, a New York law was passed that made revenge porn illegal.[38] The main requirement for violating the law is that the nude or sexually explicit images or videos be posted without the victim's consent.[39]

In other cases, users have posted revenge porn on social media websites like Facebook. For example, in the United Kingdom, Thomas Samuel posted intimate photos he had taken of his ex-girlfriend, Folami Prehaye, on a Facebook page he created in her name.[40] He invited her friends and family to become Facebook friends in order for them to be able to access her new profile. Her friends and family accepted, thinking Folami had created a second Facebook page. Samuel was prosecuted pursuant to the Malicious Communications Act of 1988. He did not receive a term of imprisonment, only a restraining order and community service. This case preceded the passage of the Criminal Justice and Courts Act of 2015. Section 33 of this act criminalized revenge porn, which it defined as "disclosing private sexual photographs and films with intent to cause distress." Paige Mitchell was the first female in the United Kingdom to be charged and convicted under the Criminal Justice and Courts Act of 2015 for engaging in revenge porn, in her case by posting intimate photos of her ex-girlfriend on Facebook.[41]

Revenge porn is explicitly prohibited on certain websites and social media platforms. Facebook explicitly prohibits the sharing of "images . . . in revenge or without permissions from the people in the images."[42] These and other sites (e.g., Instagram) also prohibit posting pornographic content and content with nudity (the latter with a few exceptions). The problem does not lie in lack of policy on revenge porn, rather in lack of effective enforcement of this policy. As with other interpersonal cybercrimes covered previously in this chapter, revenge porn content is removed at the discretion of the ISP after the content has been reported. The same holds true for cyberbullying.

CYBERBULLYING

Like other forms of interpersonal cybercrime, bullying was historically limited to the geographic location of the perpetrator and victim. The event was only witnessed by those within the vicinity where the bullying occurred. Nowadays, geographic location is unimportant. A person can be bullied by anyone, anywhere in the world. This is made possible with **cyberbullying**, which involves children's use of the Internet and digital devices to annoy, humiliate, alarm, insult, or otherwise attack other children. Cyberbullying differs significantly from ordinary bullying. It can occur at all hours of the day or night. Given today's increased reliance on technology and the Internet, this form of bullying is at times inescapable. Sometimes it can occur anonymously, making it difficult to identify the source of the comments. What is more, the bullying persists well after it has occurred, meaning that a record of the bullying often exists indefinitely online.

Cyberbullying may include bullying outside of virtual worlds. Research shows that cyberbullying may occur in tandem with traditional, in-person bullying.[43] Phoebe Prince, a fifteen-year-old girl from Massachusetts, was repeatedly bullied and cyberbullied by her peers before she committed suicide in 2010. Rebecca Ann Sedwick (discussed in Chapter 7 and Chapter 8) was bullied, physically assaulted, and cyberbullied between 2012 and 2013 by several girls. Following a year of physical and verbal abuse, she committed suicide by jumping from a three-story cement plant structure on September 10, 2013. She was twelve years old at the time of her death. Unfortunately, Phoebe and Rebecca are not the only youths to have taken their lives following bullying and cyberbullying. There have been numerous such cases. In fact, studies have shown that many victims have considered committing, attempted to commit, or actually did commit suicide in the aftermath of cyberbullying, cyberharassment, and cyberstalking.[44] In addition to suicidal thoughts, victims of cyberbullying, in particular, have reported experiencing anxiety, embarrassment, fear, humiliation, anger, sadness, and depression as a result of the attacks on them.[45] Studies on cyberbullying have provided evidence of its adverse emotional, psychological, physical, and social impact on victims.[46]

Cyberbullies use a variety of digital technologies to target victims, including computers, mobile phones, smartphones, tablets, and gaming consoles. Text,[47] instant messaging (IM) services,[48] chat rooms,[49] and social media sites such as Facebook and Twitter are the primary means used to engage in cyberbullying.[50] Other lesser-known apps and online forums, such as Kik and Voxer messenger and ask.fm, have also been used to cyberbully victims, including Rebecca Ann Sedwick.[51] Ultimately, research shows that cyberbullying is more prevalent in forums where users are anonymous and on websites where anonymous comments can be made.[52] Cyberbullies utilize these anonymous forums and websites in order to avoid real-world repercussions for their cybercrimes and antisocial behaviors.

CRIMINALIZING AND RESPONDING TO CYBERBULLYING

There is no federal cyberbullying law in the United States; only state laws exist. Fifty states have bullying laws, forty-nine of which reference bullying through electronic media. The laws may be stand-alone laws specifically designed to deal with cyberbullying. Alternatively, bullying (cyber or otherwise) is considered an issue for educational institutions. Educational institutions have created policies that deal with bullying and cyberbullying (e.g., Alaska, California, Georgia, Idaho, Illinois, Indiana, Iowa, and Maine). In other states, existing cyberharassment and cyberstalking laws have been used to prosecute cyberbullies. In 2014, New Jersey prosecuted its first juvenile pursuant to its law on cyberharassment (N.J.S.A. 2C:33-4.1) for sending an expletive-filled Facebook message to a former classmate of hers threatening to kill her and challenging her to a physical fight.[53] The juvenile, a fifteen-year-old female, was charged with one count of fourth degree cyberharassment.[54] The terms *cyberharassment* and *cyberbullying* are often used interchangeably. The main difference between the two is the age of the offender and the victim; *cyberbullying* is commonly applied to youths.

For cyberbullying, children can be imprisoned, placed on probation, fined, or given community service. Nonetheless, imprisonment is not often given as a punishment for cyberbullying. In the United Kingdom, a teenager, Keeley Houghton, was imprisoned for cyberbullying Emily Moore on Facebook by threatening, among other things, to kill her.[55] More common forms of punishment for cyberbullies are probation and community service. In North Carolina, Robert Bishop cyberbullied a boy in his school, Dillion Price, via Facebook.[56] Bishop was charged and convicted under North Carolina's cyberbullying statute, General Statute § 14-458.1(a)(1)(d), receiving four years of probation and being prohibited from using social media for a year.[57] A female cyberbully, Kaylan Ashrafi, was charged and convicted for cyberbullying a classmate on Twitter. She received four months of probation, which she successfully completed; subsequently, her charges were dismissed.[58]

In addition to measures targeting cyberbullies, parents have been held liable for their children's behavior. This is made possible through parental liability laws, which seek to hold parents responsible for their children's behavior. The basis of this is purportedly negligent parental care and supervision of a child. In *Boston et al. v. Athearn et al.* (2014),[59] a Georgia court of appeals held parents responsible for the behavior of their child. In this case, the parents of a boy became aware of a fake Facebook profile page their thirteen-year-old son created in order to defame a female student. This page posted highly offensive and sexually explicit comments supposedly made by the victim (in reality, the boy was posting these remarks). The boy also used an app to distort the appearance of the young girl. Despite being aware of this profile, the parents did not make their son delete the profile, and the page remained online for eleven months.

Victims of cyberbullying employ numerous coping strategies in response to the crime committed against them, including retaliation, ignoring the cyberbully, seeking support, and utilizing technical solutions.[60] The first coping strategy, retaliation, is not often employed and is not considered as useful as other strategies.[61] The second strategy, ignoring the cyberbully, is commonly employed, although its effects on cyberbullying are unknown.[62] The third coping strategy, seeking support, is viewed as a helpful strategy,[63] although victims differ with respect to whom they confide in when they seek support. Some victims do not seek support;[64] for those who do seek support, they often choose their peers over parents or teachers.[65] Victims that have been cyberbullied are less likely than those that have been bullied in person to discuss what happened to them with an adult, opting instead to either discuss it with peers or to deal with the cyberbullying themselves.[66] Victims often do not confide in parents, teachers, or other adults because they believe these individuals do not understand cyberbullying and the situation the victim is in, and that they might ban the victims from accessing the Internet or their mobile phones in order to stop the cyberbullying.[67] The latter, if it occurs, is particularly problematic. Any action that might be interpreted as a form of punishment (e.g., banning use of electronics or revoking computer or phone privileges) may lead the child to refrain from reporting further incidents of cyberbullying.

The fourth, and final, coping strategy is responding to cyberbullying with technical solutions. It has been argued that cyberbullying can be quickly stopped by victims by either blocking the cyberbully or having the victim change his or her identity.[68] The reality, however, is that preventing cyberbullying is not that simple. The cyberbully can continue to bully the victim through other cybermeasures and using new cyberattacks. Technical solutions, such as blocking and deleting messages from cyberbullies, work best in the short term.[69] Technical solutions do not work in the long term because a motivated cyberbully will find a way to bypass these solutions and send messages to the victim.[70]

In cyberbullying, cyberharassment, and cyberstalking cases, police may refuse to file a report or turn the victim away by saying they cannot help. Victim-blaming attitudes can be present, often turning attention to the victims' acts and asking victims what they have done to place themselves in a position to be cyberbullied, cyberharassed, or cyberstalked. Victims of cyberbullying, cyberharassment, and cyberstalking may experience secondary victimization as a result of this treatment by authorities and their responses to their victimization.[71] Additionally, the preventive efforts for these cybercrimes usually target the victim and require the victim to change account identities, close existing accounts, and block individuals, among other actions, putting the onus on the victim to stop the cyberbullying. Unfortunately, the requirement for change often falls on the victim, even though the victim has not engaged in any wrongdoing.

Rob Reiner rightly pointed out that "not all policing lies in the police."[72] This is the case with interpersonal cybercrimes, which are reported by the victims or members of the public at large to websites that contain the prohibited or offensive content. Social media platforms and other websites have policies that prohibit cyberbullying, along with cyberharassment and cyberstalking. For example, Facebook explicitly prohibits the bullying, harassing, and intimidation of others.[73] Twitter, Instagram, and Flickr have similar policies in place. As with other interpersonal cybercrimes, the ISP ultimately determines whether or not to take down content after a complaint is made concerning prohibited content. Under the Communications Decency Act of 1996, 47 U.S.C. § 230(c)(1), "No provider or user of an interactive computer service shall be treated as the publisher or speaker of any information provided by another information content provider." According to 47 U.S.C. § 230(c)(2), ISPs are also shielded from liability as long as they take "action voluntarily . . . in good faith to restrict access to or availability of material that the provider or user considers to be obscene, lewd, lascivious, filthy, excessively violent, harassing, or otherwise objectionable, whether or not such material is constitutionally protected." Another interpersonal cybercrime that takes place on social media and other online websites is sextortion.

SEXTORTION

Sexual cyberextortion (**sextortion**) occurs when a perpetrator threatens to disseminate sexually explicit photos or videos of the victim online if sexual demands are not met or if sexually explicit images or videos are not sent to the perpetrator. A common threat posed by such perpetrators is that they will send sexually explicit photos or videos to the victim's family, friends, and classmates. A now infamous case of sextortion involved Amanda Todd, a Canadian who committed suicide at the age of fifteen by hanging herself following years of cyberstalking and sextortion by a stranger and cyberbullying and in-person bullying by her classmates. The cyberstalking began after a webcam session in which a stranger convinced her to flash the camera by exposing her breasts. One year after this incident, she was contacted by an unknown user who sought to extort her by threatening to post the image of her breasts and send it to her family and friends if she did not do what he was asking. When she refused, he released the image, which went viral. Amanda was repeatedly bullied and cyberbullied by her classmates and strangers for the image. After a few failed attempts to commit suicide, she succeeded on October 10, 2012. Two years after her death, in 2014, a thirty-five-year-old Dutch citizen, Aydin Coban, was charged with and arrested for sextortion and the creation and distribution of child pornography, among other charges, in the Netherlands.[74]

In another case that targeted minors, a man in the United States gained unauthorized access to "the social media, e-mail and online shopping accounts of almost a dozen minor females and threaten[ed] that he would delete, deface, and make purchases from the accounts unless the victims sent him sexually explicit photographs of themselves."[75] Moreover, in Sweden, a man convinced young girls (the youngest age eleven) to pose naked for him via webcam.[76] He threatened one of his victims with releasing the photos online; she subsequently committed suicide. Cases such as these abound. Adult women have also been targeted by sextortionists. For instance, Michael C. Ford, a former U.S. embassy employee in London, hacked into personal e-mail and social media accounts and stole sexually explicit images and personal information from victims, which he then used to extort them by threatening to release the images if the victims did not provide him with more sexually explicit images and videos.[77]

ONLINE CHILD SEXUAL PREDATION

Pedophiles are individuals who are sexually aroused by prepubescent adolescents.[78] One study found that a valid indicator of pedophilia is an individual's accessing of **child pornography**,[79] which is the visual, audio, written, or other form of portrayal of sexual activity with a child under eighteen years of age that is designed to sexually arouse a viewer. Similarly, a 2010 study revealed that the majority of the 422 Internet sex offenders examined were convicted of downloading child pornography.[80]

Offenders use the Internet, computers, and related technology to create, collect, and distribute child pornography.[81] An Internet Watch Foundation (IWF) report found over thirteen thousand websites that contained images of sexually exploited children.[82] Moreover, the report revealed that North America (54 percent) and Europe and Russia (collectively, at 43 percent) host the majority of videos and images with sexually exploited children.[83] Child pornography can be found in and distributed through e-mails, websites, chat rooms, message boards, bulletin boards, peer-to-peer networks, and newsgroups.[84] The types of images and videos that can be found include clothed children, naked children, children in erotic poses, and children being sexually assaulted.[85] Victims involved in child pornography can range from being photographed by a perpetrator without their knowledge, surreptitiously recorded while being sexually abused, sexually abused and openly photographed and video recorded, and participating in child pornography development, for example, selecting another child for abuse.[86]

BOX 10-1 SECOND LIFE AND CHILD PORN

On Second Life (a virtual reality website), virtual sex was being solicited with the avatars of minors.[87] What was occurring is known as *sexual ageplay* (a form of virtual child pornography in which a user creates an avatar of a child and engages in sexual activities).[88] In 2007, Germany reported sexual ageplay on Second Life by revealing that avatars of children were created and virtual child pornography was being developed, disseminated, and purchased using Linden dollars (the digital currency for the virtual reality website).[89] In Germany, the possession, creation, or distribution of virtual child pornography is a criminal offense. Real child pornography was also being offered on Second Life. A user of the site was suspected of offering other users the ability to purchase child pornography depicting real children off of the site using Linden dollars.[90]

In addition to using the Internet for the proliferation of child pornography, child sex offenders have taken advantage of the Internet to communicate with like-minded individuals via chat rooms, bulletin boards, newsgroups, e-mails, peer-to-peer platforms, and social media.[91] The Internet provides unprecedented opportunities for like-minded sex offenders to network and exchange ideas and information. Child sex offenders often involve lone offenders primarily driven by self-interest; this, however, does not mean that these individuals do not interact with like-minded individuals—only that they are not primarily part of organized groups or networks.[92] Child pornography offenders have been found to trade child pornography in online communities[93] such as Dreamboard, a members-only forum that enabled the sharing of child pornography between members of the site. Internet child sex offenders have reported that the creation and sharing of child pornography images plays an important role in online communities where child pornography is traded.[94] An individual collects child pornography to develop and foster relationships with other child pornography offenders.[95] Those in the forums are judged by the quality of any new child pornography material (i.e., that which is not already traded on the platforms).[96]

Some child sex offenders have operated exclusively online.[97] Internet child sex offenders can also engage in offline child sex offending. Research on the rate in which this occurs has been mixed: some research has shown that people who engage in Internet child pornography have low rates of offending in real life,[98] but other studies have shown a high rate of offending.[99]

Typologies of Internet sex offenders have been created. For instance, Lanning distinguished between situational and preferential sex offenders.[100] The situational sex offender accesses material opportunistically and impulsively, often to satisfy a sexual need, curiosity, or for economic reasons (to obtain money through the sale of child pornography). A preferential offender is driven by sexual desires for children and will actively look for child pornography. Different Internet sex offender typologies were created by Krone.[101] Specifically, he classified Internet sex offenders into the following categories:[102]

1. *Browsers.* Offenders in this category are not actively looking for child pornography but come across it in their search for pornography and choose to save it.
2. *Private fantasy offenders.* As the name implies, these individuals fantasize about sexually abusing children and may search for images depicting sexual abuse.
3. *Trawlers.* These individuals actively seek out pornography on the Internet and are curious about child pornography.

4. *Nonsecure collectors.* Offenders in this category search and use open sources to collect, distribute, or purchase child pornography.
5. *Secure collectors.* These individuals search for and collect, distribute, or purchase child pornography using techniques designed to evade detection by authorities.
6. *Groomers.* Offenders use child pornography in the grooming process to either initiate offline sexual contact or cybersex with minors.
7. *Physical abusers.* People who are contact sex offenders and use child pornography as a supplement or souvenir to remind them of their sexual activities.
8. *Producers.* These people create child pornography for distribution.
9. *Distributors.* Individuals who have child pornography in their possession with the primary motive of distributing it (for free or for a profit).

The first five types of sex offenders can be characterized as indirect abusers because they do not engage in contact offending;[103] the other four types are considered direct abusers. By contrast, O'Connor classified Internet child sex offenders under the following categories:[104]

1. *Accidental.* Offenders in this category are unaware that they have child pornography in their possession. Most likely the pornography was downloaded accidentally during a mass download of pornographic images.
2. *Curious.* As the name implies, those within this category access child pornography out of curiosity and possess a small collection of it.
3. *Morally indiscriminate.* Individuals in this category access various forms of pornography, including extreme forms of pornography, which includes child pornography.
4. *Entrepreneurial.* Offenders that possess child pornography with the intention of distributing it for financial gain.
5. *Addicted/problem aware.* People who are unable to control their sexual fantasies of sexually abusing children and are addicted to child pornography. These offenders are aware of their addiction. This type of offender is the most likely to engage in contact sexual offenses against children.

Elliot and Beech integrated the typologies of Krone, Sullivan and Beech, and Lanning to develop four general categories of Internet sex offenders:[105]

1. *Periodically prurient.* These individuals seek out child pornography on occasion. They are motivated to engage in this behavior out of curiosity or impulsivity. They may search for "**extreme pornography**,"[106] of which child pornography is just one small part. They access child pornography impulsively or opportunistically based on the opportunities presented to them.
2. *Fantasy driven/online only.* These offenders have no known history of sex offending and seek to stimulate their sexual interest in children by viewing child pornography.[107] They have no prior criminal history but fantasize about sexually abusing children.
3. *Direct victimization.* These individuals engage in both Internet and offline child sex offenses. They utilize the Internet to lure a child offline to commit a sexual offense.[108] The Internet is one of many techniques they use in child sex offending.
4. *Commercial exploitation.* These offenders obtain and distribute child pornography for profit.[109] The primary driver for this conduct is financial.[110] These individuals sell child pornography or facilitate child sex trafficking to make a profit.

Seto, Cantor, and Blanchard, and Howitt and Sheldon found that child pornographers and child sex offenders believe that children are willing to engage in sexual activity.[111] The reality is, however, that a child cannot consent to such an activity. Children's involvement in child pornography has detrimental effects on them. Indeed, "the use of children as subjects of pornographic materials is harmful to the physiological, emotional, and mental health of the child."[112] Victims have expressed feeling fear, disgust, guilt, and shame as a result of their depiction in child pornography.[113] Children who were victims of child pornography reported that fear of the perpetrator and guilt made them reticent to report what happened to them.[114] Apart from the harms done to the victims, child pornography propagates the belief of children as sexual objects.[115] Existing child pornography can increase demand for new images, which in turn will increase the supply of child pornography.

ONLINE CHILD GROOMING

Offenders can use the Internet for child grooming. **Online child grooming** refers to the manipulation tactics an offender uses to gain the victim's trust and ultimately lead them to engage in sexual activities. It is the process whereby individuals attempt to seduce children via online forums with the intention of eventually engaging in sexual activities with them. Social media sites play a role in online grooming by providing child predators with quick and easy access to minors from multiple geographic locations.[116] They also provide offenders with access to a greater number of victims. Overall, child sex offenders use the Internet to locate, contact, target, and establish and foster online relationships with targets and otherwise promote and facilitate child sexual exploitation.[117] These predators, using social media and other websites, can take on different (and often younger) digital personas to contact minors. Child pornographers utilize the information available on social media to find vulnerable victims to exploit. Moreover, children are groomed through child pornography, which is used to desensitize them to sexual activities.[118]

According to O'Connell, online grooming involves the following sequential stages:[119] First, an offender contacts the child and tries to form a relationship with the child. The time that an offender spends in this stage (the *friendship-forming* stage) varies. In the second stage, the *relationship forming* stage, an offender seeks to, as the name implies, develop a relationship with the victim. Rapport is developed with the target by asking the target about family, friends, and school. Trust is also formed between the offender and the child. In this stage, the offender ultimately seeks to obtain personal information about the target. In the third stage (the *risk assessment* stage), the offender probes the target about information that can be used by the offender to assess the risk of being caught engaging in these acts. Questions that may be asked include the location of the computer (e.g., in the child's room or common space in the house), its use by others (e.g., by siblings or parents), and access (e.g., whether it is password protected and if the password is known by family members). In the fourth stage, the *exclusivity* stage, the offender sets and communicates the rules and expectations for the relationship with the child. Emphasis is placed on the secrecy of the relationship. The fifth and final stage, the *sexual* stage, includes discussion of intimate and sexual issues (e.g., questions on kissing and touching), sending pornographic images to the child to reduce inhibitions, or requesting an image from the child or the reenactment of a sexual fantasy, either through mutual agreement or coercion.

Williams, Elliott, and Beech provided different stages of online grooming: rapport building, sexual content, and assessment.[120] In the *rapport building* stage, the offender seeks to build a friendship with the child and develop trust. The offender asks the victim questions to learn more about the victim. The offender mirrors the child's behavior and presents himself or herself as being close to or the same age as the child. The offender portrays himself or herself in a positive light and serves as a confidant or mentor of sorts to the child. In the *sexual content* stage, as the name implies, the offender introduces the child to sexual content by discussing sexual activities. The offender maintains online sexual interactions and may escalate these interactions by increasing the frequency with which such interactions are requested. In the final stage, the *assessment* stage, the offender assesses the level of trust the target has for the offender, the opportunity of the offender to engage in sexual activities with the target, and any obstacles to engaging in that activity (e.g., the level of supervision of the target and the geographic location of the target).

Briggs, Simon, and Simonsen differentiated between online child groomers who are driven by fantasies of sexual activities with children and those who are driven by the desire to engage in contact sexual offenses with children.[121] They found that those driven by the desire to engage in contact offenses spent a limited amount of time online, only to the extent required to groom a target for offline contact. The study also revealed that offenders do not fit neatly into each category; some fantasy-driven offenders were found to seek offline contact with children. For other online sex offenders, the ultimate goal is to fulfill a fantasy, not to engage in offline sex offending.[122]

CRIMINALIZING AND RESPONDING TO INTERNET SEX OFFENDERS AND CHILD PORNOGRAPHY

In Hollywood, certain celebrities have been found to possess and distribute child pornography. Recently, a producer of *Law and Order* and the *Blacklist*, Jason "Jace" Alexander, was charged and convicted of these crimes, receiving ten years of probation.[123] His child pornography images and videos were of young girls engaging in sexual activities. The ages of the girls ranged from six to thirteen years old.[124] Jared Fogle, who became famous as the spokesperson for Subway, was charged and convicted of child pornography possession and distribution and utilizing the Internet to arrange sex with minors.[125] For his crimes, Fogle received a fifteen-year, eight-month prison sentence.[126] Russell Taylor, executive director of Fogle's foundation (The Jared Foundation), which was dedicated to fighting childhood obesity, was also found to possess and create child pornography (some of which he created in his own home) and was charged and convicted for his crimes.[127] Taylor was sentenced to twenty-seven years' imprisonment.[128]

In the United Kingdom, *Operation Yewtree* was launched by the Metropolitan Police Service to investigate allegations of child sexual exploitation and abuse by celebrities (e.g., Jimmy Savile and Rolf Harris).[129] One celebrity identified during this investigation as a child sexual predator was Paul Francis Gadd ("Gary Glitter"), a famous musician who gained notoriety for child sexual exploitation and child pornography. In addition to allegations, charges, and convictions of child sexual abuse during his career, he was found to have a vast collection of child pornography of children between the ages of three and six years old (images of infants and slightly older children were also found in his collection).[130] Apart from his child sex offenses in the United Kingdom, Glitter had also traveled to a different country (Vietnam) to sexually exploit two girls.[131] What Glitter did was engage in **child sex tourism,** where perpetrators travel to another country in order to engage in some form of child sexual exploitation. Child sex tourism is a worldwide problem. William Irey, a U.S. citizen, traveled to Cambodia with the intention of engaging in sexual activities with children and also had children from Cambodia and China flown to him to the United States.[132] Irey further recorded his sexual abuse of children in images and videos and used his child pornography to gain access to child pornography websites.[133] Irey was imprisoned for his crime and was required to register as a sex offender.

The U.S. Sex Offender Registration and Notification Act of 2006 is part of the Adam Walsh Child Protection and Safety Act of 2006. This act called for the creation of a national **sex offender registry** in which the personal details of convicted sex offenders, their location, and their prior crimes are registered in an effort to track and monitor these individuals in their communities. Subsequent amendments to laws required offenders to submit biometric information, such as fingerprints and DNA. The U.S. Jacob Wetterling Crimes Against Children and Sexually Violent Offender Act of 1994 also required states to create sex offender registries. Sex offender registries include three classifications of offenders.[134] The most dangerous sex offenders are included in Tier 3 and are required to update their information every three months on the registry and must be listed in the registry for their entire life. Tier 2 offenders must be listed in the sex offender registry for twenty-five years; these individuals are required to update their information biannually. Finally, Tier 1 offenders must be listed in the registry for fifteen years and are required to update their data annually. Other countries have similar registries in place. In the United Kingdom, convicted sex offenders are required to register with law enforcement three days after their release from imprisonment under the Sex Offenders Act of 1997 (amended by the Sexual Offences Act of 2003). For his many child sex offenses, Glitter was required to register as a sex offender for life under U.K. law.[135]

Children have been used in live webcam sex shows, in which perpetrators provide instructions on the type of abuse they are looking for and see the abuse occur in real time for a payment. The payment varies according to the website accessed and the type of request. The live webcam sex shows are more difficult to detect, as copies of the show are often not made[136] (unless, for example, the perpetrator records the show for later viewing or the site offers it for purchase). Undercover investigations have been used to identify perpetrators of this crime. Even private organizations have conducted undercover operations to reveal perpetrators involved in this crime. Terre des Hommes, a Dutch organization, carried out an undercover investigation by creating a virtual ten-year-old Filipino girl, Sweetie, and posing as the young girl in video chat rooms. The investigation revealed that over a ten-week period approximately twenty thousand men contacted her in these forums, one thousand of whom offered her money to engage in sexual acts.[137]

The prosecution of perpetrators involved in these shows and those requesting sexually explicit conduct from children depends on the laws of the countries in which these acts occur. The same holds true for child pornography. The United States requires the depiction of a real child in the image to convict an offender for this crime.[138] Several U.S. laws criminalize child pornography possession, creation, and distribution: 18 U.S.C. § 2251, 18 U.S.C. § 2251A, 18 U.S.C. § 2252, and 18 U.S.C. § 2252A.[139] The Child Pornography Prevention Act of 1996 had criminalized, among other things, "any visual depiction, including any photograph, film, video, picture, or computer or computer-generated image or picture" that visually depicts "or appears to . . . [depict] a minor engaging in sexually explicit conduct." This law also criminalized "visual depiction[s] . . . advertised, promoted, presented, described, or distributed in such a manner that conveys the impression that the material is or contains a visual depiction of a minor engaging in sexually explicit conduct." The law was struck down by the Supreme Court on the grounds that it criminalized material that does not depict a real child.[140] In 2003, the Prosecutorial Remedies and Other Tools to End the Exploitation of Children Today Act was passed, which criminalized the pandering of visual depictions of child pornography that do not involve the depiction of real children. The Supreme Court upheld the law in 2008 in *United States v. Williams*.[141]

Likewise, in Japan, under the Act on Punishment of Activities Relating to Child Prostitution and Child Pornography, and the Protection of Children of 1999, child pornography prosecutions are pursued solely for visual representations of real children; digitally altered images depicting child pornography and fictional depictions of child pornography via text, images, or other formats are excluded. The same holds true for South Korea with the Juvenile Sexual Protection Act of 2000. The same requirement does not exist in other countries, for example, in the United Kingdom. In the United Kingdom, "non-photographic pornographic images of children" are criminalized under the Coroner and Justice Act of 2009. Under Section 65(6) of the act, these images include those in which either "the impression conveyed . . . is that the person shown is a child" or "the predominant impression conveyed is that the person shown is a child despite the fact that some of the physical characteristics shown are not those of a child." Section 62 of this act covers possession of prohibited images of children. In particular, "non-photographic images (this includes computer generated images [CGI's], cartoons, manga images and drawings) and therefore specifically excludes indecent photographs, or pseudo-photographs of children, as well as tracings or derivatives of photographs and pseudo-photographs."[142]

In addition to national laws, there are regional laws in place that criminalize this conduct. For instance, the Council of the European Union's Framework Decision on Combating the Sexual Exploitation of Children, including Child Pornography (Council Framework Decision 2004/68/JHA) considers "realistic images of a non-existent child involved or engaged in . . . sexually explicit conduct, including lascivious exhibition of the genitals or the pubic area of a child" as child pornography (see Article 1). What is more, Article 3 of the Council Framework Decision 2004/68/JHA criminalized the development, distribution, provision, and possession of child pornography. Moreover, regional laws exist that call for the protection of children against sexual exploitation. A case in point is Article 16 of the African Charter on the Rights and Welfare of the Child. Article 23(l) of the African Youth Charter similarly calls for the creation and implementation of measures that specifically protect women and girls from different forms of sexual exploitation and sexual violence.

Along with national and regional laws, multilateral conventions, such as the Cybercrime Convention (discussed in Chapter 4), prohibit the possession, creation, and distribution of child pornography. Although the Cybercrime Convention largely does not include online interpersonal crimes, it does criminalize child pornography. Specifically, Article 9(1) of the Cybercrime Convention criminalizes the production, offer, distribution, procurement, and possession of child pornography and holds that signatories must ensure that laws are in place that criminalize this behavior. Article 9(2) of the Cybercrime Convention describes child pornography as "pornographic material that visually depicts . . . a minor engaged in sexually explicit conduct; . . . a person appearing to be a minor engaged in sexually explicit conduct; . . . [and] realistic images representing a minor engaged in sexually explicit conduct." A minor is considered to be an individual under the age of eighteen. There is, however, a provision under Article 9(3) of the treaty that enables member states to have laws in place that deem minors those who are seventeen or sixteen years of age (no younger than that). Moreover, Article 34(c) of the UN Convention on the Rights of the Child criminalizes child sexual exploitation "in pornographic performances and materials." Furthermore, Article 3(2)(c) of the UN Optional Protocol to the Convention on the Rights of the Child on the Sale of Children, Child Prostitution and Child Pornography criminalizes "[p]roducing, distributing, disseminating, importing, exporting, offering, selling or possessing . . . child pornography" and calls for states to ensure that such behavior is outlawed in domestic laws. The need to take action to protect children from sexual exploitation is explicitly listed under the UN Convention on the Rights of the Child, which requires signatories to "take all appropriate national, bilateral and multilateral measures to prevent . . . the inducement or coercion of a child to engage in any unlawful sexual activity . . . [and] . . . the exploitative use of children in pornographic performances and materials" (see Article 34 of the convention).

The **National Center for Missing and Exploited Children** (NCMEC), established in 1984, was created in an attempt to create a national clearinghouse for information on missing and exploited children. Through April 2015, over 139 million child pornography photographs and videos, which were part of the **Child Victim Identification Program** of NCMEC, a central repository of images and videos depicting sexually explicit behaviors and acts, had been reviewed.[143] Investigators have used information provided by the NCMEC to solve a variety of cases. A case in point is Crystal Anzaldi, who was abducted as an infant.[144] Eight years after her abduction, in 1998, an investigator examining a child abuse case in Puerto Rico accessed NCMEC files and found that the child in the investigation matched Anzaldi (a fact later confirmed with DNA testing). **PhotoDNA** is used to match images to known child pornography images that are in the NCMEC database.[145] NCMEC also created the **Cybertipline** in 1998 as an online reporting mechanism for missing children and child exploitation.[146] In 1999, in an effort to develop international public-private partnerships, the **International Centre for Missing and Exploited Children** was created to assist in the dissemination of information about missing and exploited children. It also provides training to criminal justice agents and engages in advocacy for adoptions of child exploitation laws and modifications needed to existing laws and policies. Individual countries have also created their own child sexual exploitation databases. The United Kingdom had a database in place called ChildBase, which stored images of child sexual exploitation; these images are now stored in a stand-alone system of the Child Exploitation and Online Protection Centre. INTERPOL's database, **INTERPOL Child Abuse Image Database**, also contains images of child sexual exploitation which can be consulted during investigations.[147] The **INTERPOL International Child Sexual Exploitation image database** (ICSE DB) replaced the Child Abuse Image Database.[148] Certified users are able to access the database directly irrespective of their geographic location.

Moreover, the **Virtual Global Task Force** was created "to build an effective, international partnership of law enforcement agencies that helps to protect children from online child abuse."[149] The task force (see Table 10-3) consists of law enforcement authorities from a multitude of countries working together to detect, identify, and assist sexually exploited children and investigate online child sexual exploitation.[150] An example of a case that

Table 10-3 Law Enforcement Agencies Participating in the Virtual Global Task Force

Australian Federal Police	Italian Postal and Communication Police Service
National Crime Agency's Child Exploitation and Online Protection Command, United Kingdom	Korean National Police Agency
Colombian National Police	Royal Canadian Mounted Police, The Canadian Police Centre for Missing and Exploited Children/Behavioural Science Branch
Dutch National Police, Netherlands	New Zealand Police
Europol	Ministry of Interior for the United Arab Emirates
Indonesian National Police	U.S. Immigration and Customs Enforcement's Homeland Security Investigations
INTERPOL	Cybercrime Coordination Unit Switzerland

Source: Virtual Global Task Force, "Who We Are," accessed August 15, 2016, http://www.virtualglobaltaskforce.com/who-we-are/.

members of the Virtual Global Task Force worked on together is *Operation Endeavour*. In 2014, the task force dismantled an organized crime group that promoted the live and on-demand sexual abuse of children in the Philippines. Private-sector companies have also formed a coalition, the **Financial Coalition Against Child Pornography** (see Table 10-4 for companies that are part of this coalition), to stop the proliferation of child pornography. The private sector also plays a role in investigating online sex offending. Microsoft's **Child Exploitation Tracking System** enables law enforcement authorities from all over the world to cooperate in investigations of child sexual exploitation.

Undercover investigations have been used to identify online sexual predators. Law enforcement personnel pose as children in forums known to be frequented by child sexual predators. Law enforcement agencies also use honeypots to identify online sexual predators. A **honeypot** is a fake website that serves no legitimate purpose other than to gather intelligence on criminal activity and to capture the information of child sexual predators who access the site to download child pornography. In *Operation Pin*, the United States, the United Kingdom, and Australia utilized honeypots to identify child pornographers.[151] The honeypots purportedly contained child pornography.[152] Upon accessing the content of the honeypot, a user was informed that the website was a law enforcement website and that the person had engaged in unlawful activities. The details of the individuals that accessed the website were collected by law enforcement agencies. The purpose of the website was to collect intelligence and deter child sex offenders by undermining the confidence of those who go to websites to upload, view, and download images and videos of child pornography.[153]

Another undercover law enforcement investigation, *Operation Delego*, led to the charging of seventy-two individuals with child sexual exploitation crimes (of those charged, fifteen remain at large).[154] In this case, law enforcement discovered that child pornography on the site targeted in the investigation was encrypted and access to it was limited to members that had the decryption key. In fact, this site utilized a wide variety of techniques to protect its members and limited access to its content to members only in an effort to evade

Table 10-4 Members of the Financial Coalition Against Child Pornography

AOL	Green Dot Corporation
American Express Company	HSBC – North America
Banco Bradesco	JP Morgan Chase
Bank of America	MasterCard
The Bank of New York – Mellon	Microsoft
Capital One	National Processing Company
Chase Paymentech Solutions	North American Bancard
Citigroup	PayPal
CyberSource	Premier Bankcard
Deutsche Bank Americas	ProPay
Discover Financial Services	Standard Chartered Bank
Elavon	Visa
First Data Corporation	Wells Fargo
First National Bank of Omaha	WePay
Global Payments	Western Union
GoDaddy.com	Xoom.com
Google	Yahoo!

Source: National Center for Missing and Exploited Children, "Financial Coalition Against Child Pornography," accessed August 15, 2016, http://www.missingkids.com/FCACP.

detection by law enforcement authorities. Websites like Dreamboard also provide child predators with guidance on how to evade detection by authorities.[155] Motivated child pornography offenders will find ways to adapt their methods to existing prevention and control efforts and substitute tactics to evade detection by authorities. Indeed, those seriously involved in online child pornography offending tend to use more secure applications to engage in such conduct and network with other offenders.[156]

Child sex offenders have adapted to advances in technology, using these advances to facilitate the crimes they commit.[157] As one researcher noted, the language used by online criminals is continually evolving, rendering certain detection methods unable to identify them.[158] Criminals misspell words and place spaces and symbols between letters on websites and other online forums to evade identification by detection software. Words that have been altered slightly will not be caught by this software. Similarly to antivirus and antispyware on computers and other digital devices, detection software needs to be constantly updated. Moreover, filtering software can be used to block children from accessing certain sites. Filtering software conducts a real-time analysis of content. Depending on the function of the software, it restricts or blocks access based on the type of analysis that is being performed. For example, keyword analysis software reviews content for specific words or phrases and blocks or restricts access to sites accordingly. Commercial software is available that blocks or restricts access to sites containing harmful content to minors.[159]

SEXTING

Sexting refers to the generation of sexually explicit content (e.g., nude photos) distributed through messaging services on mobile phones or via the Internet. Sexting can be either a legal or illegal act, depending on the actions of the perpetrator and the consent and age of the parties involved. When he was eighteen years old, Phillip Alpert distributed nude photographs of his sixteen-year-old girlfriend and was subsequently charged with child pornography possession and distribution, among other crimes. He pled guilty and was required to register as a sex offender.[160] A survey conducted by the Pew Research Center revealed that children between the ages of twelve and seventeen engaged in sexting, the extent of which varied primarily with age.[161] Older children were more likely to engage in sexting than younger children. The survey showed that 4 percent of the children in the survey that owned phones had engaged in sexting; 15 percent of those owning cell phones had received nude or sexually explicit images.[162] In a study by Strohmaier, Murphy, and DeMatteo, 54 percent of the 175 children surveyed revealed that they had engaged in sexting, though not all of those in this category had sent images, just messages (28 percent).[163] Some youths in the survey downplayed the seriousness of the offense. Indeed, comments of those surveyed on sexting included, "Everybody does it" and "It's not really a big deal."[164]

BOX 10-2 APPS THAT PROMOTE SEXTING

Apps for sexting are available. The Kik Sexting app is used by those who use the Kik app and are looking for other users who will trade nude pictures.[165] Snapchat is also promoted as an ideal app to facilitate sexting. Snapchat marketed its products as enabling users to send Snaps (in the form of photos and videos) that would purportedly disappear ten seconds after being opened by recipients. Receivers could, however, still take pictures of the Snaps they received.[166]

Sexting by youths results in what Leary termed "self-produced child pornography."[167] This type of child pornography is produced by an individual absent coercion or grooming and is subsequently distributed to others who may keep it for themselves or distribute the image to others.[168] In 2015, a male teenager was prosecuted for having naked images of himself (in the form of selfies) and his girlfriend on his phone.[169] Both pled guilty to misdemeanors to avoid felony charges; instead, they received probation, a fine, community service, and were prohibited from using a mobile phone for one year. Their criminal records were to be expunged if they completed the terms of their sentences. Even though images in sexting are self-produced, these images can cause significant psychological and emotional harm to minors.[170] Indeed, "those images document the user's participation in the production . . . that is exacerbated by [their] circulation throughout the Internet."[171] Children have committed suicide after sexual images of themselves were distributed online. In one case, a teenager, Rehtaeh Parsons, committed suicide after sexually explicit photographs of herself were shared among her peers without her consent.[172]

Children who have engaged in sexting have been charged with child pornography distribution. In Canada, a teenager was charged with child pornography distribution for sending sexually explicit photographs of her boyfriend's ex-girlfriend via text to others.[173] The seventeen-year-old was also charged with child pornography possession and communicating threats via text messages and social media (Facebook) to the victim.[174] Child pornography charges have also been levied against children who take naked pictures of themselves.

CONTROLLING INTERPERSONAL CYBERCRIME

Cyberbullying, cyberharassment, and cyberstalking serve no legitimate purpose, seeking only to cause harm or emotional distress to another individual. Such harm and emotional distress are also sought by Internet trolls, as well as those who engage in sextortion and revenge porn. Current laws alone cannot deal with these interpersonal cybercrimes. The key to effectively controlling interpersonal cybercrime is education. Children should be taught how to appropriately behave online and use the Internet safely (e.g., not providing personal information online). To do this, primary, secondary, and tertiary prevention education programs can be implemented.

Primary prevention programs are proactive, dealing with problems before they occur. The manner in which children are communicating with each other, especially online, illustrates the need to teach students about empathy and social value *before* they engage in bullying, harassing, stalking, or other forms of interpersonal crime. Accordingly, elementary, middle school, and high school curricula need to be augmented to include teaching students about the appropriate use of the Internet by educating them on (1) netiquette (the appropriate rules of behavior in online forums), (2) how to use the Internet safely (e.g., emphasizing the permanence of online content), and (3) online threats. With respect to netiquette, a program in Germany called Medienhelden (Media Heroes) focuses on training middle school teachers and working with them to develop programs that target students' online behavior.[175] The program is meant to provide students with information about the likely consequences of online actions to help foster proper netiquette.[176] Programs like these should be mass implemented in the United States and other countries. They should emphasize that the rules and values which guide in-person interactions should also guide online interactions. Moreover, character education is needed, which teaches students about the importance of core values. The ultimate goal of these programs should be the creation of a new online culture that rejects antisocial behavior, such as Internet trolling and interpersonal cybercrimes.

In addition to netiquette, students should be adequately prepared to use the Internet safely and responsibly. Currently, this is not the case. Today, students are primarily taught about safe and responsible Internet practices when they are undergraduates. The Department of Homeland Security has emphasized the need for elementary, middle, and high school students to be taught these practices.[177] Some states have created such programs. In Colorado, schools are encouraged to work with law enforcement agencies and nonprofit organizations to introduce Internet safety in the curricula.[178] Some countries have created websites to inform students about ways to navigate the Internet safely. Websites like these are designed to educate students about online child groomers, cyberbullying, and other cyberthreats and ways to deal with these threats. Stopbullying.gov is an example of such a website. Other countries have similarly created websites to inform children, parents, and others about ways to navigate the Internet safely (e.g., WebWise, the Irish Internet Safety Awareness Centre).[179]

(2)   Secondary prevention programs can also be created to deal with interpersonal cyber-crime. These programs target children most at risk of being bullied, harassed, stalked, or harmed in any way. Research has found that risky behaviors such as providing personal information and images or being willing to discuss sex with strangers online places them at greater risk of sexual exploitation.[180] Programs should therefore be targeted at these individuals to inform them of the risks. Specifically, children should be informed about how information and images posted online can be used by a perpetrator to engage in a wide variety of antisocial behaviors (Internet trolling) and interpersonal cybercrimes. Children should also be informed at an early age that online content can be permanent, especially posts that are not user controlled or that are mass e-mailed to others.

3.   Tertiary prevention methods (i.e., prevention after an undesirable behavior or illicit act has occurred) can be used to reactively respond to antisocial behavior and interpersonal cybercrime. Tertiary prevention programs include classical responses to antisocial behavior and interpersonal cybercrime, such as establishing laws and policies, enforcing the laws and policies, and investigating and prosecuting cybercriminals. However, these measures deal with an illicit act after the fact. What is needed are measures that seek to intervene before antisocial behavior or interpersonal cybercrimes occur. Early intervention is preferred to minimize existing risks and educate children on the risks posed by online and offline offenders. Proactive measures should be aimed at providing the new generation with information that will help them better prepare to use the Internet safely and responsibly and to use telecommunications and electronic communications to respectfully communicate with one another.

CASE STUDY

Consider the case of Curt Schilling (mentioned in the beginning of this chapter), especially his response to the Internet trolls who tweeted about his daughter. Curt Schilling took matters into his own hands by pursuing the Internet trolls.

- What is your opinion of this action? And what are the consequences of taking these matters into your own hands?
- What message do his actions send to others?

Do not forget to mention both potential personal consequences and the larger social consequences of his actions.

REVIEW QUESTIONS

1. What is the best way to respond to Internet trolls? Is public castigation appropriate?
2. Is cyberstalking difficult to investigate and prosecute? Why or why not?
3. What can a user do if cyberharassed?
4. Is revenge porn cyberharassment? Is it prosecuted as such? Please explain your response.
5. As Rob Reiner stated, "not all policing lies in the police." How does this relate to cyberbullying?
6. What is sextortion? How does it occur?
7. What types of child sex offenders operate online?
8. In what ways are children groomed for sex online?
9. In your opinion, what is the best way to deal with children engaging in sexting?
10. What are the best ways to deal with interpersonal cybercrimes?

LAWS

Act on Punishment of Activities Relating to Child Prostitution and Child Pornography, and the Protection of Children of 1999 (Japan)

Adam Walsh Child Protection and Safety Act of 2006 (United States)

African Charter on the Rights and Welfare of the Child of 1990

African Youth Charter of 2006

Child Pornography Prevention Act of 1996 (United States)

Communications of Decency Act of 1996 (United States)

Coroner and Justice Act of 2009 (United Kingdom)

Criminal Justice and Courts Act of 2015 (United Kingdom)

Criminal Justice and Immigration Act of 2008 (United Kingdom)

Cybercrime Convention of 2001 (Council of Europe; also known as Convention on Cybercrime of 2001)

First Amendment to the U.S. Constitution (United States)

Framework Decision on Combating the Sexual Exploitation of Children, including Child Pornography of 2004 (Council of the European Union)

Jacob Wetterling Crimes Against Children and Sexually Violent Offender Registration Act of 1994 (United States)

Juvenile Sexual Protection Act of 2000 (South Korea)

Malicious Communications Act of 1988 (United Kingdom)

Prosecutorial Remedies and Other Tools to End the Exploitation of Children Today Act of 2003 (United States)

Protection from Harassment Act of 2014 (Singapore)

Sex Offender Registration and Notification Act of 2006 (United States)

Sex Offenders Act of 1997 (United Kingdom)

Sexual Offences Act of 2003 (United Kingdom)

UN Convention on the Rights of the Child of 1989

UN Optional Protocol to the Convention on the Rights of the Child on the Sale of Children, Child Prostitution and Child Pornography of 2000

DEFINITIONS

Child Exploitation Tracking System. A system enabling law enforcement authorities from all over the world to cooperate in investigations of child sexual exploitation.

Child pornography. A visual, audio, written, or other form of portrayal of sexual activity with a child under eighteen years of age that is designed to sexually arouse the user.

Child sex tourism. Child sex tourism involves the traveling to another country in order to engage in some form of child sexual exploitation.

Child Victim Identification Program. A central repository of images and videos that is part of the National Center for Missing and Exploited Children depicting sexually explicit behaviors and acts.

Cyberbullying. Cyberbullying involves children's use of the Internet, computers and related technology to annoy, humiliate, alarm, insult or otherwise attack a child, preteen, or teen.

Cyberharassment. Cyberharassment refers to the use of the Internet and digital devices to intentionally alarm, annoy, attack, and verbally abuse another individual.

Cyberstalking. Cyberstalking refers to the use of the Internet and Internet-enabled technology to repeatedly threaten, harass, and/or frighten another individual.

Cybertipline. An online reporting mechanism for missing children and child exploitation that was developed by the National Center for Missing and Exploited Children.

Extreme pornography. This type of pornography depicts sexual acts with animals, dead bodies and/or that endanger a person's life or can cause extreme physical harm to breasts, genitals, and/or the anus of an individual.

Financial Coalition Against Child Pornography. A coalition created to stop the proliferation of child pornography.

Honeypot. A fake website that serves no other legitimate purpose other than to gather intelligence on online criminal activity to identify perpetrators.

International Centre for Missing and Exploited Children. A center created to develop international public-private partnerships and assist in the dissemination of information about missing and exploited children.

Internet troll. An Internet troll posts highly offensive and inflammatory remarks online in order to provoke an emotional reaction and response from other users.

INTERPOL Child Image Database. A database containing images of child sexual exploitation which can be consulted during investigations.

INTERPOL International Child Sexual Exploitation Image Database. This database replaced the Child Abuse Image Database.

National Center for Missing and Exploited Children. This center is a national clearinghouse for information on missing and exploited children.

Online child grooming. The manipulation tactics an offender uses online to gain the victim's trust and ultimately lead them to engage in sexual activities.

Pedophile. An individual who is sexually aroused by prepubescent adolescents.

PhotoDNA. PhotoDNA is used to match images to known child pornography images that are in the database of the National Center for Missing and Exploited Children.

Revenge porn. A term used to describe the use of sexually explicit photos and/or videos of the victim without the victim's consent to cause the victim distress, humiliation, and/or harm them in some way.

Sex offender registry. A registry that includes information about sex offenders and their activities and whereabouts.

Sexting. The generation and sending of sexually explicit content through messaging services on mobile phones or via the Internet.

Sextortion. Sextortion occurs when a perpetrator threatens to disseminate sexually explicit photos or videos of the victim online if sexual demands are not met or if sexually explicit images or videos are not sent to the perpetrator.

Unprotected speech. Speech that is excluded from First Amendment protection.

Virtual Global Taskforce. A taskforce of law enforcement authorities from a multitude of countries working together to detect, identify, and assist sexually exploited children and investigate online child sexual exploitation.

ENDNOTES

1. C. Moss, "Curt Schilling Destroys 2 Dudes Who Were Harassing His Daughter on Twitter," *Business Insider*, March 2, 2015, http://www.businessinsider.com/curt-schilling-tweets-about-daughter-gabby-2015-3.
2. Ibid.
3. Ibid.
4. B. Quinn, "Man Admits to Elaborate Online Stalking Campaign against Girlfriend," *Guardian*, September 20, 2011, http://www.theguardian.com/uk/2011/sep/21/man-online-stalking-girlfriend-nottingham; *Huffington Post* "Violentacrez Fired: Michael Brutsch Loses Job after Reddit Troll Identity Exposed by *Gawker*," October 16, 2012," http://www.huffingtonpost.com/2012/10/15/michael-brutsch-reddits-biggest-loses-job-identity-gawker_n_1967727.html; A. Chen, "Unmasking Reddit's Violentacrez, the Biggest Troll on the Web, *Gawker*, October 12, 2012, http://gawker.com/5950981/unmasking-reddits-violentacrez-the-biggest-troll-on-the-web.
5. Chen, "Unmasking Reddit's Violentacrez."

6. R. J. Rosen, "What Was Reddit Troll Violentacrez Thinking?" *Atlantic*, October 16, 2012, http://www.theatlantic.com/technology/archive/2012/10/what-was-reddit-troll-violentacrez -thinking/263648/.

7. CBS News, "U.K. Cops Probe Internet 'Trolls' Attacking McCanns," October 2, 2014, http:// www.cbsnews.com/news/madeleine-mccann-parents-internet-trolls-may-face-prosecution/.

8. Ministry of Law, Singapore, "Protection from Harassment Act 2014 Now in Force," 2014, https://www.mlaw.gov.sg/content/minlaw/en/news/press-releases/protection-from-harass ment-act-in-force.html.

9. *Gertz v. Welch*, 418 U.S. 323 (1974).

10. *Chaplinsky v. New Hampshire*, 315 U.S. 568 (1942).

11. *Brandenburg v. Ohio*, 395 U.S. 444 (1969).

12. *Roth v. United States*, 354 U. S. 476 (1957); *Miller v. California*, 413 U.S. 15 (1973).

13. *Harper & Row, Publishers, Inc. v. Nation Enterprises*, 471 U.S. 539 (1985).

14. *Watts v. United States*, 394 U.S. 705 (1969).

15. Quinn, "Man Admits to Elaborate Online Stalking Campaign against Girlfriend"; T. Kelly, "Student Tells How 'Caring Boyfriend' Was Malicious and Vile Stalker Who Posted Sexually Explicit Photos of Her Online," *Daily Mail*, January 13, 2014, http://www.dailymail.co.uk /news/article-2055678/Shane-Webber-stalked-girlfriend-Ruth-Jeffery-online-jailed-4-months .html#ixzz3nH7CinuI.

16. L. Riparbelli, "12-Year-Old Sentenced for Cyberstalking Classmate," *ABC News*, July 14, 2011, http://abcnews.go.com/Technology/12-year-sentenced-washington-cyberstalking-case /story?id=14072315.

17. Ibid.

18. B. Zwecker, "Rihanna's Stalker Scaring Her with Gun Threat," *Chicago Sun Times*, July 13, 2015, http://entertainment.suntimes.com/music/rihannas-stalker-scaring-gun-threats/.

19. *United States v. Kammersell*, 196 F.3d 1137 (10th Cir. 1999).

20. *Elonis v. United States*, 575 U. S. _____ (2015).

21. M.-H. Maras, "Unprotected Speech Communicated via Social Media: What Amounts to a True Threat?" *Journal of Internet Law* 19, no. 3 (2015): 3–9.

22. K. Quarmby, "How the Law Is Standing Up to Cyberstalking," *Newsweek*, August 13, 2014, http://www.newsweek.com/2014/08/22/how-law-standing-cyberstalking-264251.html.

23. Ibid.

24. Ibid.

25. L. W. Foderafo, "Private Moment Made Public, Then a Fatal Jump," *New York Times*, September 29, 2010, http://www.nytimes.com/2010/09/30/nyregion/30suicide.html?_r=0.

26. K. Hayes, "Tyler Clementi: Rutgers Student Suicide Causes Outrage, Stirs Gay Rights Groups," *CBS News*, September 30, 2010, http://www.cbsnews.com/news/tyler-clementi-rutgers-student -suicide-causes-outrage-stirs-gay-rights-groups/.

27. K. Zernike, "Jury Finds Spying in Rutgers Dorm Was a Hate Crime," *New York Times*, March 16, 2012, http://www.nytimes.com/2012/03/17/nyregion/defendant-guilty-in-rutgers-case .html; K. Zernike, "Jail Term Ends After 20 Days for ex-Rutgers Student," *New York Times*, June 19, 2012, http://www.nytimes.com/2012/06/20/nyregion/dharun-ravi-ex-rutgers-student-who -spied-leaves-jail.html?ref=topics &_r=0.

28. Ibid.

29. See Twitter's abusive behavior policy: https://support.twitter.com/articles/20169997#.

30. See Twitter Rules: https://support.twitter.com/articles/18311#.

31. See Article 3(6) and Article 3(7) of Facebook's Statement of Rights and Responsibilities, https://www.facebook.com/terms.php.

32. Twitter, "Reporting Abusive Behavior," https://support.twitter.com/articles/20169998- reporting-abusive-behavior#; E. Avey, "Making It Easier to Report Threats to Law Enforce-

ment," *Twitter*, March 17, 2015, https://blog.twitter.com/2015/making-it-easier-to-report -threats-to-law-enforcement.

33. See Flickr Community Guidelines: https://www.flickr.com/help/guidelines.

34. U.S. Attorney's Office, Central District of California, "L.A. Man Who Hacked into Email Accounts and Obtained Nude Photos for 'Revenge Porn' Website Pleads Guilty in Hacking Scheme," *Department of Justice*, July 2, 2015, http://www.justice.gov/usao-cdca/pr/la -man-who-hacked-email-accounts-and-obtained-nude-photos-revenge-porn-website -pleads.

35. A. Ronan, "Could All These New Revenge-Porn Laws Actually Be a Bad Thing?" *New York Magazine*, April 16, 2015, http://nymag.com/thecut/2015/04/why-regulating-revenge-porn -is-so-tricky.html.

36. Ronan, "Could All These New Revenge-Porn Laws Actually Be a Bad Thing?"

37. M. S. Sweeney, "What the Law Can (and Can't) Do about Online Harassment," *Atlantic*, November 12, 2014, http://www.theatlantic.com/technology/archive/2014/11/what-the-law-can -and-cant-do-about-online-harassment/382638/.

38. T. Weaver, "'Revenge Porn' Now Illegal in New York," *CBS News*, August 1, 2014, http://www .syracuse.com/news/index.ssf/2014/08/revenge_porn_now_illegal_in_new_york.html.

39. CBS News, "Cuomo Signs Amendment Strengthening Statewide Revenge Porn Ban," August 1, 2014, http://newyork.cbslocal.com/2014/08/01/cuomo-signs-amendment-strengthening statewide-revenge-porn-ban/.

40. L. Ridley, "Revenge Porn Is Finally Illegal: Who Are the Victims and Perpetrators of This Growing Phenomenon?" *Huffington Post*, February 12, 2015, http://www.huffingtonpost .co.uk/2015/04/12/revenge-porn-law_n_6630730.html.

41. Press Association, "Woman Pleads Guilty to Posting Revenge Porn Photos of Girlfriend," *Guardian*, September 1, 2015, http://www.theguardian.com/uk-news/2015/sep/01/woman -sentenced-revenge-porn-offence-explicit-photos-girlfriend.

42. See Facebook Community Standards: https://m.facebook.com/communitystandards /?section=0.

43. M. L. Ybarra and K. J. Mitchell, "Youth Engaging in Online Harassment: Associations with Caregiver-Child Relationships, Internet Use and Personal Characteristics," *Journal of Adolescence* 27, no. 3 (2004): 319–336; J. Junoven and E. F. Gross, "Extending the School Grounds? Bullying Experiences in Cyberspace," *Journal of School Health* 78, no. 9 (2008): 496–505; J. Raskauskas and A. D. Stoltz, "Involvement in Traditional and Electronic Bullying Among Adolescents," *Developmental Psychology* 43, no. 3 (2007): 564–575; P. K. Smith, J. Mahdavi, M. Carvalho, S. Fisher, S. Russell, and N. Tippett, "Cyberbullying: The Nature and Impact in Secondary School Pupils," *Journal of Child Psychology and Psychiatry* 49, no. 4 (2008): 376–385; P. K. Smith, G. Steffen, and R. Sittichai, "The Nature of Cyber Bullying and an International Network," in *Severability through the New Media: Findings from an International Network*, ed. P. K. Smith and G. Steffen (New York: Psychology Press, 2013).

44. S. Hinduja and J. Patchin, "Bullying, Cyberbullying, and Suicide," *Archives of Suicide Research* 14, no. 3 (2010): 206–221.

45. T. Beran and Q. Li, "Cyber Harassment: A Study of a New Method for an Old Behavior," *Journal of Educational Computing Research* 32, no. 3 (2005): 265–277; J. Wang, T. Nansel, and R. Ionatti, "Cyber and Traditional Bullying: Differential Association with Depression," *Journal of Adolescent Health* 48, no. 4 (2011): 415–417; F. Staude-Muller, B. Hansen, and M. Voss, "How Stressful is Online Victimization? Effects of the Victim's Personality and Properties of the Incident," *European Journal of Developmental Psychology* 9, no. 2 (2012): 100; S. Perren, J. Dooley, T. Shaw, and D. Cross, "Bullying in School in Cyberspace: Associations with Depressive Symptoms in Swiss and Australian Adolescents," *Child and Adolescent Psychiatry and Mental Health* 4, no. 28 (2010): 1–10.

46. Perren et al., "Bullying in School in Cyberspace"; D. Cross, T. Shaw, L. Hearn, M. Epstein, H. Monks, L. Lester, et al. (2009), *Australian Covert Bullying Prevalence Study*, Child Health Promotion Research Center, Edith Cowan University, Perth, Australia; A. Sourander, A. B. Klomek, M. Ikonen, J. Lindroos, T. Luntamo, M. Koskelainen, et al., "Psychosocial Risk Factors Associated with Cyberbully Among Adolescents: A Population-Based Study," *Archives of General Psychiatry* 67, no. 7 (2010): 720–728; Wang et al., "Cyber and Traditional Bullying"; P. Gradinger, D. Strohmeier, and C. Spiel, "Traditional Bullying and Cyberbullying: Identification of Risk Groups for Adjustment Problems," *Journal of Psychology* 217, no. 4 (2009):205–213; J. Raskaukas, "Text Bullying: Associations with Traditional Bullying and Depression Among New Zealand Adolescents," *Journal of School Violence* 9, no. 1 (2010): 74–97.

47. J. Pyżalski, "Electronic Aggression Among Adolescents: An Old House with a New Facade (or Even a Number of Houses)," in *Youth Culture and Net Culture: Online Social Practices*, ed. C. Hallgren, E. Dunkels, and G. M. Franberg (Hershey, PA: IGI Global, 2011), 278–295; J. Pyżalski, "From Cyberbullying to Electronic Aggression: Typology of the Phenomenon," *Emotional & Behavioural Difficulties* 17, nos. 3–4 (2012): 305–317.

48. R. M. Kowalski and S. P. Limber, "Electronic Bullying among Middle School Students," *Journal of Adolescent Health* 41, no. 6 (2007): S22–S30.

49. C. Katzer, D. Fetchenhauer, and F. Belschak, "Cyberbullying: Who Are the Victims? A Comparison of Victimization in Internet Chatrooms and Victimization in School," *Journal of Media Psychology* 21, no. 1 (2009): 25–36.

50. Pyżalski, "Electronic Aggression Among Adolescents"; Pyżalski, "From Cyberbullying to Electronic Aggression"; E. Whittaker and R. M. Kowalski, "Cyberbullying via Social Media," *Journal of School Violence* 14, no. 1 (2015): 11–29.

51. L. Alvarez, "Girl's Suicide Points to Rise in Apps Used by Cyberbullies," *New York Times*, September 13, 2013, http://www.nytimes.com/2013/09/14/us/suicide-of-girl-after-bullying-raises-worries-on-web-sites.html?_r=0.

52. Whittaker and Kowalski, "Cyberbullying via Social Media," 11–29.

53. "New Cyberbullying Law Generates First Juvenile Sentence in Union County," *Suburban News*, July 2014, http://www.nj.com/suburbannews/index.ssf/2014/07/new_cyberbullying_law_generate.html.

54. Ibid.

55. H. Carter, "Teenage Girl Is First To Be Jailed for Bullying on Facebook," *Guardian*, August 21, 2009, http://www.theguardian.com/uk/2009/aug/21/facebook-bullying-sentence-teenage-girl.

56. T. LeBoeuf, "North Carolina Appeals Court Upholds Cyberbullying Conviction Over Claims of First Amendment Violations," *SPLC*, June 29, 2015, http://www.splc.org/article/2015/06/north-carolina-appeals-court-upholds-cyberbullying-conviction-over-claims-of-first-amendment-violations.

57. F. S. Abubey, "County Convicts First Suspect Under Cyber Bullying Law," *WFMY*, February 6, 2014, http://www.wfmynews2.com/story/news/local/2014/02/06/cyber-bullying-conviction/5265675/.

58. T. Smith, "Teen Sentenced to Probation, Community Service for Cyberbullying," *WSOCTV*, March 21, 2014, http://www.wsoctv.com/news/news/local/teen-sentenced-probation-community-service-cyberbu/nfH9F/.

59. *Boston et al. v. Athearn et al.*, A140971 (Ga. Ct. App. Oct. 10, 2014).

60. S. Perren, L. Corcoran, H. Cowie, F. Dehue, D. Garcia, C. McGuckin, A. Sevcikova, P. Tsatsou and T. Vollink, "Tackling Cyberbullying: Review of Empirical Evidence Regarding Successful Responses by Students, Parents and Schools," *International Journal of Conflict and Violence* 6, no. 2 (2012): 283–293.

61. Juvonen and Gross, "Extending the School Grounds? Bullying Experiences in Cyberspace."

62. D. L. Hoff and S. N. Mitchell, "Cyberbullying: Causes, Effects, and Remedies," *Journal of Educational Administration* 47, no. 5 (2009): 652–665.

63. P. K. Smith and A. Frisén, "The Nature of Cyberbullying, and Strategies for Prevention," *Computers in Human Behavior* 29, no. 1 (2012): 26–32.

64. Juvonen and Gross, "Extending the School Grounds?"

65. E. Stacey, "Research into Cyberbullying: Student Perspectives on Cyber Safe Learning Environments," *Informatics in Education* 8, no. 1 (2009): 115–130; T. Aricak, S. Siyahhan, A. Uzunhasanoglu, S. Saribeyoglu, S. Ciplak, N. Yilmaz, and C. Memmedov, "Cyberbullying Among Turkish Adolescents," *Cyberpsychology and Behavior* 11, no. 3 (2008): 253–261; Hoff and Mitchell, "Cyberbullying: Causes, Effects, and Remedies"; Juvonen and Gross, "Extending the School Grounds?"; Smith et al., "Cyberbullying"; F. Mishna, M. Saini, and S. Solomon, "Ongoing and Online: Children and Youths' Perceptions of Cyberbullying," *Children and Youth Services Review* 31 (2009): 1222–1228; C. Topcu, O. Erdur-Baker, and Y. Capa-Aydin, "Examination of Cyberbullying Experiences Among Turkish Students from Different School Types," *Cyberpsychology and Behavior* 11, no. 6 (2008): 643–648.

66. P. K. Smith, J. Mahdavi, M. Carvalho, S. Fisher, S. Russell, and N. Tippett, "Cyberbullying: The Nature and Impact in Secondary School Pupils," *Journal of Child Psychology and Psychiatry* 49, no. 4 (2008): 376–385.

67. R. M. Kowalski, S. P. Limber, and P. W. Agaston, *Cyberbullying: Bullying in the Digital Age* (Malden, MA: Blackwell, 2008); E. Stacey, "Research into Cyberbullying: Student Perspectives on Cyber Safe Learning Environments," *Informatics in Education*, 8, (2009): 115–130; Hoff and Mitchell, "Cyberbullying: Causes, Effects, and Remedies"; Mishna, Saini, and Solomon, "Ongoing and Online: Children and Youths' Perceptions of Cyberbullying," cited in C. McGuckin, S. Perren, L. Corcoran, H. Cowie, F. Dehue, A. Sevcikova, P. Tsatsou, and T. Vollink, "Coping with Cyberbullying: How We Can Prevent Cyberbullying and How Victims can Cope with it," in *Cyberbullying through the New Media: Findings from an International Network*, ed. P. K. Smith and G. Steffen (New York: Psychology Press, 2013), 128.

68. P. Gradinger, D. Strohmeier, E. M. Schiller, E. Stefanek, and C. Spiel, "Cyber-Victimization and Popularity in Early Adolescence: Stability and Predictive Associations," in "Cyberbullying: Development, Consequences, Risk and Protective Factors," *European Journal of Developmental Psychology* 9, no. 2 (2012): 77, special issue, ed. E. Menesini and C. Spiel.

69. T. Aricak, S. Siyahhan, A. Uzunhasanoglu, S. Saribeyoglu, S. Ciplak, N. Yilmaz, and C. Memmedov, "Cyberbullying Among Turkish Adolescents," *Cyberpsychology and Behavior* 11, no. 3 (2008): 253–261; R. M. Kowalski, S. P. Limber, and P. W. Agaston, P. W., *Cyberbullying: Bullying in the Digital Age* (Malden, MA: Blackwell, 2008); Stacey, "Research into Cyberbullying: Student Perspectives on Cyber Safe Learning Environments."

70. L. Parris, K. Varjas, J. Meyers, and H. Cutts, "High School Students' Perceptions of Coping with Cyberbullying," *Youth and Society* 44, no. 2 (2012): 284–306.

71. D. Haldera and K. Jaishankar, "Cyber Gender Harassment and Secondary Victimization: A Comparative Analysis of the United States, the UK, and India," *Victims & Offenders: An International Journal of Evidence-Based Research, Policy, and Practice* 6, no. 4 (2011): 386–398.

72. R. Reiner, *The Politics of the Police*, 3rd ed. (Oxford: Oxford University Press, 2000), xi.

73. See Article 3(6) of Facebook's Statement of Rights and Responsibilities, https://www.facebook.com/terms.php.

74. CBC News, "Amanda Todd Suspect Aydin Coban Writes Open Letter Proclaiming Innocence," January 28, 2015, http://www.cbc.ca/news/canada/amanda-todd-suspect-aydin-coban-writes-open-letter-proclaiming-innocence-1.2935055.

75. U.S. Department of Justice, Office of Public Affairs, "New Hampshire Man Charged with Computer Hacking and Cyberstalking in 'Sextortion' Scheme Targeting Minors," July 16,

2015, http://www.justice.gov/opa/pr/new-hampshire-man-charged-computer-hacking-and-cyberstalking-sextortion-scheme-targeting.

76. "Cyberbully's Prison Sentence Appealed," *The Local*, November 22, 2013, http://www.thelocal.se/20131122/cyberbullys-prison-sentence-appealed.

77. U.S. Department of Justice, Office of Public Affairs, "Former U.S. Government Employee Charged in Computer Hacking and Cyber Stalking Scheme," August 19, 2015, http://www.justice.gov/opa/pr/former-us-government-employee-charged-computer-hacking-and-cyber-stalking-scheme.

78. L. R. Shapiro and M.-H. Maras, *Multidisciplinary Investigation of Child Maltreatment* (Burlington, MA: Jones and Bartlett, 2015), 311.

79. M. C. Seto, J. M. Cantor, and R. Blanchard, "Child Pornography Offenses Are a Valid Diagnostic Indicator of Pedophilia," *Journal of Abnormal Psychology* 115, no. 3 (2006): 610–615; A. Carr, "The Social Dimension of the Online Trade of Child Sexual Exploitation Material," in *Understanding and Preventing Online Sexual Exploitation of Children*, ed. E. Quayle and K. M. Ribisl (New York: Routledge, 2012), 98.

80. O. Henry, R. Mandeville-Norden, E. Hayes, and V. Egan, "Do Internet-Based Sexual Offenders Reduce to Normal, Inadequate and Deviant Groups?" *Journal of Sexual Aggression* 6, no. 1 (2010): 33–46.

81. E. Quayle and M. Taylor, "Pedophiles, Pornography and the Internet: Assessment Issues," *British Journal of Social Work* 32 (2002): 863–875; M. D. O'Brien and S. D. Webster, "The Construction and Preliminary Validation of the Internet Behaviors and Attitudes Questionnaire (IBAQ)," *Sexual Abuse: A Journal of Research and Treatment* 19 (2007): 237–256.

82. Internet Watch Foundation, *Internet Watch Foundation Annual & Charity Report 2013*, (2013), 6, https://www.iwf.org.uk/assets/media/annual-reports/annual_report_2013.pdf.pdf.

83. Ibid., 7.

84. M.-H. Maras, *Computer Forensics: Cybercriminals, Laws and Evidence*, 2nd ed. (Burlington, MA: Jones and Bartlett, 2014), 169–170; M.-H. Maras, "Inside Darknet: The Takedown of Silk Road," *Criminal Justice Matters* 98, no. 1 (2014): 22.

85. J. Davidson and S. Webster, "The Theoretical Context of Online Child Sexual Abuse," in *Online Offending Behavior and Child Victimization: New Findings and Policy*, ed. S. Webster, J. Davidson, and A. Bifulco (New York: Palgrave-Macmillan, 2015), 25; Quayle and Taylor, "Pedophiles, Pornography and the Internet"; E. Quayle and M. Taylor, "Model of Problematic Internet Use in People with a Sexual Interest in Children," *Cyberpsychology and Behavior* 6, no. 1 (2003): 93–106.

86. E. Quayle, M. Erooga, I. Wright, M. Taylor, and D. Harbinson, *Only Pictures? Therapeutic Work with Internet Sex Offenders* (Dorset, UK: Russell House, 2006); M. C. Seto, *Internet Sex Offenders* (Washington, DC: American Psychological Association, 2013), 258.

87. K. Connolly, "Germany Investigates Second Life Child Pornography," *Guardian*, May 8, 2007, http://www.theguardian.com/technology/2007/may/08/secondlife.web20.

88. C. Reeves, "Fantasy Depictions of Child Sexual Abuse: The Problem of Ageplay in Second Life," *Journal of Sexual Aggression* 19, no. 2 (2013): 238.

89. D. Rising, "Germans Investigate Child Porn in Virtual World," *NBC News*, May 10, 2007, http://www.nbcnews.com/id/18600982/ns/technology_and_science-tech_and_gadgets/t/germans-investigate-child-porn-virtual-world/#slice-2.

90. Ibid.

91. Maras, *Computer Forensics*, 169–170.

92. See Chapter 3.3, Europol, "The Internet Organised Crime Threat Assessment," 2014, https://www.europol.europa.eu/iocta/2014/chap-3-3-view1.html.

93. M. C. Seto, L. Reeves, and S. Jung, "Motives for Child Pornography Offending: The Explanations Given by the Offenders," *Journal of Sexual Aggression* 16 (2010): 177.

94. V. Sheehan and J. Sullivan, "A Qualitative Analysis of Child Sex Offenders Involved in the Manufacture of Indecent Images of Children," *Journal of Sexual Aggression* 16, no. 2 (2010): 143–168; E. Quayle and R. Sinclair, "An Introduction to the Problem," in *Understanding and Preventing Online Sexual Exploitation of Children*, ed. E. Quayle and K. M. Ribisl (New York: Routledge, 2012), 13.

95. H. L. Merdiana, C. Curtisa, J. Thakkera, N. Wilson, and D. P. Boer, "The Three Dimensions of Online Child Pornography Offending," *Journal of Sexual Aggression: An International, Interdisciplinary Forum for Research, Theory and Practice* 19, no. 1 (2013): 121–132.

96. Europol, "The Internet Organised Crime Threat Assessment."

97. E. Quayle, G. Holland, C. Linenan, and M. Taylor, "The Internet and Offending Behavior: A Case Study," *Journal of Sexual Aggression* 6, no. 1 (2000): 78–96.

98. D. Finkelhor and R. Ormrod, *Child Pornography: Patterns from the NIBRS*, Office of Justice Programs, Office of Juvenile Justice and Delinquency Prevention (Washington, DC: U.S. Department of Justice, 2004).

99. M. L. Bourke and A. E. Hernandez, "The 'Burner Study' Redux: A Report of the Incidence of Hands on Child Victimization by Child Pornography Offenders," *Journal of Family Violence* 24 (2009): 183–191; Seto et al., "Child Pornography Offenses Are a Valid Diagnostic Indicator of Pedophilia."

100. K. Lanning, *Child Molesters: A Behavioral Analysis*, 4th ed. (Arlington, VA: National Center for Missing and Exploited Children, 2001).

101. T. Krone, "Typology of Online Child Pornography Offending," *Trends and Issues in Crime and Criminal Justice*, 279 (2004): 1–6, http://www.aic.gov.au/media_library/publications/tandi _pdf/tandi279.pdf.

102. Krone, "Typology of Online Child Pornography Offending."

103. Krone, "Typology of Online Child Pornography Offending"; H. L. Merdiana, C. Curtisa, J. Thakkera, N. Wilson, and D. P. Boer, "The Three Dimensions of Online Child Pornography Offending," *Journal of Sexual Aggression: An International, Interdisciplinary Forum for Research, Theory and Practice* 19, no. 1 (2013): 121–132.

104. C. O'Connor, "Child Pornography and the Internet—A Statistical Review," *Australian Police Journal* 59, no. 4 (2005): 190–199.

105. Krone, "Typology of Online Child Pornography Offending"; K. Lanning, *Child Molesters: A Behavioral Analysis*, 4th ed. (Arlington, VA: National Center for Missing and Exploited Children, 2001); I. A. Elliot and A. R. Beech, "Understanding Online Child Pornography Use: Applying Sexual Offender Theory to Internet Offenders," *Aggression and Violent Behavior* 14 (2009): 180–193; J. Sullivan and A. R. Beech, "Are Collectors of Child Abuse Images a Risk to Children?" in *Policing Pedophiles on the Internet*, ed. A. MacVean and P. Spindler (London: New Police Bookshop, 2003), 11–20; A. R. Beech and I. A. Elliot, "Understanding the Emergence of the Internet Sex Offender: How Useful Are Current Theories in Understanding the Problem?" in *Understanding and Preventing Online Sexual Exploitation of Children*, ed. E. Quayle and K. M. Ribisl (New York: Routledge, 2012), 45.

106. Sections 63 to 67 of the Criminal Justice and Immigration Act of 2008 criminalize the possession of "pornographic images that depict acts which threaten a person's life; acts which result in or are likely to result in serious injury to a person's anus, breasts or genitals; bestiality; or necrophilia." Crown Prosecution Service, *Extreme Pornography*, http://www.cps.gov .uk/legal/d_to_g/extreme_pornography/.

107. J. Osborn, I. A. Elliot, and A. R. Beech, "The Use of Actuarial Risk Assessment Measures with UK Internet Child Pornography Offenders," *Journal of Aggression, Conflict and Peace Research* 2, no. 3 (2010): 16–24; M. C. Seto, R. K. Hanson, and K. M. Babchishin, "Contact Sexual Offending by Men with Online Sexual Offenses," *Sexual Offense: The Journal of Research and Treatment* 23, no. 1 (2011): 124–145; L. Webb, J. Craisatti, and S. Keen, "Characteristics of

Internet Child Pornography Offenders: A Comparison with Child Molesters," *Sexual Abuse: A Journal of Research and Treatment* 19, no. 4 (2007): 449–465.

108. Krone, "Typology of Online Child Pornography Offending."
109. Lanning, *Child Molesters: A Behavioral Analysis.*
110. Y. Jewkes and M. Yar, *Handbook on Internet Crime* (Cullompton, UK: Willan, 2010).
111. Seto et al., "Child Pornography Offenses are a Valid Diagnostic Indicator of Pedophilia"; D. Howitt and K. Sheldon, "The Role of Cognitive Distortions in Pedophilic Offending: Internet and Contact Offenders Compared," *Psychology, Crime and Law* 13, no. 5 (2007): 469–486; A. Carr, "The Social Dimension of the Online Trade of Child Sexual Exploitation Material," in *Understanding and Preventing Online Sexual Exploitation of Children*, ed. E. Quayle and K. M. Ribisl (New York: Routledge, 2012), 99.
112. *New York v. Ferber*, 458 US 747, 758 (1982).
113. J. Weiler, A. Haardt-Becker, and S. Schulte, "Care and Treatment of Child Victims of Child Pornographic Exploitation (CPE) in Germany," *Journal of Sexual Aggression* 16, no. 2 (2010): 211–222, cited in Seto, *Internet Sex Offenders*, 259.
114. Weiler et al., "Care and Treatment of Child Victims of Child Pornographic Exploitation (CPE) in Germany."
115. E. Quayle, L. Loof, and P. Tink, *Child Pornography and Sexual Exploitation of Children Online* (Bangkok: ECPAT International, 2008).
116. R. Choo, "Online Child Grooming: A Literature Review—On the Misuse of Social Networking Sites for Grooming Children for Sexual Offenses," *Australian Institute of Criminology Research and Public Policy Series* 103 (2009): ii–xiv.
117. A. R. Beech, I. A. Elliott, A. Birgden, and D. Findlater, "The Internet and Child Sexual Offending: A Criminological Review," *Aggression and Violent Behavior* 13, no. 3 (2008): 216–228; A. Burke, S. Sowerbutts, B. Blundell, and M. Sherry, "Child Pornography and the Internet: Policing and Treatment Issues," *Psychiatry, Psychology, and Law* 9, no. 1 (2002): 79–81; J. Stanley, "Child Abuse and the Internet," *Child Abuse Prevention Issue* 15 (Melbourne: Australian Institute of Family Studies, 2001), 2; M. Taylor and E. Quayle, *Child Pornography: An Internet Crime* (Brighton, UK: Routledge, 2003).
118. Quayle et al., *Child Pornography and Sexual Exploitation of Children Online*; P. Aftab, *The Parent's Guide to Protecting Your Children in Cyberspace* (New York: McGraw-Hill, 2002).
119. R. O'Connell, *A Typology of Cyber Sexploitation and Online Grooming Practices* (Preston, UK: University of Central Lancashire, 2003).
120. R. Williams, I. A. Elliott, and A. R. Beech, "Identifying Sexual Grooming Themes Used by Internet Sex Offenders," *Deviant Behavior* 34, no. 2 (2013): 135–152.
121. P. Briggs, W. T. Simon, and S. Simonsen, "An Exploratory Study of the Internet-Initiated Sexual Offenses and the Chat Room Sex Offender: Has the Internet Enabled a New Typology of Sex Offender?" *Sexual Abuse: A Journal of Research and Treatment* 23, no. 1 (2011): 72–91.
122. K. Sheldon and D. Howitt, *Sex Offenders and the Internet* (Chichester, UK: Wiley, 2007); K. Sheldon and D. Howitt, "Sexual Fantasy in Paedophile Offenders: Can Any Model Explain Satisfactorily New Findings from a Study of Internet and Contact Sexual Offenders?" *Legal and Criminological Psychology* 13, no. 1 (2008): 137–158.
123. NBC News, "'Law & Order' Director Jason Alexander Charged with Child Pornography: Police," July 30, 2015, http://www.nbcnewyork.com/news/local/Law-Order-Director-Jason-Alexander-Charged-Child-Pornography-319790011.html; A. Campbell, "'Law & Order' Director Arrested on Child Pornography Charges," *Huffington Post*, July 29, 2015, http://www.huffingtonpost.com/entry/law-order-director-arrested-on-child-pornography-charges_55b969fbe4b0af35367a40cb; H. Saul, "'Jace' Alexander Sentenced to 10 Years Probation for Child Abuse Images," *The Independent*, June 29, 2016, http://www.independent.co.uk

/news/people/former-law-and-order-director-jason-jace-alexander-sentenced-to-10-years -probation-for-possessing-a7109596.html.

124. Campbell, "'Law & Order' Director Arrested on Child Pornography Charges."

125. A. Phillip and S. Larimer, "Jared Fogle Charged with Paying for Sex with Minors, Possessing Child Porn," *Washington Post*, August 19, 2015, http://www.washingtonpost.com/news /morning-mix/wp/2015/08/19/jared-fogle-ex-subway-spokesman-faces-child-sex -and-child-pornography-charges/.

126. C. Isidore, "Jared Fogle Sentenced to More Than 15 Years," *CNN Money*, November 19, 2015, http://money.cnn.com/2015/11/19/news/companies/jared-fogle-jail-sentence/.

127. K. Rogers, "Jared Fogle, Ex-Subway Pitchman, to Plead Guilty to Child Sex and Pornography Charges," *New York Times*, August 19, 2015, http://www.nytimes.com/2015/08/20/business /media/jared-fogle-ex-subway-pitchman-to-plead-guilty-to-child-sex-and-pornography -charges.html?_r=0.

128. E. Chuck, "Russell Taylor, Associate of Ex-Subway Pitchman Jared Fogle, Gets 27 Years for Child Porn," *NBC News*, December 12, 2015, http://www.nbcnews.com/news/crime-courts /russell-taylor-cohort-ex-subway-pitchman-jared-fogle-gets-27-n477741.

129. BBC News, "Gary Glitter Jailed for 16 Years," February 27, 2015, http://www.bbc.com/news /uk-31657929; "Rolf Harris and Jimmy Savile 'Prowled Broadmoor Hospital Together,'" *Huffington Post UK*, July 1, 2014, http://www.huffingtonpost.co.uk/2014/07/01/rolf-harris -jimmy-savile_n_5546552.html.

130. BBC News, "Glitter Jailed over Child Porn," November 12, 1999, http://news.bbc.co.uk/2/hi /uk/517604.stm.

131. J. Pheby, "British Singer Gary Glitter Found Guilty of Child Sex Crimes," *Business Insider*, February 5, 2015, http://www.businessinsider.com/afp-british-singer-gary-glitter-found -guilty-of-child-sex-crimes-2015-2.

132. *United States v. Irey*, Human Trafficking Law Project (HTLP) database, Human Trafficking Clinic at Michigan Law School, University of Michigan, 2007, https://www.law.umich.edu /clinical/HuTrafficCases/Pages/CaseDisp.aspx?caseID=473.

133. Ibid.

134. Maras, *Computer Forensics*, 166.

135. Pheby, "British Singer Gary Glitter Found Guilty of Child Sex Crimes."

136. See Chapter 3.3, Europol, "The Internet Organised Crime Threat Assessment," accessed August 15, 2016, https://www.europol.europa.eu/iocta/2014/chap-3-3-view1.html.

137. A. Crawford, "Computer-Generated 'Sweetie' Catches Online Predators," *BBC News*, November 5, 2013, http://www.bbc.com/news/uk-24818769.

138. *Ashcroft v. Free Speech Coalition*, 535 U.S. 234 (2002).

139. Maras, *Computer Forensics*, 168.

140. *Ashcroft*.

141. *United States v. Williams*, 553 U.S. 285 (2008).

142. Crown Prosecution Service, "Prohibited Images of Children," accessed August 15, 2016, http://www.cps.gov.uk/legal/p_to_r/prohibited_images_of_children/.

143. National Center for Missing and Exploited Children, "Child Victim Identification Program," accessed August 15, 2016, http://www.missingkids.com/CVIP.

144. N. A. Dube, "Globalsearch: The International Search for Missing and Exploited Children," *International Review of Law, Computers and Technology* 13, no. 1 (1999): 71–73.

145. Seto, *Internet Sex Offenders*, 253.

146. National Center for Missing and Exploited Children, *CyberTipline*, accessed August 15, 2016, http://www.missingkids.com/cybertipline/.

147. United Nations Global Initiative to Fight Human Trafficking, 017 Workshop: Technology and Human Trafficking, The Vienna Forum to Fight Human Trafficking, Austria Center,

Vienna, February 13–15, 2008, UN.GIFT B.P.:017, 15, http://www.unodc.org/documents/human-trafficking/2008/BP017TechnologyandHumanTrafficking.pdf.

148. INTERPOL, "Victim Identification," accessed August 15, 2016, http://www.interpol.int/Crime-areas/Crimes-against-children/Victim-identification.

149. United Nations Global Initiative to Fight Human Trafficking.

150. Virtual Global Task Force, "What We Do: Making the Internet Safer for Children," accessed August 15, 2016, http://www.virtualglobaltaskforce.com/what-we-do/.

151. M. Schrage, "Outlook: Internet Honeypots," *Washington Post*, January 12, 2004, http://www.washingtonpost.com/wp-dyn/articles/A4617-2004Jan9.html.

152. United Nations Global Initiative to Fight Human Trafficking.

153. Y. Jewkes and C. Andrews, "Policing the Filth: The Problems of Investigating Online Child Pornography in England and Wales," *Policing and Society* 15, no. 1 (2005): 59.

154. U.S. Immigration and Customs Enforcement, "Massachusetts Man Gets 45 Years for 'Dreamboard' Child Pornography Role," 2013, https://www.ice.gov/news/releases/massachusetts-man-gets-45-years-dreamboard-child-pornography-role.

155. Europol, "The Internet Organised Crime Threat Assessment."

156. H. L. Merdiana, C. Curtisa, J. Thakkera, N. Wilson, and D. P. Boer, "The Three Dimensions of Online Child Pornography Offending," *Journal of Sexual Aggression: An International, Interdisciplinary Forum for Research, Theory and Practice* 19, no. 1 (2013): 121–132.

157. A. Cooper, "Sexuality and the Internet: Surfing into the New Millennium," *Cyberpsychology and Behavior* 1, no. 2 (1998): 181–187.

158. D. Crystal, *Language and the Internet* (New York: Cambridge University Press, 2006).

159. Electronic Frontiers Australia, "Internet Content Filtering and Blocking," accessed August 15, 2016, https://www.efa.org.au/Issues/Censor/cens2.html.

160. V. Mabrey and D. Perozzi, "'Sexting': Should Child Pornography Laws Apply?" *ABC News*, April 1, 2010, http://abcnews.go.com/Nightline/phillip-alpert-sexting-teen-child-porn/story?id=10252790.

161. A. Lenhart, "Sexting—Teens and Sexting," *Pew Research Center*, December 15, 2009, http://www.pewinternet.org/2009/12/15/teens-and-sexting/.

162. Ibid.

163. H. Strohmaier, M. Murphy, and D. DeMatteo, "Youth Sexting: Prevalence Rates, Driving Motivations, and the Deterrent Effect of Legal Consequences," *Sexuality Research and Social Policy* 11, no. 3 (2014): 245–255.

164. Lenhart, "Sexting—Teens and Sexting."

165. Kik Sexting, kiksexting.com/.

166. RT, "Snapchat 'Deceived Users' about Disappearing Messages, Will Be Monitored by Gov't," 2014, http://www.rt.com/usa/157960-snapchat-deceived-users/.

167. M. G. Leary, "Self-Produced Child Pornography: The Appropriate Societal Responses to Juvenile Self-Exploitation," *Virginia Journal of Social Policy and Law* 15, no. 1 (2007): 12–14; M. G. Leary, "Sexting or Self-Produced Child Pornography? The Dialogue Continues -Structured Prosecutorial Discretion with a Multidisciplinary Response," *Virginia Journal of Social Policy and Law* 17, no. 3 (2010): 492.

168. Ibid.

169. J. Walters, "Teen Prosecuted as Adult for Having Naked Images—Of Himself—On Phone," *Guardian*, September 20, 2015, http://www.theguardian.com/us-news/2015/sep/20/teen-prosecuted-naked-images-himself-phone-selfies.

170. S. Walster, "The Harm in 'Sexting'? Analyzing the Constitutionality of Child Pornography Statutes that Prohibit Voluntary Production, Possession, and Dissemination of Sexually Explicit Images By Teenagers," *Harvard Journal on Law and Gender* 33 (2010): 687–702.

171. Leary, "Sexting or Self-Produced Child Pornography? The Dialogue Continues—Structured Prosecutorial Discretion with a Multidisciplinary Response," 526.

172. R. Browne, "Canada's New Cyberbullying Law Is Targeting Teen Sexting Gone Awry," *Vice News*, May 1, 2015, https://news.vice.com/article/canadas-new-cyberbullying-law-is-targeting-teen-sexting-gone-awry.

173. "Teen Convicted of Distributing Child Porn Highlights Need for Cyberbullying Education," *Global News*, January 11, 2014, http://globalnews.ca/video/1076672/teen-convicted-of-distributing-child-porn-highlights-need-for-cyberbullying-education.

174. D. Meissner, "Sexting B.C. Teen Found Guilty of Child Pornography," *CTV News*, January 10, 2014, http://bc.ctvnews.ca/sexting-b-c-teen-found-guilty-of-child-pornography-1.1633678.

175. A. Schultze-Krumbholz, R. Wolfer, A. Jakel, P. Zagorscak, and H. Scheithauer, "The Medienhelden Program," paper presented at the International Conference on Cyberbullying, Paris, June 28–29, 2012.

176. B. Spears, A. Costabile, A. Brighi, R. Del Rey, M. Porhola, V. Sanchez, C. Spiel, and F. Thompson, "Positive Uses of New Technologies and Relationships in Educational Settings," in *Cyberbullying Through the New Media: Findings from an International Network*, ed. P. K. Smith and G. Steffen (New York: Psychology Press, 2013), 187.

177. Department of Homeland Security, "National Cyber Security Awareness Month, 2015," last updated August 5, 2016, http://www.dhs.gov/national-cyber-security-awareness-month.

178. National Conference of State Legislatures, *Cyberbullying*, accessed May 7, 2016, http://www.ncsl.org/research/education/cyberbullying.aspx.

179. See WebWise, the Irish Internet Safety Awareness Centre: http://www.webwise.ie/.

180. J. Wolak, D. Finkelhor, K. J. Mitchell, and M. L. Ybarra, "Online 'Predators' and Their Victims: Myths, Realities and Implications for Prevention and Treatment," *American Psychologist* 63, no. 2 (2008): 111–128.

CHAPTER 11

CYBERTRESPASS, CYBERVANDALISM, AND CYBERTHEFT

KEYWORDS

Abandonware
Advanced fee scam
Adware
Backdoors
Bot
Botcode
Botherder
Botnet
Catphishing
Charity fraud
Computer virus
Computer worm
Copyright
Copyright infringement
Credit card fraud
Cyberespionage
Cyberidentity theft

Cybersquatting
Data brokers
Debit card fraud
Denial of service attack
Digital wallet
Distributed denial of
    service attack
Dumps
Electronic health records
Hacking
Identity theft
Intellectual property
Intellectual property theft
Internet of Things
Keylogger
Malware
Medical identity theft

Online auction fraud
Patent
Pharming
Phishing
Rippers
Shill feedback
Signaling theory
Smishing
Social engineering
Spam
Spearphishing
Spyware
Trade secrets
Trademark
Trojan horse
Website defacement

Koobface is a form of malware that targeted Facebook users and spread through infected users to their Facebook friends. Once infected with malware, messages would be sent from the infected user's account to his or her Facebook friends. These messages would include links to websites that prompted users to download what looked like Adobe Flash Player. When the user downloaded this fake Adobe Flash Player, Koobface would infect the user's machine and take over the user's search engine, redirecting him or her to illicit websites containing various scams (e.g., fake antivirus programs and dating services). The creators and distributors of Koobface made a profit from fees retrieved from pay-per-install (i.e., the perpetrator receives funds for applications downloaded by users) and pay-per-click (i.e., the perpetrator receives a fee each time a user accesses an illicit website). In addition to Facebook, other social media sites (e.g., Twitter and MySpace) have been targeted by malware.

Cases such as this one illustrate the costs associated with using social media websites. Companies and users rely on social media, in particular, and the Internet, in general, to conduct daily activities. The Internet and digital technology have improved the efficiency of professional and personal activities. This efficiency has been made possible through the ease with which individuals and companies can communicate with others and share information. This efficiency comes at a cost, namely, the vulnerability of users and companies to threats, some of which would not have been present without the Internet. This chapter examines some of these threats, looking in particular at cybertrespass, cybervandalism (e.g., computer intrusions and computer threats), and cybertheft (e.g., online fraud, identity theft, and intellectual property theft). Finally, this chapter considers ways to control these cybercrimes.

CYBERTRESPASS AND CYBERVANDALISM

Cybertrespass involves unauthorized access into computer systems and digital devices. Cybervandalism refers to the virtual defacement of someone else's property. Cybertrespass and cybervandalism may occur for a wide variety of reasons: to gain status, acceptance, and recognition among peers, for thrills, for revenge, and for financial, ideological, political, or psychological reasons (such as addiction; see Chapter 5).[1] Those engaging in cybertrespassing or cybervandalism may seek the alteration, deletion, damage, destruction, or disruption of a computer or related technology.

HACKING

Gaining unauthorized access to a computer or related system is known as **hacking**. A well-known hacker is Kevin Mitnick, the first hacker to be placed on the FBI's most wanted list. For his cybercrimes, he received five years' imprisonment. During his sentence, he was placed in solitary confinement because officials believed he was very dangerous and could cause catastrophic harm by accessing telecommunications and electronic communications, even in prison.[2] In addition to hacking via electronic communications, telecommunications hacking (or phreaking) may occur. On February 14, 2015, Noor Aziz Uddin, who was on the FBI's most wanted cybercriminal list, was arrested in Pakistan for engaging in an international telecommunications fraud with other cybercriminals, hacking into phone lines, hijacking numbers, and using them to auto-dial premium rate numbers (belonging to the hackers), charging victims money for the calls.[3]

The primary motive of Uddin and his co-conspirators for these cybercrimes was financial gain. Other hackers engage in this conduct for their own personal amusement, which was the case for the Lizard Squad when it hacked PlayStation and Xbox networks during the 2014 Christmas holiday in order to annoy and cause disappointment to those seeking to utilize their gaming consoles.[4] And yet others are motivated by peer recognition, fame, and learning.[5] With respect to learning, these hackers break into the system purely for the challenge and do not believe that their conduct is wrong or should be considered illegal.

Such a hacker "justifies his actions by claiming that anything the computer operator can do should be permitted legally, with no regard for the privacy, property, and other interest of the owner of the system. He argues that because the system owner suffers no loss, such actions are acceptable, even praiseworthy, [as] it may result in tighter security measures against 'bad hackers.' Of course, he never considers himself to be a bad hacker."[6] This justification is akin to an individual claiming to have entered someone's property but not to take anything; therefore, a crime was not committed. However, this fails to address an obvious fact, that is, the individual trespassed onto someone's property, which, despite claims to the contrary, is considered a crime. Moreover, just because hackers claim no harmful intent does not absolve them of criminal responsibility for their actions. U.S. law criminalizes such conduct (i.e., unauthorized access) irrespective of whether or not the person intended to cause harm (Computer Fraud and Abuse Act of 1986; 18 U.S.C. § 1030). The Computer Fraud and Abuse Act of 1986 also criminalizes the exceeding of authorized access to a system and data. In a 2015 case, employees at AT&T international call centers located in Colombia, Mexico, and the Philippines exceeded their authorization by accessing, downloading, and sharing customer information (names and Social Security numbers) and selling this data to third parties.[7]

MALWARE

Malware (i.e., malicious software) exists in a zoo (i.e., a controlled laboratory) and is often spread in the wild (i.e., the Internet, computers, and related technology) through attachments and links in e-mails and websites.[8] Malware has two main components, payload (its functionality) and propagation techniques (the method by which the malware is delivered; for example, via USB). Historically, malware carried serious payloads but had ineffective propagation techniques (e.g., floppy disks). Today, malware carries both serious payloads and effective propagation techniques. Apart from its two main components, malicious software also contains a signature, a method by which to avoid detection by authorities, and some form of activation mechanism.[9] Malware can be propagated when users mistakenly download a malicious (instead of legitimate) program on websites. Malware can also be downloaded and distributed through e-mail and instant messaging. Some malware creates **backdoors** in users' systems, which enable a perpetrator to access the system at any time. These backdoors gain unauthorized remote access to a computer, bypassing existing authentication measures in order to evade detection. Malware can be designed to record keystrokes of users; this is known as keylogging software (or a **keylogger**). The distribution of malware can cause significant damage to systems worldwide. Malware writing kits are available as well. These kits can be used by those who lack the computer programming background needed to write code. Because of these kits, the speed with which malware has been released has increased.[10] In the past, only those with specialized knowledge could create malware. Today, the knowledge is available to all through the Internet.

An example of malware is a **computer virus**, a "program that is designed to spread, through user activity, to other computers and to damage or disrupt a computer, by attaching itself (or piggybacking) on files or programs."[11] To survive, viruses require hosts. A host enables the virus to replicate and potentially spread (with user activity). Indeed, upon user activity, the virus will release its payload. The payload may be benign (e.g., a joke message) or harmful to the system (e.g., deletes critical data). An example of the former is the Christmas tree virus. This virus was developed in 1987 by a student in Germany who wanted to send greetings to friends, which stated "a very happy Christmas and my best wishes for the next year. Let this run and enjoy yourself. Browsing this file is no fun at all. Just type Christmas."[12] When the users would type "Christmas," the virus would replicate and send copies of itself to others in the user's name. An example of the latter is the Chernobyl virus. This virus was created in 1998 by Cheng-Ing Han, a resident of Taiwan. It infected millions of computers and caused billions of dollars in damages. The virus overwrote critical data in infected systems, and in many instances it destroyed the basic input/output system (BIOS), which is responsible for booting the computer.[13] The creator of the Chernobyl virus was not prosecuted, because companies in Taiwan did not file a complaint, which was needed before charges could be filed against a perpetrator.

Viruses have also been found in mobile phones and smartphones. For instance, the zombie virus infected one million mobile phones in China.[14] The creators of the virus obtained subscriber identity module (SIM) card details of infected phones, which were then relayed to a server controlled by the perpetrators. The virus creators then sent messages and made phone calls from the infected phone, for which victims were charged. With respect to text messages, the malware creators sent texts from the controlled phones to other users listed in the infected phone's address book. These text messages had links to games and software that contained the malware. When users receiving these messages clicked on the links, their phones became infected with the malware.

A computer virus requires some form of user activity to execute, make copies of itself, and spread. By contrast, a **computer worm**, although similar to a computer virus, does not need any user activity to do this. In fact, it self-executes and self-propagates. Worms are often noticed because they consume resources and slow systems down. Consider the MyDoom worm, which was a mass-mailer worm detected in 2004. This worm propagated through e-mails, making over 1.8 million copies of itself; in so doing, it infected systems in 168 countries.[15] Certain versions of the worm installed keylogging software on a user's machine, while others installed backdoors. Another computer worm that caused significant damage was the Nimda worm. This worm was designed to spread very quickly, and it caused damage that surpassed the economic damage of Code Red, a worm that had infected 359,000 computers and defaced websites with the message "Hacked by the Chinese."[16] The Nimda worm spread in 2001, utilizing multiple propagation techniques, including e-mail, via browsing and compromised websites and backdoors left behind by previous worms, such as the Code Red II worm.[17]

Another form of malware, a **Trojan horse**, is designed to appear as a legitimate program but actually carries a malicious payload. An example of a Trojan horse is PC-Write, which masqueraded as a legitimate (and at the time popular) word processing program. Once a user downloaded this program, it formatted the user's hard disk to delete stored files.[18] The Storm Worm was a backdoor Trojan designed to subtly spread by attacking systems and then shutting down for a while to prevent its detection.[19] This worm infected millions of computers in Europe and the United States and spread via an e-mail containing a message about a severe weather event that targeted Europe with the subject title "230 dead as storm battles Europe."[20] Trojan horses have also infected Mac computers (e.g., Trojan Flashback). In 2012, 600,000 Mac users were infected with a Trojan that disabled key security features of systems in order to gain control of their systems and alter content.[21]

Mobile phones and smartphones have been infected by Trojan horses as well. The Skulls Trojan horse rendered all phone applications including SMS (Short Message Service) and MMS (Multimedia Messaging Service) useless and replaced desktop items with images of skulls.[22]

Moreover, some software can track individuals' online activity—legally and illegally. **Adware** collects information about users' web-browsing activities in order to provide targeted advertising content to the user based on his or her online behavior. Adware that collects information about the user without their consent can be obtained through freeware, shareware, or infected websites that users visit. **Spyware** can surreptitiously monitor users' activity and relay this activity to the person who created or distributed the malware. This form of malware can also spy on targets by activating their webcams, and in some cases, their microphones. Both adware and spyware can track users and can be used for legitimate or criminal purposes. Antivirus and antispyware programs have been developed to protect users' digital devices from malware. However, even fake antivirus and antispyware programs have been created that are installed on users' systems and notify them of purported threats found on their machines. The ultimate goal of these malicious programs is to get users to pay a fee to have the fictitious malware removed.

BOX 11-1   MOBILE APPS FOR SPYING

Hammad Akbar, a Pakistani, created the spyware app Stealth-Genie, which was designed to surreptitiously monitor telecommunications and electronic communications (e.g., calls, texts, and e-mails) on a user's phone.[23] An app created by the Japanese company Karelog ("Boyfriend Log") enabled users to download an app without the owner's permission to surreptitiously track the person via GPS.[24] Other applications reveal whether or not third parties are seeking surreptitious access to a user's phone. For instance, an app called iTrust is available that, once activated on a user's device, records any activities that a third party (e.g., spouse, roommate, boyfriend, or girlfriend) is engaging in on the user's phone (e.g., apps or messages accessed).[25]

Malware creators and distributors have claimed that their intention is not to cause damage with the malware. David Smith, who was responsible for creating and spreading the Melissa virus in 1999, claimed at his trial that he sought to minimize the damage he caused with the virus by restricting the e-mails he would send from infected systems to only the first 50 individuals listed in his or her address book.[26] In other cases, malware creators and distributors have claimed that they had not intended to release malicious software. Malware creators and distributors can be held liable even if transmission of the malware was unintentional.[27] The creators and distributors of malware can be charged with 18 U.S.C. § 1030(a)(5)(A) for intentionally causing damage or 18 U.S.C. §1030(a)(5)(B) for unintentionally causing damage. Those responsible for the creation and release of Trojan horses can be charged under 18 U.S.C. § 1030(e)(8). Finally, adware and spyware distributors and creators can be charged under 18 U.S.C. § 1030(a)(2).

DENIAL OF SERVICE AND DISTRIBUTED DENIAL OF SERVICE ATTACKS

A **denial of service attack** (DoS attack) seeks to disrupt legitimate access to a server by overwhelming its resources. A **distributed denial of service attack** (DDoS attack) utilizes multiple computers to target a system or website in order to prevent access to it by legitimate users. A recent investigation of a DDoS attack revealed that the CEO of a company hired hackers to conduct DDoS attacks against its online competitors, causing the targets approximately $2 million in losses (*Operation Cyberslam*).[28] Those seeking to conduct DoS or DDoS attacks do so for financial, personal (e.g., revenge, mischief), ideological, political (e.g., hacktivism),[29] or security reasons (e.g., as a method of protection against nefarious actors).[30] Individuals who conduct these cybercrimes violate 18 U.S.C. §1030(a)(5)(A). Charges related to DoS and DDoS attacks may also involve other cybercrimes, such as interfering with government systems (when such attacks are aimed at government systems) under 18 U.S.C. § 1362 or cyberextortion pursuant to 18 U.S.C. §1030(a)(7) when, for example, a company or organization is threatened with such attacks if payment is not provided.

The digital systems utilized in DDoS attacks can be infected with malware known as botcode. **Botcode** is malware designed to enable the remote control of digital devices. It can easily be found on the Internet.[31] Once a digital device has been infected with botcode, it can be used for multiple purposes: as a zombie device (i.e., a **bot**) to do the bidding of the **botherder** (i.e., the person or persons controlling the zombie computers); to engage in cyberattacks; or to steal information within the digital device. A **botnet** can relay information obtained through keylogging software and Trojan horses to the botherder for use in other criminal activities.[32] Those who control botnets have used information obtained from bot-infected computers in a variety of ways. Currently, these botnets are even for hire, often being advertised for use in DDoS attacks.[33] Prosecuting botherders is particularly challenging due to the sheer number of computers involved in the investigation and the resources needed to adequately conduct the investigation. Nonetheless, investigations and prosecutions have targeted botnets in order to disrupt and dismantle them and identify botherders (e.g., *Operation Bot Roast*).[34]

WEBSITE DEFACEMENT

Website defacement is a form of cybervandalism whereby a cybercriminal gains unauthorized access to a website and modifies content. Many websites of national and international agencies and private companies have been defaced for political, ideological, religious, and personal reasons.[35] When the Royal Australian Air Force website was defaced, the perpetrator posted the following message: "This site [was] hacked by Atul Dwivedi[.] Long live India[.] This is a Warning message to [the] Australian govt. immediately take all measures to stop racist attacks against Indian students in Australia else I wil [*sic*] pawn all your cyber properties like this one. Jai Hind."[36] When hacking occurs for a political reason, it is called hacktivism (see Chapter 14 for more information on this). Websites that are inadequately protected or incorrectly configured are usually targets of this form of cybercrime. In 1999, hackers defaced the U.S. Senate website.[37] In 2010, the EU presidency website was defaced as well, by replacing the image of the EU president (José Luis Rodriguez Zapatero) with that of Rowan Atkinson (best known for the fictional character he played, Mr. Bean).[38] Those involved in website defacement include skilled programmers and inexperienced users who obtain the information needed to engage in this conduct online (i.e., script kiddies). Website defacement is prohibited under the U.S. Computer Fraud and Abuse Act of 1986.

IMAGE 11-1 Screenshot of EU Presidency Website Defacement.

CYBERTHEFT

Cybertheft involves stealing personal information, medical information, financial information, or money via the Internet and digital devices for personal or other use. This data and money can be obtained through hacking, malware distribution, and online scams that seek to dupe the victim into providing personal information which will then be used by the perpetrator to conduct fraud. There are three identifiable elements common to all types of frauds: perceived pressure; perceived opportunity; and rationalization of fraud by the perpetrator (seen as acceptable according to his or her own beliefs, views, and moral and ethical codes).[39] *Perceived pressure* refers to the motive of a perpetrator based on a need. This need could be financial or personal (e.g., thrill, revenge, frustration over a workplace situation). Fraud can be committed for the individual's benefit, on behalf of a company, or against another person or company. A *perceived opportunity* is the ability to commit the activity. Research has shown that individuals will not commit fraud if the perceived risks of doing so are high; that is, whether there is a significant likelihood that the person will be detected and punished by authorities.[40] The final factor is *rationalization*. If the pressure to engage in these actions is high enough and significant opportunity exists to commit the crime, rationalization is needed to justify the conduct. In a similar fashion, individuals with questionable morals and ethical views tend to rationalize deviant behavior. These individuals, however, require high pressure and ample opportunities to be motivated to commit the criminal activity.[41]

Online fraud scams often follow similar patterns: the target of the scam believes that he or she is providing information or money to a stranger in need (e.g., a military member or a refugee), a friend, or a person from an official agency or organization (e.g., a government or a bank). The details of the stories in scams vary, but the goal remains the same: to get the victim to provide the perpetrator with something (data or money). The most well known scam is the **advanced fee scam**. In this scam, the perpetrator informs the target that an advanced fee is needed to transfer or deposit a large sum of money into a bank. The perpetrator can pretend to be a member of royalty, a government official, or a legal official. For example, the target of the scam is contacted by the scam artist pretending to be the attorney of a long-lost relative that has died in a horrific traffic accident overseas. The "attorney" informs the target that he or she has inherited the relative's money. The attorney then informs the target that a bank account number must be provided for the money to be deposited and a standard fee is needed before it can be deposited. The victim provides the attorney with the advance fee and never hears from that person again. Research has shown that individuals who score high in sensation seeking (i.e., motivation to act because of the emotional impact of the activity) may be more likely to engage in activities that turn out to be financial scams because of the prospect of gaining a large sum of money and the excitement in participating in the activity.[42]

Other scams prey on a person's emotions. This has been seen with dating scams in which perpetrators take advantage of victims, often requesting money and other items from them. Here, scammers create profiles on online dating websites and even social media websites to lure unsuspecting victims into fake relationships (i.e., **catphishing**). In some cases, after establishing a relationship and quickly "falling in love" with the victim, the scammer provides the target with a story, such as an emergency situation requiring money (e.g., money needed for travel to meet the target or money needed for unpaid bills). After providing the money, the victim may or may not hear from the perpetrator again. In the event that contact is maintained, the perpetrator may continue to engage in that conduct as long as the victim continues to provide for them. A wide assortment of dating scams have been employed. For example, in 2015, in the Hague, Netherlands, two men were arrested for perpetrating "loverboy" scams through a free online dating app, Tinder.[43] The men used fraudulent profiles to register for the app and contact women. After dating the women for a few months, the perpetrators would try to scam, extort, blackmail, or threaten them.[44] Research has shown that those with romantic beliefs and beliefs in the ideal or perfect relationship are more likely to fall victim to online dating scams.[45]

Those in need are also preyed upon by scam artists. This is especially true of employment scams offering false promises of money for work provided. Fake Section 8 housing assistance websites exist as well.[46] Unsuspecting users may access these sites believing that they are registering for lotteries and pay the registration fee; the authentic Section 8 websites do not require a registration fee. Moreover, scam artists prey on individuals' fears. For instance, there are scams whereby individuals claim to be authorities seeking to arrest the target for failing to appear for jury duty unless they pay a fine.[47] Scammers have also called unsuspecting users claiming to be the Internal Revenue Service (IRS) and threatening users with arrest if they do not pay a fine.[48] The point of these calls is to inform the target that they can pay a fee to avoid arrest.

Phishing scams involve masquerading as a legitimate entity or business in order to trick users into revealing some type of information. Phishers have pretended to be financial institutions while actually intending to harvest users' personal and financial information for later sale in online marketplaces (e.g., *Operation Cardkeeper*).[49] They have also pretended to be government institutions. For example, users have received IRS phishing e-mails. Like IRS scams in the United States, in Brazil, fraudsters have sent phishing e-mails to unsuspecting users pretending to be Receita Federal, the Brazilian tax organization, informing them that their income taxes were not received.[50] As with other phishing e-mails, the user is directed to click on a link that takes the user to a fake website or to a page with malware. In the case of Brazil and this particular phishing scam, users were taken to a page that informed them that their Adobe Flash Player needed to be updated. The unsuspecting user downloaded the executable file thinking it was an update to Adobe Flash Player. Instead, a Trojan horse was downloaded.[51] Users may also be tricked into downloading malware on their phone through **smishing** (or SMS phishing). A user receives a text that contains a link that takes the user to a website with malware or a website seeking to obtain personal information about the user.

Pharming involves spoofed websites that look identical or nearly identical to the known websites they are pretending to be. Their purpose is to harvest users' data for later use in a criminal activity. Pharmed websites for financial institutions exist as well. Brazilian cybercriminals were arrested in Spain for creating pharmed bank websites and utilizing phishing tactics to obtain usernames and passwords of bank accounts.[52] The funds obtained from these accounts were then deposited into Brazilian accounts. The websites of commercial institutions and even charity and relief organizations have also been pharmed. For example, following Hurricane Katrina, a pharmed website was created which was almost identical to the American Red Cross website. The pharmer, Jovany Desir, sought to defraud users who were willing to donate to the Hurricane Katrina relief effort (a form of **charity fraud**) by creating the pharmed website and accepting donations.[53] Victims accessing and donating to his pharmed website had their personal information, such as names, home addresses, and phone numbers, along with financial information (e.g., credit card numbers and bank account numbers), stolen. The money provided to this fake website was never actually given to those in need, of course; instead, the funds were diverted to Desir for his personal use.

Social media websites have been targeted by scammers as well. A popular social media site in Brazil, known as Orkut, has been used by cybercriminals to distribute **spam** (i.e., unsolicited e-mail) and engage in phishing.[54] Bots have also been used in spamming campaigns. The Controlling the Assault of Non-Solicited Pornography and Marketing Act of 2003 (CAN-SPAM Act of 2003) is the federal law used to criminalize spam. States have also implemented laws that can be used to prosecute spammers (see Table 11-1 for states with spam laws). Certain state laws require those sending advertisements and pornographic materials for adults to place information in the subject line of the e-mail that is representative of the contents of the e-mail.[55] The majority of the laws in place specifically prohibit misleading subject headings and e-mails and misleading sender and return addresses.[56] Other states require those sending advertisements and pornographic material to include a link that enables individuals to opt out of receiving further e-mails.[57] This requirement is particularly problematic as some spam e-mails that include these links have used individuals opting out of the spam as a way to validate the e-mail (and show that it is operational). E-mails that have been validated are worth more to spammers and those who buy and sell e-mail addresses for advertising purposes. Moreover, the opt-out links in spam may take individuals to fraudulent websites seeking personal information. Some states have updated existing provisions on spam to prevent those sending e-mails with advertisements from doing so unless individuals have specifically opted in to receive them.

There is no specific federal law criminalizing phishing; however, other federal laws can be used to prosecute phishers (e.g., wire and bank fraud statutes), depending on the type of phishing activity that has occurred. Even the CAN-SPAM Act of 2003 has been used to

Table 11-1 States With Spam Laws, 2015

Alaska	Missouri
Arizona	Nevada
Arkansas	New Mexico
California	North Carolina
Colorado	North Dakota
Connecticut	Ohio
Delaware	Oklahoma
Florida	Pennsylvania
Georgia	Rhode Island
Idaho	South Dakota
Illinois	Tennessee
Indiana	Texas
Iowa	Utah
Kansas	Virginia
Louisiana	Washington
Maine	West Virginia
Maryland	Wisconsin
Michigan	Wyoming
Minnesota	

Source: National Conference of State Legislatures, "State Laws Relating to Unsolicited Commercial or Bulk E-mail (SPAM)," accessed May 7, 2016, http://www.ncsl.org/research/telecommunications-and-information-technology/state-spam-laws.aspx.

prosecute phishers, like Sanford Wallace. Sanford Wallace (nicknamed Spam King) opened up numerous fake accounts, groups, and forums on the MySpace social media website and spammed thousands of users using these accounts.[58] Using his MySpace accounts, groups, and forums, he also sent numerous phishing e-mails designed to hijack a user's account. Once users clicked on the link in the e-mails they received, they were directed to Wallace's websites, which had a MySpace logo.[59] In addition to existing federal laws, states have laws criminalizing phishers (see Table 11-2 for state phishing laws). Some states have allowed victims to sue phishers for damages (e.g., California and Texas). The reality is that phishers and spammers do not fear being prosecuted for their activities because prosecutions are not often pursued due to the time and resources needed to prosecute these types of cases.[60]

Online commercial transactions are also not immune from fraud. Cases in point are transactions on online auction websites. On such sites, a seller posts a description of the item to be sold, usually along with a photograph and description of the item. The seller's listing is available for all on the site to see. Registered users of the site are allowed to bid on the item for a limited period (e.g., a week). **Online auction fraud** (criminalized under 18 U.S.C. § 1343) occurs when an individual bids on an item for sale on a website that is

Table 11-2 States With Phishing Laws, 2015

Alabama	Montana
Arizona	New York
Arkansas	New Mexico
California	Oklahoma
Connecticut	Oregon
Florida	Rhode Island
Georgia	Tennessee
Illinois	Texas
Kentucky	Utah
Louisiana	Virginia
Michigan	Washington
Minnesota	

Source: National Conference of State Legislatures, "State Laws Addressing 'Phishing,'" accessed May 7, 2016, http://www.ncsl.org/research/telecommunications-and-information-technology/state-phishing-laws.aspx.

misrepresented in some way by the seller in an effort to deceive the buyer in order to obtain a financial gain. Fraud that involves commercial transactions on online auction sites includes the nondelivery of purchased items and the misrepresentation of the item. The nondelivery of items may occur because the seller did not have the item listed to begin with or had no intention of shipping the item once the auction ended and funds for the items were received. His or her intentions were merely to obtain the victim's money. The individual may also misrepresent the item being auctioned. The item may be of lesser value than what is advertised or may be a counterfeit or stolen good.[61]

Often, the quality and condition of the item cannot be accurately assessed online. Accordingly, online sellers can make false claims about the quality and condition of the items sold. To encourage buyers to shop in online markets, websites have created rating scales and buyer feedback systems to attest to the reliability of sellers utilizing those sites. Buyers can judge the validity and reliability of a seller by the information they provide and the feedback about the seller on the website. Online feedback mechanisms are believed to foster good and appropriate online behavior by ensuring that business transactions are completed to the satisfaction of the buyer and the seller.[62]

Online transactions depend on trust in the seller and trust in the platform.[63] Trust refers to the confidence in the motives and intentions of other persons and can be defined as a "belief that the other side prefers mutual cooperation to exploiting one's own cooperation, while mistrust is a belief that the other side prefers exploiting one's cooperation to returning it."[64] Trust, therefore, depends on what the seller will do with the trust provided by the buyer.[65] In its most basic sense, trust is determined by the manner in which a particular person will behave in the future based on prior claims of the individual concerning his or her behavior.[66] Trust makes a consumer more willing to conduct an online transaction.

Buyers' trust institutional mechanisms in place to facilitate the success of online transactions. The feedback system is one such institutional mechanism. Feedback is a public good, it is available to all, and the benefits of this good do not diminish with each use of it. Game theorists, who examine strategic decisions of individuals when these are dependent on others' choices and decisions,[67] have studied public goods. They have found that individuals participating in online feedback systems, "instead of acting out of self-interest (e.g., using feedback without leaving any), people contribute to the public good out of a sense of fairness, public duty, and concern for community."[68] Likewise, buyers have been found to leave feedback to ensure cooperation by the seller (i.e., to ensure that they follow through with transactions for altruistic motives to contribute to the public good).[69]

Because users rely on feedback systems to determine the trustworthiness of sellers, some sellers have been known to alter feedback systems to show favorable reviews toward the seller. The seller can use different identities to rate his or her products. This process is known as **shill feedback**. For example, those trading on eBay can inflate online reputation by engaging in simple transactions between their own accounts or with the accounts of acquaintances.[70] Actually, online auction websites and other websites that have feedback systems cannot confirm that the information they provide is accurate. There are currently no mechanisms in place that can prevent the seller from creating multiple fake accounts, through which the seller can post positive feedback. These accounts can be opened because all that is needed is a valid e-mail address (e.g., e-mails can be easily acquired through e-mail providers like Hotmail, Yahoo!, and Google) and credit card. **Signaling theory** explains why specific signals are considered reliable while others are not by examining the signal and the quality it purportedly represents.[71] On the one hand, signals can be honest, intended to indicate a particular quality that the signaler possesses. On the other hand, signals can be deceptive, intended to indicate a particular quality that the signaler does not possess. In competitive situations, the interests of signalers and receivers may not align, and it may be quite beneficial for signals to be deceptive. In the same manner, misleading information is sometimes posted online to benefit the buyer or seller in some way.

Buyers are protected from losses incurred on certain auction websites. Ebay, for example, has a money-back guarantee offering to reimburse buyers for items that are purchased but not received and for items received that do not match the description posted and advertised on the site.[72] However, the request for reimbursement must be made within the required time frame.[73] PayPal has a policy that if it decides in favor of a buyer following a complaint, it may reimburse the buyer directly and then seek reimbursement from the seller, which will be obtained from the seller's PayPal account directly.[74] If the funds are not available in the seller's PayPal account when reimbursement is sought, PayPal will obtain the money from the seller when it is available.[75] In the past, PayPal accounts have been hijacked. In some instances, sellers have sold items to individuals who used funds from hijacked PayPal accounts to pay them. When the owners of the hijacked account complained to PayPal, the transaction to the seller was reversed, leaving the seller at a loss for the item provided to the user who hijacked a third party account. To protect sellers in such instances, PayPal created a new policy called a goodwill refund, which it considers granting if an incident is promptly reported to the police.[76]

CYBERIDENTITY THEFT

Identity theft occurs to when an individual assumes the identity of a target by unlawfully obtaining and using the target's name, Social Security number (SSN), bank account number, or other identifying information to commit a crime. **Cyberidentity theft** involves using **social engineering** tactics (i.e., tactics designed to deceive, manipulate, and ultimately trick users into revealing information) and other methods to steal a wide variety of data for subsequent criminal use, for example, to obtain goods and services in the target's name. Basically, cyberidentity thieves engage in identity theft using new means, namely, the Internet and digital technology. Cyberidentity theft enables criminals to commit identity theft with greater efficiency—often harvesting vast amounts of personal data, financial data, and even medical data in shorter periods than using traditional means (e.g., dumpster diving for discarded mail and documents containing personal information). Identity theft online and offline violates the U.S. Identity Theft and Assumption Deterrence Act of 1998.

Cyberidentity theft is costly. The costs incurred by victims are "lost wages, medical expenses and expenses . . . [associated with] restoring the integrity of [the person's] identity."[77] Victims may also be denied lines of credit, loans, and even credit cards. Additionally, victims can suffer a bad credit rating, resulting in an increase in the rates for credit cards and loans they seek. Individuals may further experience secondary victimization as a result of cyberidentity theft. The impact a victim experiences is directly related to the victim's ability to resolve issues that arise with cyberidentity theft and the time it takes to resolve them.[78] A person can also experience significant psychological and emotional harm if unable to quickly resolve the cost incurred from identity theft.

Data Breaches

The Internet has enabled intangible goods (e.g., data) to freely traverse networks. Identity data is a form of online currency.[79] All forms of data are valuable in legitimate markets and black markets. In the last few years, several U.S. banks have suffered data breaches resulting in the loss of clients' personal information (e.g., Chase, Citigroup, and Bank of America). In the Chase data breach, the names, home addresses, and phone numbers of an estimated seventy-six million account holders were targeted.[80] Banks are targeted because they consolidate and store vast quantities of users' personal and financial information, which cybercriminals can steal and either use themselves or sell for a price. For example, credit and debit card data can be sold on dedicated carding forums. Max Ray Vision (formerly known as Max Butler; also known as Iceman) operated an online forum, Carders-Market, where he sold magnetic strip data for credit cards to criminals for an estimated twenty dollars a card; the charges made to the cards he sold were over eighty-six million dollars.[81] For his crime, he received a thirteen-year sentence, along with a five-year subsequent supervision upon release, and was required to pay twenty-seven and a half million dollars in restitution.[82] Certain carding forums are well known to criminals. These forums often have a very difficult vetting process in order to ensure that **rippers** (i.e., fraudsters or scam artists seeking to sell fake financial information) do not make it to the site and do not defraud forum users by posting fake financial information.[83] Financial information can also be sold on vendor websites as well as on noncarding websites (i.e., sites unrelated to carding forums) to sell **dumps** (i.e., any stolen credit card or other financial information).[84]

Dump vendors are typically websites owned and run by a vendor who sells only the items that the vendor is selling.[85]

Apart from the sale of financial information online, cybercriminals engage in **credit card fraud** with stolen data in violation of 15 U.S.C. § 1644. An INTERPOL-led investigation that spanned forty-five countries revealed a credit card fraud involving the purchase of airline tickets using stolen and fake MasterCard, Visa, and American Express credit card information.[86] To prevent credit card fraud and **debit card fraud**, chip and PIN cards (a form of situational crime prevention) have been adopted by financial institutions in the United States; these cards have existed in other areas, such as Europe, for quite some time. The chip in these cards generates a unique one-time code with each transaction. This means that stolen data cannot be used by cybercriminals to clone debit or credit cards for in-person use. More specifically, cybercriminals cannot add this data to a magnetic strip of a blank card nor can they program this data into a different chip to make purchases at establishments, use the cards at ATMs, or engage in any other in-person transaction. The chip and PIN cards cannot, however, prevent fraud perpetrated via telecommunications and electronic communications. Irrespective of the tactics used by perpetrators to engage in these types of frauds, victims are protected from liability for unauthorized charges to their credit cards pursuant to the Truth in Lending Act of 1968, implemented by the Board of Governors of the Federal Reserve System's Regulation Z (12 CFR Part 226), and from debit card liability pursuant to the Electronic Funds Transfer Act of 1978, implemented by the Board of Governors of the Federal Reserve System's Regulation E (12 CFR Part 205). While there are some protections against certain frauds, victims still suffer financial and psychological harm from this form of cybercrime.[87]

BOX 11-2   DIGITAL WALLETS

A **digital wallet** enables users to engage in electronic commerce transactions by allowing them to pay using their digital devices (e.g., smartphone or computer). Digital wallets have been made available for users to consolidate credit cards, debit cards, prepaid cards, loyalty cards, and gift cards. They can be accessed by a user using a username and password. While providing convenience to the user, there are security and privacy risks associated with the use of digital wallets. If a perpetrator hacks into a digital wallet, the perpetrator will have access to all of the cards included in the wallet.

In addition to financial institutions, public agencies have suffered data breaches. In 2014, the U.S. Postal Service was hacked, compromising the personal information (e.g., name, SSN, date of birth, home address, and date of employment) of appropriately 800,000 employees.[88] The following year, the IRS website was compromised by hackers. These hackers entered taxpayers' SSN, date of birth, and tax filing status and retrieved their tax transactions, which included tax returns from previous years. These criminals subsequently filed fraudulent tax returns. The data of more than 100,000 taxpayers was taken.[89] It is believed that the attack originated in Russia.[90] Educational institutions have also been targeted. A server of the North Dakota University System was hacked, compromising the personal data (e.g., names and SSNs) of 780 faculty and staff and 209,000 current and former students.[91] Along with financial institutions, public agencies, and educational institutions, commercial institutions have experienced data breaches. EBay was hacked, compromising the personal data (i.e., e-mail and home addresses and birth dates) and encrypted passwords of 145 million users.[92] Target was hacked as well, and the personal information of 70 million people, including names, addresses, phone numbers, and e-mails, were stolen.[93] Additionally, 40 million credit and debit card users' information was obtained.[94] This information was stolen from a vulnerability in the point-of-sale (POS) system of a Target vendor. This was not the only incident of its kind. Vulnerabilities in vendors' systems have led to other cybersecurity incidents in the commercial industry. In 2014, the POS system of Dairy Queen was targeted; this time, malware infected the system. Compromised credentials of a third party vendor were used to access the POS system.[95] That same year, the POS system of Home Depot was hacked, resulting in the theft of debit and credit card information of an estimated 56 million customers.[96] Like Target and Dairy Queen, HomeDepot was hacked because of a vendor vulnerability. Target and HomeDepot offered users one year of free credit monitoring. This one-year monitoring is a form of "security theater," that is, a measure designed to make a user feel safer irrespective of whether or not such security is actually provided. In actuality, some of the data stolen cannot be easily replaced (if at all), requiring lifelong credit monitoring.

Liability claims against agencies, companies, and organizations that have had data breaches resulting in the loss or theft of individuals' data are difficult because the data often lost or stolen from breaches can easily be obtained from other online forums. In fact, Internet websites exist that consolidate users' data from a vast range of online and offline sources and offer it for a fee to anyone seeking to purchase it. Some websites include information about a person's date of birth, home address, previous addresses, names of family members, and in certain cases, the person's income. Individuals and companies that engage in this activity are known as **data brokers**. They make it easier for cybercriminals to obtain user information, which, while publicly available, cannot be obtained with the same speed and quantity as it can through data brokers. The information is utilized by criminals to obtain users' credit reports, which ask questions about information that can be found at these sites.

Besides the websites of data brokers, social media websites provide perpetrators with information about the target. Users' credentials have been stolen from several social media sites, including Facebook, Twitter, and LinkedIn. Apart from data brokers and social media websites, users' data is stored in the databases of previous employers; human resources departments of companies and organizations that users applied to for employment; credit bureaus; the Department of Veterans Affairs; the Department of Motor Vehicles (DMV); car dealerships where a user bought a car; credit reporting agencies; airline frequent flyer rewards programs; preferred customer accounts; pharmacies; supermarkets and retail stores; county recorder's offices (where house deeds are registered and recorded); county municipal halls (where marriage, birth, and death certificates can be obtained); and hospitals, doctors' offices, and other healthcare institutions where SSNs are stored.[97]

A victim of identity theft should place a fraud alert on his or her credit report with any of the three credit reporting bureaus: Equifax, Experian, and TransUnion. The victim should also view his or her credit report. Pursuant to the Fair and Accurate Credit Transactions Act of 2003, consumers are entitled to one free annual credit report, which can be obtained from annualcreditreport.com. After reviewing the report, the victim should report the identity theft to the Federal Trade Commission (FTC). The FTC report is known as the identity theft affidavit. The victim should then report the incident to the police and

FIGURE 11-1 Items Needed to Create an Identity Theft Report.

obtain a copy of the police report. An identity theft report can be created by combining the identity theft affidavit and the police report (see Figure 11-1).[98] This identity theft report serves as proof that the victim's identity was stolen.[99]

Medical Identity Theft

Medical identity theft involves the use of an individual's personal information (name and SSN) and medical insurance card data to obtain medical services. A victim may become aware of medical identity theft when he or she receives a bill for medical services that the victim did not receive, a notice from a healthcare insurance provider that the victim has reached the maximum of their benefit, or a phone call from a debt collector about unpaid medical services that have not been obtained by the victim.[100] A credit report can also reveal medical identity theft. Collection notices may appear on the individual's credit report for medical services that were not received by the victim.[101]

Medical identity theft can occur in a variety of ways. A common tactic is for a perpetrator to walk into an emergency room and provide a target's SSN to receive emergency medical services. Hospitals are required to provide emergency medical services irrespective of whether or not a person has insurance. What is provided in these cases is a user's name and SSN. Brandon Sharp was a victim of this form of medical identity theft. He found out that he was a victim when he requested a credit report to apply for a mortgage.[102] On his credit report, he saw numerous charges for emergency medical services in various states that he had not obtained. Unfortunately, cases like that of Brandon Sharp are commonplace. The reality is that stolen SSNs can lead to medical identity theft as well as financial fraud.

The consequences of medical identity theft extend beyond the financial costs; individuals can suffer significant bodily harm and even death. These harmful consequences are possible because the identity thief's medical information is included in the medical records of the victims. Depending on what this information is (e.g., blood type), it could be life threatening. Lind Weaver was a victim of medical identity theft. The thief used her information to have a foot amputated, leaving Lind with the bill. Even after Lind provided proof that she had not received a foot amputation at the hospital, the hospital still sent her bills, which were then sold to collection agencies that kept contacting her.[103] She spent most of her time and resources dealing with the financial implications of the acts of her identity thief. In addition to receiving bills for surgeries that were never performed on her, she also had her medical identity thief's medical information mixed with her information. In cases where an identity thief's information is included in the victim's medical record, the victim may be denied insurance because of a condition that the identity thief has.

When medical identity theft occurs, users should request access to their medical record and review the information within it. To correct mistakes in records, victims should first request a copy of their medical record in writing to review it for any errors. The FTC notes that there is a possibility that access to a medical record may be denied. Specifically, the FTC argues that "a provider might refuse to give you copies of your medical or billing records because it thinks that would violate the identity thief's privacy rights."[104] In the event that a healthcare provider refuses to provide an individual with access to their "record . . . within 30 days of . . . [their] written request, . . . [the FTC notes that the individual should] complain to the U.S. Department of Health and Human Services' Office for Civil Rights."[105] The FTC also recommends that individuals request an accounting of disclosures, which reveals what information was sent to others by the healthcare provider, when this data was sent, who received it, and for what purposes it was provided. The FTC further recommends that users ask for corrections in writing when errors are observed in the medical record. Even though changes to incorrect information can be requested, this does not mean that healthcare providers will make the changes.

Medical identity theft has also occurred as a result of data breaches. U.S. laws are in place that require notification of breaches that affect 500 or more individuals. Specifically, the Department of Health and Human Services posts information about breaches in the healthcare industry that affect 500 or more people pursuant to the 13042(e)(4) of the Health Information Technology for Economic and Clinical Health Act of 2009.[106] Recent breaches have involved the theft of personal and medical data of millions of users from Community Health System, Anthem, Premera Blue Cross, and CareFirst BlueCross BlueShield. Community Health System experienced a data breach compromising the personal information of approximately 4.5 million patients.[107] In 2015, Anthem (part of the Blue Cross and Blue Shield Association) was hacked, compromising 40 million users' personal information.[108] That same year, Premera Blue Cross reported being hacked. In this incident, the perpetrators accessed claims data (e.g., names, birth dates, SSNs, clinical information, and bank account numbers).[109] A couple of months later, CareFirst BlueCross BlueShield reported being hacked. In this incident, an estimated 1.1 million customers' personal data, including name, date of birth, e-mail address, and medical insurance identification numbers were stolen. Although no SSNs were obtained, the insurance identification numbers are worth more than SSNs on the black market.[110]

These breaches are concerning, especially in light of the push toward **electronic health records** (EHRs). On January 1, 2014, the United States mandated that public and private healthcare providers adopt EHRs. EHRs are basically a digital version of a patient's paper medical records and include "patient demographics, progress notes, problems, medications, vital signs, past medical history, immunizations, laboratory data and radiology reports" and have the ability to provide "evidence-based decision support, quality management, and outcomes reporting."[111] EHRs are implemented so that digital versions can be accessed by healthcare providers anywhere in the United States. The purpose of EHRs is to improve the quality of care by making a patient's medical records easily available irrespective of the patient's care provider. This EHR data is now vulnerable to hackers. Pursuant to the Health Insurance Portability and Accountability Act (HIPAA) of 1996, national standards were created that are designed to protect the integrity, confidentiality, and availability of EHRs (the HIPAA Security Rule).[112] Despite these requirements, medical and other forms of data are still at risk of cybertheft; the numerous database breaches illustrate this, as well as the many incidents reported by the Privacy Rights Clearinghouse

IMAGE 11-2 Depiction of IoT Objects and Devices.

database, where USBs, laptops, and other digital devices with users' personal, financial, and medical data were stolen, misplaced, lost, and even left on trains by employees.[113]

Internet of Things

The **Internet of Things** (IoT) refers to the connection of humans, animals, plants, and inanimate objects in the physical world to the Internet. People, animals, plants, and inanimate objects are connected to the Internet in order to monitor them remotely and in real time and collect, store, use, and share data about them with the intention of providing IoT device users with a service. IoT devices can be monitored and controlled remotely through applications that facilitate sensing, automation, and machine-to-machine communications, enabling the translation of real-time data in order to make appropriate, timely, and valuable decisions independent of the user.[114]

People can become part of the IoT by wearing clothing and accessories that can send data to digital devices; for instance, Garmin Vivoactive tracks users' exercise and health and sends the data to a user's device. The same holds true for animals. In Japan, Anicall created a plastic collar that pets can wear that sends data to an owner's iPhone or IPad via the Anicall app.[115] Unlike other pet IoT devices (e.g., those by Tagg and Whistle), Anicall uses Bluetooth. Similarly to animals, plants are part of the IoT. The Parrot Flower Power utilizes sensors to communicate via Bluetooth with a user's smartphone or tablet.[116] These sensors inform users about the plant's health and notifies them when water, fertilizer, and even repotting are needed. Finally, everyday objects have been connected to the Internet, including household appliances (e.g., coffeemakers, washers, dryers, and ovens). Security devices such as cameras, doors, and alarm systems are part of the IoT as well. Honeywell's Total Connect enables users to remotely monitor and control their security systems, door locks, thermostats, and lighting.[117] This company also has IoT devices that offer users the ability to track and monitor their vehicles and other assets.[118] Certain IoT devices can be attached to either people or objects, for example, smart sensors (e.g., Sen.se Mother).[119] These sensors can be placed on either an object or a person to track location, movements, and activities, and the history of the recorded activities can be reviewed online through proprietary apps.

It is estimated that there are billions of IoT devices currently in use by individuals and public and private sectors.[120] A sector that has adopted a wide variety of IoT devices is healthcare. For instance, NousLogic Healthcare has created soap dispensers that can inform employers when employees have not washed their hands after using facilities. To enable this function of the soap dispensers, employees must wear a Bluetooth chip designed to communicate with the object.[121] Actually, there are numerous IoT-enabled medical devices that can, for example, monitor patients' vital signs (e.g., breathing, heart rate, blood pressure, and temperature) and internal functions (e.g., blood sugar level). Some of these devices can alert medical professionals to abnormal vital signs or internal functions of a patient. The main purpose of IoT-enabled medical devices is for user convenience, savings in costs and time, and improvement in the quality of care.

The benefits associated with use of these devices come at high security costs for users. These devices, like other parts of the IoT, are vulnerable to hacking, malware, DoS attacks, DDoS attacks, and cybertheft. This becomes evident when examining instances where such devices have been compromised. Consider the use of IoT devices by the critical manufacturing sector, particularly the automobile industry. Chrysler recalled automobiles that had Uconnect dashboard computers.[122] A vulnerability was found in the computer system that enabled hackers to gain access to it. This vulnerability was found by researchers who wirelessly hacked into the system, taking over key vehicle features (e.g., steering, braking, and dashboard functions). This recall required only a software update. The company sent owners a USB that they were required to connect to the dashboard to update the software in order to prevent the existing system vulnerability from being exploited.[123]

Essentially, IoT devices have been rapidly deployed and adopted by consumers and organizations with little if any consideration for the privacy and security implications of the devices. Usually, the devices are not manufactured with security or consumer privacy in mind. In view of that, measures should be adopted to safeguard such devices and the data they collect from cyberattacks and unauthorized access, monitoring, sharing, and use of data.

INTELLECTUAL PROPERTY THEFT

Apart from fraudulent activity, other forms of theft are commonplace online, for instance, **intellectual property theft**. **Intellectual property** refers to ownership rights to intangible property such as the "creations of the mind, such as inventions; literary and artistic works; designs; and symbols, names and images used in commerce."[124] Intellectual property protection ensures that creators of intellectual property can receive recognition and financial benefit from their creations. The Internet makes possible the duplication and mass distribution of materials anywhere in the world in a matter of minutes (even seconds). This duplication and distribution may occur in violation of existing intellectual property laws. International treaties have been created and ratified that seek to regulate intellectual property to combat its misappropriation and theft. A case in point is the 1994 World Trade Organization (WTO) Agreement on Trade-Related Aspects of Intellectual Property Rights. This agreement includes regulation requirements for intellectual property among WTO members. National laws relating to intellectual property vary between countries and several countries do not adequately protect intellectual property rights. The Office of the United States Trade Representative has created a priority watch list, which is updated annually on the office's website and includes countries that are well known for failing to protect intellectual property rights. In 2015, this list included thirteen countries: China, Indonesia, Thailand, India, Pakistan, Algeria, Kuwait, Russia, Ukraine, Argentina, Chile, Ecuador, and Venezuela.

Intellectual property includes copyrights, trademarks, patents, and trade secrets. A **copyright** protects literary or artistic works (see 17 U.S.C. §§ 101-1332). The Internet and digital devices have afforded cybercriminals with the opportunity to steal a significant amount of copyrighted material, copy it, and illegally distribute it online. Online **copyright infringement** (i.e., digital piracy) occurs through illegally streaming, downloading, and distributing movies, TV shows, music, and other copyrighted works. Beta versions of games have also been stolen from companies and later distributed to the public for free, resulting in devastating economic losses for the companies. A case in point is Half-Life 2. A hacker gained unauthorized access to the gaming company's (Valve) servers and created a copy of the video game. The hacker then posted the copy on Anathema, a file-sharing site.[125] Users quickly began replicating and distributing the game.

A general motive for digital pirates is the belief that intellectual property should be free for all to access. Often those who provide pirated works for free to the public are viewed as Robin Hoods. Internet piracy has also been justified by those who provide the pirated works and those who obtain them as a response or form of protest against the rising costs of entertainment and software products. The time it takes to download content and the price of the pirated works play a role in a user's decision to engage in digital piracy. One study found that individuals are more likely to pirate works that have the smallest "price to time ratio."[126] Antibusiness sentiment fuels the demand and supply of counterfeits and pirated works.[127] To decrease supply, demand must also be targeted. It is difficult to deter consumption of pirated products due in part to a relative absence of, or at the very least minimal fear of, being caught and punished for this activity. Demand for counterfeit products can be influenced by information awareness campaigns, limiting access to such items, and increasing law enforcement responses to this illicit activity.[128]

One of the tactics owners of copyrighted works and law enforcement have used is the monitoring of sites known to distribute intellectual property and peer-to-peer (P2P) networks that have been known to serve as a platform within which digital piracy occurs. Known networks and sites that engage in this conduct have also been targeted. For example, a well-known P2P network, Limewire, was taken down for causing irreparable harm to the music industry.[129] However, these takedowns do not mean the end of such networks. Several more have been created in their place. These networks and sites learn to adapt their practices according to known monitoring techniques to avoid detection by authorities. The takedown of these sites has not been effective in combating digital piracy. The Pirate Bay takedowns illustrate this. Pirate Bay, a file-sharing website started in 2003, was notorious for illegally distributing copyright material and was shut down several times only to reappear, shortly after each takedown, hosted by a different Internet service provider (ISP).[130] For instance, after Swedish authorities shut down Piratebay.se, it reappeared "with a new logo, . . . [a] Phoenix rising from the flames," on a server located in a different country.[131] Pirate Bay prosecutions and site takedowns are like playing a game of whack-a-mole. When a site is shut down, another site shortly appears in its place, enabling the same illicit uploading, downloading, and sharing of content.

Online piracy has significant adverse economic effects on individuals and the corporations whose intellectual property is stolen, copied, or distributed without their approval. For example, the Recording Industry Association of America (RIAA) has suffered significant economic losses from music piracy.[132] The film industry has similarly suffered from movie and TV show piracy.[133] Apart from the criminalization of this conduct, companies have sued pirates for intellectual property theft. For example, single users who have downloaded copyrighted material have been sued by the RIAA in order to send the message to other copyright infringers that they can be held liable for such conduct.[134] These prosecutions are aimed at general and specific deterrence. One of the last individuals to be prosecuted for Internet piracy in the United States by the RIAA was Jammie Thomas-Rasset.[135] She was prosecuted for downloading and sharing copyrighted songs from the now defunct Kazaa (a file-sharing website). The RIAA has sued approximately eighteen thousand people for Internet piracy. In 2008, it stopped using this practice, focusing instead on other antipiracy efforts, such as targeting websites that hold the copyrighted works (e.g., Mega-upload).[136] Overall, antipiracy efforts are costly and can divert critical resources (in the form of time, personnel, and funds) away from research and development.

Those engaging in copyright infringement for financial gain or commercial advantage can be charged under 17 U.S.C. § 506(a). The No Electronic Theft Act of 1997 made it illegal to engage in copyright infringement even if no financial gain was obtained from the act. Before the implementation of this act, it was not considered illegal to distribute copyrighted content if no financial gain was obtained. Without this act, individuals or groups that had illegally copied and distributed content without profit could not be prosecuted. The "warez scene" is a place where users and groups upload, download, and otherwise share copyright material without financial gain.[137] Illicit gains by individuals and groups in the warez scene are actually discouraged and viewed in a negative light.[138] Individuals may also go to these sites to access, download, and distribute **abandonware** (software that is no longer available for use). Those who participate in the warez scene are often amateur hackers and members of hacking groups.[139] Individuals within hacking groups spend a significant portion of their time engaging in activities in the warez scene, whereas amateur hackers participate in the warez scene only on occasion.[140] Hacker groups compete in releasing their pirated works.[141] This competition is for respect, status, and notoriety in the warez scene.[142] These individuals also seek recognition from peers, which serves as an incentive to continue this behavior.[143] The goals of release groups online is to obtain copyrighted material and distribute it before it is due to be released to the public. Groups participating in the warez scene are assessed based on the quantity and quality of pirated works released on the sites.[144] Law enforcement agencies have conducted operations to take down warez sites. For example, *Operation Site Down* involved coordinated efforts by law enforcement agencies to take down online forums illegally distributing movies, software, and games.[145] The warez scene became more secretive following the arrests of major hacking groups for distributing pirated works (e.g., Pirates With Attitudes).[146]

International treaties have been implemented to protect copyrights. A case in point is the Copyright Treaty of 1996 of the World Intellectual Property Organization (WIPO).[147] Regional laws also exist with respect to intellectual property. The European Parliament and the Council of the European Union implemented Directive 2001/29/EC to harmonize intellectual property laws and to transpose WIPO's Berne Convention for the Protection of Literary and Artistic Works of 1886 and Copyright Treaty of 1996 into national law. Domestic laws have been passed to deal with copyright infringement as well. In the United States, the Digital Millennium Copyright Act (DMCA) of 1998 makes it illegal for individuals to bypass digital rights management mechanisms that are in place to prevent digital piracy. DrinkorDie was an infamous piracy group that illegally stripped copyrighted works of their protection, checked content to see if it worked after the removal of the protection, and then distributed the content to sites which were accessible to the public.[148] In addition, the DMCA enabled copyright holders to have removed from the Internet content that violated their copyright. DMCA takedown notices are used to remove content. The DMCA further included safe harbor provisions for ISPs, which minimize or remove liability of ISPs for content they host, provided that the ISPs act in good faith. Specifically, 17 U.S.C. § 512(c) shields ISPs from liability as long as the ISPs were unaware of the illicit content. If ISPs become aware of illegal content (e.g., through reporting), the content must be removed in a timely manner.

A **trademark** protects symbols and names associated with a particular good or service (15 U.S.C. § 1127). Apart from the theft or illicit use of trademarks, individuals have sought to exploit known trademarks by registering domain names similar to that of the business targeted. This is known as **cybersquatting**. Cybersquatters have registered, sold, and otherwise profited from businesses' trademarks. The purpose of cybersquatting is to have the target business buy the domain names from the perpetrator. Individuals with trademarks can sue cybersquatters pursuant to the Anticybersquatting Consumer Protection Act of 1999. International laws exist to protect trademarks around the world. The Trademark Law Treaty of 1994 sought to protect trademarks by harmonizing the application and registration procedure for trademarks in contracting states. The Singapore Treaty on the Law of Trademarks of 2006 was implemented to update the Trademark Law Treaty and remove the existing provision for paper applications for trademarks, allowing for electronic application and registration instead. This treaty also removed existing barriers which prevented trademark holders from exercising their rights due to existing strict mandatory licensing recording provisions in certain contracting states. Relief measures were also made available to trademark holders that failed to comply with the existing specified time limit for the application process.

Pursuant to 35 U.S.C. § 271(a), a **patent** is obtained to protect an invention. Like the trademark treaties, the Patent Cooperation Treaty of 1970, as amended in 1979 and modified in 1984 and 2001, created a unified patent application procedure to protect patent applications and owners in contracting states. The treaty enabled users to file one international application that could be used for one patent to protect the invention in the 148 contracting states. The Patent Law Treaty of 2000 sought to harmonize and create a system that enables patent applicants and owners to maintain their patent rights around the world. The Patent Law Treaty modified rules for filing international applications pursuant to the Patent Cooperation Treaty of 1970.

The final type of intellectual property is the **trade secret**. Trade secrets include "all forms and types of financial, business, scientific, technical, economic, or engineering information, including patterns, plans, compilations, program devices, formulas, designs, prototypes, methods, techniques, processes, procedures, programs, or codes, whether tangible or intangible, and whether or how stored, compiled, or memorialized physically, electronically, graphically, photographically, or in writing" (see 18 U.S.C. § 1839(3)). Trade secrets are protected under the Economic Espionage Act of 1996 if the trade secret is not generally known or easily accessible to the public, and if the owner of the trade secret has taken reasonable measures to keep the information secret.[149] Trade secrets require protection because they are "an integral part of virtually every aspect of U.S. trade, commerce, and business."[150]

The theft of a trade secret for the benefit of an individual, corporation, or government is known as economic espionage.[151] When this occurs utilizing the Internet, computers, and related technology, it is known as **cyberespionage**. Those engaging in cyberespionage seek to gain unauthorized access to a system or information for their benefit or the benefit of others. Various methods have been used to engage in cyberespionage for personal benefit or for the benefit of a company (government or government-directed trade secret theft is covered in Chapter 14). Currently, two IoT companies, Jawbone and FitBit, are engaged in a lawsuit; purportedly, FitBit contacted and subsequently hired employees from Jawbone.[152] The hired employees allegedly copied trade secrets which were then distributed to FitBit.

A common technique used in cyberespionage is **spearphishing**, which involves sending e-mails from what looks like a higher-level official within an organization, making it more likely that employees will fall victim to the scam. One such attack involved twenty-five companies in Dallas, Texas.[153] The e-mails sent to employees of these companies looked like they came from higher-level executives in the same company (the e-mails were similar but not identical to the original; for example, they may have been missing a letter in the e-mail address). The spearphishing incident was uncovered when an employee contacted one of the higher-level executives who supposedly sent the e-mail for clarification on the instructions included in the message. The e-mails sent in this particular incident instructed employees to process payments and included wire transfer information.[154] Regardless of the method used to obtain them, trade secrets must be adequately protected because their exposure or loss can adversely affect a nation's economy and the security and well-being of its citizens.

CONTROLLING CYBERTRESPASS, CYBERVANDALISM, AND CYBERTHEFT

The responsibility for the control of cybertrespassing, cybervandalism, and cybertheft often lies with the company or user. Incidents of cybertrespass, cybervandalism, and cybertheft can cause significant damage or harm. To protect against these types of cybercrimes, companies have implemented cybersecurity policies and measures designed to prevent or at the very least mitigate disruption to systems and operations and theft, alteration, or deletion of stored data. These measures should include training employees on threats and vulnerabilities to these threats; limiting access to the system and information to only those who need it and are authorized to access it; limiting what individuals can do once when they access the system and monitoring this access; and implementing strong authentication measures. An example of an authentication measure is a password. Passwords should be selected by the user, kept secret, and changed periodically. Users that select their own passwords may choose fairly obvious ones (like the name of their pet or their initials or birthdate). To be an effective authentication measure, passwords should (1) be at least eight characters long; (2) be randomly generated; (3) not include any information that has a personal connection to the user; (4) remain secret; and (5) be changed every three months (at a minimum). Companies should implement best practices when it comes to passwords.

In addition to passwords, timed or delayed lockouts of accounts should occur when the allotted log-in attempts are exceeded. Moreover, personnel security and physical security measures are required to prevent data loss. Personnel security seeks to ensure that employees safeguard the information they have access to by managing the risk of employees gaining unauthorized access or exceeding authorized access to an organization's assets (e.g., information). Physical security measures include access control systems (which enable an authority to control individual access to areas and resources in a database), identifications, and surveillance systems, to name a few. Furthermore, policies must exist that cover unauthorized access, theft, manipulation, and destruction of data by employees. These policies should be communicated to employees, along with the consequences of violating these policies.

Users should further be educated on how to navigate the Internet safely and protect their systems from malware. Malware exposure and distribution is often believed to be primarily the fault of users. However, this is not the case. Software and manufacture vulnerabilities play a large role in malware distribution. Accordingly, the role of the end user in the spreading of malware should be emphasized but not exaggerated or focused on exclusively. The best way to avoid malware is to avoid clicking on any links or attachments from unknown users; back up files daily; access the Internet from digital devices that do not contain private and sensitive information and files; and avoid using the administrator account on a computer when searching the Internet. A secondary account that does not have personal information stored on it should be created and used to browse the Internet. Files should also be backed up on external drives. In addition, users should have up-to-date antivirus and antispyware programs on their systems. These programs are designed to check the malware database (which should be updated daily) to determine if there are any known malicious software programs on the user's system. Antivirus programs need to be continuously updated so that their databases include known computer viruses, worms, and other forms of malware. Antivirus programs also scan systems for patterns that may indicate any new, unknown malware infections.

Finally, users should be educated on cybertheft; particularly, intellectual property theft, scams, and fraudulent activity online. Here, users should be informed that they should minimize their digital footprint online as much as possible. Even though users cannot control the vast amount of information about them, they can minimize their own contributions by refraining from posting personal information about themselves online. Nonetheless, the reality is that what makes users vulnerable online is often the activities of others. This is most pronounced with identity theft when users' data is stored in and stolen from third party databases far removed from the individual's control. Although the onus for security against cybertrespassing, cybervandalism, and cybertheft is often placed on individuals, the fault of these breaches has been attributed to third parties on numerous occasions.

CASE STUDY

Ralph gains unauthorized access to a company's computer system. He later sends a message to the company informing it of the vulnerability that enabled him to gain access to the system.

1. What type of hacker is he?
2. Was a cybercrime committed? Why do you think so?
3. What general cybersecurity practices can the company implement to protect against unauthorized access to the company's computer system in the future?

REVIEW QUESTIONS

1. What is cybertrespassing? Provide examples of cybercrimes that could fall into this category.
2. How does cybervandalism occur?
3. What cybercrimes are considered a form of cybertheft?
4. What are the common elements of all types of fraud? Describe them in detail.
5. In what ways can personal data be obtained legally and illegally online?
6. What are the ways in which medical identity theft is conducted?
7. What should an individual do after uncovering that he or she is a victim of identity theft? What about medical identity theft?
8. What is the Internet of Things? What are the privacy and security consequences of the IoT?
9. What is digital piracy? How does it occur?
10. In your opinion, what is the best way to deal with intellectual property theft?

LAWS

Agreement on Trade-Related Aspects of Intellectual Property Rights of 1994 (WTO)
Anticybersquatting Consumer Protection Act of 1999 (United States)
Berne Convention for the Protection of Literary and Artistic Works of 1886 (WIPO)
Computer Fraud and Abuse Act of 1986 (United States)
Controlling the Assault of Non-Solicited Pornography and Marketing Act of 2003 (CAN-SPAM Act of 2003)
Copyright Treaty of 1996 (WIPO)
Digital Millennium Copyright Act of 1998 (United States)
Directive 2001/29/EC on the Harmonisation of Certain Aspects of Copyright and Related Rights in the Information Society (European Union)
Economic Espionage Act of 1996 (United States)
Electronic Funds Transfer Act of 1978 (United States)
Fair and Accurate Credit Transactions Act of 2003 (United States)
Health Information Technology for Economic and Clinical Health Act of 2009 (HITECH Act of 2009) (United States)
Health Insurance Portability and Accountability Act of 1996 (United States)
Identity Theft and Assumption Deterrence Act of 1998 (United States)
No Electronic Theft Act of 1997 (United States)
Patent Cooperation Treaty of 1970 (WIPO)
Patent Law Treaty of 2000 (WIPO)
Singapore Treaty on the Law of Trademarks of 2006 (WIPO)
Trademark Law Treaty of 1994 (WIPO)
Truth in Lending Act of 1968 (United States)

DEFINITIONS

Abandonware. Software that is no longer available for use.
Advanced fee scam. In this scam, the perpetrator informs the target that an advanced fee is needed to transfer or deposit a large sum of money into a bank. The perpetrator may pretend to be a member of royalty, a government official, or a legal official.

Adware. Software that collects information about a user's web-browsing activities in order to provide targeted advertising content to the user based on the user's online behavior.

Backdoors. Backdoors enable a perpetrator to access a user's system at any time.

Bot. A zombie device.

Botcode. Malware designed to enable the remote control of digital devices.

Botherder. The person or persons controlling zombie computers.

Botnet. A network of botcode-infected digital devices.

Catphishing. Scammers create profiles on online dating websites and even social media websites to lure unsuspecting victims into fake relationships. After establishing a relationship and quickly "falling in love" with the victim, the scammer provides the target with a story, such as an emergency situation requiring money (e.g., money needed for travel to meet the target or money needed for unpaid bills).

Charity fraud. A form of fraud in which a perpetrator dupes users into thinking that they are providing funds or donations to legitimate charities.

Computer virus. A form of malware that spreads through user activity to systems with the intention of causing damage or disruption to a computer by attaching itself to files or programs.

Computer worm. A form of malware that spreads independent of user activity with the intention of causing damage or disruption to a computer.

Copyright. A copyright protects literary or artistic works.

Copyright infringement. The illegal streaming, downloading, and distributing of movies, TV shows, music, and other copyrighted works.

Credit card fraud. Theft and/or subsequent illicit use of credit cards.

Cyberespionage. The theft of trade secrets illicitly obtained through the use of the Internet, computers, and related technologies.

Cyberidentity theft. The use of social engineering tactics (i.e., tactics designed to deceive, manipulate, and ultimately trick users into revealing information) and other methods to steal a wide variety of data for subsequent criminal use, for example, to obtain goods and services in the target's name.

Cybersquatting. The process of exploiting a known trademark by registering a domain name similar to that of the business targeted with the intention of selling the domain to the business.

Data brokers. Individuals and companies that consolidate users' data from a vast range of online and offline sources and offer it for a fee to anyone seeking to purchase it.

Debit card fraud. Fraud involving the theft or illicit use of debit cards.

Denial of service attack. A disruption of legitimate access to a server by overwhelming its resources.

Digital wallet. A digital wallet enables users to engage in electronic commerce transactions by allowing users to consolidate credit cards, debit cards, prepaid cards, loyalty cards, and gift cards on their digital devices and pay through them.

Distributed denial of service attack. An attack utilizing multiple computers to target a system or website in order to prevent access to it by legitimate users.

Dump. Any stolen credit card or other financial information.

Electronic health records. A digital version of a patient's paper medical records.

Hacking. Gaining unauthorized access to a computer or related system.

Identity theft. Theft in which the perpetrator assumes the identity of a target by unlawfully obtaining and using the target's name, Social Security number, bank account number, or other identifying information to commit a crime.

Intellectual property. Ownership rights to intangible property.

Intellectual property theft. Theft of intangible property.

Internet of things. The connection of human, animals, plants, and inanimate objects in the physical world to the Internet.

Keylogger. Malware that is designed to record the keystrokes of users.

Malware. Malicious software.

Medical identity theft. Use of an individual's personal information and medical insurance card data to obtain medical services.

Online auction fraud. A fraud in which the perpetrator bids on an item for sale on a website that is misrepresented in some way by the seller in an effort to deceive the buyer in order to obtain a financial gain.

Patent. An exclusive right granted for an invention.

Pharming. Spoofed websites designed to look identical or nearly identical to the known websites they are pretending to be.

Phishing. Masquerading as a legitimate entity or business in order to trick users into revealing some type of information

Rippers. Fraudsters or scam artists seeking to sell fake financial information.

Shill feedback. A form of feedback that has been altered by the seller in some way to dupe buyers into thinking the seller is legitimate and reputable.

Signaling theory. A theory that examines signals and the quality they purportedly represent to determine the signaler's reliability.

Smishing. A scam via text messaging whereby a user receives a text with a link to a website with malware or a website seeking to obtain personal data from the user.

Social engineering. Use of tactics designed to deceive, manipulate, and ultimately trick users into revealing information.

Spam. Unsolicited e-mail sent en masse.

Spearphishing. A scam involving sending e-mails from what looks like a higher-level official in an organization, making it more likely that employees will fall victim to the scam.

Spyware. Software that surreptitiously monitors a user's computer activity.

Trade secrets. Under 18 U.S.C. § 1839(3), trade secrets are defined as "All forms and types of financial, business, scientific, technical, economic, or engineering information, including patterns, plans, compilations, program devices, formulas, designs, prototypes, methods, techniques, processes, procedures, programs, or codes, whether tangible or intangible, and whether or how stored, compiled, or memorialized physically, electronically, graphically, photographically, or in writing."

Trademark. A sign, design, or expression that provides legal protection for symbols and names associated with a particular good or service.

Trojan horse. Software designed to appear to be a legitimate program but actually carrying malicious payloads.

Website defacement. Website defacement occurs when a cybercriminal gains unauthorized access to a website and modifies the content.

ENDNOTES

1. S. C. McQuade III, *Understanding and Managing Cybercrime* (Upper Saddle River, NJ: Pearson Education, 2006); D. S. Wall, *Cybercrime: The Transformation of Crime in the Information Age* (Cambridge, UK: Polity, 2007); M. Yar, *Cybercrime and Society* (Thousand Oaks, CA: Sage, 2006); D. Maimon, M. Alper, B. Sobesto, and A. Cukier, "Restrictive Deterrent Effects of a Warning Banner in an Attacked Computer System," *Criminology* 52, no. 1 (2014): 34.

2. T. W. Coleman, "Kevin Mitnick: The Hacking Hamburglar," *Forbes*, April 11, 2013, http://www.forbes.com/sites/singularity/2013/04/11/kevin-mitnick-the-hacking-hamburglar/; CNN, "A Convicted Hacker Debunks Some Myths," October 13, 2005, http://www.cnn.com/2005/TECH/internet/10/07/kevin.mitnick.cnna.

3. FBI, "Cyber's Most Wanted," accessed August 15, 2016, https://www.fbi.gov/wanted/cyber; E. Markowitz, "The Inside Story of How Pakistan Took Down the FBI's Most-Wanted Cyber-

criminal," *International Business Times*, March 30, 2015, http://www.ibtimes.com/inside-story-how-pakistan-took-down-fbis-most-wanted-cybercriminal-1860808.

4. B. Krebs, "Cowards Attack Sony PlayStation, Microsoft Xbox Networks," December 14, 2014, http://krebsonsecurity.com/2014/12/cowards-attack-sony-playstation-microsoft-xbox-networks/.

5. P. A. Taylor, *Hackers: Crime in the Digital Sublime* (New York: Routledge, 2000).

6. E. H. Freeman, "Prosecution of Computer Virus Authors," *Information Systems Security* 12, no. 1 (2003): 8.

7. K. Gough, "AT&T Privacy Rights Clearinghouse," April 10, 2015, https://www.privacyrights.org/node/61543.

8. L. A. Hughes and G. J. DeLone, "Viruses, Worms, and Trojan Horses: Serious Crimes, Nuisance, or Both?" *Social Science Computer Review* 25, no. 1 (2007): 84.

9. M. Milone, "Hacktivism: Securing the National Infrastructure," *Knowledge, Technology, & Policy* 16, no. 1 (2003): 78.

10. Hughes and DeLone, "Viruses, Worms, and Trojan Horses," 80.

11. M.-H. Maras, *Computer Forensics: Cybercriminals, Laws and Evidence*, 2nd ed. (Burlington, MA: Jones and Bartlett, 2014), 4.

12. J. Burgess, "Prankster's Christmas Greeting Generates Few Ho-Ho-Hos at IBM," *Washington Post*, December 18, 1987, http://www.washingtonpost.com/archive/business/1987/12/18/pranksters-christmas-greeting-generates-few-ho-ho-hos-at-ibm/9a3d7d56-ff65-4b27-9477-06f0838270b2/.

13. J. Cluley, "Memories of the Chernobyl Virus," *Naked Security*, April 26, 2011, https://nakedsecurity.sophos.com/2011/04/26/memories-of-the-chernobyl-virus/.

14. J. Maddox, "'Zombie' Virus Attacks More Than 1 Million Cell Phones in China," *CNN*, November 11, 2010, http://www.cnn.com/2010/TECH/mobile/11/11/china.cell.phone.virus/.

15. CNN, "Security Firm: MyDoom Worm Fastest Yet," January 28, 2004, http://www.cnn.com/2004/TECH/internet/01/28/mydoom.spreadwed/.

16. C. Meinel, "Code Red: Worm Assault on the Web," *Scientific American*, October 28, 2002, http://www.scientificamerican.com/article/code-red-worm-assault-on/.

17. K. Poore, *Nimda Worm—Why Is It Different?* SANS Institute InfoSec Reading Room, 2001, 2, https://www.sans.org/reading-room/whitepapers/malicious/nimda-worm-different-98.

18. Hughes and DeLone, "Viruses, Worms, and Trojan Horses," 81.

19. S. Luco, *Research Note: Malware Analysis—A Look into the Past and Future*, ASA Institute for Risk & Innovation, November 2012, http://anniesearle.com/web-services/Documents/Research Notes/ASA_Research_Note_MalwareAnalysis-ALookIntothePastandFuture_November 2012.pdf.

20. D. Kawamoto, "'Storm Worm' Rages Across the Globe," *CNET*, April 13, 2007, http://www.cnet.com/news/storm-worm-rages-across-the-globe/; Luco, *Research Note: Malware Analysis*, 5.

21. R. Pegoraro, "Secure Your Mac from Flashback Infection," *USA Today*, April 7, 2012, http://usatoday30.usatoday.com/tech/products/story/2012-04-06/pegoraro-secure-mac-flashback-trojan/54087366/1.

22. I. Marson, "Mobile Trojan Launches Skulls Attack," *CNET*, January 6, 2005, http://www.cnet.com/news/mobile-trojan-launches-skulls-attack/.

23. Department of Justice, Office of Public Affairs, "Pakistani Man Indicted for Selling 'Stealth genie' Spyware App," September 29, 2014, http://www.justice.gov/opa/pr/pakistani-man-indicted-selling-stealthgenie-spyware-app.

24. M. Gregg, "Spouse-Busting: Intimacy, Adultery, and Surveillance Technology," *Surveillance & Society* 11, no. 3 (2013): 302.

25. Ibid.

26. E. H. Freeman, "Prosecution of Computer Virus Authors," *Information Systems Security* 12, no. 1 (2003): 6.

27. L. J. Nicholson, "Computer Crimes," *American Criminal Law Review* 37 (2000): 207.

28. K. Poulsen, "FBI Busts Alleged DDoS Mafia," *SecurityFocus*, August 26, 2004, http://www.securityfocus.com/news/9411.

29. Hacktivism is explored in Chapter 14 in further detail.

30. K. Dunham and J. Melnick, *Malicious Bots: An Inside Look into the Cyber-Criminal Underground of the Internet* (Boca Raton, FL: CRC Press, 2009), 60.

31. Ibid., 33.

32. Ibid., 72.

33. Ibid., 3, 57.

34. FBI, "Operation: Bot Roast—'Bot-Herders' Charged as Part of Initiative," June 2007, https://www.fbi.gov/news/stories/2007/june/botnet_061307.

35. H. Woo, Y. Kim, and J. Dominick, "Hackers: Militants or Merry Pranksters? A Content Analysis of Defaced Web Pages," *Media Psychology* 6, no. 1 (2004): 63–82.

36. A. Moses, "Indian Hacks RAAF Website over Student Attack," *Sydney Morning Herald*, July 16, 2009, http://www.smh.com.au/technology/security/indian-hacks-raaf-website-over-student-attacks-20090716-dmgo.html.

37. Associated Press, "Hackers Deface Senate Web Page and Force FBI to Close Its Site," *Los Angeles Times*, May 28, 1999, http://articles.latimes.com/1999/may/28/news/mn-42018.

38. BBC News, "Mr Bean Replaces Spanish PM on EU Presidency Site," last updated January 4, 2010, http://news.bbc.co.uk/2/hi/8440554.stm; G. Tremlett, "Mr Bean Ousts Zapatero from Spain's EU Website," *Guardian*, January 5, 2010, http://www.theguardian.com/technology/2010/jan/05/mr-bean-hacker-zapatero.

39. W. S. Albrecht, C. C. Albrecht, and C. O. Albrecht, *Fraud Examination*, 2nd ed. (Mason, OH: Thompson-Southwestern, 2006); W. S. Albrecht, C. Albrecht, and C. C. Albrecht, "Current Trends in Fraud and its Detection," *Information Security Journal: A Global Perspective* 17, no. 1 (2008): 2–12; W. S. Albrecht, N. C. Hill, and C. C. Albrecht, "The Ethics Development Model Applied to Declining Ethics in Accounting," *Australian Accounting Review* 16, no. 38 (2006): 30–40.

40. Albrecht, Albrecht, and Albrecht, *Fraud Examination*.

41. Albrecht, Hill, and Albrecht, "The Ethics Development Model."

42. S. Lea, P. Fischer, and K. Evans, *The Psychology of Scams: Provoking and Committing Errors of Judgement—A Report for the Office of Fair Trading*, May 2009, 29, http://mastersofmindcontrol.com/psychology_of_scams2.pdf.

43. J. Pieters, "Digital Loverboy Arrests Revealed; Police Warn Tinder Women," *NL Times* (Netherlands), February 11, 2015, http://www.nltimes.nl/2015/02/11/digital-loverboy-arrests-revealed-police-warn-tinder-women/.

44. Ibid.

45. T. Buchanan and M. T. Whitty, "The Online Dating Romance Scam: Causes and Consequences of Victimhood," *Psychology, Crime and Law* 20, no. 3 (2014): 278.

46. L. Lake, "Section 8 Scammers Cheat People Seeking Housing," Federal Trade Commission, June 5, 2015, https://www.consumer.ftc.gov/blog/section-8-scammers-cheat-people-seeking-housing.

47. Better Business Bureau, "BBB Top Ten Scams of 2014," January 27, 2015, https://www.bbb.org/council/news-events/consumer-tips/2015/01/bbb-top-ten-scams-of-2014/.

48. IRS, "Phone Scams Continue To Be Serious Threat, Remain on IRS 'Dirty Dozen' List of Tax Scams for the 2015 Filing Season," January 22, 2015, http://www.irs.gov/uac/Newsroom/Phone-Scams-Continue-to-be-Serious-Threat-and-Remain-on-IRS-Dirty-Dozen-List-of-Tax-Scams-for-the-2015-Filing-Season.

49. R. Lemos, "FBI Nabs Suspected Identity-Theft Ring," *SecurityFocus*, November 3, 2006, http://www.securityfocus.com/brief/347.

50. J. Graham, ed., *Cyber Fraud: Tactics, Techniques, and Procedures* (Boca Raton, FL: CRC Press, 2009), 157.
51. Ibid., 157–158.
52. Ibid., 167.
53. Associated Press, "Miami Man Pleads Guilty in Katrina Relief Scam That Used Fake Websites," *Metro*, January 10, 2008, http://www.metro.us/news/miami-man-pleads-guilty-in-katrina-relief-scam-that-used-fake-websites/tmWhak---adJSUVUPkpLE/.
54. Graham, *Cyber Fraud*, 165.
55. R. A. Ford, "Preemption of State Spam Laws by the Federal CAN-SPAM Act," *University of Chicago Law Review* 72 (2005): 355, 364–365; D. E. Sorkin, "Spam Legislation in the United States," *John Marshall Journal of Information Technology and Privacy Law* 22, no. 1 (2003): 3, 5–6.
56. Ford, "Preemption of State Spam Laws," 364.
57. Sorkin, "Spam Legislation," 6.
58. S. Musil, "MySpace Wins $234 Million Antispam Judgment," *CNET*, October 29, 2009, http://www.cnet.com/news/myspace-wins-234-million-antispam-judgment/.
59. *MySpace Inc. v. Sanford Wallace*, F. Supp. 2d 1293 (2007).
60. J. E. McNealy, "Angling for Phishers: Legislative Responses to Deceptive E-Mail," *Communication Law and Policy* 13, no. 2 (2008): 291.
61. N. Delener, "International Counterfeit Marketing: Success without Risk," *Review of Business* 21, nos. 1–2 (2000): 16–20; D. G. Gregg and J. E. Scott, "The Role of Reputation Systems in Reducing On-Line Auction Fraud," *International Journal of Electronic Commerce* 10, no. 3 (2006): 95–120.
62. I. MacInnes, Y. Li, and W. Yurcik, "Reputation and Dispute in eBay Transactions," *International Journal of Electronic Commerce* 10, no. 1 (2005): 30.
63. Y. Tan and W. Theon, "Toward a Generic Model of Trust for Electronic Commerce," *International Journal of Electronic Commerce* 5, no. 2 (2000–2001): 61–76.
64. A. H. Kydd, *Trust and Mistrust in International Relations* (Princeton, NJ: Princeton University Press, 2005), 6.
65. M.-H. Maras, "What Happens When We Become the 'Others'? The Social Consequences of a Mass Surveillance," *International Journal of Law, Crime and Justice* 40, no. 2 (2012): 69.
66. D. Good, "Individuals, Interpersonal Relations, and Trust," in *Trust: Making and Breaking Cooperative Relations*, ed. D. Gambetta (Oxford, UK: Basil Blackwell, 1988), 33, cited in Maras, "What Happens When We Become the 'Others'?, 70.
67. J. von Neumann and O. Morgenstern, *Theory of Games and Economic Behavior* (Princeton, NJ: Princeton University Press, 1944).
68. S. H. Schwartz, "Moral Decision Making and Behavior," in *Altruism and Helping Behavior*, ed. J. Macauley and L. Berkowitz (New York: Academic Press, 1970), 127–141; Gregg and Scott, "The Role of Reputation Systems in Reducing On-Line Auction Fraud," 98–99.
69. J. Andreoni, "Impure Altruism and Donations to Public Goods: A Theory of Warm-Glow Giving," *Economic Journal* 100 (1990): 464–477; C. Dellarocas, M. Fan, and C. A. Wood, "Self-Interest, Reciprocity, and Participation in Online Reputation Systems," working paper 205, MIT Center for Digital Business, 2004; A. Diekmann, B. Jann, W. Przepiorka, and S. Wehrli, "Reputation Formation and the Evolution of Cooperation in Anonymous Online Markets," *American Sociological Review* 79, no. 1 (2014): 65–85.
70. MacInnes et al., "Reputation and Dispute in eBay Transactions," 31.
71. B. L. Connelly, S. T. Certo, R. D. Ireland, and C. R. Reutzel, "Signaling Theory: A Review and Assessment," *Journal of Management* 37, no. 1 (2011): 39–67.
72. eBay, "eBay Money Back Guarantee," accessed August 15, 2016, http://pages.ebay.com/help/policies/money-back-guarantee.html.
73. Ibid.
74. eBay, "About Reimbursement," accessed August 15, 2016, http://pages.ebay.com/help/sell/reimbursement.html.

75. Ibid.

76. M. Brignall, "When PayPal Refuses Buyers Protection Against Ebay Fraud," *Guardian*, August 9, 2014, http://www.theguardian.com/money/2014/aug/09/paypal-buyer-protection -ebay-fraud.

77. J. Jefferson, "Police and Identity Theft Victims—Preventing Further Victimisation," Austral-asian Centre for Policing Research, 2004, https://www.ncjrs.gov/App/publications/abstract .aspx?ID=205618; L. M. LoPucki, "Human Identification Theory and the Identity Theft Prob-lem," *Texas Law Review* 80 (2001): 89–135; Identity Theft Resource Centre, *Identity Theft: The Aftermath 2003*, accessed August 15, 2016, http://www.idtheftcenter.org/images/surveys_ studies/Aftermath2013.pdf; Identity Theft Resource Centre, *Identity Theft: The Aftermath 2004*, accessed August 15, 2016, http://www.idtheftcenter.org/images/surveys_studies/After math2014FINAL.pdf.

78. T. Sharp, A. Shreve-Neiger, W. Fremouw, J. Kane, and S. Hutton, "Exploring the Psychological and Somatic Impact of Identity Theft," *Journal of Forensic Sciences* 49, no. 1 (2004): 131–136.

79. J. Crosby, *Challenges and Opportunities in Identity Insurance* (London: HM Treasury, 2008).

80. S. Rosenblatt, "JPMorgan Hackers Altered, Deleted Bank Records, Says Report," *CNET*, August 28, 2014, http://www.cnet.com/news/jpmorgan-hackers-altered-deleted-bank-records-says -report/.

81. K. Poulsen, "Superhacker Max Butler Pleads Guilty," *Wired*, June 29, 2009, http://www.wired .com/2009/06/butler_court/.

82. K. Poulsen, "Record 13-Year Sentence for Hacker Max Vision," *Wired*, February 12, 2010, http://www.wired.com/2010/02/max-vision-sentencing/.

83. Graham, *Cyber Fraud*, 28.

84. Ibid., 31.

85. Ibid., 30.

86. INTERPOL, "Global Action Against Online Fraud in the Airline Sector Nets 118 Arrests," November 28, 2014, http://www.interpol.int/News-and-media/News/2014/N2014-228.

87. A. W. Brugess, C. Regehr, and A. R. Roberts, *Victimology: Theories and Applications* (Burlington, MA: Jones and Bartlett, 2010), 383.

88. E. Nakashima, "China Suspected of Breaching U.S. Postal Service Computer Networks," *Washington Post*, November 10, 2014, https://www.washingtonpost.com/news/federal-eye /wp/2014/11/10/china-suspected-of-breaching-u-s-postal-service-computer-networks/.

89. B. Krebs, "IRS: Crooks Stole Data on 100k Taxpayers via 'Get Transcript' Feature," *Krebson-Security*, May 15, 2015, http://krebsonsecurity.com/2015/05/irs-crooks-stole-data-on-100k -taxpayers-via-get-transcript-feature/.

90. C. Frates, "IRS Believes Massive Data Theft Originated in Russia," *CNN*, June 4, 2015, http:// www.cnn.com/2015/05/27/politics/irs-cyber-breach-russia/index.html.

91. K. Gough, "North Dakota University," *Privacy Rights Clearinghouse*, March 7, 2014, https:// www.privacyrights.org/content/north-dakota-university.

92. eBay, "Frequently Asked Questions on eBay Password Change," May 21, 2014, http://www .ebayinc.com/in_the_news/story/faq-ebay-password-change.

93. B. Krebs, "Target: Names, Emails, Phone Numbers on Up To 70 Million Customers Stolen," *KrebsonSecurity*, January 14, 2014, http://krebsonsecurity.com/2014/01/target-names-e-mails -phone-numbers-on-up-to-70-million-customers-stolen/.

94. C. Timberg, J. L. Yang, and H. Tsukayama, "Target Says 40 Million Credit, Debit Cards May Have Been Compromised in Security Breach," *Washington Post*, December 19, 2013, http:// www.washingtonpost.com/business/technology/target-data-breach-affects-40-million -accounts-payment-info-compromised/2013/12/19/5cc71f22-68b1-11e3-ae56-22de072140a2 _story.html.

95. B. Krebs, "DQ Breach? HQ Says No, But Would it Know?" *KrebsonSecurity*, August 26, 2014, http://krebsonsecurity.com/2014/08/dq-breach-hq-says-no-but-would-it-know/.

96. S. Li, "Possible Data Breach at Home Depot Highlights Retailers' Vulnerability," *Los Angeles Times*, September 4, 2014, http://www.latimes.com/business/la-fi-retail-hacking-20140904 -story.html.

97. Experian, "How Your Identity Is Stolen," accessed August 17, 2016, https://www.protect myid.com/identity-theft-protection-resources/identity-basics/how-thieves-operate.aspx.

98. See Federal Trade Commission, https://www.identitytheft.gov/.

99. Ibid.

100. Federal Trade Commission, "Medical Identity Theft," accessed August 17, 2016, http://www .consumer.ftc.gov/articles/0171-medical-identity-theft.

101. Ibid.

102. W. Konrad, "Medical Problems Could Include Identity Theft," *New York Times*, June 12, 2009, http://www.nytimes.com/2009/06/13/health/13patient.html?_r=0.

103. L. Laird, "Federal Medical-Privacy Law Frustrates ID Theft victims," *ABA Journal*, September 1, 2014, http://www.abajournal.com/magazine/article/federal_medical-privacy_law _frustrates_id_theft_victims/.

104. Federal Trade Commission, "Medical Identity Theft."

105. Ibid.

106. For database, see https://ocrportal.hhs.gov/ocr/breach/breach_report.jsf.

107. B. Hardekopf, "The Big Data Breaches of 2014, *Forbes*, January 13, 2015, http://www.forbes .com/sites/moneybuilder/2015/01/13/the-big-data-breaches-of-2014/.

108. E. Viebeck, "Analysis: Anthem Attack May Have Started in April," *The Hill*, February 10, 2015, http://thehill.com/policy/cybersecurity/232285-analysis-anthem-attack-may-have -started-last-april.

109. J. Finkle, "Premera Blue Cross Hacked, Medical Information of 11 Million Customers Exposed," *Huffington Post*, March 17, 2015, http://www.huffingtonpost.com/2015/03/17 /premera-blue-cross-cybera_n_6890194.html.

110. S. Dance, "Cyberattack Affects 1.1 million CareFirst Customers," *Baltimore Sun*, May 20, 2015, http://www.baltimoresun.com/health/bs-bz-carefirst-data-breach-20150520-.

111. Healthcare Information and Management Systems Society, "Electronic Health Records," accessed August 17, 2016, http://www.himss.org/library/ehr/.

112. U.S. Department of Health and Human Services, "Health Information Privacy: The Security Rule," accessed August 17, 2016, http://www.hhs.gov/ocr/privacy/hipaa/administrative /securityrule/.

113. For database, see http://www.privacyrights.org/data-breach.

114. M.-H. Maras, "Internet of Things: Security and Privacy Implications," *International Data Privacy Law* 5, no. 2 (2015): 100.

115. A. Patrizio, "New 'Internet of Animals' Actually Seems Useful for Pet Owners," *NetworkWorld*, May 28, 2015, http://www.networkworld.com/article/2927442/microsoft-subnet /new-internet-of-animals-iot-actually-seems-useful-for-pet-owners.html.

116. For information on the device, see http://www.parrot.com/usa/products/flower-power/.

117. For information on this, see http://www.homesecurity.honeywell.com/mobile.html.

118. Ibid.

119. For information on the device, see https://sen.se/mother/.

120. D. Evans, "The Internet of Things: How the Next Evolution of the Internet Is Changing Everything," CISCO white paper, 2011, http://www.cisco.com/web/about/ac79/docs/innov /IoT_IBSG_0411FINAL.pdf.

121. M. Brown, "These 7 Internet of Things–Powered Devices Will Change Your Life," *International Business Times*, October 10, 2015, http://www.ibtimes.com/these-7-internet -things-powered-devices-will-change-your-life-2135607.

122. A. Greenberg, "After Jeep Hack, Chrysler Recalls 1.4M Vehicles for Bug Fix," *Wired*, July 24, 2015, http://www.wired.com/2015/07/jeep-hack-chrysler-recalls-1-4m-vehicles-bug-fix/.

123. Ibid.
124. World Intellectual Property Organization, "What Is Intellectual Property?" http://www
    .wipo.int/about-ip/en/.
125. J. Howe, "The Shadow Internet," *Wired*, January 1, 2015, http://archive.wired.com/wired
    /archive/13.01/topsite.html.
126. J. R. Schultz, "Warez Everyone Going: An Exploratory Look at Online Piracy," May 2005,
    http://www.csulb.edu/colleges/cba/honors/thesis/documents/Joshua_Schultz_Thesis.pdf.
127. P. E. Chaudry, S. S. Chaudry, S. A. Stumpf, and H. Sudler, "Piracy in Cyberspace: Consumer
    Complicity, Pirates and Enterprise Enforcement," *Enterprise Information Systems* 5, no. 2
    (2011): 260.
128. Ibid., 257.
129. J. Halliday, "LimeWire Shut Down by Federal Court," *Guardian*, October 27, 2010, http://
    www.theguardian.com/technology/2010/oct/27/limewire-shut-down.
130. A. Griffin, "Pirate Bay Resurrected by Rival, as Hackers Leak Government E-Mails in Re-
    sponse to Swedish Raid," *Independent*, December 15, 2014, http://www.independent.co.uk
    /life-style/gadgets-and-tech/news/pirate-bay-resurrected-by-rival-as-hackers-leak-govern
    ment-e-mails-in-response-to-swedish-raid-9924925.html.
131. A. Newcomb, "The Pirate Bay Rises Again, Back Online Two Months after Swedish Police
    Raid," *ABC News*, February 2, 2015, http://abcnews.go.com/Technology/pirate-bay-rises
    -back-online-months-swedish-police/story?id=28662407.
132. RIAA, "Scope of the Problem," accessed November 13, 2015, https://www.riaa.com/physi
    calpiracy.php?content_selector=piracy-online-scope-of-the-problem.
133. D. Lodderhose, "Movie Piracy: Threat to the Future of Films Intensifies," *Guardian*, July 17,
    2014, http://www.theguardian.com/film/2014/jul/17/digital-piracy-film-online-counterfeit
    -dvds.
134. P. E. Chaudry, S. S. Chaudry, S. A. Stumpf, and H. Sudler, "Piracy in Cyberspace: Consumer
    Complicity, Pirates and Enterprise Enforcement," *Enterprise Information Systems* 5, no. 2
    (2011): 263.
135. ABC News, *Jammie Thomas-Rasset News*, August 3, 2009, http://abcnews.go.com/topics
    /news/jammie-thomas-rasset.htm.
136. A. Holpuch, "Minnesota Woman to Pay $220,000 Fine for 24 Illegally Downloaded Songs,"
    Guardian, September 11, 2012, http://www.theguardian.com/technology/2012/sep/11
    /minnesota-woman-songs-illegally-downloaded.
137. L. Gomes, "FBI Probe of Alleged Software Piracy via Internet Brings Arrest of 17 People,"
    Wall Street Journal, May 5, 2000, http://www.wsj.com/articles/SB957492236169474418.
138. D. Décary-Hétu, C. Morselli, and S. Leman-Langlois, "Welcome to the Scene: A Study of
    Social Organization and Recognition Among Warez Hackers," *Journal of Research in Crime
    and Delinquency* 49, no. 3 (2012): 364.
139. P. Craig, *Software Piracy Exposed* (Rockland, MA: Syngress, 2005); Décary-Hétu et al., "Wel-
    come to the Scene," 359–382.
140. Craig, *Software Piracy Exposed*; Décary-Hétu et al., "Welcome to the Scene," 359–382.
141. A. Rehn, "The Politics of Contraband: The Honor Economies of the Warez Scene," *Journal of
    Socio-Economics* 33 (2003): 359–374; Décary-Hétu et al., "Welcome to the Scene," 359–382.
142. Craig, *Software Piracy Exposed*; Décary-Hétu et al., "Welcome to the Scene," 359–382.
143. P. T. Leeson and C. Coyne, "The Economics of Computer Hacking," *Journal of Law, Economics
    and Policy* 1, no. 5 (2005): 11–32.
144. Décary-Hétu et al., "Welcome to the Scene," 359–382.
145. J. Healey, "Digital Piracy Raids Net Arrests," *Los Angeles Times*, July 1, 2005, http://articles
    .latimes.com/2005/jul/01/business/fi-piracy1.
146. D. Décary-Hétu, "Police Operations 3.0: On the Impact and Policy Implications of Police
    Operations on the Warez Scene," *Policy & Internet* 6, no. 3 (2014): 315–340.

147. The World Intellectual Property Organization is a United Nations agency that is dedicated to intellectual property information, cooperation, protection, and services.

148. R. Broadhurst, P. Grabosky, M. Alazab, and S. Chon, "Organizations and Cyber Crime: An Analysis of the Nature of Groups Engaged in Cyber Crime," *International Journal of Cyber Criminology* 8, no. 1 (2014): 11.

149. 18 U.S.C. § 1839(3).

150. P. Kelley, "The Economic Espionage Act of 1996," *FBI Law Enforcement Bulletin*, July 1997, http://www2.fbi.gov/publications/leb/1997/july976.htm.

151. Maras, *Computer Forensics*, 127.

152. M. Taves, "Jawbone Lawsuit Accuses Fitbit of Trade Secret Theft," *CNET*, May 27, 2015, http://www.cnet.com/news/jawbone-lawsuit-accuses-fitbit-of-trade-secret-theft/.

153. R. Simon, "Hackers Trick Email Systems into Wiring Them Large Sum," *Wall Street Journal*, July 29, 2015, http://www.wsj.com/articles/hackers-trick-e-mail-systems-into-wiring-them -large-sums-1438209816.

154. Ibid.

CHAPTER 12

DEVIANT CYBERACTS AND PUBLIC ORDER CYBERCRIMES

Paraphilia, Prostitution, Substance Abuse, and Gambling

KEYWORDS

Adultery
Anorexia
Asphyxiophilia
Bestiality
Brothel
Bulimia
Call girl
Child sex trafficking
Coprophilia
Crime against nature
Cyberdildonics
Cyberpornography
Cyberprostitution
Cybersex
Deviance
Escort

Exhibitionism
Fetishism
Frotteurism
Johns
Juvenile prostitution
Madam
Malum in se
Masochism
Morality
Necrophilia
Paraphilia
Pedophilia
Pimp
Pornography
Prohibition
Prostitution

Psychoactive substances
Punter
Sadism
Sadomasochism
Scoptophilia
Sexual deviance
Sodomy
Streetwalker
Urophilia
Verified Internet Pharmacy
　　Practice Sites
Veterinary-Verified Internet
　　Pharmacy Practice Sites
Voyeurism
Zoophilia
Zoosadism

Rentboy was an Internet escort website that marketed its services to gay men. Escorts paid to advertise services and fees by posting profiles on the website. The amount paid by the escorts varied between $59.95 and $299.95 based on how visible their profiles were.[1] The website had a disclaimer that users were required to acknowledge before accessing the site. The disclaimer included the following statement: "This site may not be used for the advertising of sexual services or to engage in activities requiring the payment of money for sex or other illegal activities."[2] Visitors gaining access to the website could peruse the profiles to choose an escort based on sexual services and fees provided. The escorts would list sexual preferences (fetishes, role-playing, etc.) and post preferred sexual positions.[3] Reviews of these escorts by consumers were available on separate websites (e.g., DaddysReview.com).[4]

In 2016, U.S authorities indicted the chief executive officer, Jeffrey Hurant, on prostitution charges.[5]

This chapter examines use of the Internet, computers, and related technology to facilitate prostitution. The overall emphasis of this chapter is the exploration of deviant and criminal behavior online, particularly paraphilias, prostitution, substance abuse, and gambling. Furthermore, it considers the measures needed to control these crimes and deviant behaviors.

THE RELATIONSHIP BETWEEN LAW AND MORALITY

Law and morality seek to protect the public and preserve order and peace. Law refers to the system of rules that regulate the public's actions and provide penalties for noncompliance. To uphold moral standards, laws were created criminalizing conduct believed to threaten the moral fabric of society. Crimes that violate the moral principles of society are known as **malum in se** offenses. **Morality** refers to the values and principles of conduct that distinguish between right and wrong behavior, and represents the standards with which behavior is assessed. Moral behavior is that which restrains people from causing some form of harm to others.

In addition to immoral acts that are criminalized by law, there are immoral acts that cause harm but are not prohibited by law. The immoral acts considered illegal have changed over time. Consider **adultery**, which has been decriminalized in Europe, various parts of Latin America, and certain states in the United States. In the states that do have adultery laws in place, prosecutions are rare. Today, even with these laws in place, there are websites that promote and encourage adultery. A case in point is Ashley Madison, a website which enables users seeking to engage in adultery to meet, communicate, and connect with other like-minded individuals. Married users can meet other married or nonmarried users for the purpose of engaging in an affair.

Moral behavior is also considered to be behavior that is restrained to prevent causing some form of offense to others. Indeed, some acts that may be deemed immoral are those considered offensive. A case in point is **pornography**, which involves the visual, audio, written, or other form of portrayal of sexual activity designed specifically to cause sexual arousal in the user. The next section examines the acts that violate conventional moral principles or threaten the well-being of the public.

CYBERDEVIANCE

Deviance refers to behavior that violates social norms and expectations. Individuals, groups, and societies label a particular act as deviant and react to it with repulsion. Deviant acts are not necessarily illegal acts. Consider eating disorders and acts of self-harm, both physical (e.g., cutting) and psychological harm (e.g., suicidal thoughts). Numerous groups and websites online promote both of these negative behaviors; for example, some websites encourage those with eating disorders (termed *pro ana* and *pro mia*), such as **anorexia** (i.e., anorexia nervosa; a condition where an individual engages in self-starvation or eats very little food due to fear of gaining weight, and has a distorted perception of body/weight) and **bulimia** (i.e., bulimia nervosa; the binging and then purging of food through self-induced vomiting), to continue these behaviors rather than attempt recovery.

Sexual deviance refers to sexual behavior that violates social norms and expectations. Specifically, it involves sexual gratification through atypical or socially unacceptable ways. For instance, there are individuals who actually seek others with sexually transmitted diseases to become infected themselves.[6] What is considered sexual deviance depends on those defining the behavior (the individual, group, community or society), and who and /or what is involved in the sexual act. Some sexually deviant acts are considered crimes (e.g., rape). Other sexually deviant acts are also considered crimes; for some acts of sexual deviance, this depends on the state or country defining and criminalizing that behavior. For instance, **sodomy** (or "buggery") is considered a crime in certain countries. Buggery was viewed as an unlawful act and a **crime against nature** (or an unnatural act) in Ireland until it was decriminalized between adults with the passage of the Criminal Law (Sexual Offences) Act of 1993. In its 2003 decision in *Lawrence v. Texas* (2003),[7] the Supreme Court invalidated sodomy laws in the United States, rendering them unconstitutional.

Cyberdeviance involves use of the Internet to engage in conduct that violates social norms and expectations. The Internet enables, propagates, and fosters deviant behavior through the accessibility of information on aberrant behavior and images depicting different forms of sexual deviance and through the abundance of like-minded individuals, often reinforcing behaviors that society has deemed to be immoral and unacceptable.[8] Forums can reinforce abnormal behavior by providing encouragement and tips for the behavior and ways to avoid detection by family, friends, and law enforcement. Furthermore, the Internet has created new opportunities for sexual deviants to access material and act upon their desires. The types of pornography available are conventional forms (e.g., those available on most pornographic websites and in print materials, such as magazines), hardcore pornography, and extreme or bizarre pornography. The next section focuses on sexually deviant behaviors known as paraphilias, which are abnormal sexual desires and behaviors.

PARAPHILIA ONLINE

Paraphilia is an umbrella term used for a wide variety of psychosexual disorders, including those listed below. It involves unusual legal or illegal sexual activities and practices. More specifically, it is a term used to describe those who engage in abnormal sexual activities that involve animals, humans, or objects or receive sexual gratification from viewing such activities. Studies have not shown any significant differences in ethnicity, socioeconomic status, intelligence, or sexual orientation between those with paraphilias and those without them.[9]

 Fetishism. An individual with a fetish derives sexual gratification and pleasure from an inanimate object or a nongenital body part.
 Frotteurism. With frotteurism, sexual arousal and pleasure are obtained by rubbing or touching another, nonconsenting individual in a public space.
 Exhibitionism. Exhibitionism refers to the exposure of one's genitals to an unsuspecting and unwilling person. Sexual pleasure is derived from exposing oneself to arouse shock, surprise, and often dismay in an unsuspecting party.
 Sadomasochism. Sadomasochism refers to the process of giving and receiving sexual arousal and pleasure from inflicting and receiving pain. With **masochism**, sexual arousal and pleasure are obtained from self-inflicted pain or pain inflicted by others, whereas with **sadism**, sexual arousal and pleasure are obtained by inflicting

pain on others. Studies have shown that paraphilias, with the exception of sado-masochism, are rare in women.[10]

Pedophilia. A pedophile is sexually aroused and derives pleasure from child sexual exploitation. Pedophilia is the most widely studied deviant behavior (see Chapter 10 for more information on this paraphilia).

Zoophilia. An individual with this paraphilia is sexually attracted to animals or seeks a sexual relationship with animals. **Bestiality** refers to sexual activity between a human and an animal. In most countries, bestiality is criminalized as a crime against nature and, to a lesser extent, as an abuse of animals prohibited under animal cruelty laws. In South Africa, sexual acts with animals are explicitly prohibited under Section 13 of the Criminal Law (Sexual Offences and Related Matters) Amendment Act of 2007. Laws also exist that criminalize the possession of pornography involving bestiality. In the United Kingdom, Section 63 of the Criminal Justice and Immigration Act of 2008 criminalizes the possession of pornographic images that depict bestiality.[11]

BOX 12-1   ZOOSADISM AND ANIMAL CRUSH VIDEOS

Zoosadism is considered illegal in the United States pursuant to the Animal Crush Video Prohibition Act of 2010. Zoosadists receive sexual gratification from watching animals being tortured or killed. The videos depicting animal cruelty, torture, and killings are known as animal crush videos. According to the Department of Justice, these videos often depict "women . . . , usually barefoot or in high heels, stepping on (or crushing), torturing and killing different species of animals, ranging from crawfish, crabs and insects to rodents, rabbits, kittens, puppies, cats, dogs and other mammals."[12] In 2015, Ashley Richards was convicted for creating and distributing numerous animal crush videos. In one of the many vile and horrific videos she created, starred in, and distributed, "Richards is seen torturing and killing a blue Pit Bull-mix puppy in a kitchen. The defenseless dog's mouth is closed with duct tape and he struggles as Richards strikes the dog numerous times with a meat cleaver. In the video, Richards chops off one of the puppy's paws, then hacks at his head and neck. Richards is later seen severing the dog's head and urinating on its body."[13] She was the first person to be convicted under the Animal Crush Video Prohibition Act of 2010.

Necrophilia. A necrophiliac receives sexual arousal and pleasure from viewing or having sexual intercourse with corpses. In South Africa, Section 14 of the Criminal Law (Sexual Offences and Related Matters) Amendment Act of 2007 criminalizes sexual acts with a corpse. In the United Kingdom, necrophilia was made illegal with the passage of the Sexual Offences Act of 2003. The possession of pornographic images that depict necrophilia is illegal in the United Kingdom under Section 63 of the Criminal Justice and Immigration Act of 2008. In the United States, there is no federal law prohibiting necrophilia, but state laws exist that consider this act either a misdemeanor (e.g., New York Penal Law § 130.20) or felony crime (e.g., Florida Law, § 872.06).

BOX 12-2   NECROPHILIA, ASPHYXIOPHILIA, AND MURDER

Graham Coutts, a necrophiliac and asphyxiophile (a person who receives sexual gratification and pleasure from the intentional restriction of oxygen to the brain of others or themselves), subscribed to a variety of online websites that were dedicated to necrophilia, female **asphyxiophilia**, and rape. He murdered the best friend of his lover, Jane Longhurst, via asphyxiation.[14] He kept her body for several weeks, often visiting the corpse, first in the shed in his home where he placed it after he killed her and then in a storage unit where he kept it until the odor from the decomposing body was such that he risked being caught by authorities. When he removed the body from storage, he set it on fire. He received life imprisonment for his crime.[15]

Voyeurism. Voyeurism is a form of paraphilia, a coercive form, because it violates an individual's privacy by engaging in unauthorized surveillance of the person. Male voyeurs are also known as peeping Toms. Individuals engage in this act to receive sexual gratification and excitement by watching unsuspecting users undress, shower or bathe, engage in other day-to-day activities, have sex or engage in other sexual acts (i.e., **scoptophilia**), and in some cases, even urinate (i.e., **urophilia**) and defecate (i.e., **coprophilia**). The risk of getting caught watching the targets also excites them. Voyeurs can engage in these activities either through real-world or online monitoring. Hidden cameras can enable these individuals to engage in surreptitious surveillance of users. Voyeurs have also been known to gain unauthorized access to a user's computer (or other digital device) by surreptitiously downloading malware to enable him or her to spy from a webcam. This is what Mark Wayne Miller did when he hacked into underage girls' webcams and recorded them.[16] Another voyeur, Mahmoud Abdo, contacted the victim of his unauthorized surveillance, Chelsea Clark, by sending her a Facebook message, "Really, cute couple," with an image of herself and her boyfriend watching TV online.[17] In one incident in the United Kingdom, Andrew Meldrum even pretended to be a repairman to gain access to a victim's computer and secretly installed spyware on her system to enable remote monitoring via her webcam.[18] The reality is that there are numerous websites with videos from purported hidden cameras which are advertised to voyeurs.

PUBLIC ORDER CYBERCRIMES

Public order crime offends the public's shared norms, morals, values and customs. Acts within this category are deemed harmful to society, even though they may not have an identifiable victim (other than the perpetrator). These crimes are purportedly perpetrated by willing victims. The term *victimless crime*, which is often used to describe public order crimes, is inappropriate because this crime affects secondary victims, such as strangers and the perpetrator's family, friends, acquaintances, and community. Public order cybercrimes are public order crimes, such as prostitution, substance abuse, and gambling, committed or facilitated online.

PROSTITUTION

Prostitution involves engaging in a sexual activity for some form of remuneration. Remuneration for sexual services can take many forms, including money, basic necessities (e.g., food, shelter, clothing, and protection), and addictive products (e.g., drugs and cigarettes).[19] Three factors are present in prostitution: offer or agreement to engage in a sexual act, engagement in a sexual act, and a fee. Prostitutes can work independently or under the control, direction, or management of a **pimp** (a person who is in charge of and controls a prostitute or prostitutes) or a **madam** (a woman who is in charge of prostitutes in a **brothel**—a house of prostitution).

Pimps, madams, and prostitutes working independently or in concert facilitate, manage, and advertise sexual acts for a profit (a portion or all of the proceeds). Pimps and madams use money to control prostitutes. For example, prostitutes are required to pay a sum of money to pimps in the form of fixed sums considered as daily or weekly fees, a percentage of the money earned per client, and fines in the event that the prostitute violates any rules set by her pimp.[20] In one recent case, Otasowie Christopher Asuen required that the prostitutes working for him pay him 40 percent of their proceeds.[21]

Johns, men who seek sexual services from female and male prostitutes for a fee, are motivated by different desires: to engage in socially undesirable activity and unfamiliar sex; to have a sexual partner who has attributes they find desirable; to be able to specify sex acts to be performed by the prostitute; to engage in sex acts with numerous or different people; and to not be involved emotionally with the sexual partner.[22] A 2011 study by Farley revealed that men who purchase women for sexual activities view them as subhuman or inhuman.[23] These individuals lack empathy for sex workers and may have negative emotions toward them (e.g., contempt).[24] Men who learn about sexual activity through pornography tend to have unrealistic expectations about sexual relations, particularly that women enjoy engaging in sexual behaviors that are aggressive or degrade and humiliate them.[25]

Prostitution is differentiated from other forms of sex work, particularly sex trafficking, which involves the third-party facilitation of an individual's participation in the illicit sex industry via coercion, because it is a practice that a person engages in voluntarily. Women are not believed to make the decision to enter into sex work autonomously, but rather because they succumb to existing economic and societal pressures and lack of educational and employment opportunities. Individuals who were part of a Cambodian brothel explained that their motives for engaging in prostitution included "economic incentives, desire for an independent lifestyle, and dissatisfaction with rural life and agricultural labor."[26]

Sex work is viewed as a form of female oppression. In fact, feminists view prostitution as the result of male oppression seeking to subjugate women in an attempt to maintain a power imbalance.[27] Certain academics have viewed prostitution as the use of a woman as an object.[28] Here, women are considered a commodity—to be advertised, rated, commented on, bought, and even rented for sex. This good is available to men for consumption for a price. Nonetheless, the reality is that some women's role in the sex industry is not just that of an object of sex but also as the buyer and manager of sex.[29] As the buyer, women too can purchase a woman or man for sex. As a manager of sex, they can serve as madams of brothels, arranging meetings, taking care of prostitutes, and meeting their clients' needs. Prostitution has been labeled a victimless crime. Many theorists argue against the use of this description for prostitution due to the trauma experienced by the prostitute with each sex act to her body and dignity.[30] By contrast, others view it as a form of empowerment to have power over men through a sex act. Nevertheless, the act is not truly empowering for a number of obvious reasons: prostitutes may not be in control of how and how often their bodies are used; they are subjected to disease and physical abuse, including rape; and they are routinely shamed and stigmatized by society.

Prostitution is viewed by some societies as a violation of social norms and as an illicit behavior. The United States criminalizes prostitution, with the exception of certain counties in Nevada. In the People's Republic of China, prostitution is criminalized under Article 41 of the Law Safeguarding Women's Rights and Interests of 1992. Specifically, this law makes it illegal "for anyone to organize, force, seduce, shelter or introduce a woman to engage in prostitution or employ or shelter a woman to engage in obscene activities with others." In other countries, like the Netherlands, prostitution is legal and is not considered a public order crime. Sweden does not punish those who sell sexual services under the Law

That Prohibits the Purchase of Sexual Services of 1999; instead, it punishes those who purchase it. In Finland, the purchasing of sex from prostitutes is not illegal; it is, however, illegal to purchase sex from trafficked victims. In other countries, prostitution has been decriminalized but only if it occurs in places that have been authorized by existing regulation. For example, in Greece, prostitution is regulated by the government and can be practiced in licensed brothels (e.g., the red light district of Chania in Crete). The same holds true in the Nevada counties where prostitution is legal. Overall, countries conflict in their views on the legality of prostitution, even the legality of certain facets of prostitution.

Facilitation of Prostitution via the Internet

Before the Internet, customers knew very little about the types of services provided by prostitutes and the quality of these services. The Internet readily provides this information. It provides greater ease with which individuals can shop for men, women, and even children with whom to engage in sexual activities. Websites are interactive, enabling users to search for what they are looking for, and they may include price lists for services provided.[31] The Internet further provides clients with a wide variety of potential prostitutes from which to choose. It has made it easier for a client to find the type of person he or she wants for the sex act. The physical characteristics of prostitutes can be evaluated by the client to determine whether the prostitute fits his or her desired type of sexual partner. Prostitutes who offer niche services or have a look or personal features that are in high demand can charge a premium for them. The Internet is also used by prostitutes to promote their services. Their profiles include information that potential clients can use to determine whether they will purchase the services provided by a prostitute. Individuals may look for specific physical characteristics and personality traits.[32] The websites where prostitutes advertise differ in appearance and content. The pictures may be head shots, full body (clothed), nude, seminude, or include sexually provocative poses.

The Internet is widely utilized by pimps, madams, and prostitutes. Pimps and madams use it to communicate with one another and clients; schedule and arrange times and places for clients to meet with prostitutes; and advertise services provided. In one such case, Laurie Lynn McConnell, a former employee of the U.S. Department of Agriculture, and her co-conspirator, John Miller, ran the online prostitution businesses Darc Phoenix and USA Honies and placed advertisements for services offered on websites and in newspapers.[33]

Brothels also advertise their services online. The federal and state governments of the United States, with the exception of certain counties in Nevada, have statutes that criminalize prostitution. Brothels in these counties in Nevada advertise online prostitutes and the services they provide, along with images of the women, and even allow clients to book appointments through websites, e-mail, or phone. Certain brothel websites have message boards where clients can post general inquiries. Clients can also offer feedback for services provided. Brothels review the feedback to determine if clients are pleased with services provided and to respond to any unsatisfied customers.[34] In China, brothels advertise their services online and even have search engines dedicated to prostitution websites, despite the fact that prostitution is illegal.[35] The websites of brothels in Greece and Slovenia include languages other than the main languages of the host countries, indicating that sex tourism (i.e., travel to foreign countries for the sole purpose of engaging in sexual activities with prostitutes) is occurring in these countries.[36] Pimps and madams have also used the Internet to recruit prostitutes from anywhere in the world via e-mail, chat rooms, bulletin boards, classified ads, social media, and other websites. For instance, Otasowie Christopher Asuen, who ran an online prostitution enterprise employing over 500 prostitutes, recruited prostitutes to his business from advertisements on Backpage and Craigslist.[37]

Prostitutes that work independently of any pimp, madam, or other entity also utilize the Internet and digital technology to facilitate prostitution in some way, whether coordinating and scheduling actions, communicating with clients, or advertising services. In 2013, the AIM Group found that advertising websites such as AdultSearch, Backpage, CityVibe, Eros, and MyRedbook had ads posted that promoted prostitution.[38] In the United States, in 2003, 104 johns were arrested for using Backpage to arrange meetings with undercover police officers posing as prostitutes.[39] In another incident in the United States, prostitutes that advertised their services online on Backpage were arrested when they agreed to perform sexual services on individuals that turned out to be undercover police officers.[40] Social media websites have also been found to advertise prostitution. Consider LinkedIn, a professional social networking site. Nevada prostitutes used this site to promote their services, which were considered legal in the county in Nevada where they were located. LinkedIn removed their profiles because the website's policy is that LinkedIn could not be used to promote anything unlawful.[41] Irrespective of LinkedIn's policy and removal of certain profiles of prostitutes advertising their services, profiles of prostitutes are still available on the website. Dating websites whose primary purpose is dating services have also been found to house profiles advertising sexual services for a fee.[42]

E-mail exchanges are used to screen clients. Prostitutes can determine what type of customer is requesting their services from the manner in which the e-mail is phrased.[43] Websites are also used to advertise the sexual services they provide. Some "massage parlors" (i.e., establishments that are really a front for prostitution or a brothel) openly advertise erotic services online but not sexual activities or remuneration, and others openly advertise sexual services online. Law enforcement agencies deal with the advertisement of prostitution online through undercover operations, as was the case for the massage parlor A1 Therapy and Spa on Highway 69 South, Tuscaloosa, Alabama, where the women working at the establishment were arrested for soliciting prostitution.[44]

Websites on which prostitutes can create profiles and allow customers to contact them are also used by prostitutes to exchange information with one another. In addition, there are websites that verify prostitution websites, rate them, and provide feedback about their services. Clients often describe in detail the sexual activities performed by the prostitute, usually using cruel and degrading language, which further demeans, humiliates, and traumatizes those in the sex industry. Some of the women are also videotaped and photographed without their knowledge by clients who keep the videos or photographs for souvenirs or trophies. A now defunct site known as MyRedBook enabled sex workers to advertise services and chat with clients; the services of sex workers were also reviewed.[45] Some websites record information about clients who are abusive or do not pay for services. Others are used to vouch for certain clients to minimize risks to prostitutes for infectious disease and harm by violent clients.

CAN A WEBSITE BE A HOUSE OF PROSTITUTION? Southwest Companions was a website where prostitutes and clients could arrange meetings, discuss fees and services, and provide ratings of their experiences. Individuals gained access to the site through prostitutes. After sleeping with a prostitute, a client would be given access to the password-protected site. Southwest Companions had three levels of membership: probation, verified, and trust:[46] A client started on probation status. The client was removed from probation after engaging in a sex act with a prostitute if the prostitute sent the website administrator positive feedback regarding the behavior of the client (e.g., demeanor and whether he paid). The client then moved to verified status, which enabled the client to access different prostitutes on the website. After the client arranged and paid for several sexual liaisons with prostitutes and the administrator received positive feedback concerning the client, he was promoted to trusted status. At this level, the client could give feedback on personal experiences with various prostitutes.

On Southwest Companions, prostitutes were purportedly paid up to $200 for certain sexual acts and $1,000 for a full hour with a client,[47] although no money was ever exchanged on the website. At the time the website was taken down, there were fourteen thousand members, two hundred of whom were prostitutes.[48] David Flory, a retired physics professor from Fairleigh Dickinson University, and Chris Garcia, a former president of the University of New Mexico, ran the website.[49] The government claimed that the website operated like a brothel. The court, however, disagreed, finding that the website was "not a place where prostitution was practiced, encouraged, or allowed."[50] Many websites similar to Southwest Companions serve primarily to screen clients and prostitutes. They serve as a way to link prostitutes with a customer base. Such sites are not considered illegal per se, at least not according to existing U.S. laws.

PROSTITUTION: THERE IS AN APP FOR THAT In Germany, an app was created which used the global positioning system (GPS) capabilities of a digital device in order to link a paying client (i.e., **punter**) with a prostitute. In Berlin, there is an app known as Peppr that enables users to locate prostitutes. This app works by enabling users to type in their location and then a list of prostitutes in the area appears with their photos, physical characteristics, and prices for services. Prostitution and its advertisement has been legal in Germany since 2002. The app enables users to filter through the list and book services with a prostitute for a fee. An app by the name of AdultWork in the United Kingdom enables a **call girl** to advertise services and a customer to purchase their services.[51] Call girls, unlike **streetwalkers**, are prostitutes who do not display their profession publicly (i.e., in the streets); instead, they arrange meetings with clients over the phone or online and are able to charge high fees for their sexual services.[52] There are also apps that promote and facilitate sexual acts without remuneration. New websites and apps in the United States provide women and men with information regarding individuals who are similarly seeking to engage in sexual activities without payment (e.g., Disckreet and Pure).[53] Another app, Mixxer, also enables users to meet with others to engage in sex acts without remuneration.[54]

Escorts: Prostitutes With a Different Name?

Escort agency websites primarily provide nonsexual services for a fee. Provision of such services for a fee is not illegal. However, escort websites have been found to offer their clients the opportunity to discretely purchase sexual services from escorts. Escorts who provide sexual services to another person for remuneration are engaging in prostitution. Escorts are paid to go on dates with clients. They are not paid to have sex with them, even if sex occurs after the date. Escort services are advertised as providing companionship and not sexual services for a fee. No fees for sexual services are given, negotiated, or discussed

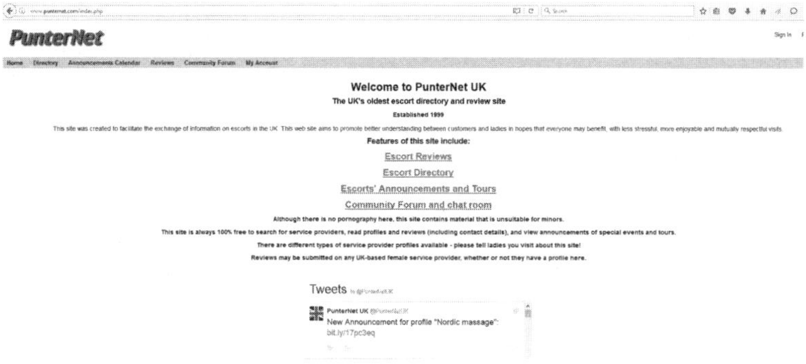

IMAGE 12-1   Screenshot of PunterNet.

on the phone when contacting the agency; this enables the escort agency to claim that an escort was acting on his or her own volition and not under the direction of the agency if the escort engaged in sex with the client. The reality is that not all escorts are prostitutes. Some do not engage in sexual activities with their clients.[55] Nonetheless, in numerous instances escort sites and agencies have been used for prostitution. These agencies use the word "escort" so as not to draw the attention of authorities.

Websites offering commercial sex have used the word escort instead of prostitute. A case in point is PunterNet, one of "the oldest escort directory and review site[s] in the United Kingdom," which includes "a very active community forum for both clients and service providers."[56] PunterNet is a website that enables escorts and prostitutes to advertise their services and users to find and evaluate prostitutes in the United Kingdom.[57] The EroticReview is a website where clients can provide and review feedback on sex workers and experiences with them. The website describes itself as a "top community of escorts, hobbyists and service providers."[58] In the United States, the website Classy DC Escorts was found to be a front for prostitution. Kuraye Tamunoibi Akuiyibo employed over one hundred prostitutes in the United States and abroad via the website.[59] Another U.S. website, Escort.com, was found to facilitate interstate prostitution.[60] The Mann Act of 1910 (18 U.S.C. § 2421 et seq.) criminalizes the facilitation of interstate prostitution by either enticing or transporting a person (adult or child) across state lines to engage in prostitution. This activity is considered illegal under the Mann Act even if the person, considered a victim under this law, is able to legally consent to engage in sexual acts.

Escorts communicate with clients and negotiate prices and services via e-mail, social networking websites, or dating websites. The escorts show their picture and give their personal information, including name (usually not their real name), sexual orientation (straight, gay, lesbian, bisexual), types of sexual activities they are willing to engage in (individual sex, group sex, submissive sexual practices, vaginal sex, anal sex, fellatio, cunnilingus, etc.), and the desired gender of the potential client. The physical characteristics and personality of the person are also included. Sometimes other information is included on the escort website (favorite foods, music, movies, actors, authors, among other things). Male escorts are more likely to include this information on their online profile than are female escorts.[61] Male escorts tend to provide information about their penis length and girth and whether they are circumcised. Some male escort websites include information similar to that included on dating websites, such as hobbies, likes and dislikes, and recreational interests.[62] Castle and Lee found that of the escort websites they reviewed, the ones offering female escorts provided more detailed information about their physical appearance to potential clients. These websites also included detailed customer reviews of the services provided by the female escorts.[63]

Research has shown that male escort services that target female clients are subtle in their advertisements, making the websites resemble dating websites.[64] The male escort websites targeting male clients are explicit in the offered services and graphic in the descriptions of these services, often including photographs.[65] The audience to which these sites are geared can be determined from the words used to describe the men's sexual preferences with respect to position (top, bottom, or both; active, passive, or versatile). As Lee-Gonyea, Castle, and Gonyea pointed out, these terms are commonly used by homosexual men to indicate their preferred sexual roles.[66] In the sites on which male prostitutes cater only to male clients, there is no pretense as to what is being advertised and sold, namely, sexual services. This primarily is not the case with male escort websites targeting services to female clients.

Juvenile Prostitution

Juvenile prostitution refers to the engagement of children in sexual acts for some form of remuneration. A juvenile can be enticed to enter into prostitution or may engage in sex acts to meet basic needs of food, shelter, and income. Those engaging in this type of behavior do so to earn money out of necessity (e.g., homeless youth, runaways), relying on the income to find food and shelter, or just to have an income (but not out of necessity).[67] Some of them may still be living at home with parents or guardians. Others may engage in this conduct through pimps, brothels, and other services (such as escort services, massage parlors, and strip clubs). Children cannot legally consent to engage in sexual acts. Therefore, what is occurring is considered by society to be **child sex trafficking**, which involves inducing, recruiting, harboring, transporting, providing, or obtaining a child under the age of eighteen for the purpose of commercial sex. Children have also facilitated the prostitution of other children. A case in point involved a seventeen-year-old girl who was charged with trafficking for running a prostitution ring in which her clients had sex with underage girls.[68]

Some children have been lured into the sex trade on false promises: love, work, to be famous. For instance, in four separate cases, each perpetrator (Christopher Tyrone Young, Marvin Chavelle Epps, Jamaal Watkins, and Alan Townsend) lured underage girls from social media websites MySpace and Urbanchat.com on false promises and ultimately forced them into prostitution.[69] Factors affecting children's vulnerability include emotional dependence, lack of identity documents, difficult family circumstances, threats, financial difficulty, drug addiction, sexual abuse, and homelessness.[70] The methods used to target vulnerable girls are more or less the same. Perpetrators peruse social media websites to find potential victims. Once they find a target, they contact the target and compliment the child on his or her appearance (e.g., handsome/pretty face, attractive body). Depending on the interaction, they might also offer the target the opportunity to make money (e.g., as a model). The perpetrators shower the target with affection and seek to lure the victim into a meeting offline. The ultimate goal is to get the girl or boy to engage in prostitution. Street gangs have utilized social media in this manner to recruit girls into prostitution. This was the case with Underground Gangster Crips, which used the Internet to recruit young girls to their prostitution business.[71]

Cyberprostitution, Cybersex, and Cyberpornography

Researchers vary in their interpretation of **cyberprostitution**. Some contend that cyber-prostitution occurs through live sex shows where individuals pay those engaging in these acts or performances either to masturbate or perform sex acts with others.[72] With cyber-prostitution, the Internet acts as pimp or madam and facilitator. Other researchers argue that cyberprostitution takes place in real time but does not involve physical penetration of the prostitute by the client.[73] What is missing with cyberprostitution is physical proximity of the client to the prostitute. The term *cyberprostitution* has also been used to refer to the means with which individuals use the Internet to advertise, communicate, and arrange meetings with clients.[74] Sharp and Earle argued that cyberprostitution takes three forms:[75]

1. *Escort services*, whose clients are considered part of the upper class.
2. *Independents*, who work on their own independent of any pimp or brothel.
3. *Massage parlors*, where prostitutes work for an establishment and the focus of the site is on the agency and its services.

Cyberprostitution has also been characterized as paid **cybersex**.[76] Cybersex is viewed by some as requiring some form of genital stimulation or even penetration—this has been made possible by the advent of apps (e.g., Sexy Vibes, which turns phones into vibrators) and sexual instruments such as **cyberdildonics**. Cybersex can be facilitated either through text messages, video streaming services (where participants watch each other perform sex acts), or cyberdil-donics (where sex toys are controlled by those seeking to engage in cybersex with the user).[77]

A type of Internet addiction is cybersex addiction, which involves both engaging in cy-bersex and accessing and viewing **cyberpornography**.[78] Drivers for cybersex and access and viewing of cyberporn are the affordability of Internet services, the accessibility of sexualized content online, and the anonymity afforded by the Internet.[79] The Internet reduces individu-als' inhibitions.[80] Indeed, individuals tend to engage in conduct online that they might not engage in offline without the same level of anonymity. Websites and peer-to-peer networks enable the downloading, uploading, and sharing of pornographic images and videos. Com-pulsive behaviors are developed due to the availability and ease with which pornography can be accessed online.[81] Cooper et al. posited three categories of users who utilize the Inter-net for sexual purposes:[82] *recreational users*, those who are curious about sex or seek sexually related materials online for entertainment; *at-risk users*, who are likely to develop addictive behaviors due to existing personality factors and because of the accessibility, affordability, and anonymity afforded to them by the Internet with respect to sexually related materials; and *sexually compulsive users*, who utilize the Internet to fulfill their sexual impulses, many or all of which are often characterized as an abnormal sex drive or obsession with sex.

Some researchers contend that live sex shows are cyberpornography and not cyber-prostitution.[83] Others argue that prerecorded peep and sex shows are cyberpornography; sexual acts performed in real time for remuneration, however, are characterized as cyber-prostitution. The cyberprostitute is directed by the client to perform the acts the client wants. Those engaged in sexual activity through these webcams may be doing so voluntarily or under coercion. If by coercion, the individuals are deemed victims of trafficking.

Some websites also enable users to watch live sex shows (some of which have interactive capabilities). CamGirls and CamBoys are sites that offer live explicit pornographic content (both fee and nonfee based). Interactive live sex shows enable clients to make requests through typing or speaking. Once audio and video live transmission became available through digital devices, pimps exploited the technology by offering live peep and sex shows for a fee. Live strip shows are also available for purchase; these shows can be interactive. Even live videos of women being raped or tortured are available online.[84]

Pimps and madams can also use technology like webcams to monitor prostitutes. Other websites offer live webcam streaming of prostitutes engaging in day-to-day activities for a fee. To provide these live streams, cameras are placed all over the prostitutes' home (similar to reality shows like *Big Brother*). Prostitutes are watched when they eat, sleep, dress, cook, watch TV, take a shower, or use the toilet. This live video streaming enables voyeurism to occur. Other voyeuristic technologies are available which further invade the bodies of women in the sex industry. Specifically, there are certain sex toys that are advertised on sex industry websites that contain tiny cameras that can see inside a woman's body during use.

SUBSTANCE ABUSE AND DRUGS ONLINE

Psychoactive substances affect the mental state of individuals who consume them, altering cognition, mood, and perception.[85] These substances can be either legal (e.g., alcohol and tobacco) or illegal (e.g., heroin). Psychoactive substances include *depressants* (e.g., alcohol and opiates), *stimulants* (e.g., caffeine and amphetamines), and *hallucinogens* (e.g., mescaline and LSD).[86] Users may abuse these substances, especially when the substances are illegal and consumption occurs without medical oversight. Substance abuse occurs from the harmful and frequent use of addictive psychoactive substances (e.g., drugs and alcohol). This repeated and often excessive use of a substance can have a detrimental effect on one's health. It may also adversely affect a user's work and home life. The overindulgence and frequent use of a substance can lead to dependency on the substance. Dependency manifests itself in the form of an intense desire to take the drug and inability or extreme difficulty in controlling its potential withdrawal symptoms when the substance is not consumed. It results in the increased use of a substance over a period of time, continued use even if adverse effects are experienced, and increased tolerance when using the substance, resulting in the need to use greater quantities of the substance to receive the same effects experienced with smaller doses or amounts consumed. Ultimately, when a user is dependent on a substance, it increasingly becomes a priority to a user and takes precedent over other day-to-day activities.

The Internet provides users around the globe with the opportunity to buy drugs. Indeed, the Internet has made drugs more accessible to users. Specifically, users are able to obtain drugs more easily online than in person, especially users who do not know where or whom to go to obtain drugs offline. Both licit and illicit psychoactive substances can be sold online. This chapter covers pharmaceuticals (i.e., medical drugs) sold online (Chapter 13 covers other drugs regulated and prohibited by governments). Pharmaceuticals are categorized into over the counter and prescription only; the latter requires approval for use by a doctor before purchase and use. Users can access drugs in a number of forums, bulletin boards, chat rooms, and social media websites. The most widely used sites to purchase drugs online are Internet pharmacies, which are prevalent online. The reliability of the website and the quality of the products on the website are advertised in order to solicit new and maintain existing customers anywhere in the world with an Internet connection.

Online Pharmacies

There are three types of online pharmacies: legal, illegal, and fake.[87] The legal pharmacies follow existing legal frameworks and provide prescription medications only if valid prescriptions are provided. Certain Internet pharmacies are owned and operated by well-known pharmacies. Accordingly, the same rules apply to online stores as those in the physical world. In the United States, in order to obtain drugs from these online pharmacies, a prescription from a doctor is required before purchasing and shipping drugs. The Ryan Haight Online Pharmacy Consumer Protection Act of 2008 mandates that a prescription not be given without a patient's physical visit to a physician. Specifically, 21 U.S.C. § 829(e)(1) criminalizes the delivery, distribution, or dispensing of "a prescription drug as determined under the Federal Food, Drug, and Cosmetic Act [21 U.S.C. § 301 et seq.] . . . without a valid prescription." This law was named after a teenager (Ryan Haight) who died after an overdose resulting from a mix of prescription drugs that he had obtained online without prescriptions.[88] Unfortunately, there have been many cases of individuals who have died after consuming drugs purchased from online pharmacies.

The second type, illegal pharmacies, provide drugs in violation of existing laws. Specifically, these online pharmacies do not require a valid prescription to dispense drugs approved by the Food and Drug Administration (FDA) or non-FDA-approved drugs, in violation of U.S. law. In these online forums, all a person has to do is fill out an online questionnaire in order to obtain prescription drugs. No face-to-face interviews, physical examination, or a doctor's diagnosis is required to obtain the drugs. What is more, the information the individual provides on the website is not authenticated. The information included is an address to which the drugs are to be shipped, the user's date of birth, the height and weight of the individual, and a method of payment. Illegal fulfillment pharmacies also exist. These pharmacies carry the drug inventory for online pharmacies and are usually responsible for shipping orders.[89]

The last type, fake online pharmacies, are made to look like legitimate online pharmacies in physical appearance and content, even with fake testimonies and logos of accrediting and licensing agencies. The fake online pharmacies are meant to defraud customers by obtaining their personal information. Fake websites can be "pharmed" websites, which are designed to look like existing legitimate online pharmacies. Those running fake online pharmacies have been known to engage in shill feedback, posting positive comments not only on their website but also other forums where their website is advertised and where online pharmacies are discussed.[90] The purpose of these fake websites is to dupe users of existing legitimate pharmacies into accidentally posting personal and financial information on the fake websites. The main purpose of the websites is to defraud users. These websites may steal users' personal and financial information and use the data for other illicit purposes (e.g., identity theft and fraud).

Some fake online pharmacies also sell counterfeit medications, both over the counter and prescription only. Counterfeit pharmaceuticals are marketed online as legitimate.

Indeed, users are duped into thinking that drugs sold on online pharmacies are of exactly the same quality as those sold in offline U.S. pharmacies. The reality is that users may receive counterfeit and substandard versions of the drugs they purchase online.[91] A case in point involved Hi-Tech Pharmaceuticals, which purportedly sold drugs such as Viagra that were developed in unsanitary and unsafe conditions in Belize.[92] Studies have shown that lifestyle drugs, such as those given for erectile dysfunction, have been counterfeited and sold online.[93] Similarly, studies have shown that counterfeit anti-HIV drugs have been sold online as well.[94] Drugs sold on these websites may contain different ingredients from those advertised, which in consequence can have a harmful effect on users. In other cases, drugs sold on these websites may not have the active ingredient or may contain an improper dose of the active ingredient or ingredients. There are significant health risks associated with consuming counterfeit pharmaceuticals, the ultimate of which is death.[95] Users should be educated on what they are purchasing online and the risks associated with purchasing substandard and counterfeit drugs.

DIFFERENTIATING LICIT, ILLICIT, AND FAKE ONLINE PHARMACIES Finding legitimate online pharmacies is not an easy feat, as they exist alongside fraudulent websites and websites with counterfeit and expired medications seeking to take advantage of unsuspecting users. Fraudulent websites often provide a limited number of prescription drugs (e.g., Viagra).[96] Online pharmacies should be checked for legitimacy before providing any personal, financial, or health information on the website.

The FDA has a website that enables users to verify that online pharmacies have state licenses. This, of course, can only occur if the user is purchasing drugs from a U.S. online pharmacy. The FDA recommends buying prescription drugs from U.S.-licensed online pharmacies. The FDA provides users with guidelines on how to find approved and safe online pharmacies.

The National Association of Boards of Pharmacy (NABP) created the **Verified Internet Pharmacy Practice Sites** (VIPPS) program, which "accredits online pharmacies that dispense prescription drugs."[97] This program requires online pharmacies to meet U.S. licensing requirements of the state where its offline headquarters are located and every state where it dispenses prescription drugs.[98] The NABP has listed eleven thousand websites that are not recommended for use by individuals. These websites "are those Internet drug outlets that appear to be out of compliance with state and federal laws or NABP patient safety and pharmacy practice standards. Ordering drugs from these websites . . . [is believed to put the patient and his or her family] at risk. NABP has reviewed over 11,000 sites and found 96% of those sites to be out of compliance. NABP recommends that patients use sites accredited through the VIPPS program or sites that use a pharmacy domain name when purchasing drugs online."[99] The Better Business Bureau (BBB) also has a seal that online sites can use once they have been verified by the BBB and meet their membership standards.[100] Both of these programs serve as a way for users to verify the legitimacy of online pharmacies before purchasing over-the-counter and prescription drugs. Participation in VIPPS and the BBB's Online Reliability program is voluntary. Other ways to verify the authenticity of the online pharmacy is through the VeriSign Secure Site Program. If a site has a VeriSign Secure Site logo, the user can click on the logo and be led to "a validation page," which gives the "location of the company represented on the Web site, the organization name, and a verification of proof that the organization has the right to use the name."[101]

IMAGE 12-2   An Image of a Legitimate Online Pharmacy.

The VIPPS has an equivalent accreditation method for veterinarian pharmacies. Online pharmacies that disperse medications for pets can be accredited by **Veterinary-Verified Internet Pharmacy Practice Sites** (Vet-VIPPS). These accreditation programs seek to minimize the risks associated with prescription drugs from unlicensed websites that contravene existing laws.[102] Legitimate online pharmacies for pet medications require a prescription from a veterinarian. To avoid raising potential buyers' suspicion, illicit websites claim that a prescription for a drug requested is not needed in other countries and that is why it is not requested. Other pharmacies, domestic or foreign, may claim they have a veterinarian who will go over information provided by the patient about their pet and then prescribe the drug. The FDA warns that a veterinarian should physically examine pets before making a diagnosis. An FDA investigation revealed that online pharmacies dispensing pet medications made false claims about the purported benefits of a drug and sold counterfeit drugs, expired drugs, and drugs without a prescription.[103] Users can consult veterinarians to find legitimate online pharmacies. The veterinarian may work with state-licensed online pharmacies.[104] Users are advised to buy pet pharmaceuticals from sites accredited through Vet-VIPPS,[105] which are provided with a seal to be placed on the website.

Another warning sign for users that a website may be illegal or fake is the price of the product. If the price is significantly lower than the offline cost of the medication, a user should be wary of the website. The adage "if it is too good to be true, then it probably isn't true" applies here and should be utilized for good measure.[106] The cost of many medications is prohibitive, leading some people to turn to online pharmacies to save on the cost.

Individuals in the United States also purchase prescription drugs online from Canadian pharmacies. Nevertheless, websites have falsely advertised that they are Canadian pharmacies.[107] The reason users purchase prescription drugs from these websites is that drug sales in Canada are regulated by the government; so too are prices of the drugs. The same price controls do not exist in the United States. Pharmaceutical companies receive a significant amount of money for drugs, many of which, especially those requiring a prescription, are economically prohibitive without insurance. Pharmaceutical companies in the United States can charge whatever they want for prescription drugs. Some buyers, therefore, purchase their prescription drugs from Canadian pharmacies because they are significantly cheaper than similar drugs sold in the United States. However, the safety of foreign-produced and foreign-distributed drugs imported to the United States cannot be established. Furthermore, the importation of these drugs violates existing laws.

Companies have illegally advertised and facilitated the advertisement of foreign online pharmacies. A case in point is Google. Google's AdWords program enables companies to advertise on Google for free and only pay Google each time a user clicks on an advertisement to visit the company's website or calls the company pursuant to the advertisement. Google allowed Canadian pharmacies to use AdWords to advertise services to U.S. customers. Due to these advertisements, U.S. customers ordered drugs from these pharmacies, resulting in the importation of drugs to the United States in violation of the Federal Food, Drug, and Cosmetic Act of 1938. Online Canadian pharmacies were found to be selling prescription drugs without a valid prescription by a doctor. The only requirement was completing an online consultation; a premium was also provided for this service. Because Google allowed Canadian pharmacies to advertise to U.S. citizens, it was required to forfeit $500 million in proceeds from Canadian pharmacies.[108] In addition to the forfeiture of proceeds, Google was required to implement measures to ensure that a similar incident does not happen in the future.

INTERNET GAMBLING

The Internet has enabled gamblers with digital devices and an Internet connection to place a bet from one country to any country in the world with an online gambling site and Internet connection. The rise of online gambling can be attributed to the availability of a multitude of websites that could be accessed easily to engage in the activity conveniently from the comfort of one's home or work environment. Studies have shown that the convenience of online gambling and its twenty-four-hour availability are motivating factors for using these sites.[109] The anonymity afforded to users has also been reported as a motivating factor for using online sites rather than in-person casinos.[110] Motivations for gambling include "demonstrating one's worth, social acceptance, rebelling against others, relieving negative emotions and feelings, hoping to win, beating the odds, excitement, passing time, and having fun."[111] The motivations differ depending on the site chosen for gambling—online or offline.[112] Motivations for gambling also differ by gender.[113]

A negative consequence of online gambling is addiction.[114] Indeed, studies have shown that behaviors such as sex and gambling can be addictive.[115] Addiction is characterized by "salience, mood modification, tolerance, withdrawal, conflict, and relapse;"[116] if all of these factors are present, then a person is considered to be addicted. *Salience* exists when something dominates a person's thinking, feelings, and even their behavior. The cyberactivity individuals engage in is considered the most important thing in their lives. Salience is present when an individual becomes consumed with an activity (e.g., thoughts or behavior). The activity results in a change in the mood of the person (*mood modification*), which can be adversely affected when he or she is unable to engage in the activity or does so with limited frequency. A person can build a *tolerance* to the activity, especially if engaging in that activity in great frequency. *Conflict* arises between the person engaging in the activity and those around him or her because of the individual's engagement in the online activity. Finally, an addicted person may revert to previous behaviors concerning the activities (i.e., *relapse*). Addiction to online gambling is a concern due to the ease of use and accessibility of such websites on a continuous basis as long as funds are available to play and the user is of age (though the latter depends on the type of site one uses—licensed or unlicensed). Other negative consequences of Internet gambling are the loss of money, lies told to family, negligence of family, and creation of conflict in the household.[117] Indeed, relationships can be damaged by Internet gambling, especially if one of the parties has a gambling problem.[118] Work has also been found to be adversely affected by gambling, owing to lost productivity and sometimes even a job.[119]

Licit and Illicit Online Gambling Sites

Internet gambling sites have a wider clientele base and fewer start-up, maintenance, and lower operating costs than offline gambling sites; as such, they are lucrative businesses.[120] For those seeking to set up online gambling sites, there are few barriers to entering the market. Several countries enable those seeking to run online gambling operations to do so after obtaining a license and paying a license fee. For instance, Gibraltar requires Internet gambling sites to purchase a license under the Gambling Act of 2005. Some countries do not require the same checks that other countries do in order to obtain a license and run remote gambling services. By contrast, other countries strictly regulate Internet gambling. Australia is well known for its reputable online gambling sites due to its extensive regulation and oversight of those who have licenses to provide these services to Australians. In fact, Australia restricts access to its licenses in an effort to strictly regulate online gaming sites in order to protect consumers.[121] This restriction has made these licenses extremely valuable because consumers are more likely to use licensed websites since they believe their winnings will be paid to them and their personal and financial information will be adequately protected by the sites.[122]

Unlicensed online gambling sites, however, may have rigged games to cheat consumers out of their money, and payment of winnings is not guaranteed. Research has also shown that criminal activities, such as money laundering, theft of personal and financial data, and theft of money, among other illicit activities, occurs on unlicensed gambling sites.[123] Fraudulent gambling websites also exist. To get new players to these types of websites, incentives are usually provided in the form of credits or free games. Cybercriminals can easily create a website that looks similar to legitimate licensed websites, even using logos from Gaming or Gambling Commissions, among other organizations, to dupe users into thinking that they are trustworthy sites. Users who deposit money into accounts on these sites may have their money stolen or they may be forced to deplete their deposits through gambling if they are prevented from withdrawing money from the account.[124] Indeed, studies have shown that theft and fraud may occur on online gambling sites involving users' winnings and deposits and the unauthorized use of personal and financial data submitted to the website during registration.[125] Certain online gambling sites actually include existing Terms of Service and wager requirements that prevent users from being able to withdraw their money unless certain criteria are met (e.g., minimum play amount).[126] Moreover, unlicensed websites may sell users' data to other unlicensed websites and enable perpetrators to use this data to try to obtain additional information from users through phishing activities or some other form of cybercrime (e.g., malware distribution).

Regulating Internet Gambling

Countries differ in their perspectives on online gambling. Some countries have legalized certain types of online gambling. European Community law does not regulate Internet gambling, leaving it instead up to member states to determine if Internet gambling should be regulated and to what extent.[127] In Greece, Law 4002/2011 legalized online gambling. In Norway, state-owned gambling companies are the only ones authorized to provide online gambling. In Belgium, a license is required, and the license must be linked to an offline gambling site. The Gambling Act of 2005 regulates online gambling in the United Kingdom. The act was implemented to, among other things, ensure that gambling is conducted in a fair manner and is not used to harm children or vulnerable persons. The United Kingdom regulates and taxes the online gambling industry. In contrast, in South Korea, online gambling is prohibited. The same holds true in Taiwan, where those who engage in online gambling and the operators of the websites can be prosecuted.

U.S. states vary in their views on the legality of Internet gambling. New Jersey now authorizes a variety of gambling services online (e.g., poker, blackjack, roulette, and slot machines). Online gambling was legalized in New Jersey through Assembly Bill 2578. New Jersey gambling websites have an authentication procedure in place to verify the Social Security number and identity of users before they can play.[128] If the Social Security number of users is verified but not their age, identity, and location, they can provide a valid photo ID with the date of birth (e.g., driver's license) and a recent utility bill with their home address listed to verify age, identity, and location.[129] The law does not require players to be residents of New Jersey; however, they must be in New Jersey when playing. Even New Jersey residents cannot play if they are not physically in the state. To verify location, geolocation and IP verification are used. The only casinos allowed to provide gambling services in New Jersey are those that have land-based casinos. They must be licensed and approved by the New Jersey Division of Gaming Enforcement. New Jersey casinos are required by law to keep players' money in secure accounts, safeguard personal information, and ensure the fairness of games.[130]

In the past, Internet gambling was prohibited under the U.S. Interstate Wire Act (Wire Act) of 1961. In *Thompson v. MasterCard International et al.* (2002),[131] the court interpreted the Wire Act as only applying to online sports gambling. This view differed from that of the Department of Justice, which held that the Wire Act prohibits all but one form of Internet gambling, namely, online horseracing betting pursuant to the Interstate Horseracing Act of 1978. This law enables users to engage in remote horseracing betting, specifically interstate off-track wagers. Under 15 U.S.C. § 3002(3), an "interstate off-track wager" is defined as "a legal wager placed or accepted in one State with respect to the outcome of a horserace taking place in another State and includes pari-mutuel wagers, where lawful in each State involved, placed or transmitted by an individual in one State via telephone or other electronic media and accepted by an off-track betting system in the same or another State, as well as the combination of any pari-mutuel wagering pools." Certain states allow residents to place bets for horseraces online (e.g., California, Oregon, Nevada, and South Dakota). This remote gambling was authorized for individuals as long as the services were provided within the United States. As such, the provision of remote gambling and betting services by other countries to U.S. residents was considered illegal.

Antigua and Barbuda argued that the practices of the United States targeting foreign online gambling and betting sites that offered their services to citizens of the United States violated the General Agreement on Trade in Services of 1995 (hereafter GATS).[132] The United States claimed that its practices regarding gambling and betting were in pursuit of the protection of public morals.[133] Antigua and Barbuda pointed out the contradictions in U.S. claims because gambling is legal in certain states; what is illegal is online gambling (with the exception of horseracing betting).[134] The World Trade Organization (WTO)[135] agreed with Antigua and Barbuda and held that the remote gambling provisions authorized by the Interstate Horseracing Act of 1978 discriminated against foreign Internet gambling providers. Under Article XIV of the GATS, countries cannot implement measures that "are . . . applied in a manner which would constitute a means of arbitrary or unjustifiable discrimination between countries where like conditions prevail, or a disguised restriction on trade in services." The United States has not yet complied with the ruling of the WTO on this matter.

In 2011, the United States did, however, clarify the confusion that existed concerning the Wire Act and its prohibition on Internet gambling. The Department of Justice Office of Legal Counsel stated that the Wire Act of 1961 limits only sports betting online.[136] By contrast, this type of gambling is considered legal in certain countries. Spain, for instance, legalized various forms of online gambling pursuant to Law 13/2011 on Gambling, and online sports gambling is considered legal. These differences in laws complicate the cooperation and coordination of investigations of online gambling in countries that consider it an illegal activity. Given that online gambling sites outside of nations that criminalize this conduct are available, taking down these websites and prosecuting those responsible for them are extremely difficult, especially in light of the varied views on the legality of this activity.

CONTROLLING CYBERDEVIANCE AND PUBLIC ORDER CYBERCRIMES

Views on the legality of cyberdeviance and public order cybercrimes differ by country, state, and in some cases, counties. This makes controlling cyberdeviance and public order cybercrimes particularly challenging. In regard to cyberdeviance, the proliferation of websites, newsgroups, chat rooms, and other online forums dedicated to illicit forms of paraphilia make this content extremely difficult to control. The reality is that law enforcement has prioritized investigations of pedophilia. Other forms of illicit cyberdeviance practices do not receive the same attention unless they involve some other serious crime, such as murder, as in the case of the necrophiliac and asphyxiophile Graham Coutts, discussed earlier. The family of the victim in the Coutts trial called for a more aggressive response than the current practice toward websites and other online forums that target those who receive sexual gratification from harm committed against individuals (e.g., rape and necrophilia). The criminalization of websites that contain this content varies by country. The take down of these websites serves as a temporary, albeit necessary, fix to a larger widespread problem. The reality is that websites can be hosted on servers located in countries that do not criminalize this conduct, making it impossible to get them taken down, absent the implementation of some form of censorship, which is not a desirable result. Ultimately, illicit forms of cyberdeviance and public order cybercrimes can only be controlled through harmonized laws and enforcement strategies. This, however, is not the current practice. What is more, existing public disobedience of laws relating to criminal forms of cyberdeviance (with the exception of certain paraphilias) and public order cybercrimes (with few exceptions, for example, sports gambling operations by organized crime networks) can be attributed to the lack of priority and the lack of robust enforcement of laws.

Consider, for example, gambling and prostitution and the facilitation of these actions online. These acts are not considered crimes in several countries. For instance, Internet gambling has been decriminalized in some countries. As long as local laws are respected and licenses are obtained, gambling sites can legally operate and market services to clientele in countries where a license has been obtained. By contrast, other countries prohibit some or all forms of Internet gambling. The upshot is that Internet gambling can only be controlled if there is a widespread global prohibition of it or if it is decriminalized and regulated in all countries. In the current state, the practices between countries differ significantly, making enforcement of laws that criminalize this behavior extremely difficult. Moreover, lack of harmonized regulation and enforcement has led to the flourishing of illicit gambling sites.

Likewise, countries have conflicting perspectives on how to deal with prostitution. Some argue that the entire sex industry should be eradicated. This view is held by those who subscribe to an *abolitionist* perspective on prostitution. Abolitionists seek to eradicate the sex work industry by punishing the purchasing of sex and by assisting prostitutes in leaving the sex industry.[137] The abolitionist perspective views those in prostitution as victims. Other countries follow a *prohibitionist* view, outlawing prostitution on moral grounds. This view characterizes prostitution as a vice, a public order crime which must be prosecuted. These crimes offend the existing moral order by coming into conflict with accepted social norms and principles. A prohibitionist views all those who participate in the sex trade as criminals: prostitutes, pimps, madams, and clients (i.e., johns).

Others believe that the abolition of sex work and its illegality will cause sex workers to work under deplorable conditions, placing them in harm's way. Instead, sex work should be viewed as voluntary paid work (when individuals freely engage in it absent coercion).[138] Governments have sought to regulate the industry for those who seek to voluntarily engage in sex work. The *regulationist* perspective seeks to control the sex industry, requiring it to comply with existing laws. Here, the sex industry is seen as a source of revenue and is taxed by the government. The regulationist perspective also holds that prostitution can be regulated to protect the public from its harmful effects (e.g., health consequences). This approach seeks to minimize the spread of STDs and other diseases by regulating the industry and requiring sex workers to receive regular medical checkups.

Another view is the legalization perspective, which approaches and views prostitution as a form of commerce. Other countries have viewed the futility of abolishing and controlling prostitution and have decriminalized it. Decriminalization enables prostitutes to advertise and expand their services free from existing laws and regulations that criminalize prostitution and seek to regulate it. New Zealand is one country that has decriminalized prostitution. Decriminalization has also been promoted for certain psychoactive substances, often on the grounds that prohibition of other psychoactive substances has failed in the past. An example often used is **Prohibition**, which outlawed alcohol sale and consumption in the United States between 1920 and 1933. During this time, the Eighteenth Amendment to the U.S. Constitution was passed, which prohibited "the manufacture, sale, or transportation of intoxicating liquors within, the importation thereof into, or the exportation thereof from the United States and all territory subject to the jurisdiction thereof for beverage purposes." The National Prohibition Act of 1919, better known as the Volstead Act, was also passed to assist federal agencies in enforcing Prohibition. Prohibition failed to prevent the manufacture, sale, and distribution of alcohol, however, and in 1933, the Twenty-First Amendment to the U.S. Constitution repealed the Eighteenth Amendment. Those opposing prohibition believe that the criminalization of psychoactive substances has negative consequences, possibly pushing this activity further underground and beyond the reach of law enforcement agencies. In reality, unless countries have similar views on public order cybercrimes and illicit forms of cyberdeviance, cooperation in investigations and the prosecution of perpetrators is difficult (if at all possible).

CASE STUDY

Tina lives in New Jersey and regularly plays online poker from her home.

1. Is playing poker online considered a cybercrime? Why do you think so?
2. Did Tina engage in a cybercrime? Why or why not? Please explain your response.

REVIEW QUESTIONS

1. What is cyberdeviance? Provide examples of it.
2. Can cyberdeviance be controlled? If so, in what ways?
3. How is the Internet used to facilitate prostitution?
4. Can a website be a house of prostitution?
5. What are the differences between prostitutes and escorts?
6. In what ways has the Internet facilitated juvenile prostitution?
7. What are the differences between cyberprostitution, cybersex, and cyberpornography?
8. Name and describe three types of online pharmacies. How can one differentiate between licit, illicit, and fake online pharmacies?
9. What are the differences between legal and illegal Internet gambling websites?
10. Can public order cybercrime be controlled? If so, in what ways?

LAWS

Animal Crush Video Prohibition Act of 2010 (United States)
Assembly Bill 2578 (New Jersey)
Criminal Justice and Immigration Act of 2008 (United Kingdom)
Criminal Law (Sexual Offences) Act of 1993 (Ireland)
Criminal Law (Sexual Offences and Related Matters) Amendment Act of 2007 (South Africa)
Eighteenth Amendment to the U.S. Constitution (United States)
Federal Food, Drug, and Cosmetic Act of 1938 (United States)
Gambling Act of 2005 (Gibraltar)
Gambling Act of 2005 (United Kingdom)
General Agreement on Trade in Services of 1995 (WTO)
Interstate Horseracing Act of 1978 (United States)
Interstate Wire Act of 1961 (United States)

Law 13/2011 on Gambling (Spain)
Law 4002/2011 (Greece)
Law Safeguarding Women's Rights and Interests of 1992 (People's Republic of China)
Law That Prohibits the Purchase of Sexual Services of 1999 (Sweden)
Mann Act of 1910 (United States)
National Prohibition Act of 1919 (United States; also known as Volstead Act of 1919)
Ryan Haight Online Pharmacy Consumer Protection Act of 2008 (United States)
Sexual Offences Act of 2003 (United Kingdom)
Twenty-First Amendment to the U.S. Constitution (United States)

DEFINITIONS

Adultery. Engaging in sexual intercourse with a person other than one's spouse.
Anorexia. Anorexia nervosa; a condition in which an individual engages in self-starvation or eats very little food due to fear of gaining weight and has a distorted perception of body /weight.
Asphyxiophilia. The sexual gratification and pleasure received from the intentional restriction of oxygen to the brain of others or oneself.
Bestiality. Sexual acts between a human and an animal.
Brothel. A house of prostitution.
Bulimia. Bulimia nervosa; the binging and then purging of food through self-induced vomiting.
Call girl. A prostitute who does not display her profession publicly, but instead advertises services and arranges meetings with clients over the phone or online, independently or as part of an escort service.
Child sex trafficking. Inducing, recruiting, harboring, transporting, providing, or obtaining a child under the age of eighteen for commercial sex.
Coprophilia. The act of receiving sexual gratification and pleasure by watching others defecate.
Crime against nature. An unnatural act.
Cyberdildonics. Sexual instruments that individuals may utilize for genital stimulation or even penetration during cybersex.
Cyberpornography. The visual and audio portrayal of sexual activity online (through, for example, prerecorded live sex shows) that is specifically designed to cause sexual arousal in the user.
Cyberprostitution. Sexual acts performed online in real time for remuneration.
Cybersex. The use of the Internet and digital technology to sexually arouse another user through text messages, video streaming services, or the use of cyberdildonics.
Deviance. A behavior that violates social norms and expectations.
Escort. One who provides nonsexual services to other individuals, such as companionship, for a fee.
Exhibitionism. The act of exposing one's genitals to an unsuspecting and unwilling person.
Fetishism. A condition in which one derives sexual gratification and pleasure from an inanimate object or a nongenital body part.
Frotteurism. A condition in which one is sexually aroused and receives pleasure from rubbing or touching another nonconsenting individual in a public space.
Johns. Men who seek sexual services from female and male prostitutes for a fee.
Juvenile prostitution. The engagement of children in sexual acts for some form of remuneration.
Madam. A woman in charge of prostitutes in a brothel (or a house of prostitution).
Malum in se. An offense that violates the moral principles of society.

Masochism. A condition whereby an individual obtains sexual pleasure and gratification from self-inflicted pain or pain inflicted by others.

Morality. A society's values and principles of conduct that distinguish between right and wrong behavior, and represents the standards with which behavior is assessed.

Necrophilia. A condition whereby an individual receives sexual arousal and gratification by viewing or having sexual intercourse with corpses.

Paraphilia. Conditions characterized by unusual legal and illegal sexual desires and activities.

Pedophilia. A condition whereby an individual is sexually aroused and derives pleasure from child sexual exploitation.

Pimp. A male who is in charge of and controls a prostitute.

Pornography. A visual, audio, written, or other form of portrayal of sexual activity designed specifically to cause sexual arousal in the user.

Prohibition. In the United States, the outlawing of alcohol sale and consumption between 1920 and 1933.

Prostitution. Engaging in sexual acts for some type of remuneration.

Psychoactive substances. Chemical substances that affect the mental state of individuals who consume them, altering cognition, mood, and perception.

Punter. A client who pays for prostitution.

Sadism. A condition whereby an individual is sexually satisfied when inflicting pain on others.

Sadomasochism. The process of giving and receiving sexual arousal and pleasure from inflicting and receiving pain.

Scoptophilia. The process of receiving sexual gratification and pleasure by watching others engage in sexual acts without their knowledge.

Sexual deviance. Sexual behavior that violates social norms and expectations.

Sodomy. Anal or oral penetration by a penis.

Streetwalker. A prostitute that displays her profession by soliciting clients in the street.

Urophilia. The process of receiving sexual gratification and pleasure by watching others urinate.

Verified-Internet Pharmacy Practice Sites. A program that accredits online pharmacies that dispense prescription drugs.

Veterinary-Verified Internet Pharmacy Practice Sites. A program that accredits websites which provide medications for pets.

Voyeurism. A form of paraphilia, a coercive form, because it violates an individual's privacy by engaging in unauthorized surveillance of the person.

Zoophilia. A condition whereby an individual is sexually attracted to animals or seeks a sexual relationship with animals.

Zoosadism. A paraphilia in which individuals receive sexual gratification from watching animals being tortured or killed.

ENDNOTES

1. L. Ferrigno, "CEO, 6 Others From 'World's Largest Male Escort Site' Arrested," *CNN*, August 26, 2015, http://www.cnn.com/2015/08/25/us/male-escort-site-arrests-rentboy-com/.
2. Ibid.
3. S. Clifford, "7 Charged with Promoting Prostitution by Working on Rentboy.Com, an Escort Website," *New York Times*, August 25, 2015, http://www.nytimes.com/2015/08/26/nyregion/7-charged-with-promoting-prostitution-by-working-on-rentboycom-an-escort-website.html?_r=0.
4. *Daddy* is a term used by gay men to describe older men who desire or have a sexual relationship with younger men.

5. R. D. O'Brien, "Rentboy.com CEO, Business Indicted," *Wall Street Journal*, January 27, 2016, http://www.wsj.com/articles/rentboy-com-ceo-faces-indictment-1453945668.
6. C. Grov, "'Make Me Your Death Slave': Men Who Have Sex with Men and Use the Internet to Intentionally Spread HIV," *Deviant Behavior* 25, no. 4 (2004): 329.
7. *Lawrence v. Texas*, 539 U.S. 558 (2003).
8. T. H. Deshotels and C. J. Forsyth, "Postmodern Masculinities and the Eunuch," *Deviant Behavior* 28, no. 3 (2007): 201–218; K. Durkin, C. J. Forsyth, and J. F. Quinn, "Pathological Internet Communities: A New Direction for Sexual Deviance Research in a Post Modern Era," *Sociological Spectrum* 26, no. 6 (2006): 595–606.
9. L. Seligman and S. Hardenburg, "Assessment and Treatment of Paraphilias," *Journal of Counseling and Development* 78, no. 1 (2000): 107–113.
10. A. Blum, "When Sex Fantasies Turn Lethal," *Forensic Panel Letter* 5, no. 3 (2001): 18–19.
11. Crown Prosecution Service, "Extreme Pornography," in *The Code for Crown Prosecutors*, January 2013, http://www.cps.gov.uk/legal/d_to_g/extreme_pornography/.
12. Department of Justice, Office of Public Affairs, "Houston Woman Convicted of Producing and Distributing Animal Crush Videos," September 8, 2015, https://www.justice.gov/opa/pr/houston-woman-convicted-producing-and-distributing-animal-crush-videos.
13. B. Rogers, "Videographer Gets 50 Years in Animal Crush Videos," *Houston Chronicle*, February 16, 2016, http://www.chron.com/news/houston-texas/houston/article/Videographer-gets-50-years-in-animal-crush-videos-6833505.php.
14. R. Cowan, "'I Want to Stop Another Murder,'" *Guardian*, September 16, 2004, http://www.theguardian.com/technology/2004/sep/16/g2.onlinesupplement.
15. BBC News (2007), "Mother's Relief as Killer Jailed," July 5, 2007, http://news.bbc.co.uk/2/hi/uk_news/england/6274330.stm.
16. S. Gaudin, "Ohio Man Gets 25 Years for Hacking into Webcams, Recording Minors," *Information Week*, July 12, 2007, http://www.informationweek.com/ohio-man-gets-25-years-for-hacking-into-webcams-recording-minors/d/d-id/1057017?.
17. P. Muncaster, "Webcam Voyeur Hacks Laptop to Spy on Toronto Couple," *Infosecurity Magazine*, August 17, 2015, http://www.infosecurity-magazine.com/news/webcam-voyeur-hacks-laptop-spy/.
18. T. Porter, "IT Expert Andrew Meldrum Spied on Women Using Their Own PC Webcams," *International Business Times*, May 31, 2014, http://www.ibtimes.co.uk/it-expert-andrew-meldrum-spied-women-using-their-own-pc-webcams-1450723.
19. C. Ashford, "Sex Work in Cyberspace: Who Pays the Price?" *Information & Communications Technology Law* 17, no. 1 (2008): 39.
20. M. Viuhko, "Human Trafficking for Sexual Exploitation and Organized Procuring in Finland," *European Journal of Criminology* 7, no. 1 (2010): 70.
21. U.S. Attorney's Office, Eastern District of Virginia, "Owner of D.C.-Based Online Prostitution Enterprise Pleads Guilty to Money Laundering, Racketeering Offenses," U.S. Department of Justice, June 7, 2012, https://www.fbi.gov/washingtondc/press-releases/2012/owner-of-d.c.-based-online-prostitution-enterprise-pleads-guilty-to-money-laundering-racketeering-offenses.
22. T. M. Groom and R. Nandwani, "Characteristics of Men Who Pay for Sex: A UK Sexual Health Clinic Survey," *Sexually Transmitted Infections* 82, no. 5 (2006): 366; M. D. Hughes, *Best Practices to Address the Demand Side of Sex Trafficking* (Providence: University of Rhode Island, 2004); J. Macleod, M. Farley, L. Anderson, and J. Golding, *Challenging Men's Demand for Prostitution in Scotland: A Research Report Based on Interviews with 110 Men Who Bought Women in Prostitution* (Glasgow: Women's Support Project, 2008), 14–18; N. McKeganey and M. Barnard, *Sex Work on the Streets: Prostitutes and Their Clients* (Buckingham, UK: Open University Press, 1996), 50.

23. M. Farley, "Comparing Sex Buyers with Men Who Don't Buy Sex," *Newsweek* 158, no. 4 (2011): 61.

24. Ibid.

25. L. Bennetts, "The John Next Door: The Men Who Buy Sex Are Your Neighbors and Colleagues—A New Study Reveals How the Burgeoning Demand for Porn and Prostitutes Is Warping Personal Relationships and Endangering Women and Girls," *Newsweek* 158, no. 4 (July 25, 2011): 61; K. Beckham and A. Prohaska, "Deviant Men, Prostitution, and the Internet: A Qualitative Analysis of Men Who Killed Prostitutes Whom They Met Online," *International Journal of Criminal Justice Sciences* 7, no. 2 (2012): 635–648.

26. J. Busza, S. Castle, and A. Diarra, "Trafficking and Health," *British Medical Journal* 328 (2004): 1370.

27. A. Dworkin, *Pornography: Men Possessing Women* (New York: E. P. Dutton, 1989).

28. S. Jeffreys, "Sex Tourism: Do Women Do It Too?" *Leisure Studies* 22, no. 3 (2003): 223–238; C. Pateman, "'The Disorder of Women': Women, Love, and the Sense of Justice," *Ethics* 91, no. 1 (1980): 20–34; D. Satz, "Markets in Women's Sexual Labor," *Ethics* 106, no. 1 (1995): 63–85; M. Pajnik, N. Kambouri, M. Renault, and I. Šori, "Digitalising Sex Commerce and Sex Work: A Comparative Analysis of French, Greek and Slovenian Websites," *Gender, Place & Culture: A Journal of Feminist Geography* (Published online: Mar 2, 2015), 2.

29. The number of women in these roles compared to men is minimal.

30. M. Farley, I. Baral, M. Kiremire, and U. Sezgin, "Prostitution in Five Countries: Violence and Posttraumatic Stress Disorder," *Feminism and Psychology* 8, no. 4 (1998): 405–426; D. M. Hughes, "Prostitution Online," *Journal of Trauma Practice* 2, nos. 3–4 (2004): 127.

31. Pajnik et al., "Digitalising Sex Commerce and Sex Work," 1–20.

32. N. McKeganey and M. Barnard, *Sex Work on the Streets: Prostitutes and Their Clients* (Buckingham, UK: Open University Press, 1996), 52.

33. FBI, St. Louis Division, "Former Department of Agriculture Employee and Associate Indicted on Charges Involving an Online Prostitution Business," January 14, 2009, https://www.fbi .gov/stlouis/press-releases/2009/sl011409.

34. Ashford, "Sex Work in Cyberspace," 37–49.

35. M. Chan, C. Leung, C. Ng, and C. Chow, *Oldest Profession in the New Economy: A Study of Online and Cyberprostitution in the Netherlands, the United States, China, and Hong Kong*, 2005, http://newmedia.cityu.edu.hk/cyberlaw/gp22/intro.html.

36. Pajnik et al., "Digitalising Sex Commerce and Sex Work," 1–20.

37. U.S. Attorney's Office, Eastern District of Virginia, "Owner of D.C.-Based Online Prostitution Enterprise Pleads Guilty to Money Laundering, Racketeering Offenses."

38. AIMGroup, "Backpage Rebound Leads to Record Month for Prostitution Ad Revenue," February 28, 2013, http://aimgroup.com/2013/02/28/backpage-rebound-leads-to-record-month -for-prostitution-ad-revenue/.

39. ABC News Local, "Long Island Prostitution Sting Leads to More Than 100 Arrests," June 3, 2013, http://abc7ny.com/archive/9125178/.

40. N. Shepherd, "Online Sting Nets Six Arrests for Prostitution," *Time News*, August 21, 2015, http://www.timesnews.net/article/9091257/online-sting-nets-six-arrests-for-prostitution.

41. F. Love, "'How Dare You Ban Prostitutes from Linkedin!,' Say Prostitutes," *Business Insider*, May 16, 2013, http://www.businessinsider.com/linkedin-prostitution-ban-2013-5.

42. Pajnik et al., "Digitalising Sex Commerce and Sex Work," 1–20.

43. T. Sanders, *Sex Work: A Risky Business* (Cullompton, UK: Willan, 2005), 69; Ashford, "Sex Work in Cyberspace," 37–49.

44. S. Dethrage, "Tuscaloosa Police Arrest 3 Georgia Women at Massage Parlor after Finding Ads for Prostitution Online," February 2015, http://www.al.com/news/tuscaloosa/index.ssf /2015/02/tuscaloosa_police_arrest_3_geo.html.

45. E. Steuer, "The Rise and Fall of Redbook, the Site That Sex Workers Couldn't Live Without," *Wired*, February 24, 2015, http://www.wired.com/2015/02/redbook/.

46. D. Porter, "NJ Professor Accused of Running Prostitution Site," *ABC News Local*, June 21, 2011, http://abc7.com/archive/8202687/.

47. R. Contreras, "F. Chris Garcia and David Flory Cleared in Online Prostitution Case: Experts Say Laws out of Date," *Huffington Post*, August 20, 2012, http://www.huffingtonpost.com/2012/08/20/f-chris-garcia-david-flory-online-prostitution-_n_1810147.html.

48. R. Contreras, "F. Chris Garcia, Former University of New Mexico President, Cleared of Criminal Charges Concerning 'Southwest Companions,'" *Huffington Post*, June 20, 2012, http://www.huffingtonpost.com/2012/06/20/f-chris-garcia-prostitution-ring_n_1613009.html.

49. A. Koloff, "Prostitution-Ring Case Involving Retired Fairleigh Dickinson Professor Headed to New Mexico High Court," January 2, 2013, http://www.northjersey.com/news/prostitution-ring-case-involving-retired-fairleigh-dickinson-professor-headed-to-new-mexico-high-court-1.351580.

50. R. Contreras, "Experts: Laws on Online Prostitution Outdated," *Albuquerque Journal*, August 20, 2012, http://www.abqjournal.com/125360/news/experts-laws-on-online-prostitution-outdated.html.

51. M. Jefferies, "Call Girls Can Be Ordered on Mobile Phone App for Up to £500 an Hour," *Mirror*, May 17, 2015, http://www.mirror.co.uk/news/uk-news/call-girls-can-ordered-mobile-5715004.

52. M. Celizic, "Former Call Girl Opens Up about the Industry," *Today*, March 12, 2008, http://www.today.com/news/former-call-girl-opens-about-industry-2D80555180.

53. A. Gabbatt, "Popularity of 'Hookup Apps' Blamed for Surge in Sexually Transmitted Infections," *Guardian*, May 28, 2015, http://www.theguardian.com/us-news/2015/may/28/hookup-apps-stds-tinder-grindr.

54. S. Lazzaro, "New X-Rated Hookup App Is Basically Naked Tinder," *Observer*, July 23, 2014, http://observer.com/2014/07/new-x-rated-hookup-app-is-basically-naked-tinder/.

55. There are also call girls who do not have sex with clients but may engage in other acts, such as fetish behavior, or simply spend time with a john by having a meal or conversation with him.

56. www.punternet.com.

57. J. Taylor, "Punter Net Prostitutes Thank Harriet Harman for Publicity Boost," *Independent*, October 2, 2009, http://www.independent.co.uk/news/uk/home-news/punter-net-prostitutes-thank-harriet-harman-for-publicity-boost-1796759.html.

58. www.theeroticreview.com.

59. U.S. Attorney's Office, Eastern District of Virginia, "Owner of D.C.-Based Online Prostitution Enterprise Pleads Guilty."

60. U.S. Attorney's Office, Middle District of Pennsylvania, "Millions Forfeited from Online Prostitution Enterprise Distributed to State and Local Law Enforcement," March 28, 2013, http://www.justice.gov/usao-mdpa/pr/millions-forfeited-online-prostitution-enterprise-distributed-state-and-local-law.

61. Ashford, "Sex Work in Cyberspace," 37–49.

62. J. A. Lee-Gonyea, T. Castle, and N. E. Gonyea, "Laid to Order: Male Escorts Advertising on the Internet," *Deviant Behavior* 30, no. 4 (2009): 336.

63. T. Castle and J. Lee, "Ordering Sex in Cyberspace: A Content Analysis of Female Escort Websites," *International Journal of Cultural Studies* 11, no. 1 (2008): 97–111; Lee-Gonyea, Castle, and Gonyea, "Laid to Order," 322–323.

64. Lee-Gonyea, Castle, and Gonyea, "Laid to Order," 342.

65. Ibid.

66. Ibid., 343–344.

67. K. J. Mitchell, D. Finkelhor, and J. Wolack, "Conceptualizing Juvenile Prostitution as Child Maltreatment: Findings from the National Juvenile Prostitution Study," *Trauma Treatment* 15, no. 1 (2010): 18–36.

68. J. Roy, "17-Year-Old Girl Arrested for Running Facebook Prostitution Ring," *New York Magazine*, November 25, 2014, http://nymag.com/daily/intelligencer/2014/11/teen-arrested-for-facebook-prostitution-ring.html.

69. K. Poulsen, "Alleged Pimp Charged with Recruiting Teen Runaway on MySpace," *Wired*, April 15, 2009, http://www.wired.com/2009/04/pimping-2/.

70. A. van den Borne and K. Kloosterboer, "Investigating Exploitation: Research into Trafficking in Children in the Netherlands," 2005, http://www.childtrafficking.com/Docs/stichting_defence_0870.pdf.

71. FBI, "Teen Prostitution: Gang Used Social Media Sites to Identify Potential Victims," September 2012, https://www.fbi.gov/news/stories/2012/september/teen-prostitution/teen-prostitution.

72. B. Campell, "Is Cyberprostitution Prostitution? New Paradigm, Old Crime," 2009, http://web.law.columbia.edu/sites/default/files/microsites/law-culture/files/2009-files/Campbell-paper.pdf.

73. Chan et al., *Oldest Profession in the New Economy.*

74. Campell, "Is Cyberprostitution Prostitution?"

75. K. Sharp and S. Earle, "Cyberpunters and Cyberwhores: Prostitution on the Internet," in *Dot.cons: Crime, Deviance and Identity on the Internet*, ed. Y. Jewkes (Cullompton, UK: Willan, 2003), 37.

76. Chan et al., *Oldest Profession in the New Economy.*

77. N. Doring, "Feminist Views of Cybersex: Victimization, Liberation, and Empowerment," *Cyberpsychology and Behaviour* 3, no. 5 (2000): 863–884.

78. K. Young, "Internet Addiction: Evaluation and Treatment," *Student British Medical Journal* 7 (1999): 351–352.

79. A. Cooper, "Sexuality and the Internet: Surfing into the New Millennium," *Cyberpsychology and Behavior* 1, no. 2 (2009): 181–187.

80. A. Joinson, "Causes and Implications of Disinhibited Behavior on the Internet," in *Psychology and the Internet: Intrapersonal, Interpersonal, and Transpersonal Implications*, ed. J. Gackenback (New York: Academic Press, 1998), 43–60.

81. K. S. Young, E. Griffin-Shelley, A. Cooper, J. O'Mara, and J. Buchanan, "Online Infidelity: A New Dimension in Couple Relationships with Implications for Evaluation and Treatment," in *Cybersex: The Dark Side of the Force*, ed. A. Cooper (Philadelphia: Brunner/Routledge, 2000), 59–74.

82. A. Cooper, D. E. Putnam, L. A. Planchon, and S. C. Boies, "Online Sexual Compulsivity: Getting Tangled in the Net," *Sexual Addiction & Compulsivity: The Journal of Treatment and Prevention* 6, no. 2 (1999): 79–104; M. Griffiths, "Sex on the Internet: Observations and Implications for Internet Sex Addiction," *Journal of Sex Research* 38, no. 4 (2001): 333–342.

83. J. Wallace and M. Mangan, *Sex, Laws, and Cyberspace* (New York: Henry Holt, 1996); M. Green, "Comment: Sex on the Internet: A Legal Click or an Illicit Trick?" *California Western Law Review* 38 (2002): 527.

84. D. M. Hughes, "Welcome to the Rape Camp: Sexual Exploitation and the Internet in Cambodia," *Journal of Sexual Aggression* 6, nos. 1/2 (2000): 29–51, cited in Hughes, "Prostitution Online," 119.

85. WHO, "Psychoactive Substances," accessed August 15, 2016, http://www.who.int/substance_abuse/terminology/psychoactive_ substances/en/.

86. Australian Department of Health, "Classifying Drugs by Their Effect on the Central Nervous System," 2004, http://www.health.gov.au/internet/publications/publishing.nsf/Content/drugtreat-pubs-front6-wk-toc~drugtreat-pubs-front6-wk-secb~drugtreat-pubs-front6-wk-secb-3~drugtreat-pubs-front6-wk-secb-3-1.

87. D. DiGorgio, *Counterfeit Medicines: Facts and Practical Advice* (Milan: EDQM-AIFA, 2011), cited in A. Lavorgna, "The Online Trade in Counterfeit Pharmaceuticals: New Criminal Opportunities, Trends and Challenges," *European Journal of Criminology* 12, no. 2 (2015): 227.

88. M. P. Flaherty and G. M. Gaul, "Experimentation Turns Deadly for One Teenager," *Washington Post*, October 21, 2003, http://www.washingtonpost.com/wp-dyn/content/article/2007/06/28/AR2007062801395.html.

89. *United States v. FedEx Corporation, FedEx Express Inc., and FedEx Corporate Services, Inc.*, Indictment No. 14 CR 380, Northern District Court of California, San Francisco, 2014, 2.

90. Lavorgna, "The Online Trade in Counterfeit Pharmaceuticals," 237.

91. FDA, "FDA Targets Illegal Online Pharmacies in Globally Coordinated Action," May 22, 2014, http://www.fda.gov/NewsEvents/Newsroom/PressAnnouncements/ucm398499.htm.

92. M.-H. Maras, *Computer Forensics: Cybercriminals, Laws, and Evidence*, 2nd ed. (Burlington, MA: Jones and Bartlett, 2012), 19.

93. DiGorgio, *Counterfeit Medicines*; R. F. Forman, G. E. Woody, T. McLellan, and K. G. Lynch, "The Availability of Web Sites Offering to Sell Opioid Medication Without Prescriptions," *American Journal of Psychiatry*, 163, no. 7 (2006): 1233–1238; C. Raine, D. J. Webb, and S. R. Maxwell, "The Availability of Prescription-Only Analgesics Purchased from the Internet in the UK," *British Journal of Clinical Pharmacology* 62, no. 2 (2008): 250–254.

94. H. Sklamberg, "Counterfeit Drugs: Fighting Illegal Supply Chains," *FDA*, February 27, 2014, http://www.fda.gov/NewsEvents/Testimony/ucm387449.htm.

95. J. Harris, P. Stevens, and J. Morris, *"Keeping It Real. Combating the Spread of Fake Drugs in Poor Countries* (Washington, DC: International Policy Network, 2009); International Medical Products Anti-Counterfeiting Taskforce (IMPACT), *Counterfeit Drugs Kill*, (Geneva: World Health Organization, 2008); R. Bate, "The Deadly World of Fake Medicine," *CNN*, July 17, 2012, http://www.cnn.com/2012/07/17/health/living-well/falsified-medicine-bate/.

96. C. Walsh, "Drugs, the Internet and Change," *Journal of Psychoactive Drugs* 43, no. 1 (2011): 41.

97. National Association of Boards of Pharmacy, "VIPPS," accessed August 17, 2016, http://www.nabp.net/programs/accreditation/vipps.

98. Ibid.

99. National Association of Boards of Pharmacy, "Not Recommended Sites," accessed August 17, 2016, http://www.nabp.net/programs/consumer-protection/buying-medicine-online/not-recommended-sites.

100. V. A. Lingle, "Prescription Drug Services on the Internet," *Health Care on the Internet*, 5, no. 1 (2001): 44.

101. Ibid.

102. National Association of Boards of Pharmacy, "Find a VIPPS Online Pharmacy," accessed August 17, 2016, http://www.nabp.net/programs/accreditation/vipps/find-a-vipps-online-pharmacy.

103. FDA, "Purchasing Pet Drugs Online: Buyer Beware," March 11, 2010, http://www.fda.gov/ForConsumers/ ConsumerUpdates/ucm048164.htm.

104. Ibid.

105. Ibid.

106. Lingle, "Prescription Drug Services on the Internet," 42.

107. FDA, "FDA Takes Action to Protect Consumers from Dangerous Medicines Sold by Illegal Online Pharmacies," June 27, 2013, http://www.fda.gov/NewsEvents/Newsroom/PressAnnouncements/ucm358794.htm.

108. Department of Justice, Office of Public Affairs, "Google Forfeits $500 Million Generated by Online Ads & Prescription Drug Sales by Canadian Online Pharmacies," August 24, 2011, http://www.justice.gov/opa/pr/google-forfeits-500-million-generated-online-ads-prescription-drug-sales-canadian-online.

109. R. T. Wood, and R. J. Williams, *Internet Gambling: Prevalence, Patterns, Problems, and Policy Options*, final report prepared for the Ontario Problem Gambling Research Centre, Guelph, Ontario, 2009, 9.

110. Ibid.

111. J. Cotte, "Chances, Trances, and Lots of Slots: Gambling Motives and Consumption Experiences," *Journal of Leisure Research* 29, no. 4 (1997): 380–406; M. Dumont and R. Ladouceur, "Evaluation of Motivation among Video-Poker Players," *Psychological Reports* 66, no. 1 (1990): 95–98; Productivity Commission, *Australia's Gambling Industries: Final Report* (Canberra: Government Press, 1999); R. Corney and J. Davis, "Female Frequent Internet Gamblers: Qualitative Study Investigating the Role of Family, Social Situation and Work," *Community, Work & Family* 13, no. 3 (2010): 292.

112. M. Griffiths and A. Barnes, "Internet Gambling: An Online Empirical Study Among Student Gamblers," *International Journal of Mental Health Addiction* 6 (2008): 194–204; G. Valentine and K. Hughes, *New Forms of Participation: Problem Internet Gambling and the Role of the Family* (Leeds: University of Leeds, 2008); Corney and Davis, "Female Frequent Internet Gamblers," 292.

113. K. Legge, "Jackpot Society," in *Place Your Bet: Gambling in Victoria*, ed. M. Cathcart and D. K. Smith (Melbourne: The Australian Centre, University of Melbourne, 1996), 103–111; H. Lesieur, "Female Pathological Gamblers and Crime," in *Gambling Behavior and Problem Gambling* (Las Vegas: University of Nevada Press, 1993), 495–515; H. R. Lesieur and S. B. Blume, "When Lady Luck Loses: Women and Compulsive Gambling," in *Feminist Perspectives on Treating Addictions*, ed. N. van den Burgh (New York: Springer, 1991), 181–197; E. D. Scannell, M. M. Quirk, K. Smith, R. Maddern, and M. Dickerson, "Females' Coping Styles and Control over Poker Machine Gambling," *Journal of Gambling Studies* 16, no. 4 (2000): 417–432; Corney and Davis, "Female Frequent Internet Gamblers," 292.

114. R. Kalischuk, N. Nowatzki, K. Cardwell, K. Klein, and J. Solowoniuk, "Problem Gambling and its Impact on Families: A Literature Review," *International Gambling Studies* 6, no. 1 (2006): 31–60.

115. M. D. Griffiths, "Behavioural Addictions: An Issue for Everybody?" *Journal of Workplace Learning* 8, no. 3 (1996): 19–25; I. Marks, "Non-Chemical (Behavioural) Addictions," *British Journal of Addiction* 85, no. 11 (1990): 1389–1394; J. Orford, *Excessive Appetites: A Psychological View of the Addictions* (Chichester, UK: Wiley, 1985).

116. Griffiths, "Behavioural Addictions," 19–25; M. D. Griffiths, "Nicotine, Tobacco, and Addiction," *Nature* 384 (1966): 18; M. Griffiths, "Sex on the Internet: Observations and Implications for Internet Sex Addiction," *Journal of Sex Research* 38, no. 4 (2001): 335.

117. Corney and Davis, "Female Frequent Internet Gamblers," 292.

118. V. C. Lorenz and R. A. Yaffee, "Pathological Gambling: Psychosomatic, Emotional and Marital Difficulties as Reported by the Gambler," *Journal of Gambling Behavior* 2, no. 1 (1986): 40–49; V. C. Lorenz and R. A. Yaffee, "Pathological Gambling: Psychosomatic, Emotional and Marital Difficulties as Reported by the Spouse," *Journal of Gambling Behavior* 4, no. 1 (1988): 13–26.

119. R. M. Politzer, J. S. Morrow, and S. B. Leavey, "Report on the Societal Cost of Pathological Gambling and the Cost-Benefit/Effectiveness of Treatment," paper presented at the Fifth Annual Conference on Gambling and Risk-Taking, Lake Tahoe, NV, 1981.

120. R. Clarke and G. Dempsey, "The Feasibility of Regulating Gambling on the Internet," *Managerial and Decision Economics* 22, nos. 1–3 (2001): 125–132.

121. J. McMillen, "Online Gambling: Challenges to National Sovereignty and Regulation," *Prometheus: Critical Studies in Innovation* 18, no. 4 (2000): 393.

122. Ibid., 394.

123. J. McMullan and A. Rege, "On Line Crime and Internet Gambling," *Journal of Gambling Issues* 24 (2010): 54–85.

124. J. Banks, "Edging Your Bets: Advantage Play, Gambling, Crime and Victimization," *Crime, Media, Culture* 9, no. 2 (2013): 178.

125. Ibid.

126. Ibid., 179.

127. M. Hamilton and K. M. Rogers, "Internet Gambling: Community Flop or the Texas Hold'em Poker Rules," *International Review of Law, Computers & Technology* 22, no. 3 (2008): 224.

128. S. Ruddock, "Ever Wonder Why New Jersey's Legal Online Casinos Ask for Your Social Security Number?" April 6, 2015, https://www.playnj.com/news/nj-online-casino-identity-verification-process/2045/.

129. S. Ruddock, "Player Requirements for Online Gambling in New Jersey," September 24, 2013, http://www.nj.com/onlinegamblingnj/index.ssf/2013/09/player_requirements_for_online.html; Borgata Hotel Casino and Spa, "Top Questions," accessed August 17, 2016, https://casino.theborgata.com/support/faq.html.

130. C. Grove, *Legal New Jersey Online Casinos: Fact Sheet and FAQs*, accessed May 7, 2015, http://www.onlinepokerreport.com/nj-online-casinos/.

131. *Thompson v. MasterCard International et al.*, 313 F.3d 257 (5th Cir. 2002).

132. T. Magder, "Gambling, the WTO, and Public Morals: A Short Review of Antigua versus the United States," *Television & New Media* 7, no. 1 (2006): 57.

133. Ibid., 52.

134. S. Jackson, "Small States and Compliance Bargaining in the WTO: An Analysis of the Antigua–US Gambling Services Case," *Cambridge Review of International Affairs* 25, no. 3 (2012): 378; Magder, "Gambling, the WTO, and Public Morals," 62.

135. This organization is responsible for global rules of trade and resolving trade disputes between nations.

136. Memorandum Opinion for the Assistant Attorney General, Criminal Division, *Whether Proposals by Illinois and New York to Use the Internet and Out-Of-State Transaction Processors to Sell Lottery Tickets to In-State Adults Violate the Wire Act*, September 31, 2011, http://www.justice.gov/sites/default/files/olc/opinions/2011/09/31/state-lotteries-opinion.pdf.

137. Pajnik et al., "Digitalising Sex Commerce and Sex Work," 1–20.

138. L. M. Augustín, "Migrants in the Mistress's House: Other Voices in the Trafficking Debate," *Social Politics: International Studies in Gender, State and Society* 12, no. 1 (2005): 96–117; L. M. Augustín, *Sex at the Margins: Migration, Labour Market and the Rescue Industry* (London: Zed Books, 2007); F. Delacoste and P. Alexander, eds., *Sex Work: Writings by Women in the Sex Industry* (San Francisco: Cleis Press, 1998); K. Kempadoo and J. Doezema, eds., *Global Sex Workers* (New York: Routledge, 1998).

CHAPTER 13

ORGANIZED CYBERCRIME

KEYWORDS

Bitcoin
Bulletproof hosting
Centralized digital
   currency
Cigarette trafficking
Controlled substances
Crime as a Service
Crimeware
Cryptocurrency
Cryptoransomware
Darknet
Debt bondage
Decentralized digital
   currency
Deep web
Drug trafficking

Fauna
Federal firearms license
Firearms trafficking
Flora
Forced labor
Hidden wiki
Human smuggling
Human trafficking
Labor trafficking
Memex
Microlaundering
Money laundering
Money mule
Organized cybercrime
   group
Organ transplant tourism

Organ trafficking
Pay-per-install services
Ransomware
Schedule I drugs
Schedule II drugs
Schedule III drugs
Schedule IV drugs
Schedule V drugs
Sex trafficking
Silk Road
Tor
Virtual currency
Visible web
Wildlife trafficking

In 2013, a coordinated investigation between law enforcement agencies of different countries titled *Unlimited Operation* resulted in the arrest of a cell connected to an international organized cybercrime group that targeted financial institutions. In this incident, an estimated $45 million was stolen from two Middle Eastern banks, the Bank of Muscat of Oman and the National Bank of Ras Al-Khaimah (RAKBANK) of the United Arab Emirates.[1] This cybertheft, which spanned twenty-seven countries,[2] was made possible by the hacking of credit card–processing systems and the subsequent increasing of available balances and withdrawal limits on prepaid MasterCard debit cards that were issued by the banks. The cybercriminals then created and distributed counterfeit debit cards to cashers around the world, enabling them to siphon millions of dollars from ATMs within hours.

This case is but one example of how organized cybercriminals utilize the Internet to commit illicit activities. This chapter covers organized cybercrime and the activities of organized cybercriminals. Specifically, it explores organized cybercriminals' engagement in the selling of illicit services, money laundering, and trafficking in drugs, humans, firearms, cigarettes, and wildlife. Special emphasis is placed on the "underworld of cyberspace" (the Darknet) and the trafficking crimes committed within this space and other areas of the World Wide Web. The chapter includes the ways in which organized cybercrime and various forms of trafficking can be controlled.

ORGANIZED CYBERCRIME: AN INTRODUCTION

Under Article 2(a) of the United Nations Convention against Transnational Organized Crime, an "organized criminal group" refers to "a structured group of three or more persons, existing for a period of time and acting in concert with the aim of committing one or more serious crimes or offences established in accordance with this Convention, in order to obtain, directly or indirectly, a financial or other material benefit." In light of this definition, an **organized cybercrime group** can be described as a structured group of three or more persons that act in concert with the goal of committing a serious cybercrime or cybercrimes for financial gain using the Internet.

Organized cybercrime involves the planning and execution of illegal business ventures online by either hierarchical groups or decentralized networks. There exists insufficient evidence about the type of structure most prevalent in online organized cybercrime groups (e.g., formal hierarchical organizations or loosely associated groups or networks).[3] Research has shown the existence of an identifiable hierarchy in some forums,

> with designated roles and responsibilities, [which] allow . . . forums to effectively police themselves, controlling population levels, and rooting out unwanted or troublesome members. Forums are run by Administrators who manage . . . hosting, determine the general purpose and direction of the forum and set rules for recruitment and behaviour. Each subforum is generally overseen by one or more Moderators. These are trusted individuals who are often subject matter experts for their particular subforum topic and who manage content and disputes within their area. Each forum will also have a multitude of Vendors with services and products to trade with the forum membership. Vendor status typically requires providing samples to the Moderators for review. Furthermore [Vendors'] products . . . [are] continuously . . . reviewed and rated by customers.[4]

A case in point is DarkMarket (created in 2005, closed in 2008), an online website where users could engage in illicit activities such as buying and selling stolen financial data and other illicit goods (e.g., malicious software).[5] DarkMarket was characterized as a highly organized site because of its vetting process, the requirement of new members to be nominated by existing members, the administrator active on the site to monitor transactions, and the requirement of vendors to prove the validity of their data. This site also required vendors seeking to sell data on their site to prove that the data sold could be used by those who purchased it.[6] Other organized cybercrime groups do not have the hierarchical structure of traditional organized crime groups and instead coalesce to achieve some goal, for example, to conduct a DDoS attack or to steal data or money from online accounts. Instead of a hierarchical structure, they consist of a network of separate cells.

ACTIVITIES OF ORGANIZED CYBERCRIMINALS

Like traditional organized crime groups, organized cybercriminals sell a form of "protection" to users. The main difference between traditional organized crime and organized cybercrime is that the protection one purchases with traditional organized crime is against the organized crime group itself. Those who threaten organized cybercrime groups' livelihood are either targeted for a cyberattack or threatened with violence. An online "hit" may entail rendering a site unusable using DDoS attacks. Violence is threatened only against those who endanger the criminal enterprise (i.e., "any individual, partnership, corporation, association, or other legal entity, and any union or group of individuals associated in fact although not a legal entity")[7] as a whole.

Organized cybercrime groups have functioned as a criminal enterprise and engaged in racketeering activities such as "gambling, . . . extortion, . . . or dealing in a controlled substance."[8] Furthermore, utilizing the Internet and technology, organized cybercriminals have, among other illegal acts, illicitly obtained personal and financial information with the intention of committing some form of fraud or theft; illegally possessed, copied, and transferred copyrighted material; stolen trade or military secrets for subsequent blackmailing, extortion, or sale to a third party; used malicious software with the intention of stealing information for later use to engage in a subsequent criminal activity, such as ransom or identify theft; sold data, hacking and malware products, and services for a fee; and engaged in money laundering. The next sections focus on crime as a service and money laundering.

CRIME AS A SERVICE

Members of organized cybercrime groups (irrespective of structure) are primarily chosen not based on social factors but on their skills. The knowledge, skills, and abilities of actors and groups engaged in organized cybercrime varies. In organized cybercrime groups, labor is divided according to individuals' skills in order to develop goods and services that can be utilized by all, irrespective of background, for a fee. These goods and services enable anyone to engage in cybercrime irrespective of their technical abilities. In the past, barriers existed in the use of such goods and services due to the highly technical skills needed to create and use them. Today, individuals (and even traditional organized crime groups) can engage in cybercrime without the necessary technical knowledge and abilities needed to conduct some of these illicit activities by purchasing the goods and services required to conduct the cybercrime.

Europol, a European law enforcement agency that disseminates intelligence about cybercrime (among other crimes) and assists countries in their investigations of this crime, has found that organized cybercriminals often operate under a **crime as a service** (CaaS) business model, whereby they offer a variety of services that facilitate virtually any cybercrime.[9] Indeed, the 2014 Internet Organised Crime Threat Assessment identified the following types of services that organized cybercriminals provide: stolen data; malicious software toolkits and services to engage in attacks; hacking services; pay-per-install services; and infrastructure with which cybercriminals can protect illicit goods and services and launch cyberattacks.[10]

Stolen Data. Data is a highly sought after commodity online. Organized cybercrime groups sell this data en masse. The data that is bought and sold includes personal data (e.g., Social Security number, home address, e-mail address), financial data (e.g., credit and debit card data), health data (e.g., medical insurance data), banking credentials (e.g., username and password), and other account data (e.g., usernames and passwords of social networking accounts). In *Operation Shrouded Horizon*, law enforcement agencies targeted and took down a password-protected site known as Darkode. Darkode served as a marketplace for stolen data and provided members of the forum with access to information and tools that would enable them to victimize individuals around the world. The investigation of this site resulted in the arrest of approximately seventy members by law enforcement agencies from twenty countries.[11] Some dark markets, such as Darkode, operate by invitation only. In this manner, they have taken a page out of the playbook of traditional organized crime groups, which require new members to be sponsored by an existing member (to prevent infiltration by law enforcement). Active members of Darkode and similar dark markets would then review the prospective member and the information the individual provided about his or her "past criminal activity, particular cyber skills, and potential contributions to the forum."[12] Existing members would then determine whether to grant the individual access to the forum.

Malicious Software Toolkits and Services. Organized cybercriminals provide malware as a service. Those engaging in this service often operate like a legitimate software developer and distributor with troubleshooting services and customer care to enable users to utilize the product more effectively and efficiently. Individuals can purchase a wide variety of services for a fee. Examples of this malware are crimeware and ransomware. **Crimeware** is malware designed to facilitate a cybercrime and can be modified to users' needs (e.g., with respect to language and currency). An example of crimeware is Zeus, a banking Trojan. Evgeniy Mikhailovich Bogachev[13] is part of an organized cybercriminal organization that was responsible for the release of the Zeus malware designed to surreptitiously collect users' financial data, including bank account numbers and passwords.[14] His co-conspirators sent spam and phishing e-mails directing individuals to a website infected with the malware. GameOver Zeus (a modified version of Zeus Trojan) infected an estimated one million computers.

Ransomware is a particular type of crimeware that warns users of the existence of unlicensed applications, child pornography, and other forms of illicit activity on the user's system. Ransomware pretends to be from an authority informing the user of illegal activity. The warning is followed by a demand to pay a fine, purportedly to a law enforcement agency, threatening arrest for nonpayment. The payment demanded is either through MoneyPak (a prepaid card that is now discontinued) or **Bitcoin** (highly volatile **virtual currency** or digital currency). A case in point is the Reveton ransomware.[15] Ransomware seeks to cause fear, distress, or shame in targets to get them to pay the ransom.[16] Users become infected with ransomware through phishing e-mails and pharmed websites.

Another form of crimeware is **cryptoransomware**. This form of crimeware is a Trojan horse designed to encrypt data on a victim's system and extort money from victims to release information. Cryptolocker, a form of cryptoransomware, demanded that users pay a ransom in seventy-two hours or the decryption keys would be destroyed. The files might or might not be decrypted upon payment. There is an incentive for cybercriminals to decrypt data after payment because users will not pay the ransom if it becomes known that cybercriminals do not decrypt the data following the rendering of payment. If a user does not pay, access to the files will not be given. Although paying the ransom may provide users with access to the files, the more cybercriminals benefit from these schemes, the more likely they are to continue. Cryptolocker was distributed though spam e-mails that contained malicious links and attachments. The user would either go to a compromised website or click on some e-mail with a malicious link. A variation of Crytpolocker was discovered in smartphones. It was called Simplocker and encrypted data on Android phones, threatening the destruction of files unless a ransom was paid.[17]

"Exploit" kits take advantage of existing vulnerabilities in software. Java has been a primary target of these exploits. The primary purpose of these kits is to deliver a malicious payload. The most well-known exploit kit is Blackhole. A compromised site or e-mail link sends a user to the landing page of the Blackhole servers. The kit is designed to load exploits onto a victim's machine based on the content of the system. It takes advantage of existing vulnerabilities to download relevant exploits; that is, it utilizes the exploits to download a malicious payload to a user's system. Those whose systems are infected with malware are not only at risk that their data will be compromised but may also become infected with botcode, becoming part of a botnet, which can subsequently be used in a DDoS attack. Additionally, once infected with botcode, a computer can be used to engage in a wide variety of cybercrimes (e.g., malware distribution). Furthermore, organized cybercriminals rent botnets for a fee. Users can utilize botnets to engage in DDoS attacks. Smartphones can also be part of a mobile botnet and can be used to send spam via SMS.[18]

Hacking Services. Organized cybercriminals further engage in hacking as a service. Here, members of the organized cybercrime group or network are hired to hack into a user's account in order to surreptitiously access his or her account and data. The hacking services may be for multiple users and may involve a wide variety of illicit activities, beyond those limited to illegal data access.

Pay-Per-Install Services. Organized cybercriminals provide **pay-per-install services** whereby members of the group or network get paid each time a user downloads the malware or accesses a site with malware.

Infrastructure. Organized cybercriminals provide hosting services for a fee to enable users to store illicit goods and services and utilize them to attack targets. Examples of sought-after infrastructure services include **bulletproof hosting** (i.e., a service that allows users to upload content and promises not to remove users' content even if it is illegal) and proxy servers (i.e., an intermediary server that enables indirect access to the content of other servers). This infrastructure protects users from detection by law enforcement authorities.

These goods and services are advertised by organized cybercriminals (though not exclusively) on websites and other online forums. These forums also serve as a place to network and share information about illicit activity and how to evade detection by authorities. Moreover, these forums can focus on sharing information and buying and selling cybercrime goods and services. Whatever the focus of these forums, they provide the logistics necessary for users to engage in different types of cybercrime.

MONEY LAUNDERING

Organized cybercriminals take advantage of the ease with which funds are transferred and exchanged online. **Money laundering** can be described as the process whereby criminals conceal and legitimate illicit funds. The U.S. Money Laundering Control Act of 1986 made it a federal crime to commit money laundering. Pursuant to 18 U.S.C. § 1956(a)(1),

> Whoever, knowing that the property involved in a financial transaction represents the proceeds of some form of unlawful activity, conducts or attempts to conduct such a financial transaction which in fact involves the proceeds of specified unlawful activity— . . . with the intent to promote the carrying on of specified unlawful activity; or . . . knowing that the transaction is designed in whole or in part— . . . to conceal or disguise the nature, the location, the source, the ownership, or the control of the proceeds of specified unlawful activity; or . . . to avoid a transaction reporting requirement under State or Federal law . . . [violates the federal money laundering statute].

Cybercriminals engage in money laundering to hide the original source of money, that is, how it was illicitly obtained. If money was used from ill-gotten gains, it would be traced back to them. There are three stages of money laundering: placement, layering, and integration. During the placement stage, the cybercriminal places money from illicit activities in either regulated or unregulated financial systems. At this stage, placing funds in regulated financial systems is risky and the individual may be detected by authorities. By contrast, unregulated financial systems are often used to evade detection by authorities. The cybercriminals then send the funds placed in the regulated or unregulated financial system through several transactions in order to make the money hard to trace. The next stage is layering. In this stage, money can be sent to accounts in different countries that have different names associated with the accounts or could be used to purchase goods. One trend is to launder large amounts of money by engaging in numerous small transactions, which is known as **microlaundering**. An example of microlaundering is as follows: A user creates a fake job advertisement and lists the purported pay. The user then creates another account with a different (but fake) name bidding on the job advertisement. The user completes the application for the fictitious work, is awarded the position, and subsequently retrieves the funds for the job. The process is similar for online auction sites: the seller and the buyer could be the same person using different accounts and online personas because fictitious information can be used to open PayPal accounts. In integration, the money is reintroduced into the economy from a legitimate transaction.

Money can be laundered through bank accounts under fictitious names, PayPal accounts, prepaid debit and credit cards, gift cards, Paysafecards (i.e., a form of web-based currency exchange that enables users to pay for items online without requiring personal details in transactions), and digital currencies. With respect to the latter, organized cybercriminals exploit the anonymity and protection afforded to them by the use of digital currencies in illicit activities. There are centralized and decentralized digital currencies.

Centralized digital currency works as follows: a single entity is responsible for transferring units between users. Users with a Perfect Money online payment account can transfer units to others with accounts. Third party exchanges enable users to cash out or obtain bank credit with an online vendor that accepts this currency. Centralized digital currency has more stability than **decentralized digital currency** and is managed by a single entity in a manner equivalent to the banking industry, although these services are unregulated by the financial industry. According to the 2015 National Money Laundering Risk Assessment, WebMoney was used to launder money obtained using stolen data.[19] WebMoney has a fixed value. Transactions of up to one hundred euros can be made without providing any personal information. WebMoney does not require a back account or credit card. Fake IDs can also be used to open up accounts and launder money. A well-known form of digital currency was the Liberty Reserve Dollar and Liberty Reserve Euro. Through Liberty Reserve, a user could convert a Liberty Reserve Dollar and Liberty Reserve Euro, which could be anonymously transferred or received by a user. The individual could cash out this digital currency to obtain U.S. dollars or euros. This site was shut down by the U.S. government, and those responsible for this digital currency were charged with money laundering, among other cybercrimes.[20]

An example of a decentralized digital currency is **cryptocurrency**. Cryptocurrencies are virtual currencies that utilize cryptography for security reasons. They can be bought and sold online outside of the traditional regulatory system and are stored in digital wallets. Cryptocurrencies include Bitcoin, Darkcoin, Dogecoin, Feathercoin, Litecoin, Namecoin, and Peercoin. The most well-known and widely utilized cryptocurrency is Bitcoin. Bitcoins can be obtained for purchase on websites and even physical Bitcoin stores. They can also be obtained by solving complex mathematical algorithms. When such algorithms are solved, a new batch of Bitcoins is released. The algorithm subsequently becomes much harder to solve to prevent the supply of Bitcoins from timing out. Bitcoin transactions occur through Bitcoin wallets, which are basically apps that a user can download to a computer or digital device, such as a smartphone. E-wallets (or digital wallets) containing cryptocurrencies allow a user to mix laundered funds that were converted into cryptocurrencies with legitimate funds. The user's funds are (sans a commission) deposited in a new e-wallet, making the tracing of the original source of the funds extremely difficult. Currency exchanges and purchases made utilizing these crytpocurrencies are difficult to trace by law enforcement agencies. Cryptocurrencies are distributed peer to peer without third party oversight or interaction in the transfer of funds; as such, they can be sent to members of organized cybercriminals around the world, who can exchange them for real money.

Organized cybercrime groups not only engage in money laundering but also offer money laundering services for a fee. To engage in money laundering, organized cybercriminals often utilize both online and offline tactics. Money mules play a key role in online and offline money laundering tactics. A **money mule** is an individual who obtains and transfers money illegally upon request and payment by other users. Money mules may be witting or unwitting participants in organized cybercrime. Those who are witting participants know that they are engaging in illicit activities when obtaining goods or funds and then transferring these to the group for a fee. Those mules who are knowledgeable of the criminal operation are usually protected by the organization. On the other hand, unsuspecting users taking part in the cybercriminal activity, known as a drops, are considered expendable because they are viewed as being easy to replace. These individuals do not know that they are transferring funds and goods to and from organized cybercriminals. They may be working for an online company that they believe is legitimate. The goods or funds being transferred may be disguised as a legitimate work-at-home employment opportunity.

Moreover, money can be laundered through online gambling (e.g., unlicensed gambling sites),[21] gaming, and virtual world sites. Several online unlicensed gambling sites allow users to open gambling accounts without requiring them to reveal their real identity and location.[22] These sites also enable users to use Paysafecards and virtual currencies. Indeed, there are online gambling sites that promote their anonymous services and their use of cryptocurrencies. In online gaming and virtual world sites (e.g., Second Life), users can create multiple user accounts with fictitious information and conduct multiple transactions. The organized cybercriminal can use some of the accounts to acquire goods and services from his or her other accounts. The person can then transfer the proceeds obtained in the forums to some of these accounts. The person can then withdraw these funds.

In addition to money laundering, organized cybercriminals have engaged in drug trafficking online. The nature and extent of their engagement in other forms of trafficking (e.g., human, firearms, cigarettes, and wildlife) is currently unknown. What is also unknown is the extent to which these operations are conducted by traditional organized crime groups using technology to facilitate operations, organized cybercriminals, or lone sellers taking advantage of the opportunities provided by the Internet to engage in these illicit forms of trafficking. What *is* known is that organized crime groups have used the Internet to facilitate trafficking. Due to the scope of trafficking activities occurring online and the increasing use of the Internet and related technology in the engagement in trafficking, these crimes receive further attention in this chapter.

DRUG TRAFFICKING

Drug trafficking involves the unlawful distribution and sale of drugs in violation of existing national and international laws. Drug traffickers have access to more individuals online than offline.[23] With the Internet, they can market their drugs worldwide. Drug trafficking is criminalized under 21 U.S.C. § 841(a). According to this law, it is considered illegal for a person "to manufacture, distribute, or dispense, or possess with intent to manufacture, distribute, or dispense, a controlled substance; or . . . to create, distribute, or dispense, or possess with intent to distribute or dispense, a counterfeit substance." Another law that criminalizes the sale of certain drugs, particularly the sale of **controlled substances**, is the U.S. Controlled Substances Act of 1970 (Title II of the U.S. Comprehensive Drug Abuse Prevention and Control Act of 1970, codified at 21 U.S.C. § 801 et seq.). In this act, controlled substances are categorized under five schedules, based on medical use, potential for abuse, and probability of causing drug dependency.[24] **Schedule I** drugs have the greatest potential for abuse and are the only drugs listed in the act that have no medical use (e.g., heroin, LSD, and ecstasy). Drugs in **Schedule II** have a medical use, but those who use these substances are at great risk for abuse of these drugs because their use can result in physical or psychological dependency (e.g., morphine, cocaine, and methadone). **Schedule III** drugs may possibly lead to moderate and low dependency on drugs by users (e.g., anabolic steroids, Tylenol with codeine, and ketamine). **Schedule IV** drugs have a lower likelihood for abuse and dependency than those listed in Schedule III (e.g., Ambien, Valium, and Xanax). Finally, **Schedule V** lists drugs with the lowest likelihood for abuse and dependency than the drugs listed in previous schedules (e.g., Lyrica and Robitussin AC).

It is illegal to possess controlled substances with the intent to distribute them unless this possession and distribution is in accordance with existing laws. The controlled substances listed in the Controlled Substances Act cannot be lawfully possessed, with one exception: a prescription is given for the drugs to be used for medical reasons and the purchase of the drugs with the prescription occurs in a lawful manner. This, of course, only applies to those drugs that have a medical use and can be prescribed by doctors. This means that Schedule I drugs are excluded. Marijuana is listed as a Schedule I drug. Despite the fact that some states have authorized its use for limited medical purposes (e.g., California, Illinois, New York, and Vermont), others have decriminalized possession of small quantities of this controlled substance (e.g., Minnesota, Nebraska, North Carolina, and Ohio), and a couple of states have legalized its recreational use (e.g., Colorado, Washington, Alaska, and Oregon), federal law does not acknowledge any medical use of marijuana nor authorize its possession in any amount. Online sales of marijuana could thus violate the Controlled Substances Act. States (e.g., Washington) do not allow the online sale of marijuana.[25] Search engines (e.g., Google, Yahoo, and Bing) and social media sites (e.g., Facebook and Twitter) also do not authorize the advertising of marijuana and other drugs on their site. Their advertising policies clearly ban the promotion of drugs and drug paraphernalia.

BOX 13-1 MAIL COURIERS AND DRUG TRAFFICKING

FedEx was charged with money laundering and drug trafficking for knowingly delivering drugs from online pharmacies that were illegally selling drugs without prescriptions to consumers. The indictment notes that FedEx was aware that two online pharmacies, Chhabra-Smoley Organization and Superior Drugs, were providing users with controlled substances in violation of existing laws. In particular, these two online pharmacies were issuing controlled substances to users without a doctor's prescription; all users had to do was fill out an online form.[26] The indictment further pointed out that FedEx continued to mail drugs from these online pharmacies even after they were made aware of the pharmacies' illicit activities. Specifically, multiple agencies and members of legislature informed FedEx of the illegal sale and distribution of drugs by these sites. Such awareness of illegal activities from these sites was evident in the online pharmacy credit policy that was distributed to the managing directors of sales of FedEx about these online pharmacies, which stated, "Many of these companies operate outside federal and state regulations over the sale of controlled drugs, which require diagnosis and prescription by a licensed physician. Drugs purchased from the sites may be diluted or counterfeit. Several sites have been shut down by the government without warning or simply disappeared leaving large balances . . . [owed] to FedEx."[27] This was not the first time a delivery service was charged for knowingly delivering illicit products from online pharmacies. UPS was required to forfeit $40 million of its gains for shipping products from an online pharmacy that illegally sold prescription drugs and controlled substances.[28]

Despite these bans, the Internet has been used to promote the sale of marijuana, along with other drugs, both old (e.g., heroin, cocaine, ecstasy, methamphetamines, hallucinogens, and anabolic steroids) and new drugs (e.g., flakka and bath salts).[29] Counterfeit prescription drugs have also been trafficked. A case in point involved Michael Markiewicz, a pharmacist who bought counterfeit prescription drugs (Viagra and Cialis) online and sold them in his pharmacy. The tablets were ordered online and shipped from China. The counterfeit drugs were packaged in boxes that were labeled as gift pens; the drugs were included within the package, underneath the pens in clear plastic bags that did not have a label.[30] In addition to the sale of drugs in online pharmacies,[31] drugs can be sold on websites (both password protected and open access) and online advertisements. Social networking sites have been used in the advertisement and sale of a variety of drugs as well.[32] Moreover, the Internet has enabled users to obtain the "know how" to create, sell, and distribute drugs. This is especially true for the **deep web**.

SURFACE WEB VS. DEEP WEB

The web can be conceptualized as an iceberg in the ocean that includes a visible part above the water and an invisible part underneath the water. The part above the water is the **visible web**. The visible web is open to all, anyone can access it—whether a criminal or a law-abiding citizen. The visible web consists of a collection of indexed sites that users can find through search engines, such as Google or Bing. By contrast, the deep web is made up "of a collection of nonindexed sites . . . [that] cannot be found through search engines"[33] and are not easily accessed by the general public. The number of sites on the deep web are unknown. The deep web includes sites that are password protected, intranets, and sites that are part of what is known as **Darknet**.

Darknet: The Underworld of Cyberspace

The deep web has been used by activists to evade persecution by totalitarian governments. For instance, dissidents in the Arab Spring used the deep web to communicate undetected by law enforcement authorities.[34] Along with its positive uses, the deep web has been used to engage in criminal activity; this has been observed in the Darknet. *Darknet* is a term used to describe the underworld of cyberspace.[35]

Many criminal activities have been observed on the Darknet, some of which include the buying and selling of counterfeit money, counterfeit documents (e.g., national IDs, driver's licenses, and passports), counterfeit and stolen goods (e.g., jewelry), weapons, drugs, precious metals and stones, hacking services (e.g., to hack into a user's social media account), malware code, and copyrighted works (e.g., books, music, and movies). Other sites provide a wealth of counterfeit goods, such as accessories (e.g., handbags and watches), clothing, and electronics. How-to books on killing, spying, hacking WiFi, creating explosives, and evading detection by authorities, among other topics, are also available on Darknet. One seller on the now closed Evolution Darknet site had posted hacked tax accounts from the likes of TurboTax, H&R Block, TaxAct, and TaxHawk sites.[36] Another seller, Beau Wattigney, sold counterfeit coupons on a Darknet site that was taken down by law enforcement authorities. Those who purchased these coupons obtained significant discounts from the stores targeted in the fraud.[37] What is also sold on dark markets and Darknet sites is mobile data; some of the best-selling commodities in these forums are lists of phone contacts, IMEI (international mobile equipment identity) numbers, information about installed apps on devices, and WiFi details. Cryptocurrencies, such as Bitcoins, are used to purchase illicit items on Darknet sites. Bitcoins have been used on sites on the visible web and Darknet for some time, but other businesses have started to accept them for payment (e.g., restaurants and markets).

BOX 13-2 ASHLEY MADISON HACK AND DARKNET

In 2015, Ashley Madison was hacked by a group called the Impact Team. This website promoted and enabled extramarital affairs, which was evident in its tagline: "Life is short. Have an affair." The group threatened to release user data if the site was not shut down. The site did not shut down in response to the threat. Staying true to their word, the Impact Team released personal information about users of the site (e.g., names, e-mail addresses, and personal preferences), resulting in significant personal consequences for those identified as users of the site, along with the potential financial consequences for Ashley Madison that may ensue from lawsuits by those who used the site.[38] The information about users was first released on Darknet.[39] Subsequently, the data was placed on websites on the visible web to enable users to access the data with greater ease.[40] In total, information from more than thirty million users' accounts was published online.[41]

IMAGE 13-1   Screenshot of Tor Browser.

To access certain Darknet sites, such as the onion sites hidden on **Tor** ("The Onion Router") network (i.e., Onionland), the Tor browser is needed. Tor is "an anonymous Internet communication system that provides individuals (and organizations) with the ability to share information and communicate over public networks without compromising their privacy."[42] Tor was designed to secure communications and information exchange between senders and receivers. With Tor, messages are protected as they traverse networks, whereby "each onion router removes a layer of encryption to uncover routing instructions, and sends the message."[43] Tor also enables anonymous browsing; nevertheless, even the Tor site where a user can download the browser informs the user that the browser is not all that is needed to engage in anonymous browsing.[44] For users without any technical knowledge, skills, and abilities, sites like YouTube provide step-by-step guidelines on how to access Darknet using Tor.[45] Outside of Tor, Freenet and the Invisible Internet Project (I2P) also provide users with access to Darknet sites.

In the past, access to Darknet sites was made possible if the user knew the URL of the site the user sought to access. Today, search engines on Darknet enable users to search for Darknet sites. A well-known example is Grams (a Darknet market search engine). Grams, whose main page looks like the Google search page (and its results mirror Google's too), enables users to check Darknet sites for drugs. Once a search is conducted, the user can see the search results and news updates (on the left side of the screen) along with an advertisement; usually, news and advertisements focus on new sites and goods. Onion City is another well-known search engine where users can search for a wide variety of licit and illicit items on Darknet.

Information about Darknet sites can be found on a **hidden wiki**,[46] which includes information and links to commercial and noncommercial and Darknet sites. Noncommercial sites include information about illicit items, for example, drugs. More specifically, noncommercial sites contain information about drug chemistry, how to grow and create illicit substances, and pharmacology. Commercial sites, as the name implies, enable the sale of such items and include the sites of suppliers and vendors along with the products sold on the sites. The commercial sites that sell controlled substances look like traditional

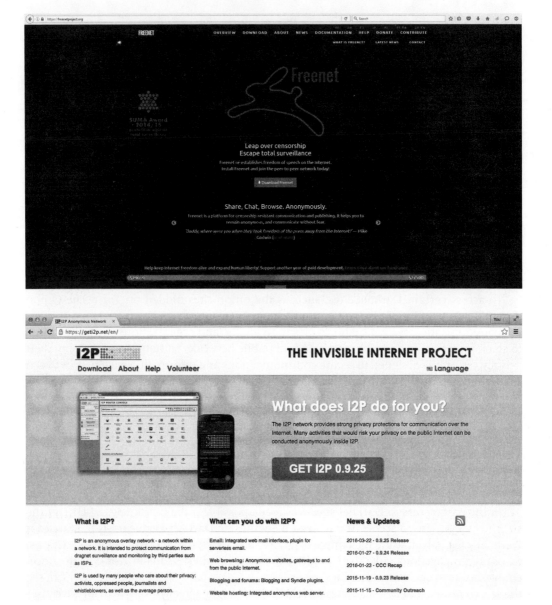

IMAGE 13-2   Screenshots of Freenet and I2P.

online sites that sell goods on the visible web (e.g., Amazon); the main difference is that what is sold on the former Darknet sites is predominantly illegal.

On the Darknet, cybercriminals and organized cybercriminals use hidden services such as underground forums and criminal marketplaces.[47] Underground forums on the Darknet mimic those on the visible web. They serve as a virtual meeting place in which to communicate about and trade illicit goods and services. Sexual predators also use Darknet

IMAGE 13-3 Screenshot of Silk Road.

to view, download, and distribute child pornography. They exchange information in hidden services on how to evade detection by law enforcement authorities (such as modifying backgrounds in pictures and deleting EXIF[48] in photos).[49] Hidden services forums may have VIP sections which can only be accessed after the vetting of potential members. With child sexual predators, this process may include the production of child pornography, detailed descriptions of the predator's experiences, and ways to victimize children. One infamous (but now defunct) criminal marketplace on the Darknet was **Silk Road**.

SILK ROAD News reports and successful law enforcement investigations of Darknet sites brought worldwide attention to the deep web.[50] Silk Road was an onion site on the Darknet that served primarily as an online drug bazaar (although other illicit and licit goods were sold on the site). The public-facing site of Silk Road had no identifying information. To get to the site, the user needed to know the URL. The public-facing site was a black screen, with user name and passphrase boxes, a CAPTCHA (Completely Automated Public Turing Test to Tell Computers and Humans Apart) image and text box, and a "click to join" link. To enter the site, returning users merely needed to input their user name and passphrase and type what they saw in the CAPTCHA image. New users could easily create a profile. After accessing the "click to join" link, the site asked for the user name, passphrase, and location of the user (which was not authenticated). Upon creating an account, the user typed in his or her details and whatever was depicted in the CAPTCHA image to gain access to the site. When users accessed the site, they saw a website similar to those that sells goods on the visible web, with an important difference—what was primarily sold were drugs and other illicit goods, with Bitcoins as the currency of choice.

Silk Road operated as an organized criminal network. With traditional organized crime groups, when the livelihood of an organized crime group is threatened, violent actions are taken to protect the criminal enterprise[51] from those who threaten it. Those in charge of illegal online criminal enterprises have resorted to threats of violence (with the intention of having them carried out) in order to protect their enterprise. This was evident in the case of Silk Road, where the administrator, seeking to resort to violence to protect his enterprise, solicited murderers for hire to deal with an individual who threatened his operation.[52] The administrator of Silk Road, Dread Pirate Roberts, was Ross William Ulbricht. He was charged and convicted of running a criminal enterprise on the Darknet.[53] During his term as a site administrator, he received an estimated eighty million dollars in commission.[54]

Sites like Silk Road enable drugs to be sold by the producers to consumers without any involvement by other individuals. These forums also remove the need for face-to-face contact between purchasers and suppliers. With the creation of Silk Road, the barriers to entering the underground economy were lowered, making it easier for buyers and sellers to participate in the drug trade. At Ulbricht's trial, a heroin dealer of the now defunct Silk Road testified that to deal heroin, he

> merely had to procure a supply of drugs (which he bought from his existing personal supplier on the street), and Silk Road provided the rest: an anonymous online sales portal, a huge preexisting customer base, how-to advice from the "Seller's Guide" and Silk Road discussion forum, and an escrow system enabling him to collect payment from his customers remotely . . . [He further] testified . . . [that] he never would have been able to become a drug dealer so easily and surreptitiously in real space; he was only able to do so online, through the facilitating technology of Silk Road.[55]

The government argued that Ulbricht "developed a blueprint" that others subsequently used to develop criminal marketplaces similar to Silk Road but offering an even wider variety of goods and services (even some that were banned on Silk Road, for example, weapons and child pornography).[56] For his crimes and for paving the way for others to engage in similar conduct, Ulbricht was given the maximum penalty, life imprisonment. This sentence was provided by the government in the interest of general deterrence:[57] Those seeking to develop, maintain, and monitor for a profit an illegal online enterprise will do so at a high cost, namely, life imprisonment. This significant penalty was thus meted to deter others from engaging in similar conduct.[58] In May 2015, in addition to the administrator of Silk Road, others were charged and convicted for crimes committed in this forum. Cornelius Jan Slomp received a ten-year term of imprisonment in exchange for a guilty plea for engaging in drug trafficking on Silk Road.[59]

Silk Road was well known for having an administrator (Dread Pirate Roberts) that closely monitored the site to ensure that buyers and sellers were behaving in a manner that was beneficial to both parties. When a buyer purchased an item from Silk Road with Bitcoins, his or her payment would remain in escrow until the item was delivered. Once the item was delivered, the money was released from escrow and provided to the seller. Dread

Pirate Roberts also vetted buyers and sellers and removed anyone from the site that was not following site rules. The same holds true for other Darknet sites. However, Darknet sites, even Silk Road, had issues with sellers. For instance, on Silk Road, some vendors threatened customers with revealing their address information if they failed to provide a positive rating for the seller on the site.[60] Vendors sought positive ratings because a vendor with higher positive feedback from users tended to attract more customers. Indeed, in dark markets, sellers seek to build a reputation for being reliable and ensuring product delivery. Darknet sites provide information about the quality of transactions; quality involves not only successful transactions in that they arrive to their intended target but also that the quality of goods or services is as advertised.

Darknet sites are successful because they enable sellers to build a reputation through the customer rating and feedback provisions on the site and are built on creating trust among users. Trust is critical when relying on others in high risk and vulnerable situations to deliver goods and services, especially when the transactions are illicit in nature. Victims of nondelivery or counterfeit items cannot report this to the police, because they have engaged in unlawful conduct.[61] Accordingly, the dark markets on the invisible web are largely dependent on trust.

The scam markets revealed on the Darknet created distrust. Before Dread Pirate Roberts' arrest, there were three major Darknet players: Silk Road, BlackMarketReloaded, and Atlantis. Atlantis closed its site in response to purported security concerns, taking users' Bitcoins with it. This scam market was a cause for concern among Darknet users, and as these users found out, this scam market site was by no means unique. Following the closure of Atlantis, the leading markets were Silk Road and BlackMarketReloaded. After the shutdown of Atlantis, Dread Pirate Roberts' arrest, and the seizure of Silk Road, BlackMarketReloaded became the major player. BlackMarketReloaded had a bad reputation for the scammers that used its site. Because of this, following the closure of Atlantis and Silk Road, some of the customers from Atlantis and Silk Road sought an alternative site to BlackMarketReloaded, namely, Sheep. Sheep, however, turned out to be a scam market. BlackMarketReloaded also closed due to its inability to handle and vet the influx of buyers and sellers to the market in the aftermath of the Silk Road closing and the Atlantis and Sheep scam markets.

During this time (after Silk Road was taken down), Silk Road 2.0 was launched. Before it was launched, an announcement was posted on Twitter. The announcement was from the new administrator, also named Dread Pirate Roberts. The name Dread Pirate Roberts was taken from the character in *The Princess Bride* with the same name. The name is a pseudonym inherited by successors. Each successor inherits not only the name but also the reputation of those who bore the name before them. Silk Road 2.0 had more buyers and sellers of drugs on its site than Silk Road because of the good reputation of Silk Road and the Darknet scam markets.

Silk Road 2.0, Pandora, and Tormarket subsequently became the leading Darknet sites. TorMarket was also a scam market and closed its site without returning or allowing users to withdraw their Bitcoins. After TorMarket shut down its site, the leading competitors of Silk Road 2.0 were Pandora, Evolution, and Agora. Following the arrest of the administrator of Silk Road 2.0, Defcon became the new administrator of the site. Silk Road 2.0 experienced a hack in which users' Bitcoins were stolen. Customers with Bitcoins on the site feared that it was a scam market, like Sheep, Atlantis, and TorMarket.[62] Pandora, another leading Darknet competitor, was also hacked. Both Pandora and Silk Road 2.0 provided a reimbursement payment plan for users in response to the hacking incidents. Because of the payment plan, they distanced themselves from scam markets and were able to rebuild trust with buyers and sellers using their sites. Nonetheless, Silk Road 2.0 and Pandora were later seized by law enforcement authorities.[63] Evolution also turned out to be a scam market, shutting down its site and stealing users' Bitcoins.[64]

A new version of Silk Road is now hosted on I2P. This version of Silk Road, Silk Road Reloaded, is not connected to the original Silk Road or Silk Road 2.0. Users can buy and sell items on Silk Road Reloaded using a variety of cryptocurrencies. Along with I2P, Freenet also provides users with access to Darknet sites. The leading drug market up until August 2015 was Agora, which closed its site at the end of August 2015 for security reasons.[65] There are many similar known sites that sell numerous illicit items. The reality is that authorities do not know the nature and extent of illicit activities occurring on the Darknet. The role of law enforcement here is central to uncovering operations occurring on the deep web; this is evident by the takedown of several Darknet sites over the last couple of years.

Law enforcement can conduct undercover operations on the Darknet to uncover new sites and monitor existing ones for subsequent arrest of those engaging in illicit conduct. In addition to undercover investigations and the takedown of sites, they can also work with the United States Postal Service and private mail couriers to intercept packages with illicit items. This recommendation is extremely difficult to implement because of the daily volume of mail and packages sent. The postal and courier industry does not have the necessary time and financial and human resources to screen every letter or package (nor is such a practice desirable). Accordingly, only a limited number of items can be screened. What is more, the concealment tactics used by cybercriminals have improved. Sites on the Darknet provide information to sellers on how they can avoid having packages intercepted by authorities. Buyers are also informed on how to protect their letter and parcels from being intercepted and traced back to them. Furthermore, Darknet sites have message boards on which users can share information on a wide variety of topics, including how to evade detection by law enforcement authorities.

HUMAN TRAFFICKING

Human smuggling has been used interchangeably with **human trafficking**, albeit incorrectly. They are two distinct concepts. According to Article 3(a) of the UN Protocol against the Smuggling of Migrants by Land, Sea and Air of 2000, supplementing the UN Convention against Transnational Organized Crime of 2000, human smuggling (i.e., migrant smuggling) is "the procurement, in order to obtain, directly or indirectly, a financial or other material benefit, of the illegal entry of a person into a State Party of which the person is not a national or a permanent resident." The smuggler agrees to assist an individual to gain entry into a country. Once the person is smuggled into the country, the relationship between the smuggler and the individual supposedly ends. However, this is not always the case. The smuggler may request additional fees from the person either en route or upon arrival at the destination. The smuggler may seek to extort money from the person, threatening to force the person into **forced labor** (i.e., involuntary servitude) or to engage in sexual activities if the person does not comply. Individuals who have been smuggled have also been the victims of violent crimes (e.g., assault, rape, and murder).

Someone willingly participates in human smuggling, which involves illegally entering a country. The person is aware that the act is illegal. In contrast, individuals who are trafficked are coerced and forced into engaging in commercial sex or forced labor against their will. Human trafficking is defined in Article 3(a) of the UN Protocol to Prevent, Suppress and Punish Trafficking in Persons of 2000 as

> the recruitment, transportation, transfer, harbouring or receipt of persons, by means of the threat or use of force or other forms of coercion, of abduction, of fraud, of deception, of the abuse of power or of a position of vulnerability or of the giving or receiving of payments or benefits to achieve the consent of a person having control over another person, for the purpose of exploitation. Exploitation shall include, at a minimum, the exploitation of the prostitution of others or other forms of sexual exploitation, forced labour or services, slavery or practices similar to slavery, servitude or the removal of organs.

In the United States, **sex trafficking** and **labor trafficking** are characterized as severe forms of trafficking in persons. According to the National Human Trafficking Resource Center, trafficking involves inducing, recruiting, harboring, transporting, providing, or obtaining a person by means of fraud, force, or coercion for the purpose of commercial sex or labor.[66] Sex trafficking involves a third party facilitation of an individual's participation in the illicit sex industry. The person engaging in this conduct is doing so under coercion, and not under their own volition. Those trafficked are often duped into traveling to the trafficker's location. In 2014, Cameroon reported that women were lured to other countries by fraudulent marriage proposals via the Internet and subsequently forced into prostitution.[67] Perpetrators may take a victim's identifying documents and threaten or use violence against victims to keep them from escaping or leaving. Sex trafficking can also occur through **debt bondage**,[68] wherein a trafficker informs the victim that he or she must engage in sexual activities until a debt is paid (e.g., travel costs to the country).

Under Section 103(8)(A) of the Trafficking Victims Protection Act of 2000, any person under the age of eighteen who is induced into engaging in prostitution is considered a trafficked victim.[69] Juan A. Moreno, a convicted sex offender, kidnapped, harbored, and beat, drugged, and sexually abused (along with others) a thirteen-year-old girl while she was tied to a bed. After a few weeks she escaped. Moreno received life imprisonment without parole for his crimes.[70] Not all sex trafficking cases involving minors result in a severe sentence for traffickers. A now infamous case of child sex trafficking involves a hedge fund mogul, Jeffrey Epstein. Epstein trafficked many underage girls to his home to engage in various sexual services; for his numerous sexual crimes against minors, he received a paltry eighteen months' imprisonment (he served only thirteen months of the sentence).[71]

Labor trafficking refers to "the recruitment, harboring, transportation, provision, or obtaining of a person for labor or services, through the use of force, fraud, or coercion for the purpose of subjection to involuntary servitude, peonage, debt bondage, or slavery."[72] Labor trafficking can take many forms, one of which is domestic servitude. Those subjected to this form of trafficking are coerced and isolated. Children have been forced into domestic servitude and other forms of forced labor. Labor trafficking can also occur through debt bondage, in which a smuggled individual is forced into labor by the smuggler to pay off his or her debt or purported additional costs incurred during transport. Those engaged in labor trafficking often deceive individuals through false promises of employment opportunities in a different country.[73]

NATURE AND EXTENT OF HUMAN TRAFFICKING

An accurate assessment of the nature and extent of human trafficking does not exist, especially in regard to the scope of this activity online. Measuring human trafficking is difficult due to its clandestine nature.[74] Persons involved in trafficking are part of what is known as "hidden populations," "membership [in which] often involves stigmatized or illegal behavior, leading individuals to refuse to cooperate, or give unreliable answers to protect their privacy."[75] And because trafficking victims fear potential violence or other repercussions from governmental agencies (e.g., deportation) or retaliation by the trafficker (e.g., harm to family), they are hesitant to report the crime.[76] Moreover, several countries that serve as a source, transit, or destination country may not adequately collect, if at all, data on this crime.[77] Also, the data collected by countries is "generally not available, reliable, or comparable."[78] For these reasons, the Government Accountability Office concluded that the estimates of human trafficking suffer from "methodological weaknesses, testing data, and numerical discrepancies."[79] To date, no country has "established an effective mechanism for estimating the number of victims."[80] Those who record data also differ in their methodologies and reporting. Another problem identified by the Government Accountably Office is that countries tend to combine data for "trafficking, smuggling and illegal immigration."[81] However, these crimes differ significantly; the latter two do not involve coerced activity. Human trafficking has been misidentified as human smuggling and prostitution.[82] This misreporting contributes to an inadequate picture of this crime. This variation accounts for differences in estimates in annual reports. A tool, **Memex**, has been developed that seeks to shed light on the dark figure of this crime due to underreporting and ineffective reporting mechanisms. Memex is a deep web search tool created by the Defense Advanced Research Project Agency that targets, among other crimes, the illicit purchasing, selling, and advertising of humans.[83] Memex was first used on deep web sites suspected of facilitating human trafficking in some way.[84] Irrespective of this tool, reporting mechanisms should be harmonized between countries and improved.

HUMAN TRAFFICKERS: TARGETS AND TACTICS OF CONTROL

Traffickers facilitate, manage, and advertise the sexual acts of others for a profit (a portion or all of the proceeds). Trafficking is perpetrated by organized crime groups and may be the focus or one of several illegal activities they conduct.[85] Terrorist groups have also engaged in human trafficking. Boko Haram, a religious terrorist group based in Nigeria (though it is also active in other African countries, for example, Cameroon, Chad, and Niger), has sold trafficked women and girls into slavery for sex and labor and has enlisted children as soldiers.[86]

The targets of traffickers include those who are economically disadvantaged.[87] Traffickers take advantage of victims who cannot satisfy their basic needs by providing them with food, shelter, and clothing. These needs were identified by Abraham Maslow in 1943 in his "hierarchy of needs."[88] Maslow specified five types of needs that humans seek to fulfill: physiological (e.g., hunger and thirst); safety and security (e.g., stability, protection, and need for structure); love and belongingness (e.g., fitting in with groups); esteem (i.e., esteem for oneself and the respect one receives from others, for example, status, competence, prestige, and recognition); and self-actualization (i.e., one's desire to reach his or her full potential). Individuals must fulfill, for example, the physiological need before fulfilling the next need in the hierarchy (i.e., safety and security), and so on. If individuals cannot satisfy basic physiological needs using legal means, they will do so using illegal measures.

In 2014, the *Trafficking in Persons Report* revealed that in South Korea an estimated two hundred thousand girls were sexually exploited to fulfill their basic needs of food and shelter.[89] Traffickers have been found to fulfill other needs as well, such as safety and security, love and belongingness, and esteem needs. Deceptive recruitment is also utilized by traffickers to fulfill victims' security and even esteem needs by falsely promising acting or modeling jobs. Love and belongingness are fulfilled by traffickers who pretend to be a boyfriend or father figure in the victim's life. Ultimately, the victim's needs are met only until the trafficker obtains his or her desired outcomes.

Consider the loverboy scam, which is used by traffickers in the Netherlands to lure victims. There are several variations of the loverboy scam, but they all more or less follow this scenario:[90] The perpetrator singles out a vulnerable child and tries to gain the child's love by pretending to have a relationship with the child. The perpetrator cares for the victim and provides the victim with money and material things (e.g., clothes or a mobile phone). Those individuals targeted are usually insecure and have low self-esteem. They may come from broken homes but not necessarily. The victims are basically seduced by the perpetrator, who showers them with attention and compliments, which before the perpetrators' arrival were lacking. A child may be lured by promises of excitement and adventure. After gaining the victim's trust, the "loverboy" gets the victim to engage in drug use and sexual activities with the loverboy, and subsequently with others. The victim is guilted into compliance or threatened with violence for noncompliance with the perpetrator's requests. The length of the grooming process varies. What has been observed is that when the grooming process is shortened, the offender often resorts to threats and violence to gain victim compliance. Here, the victim may be physically or psychologically abused or blackmailed through exposure of the sexual relationship with the perpetrator or the release of any nude or sexually provocative images or videos taken of the victim or any images or photos depicting sexual activity of the victim. In one investigation, Dutch girls who fell victim to the loverboy scam reported being in vulnerable positions.[91] The loverboys filled their physiological, security, love and belongingness, and self-esteem needs (albeit temporarily).[92]

In addition to meeting victim's needs, Shared Hope International identified several other ways in which traffickers control victims (see Figure 13-1), particularly through intimidation (e.g., engaging in harm against other victims and displaying a weapon to the victim); coercion (e.g., threatening harm to the victim or the victim's family); psychological abuse (e.g., calling the victim worthless and saying that the victim is unwanted); physical abuse (e.g., punching, slapping, or kicking the victim for noncompliance); sexual abuse (e.g., forcing sexual acts on victim as a form of punishment); economic abuse (e.g., limiting the victim's access to money or taking the victim's money); blaming (e.g., blaming the victim for treatment); minimizing (e.g., downplaying the seriousness of the acts); denial (e.g., denying that anything wrong or illegal is occurring); and isolation (e.g., isolating the victim from family and friends).[93]

Other studies have found that traffickers use psychological coercion to control victims.[94] Albert Biderman studied psychological coercion in the context of confinement. His study has been applied to the study of human trafficking.[95] Biderman identified the

FIGURE 13-1 Ways in Which Traffickers Control Victims.
Source: This information depicted was obtained from the wheel adapted from the Duluth Model Power and Control Wheel by the Domestic Abuse Intervention Project included in the Anti-Trafficking in Persons Division, Office of Refugee Resettlement, U.S. Department of Health and Human Services (HHS), http://www.doj.state.wi.us/sites/default/files/ocvs/ht-power-control-wheel.pdf

following coercive methods that can be used to gain compliance from individuals: isolation (i.e., when individuals are isolated, they are deprived of any form of social support); monopolization of perception (allowing the victim to experience only stimuli controlled by the trafficker and frustrating any attempt by the victim to engage in noncompliance); induced debility and exhaustion (i.e., the victim is rendered mentally and physically incapable of resistance); threats (i.e., the trafficker focuses on making the victim fearful to compel compliance); occasional indulgences (i.e., the trafficker intermittently engages in positive reinforcement[96] for compliant behavior); demonstration of omnipotence (i.e., the trafficker demonstrates brute force to illustrate the repercussions of noncompliance and the futility of resisting the trafficker); degradation (i.e., the trafficker subjects the victim to cruel and inhumane treatment); and enforcement of trivial demands (i.e., the trafficker seeks to develop compliance by the victim by enforcing trivial demands).[97] In one study, labor trafficking victims in Los Angeles revealed that they were subjected to conditions of psychological coercion similar to those described in Biderman's work.[98] Specifically, victims were prevented from seeing or speaking to others; deprived of basic needs such as food, medical care and treatment, and even sleep; threatened with violence, death threats, threats against family, arrest, and deportation; given occasional material or emotional rewards; humiliated; physically and sexually assaulted; and required to comply with petty demands.[99]

HUMAN TRAFFICKERS: ONLINE TACTICS

The increase in the use of the Internet and technology by human traffickers can be attributed (at least in part) to greater Internet accessibility in countries all over the globe.[100] Technology is used in innovative ways to facilitate the advertisement, sale, and delivery of individuals for sexual exploitation and labor.[101] Traffickers use smartphones and mobile phones in their activities, especially prepaid mobile phones because they do not require user registration and do not authenticate a user's identity.[102] Human traffickers have also used the Internet to communicate with one another and clients; advertise trafficked victims and services provided; schedule and arrange times and places for clients to meet trafficked victims (motels, hotels, private parties, homes, and cars);[103] and exploit a greater number of victims anywhere in the world with an Internet connection. Moreover, traffickers utilize e-mails, websites, message boards, bulletin boards, chat rooms, social media sites, newsgroups, and peer-to-peer (P2P) networks, as well as online advertising and classified websites, to advertise, recruit, and sell human beings for a wide variety of sexual and labor-related activities.[104]

Traffickers use online classified sites such as Craigslist and Backpage to advertise trafficked victims.[105] In the United States, underage and adult victims of human trafficking are lured by false promises, and once they are in the possession of traffickers, they are advertised for sexual services.[106] For instance, in 2010, authorities rescued a twelve-year-old girl in the United States who was in the sex trade and whose sexual services were being advertised on Craigslist.[107] Marcus Sewell, between 2005 and 2006, advertised two minor females on websites, such as Craigslist, as escorts.[108] In another case, Thomas Cramer, between April and December 2011, used Backpage to facilitate the trafficking of six underage girls.[109] Due to the proliferation of the advertising of trafficked victims on Backpage and the site's refusal to acknowledge and deal with these activities on its site, major credit card companies, such as Visa, MasterCard, and American Express, now prohibit the use of their cards to purchase adult ads on that site.[110] However, Backpage responded to this block by offering advertisements for adult services on its site for free.[111] As of 2015, users of Backpage were able to use Bitcoins for payment.[112]

Other countries have also reported the use of online advisements and classified websites by human traffickers. For instance, in Russia, the Internet is used by traffickers to advertise sexual services with minors.[113] Also, France has reported "a noticeable increase" in the posting of online advertisements of trafficked victims for sexual services by Russian and Bulgarian organized crime networks.[114] Other organized crime groups have engaged in similar activity. In the United States, the Gambino organized crime family was known for engaging in sex trafficking and advertising commercial sex via online advertisement sites (e.g., Craigslist) and other websites.[115] On these sites perpetrators indirectly advertise sexual services using codes to avoid detection by authorities.[116] Like traffickers, human smugglers advertise their services online. To draw a larger clientele through these advertisements, which also exist on social media sites like Facebook and Twitter, they use similar language to that found in tourism brochures and advertisements.[117] In the past, human smugglers did not openly communicate or post information about their operations. Today, certain groups publish their names, numbers, prices, and schedules for trips to countries openly on social media sites.[118]

The Internet has additionally been used by traffickers to recruit women. Victims are recruited via the Internet for both sex trafficking and labor trafficking. Traffickers recruit victims via social media websites, marriage agencies, dating sites, and employment sites with advertisements for nannies, maids, models, actors, musicians, dancers, waitresses, hostesses, bartenders, and even factory, construction, and agricultural workers.[119] In Pakistan, traffickers use social media as a recruitment tool for potential trafficked victims.[120] Marriage agency websites are also utilized by traffickers. For instance, they are used to lure victims from foreign countries on false promises of love.[121] Marriage agencies are employed not only to recruit women but also to advertise the sale of sexual services.[122] Likewise, some mail order bride sites have been found to serve as a front for human trafficking.[123] Russian and Asian organized crime groups utilize marriage agencies and mail order bride sites to facilitate human trafficking operations.[124] In Vietnam, traffickers (young men) lure victims (both women and girls) through online dating websites.[125] They gain a victim's trust through online dating and subsequently convince the victim to travel to the trafficker's location. Once there, the victim may be forced into sex or labor.

Trafficked victims are also lured through false promises of work or work that has been misrepresented in the advertisement. In one incident, Japanese women were lured to Hawaii through an online advertisement for nude models.[126] Once there, they were forced to create pornography and engage in live sex shows streamed through the Internet aimed at a Japanese audience. Traffickers from Mongolia utilize online advertisement and social media websites to post fake job advertisements to lure unsuspecting victims.[127] In 2014, Cameroon reported that women were lured to other countries by fraudulent offers for domestic work via the Internet.[128] Once they arrived at the destination country, Switzerland, France, or Russia, they became victims of forced labor.[129] Men in Cameroon were similarly exploited by being lured to Sweden on false work offers, only to be forced into forestry labor upon their arrival.[130] In Croatia, women and girls have fallen victim to fraudulent job advertisements as well.[131]

Countries have taken specific measures to deal with human trafficking. For instance, in Bangladesh, to help prevent individuals from becoming victims of labor trafficking, the government passed the Overseas Employment Act of 2013. This law requires stringent licensing requirements for job recruiters. The law also made it mandatory that job seekers outside of the country register in a database and required employers to hire only those listed in the database.[132] Education in human trafficking and the tactics that traffickers use is also essential to combating this crime. The Polaris Project provides useful information and resources about human trafficking. It also has a data analysis program that it uses to detect human trafficking operations in order to stop traffickers and assist victims.[133] Governments have also taken special measures to inform citizens of trafficking. In China, the government uses social media to educate the public about traffickers and receive information from the public about suspected trafficking.[134] Moreover, regional organizations have called for education in human trafficking. The Council of Europe's Convention on Action against Trafficking in Human Beings holds that each party to the convention must "establish and/or strengthen effective policies and programmes to prevent trafficking in human beings, by such means as: research, information, awareness raising and education campaigns, social and economic initiatives and training programmes, in particular for persons vulnerable to trafficking and for professionals concerned with trafficking in human beings." To disseminate information about worldwide cases on human trafficking, the United Nations Office on Drugs and Crime developed the Human Trafficking Case Law Database.[135]

The need to take action to protect children from trafficking is also explicitly listed under Article 5(5) of the Council of Europe Convention on Action against Trafficking in Human Beings. Moreover, the Convention on the Rights of the Child requires signatories to have "national, bilateral and multilateral measures to prevent the abduction of, the sale of or traffic in children for any purpose or in any form" (see Article 35 of the convention). Special measures have been taken that particularly target child trafficking. Microsoft's Child Exploitation Tracking System enables law enforcement authorities from all over the world to cooperate in investigations of child sexual exploitation. The National Center for Missing and Exploited Children and the International Centre for Missing and Exploited Children similarly assist law enforcement agencies with child trafficking cases. Furthermore, INTERPOL's database, the INTERPOL International Child Sexual Exploitation image database (ICSE DB), contains images of child sexual exploitation that can be consulted during child trafficking investigations.[136]

ORGAN TRAFFICKING

The Internet is also utilized for another form of human trafficking—selling the organs and body parts of people, rather than the people themselves.[137] Recruitment for **organ trafficking** occurs through chat rooms, newsgroups, social media, websites, online advertisements, and even auction websites.[138] In 1999, a kidney was auctioned on eBay at a starting bid of $25,000.[139] The auction posting was removed by eBay. At the time of removal, bids for the kidney had reached $5,750,100.[140] In 2006, a man tried to sell his amputated leg on an auction site known as TradeMe; the site quickly took down his post.[141] In 2013, a man from New Zealand using the TradeMe site tried to sell his kidney.[142] TradeMe took down the post before the item was sold. That same year, in the United States, a man was arrested for selling stolen brain matter and human tissue online. The jars containing the brains and tissue were taken from the Indiana Medical History Museum and sold on eBay.[143] The theft and sale of these items on eBay was uncovered only after an individual who purchased jars of brain and tissue contacted the executive director of the museum and informed them of the purchase after he suspected that the items might have been stolen.[144] This material was bought and sold on eBay even though the website has a strict "human remains and body parts policy," which states: "We don't allow humans, the human body, or any human body parts or products to be listed on eBay, with two exceptions. Sellers can list items containing human scalp hair, and skulls and skeletons intended for medical use."[145] The problem with organ trafficking is not with the policies in place but with their actual enforcement. These websites take down illicit content only after being alerted to its presence. Nonetheless, the action taken largely depends on the website and whether the content is believed to violate the site's Terms of Service policy. Proactive monitoring of these sites does not occur, nor is it required by law.

Most countries prohibit the sale of organs, with few exceptions (e.g., China and Iran allow for the sale of certain organs in limited circumstances).[146] Despite this, organs are still bought and sold online due in large part to the prohibitive costs of organ transplants, the extensive wait for organs on the transplant list, and the short supply of organs.[147] Currently, the demand for organs far exceeds existing supply, causing individuals to seek organs elsewhere. The places where organs are sought are usually countries with high poverty and unemployment rates. In these countries, organ transplant tourism occurs. **Organ transplant tourism** involves the recruitment of poor individuals to provide/supply organs to those in need from a wealthy country in exchange for a fee.[148] The donors may not receive the fee or the full fee for the organs.[149] Countries with high poverty rates and weak enforcement of organ trafficking laws advertise organ transplant and transplant surgery packages online.[150] For example, kidney transplant packages can range anywhere from $70,000 to $160,000.[151] These websites are available to the public and can be found using simple word searches. The existence of these websites illustrates the need for better enforcement of organ trafficking laws and the need to deal with the structural issues that underlie organ trafficking (e.g., poverty and unemployment).

FIREARMS TRAFFICKING

The Internet has enabled the sale of firearms on a mass scale. They are sold online in several ways. Offline stores that sell firearms also have websites where these items can be purchased. In addition, there are other websites that serve as intermediaries whereby private sellers can post weapons for sale. Apart from these websites, firearms can be bought and sold in multiple forums, such as online classified websites, bulletin boards, and chat rooms.[152] Arrests of firearms traffickers have revealed that this crime is perpetrated on both the visible and invisible web. With respect to the former, in 2014, the French police arrested forty-four individuals with ties to an online **firearms trafficking** ring.[153] With respect to the latter, when Silk Road was first created, firearms were sold on the site. In 2012, the administrator of Silk Road, Ross William Ulbricht, moved the sales of firearms (even military-grade weapons) to a now defunct site he created and ran, known as The Armory.[154]

Firearms are strictly regulated by U.S. laws; ammunition (with the exception of armor-piercing ammunition),[155] however, is not, due to the passage of the Firearm Owners' Protection Act of 1986. The U.S. Gun Control Act of 1968 (hereafter GCA) prohibits the sale, delivery, or receipt of firearms via interstate commerce by the following persons: convicted criminals having served a sentence of more than one year; fugitives from justice; illegal drug users or addicts; the mentally ill (adjudicated as such or committed to a mental institution); illegal aliens; those dishonorably discharged from military; persons that have renounced their U.S. citizenship; and individuals under court order restraining them from engaging in antisocial behavior, such as harassment, stalking, intimate partner violence, or threats against intimate partners.[156] The GCA also prohibits the sale, delivery, shipment, or possession of firearms or ammunition by those under felony indictment.[157] It further prohibits the sale, transfer, or receipt of a firearm by a minor, defined by the statute as a person under eighteen years of age.[158] In reality, these restrictions have not prevented individuals within these classes from accessing firearms.

The GCA, while not explicitly covering online activities, can be applied to online firearms trafficking because the law covers interstate and foreign commerce, and it has long been established that communications networks and the Internet are considered channels of interstate and foreign commerce. The sale of firearms online provides those who would otherwise be considered prohibited purchasers with the opportunity to obtain them. In 2012, Zina Daniel obtained a restraining order against her husband, Radcliffe Haughton. The order prohibited Haughton from, among other things, purchasing a firearm. Haughton accessed an online site that sold firearms, Armslist.com, and purchased a handgun. He used the handgun to shoot and kill Zina at the place of her employment in Brookfield, Winsconsin. Along with his wife, he shot and killed two other women in the spa where she worked and injured four others before turning the gun on himself and committing suicide.[159] That same year, 2012, Jitka Vesel was killed by her stalker, Dmitry Smirnov (a man she had previously dated), in her workplace parking lot with a gun he illegally purchased on Armslist.com.[160] In another stalking incident, Rochelle Inselman, who stalked a man she had previously dated, Bret Struck, violated a restraining order prohibiting her from purchasing a firearm by buying a 9mm handgun online from a private seller. She subsequently used this handgun to kill Bret.[161]

To import, manufacture, or sell firearms, one must be approved for a license, the **federal firearms license** (FLL). In 2015, Michael Albert Focia was convicted of firearms trafficking for serving as a firearms vendor on two Darknet sites, BlackMarketReloaded (no longer operational) and Agora (no longer operational), without an FFL and selling and shipping firearms to out-of-state residents.[162] Individuals who engage in "occasional sales, exchanges, or purchases of firearms for the enhancement of the personal collection or for a hobby, or who sells all or part of his personal collection of firearms" are exempted from being required to apply and be approved for an FFL.[163] In 2011, a New York City investigation (under then mayor Michael Bloomberg) revealed that out of 125 sellers advertising firearms online, 77 had sold and shipped the firearm to a person that admitted that he or she could not pass a background check.[164] According to existing U.S. law, a person must not knowingly sell or ship a firearm to a person they know or have reason to believe is prohibited by law from purchasing the firearm.[165] Despite this requirement, these private sellers are not required to maintain a record of sales of firearms, nor are they required to conduct background checks on buyers. There are, however, certain states that serve as an exception to this rule, mainly because they require a background check for every firearm purchase. Cases in point are California, the District of Columbia, and Rhode Island. Other states, for example, Connecticut, require a background check for handguns but not for long guns, such as shotguns.[166]

Private sellers are only allowed to sell firearms to buyers in their states; here, the private seller can either meet the purchaser in person to provide the firearm or mail it to the individual. Under 18 U.S.C. § 922(a)(2), shipping firearms (excluding shotguns and rifles) via the United States Postal Service is prohibited, except when such a shipment occurs for law enforcement purposes. The same restrictions do not apply to a common courier such as UPS or FedEx.[167] Firearms may be mailed through these couriers as long as they are disclosed and follow the rules of the common carriers.[168] To sell a weapon out of state, sellers must follow the same process as those with an FFL.

A firearms store or dealer with an FFL seeking to advertise the selling and supplying of firearms online must follow the same rules as those advertising in print materials. As such, they are still prohibited from selling and shipping firearms directly to those without an FFL (non-FFLs). Particularly, those with FFLs are prohibited from selling a firearm to individuals listed under 18 U.S.C. § 922(d). The Bureau of Alcohol, Tobacco, Firearms and

Explosives (ATF) created an eZ Check website to enable firearms dealers to verify the validity of FFLs.[169] If a non-FFL (unlicensed) buyer of firearms is located in a different state from the firearm store or dealer with an FFL, the licensed store or dealer must first arrange to have the firearms shipped to a licensed store or dealer in the buyer's state, where the buyer will then be subjected to a background check before purchasing the firearm. Background checks can be conducted in a manner of minutes (this includes the time needed to complete the paperwork). This swiftness in background checks has been made possible by the National Instant Criminal Background Check System.

Websites that facilitate the sale of firearms should include appropriate transparency and authentication measures to enable the adequate identification of buyers and sellers and require them to not only verify their identities but also to mandate that visitors to sites that sell firearms register (and in turn authenticate the information provided) before viewing content on the sites or posting ads.[170] Without such authentication measures, it would be difficult to prevent the purchase of firearms by those who cannot lawfully possess them. Even with these authentication measures in place, individuals prohibited from obtaining firearms may still be able to purchase them on the Darknet.

CIGARETTE TRAFFICKING

Cigarette trafficking is often conducted to evade the cost of cigarettes, which is high in many states due to high taxation rates. A case in point is New York, where the tax on cigarettes as of 2015 was $4.35 per package of twenty, except for New York City, which had a tax rate of $5.85 per package of twenty.[171] Traffickers can significantly profit from this form of trafficking. In fact, this type of trafficking is considered more profitable than other forms of trafficking.[172] In addition, the costs associated with punishment for this crime are low under 18 U.S.C. § 2344. Specifically, anyone who "knowingly. . . ship[s], transport[s], receive[s], possess[es], sell[s], distribute[s], or purchase[s] contraband cigarettes or contraband smokeless tobacco"[173] can "be fined under this title or imprisoned not more than five years, or both."[174] By contrast, the penalties for human and drug trafficking are severe, and those prosecuted for these crimes can receive life imprisonment.[175]

Cigarette trafficking also includes the sale of cigarettes with counterfeit tax stamps and counterfeit cigarettes. Counterfeit cigarettes and tobacco products may be bought and sold online, the consumption of which can pose significant health risks. The Prevent All Cigarette Trafficking (PACT) Act of 2009 was passed due to an increase in foreign and domestic Internet vendors that sold cigarettes and other tobacco products to individuals in the United States without the necessary regulation and tax of such sales.[176] Websites operating outside of existing regulations were primarily based in foreign countries, Native American Indian reservations, and states with low cigarette taxes.[177] The sales have had an adverse impact on interstate commerce.[178] Accordingly, PACT made the sale of cigarettes online illegal unless the taxes levied by the state from which the cigarettes are shipped are paid. To evade taxes, online tobacco sellers do not report sales to the proper state revenue agencies.

PACT also curbed the mailing of most cigarettes and smokeless tobacco products by USPS, both domestically and abroad.[179] For commercial mailers such as UPS, cigarettes can only be mailed by those licensed and authorized to do so pursuant to existing laws.[180] Existing domestic laws further prohibit Native American tribes from selling nontaxed cigarettes to nontribe members. Despite these laws, in 2013, the Seneca Nation territory was still delivering untaxed cigarettes to individuals across the United States.[181] The Framework Convention on Tobacco Control of 2003, which was drawn up by the World Health Organization (WHO) and entered into force February 27, 2005, addressed cigarette trafficking on a global scale. Among other things, this WHO convention requires cigarette manufacturers to be licensed; cigarette packages to include traceable markings; tracing of Internet sales; and cooperation in international investigations of this form of trafficking. There are currently 180 signatories to this convention.[182] PACT also addresses issues listed in the WHO convention.

The success of cigarette trafficking is largely attributed to the marketing of the cigarettes sold as no tax or low tax cigarettes. There is a high demand for cigarettes from states (and countries) that have high cigarette tax rates. Cigarette traffickers advertise the goods they sell online to reach more potential clients. They may also sell counterfeit cigarettes to unsuspecting victims. Cigarettes are also trafficked on the Darknet. What is currently unknown is the scope of these operations, on both the visible web and the invisible web.

WILDLIFE TRAFFICKING

Fauna (animal species in a particular region) and **flora** (plant species in a particular region) trafficking, also known as **wildlife trafficking**, refers to the illegal capture, trade, and possession of endangered species, protected wildlife, and parts and products thereof.[183] This form of trafficking can include live plants, animals, parts of animals, and products of animals and plants. The demand for wildlife trafficking persists due to wildlife's use as "food, fodder (i.e., feed for livestock), fashion (e.g., leather and fur clothing), collections (e.g., individual private collections and museums), sport (e.g., falconry and trophy hunting), healthcare (e.g., medicinal purposes), religion (e.g., [religious rituals involving] animals and plants and [their] derivatives . . .), fuel (e.g., wood for cooking), and building materials (e.g., timber to create furniture)."[184] Apart from damage to the ecosystem, the illegal import of wildlife can lead to the spread of infectious diseases. This danger has been highlighted with the seizure of wildlife carrying infectious diseases (e.g., in 2004, two eagles that were carrying the H5N1 virus were seized in Belgium).[185]

United States law enforcement investigations have revealed the use of the Internet by wildlife traffickers to facilitate operations. Christopher Hayes was arrested and subsequently pleaded guilty in 2015 to wildlife trafficking, and more specifically, trafficking in elephant ivory, black rhinoceros horns (and objects made from it), and a form of protected coral.[186] He advertised these wildlife products on his Facebook page. His arrest was part of the ongoing *Operation Crash*, led by the U.S. Fish and Wildlife Service, which also targeted others engaging in online wildlife trafficking: Michael Slattery (rhino horns); Qing Wang (rhino horns and elephant ivory); Jimmy and Felix Kha (rhino horns); Jin Zhao Feng (black rhino horn); David Hausman (rhino heads and rhino horns, including black rhino horns); Shusen Wei (rhino horns); Zhifei Li (rhino horns and objects made from elephant ivory and rhino horns); and Jarrod Wade Steffen (rhino horns).[187] Although it is not a crime to possess antique rhinoceros horns, possession is allowed only in limited circumstances, requires a permit, and is strictly regulated by the U.S. Endangered Species Act of 1973. Another operation, *Operation Cyberwild*, targeted Internet advertisements placed by sellers of wildlife, wildlife parts, and wildlife objects in California and Nevada.[188] Agents recovered "live endangered fish, protected migratory birds, and all kinds of products made from endangered animals, including an elephant foot, skins from a tiger, a polar bear, a leopard and other animals, plus some boots made of the skin of threatened sea turtles."[189]

Traffickers have used both online platforms and international postal and courier systems to commit criminal offenses. The postal system is used to transport wildlife, wildlife parts, and wildlife products.[190] The means through which wildlife and wildlife products trafficking occurs are through mail, in person, or through some mode of transportation (e.g., bus, car, plane, ship, and train).[191] Elephant ivory, which is the most trafficked wildlife object online (at least according to available evidence), enters and exits the country through legal imports and exports, illegally through airports by individuals, legally and illegally through postal and courier services, and illegally through container ports.[192]

The Lacey Act of 1900 (16 U.S.C. §§ 3371-3378) prohibits the trafficking of wildlife. Under 16 U.S.C. § 3372(a)(1), it is considered illegal "to import, export, transport, sell, receive, acquire, or purchase any fish or wildlife or plant taken, possessed, transported, or sold in violation of any law, treaty, or regulation of the United States or in violation of any Indian tribal law." It is also considered unlawful under 16 U.S.C. § 3372(a)(2) "to import, export, transport, sell, receive, acquire, or purchase in interstate or foreign commerce . . . any fish or wildlife taken, possessed, transported, or sold in violation of any law or regulation of any State or in violation of any foreign law; . . . any plant taken, possessed, transported, or sold in violation of any law or regulation of any State; . . . any prohibited wildlife species." The 1973 Convention on the International Trade in Endangered Species of Wild Fauna and Flora (CITES) also criminalizes wildlife trafficking. This convention is legally binding for signatories and regulates the trade of these species in a manner that does not threaten their existence. Appendix I of CITES contains animals and plants that are threatened by extinction. The species listed in this appendix cannot be part of international trade, with very limited exceptions. Appendix II of CITES contains species that are not yet threatened by extinction but may become extinct if their trade is not closely monitored and controlled by authorities. Currently, 171 countries are parties to CITES. Traffickers can build a clientele base from anywhere in the world. An investigation of several New Zealand websites revealed the sale of Appendix I species, such as elephant products (ivory), turtle products, and big cat (e.g., tigers) products, and Appendix II species, including reptile (e.g., crocodiles/alligators/pythons) and bear products.[193]

In 2014, an investigation conducted by the International Fund for Animal Welfare (IFAW) revealed that over 33,000 endangered wildlife species, wildlife parts, and wildlife products listed under Appendix I and II of the CITES were being sold online.[194] The IFAW monitored over 280 online sites and 9,482 advertisements from these sites.[195] Of the 9,482 ads surveyed, 7,436 ads included species listed under Appendix I of CITES and 2,046 ads included species listed under Appendix II.[196] Ultimately, the investigation revealed that 54 percent of the wildlife advertisements were for live animals and 46 percent were for wildlife parts and products (see Table 13-1 for the type of wildlife sold on these sites and the countries from which they were sold).

Between November 2004 and January 2005, the IFAW UK monitored the Internet for the sale of wildlife, wildlife parts, and wildlife products in online advertisements.[197] The investigation revealed over 9,000 such items for sale.[198] Some of the items sold via online auction sites, classified advertisement websites, chat rooms, and wholesale and private seller websites included wild cats (e.g., Siberian tigers and lions) and wild cat products

Table 13-1 Type of Wildlife Sold Online and Countries From Which Wildlife Sold

Bahrain	exotic birds and primates
Belarus	exotic birds (i.e., Amazon parrots and macaw) and bears (i.e., polar bear skin)
Belgium	ivory and suspected ivory; exotic birds; owls; turtles and tortoises; snakes; frogs; birds of prey; crocodiles and alligators; rheas; sharks; and whales
Canada	exotic birds; ivory and suspected ivory; bears (e.g., polar bear and grizzly bear skins and rugs); cats; snakes; crocodiles and alligators; whales; and elephants (not ivory)
China	ivory and suspected ivory; rhinoceros (e.g., horns); turtles and tortoises; exotic birds; cats (e.g., snow leopard teeth and tiger claws); bears; antelopes; crocodiles and alligators; lizards; sharks; pangolins; snakes; primates; whales; and hippopotamuses
France	ivory and suspected ivory; exotic birds; turtles and tortoises; cats; snakes; birds of prey; wolves; owls; whales; sharks; sturgeons; amphibians; primates; crocodiles and alligators; rhinoceros; and elephant (not ivory)
Germany	turtles and tortoises; exotic birds; snakes (e.g., emerald tree boa); frogs (e.g., poison dart frog); cats; ivory and suspected ivory; owls; birds of prey; lizards; giant clams; wolves; crocodiles and alligators; bears; newts; elephant (non-ivory); primates; stony corals; and seahorses
Kazakhstan	exotic birds (e.g., Amazon parrots, macaws, and cockatoos); lizards; and turtles and tortoises
Kuwait	exotic birds; birds of prey; and cats
Netherlands	frogs (e.g., phantasmal poison frog and various types of poison dart frogs); lizards (e.g., Madagascar giant day gecko and panther chameleons); exotic birds (e.g., hornbills and toucans); birds of prey; turtles and tortoises; ivory and suspected ivory; owls; cats; seahorses; sharks; snakes; crocodiles and alligators; wolves; bears; rheas; hippopotamus; finches; giant clams; whales; primates; and walruses
Poland	turtles and tortoises; primates (e.g., common marmosets, Barbary apes, savanna and patas monkeys); exotic birds (e.g., horned parakeets and Bali starling); wolves (e.g., fur coats); fish; birds of prey; ivory and suspected ivory; owls; bears; cats; and sturgeons
Qatar	cats and exotic birds
Russia	exotic birds (e.g., Amazons, macaws, and cockatoos); cats (e.g., tigers, jaguars, panthers, and pumas); primates (e.g., chimpanzees, orangutan, marmosets, and mangabeys); ivory and suspected ivory; crocodiles and alligators; antelopes (e.g., Saiga antelope); turtles and tortoises; owls; bears (e.g., polar bear products and Asian black bears); snakes; birds of prey (e.g., peregrine and saker falcons); lizards; conches; red panda; frogs; newts; rhinoceros; giant clams; and other species
Ukraine	exotic birds (e.g., macaws and cockatoos); primates (e.g., lorises, tamarins, condensed these); ivory and suspected ivory; pheasants; cats (e.g., caracal, ocelots, and tigers); cranes; birds of prey; crocodiles and alligators (e.g., Nile crocodiles); otters; snakes; bears (e.g., Asian black bears); turtles and tortoises; pelicans; conches; geese; whales; bustards; wallabies; penguins; and wolves
United Arab Emirates	exotic birds; primates (e.g., hamadryas baboons and chimpanzees); antelopes (e.g., Arabian oryx and gazelles); birds of prey; cats (e.g., cheetahs, caracals, leopards, and tigers); snakes; ibis; owls; mynas; foxes; sturgeons; and crocodiles and alligators
United Kingdom	ivory and suspected ivory; turtles and tortoises; owls; cats (e.g., leopard skin clothing and rugs); exotic birds; crocodiles and alligators; elephants (non-ivory); primates; birds of prey; bears; sharks; rhinoceros; whales; lizards; snakes; and otters

Source: International Fund for Animal Welfare, *Wanted—Dead or Alive: Exposing Online Wildlife Trade*, 2014, 26–57, http://www.ifaw.org/sites/default/files/IFAW-Wanted-Dead-or-Alive-Exposing-Online-Wildlife-Trade-2014.pdf.

(e.g., claws, skulls, and skin), shark fins, elephant products (e.g., skin and ivory), primates (e.g., lemurs and gibbons), turtle and tortoise shells, and other reptile products (e.g., products from crocodiles, alligators, and cobras).[199] Lack of effective oversight and monitoring of sites that facilitate wildlife trafficking was noted in other studies, such as those conducted by the IFAW in March 2004.[200] This was also revealed in the 2004 report by the Royal Society for the Protection of Animals (RSPCA) in the United Kingdom titled *Handle with Care.*[201]

A 2008 investigation of the IFAW revealed that 183 websites in 11 countries offered the sale of wildlife, wildlife products, and wildlife parts.[202] Within these websites, 7,122 advertisements, communiqués, and auctions were found that sold a variety of wildlife and wildlife products belonging to species listed under Appendixes I and II of the CITES (see Table 13-2 for the type of wildlife sold on these sites and the countries from which they were sold).[203]

Special themed websites with chat rooms have advertised the sale of CITES-listed species.[204] Additionally, wildlife objects have been illegally sold on online auction websites. Online auction sites are used by individual cybercriminals and organized cybercriminals because they "are always open, unregulated, and anonymous (anybody with an e-mail account can sign up to become a bidder), which makes them a conduit for illicit trade."[205] In Canada, law enforcement traced seized wildlife objects to an Internet auction business located in New York City.[206] An investigation conducted by the IFAW in 2014 focused on tracking ivory sales on two auction aggregator sites, LiveAuctioneers.com and AuctionZip.com (other aggregator auction sites, such as OnlineAuction.com, Invaluable.com, The-Saleroom.com, and online market platforms like Amazon and eBay were excluded from the investigation).[207] Tracking 340 online auction sites, the

Table 13-2 Type of Wildlife Sold Online and Countries From Which Wildlife Sold

Country	Wildlife, Wildlife Part, or Wildlife Product
Argentina	reptiles; elephants; several other species (not specifically identified in the report)
Australia	birds; elephants; ungulate; reptiles; sharks; marsupials; big cats; tapir; caviar; otters
Canada	elephants; birds; big cats; caviar; primates; reptiles; sharks; bears; rhinoceroses
China	elephants; reptiles; big cats; birds; rhinoceroses; caviar; primates
Colombia	primates; birds
France	elephants; big cats; birds; caviar; reptiles; rhinoceroses; oryx; sharks; primates; and addax
Germany	elephants; birds; caviar; big cats; primates; reptiles; miscellaneous (several other species)
Mexico	birds; elephants; several other species (not specifically identified in the report)
Russia	birds; elephants; big cats; reptiles; caviar; primates; rhinoceroses; bears; sharks; miscellaneous (several other species)
United Kingdom	elephants; birds; reptiles; big cats; primates; and sharks
United States	elephants; birds; big cats; primates; reptiles; rhinoceroses

Source: International Fund for Animal Welfare, *Killing with Keystrokes*, 2008, 22–38, http://www.ifaw.org/sites/default/files/Killing%20with%20Keystrokes.pdf

IFAW investigation found that 4,186 ivory products were being sold on online auction sites.[208] Sellers in China primarily provided a social media handle from WeChat as a way to be contacted by buyers in order to engage in private communications.[209] The above-mentioned investigations by the IFAW and the RSPCA focused on well-known publicly available websites. These websites are only a fraction of those on the World Wide Web. It is entirely possible that criminals are using password-protected sites and other sites on the deep web (potentially even Darknet) to engage in wildlife trafficking.

With respect to the wildlife trafficking via the Internet, the following measures should be implemented: (1) existing national and international laws regulating wildlife and wildlife products need to be amended to include online trade; (2) an e-permit system needs to be created by all signatories of the CITES; (3) these e-permits should be logged in a CITES database, which countries can check to confirm authenticity.[210] There are several challenges in identifying wildlife trafficking. Gaps in national and international legislation on wildlife trafficking and the challenges in enforcing these laws have created an environment in which criminals can engage in this form of high reward illicit activity with a low risk of detection by authorities. The sale of wildlife online further complicates issues by failing to require sellers to prove that their wildlife products comply with national and international laws.[211] Currently, those who post wildlife and wildlife products online are largely not required to prove that they are legally able to do so. An exception to this is the Czech Republic. It has created an obligation for an online seller of wildlife or wildlife objects to provide valid CITES documentation with the sale—an e-permit issued by the Czech CITES Management Authorities.[212] Sellers in the Czech Republic are required to inform buyers of existing regulations and obligations (e.g., to register specimens), and website owners and operators in the country are required to ensure that the content posted on their site complies with existing regulatory requirements and that all obligatory information is posted.[213] Other countries should similarly mandate that proper documentation be posted on sites where the buying and selling of wildlife products and parts occurs; at the very least, information should be posted warning users of the potential illegality of conduct concerning the buying and selling of wildlife, wildlife parts, and wildlife products.[214]

Website owners and operators in many countries cannot be legally required to cooperate with law enforcement authorities (unless pursuant to existing laws) or develop policies criminalizing the sale of wildlife and wildlife products due to existing laws that do not hold Internet Service Providers (ISPs) responsible for content. While obligations cannot be imposed on ISPs in several countries, the ISPs can be encouraged to adopt policies that prohibit the sale of wildlife and wildlife products on their website and remove advertisements selling wildlife and wildlife products that are not in accordance with the law. In fact, in 2007, eBay created a policy that prohibits the trade of elephant ivory on its sites.[215] Like eBay, Craigslist does not allow the sale of animal parts on the site; however, it does allow individuals to sell pets.[216] Despite this policy, the IFAW found that there were 122 listings for CITES species on Craigslist.[217] Scammers also use these sites to trick users into paying for animals or animal products that are never delivered.[218] Some websites advertise being able to ship wildlife to a buyer's doorstep. A case in point is the Russian website Animal simport.ru.[219]

Another study conducted by the IFAW examining the selling of endangered species online found 282 wildlife listings on 14 websites, many of them on eBay Australia.[220] The investigation found listings for elephant ivory on eBay sites in Australia, Canada, China,

France, Germany, the Netherlands, the United Kingdom, and the United States.[221] These sites had policies prohibiting the sale of wildlife and parts of wildlife that are protected under CITES. Even when policies prohibit such sales, enforcing the policies proves difficult. The burden of enforcement lies primarily with the public, which reports violations of Terms of Service to the websites.

The IFAW recommends a quick response to any illicit activity concerning wildlife that is brought to website owners' and operators' attention.[222] The reality is that the takedown policies of sites are neither adequately not swiftly enforced (with limited exceptions). For example, the takedown policy of eBay France was not followed after illicit wildlife items were reported by the IFAW. Despite eBay France's having a policy in place stating that illicit ivory products would be removed within twenty-four to thirty-six hours of reporting, the IFAW found that the listings with the reported 200 ivory items had not been removed, even after the allotted time frame had lapsed.[223] By contrast, eBay Germany quickly removed the reported items pursuant to its policy.[224] Like eBay France, the eBay UK policy is to remove reported prohibited items within twenty-four to thirty-six hours; nevertheless, after forty-eight hours, the IFAW observed that 75 out of the 105 prohibited items reported were still listed on eBay.[225] The IFAW also found that a prohibited item that was reported was reposted under a different description after the listing was taken down by eBay. This calls into question the efficacy of the takedown policy if follow-up monitoring of the seller does not occur to ensure that the seller does not simply repost the item. These sites should devote resources to effectively monitoring listings.[226] This is a recommendation that the IFAW has repeatedly identified in its reports on online wildlife trafficking. Finally, filters should be used to detect wildlife trafficking online. Even though certain websites use filters to detect wildlife trafficking, sellers of illicit items on these sites have found ways to evade detection, such as misspelling or using creative words for their goods, for example, for the word "ivory," a seller might use "ivoree," "ivori," "i v o ry" or "iv*ry."[227] The recommendation by the IFAW is to develop new filters for these sites in order to detect wildlife trafficking.[228]

CONTROLLING ORGANIZED CYBERCRIME

Law enforcement authorities strive to keep up with criminals' use of rapid and secure means of communicating with each other and sharing information. Authorities should be well trained in the methods, along with how to conduct online investigations of such activities. The training programs should include information about the different types of organized cybercrime activities perpetrated online, how to detect organized cybercriminals, and the ways to identify victims. Training law enforcement agencies in organized cybercrime activities is essential to combating this threat.

Along with law enforcement agencies, non-governmental organizations (NGOs), private organizations, and the public should be educated on organized cybercrime, especially since uncovering many of these crimes relies on the public's reporting them. Given the global nature of this crime, international cooperation is critical. Here, law enforcement agencies need to foster and build relations with national and international agencies that have a role in organized crime and different forms of trafficking. Furthermore, legislation among nations should be harmonized to ensure the flow of information and sharing of evidence in cross-border cases for use in domestic courts.

Even with these laws in place, the reality is that there is a need for better enforcement of existing regulations targeting organized cybercriminals and traffickers online. Enforcing these laws can serve to deter illicit behavior. Enforcement ensures that the perpetrators of these crimes are punished. Such punishment should be visible to deter future criminals, cybercriminals, organized cybercriminals, and organized criminals from engaging in similar conduct. Certain crimes have severe penalties but lack the appropriate enforcement, leading to few prosecutions. This means that certainty in punishment is lacking. And yet, other forms of trafficking (e.g., cigarette trafficking) do not even have severe penalties, sending the message to those engaging in this conduct that it is a high reward and low risk crime.

CASE STUDY

Suzie, a fifteen-year-old girl, goes to the mall one day and is approached by an eighteen-year-old boy, Danny, who tells her she is beautiful. This is the first time a boy has called her beautiful. In fact, in school she is often ridiculed and bullied by her peers. Danny asks for her number and calls her later on that same day. During the call, he asks to meet with her the next day. When Danny meets her, he brings her a gift and tells her she is special. They start to spend increasingly more time together, continually texting and calling each other in between their physical meetings. Suzie finds herself spending less and less time with her friends and family. She falls in love with Danny, who constantly showers her with attention and provides her with lavish gifts. As their "relationship" progresses, she is intimate with Danny. Shortly after, their relationship starts to change. Danny becomes angry with her for not immediately returning texts or missed calls. He also informs her of a very difficult situation he is experiencing in an attempt to explain the emotional outbursts. He tells her that he is in serious financial trouble. He then asks her to have sex with someone who he knows who would be willing to give him the money he needs. He assures her that it would only be this one time. Suzie reluctantly agrees, and he expresses his love and gratitude to her. After she engages in sexual intercourse with a stranger, he lavishes her with more affection and tells her how much he loves her. Danny then comes up with another story as to why he needs her to engage in sexual activities with another person. When she refuses, he threatens her with violence, and when this does not work, he physically abuses her until she complies.

1. What measures of control is the perpetrator using?
2. What can be done to prevent girls like Suzie from becoming a victim of human trafficking?

REVIEW QUESTIONS

1. What are the similarities and differences between traditional organized crime groups and organized cybercrime groups?
2. Organized cybercriminals provide a variety of illicit goods and services. Explain three of them.
3. Describe how money laundering occurs online. What are the obstacles to preventing online money laundering?
4. Describe the ways in which drugs are illegally sold online?
5. What illicit activities occur on Darknet?
6. Name and describe the types of human trafficking. In what ways are human trafficking victims advertised and recruited online?
7. What can be done to prevent the sale of organs online?
8. The United States has laws that criminalize the sale of firearms to particular individuals. This chapter showed that firearms are still being obtained by these individuals. How is this occurring? What can be done to prevent this?

9. How are cigarettes trafficked online? What measures are in place to prevent this form of trafficking? Do you think these measures are effective?
10. Wildlife trafficking occurs in a variety of online forums. What measures can be taken to prevent the illicit sale of wildlife?

LAWS

Appendix I of CITES
Appendix II of CITES
Comprehensive Drug Abuse Prevention and Control Act of 1970 (United States)
Controlled Substances Act of 1970 (United States)
Convention on Action against Trafficking in Human Beings of 2005 (Council of Europe)
Convention on the International Trade in Endangered Species of Wild Fauna and Flora (CITES) of 1973
Endangered Species Act of 1973 (United States)
Firearm Owners' Protection Act of 1986 (United States)
Framework Convention on Tobacco Control of 2003 (World Health Organization)
Gun Control Act of 1968 (United States)
Lacey Act of 1990 (United States)
Money Laundering Control Act of 1986 (United States)
Overseas Employment Act of 2013 (Bangladesh)
Prevent All Cigarette Trafficking Act of 2009 (United States)
Racketeer Influenced and Corrupt Organizations (RICO) Act of 1970 (United States)
Trafficking Victims Protection Act of 2000 (United States)
UN Convention against Transnational Organized Crime of 2000
UN Protocol against the Smuggling of Migrants by Land, Sea and Air of 2000
UN Protocol to Prevent, Suppress and Punish Trafficking in Persons of 2000

DEFINITIONS

Bitcoin. A form of digital currency bought and sold outside of the traditional financial regulatory systems.
Bulletproof hosting. A service that allows users to upload content and promises not to remove users' content even if it is illegal.
Centralized digital currency. A centralized digital currency involves a single entity that is responsible for transferring units between users.
Cigarette trafficking. Cigarette trafficking occurs when individuals, groups, or businesses seek to sell cigarettes in a manner that evades existing laws and taxation rates or sell counterfeit cigarettes and cigarettes with counterfeit tax stamps.
Controlled substances. Substances considered to be illegal to possess with the intent to distribute unless this possession and distribution are in accordance with existing laws.
Crime as a service. A variety of services that facilitate virtually any cybercrime.
Crimeware. Malware designed to facilitate a cybercrime and which can be modified to users' needs.
Cryptocurrency. A virtual or digital currency that utilizes cryptography for security reasons.

Cryptoransomware. A form of crimeware designed to encrypt data on victims' systems and extort money from the victims to release information.

Darknet. The term used to describe the underworld of cyberspace due to the illicit activity that occurs there.

Debt bondage. Debt bondage occurs when a trafficker informs a victim that he or she must engage in some form of labor or sexual activities until a debt is paid.

Decentralized digital currency. A form of e-currency distributed peer to peer without third party oversight or interaction in the transfer, enabling them to be bought and sold online outside of the traditional regulatory system. See also *virtual currency*.

Deep web. The deep web includes nonindexed sites that the public cannot reach through search engines on the visible web.

Drug trafficking. The unlawful distribution and sale of drugs in violation of existing national and international laws

Fauna. The animal species in a particular region.

Federal firearms license. In the United States, this license is required to import, manufacture, or sell firearms.

Firearms trafficking. The sale and delivery of firearms in violation of existing laws.

Flora. The plant species in a particular region.

Forced labor. A form of involuntary servitude.

Hidden wikis. Hidden wikis operate as Tor-hidden services and enable users to upload, modify, or delete content anonymously.

Human smuggling. The process of facilitating the illicit entry of a noncitizen or nonpermanent resident into a country for some form of remuneration.

Human trafficking. Inducing, recruiting, harboring, transporting, providing, or obtaining a person by means of fraud, force, or coercion for the purposes of commercial sex or labor.

Labor trafficking. Inducing, recruiting, harboring, transporting, providing, or obtaining a person by means of fraud, force, or coercion for the purposes of labor.

Memex. A deep web search tool created by the Defense Advanced Research Project Agency that targets, among other crimes, the illicit purchasing, selling, and advertising of humans.

Microlaundering. A process whereby criminals launder large amounts of money by engaging in numerous small transactions.

Money laundering. The process whereby criminals conceal and legitimate illicit funds.

Money mule. An individual who obtains and transfers money illegally upon request and payment by other users.

Organized cybercrime group. A structured group of three or more persons that act in concert with the goal of committing a serious cybercrime or cybercrimes for financial gain using the Internet, computers, and related technology.

Organ trafficking. Organ trafficking involves the illicit procurement, sale, and delivery of human organs and body parts.

Organ transplant tourism. The recruitment of poor individuals to provide/supply organs to those in need from a wealthy country in exchange for a fee.

Pay-per-install services. Services that enable users to be paid each time a target downloads certain malware or accesses a site with malware.

Ransomware. A form of crimeware masquerading as a message from an authority which warns a user of the existence of unlicensed applications, child pornography, or other forms of illicit activity on the user's system and demands payment of a fine, threatening arrest for nonpayment.

Schedule I drugs. Drugs listed in the Controlled Substances Act of 1970. Drugs in this schedule have the greatest potential for abuse and are the only drugs listed in the act that have no medical use.

Schedule II drugs. Drugs listed in the Controlled Substances Act of 1970. Drugs in this schedule have a medical use, but those who use these substances are at great risk for abuse of these drugs because their use can result in physical and psychological dependency.

Schedule III drugs. Drugs listed in the Controlled Substances Act of 1970. Drugs in this schedule may possibly lead to moderate and low dependency on drugs by users.

Schedule IV drugs. Drugs listed in the Controlled Substances Act of 1970. Drugs in this schedule have a lower likelihood for abuse and dependency than those listed in Schedule III.

Schedule V drugs. Drugs listed in the Controlled Substances Act of 1970. Drugs in this schedule have the lowest likelihood for abuse and dependency of all the drugs in previous schedules.

Sex trafficking. Sex trafficking involves a coerced third party facilitation of an individual's participation in the illicit sex industry.

Silk Road. An infamous (and now defunct) Darknet drug bazaar.

Tor. Tor (The Onion Router) enables secure communications and information exchange between senders and receivers as these traverse networks.

Virtual currency. A form of e-currency distributed peer to peer without third party oversight or interaction in the transfer, enabling them to be bought and sold online outside of the traditional regulatory system. See also *decentralized digital currency*.

Visible web. The visible web can be accessed by those with an Internet connection and consists of a collection of indexed sites that users can find through search engines.

Wildlife trafficking. The illegal capture, trade, and possession of endangered species, protected wildlife, and parts and products thereof.

ENDNOTES

1. U.S. Attorney's Office, Eastern District of New York, "Eight Members of New York Cell of Cybercrime Organization Indicted in $45 Million Cybercrime Campaign," *Department of Justice*, May 9, 2013, http://www.justice.gov/usao-edny/pr/eight-members-new-york-cell-cybercrime-organization-indicted-45-million-cybercrime.

2. A. Hübner, "Germany Arrests Two Dutch Citizens in Cyber Bank Heist," *Reuters*, May 10, 2013, http://www.reuters.com/article/2013/05/10/us-usa-crime-cybercrime-idUSBRE9480 PZ20130510.

3. J. Lusthaus, "How Organised Is Organised Cybercrime?" *Global Crime* 14, no. 1 (2013): 52–60.

4. See Chapter 3.1, Europol, "The Internet Organised Crime Threat Assessment," accessed August 17, 2016, https://www.europol.europa.eu/iocta/2014/chap-3-1-view1.html.

5. The techniques used to obtain the data that was sold on these sites were from skimmers, social engineering, and unauthorized access to the information.

6. R. Broadhurst, P. Grabosky, M. Alazab, and S. Chon, "Organizations and Cybercrime: An Analysis of the Nature of Groups Engaged in Cyber Crime," *International Journal of Cyber Criminology* 8, no. 1 (2014): 1–20.

7. 18 U.S.C. § 1961(4).

8. Racketeer Influenced and Corrupt Organizations (RICO) Act, 18 U.S.C. § 1961(1).

9. Europol, "Organized Crime Groups Exploiting Hidden Internet in Online Criminal Service Industry," accessed August 17, 2016, https://www.europol.europa.eu/newsletter/organised-crime-groups-exploiting-hidden-internet-online-criminal-service-industry.

10. See Chapter 3.1, Europol, "The Internet Organised Crime Threat Assessment."

11. D. Victor, "Authorities Shut Down Darkode, a Marketplace for Stolen Personal Data," *New York Times*, July 15, 2015, http://www.nytimes.com/2015/07/15/technology/authorities-shut-down-darkode-a-marketplace-for-stolen-personal-data.html?smprod=nytcore-ipad&smid=nytcore-ipad-share&_r=0.

12. FBI, "Cyber Criminal Forum Taken Down," July 2015, https://www.fbi.gov/news/stories/2015/july/cyber-criminal-forum-taken-down/cyber-criminal-forum-taken-down.

13. Bogachev is on the FBI's most wanted cybercriminals list. He is believed to be residing in Russia.

14. FBI, "Cyber's Most Wanted," accessed August 17, 2016, https://www.fbi.gov/wanted/cyber.

15. FBI, "Reveton Ransomware," August 10, 2012, https://www.fbi.gov/news/podcasts/thisweek/reveton-ransomware/view.

16. T. Newcombe, "Wages of Fear," *Government Technology* 27, no. 8 (2014): 46–48; N. MacEwan, "A Tricky Situation: Deception in Cyberspace," *Journal of Criminal Law* 77, no. 5 (2013): 417–432.

17. J. E. Dunn, "Simplocker Ransom Trojan Returns with More Dangerous Encryption," *Techworld*, February 10, 2015," http://www.techworld.com/news/security/simplocker-ransom-trojan-returns-with-more-dangerous-encryption-3597445/.

18. J. Kirk, "Android Botnet Sends SMS Spam through Android Phones," *Computer World*, December 17, 2012, http://www.computerworld.com/article/2494025/malware-vulnerabilities/android-botnet-sends-sms-spam-through--android-phones.html.

19. U.S. Department of the Treasury, *National Money Laundering Risk Assessment, 2015*, December 2015, 63, http://www.treasury.gov/resource-center/terrorist-illicit-finance/Documents/National%20Money%20Laundering%20Risk%20Assessment%20-%2006-12-2015.pdf.

20. U.S. Attorney's Office, Southern District of New York, "Founder of Liberty Reserve Arthur Budovsky Pleads Guilty in Manhattan Federal Court to Laundering Hundreds of Millions of Dollars through His Global Digital Currency Business," January 29, 2016, https://www.justice.gov/usao-sdny/pr/founder-liberty-reserve-arthur-budovsky-pleads-guilty-manhattan-federal-court.

21. See Chapter 12 of this book for further information on this.

22. J. Cosgrave, "Online Gambling: The New Home for Money Launderers?" *CNBC*, April 25, 2014, http://www.cnbc.com/2014/04/25/online-gambling-the-new-home-for-money-launderers.html.

23. Due to the geographic restrictions in physical locations.

24. Drug dependency refers to addiction to a drug; specifically, the body's physical need of a drug.

25. R. W. Wood, "Despite Legal Marijuana Rules in 20 States Feds Won't Play Ball," *Forbes*, October 19, 2013, http://www.forbes.com/sites/robertwood/2013/10/19/despite-legal-marijuana-rules-in-20-states-feds-wont-play-ball/.

26. *United States v. FedEx Corporation, FedEx Express Inc., and FedEx Corporate Services, Inc.*, Indictment No. 14 CR 380 (Northern District Court of California, San Francisco, 2014), 3.

27. Ibid., 5.

28. P. Blumberg, "FedEx Argues US Law Bars Prosecution from Drug Shipments," *Bloomberg*, March 25, 2015, http://www.bloomberg.com/news/articles/2015-03-26/fedex-seeks-dismissal-of-charges-over-web-drugstore-deliveries.

29. Flakka is the street name for a dangerous new synthetic drug known as alpha-PVP. This drug is a synthetic version of cathinone (an amphetamine-like stimulant). The chemicals used are similar to those in bath salts (another synthetic drug). Those who have taken flakka and bath salts have exhibited "bizarre and uncontrollable behavior." J. Firger, "What Is Flakka? Florida's Dangerous New Drug Trend," *CBS News*, April 2, 2015, http://www.cbsnews.com/news/flakka-floridas-dangerous-new-drug-trend/. In the case of flakka, Florida reported that the drug caused "exaggerated strength and dangerous paranoid hallucinations." F. Robles, "Police in Florida Grapple with a Cheap and Dangerous New Drug, *New York Times*, May 24, 2015, http://www.nytimes.com/2015/05/25/us/police-in-florida-grapple-with-flakka-a-cheap-and-dangerous-new-drug.html.

30. U.S. Attorney's Office, Northern District of Illinois, "Suspended North Side Pharmacist Pleads Guilty to Trafficking Counterfeit Viagra," April 2, 2015, http://www.justice.gov/usao-ndil/pr/suspended-north-side-pharmacist-pleads-guilty-trafficking-counterfeit-viagra.

31. See Chapter 12 of this book for further information on this.

32. P. A. Watters, and N. Phair, "Detecting Illicit Drugs on Social Media Using Automated Social Media Intelligence Analysis (ASMIA)," in *Cyberspace Safety and Security* (Fourth International Symposium December 12–13, 2012, *Proceedings*), ed. Y. Xiang, J. Lopez, C.-C. J. Kuo, and W. Zhou (Melbourne, Australia: Springer), 74.

33. M.-H. Maras, "Inside Darknet: The Takedown of Silk Road." *Criminal Justice Matters* 98, no. 1 (2014): 22.

34. NPR, "Going Dark: The Internet behind the Internet," *NPR*, May 25, 2014, http://www.npr.org/sections/alltechconsidered/2014/05/25/315821415/going-dark-the-internet-behind-the-internet.

35. Maras, "Inside Darknet," 22.

36. The veracity of the seller's claim of authenticity was not established.

37. U.S. Attorney's Office, Eastern District of Louisiana, "Leader of Coupon Counterfeiting Ring on Silk Road Websites Pleads Guilty," July 22, 2015, http://www.justice.gov/usao-edla/pr/leader-coupon-counterfeiting-ring-silk-road-websites-pleads-guilty.

38. P. Callan, "Ashley Madison Hack: Costly End of the Affair," *CNN*, August 25, 2015, http://www.cnn.com/2015/08/24/opinions/callan-ashley-madison-hack/.

39. S. Mlot, "Treasure Trove of Ashley Madison Data Dumped Online, *PC Mag*, August 19, 2015, http://www.pcmag.com/article2/0,2817,2489745,00.asp.

40. C. Paton, "Ashley Madison Hack List: How to Check If Your Home Address Is Part of Data," *International Business Times*, August 28, 2015, leakhttp://www.ibtimes.co.uk/ashley-madison-hack-list-how-check-if-your-home-address-part-data-leak-1517487.

41. C. Baraniuk, "Ashley Madison: Two Women Explain How Hack Changed Their Lives," *BBC News*, August 27, 2015, http://www.bbc.com/news/technology-34072762.

42. M.-H. Maras, *Computer Forensics: Cybercriminals, Laws, and Evidence,* 2nd ed. (Burlington, MA: Jones and Bartlett, 2014), 297.

43. M. Chertoff and T. Simon, *The Impact of the Dark Web on Internet Governance and Cyber Security*, Paper Series No. 6, February 2015, Global Commission on Internet Governance, Chatham House, The Royal Institute of International Affairs, 4.

44. In fact, the Tor browser site provides users with tips on how to engage in anonymous browsing.

45. See, for example, https://www.youtube.com/watch?v=NQrUZdsw2hA.

46. A wiki refers to a web application that enables users to upload, modify, or delete content in collaboration with others. A hidden wiki is a wiki that operates as a Tor hidden service.

47. Chapter 3.1, Europol, "The Internet Organised Crime Threat Assessment."

48. EXIF (i.e., exchangeable image file format) data contains information about the camera and potentially global positioning system (GPS) data, such as latitude and longitude of where a picture was taken.

49. See Chapter 3.3, Europol (2014), "The Internet Organised Crime Threat Assessment," accessed August 17, 2016, https://www.europol.europa.eu/iocta/2014/chap-3-3-view1 .html.
50. *United States v. Ross William Ulbricht*, criminal complaint, sworn statement of FBI agent Christopher Tarbell, Southern District Court of New York, 2013; A. Greenberg, "Meet the Dread Pirate Roberts, the Man Behind Booming Black Market Drug Website Silk Road," *Forbes*, September 2, 2013, http://www.forbes.com/sites/andygreenberg/2013/08/14/meet-the-dread-pirate-roberts-the-man-behind-booming-black-market-drug-website-silk-road/; A. Greenberg, "At Least Two Moderators of 'Silk Road 2.0' Drug Site Forums Arrested," *Forbes*, December 20, 2013, http://www.forbes.com/sites/andygreenberg/2013/12/20/at-least-two-moderators-of-the-silk-road-2-0-drug-site-forums-arrested/; A. Greenberg, "Silk Road Creator Ross Ulbricht Sentenced to Life in Prison," *Wired*, May 29, 2015, http://www.wired .com/2015/05/silk-road-creator-ross-ulbricht-sentenced-life-prison/.
51. A criminal enterprise refers to "any individual, partnership, corporation, association, or other legal entity, and any union or group of individuals associated in fact although not a legal entity" 18 U.S.C. § 1961(4).
52. *United States v. Ross William Ulbricht*, government sentencing submission (Southern District Court of New York, 2015), 15.
53. He was twenty-nine years old at the time of his arrest.
54. T. Hume, "How FBI Caught Ross Ulbricht, Alleged Creator of Criminal Marketplace Silk Road," *CNN*, October 5, 2013, http://www.cnn.com/2013/10/04/world/americas /silk-road-ross-ulbricht/.
55. *United States v. Ross William Ulbricht*, government sentencing submission (Southern District Court of New York, 2015), 2–3.
56. Ibid., 13.
57. Ibid., 1.
58. See government argument in this regard. *United States v. Ross William Ulbricht*, government sentencing submission (Southern District Court of New York, 2015), 14.
59. J. Meisner, "Biggest Dealer on Underground Silk Road Given 10 Years in Prison," *Chicago Tribune*, May 29, 2015, http://www.chicagotribune.com/news/local/breaking/ct-silk-road -drug-trafficking-met-20150528-story.html
60. *United States v. Ross William Ulbricht*, 11.
61. In reality, they could, but they would certainly be punished for it.
62. Digital Citizens Alliance, *Busted, but Not Broken: The State of Silk Road and the Darknet Marketplaces*, a Digital Citizens Alliance Investigative Report, 2014, 15.
63. Digital Citizens Alliance, *Darknet Marketplace Watch—Monitoring Sales of Illegal Drugs on the Darknet*, 2014, http://www.digitalcitizensalliance.org/cac/alliance/content.aspx?page=Darknetq 42014.
64. Digital Citizens Alliance, *Darknet Marketplace Watch—Monitoring Sales of Illegal Drugs on the Darknet* (Q1), 2015, http://www.digitalcitizensalliance.org/cac/alliance/content.aspx?page =Darknet.
65. J. Stone, "Agora Shuts Down: Dark Net's Most Popular Drug Site to Update Security as Users Scramble for Bitcoin," *International Business Times*, August 26, 2015, http://www.ibtimes.com /agora-shuts-down-dark-nets-most-popular-drug-site-update-security-users-scramble -2069598.
66. National Human Trafficking Resource Center, *Sex Trafficking*, accessed August 19, 2016, http://www.traffickingresourcecenter.org/type-trafficking/sex-trafficking.
67. U.S. Department of State, *Trafficking in Persons Report 2014: Country Narratives: A-C*, 123, accessed August 19, 2016, http://www.state.gov/documents/organization/226845.pdf.
68. Debt bondage refers to the pledge of an individual to engage in some form of labor or some form of other service in order to repay an existing debt.

69. Section 103(8)(A) of Trafficking Victims Protection Act of 2000.
70. *State v. Juan A. Moreno*, https://www.law.umich.edu/clinical/HuTrafficCases/Pages/CaseDisp.aspx?caseID=735.
71. C. Sarnoff, "Hedge Fund Sex Offender Triggers a New Defense for Pedophiles," *Business Insider*, August 19, 2010, http://www.businessinsider.com/epstein-defense-for-pedophiles-2010-8.
72. Section 103(8)(B) of the Trafficking Victims Protection Act of 2000.
73. M. Latonero, *Human Trafficking Online: The Role of Social Networking Sites and Online Classifieds*, University of Southern California, Center on Communication Leadership and Policy Research Series, September 2011, 18, https://technologyandtrafficking.usc.edu/files/2011/09/HumanTrafficking_FINAL.pdf.
74. S. Stefannizzi, "Measuring the Non-Measurable: Toward the Development of Indicators for Measuring Human Trafficking," in *Measuring Human Trafficking: Complexities and Pitfalls*, ed. Ernesto U. Savona and Sonia Stefanizzi (New York: Springer, 2003), 50.
75. G. Tyldum and A. Brunovskis, "Describing the Unobserved: Methodological Challenges in Empirical Studies on Human Trafficking," *International Migration* 43, nos. 1–2 (2005): 18.
76. A. J. Nichols and E. C. Heil, "Challenges to Identifying and Prosecuting Sex Trafficking Cases in the Midwest United States," *Feminist Criminology* 10, no. 1 (2015): 29.
77. Latonero, *Human Trafficking Online*, 11.
78. Government Accountability Office, *Human Trafficking: Better Data, Strategy, and Reporting Needed to Enhance U.S. Antitrafficking Efforts Abroad*, report to the chairman, Committee on the Judiciary, and the chairman, Committee on International Relations, House of Representatives, GAO-06-825, 20006, 10, http://www.gao.gov/new.items/d06825.pdf.
79. Ibid.
80. Ibid.
81. Ibid., 16.
82. E. K. Hopper, "Underidentification of Human Trafficking Victims in the United States," *Journal of Social Work Research and Evaluation* 5, no. 2 (2004): 125–136; J. Raphael, J. Reichert, and M. Powers, "Pimp Control and Violence: Domestic Sex Trafficking of Chicago Women and Girls," *Women & Criminal Justice* 20, no. 1 (2010): 89–104; Nichols and Heil, "Challenges to Identifying and Prosecuting Sex Trafficking Cases," 11.
83. CBS News, "New Search Engine Exposes the "Dark Web," February 8, 2015, http://www.cbsnews.com/news/new-search-engine-exposes-the-dark-web/; L. Greenemeier, "Human Traffickers Caught on Hidden Internet," *Scientific American*, February 8, 2015, http://www.scientificamerican.com/article/human-traffickers-caught-on-hidden-internet/.
84. K. Zetter, "Darpa Is Developing a Search Engine for the Dark Web," *Wired*, February 10, 2015, http://www.wired.com/2015/02/darpa-memex-dark-web/.
85. Section 102(b)(8) of the Trafficking Victims Protection Act of 2000.
86. Bureau of International Labor Affairs, *Nigeria: Findings on the Worst Forms of Child Labor*, U.S. Department of Labor, accessed May 7, 2016, http://www.dol.gov/ilab/reports/child-labor/nigeria.htm.
87. Section 102(b)(4) of the Trafficking Victims Protection Act of 2000.
88. A. H. Maslow, "A Theory of Human Motivation," *Psychological Review* 50, no. 4 (1943): 370–396.
89. U.S. Department of State, *Trafficking in Persons Report 2014: Country Narratives: J–M*, 232, accessed August 19, 2016, http://www.state.gov/documents/organization/226847.pdf.
90. U.S. Department of State, *Trafficking in Persons Report 2014: Country Narratives: N–S*, 290, accessed August 19, 2016, http://www.state.gov/documents/organization/226848.pdf.
91. A. van den Borne and K. Kloosterboer, eds., *Investigating Exploitation: Research into Trafficking in Children in the Netherlands*, ECPAT Netherlands, 2005, 42, http://www.childtrafficking.com/Docs/stichting_defence_0870.pdf
92. Ibid., 28–29.

93. This information was obtained from the wheel adapted from the Duluth Model Power and Control Wheel by the Domestic Abuse Intervention Project included in the Anti-Trafficking in Persons Division, Office of Refugee Resettlement, U.S. Department of Health and Human Services (HHS), accessed August 19, 2016, http://www.doj.state.wi.us/sites/default/files/ocvs/ht-power-control-wheel.pdf.

94. K. Kim, "Psychological Coercion in the Context of Modern-Day Involuntary Labor: Revisiting United States v. Kozminski and Understanding Human Trafficking" (Loyola Law School Legal Studies, Paper No. 2007-40, 2007), http://www.lexisnexis.com/documents/pdf/20090113050700_large.pdf, in "Psychological Coercion and Human Trafficking: An Application of Biderman's Framework," ed. S. B. Baldwin, A. E. Fehrenbacher, and D. P. Eisenman, *Qualitative Health Research* 25, no. 9 (2014): 1171–1181.

95. A. Biderman, "Communist Attempts to Elicit False Confessions from Air Force Prisoners of War," *Bulletin of the New York Academy of Medicine* 33 (1957): 616–625.

96. Positive reinforcement involves adding a positive stimulus following a desired behavior (e.g., privileges and showing of affection). See Chapter 7 for further information on positive reinforcement.

97. Biderman, "Communist Attempts to Elicit False Confessions," 616–625; Baldwin et al., "Psychological Coercion and Human Trafficking," 1171–1181.

98. S. B. Baldwin, D. P. Eisenman, J. N. Sayles, K. Chuang, and G. Ryan, "Identification of Human Trafficking Victims in Health Care Settings," *Health and Human Rights* 13 (2011): 1–8, http://www.hhrjournal.org/wp-content/uploads/sites/13/2013/07/8-Baldwin.pdf; Baldwin et al., "Psychological Coercion and Human Trafficking," 1172.

99. Baldwin et al., "Psychological Coercion and Human Trafficking," 1173–1177.

100. R. Skinner and C. Maher, *Child Trafficking and Organized Crime: Where Have All the Young Girls Gone?* Youth Advocacy International (YAPI) Resource Paper, 4, accessed August 19, 2016, http://yapi.org/wp-content/uploads/2014/01/report-child-trafficking.pdf; United Nations Global Initiative to Fight Human Trafficking, 017 Workshop, "Technology and Human Trafficking," The Vienna Forum to Fight Human Trafficking, Austria Center Vienna, February 13–15, 2008, UN.GIFT B.P.:017, 2, http://www.unodc.org/documents/human-trafficking/2008/BP017TechnologyandHumanTrafficking.pdf.

101. D. M. Hughes, *The Impact of the Use of New Communications and Information Technologies on Trafficking in Human Beings for Sexual Exploitation: A Study of the Users* (Council of Europe, Strasbourg, France, 2001); T. Buzzell, "The Effects of Sophistication, Access and Monitoring on Use of Pornography in Three Technological Contexts," *Deviant Behavior* 26, no. 2 (2005): 109–132.

102. United Nations Global Initiative to Fight Human Trafficking, "Technology and Human Trafficking."

103. Nichols and Heil, "Challenges to Identifying and Prosecuting Sex Trafficking Cases," 24.

104. United Nations Global Initiative to Fight Human Trafficking, "Technology and Human Trafficking," 4–5; A. Farrell, J. McDevitt, R. Pfeffer, S. Fahy, C. Owens, M. Dank, and W. Adams, *Identifying Challenges to Improve the Investigation and Prosecution of State and Local Human Trafficking Cases* (Washington, DC: National Institute of Justice, 2012); K. Kotrla, "Domestic Minor Sex Trafficking in the United States," *Social Work* 55, no. 2 (2010): 181–187; E. Kunze, "Sex Trafficking via the Internet: How International Agreements Address the Problem and Fail to Go Far Enough," *Journal of High Technology Law* 10, no. 2 (2010): 241–289; J. A. Reid, "Door Wide Shut: Barriers to the Successful Delivery of Victim Services for Domestically Trafficked Minors in a Southern US Metropolitan Area," *Women & Criminal Justice* 20 (2010): 147–166; Nichols and Heil, "Challenges to Identifying and Prosecuting Sex Trafficking Cases," 4–25.

105. Domestic Minor Sex Trafficking: Hearings on H.R. 5575 (2010), Before the Subcommittee on Crime, Terrorism, and Homeland Security of The Committee on The Judiciary House of

Representatives, 111th Congress, Second Session, September 15, 2010, Serial No. 111-146, http://www.gpo.gov/fdsys/pkg/CHRG-111hhrg58250/html/CHRG-111hhrg58250.htm.

106. U.S. Department of State, *Trafficking in Persons Report 2014: Country Narratives: T–Z and Special Case*, 399, accessed August 19, 2016, http://www.state.gov/documents/organization/226849.pdf.

107. S. Turnham and A. Lyon, "Online Sex Ads Complicate Crackdowns on Teen Trafficking," *CNN*, September 15, 2010, http://www.cnn.com/2010/CRIME/09/14/us.craigslist.sex.ads/; Latonero, *Human Trafficking Online*, iv; U.S. Immigration and Customs Enforcement, "Maryland Man Pleads Guilty in Sex Trafficking Conspiracy Involving Three Minor Girls," 2009, https://www.ice.gov/news/releases/maryland-man-pleads-guilty-sex-trafficking-conspiracy-involving-3-minor-girls; K. Poulsen, "Pimps Go Online to Lure Kids into Prostitution," *Wired*, February 25, 2009, http://www.wired.com/2009/02/pimping/; S. Turnham and A. Lyon, "Sold on Craigslist: Critics Say Sex Ad Crackdown Inadequate," *CNN*, August 4, 2010, http://www.cnn.com/2010/CRIME/08/03/ craigslist.sex.ads/.

108. Sharing Electronic Resources and Laws on Crime (SHERLOC), (database), https://www.unodc.org/cld/case-law-doc/traffickingpersonscrimetype/usa/united_states_v_marcus_sewell.html.

109. U.S. Immigration and Customs Enforcement, "New York Man Sentenced to 30 Years for Sex Trafficking of Minors," February 21, 2014, https://www.ice.gov/news/releases/new-york-man-sentenced-30-years-sex-trafficking-minors.

110. A. Sweeney, "Visa, MasterCard: Cards Can't Be Used to Pay for Backpage.com Adult Ads," *Chicago Tribune*, July 1, 2015, http://www.chicagotribune.com/news/ct-sheriff-prostitution-visa-mastercard-met-20150630-story.html; "Credit Card Companies Abandon Backpage.com over Sex Trafficking Complaints," *San Francisco Sun Times*, July 1, 2015, http://sanfrancisco.suntimes.com/sf-business/7/74/203166/credit-card-companies-abandon-backpage-com-over-sex-trafficking-complaints-2.

111. P. M. Zollman, "Sheriff's Backpage Credit Cutoff Backfires; Site Drops Charges for Adult-Services Ads," *AIM Group*, July 9, 2015, http://aimgroup.com/2015/07/09/sheriffs-backpage-credit-cutoff-backfires-site-drops-charges-for-adult-services-ads/; A. Madhani, "Backpage.com Thumbs Nose at Sheriff after Visa, Mastercard Cut Ties," *USAToday*, July 9, 2015, http://www.usatoday.com/story/money/2015/07/09/backpage-free-adult-services-ads-mastercard-visa/29931651/.

112. K. Bellware, "Credit Card Companies Abandon Backpage.com over Sex Trafficking Complaints," *Huffington Post*, July 1, 2015, http://www.huffingtonpost.com/2015/07/01/backpagecom-credit-cards_n_7705708.html.

113. U.S. Department of State, *Trafficking in Persons Report 2014: Country Narratives: N–S*, 324.

114. U.S. Department of State, *Trafficking in Persons Report 2014: Country Narratives: D–I*, 177, accessed August 19, 2016, http://www.state.gov/documents/organization/226846.pdf.

115. U.S. Attorney's Office, Southern District of New York, "Last of 14 Gambino Crime Family Members and Associates Plead Guilty to Racketeering, Murder Conspiracy, Extortion, Sex Trafficking, and Other Crimes," January 10, 2011, https://www.fbi.gov/newyork/press-releases/2011/last-of-14-gambino-crime-family-members-and-associates-plead-guilty-to-racketeering-murder-conspiracy-extortion-sex-trafficking-and-other-crimes/.

116. Nichols and Heil, "Challenges to Identifying and Prosecuting Sex Trafficking Cases," 17.

117. M. Vella and J. Balzan, "Human Traffickers Use Social Media to Advertise Trips to Italy," *MaltaToday*, May 11, 2015, http://www.maltatoday.com.mt/news/national/52783/human_traffickers_use_social_ media_to_advertise_trips_to_italy#.VcaszvlPGFV.

118. P. Kingsley, "People Smugglers Using Facebook to Lure Migrants into 'Italy Trips,'" *Guardian*, May 8, 2015, http://www.theguardian.com/world/2015/may/08/people-smugglers-using-facebook-to-lure-migrants-into-italy-trips.

119. United Nations Global Initiative to Fight Human Trafficking, "Technology and Human Trafficking," 8.

120. U.S. Department of State, *Trafficking in Persons Report 2014: Country Narratives: N–S*, 302.

121. A. P. Sykiotou, *Trafficking in Human Beings: Internet Recruitment* (Council of Europe, Director-ate General of Human Rights and Legal Affairs, 2007); Latonero, *Human Trafficking Online*; S. Sarkar "Use of Technology in Human Trafficking Networks and Sexual Exploitation: A Cross-Sectional Multi-Country Study," *Transnational Social Review: A Social Work Journal* 5, no. 1 (2015): 59.

122. United Nations Global Initiative to Fight Human Trafficking, "Technology and Human Trafficking," 9.

123. S. H. Jackson, "Human Trafficking: Mail Order Bride Abuses," testimony of Suzanne H. Jackson, hearing before the Committee on Foreign Relations, United States Senate, July 13, 2004, 2; United Nations Global Initiative to Fight Human Trafficking, "Technology and Human Trafficking," 9.

124. S. Millar, "Sex Gangs Sell Prostitutes over the Internet," *Guardian*, July 16, 2000, http://www.theguardian.com/technology/2000/jul/16/internetnews.theobserver1; A. O'Neill and A. Richard, *International Trafficking in Women to the United States: A Contemporary Manifestation of Slavery and Organized Crime*, DCI Exceptional Intelligence Analyst Program: An Intelligence Monograph, 1999, 8, https://www.cia.gov/library/center-for-the-study-of-intelligence/csi-publications/books-and-monographs/trafficking.pdf; Jackson, "Human Trafficking: Mail Order Bride Abuses," 2; United Nations Global Initiative to Fight Human Trafficking, "Technology and Human Trafficking," 9.

125. U.S. Department of State, *Trafficking in Persons Report 2014: Country Narratives: T–Z and Special Case*, 408, accessed August 19, 2016, http://www.state.gov/documents/organization/226849.pdf.

126. Council of Europe Document EG-S-NT (2002) 9 rev., *Group of Specialists on the Impact of the Use of New Information Technologies on Trafficking in Human Beings for the Purpose of Sexual Exploitation* (Strasbourg, France, February 17, 2003), 28–29; United Nations Global Initiative to Fight Human Trafficking, "Technology and Human Trafficking," 12.

127. U.S. Department of State, *Trafficking in Persons Report 2014: Country Narratives: J–M*, 277.

128. U.S. Department of State, *Trafficking in Persons Report 2014: Country Narratives: A–C*, 123.

129. Ibid.

130. Ibid.

131. U.S. Department of State, *Trafficking in Persons Report 2014: Country Narratives: A-C*, 147.

132. U.S. Department of State, *Trafficking in Persons Report 2014: Country Narratives: A–C*, 92.

133. For more information, see: http://www.polarisproject.org/what-we-do/data-analysis-program.

134. U.S. Department of State, *Trafficking in Persons Report 2014: Country Narratives: A–C*, 134.

135. United Nations Office on Drugs and Crime, *UNODC on Human Trafficking and Migrant Smuggling*, accessed August 19, 2016, https://www.unodc.org/unodc/human-trafficking/.

136. United Nations Global Initiative to Fight Human Trafficking, "Technology and Human Trafficking," 15.

137. Ibid., 4.

138. A. M. Capron and F. L. Delmonico, "Preventing Trafficking in Organs for Transplantation: An Important Facet of the Fight Against Human Trafficking," *Journal of Human Trafficking* 1, no. 1 (2015): 78.

139. A. Harmon, "Auction for a Son Ebay's Site," *New York Times*, September 3, 1999, http://www.nytimes.com/1999/09/03/us/auction-for-a-kidney-pops-up-on-ebay-s-site.html.

140. Ibid.

141. R. Su, "Man Attempts to Sell Own Kidney on Auction Site to Support Family, Blames High Cost of Living in New Zealand," *International Business Times*, August, 2, 2013, http://www.ibtimes.com.au/man-attempts-sell-own-kidney-auction-site-support-family-blames-high-cost-living-new-zealand-1313956.

142. Ibid.
143. L. Mungin and D. Debucquoy-Dodley, "Man Tries to Sell Stolen Brains on Ebay, Police Say," *CNN*, January 3, 2014, http://www.cnn.com/2014/01/03/us/indianapolis-stolen-brains-ebay/.
144. Ibid.
145. eBay, "Human Remains and Body Parts Policy," accessed August 19, 2016, http://pages.ebay.com/help/policies/remains.html.
146. M.-H. Maras, *Transnational Security* (Boca Raton, FL: CRC Press, 2014), 111.
147. Ibid., 111–112.
148. Capron and Delmonico, "Preventing Trafficking in Organs for Transplantation," 57.
149. Ibid., 58.
150. D. Ghosh, "Kidney Trade Thrives in Bengal," *Times of India*, July 23, 2014, retrieved from http://www.timesofindia.indiatimes.com/toireporter/author-Dwaipayan-Ghosh.cms; Capron and Delmonico, "Preventing Trafficking in Organs for Transplantation," 57–58.
151. Ibid., 58.
152. City of New York, *Point, Click, and Fire: An Investigation of Illegal Online Gun Sales*, December 14, 2011, 6 http://everytown.org/documents/2014/10/point-click-fire.pdf.
153. RFI, "French Police Break Up Online Arms Trafficking Ring," October 8, 2014, http://www.english.rfi.fr/france/20141008-french-police-break-online-arms-trafficking-ring; Euronews, "French Police Foil Online Arms Trafficking Network," October 8, 2014, http://81.92.237.180/2014/10/08/french-police-foil-online-arms-trafficking-network/.
154. *United States v. Ross William Ulbricht*, 2.
155. 18 U.S.C. § 922(a)(8).
156. 18 U.S.C. § 922(g).
157. 18 U.S.C. § 922(n).
158. 18 U.S.C. § 922(x).
159. Mayors Against Illegal Guns, *Felon Seeks Firearm, No Strings Attached*, June 11, 2014, 9, http://everytown.org/documents/2014/10/investigations-of-online-sales.pdf.
160. Ibid., 8.
161. Ibid., 11.
162. U.S. Attorney's Office, Middle District of Alabama, "Montgomery Man Convicted for Illegal Gun Sales On Darknet Sites," June 24, 2015, https://www.atf.gov/news/pr/montgomery-man-convicted-illegal-gun-sales-darknet-sites.
163. See 18 U.S.C. § 921(a)(21)(c).
164. City of New York, *Point, Click, and Fire*, 10.
165. Ibid., 3.
166. Connecticut General Statute 29–33(c), 2011.
167. 18 U.S.C. § 922(a)(2)(A) & 922(3); 27 CFR 178.31.
168. Guidelines for UPS: http://www.ups.com/content/us/en/resources/ship/packaging/guidelines/firearms.html; Guidelines for FedEx: http://www.fedex.com/us/freight/rulestariff/prohibited_articles.html.
169. City of New York, *Point, Click, and Fire*, 8.
170. Mayors Against Illegal Guns, *Felon Seeks Firearm*, 13; City of New York, *Point, Click, and Fire*, 3.
171. New York State, Department of Taxation and Finance, "Cigarette and Tobacco Products Tax," accessed August 19, 2016, http://www.tax.ny.gov/bus/cig/cigidx.htm.
172. "Cigarette Smuggling: The Urge to Smurf," *Economist*, November 24, 2012, http://www.economist.com/news/united-states/21567111-when-government-gets-greedy-some-people-turn-crime-urge-smurf.
173. 18 U.S. Code § 2342(a).
174. 18 U.S. Code § 2344(a).

175. Pursuant to 21 U.S.C. § 841(b), a perpetrator can receive a sentence of life imprisonment for drug trafficking. Under 18 U.S.C § 1591(b), a perpetrator can receive a sentence of life imprisonment for "sex trafficking of children or by force, fraud, or coercion."

176. See Section 1 of PACT.

177. Government Accounting Office, *Illicit Tobacco: Various Schemes Are Used to Evade Taxes and Fees,* report to congressional committees, GAO-11-313, 2011, 17, http://www.gao.gov/new.items/d11313.pdf; see also Government Accounting Office, *Internet Cigarette Sales: Giving ATF Investigative Authority May Improve Reporting and Enforcement,* report to congressional requesters, GAO-02-743, 2002, 18, http://www.gao.gov/new.items/d02743.pdf.

178. See Section 1 of PACT.

179. USPS, "Shipping Restrictions," accessed August 19, 2016, https://www.usps.com/ship/shipping-restrictions.htm.

180. UPS, "Shipping Tobacco," accessed August 19, 2016, http://www.ups.com/tobacco.

181. "US Law Didn't Halt Untaxed Tobacco Sales," *Boston Globe,* December 2, 2013, https://www.bostonglobe.com/news/nation/2013/12/02/law-didn-halt-cigarette-flow-from-tribes/0gLQZPru5w8mBxTc0lfBWN/story.html.

182. For parties to the WHO Convention, see http://www.fctc.org/about-fca/tobacco-control-treaty/latest-ratifications/parties-ratifications-accessions.

183. T. Wyatt, "Exploring the Organization of Russia Far East's Illegal Wildlife Trade: Two Case Studies of the Illegal Fur and Illegal Falcon Trades," *Global Crime* 10, no. 1 (2009): 145.

184. TRAFFIC, *Wildlife Trade: What Is It?* accessed August 19, 2016, http://www.traffic.org/trade/, cited in Maras, *Transnational Security,* 121–122.

185. S. VanBorm et al., "Highly Pathogenic H5N1 Influenza Virus in Smuggled Eagles, Belgium," *Emerging Infectious Diseases* 11, no. 5 (2005): 702–705; International Fund for Animal Welfare, *Click to Delete: Endangered Wildlife for Sale in New Zealand,* 2014, 2, http://www.ifaw.org/sites/default/files/IFAW_Internet%20Trade%20Report_NZ%20web.pdf.

186. U.S. Attorney's Office, Southern District of Florida, "Auction House and Corp. President Plead Guilty to Wildlife Smuggling Conspiracy," January 14, 2015, http://www.justice.gov/usao-sdfl/pr/auction-house-and-corp-president-plead-guilty-wildlife-smuggling-conspiracy.

187. U.S. Fish and Wildlife Service, *Operation Crash,* March 2014, http://www.fws.gov/home/feature/2014/3-31-14-Operation-Crash-Overview.pdf.

188. J. Kandel, "12 Charged in Sales of Endangered Species," *NBC News,* January 6, 2012, http://www.nbclosangeles.com/news/local/Dozen--136824738.html.

189. D. Kuipers, "Operation Cyberwild Busts Internet Endangered Species Sales," *Los Angeles Times,* January 13, 2012, http://articles.latimes.com/2012/jan/13/local/la-me-gs-operation-cyberwild-20120113.

190. International Fund for Animal Welfare, *Caught in the Web: Wildlife Trade on the Internet,* 2005, 23, http://www.ifaw.org/sites/default/files/Report%202005%20Caught%20in%20the%20web%20UK.pdf.

191. INTERPOL Environmental Crime Programme, *Project Web: An Investigation into the Ivory Trade over the Internet within the European Union,* 2013, 20, http://www.ifaw.org/sites/default/files/Project%20Web%20-%20PUBLIC.pdf.

192. Ibid., 6; International Fund for Animal Welfare, *Elephants on the High Street: An Investigation into Ivory Trade in the UK,* 2004, 5–7. http://www.ifaw.org/sites/default/files/Elephants%20on%20the%20high%20street%20an%20investigation%20into%20ivory%20trade%20in%20the%20UK%20-%202004.pdf.

193. International Fund for Animal Welfare, *Click to Delete: Endangered Wildlife for Sale in New Zealand,* 4.

194. International Fund for Animal Welfare, *Wanted—Dead or Alive: Exposing Online Wildlife Trade,* 2014, http://www.ifaw.org/sites/default/files/IFAW-Wanted-Dead-or-Alive-Exposing-Online-Wildlife-Trade-2014.pdf.

195. Ibid., 4.
196. Ibid., 17.
197. International Fund for Animal Welfare, *Caught in the Web: Wildlife Trade on the Internet*, 2.
198. Ibid., 3.
199. Ibid., 2–4.
200. International Fund for Animal Welfare, *Elephants on the High Street*.
201. International Fund for Animal Welfare, *Caught in the Web*, 5.
202. International Fund for Animal Welfare, *Killing with Keystrokes*, 2008, 2, http://www.ifaw.org/sites/default/files/Killing%20with%20Keystrokes.pdf.
203. Ibid.
204. J. Wu, "World Without Borders: Wildlife Trade on the Chinese-Language Internet," *TRAFFIC Bulletin* 21, no. 2 (2007): 75–84.
205. International Fund for Animal Welfare, *Bidding against Survival: The Elephant Poaching Crisis and the Role of Auctions in the U.S. Ivory Market*, 2014, 15, http://www.ifaw.org/sites/default/files/IFAW-Ivory-Auctions-bidding-against-survival-aug-2014_0.pdf.
206. Department of Justice, Office of Public Affairs, "Canadian Antiques Dealer Sentenced to 30 Months in Prison for Smuggling Rhinoceros Horns, Elephant Ivory and Coral," March 25, 2015, http://www.justice.gov/opa/pr/canadian-antiques-dealer-sentenced-30-months-prison-smuggling-rhinoceros-horns-elephant-ivory.
207. Sites beyond the reach of the general public were also excluded from this investigation. International Fund for Animal Welfare, *Bidding Against Survival*, 15.
208. Ibid., 15.
209. International Fund for Animal Welfare, *Wanted—Dead or Alive*, 35.
210. INTERPOL Environmental Crime Programme, *Project Web*, 26.
211. Ibid., 15.
212. Ibid., 16.
213. Ibid., 16.
214. International Fund for Animal Welfare, *Bidding against Survival*, 3.
215. Convention on International Trade in Endangered Species of Fauna and Flora, "Wildlife Trade on the Internet," *CITES Newsletter* 19, no. 6 (2010), https://cites.org/eng/news/world/19/6.php.
216. See Craigslist policy: http://www.craigslist.org/about/prohibited.
217. International Fund for Animal Welfare, *Killing with Keystrokes*, 2008, 21.
218. Ibid., 23.
219. Ibid., 33.
220. International Fund for Animal Welfare, *Click or Delete: Australian Website Selling Endangered Wildlife*, 2014, 3.
221. International Fund for Animal Welfare, *International Survey Bidding for Extinction*, 2007, 5–12, http://www.ifaw.org/sites/default/files/Report%202007%20Bidding%20for%20Extinction.pdf.
222. International Fund for Animal Welfare, *Elephants on the High Street*, 25.
223. International Fund for Animal Welfare, *International Survey Bidding for Extinction*, 8.
224. Ibid., 9.
225. Ibid., 11.
226. Ibid., 16.
227. International Fund for Animal Welfare, *Killing with Keystrokes*, 15.
228. Ibid., 18.

CHAPTER 14

POLITICAL CYBERCRIME

KEYWORDS

Advanced persistent threats
Brinkmanship
Collective punishment
Cyberdefensive tactics
Cyberoffensive tactics
Cyberterrorism
Cybervigilante
Cyberwarfare
Espionage
Extremism
Game theory

Hackback
Hacktivist
Incitement to violence
Just war theory
Left-wing terrorism
Liberalism
Mutually assured
   destruction
Nationalist-separatist
   terrorism
Realism

Religious terrorism
Reprisal
Retorsion
Right-wing terrorism
Security dilemma
Special-interest terrorism
Terrorism
Watering hole attack

The Syrian Electronic Army (SEA) is well known for conducting cyberattacks against U.S. targets, particularly cybervandalism. A recent attack involved the websites the U.S. Marine Corps uses for recruiting. The SEA posted "pictures of people wearing U.S. military uniforms holding signs in front of their faces with short declarations like 'I didn't join the Marine Corps to Fight for al Qaeda in a Syrian civil war.'"[1] It also posted the following message: "The Syrian army should be your ally not your enemy. . . . Refuse your orders and concentrate on the real reason every soldier joins their military, to defend their homeland. You're more than welcome to fight alongside our army rather than against it."[2] The SEA also hacked and defaced the website of the U.S. Army, publicly acknowledging the incident via its Twitter account.[3] The SEA was further responsible for hacking into media websites (e.g., the *New York Times* and *Washington Post*) and social media accounts.[4] An infamous incident of the SEA involved hacking the Twitter account of the Associated Press. The SEA hacked the AP Twitter account and tweeted "Breaking News: two explosions in the White House and Barack Obama is injured."[5] This false post resulted in a dramatic plunge of the

IMAGE 14-1   Screenshot of SEA Website Defacement.

stock market—a staggering $136 billion in losses.[6] The market recovered shortly thereafter, but the incident showed the significant dangers associated with such incidents.[7]

This chapter explores political cybercrime, looking in particular at hacktivism, cyberespionage (for the benefit of a foreign government, foreign instrumentality, or foreign agent), cyberterrorism, and cyberwarfare. Special attention is paid to investigations of recent incidents of foreign nationals stealing trade secrets and engaging in cyberespionage in the United States. The chapter further covers incidents that have been labeled cyberterrorism and measures that have been implemented to deal with cyberterrorism. The chapter concludes by analyzing cyberwarfare, incidents that have been labeled cyberwarfare, and the offensive and defensive measures taken in different countries to protect against cyberwarfare.

TYPES OF POLITICAL CYBERCRIMES

Political cybercrime refers to a cybercrime committed by individuals, groups, and countries in furtherance of some political goal or agenda. Political cybercriminals engage in hacking, malware distribution, denial of service (DoS) attacks, and distributed denial of service (DDoS) attacks, among other cybercrimes, online and on computers and digital devices to interfere with their use. Their targets, tactics, modus operandi, motives, and intent are examined to determine the type of cyberthreat. The tactics, targets, and even modus operandi of political cybercriminals may be similar in nature. What distinguishes these perpetrators is their motive and intent. Political cybercrimes include hacktivism, cyberespionage, cyberterrorism, and cyberwarfare.

HACKTIVISM

Vigilantes seek to right a perceived wrong to society, operating without legal authority. They engage in these acts for a variety personal, political, or ideological reasons.[8] A **cybervigilante** engages in cybercrime in furtherance of self-perceived justice to draw attention to his or her cause. A **hacktivist,** one type of cybervigilante, uses the Internet to gain access or exceed authorized access to a system in order to modify, delete, or render it temporarily or permanently unusable in furtherance of a political goal.

A well-known hacktivist group is Anonymous, a leaderless, diffuse, and loose collective of individuals with a shared vision, ethos, and disdain for authority who engage in acts to protest actions by groups or nations.[9] The individuals in Anonymous join together to conduct operations in response to what they perceive as injustices. Anonymous has engaged in many cyberoperations, one of which (#OpKKK) was launched in 2014 in retaliation for the Ku Klux Klan (KKK), a right-wing terrorist organization that engages in violent campaigns of hatred against its targets, threatening to use force against protesters in Missouri after the *Ferguson* decision,[10] in which a grand jury decided not to press charges against a police officer, Darren Wilson, who shot Michael Brown, an unarmed African American teenager.[11] Specifically, the KKK tweeted, "We will not sit by and allow you to harm our families, communities, property, nor to disrupt our daily lives. Your right to freedom of speech does not give you the right to terrorize citizens. We will use lethal force as provided under Missouri law to defend ourselves."[12] In retaliation, Anonymous hacked the Twitter account of the KKK and revealed the identity of members of the KKK. Along with posting the hashtag #HoodsOff, Anonymous engaged in doxing (publishing personal information for malicious purposes) the KKK, revealing the identity of its members in the St. Louis area.[13] In response, the KKK made the following tweet: "'Our Kommunity is not at all scared of the threats from anonymous. Just try us. You'll regret it. #WhitePrideWorldWide.' Anonymous replied in true vigilante style . . . by taking control of the KKK Twitter account and replacing the logo with its own."[14] The public tweeted its support for this action against the KKK.[15]

The acts that hacktivists engage in have been described by them as a form of civil disobedience. Civil disobedience involves actions that constitute a nonviolent intentional breach of law. This means that those engaged in civil disobedience are willing to accept the consequences for their actions. In fact, protesters have historically engaged in illegal action in protest of what they believe to be an unjust law. They acknowledge, however, that what they are doing is against the law. By contrast, hacktivists view their tactics as a form of legitimate political protest.[16] They claim to engage in cybercrimes to protest corruption, promote transparency in the public and private sector, and advocate for freedom of information irrespective of any copyright. The reality is that the tactics many hacktivists use are

IMAGE 14-2 Screenshot of #OpKKK Tweet.

not similar to lawful offline forms of political protest. Their protests are usually authorized in designated areas and are announced before the protest to minimize disruption of services and activities. These types of protests occur in areas that are open and accessible to the public. The websites and servers targeted are privately owned and not equivalent to those sites used in offline protests. Accordingly, this cannot be considered a form of legitimate protest, as it does not occur in a public space but on private property to which authority for access was not granted.

The following cybercrimes that hacktivists engage in have been equated with online civil disobedience: website defacement, redirecting websites, blockades, e-mail campaigns, malware distribution, and data theft and disclosure. Website defacement, a form of cybervandalism, cannot be considered a legitimate form of protest. It is akin to a real-world protester going up to a building and spraying graffiti on the walls or taking a sledgehammer to the exterior. This is not a legitimate form of political protest. Why would such destruction online be viewed differently? Another technique used by hacktivists is website redirects. In offline protests, protesters can stop individuals seeking to enter an establishment and divert them through verbal communications. Website redirects are not the same, because a user's ability and choice to access the website are removed.

Hacktivists also conduct blockades to prevent people from accessing and utilizing websites. Blockades occur in the form of a DDoS attack, which prevents legitimate traffic from reaching a site. This act also inconveniences users by preventing them from accessing websites. Hacktivists view DDoS attacks as a form of virtual sit-in,[17] which seek to disrupt normal operations and as a result draw attention to the protester's cause. These cyberattacks can prevent all legitimate access to a site and take it offline for hours, sometimes days. The Electronic Disturbance Theater, a hacktivist group, used a program called FloodNet to target websites in order to prevent legitimate traffic from accessing them.[18] The group remains active today; a recent attack involved cybervandalism of the website of Mexican president Enrique Peña Nieto.[19] Hacktivists view virtual sit-ins as a form of legitimate protest.[20] Anonymous filed a petition with the U.S. government—which did not receive enough signatures—to legalize DDoS attacks (virtual sit-ins) as a form of online protest.[21] The reality is that legal forms of protest online are limited to organizing offline activities, signing online petitions, and promoting awareness of one's cause through websites, blogs, chat rooms, and social media sites.[22] Other nondisruptive actions include setting up websites to distribute information, communicating with other activists, and sending mass e-mails and publications. The latter is legal only if it is not aimed at causing harm to a target.

An illegal e-mail campaign occurred when an Internet service provider (ISP) was targeted for hosting a journal about a terrorist group. Hacktivists launched the campaign against the Institute for Global Communications (IGC) for hosting the *Euskal Herria Journal*, which covered the Basque conflict.[23] Protesters argued that IGC was supporting terrorism because it included information about the Euskadi Ta Askatasuna, or ETA, a terrorist group whose ultimate goal is to create an independent homeland in provinces in Spain and France that make up the Basque region. To get this information taken down from the webpages, protesters conducted mass e-mail campaigns bombarding IGC users to hinder access to servers and flood call and e-mail centers of the ISP with requests for assistance.

Hacktivists also use malware, such as worms and viruses, to protest actions. Antinuclear protesters created and released the WANK worm against the U.S. National Aeronautics and Space Administration.[24] E-mails with attachments infected with viruses were sent to various academic institutions, government agencies, and businesses during the Kosovo conflict.[25] In 2012, a piece of malware, the Shamoon virus, infected thirty thousand computers of a Saudi Arabian oil company, Aramco, overwriting data.[26] A hacktivist group called the Cutting Sword of Justice claimed responsibility for the attack:

> We penetrated a system of Aramco company by using the hacked systems in several countries and then sended [sic] a malicious virus to destroy thirty thousand computers networked in this company. . . .This is a warning to the tyrants of this country and other countries that support such criminal disasters with injustice and oppression . . . We invite all anti-tyranny hacker groups all over the world to join this movement. We want them to support this movement by designing and performing such operations, if they are against tyranny and oppression.[27]

In Qatar, RasGas suffered a similar malware attack two weeks after the Aramco incident.[28]

Finally, hacktivists steal information and widely disseminate it either to publicly expose a group or to promote free access to and sharing of information. For example, in order to protest a bill that sought to legalize illegal immigration profiling, hacktivists gained unauthorized access to the system of the Arizona Department of Public Safety and stole home addresses and Social Security numbers of police officers.[29] Another group utilizing this tactic is Anonymous, which retaliated against the SEA for publishing information revealing individuals in opposition groups to Bashar al-Assad (the president of Syria) by exposing the identities of SEA members. Anonymous also used this tactic in response to an incident that involved Wikileaks (a journalistic organization founded by Julian Assange that is well known for publishing secret information). Wikileaks released secret information between the Department of State and the staff of the U.S. embassies overseas. Following this incident, PayPal, Visa, and MasterCard, which prior to the leaks were processing donations to Wikileaks, withdrew their services from the site. Anonymous subsequently launched DDoS attacks against the websites of these companies. Hacktivists also used this tactic in Operation Payback to actively target those who oppose Internet piracy. This operation was a response to DDoS attacks targeting torrent sites, which were responsible for enabling the uploading, downloading, and sharing of pirated works. In retaliation, Anonymous targeted antipiracy and copyright organizations; namely, the Recording Industry Association of America, Motion Picture Association of America, International Federation of the Phonographic Industry, and British Phonographic Industry.[30]

CYBERESPIONAGE

In 2014, the U.S. Investigative Services, a company that provides employee background investigations for prospective government employees, was hacked. The perpetrators gained access to the personal information, such as date of birth, Social Security number, employment history, criminal history, and information about family and friends of employees of the U.S. Department of Homeland Security, including Customs and Border Protection, Immigration and Customs Enforcement, as well as other federal agencies.[31] After the breach and theft of data, the Office of Personnel Management (OPM) declared that it would not renew its contract with the U.S. Investigative Services.[32] The following year, two OPM hacks exposed information about OPM employees, including employment positions, performance reviews, and the type of training received.[33] Information about family members, friends, and any other people listed as references on security clearance applications was also revealed.[34] The information obtained was subsequently estimated to affect eighteen million individuals, including those that applied but were not hired.[35] Subsequently, class action lawsuits were filed against OPM for failing to deal with the cybersecurity deficiencies identified by the Office of Inspector General before the incidents.[36] China is believed to be linked to the hacking incidents, although the U.S. government did not officially blame China.[37]

The information obtained in the OPM hack could be used in espionage operations. **Espionage** is the practice of spying or using spies, typically by a government, to obtain economic, political, or military information. In 2015, the United States accused Israel of spying on its negotiations concerning Iran's nuclear program and utilizing the information stolen to interfere with the negotiations by using it to undermine talks.[38] Under 18 U.S.C. § 1831, economic espionage occurs when someone knowingly targets or acquires a trade secret to "benefit any foreign government, foreign instrumentality, or foreign agent." Pursuant to 18 U.S.C. § 1839(1), a foreign instrumentality is defined as "any agency, bureau, ministry, component, institution, association, or any legal, commercial, or business organization, corporation, firm, or entity that is substantially owned, controlled, sponsored, commanded, managed, or dominated by a foreign government." Under 18 U.S.C. § 1839(2), a foreign agent is "any officer, employee, proxy, . . . delegate, or representative of a foreign government." A person can be charged with economic espionage even if the theft of a trade secret is not for the benefit of any foreign government, foreign instrumentality, or foreign agent (see Chapter 11).

Cyberespionage is considered a political cybercrime when it occurs for the benefit of a foreign government, foreign instrumentality, or foreign agent. In 2015, five members of the People's Liberation Army of the People's Republic of China—Gu Chunhui, Wang Dong, Sun Kailiang, Wen Xinyu, and Huang Zhenyu—were charged with cyberespionage, among other criminal activities, in the United States.[39] The indictment alleged that the members of the PLA gained unauthorized access to the computer systems of several American companies that were engaged in some form of negotiation, transaction, or venture with state-run companies in China and illicitly obtained trade secrets and other information that would benefit companies owned by China in the negotiations, transactions, or ventures.[40] Cyberespionage undermines national security and economic security because it threatens U.S. businesses and places the economy in jeopardy.

The targets of those engaging in cyberespionage are individuals, corporations, and governments. Those engaging in cyberespionage utilize a variety of tools to obtain trade secrets, one of which is a watering hole attack. A **watering hole attack** is utilized when the target is a particular organization. The cybercriminal monitors and determines the websites most frequented by members of a particular organization and infects those websites with malware in an attempt to gain access to the networks of the organization. Social media websites of businesses and their employees are targeted to obtain information that can be used by those engaging in cyberespionage against their targets. Another tool used to engage in cyberespionage is malware. In 2008, the U.S. Department of Defense suffered a cyberespionage attack by a foreign intelligence agency. The foreign agency infected a flash drive with malware that was subsequently inserted into a laptop at a U.S. military installation located in the Middle East, ultimately spreading to classified and unclassified networks.[41]

In addition to the United States, various Middle Eastern countries have been targeted with malware intended for cyberespionage. In 2011, the Stars malware targeted Iran's nuclear sector.[42] This malware had a dual purpose: to steal data and damage systems. That same year, Duqu infected Iran's nuclear sector. This malware was designed to spy and gather information from infected systems. In 2012, Flame infected systems in several countries in the Middle East and North Africa, including Iran and Syria.[43] Among other systems, Flame infected the machines belonging to the Iranian Oil Ministry and the National Iranian Oil Company and stole and deleted their data. In 2015, Duqu 2.0 targeted Kaspersky Lab and was found in systems in hotels in Europe where the P5+1[44] talks were held.[45]

In the United States, in 1998, "a pattern of probing of computer systems at the Pentagon, NASA, the U.S. Department of Energy, private universities, and research labs" was revealed; this incident, called Moonlight Maze, involved the accessing and viewing of approximately ten thousand files and was traced to Russia by the U.S. Department of Defense (Russia did not claim responsibility for the incident).[46] A cyberespionage ring, Titan Rain, which had targeted military data since 2003, was also uncovered by U.S. authorities.[47] In addition to groups, individuals have also engaged in cyberespionage for the benefit of a foreign government, foreign instrumentality, or foreign agent. For instance, in 2013, Liu Sixing stole files on U.S. military technologies from a U.S. company, L-3, and provided them to the PRC.[48] In 2014, Lockheed Martin's computer network was breached by an owner of an aviation firm in China who intended to steal information about U.S. military aircraft.[49] The Office of the National Counterintelligence Executive revealed that foreign collectors of intelligence targeting the United States were interested in information regarding:[50] information and communication technologies, natural resources, military technologies, and civilian and dual-use technologies, especially in critical infrastructure sectors such as healthcare and energy.

Advanced persistent threats (APTs) refer to groups with both the capability and intent to persistently and effectively target a specific entity. APTs target systems to gain unauthorized access by exploiting vulnerabilities and stealing information. Damage or disruption is not the goal of these cybercrimes, only the theft of data. APTs engage in a multitude of cyberattacks designed to identify vulnerabilities in systems. Once vulnerabilities are identified, various methods are used to exploit them, including hacking, installing malware, and social engineering. The ultimate aim of the cyberattacks is to gain access to systems. Once such access is obtained, the compromised network will be examined and valuable information will be gathered for subsequent use. The malware NetTraveler, launched by an APT, targeted "Tibetan/Uyghur activists, universities, oil industry companies, scientific research centers, private companies, military contractors, and governments and governmental institutions."[51] Targets were infected through spearphishing e-mails that contained malicious Microsoft attachments.

A 2011 report from the Office of the National Counterintelligence Executive concluded that China is a persistent collector of U.S. economic trade secrets.[52] This collection occurs primarily through cyberspace. However, there is a great attribution problem, making it difficult to directly link certain attacks back to China. In 2013, a report by the U.S. China Economic and Security Review Commission revealed that the U.S. industry and a wide range of government and military targets faced repeated exploitation attempts by Chinese hackers.[53] The same holds true for international organizations and nongovernmental groups, including Chinese dissident groups, activists, religious organizations, rights groups, and media institutions.[54] In 2013, a cybersecurity company known as Mandiant released a report that claimed evidence existed showing that China was engaging in a global cyberespionage campaign.[55] Specifically, the report claimed to have evidence that linked Unit 61398 of the People's Liberation Army (the land, sea, and air military units of the People's Republic of China) to cyberespionage attacks against 150 U.S. companies. These attacks were designed to steal economic trade secrets. Russia is also viewed as a persistent collector.[56] Allies have further been accused of espionage (cyber or otherwise). For example, Germany views France and the United States as the main perpetrators of economic espionage, whereas France views China and the United States as the main perpetrators.[57]

The Obama administration implemented a new strategy to combat trade secret theft on February 20, 2013.[58] Internationally, this strategy called for focusing diplomatic efforts on protecting trade secrets overseas, which includes promoting a sustainable coordinated effort to discourage trade secret theft from foreign trade partners. These efforts also include policies and measures designed to ensure adequate protection of trade secrets and the enhancement of national law enforcement agencies. To enhance enforcement operations in cyberespionage, investigations and prosecutions of trade secret theft should be made a top priority. Given that many trade secrets are primarily held by private organizations, this requires cooperation and collaboration between the public and private sectors. Sustained and coordinated international engagement with trading partners is also required. Nationally, the Office of the Director of National Intelligence through the Office of the National Counterintelligence Executive seeks to counter cyberespionage by "sharing threat warnings and awareness information with the private sector."[59]

CYBERTERRORISM

Terrorism refers to engaging in coercive tactics to cause fear, destruction, harm, or death with the intention of effecting some form of change in the government or population in pursuit of a political, ideological, or religious goal.[60] **Religious terrorism** involves the use of coercive acts in pursuit of what individuals believe to be divinely commanded purposes, representing extremists' interpretations of their faith.[61] Al-Qaeda, Al-Qaeda in the Arabian Peninsula (AQAP), Al-Qaeda in the Islamic Maghreb (AQIM), the Islamic State of Iraq and Syria (ISIS or Islamic State), al-Shabaab, Boko Haram, the Lord's Resistance Army, and Kach and Kahane Chai, among others, are examples of religious terrorist groups. These terrorists target all of those who are not part of or who oppose their extremist interpretations of their religion. Apart from religious terrorism, other types of terrorism include left-wing, right-wing, nationalist-separatist, and special-interest terrorism. **Left-wing terrorism** refers to the use of coercive tactics to provoke fear and cause harm or damage with the intention of replacing a capitalist regime with a socialist or communist regime. Terrorist groups that fall under this category are the Shining Path (Peru) and the Revolutionary Armed Forces of Colombia. **Right-wing terrorism** refers to the use of threats or acts of violence against a particular group that is motivated by notions of racial supremacy or antigovernment and antiregulatory beliefs. A group that harbors racial superiority beliefs is the Ku Klux Klan. A U.S. terrorist group that harbors antigovernment beliefs is the Sovereign Citizens Movement. **Nationalist-separatist terrorism** refers to the use of coercive tactics by an ethnic or religious group that believes it is, or in fact is, persecuted by a majority in order to create an independent homeland.[62] Examples of nationalist-separatist terrorist groups are the Continuity Irish Republican Army, Real Irish Republican Army, and ETA (discussed earlier in the chapter). Finally, **special-interest terrorism** refers to the use of coercive tactics in order to resolve a specific issue that a group believes warrants immediate attention.[63] These groups and terrorists engage in acts of violence in order to draw attention and gain publicity for their cause. Special-interest terrorists "occupy the extreme fringes of animal rights, pro-life, environmental, anti-nuclear, and other political and social movements."[64] Examples of special interest terrorists in the United States include the Animal Liberation Front, Earth Liberation Front, and the Army of God.

All types of terrorists utilize the Internet to further their goals. They communicate with likeminded individuals through e-mails, social media, bulletin boards, and chat rooms in order to plan an attack, raise funds for their operations, obtain followers and supporters for their cause, spread propaganda, gain new supplies, receive and give training through videos uploaded on platforms such as YouTube, and engage in psychological warfare against their enemies to demoralize them and show strength in numbers.[65] Primarily, intelligence gathering tactics and undercover investigations have been used to monitor terrorist acts online and ultimately, pursue terrorist prosecutions. The issue with the use of the Internet in facilitating terrorists' operations is that particular acts conducted by them online are not considered criminal in certain countries, making the prevention of these activities particularly challenging. For instance, encouraging terrorism is considered a criminal offense in the United Kingdom. Specifically, Section 1 of the Terrorism Act of 2006 prohibits the publishing of a statement the intention of which is to cause "members of the public to be directly or indirectly encouraged or otherwise induced by the statement to commit, prepare or instigate acts of terrorism or Convention offences; or . . . is reckless as to whether members of the public will be directly or indirectly encouraged or otherwise induced by the statement to commit, prepare or instigate such acts or offences." By contrast, in the United States, encouraging terrorism is not considered a crime; what is considered a crime is **incitement to violence**. Incitement to violence refers to speech that is intended to incite or is likely to incite imminent lawless, violent action. This form of speech is not protected under the First Amendment to the U.S. Constitution.[66]

In countries like the United Kingdom, the dissemination of terrorist publications constitutes a criminal offense. Under Section 2(2) of the Terrorism Act of 2006, the dissemination of terrorist publications includes "distribut[ing] or circulat[ing] a terrorist publication;" "giv[ing], sell[ing] or lend[ing of] such a publication;" "offer[ing] such a publication for sale or loan;" "provid[ing] a service to others that enables them to obtain, read, listen to or look at such a publication, or to acquire it by means of a gift, sale or loan;" "transmit[ting] the contents of such a publication electronically;" or possessing such a publication with the intention of disseminating it. To be charged with this offense pursuant to Section 2(1) of the act, a person either intentionally or recklessly engages in conduct that directly or indirectly encourages or induces "the commission, preparation or instigation of acts of terrorism" or provides "assistance in the commission or preparation of such acts." Moreover, Section 3 of the act criminalizes the encouragement of terrorism and dissemination of terrorist publications online. Alaa Abdullah Esayed was prosecuted pursuant to this act for encouraging terrorism and disseminating terrorist publications online through Twitter and Instagram by sharing photographs, videos, and links to terrorist speeches and propaganda. The government contended that between June 2013 and May 2014, "she intended, or was reckless as to whether, members of the public would be directly or indirectly encouraged or otherwise induced by the statement to commit, prepare or instigate acts of terrorism or convention offences."[67] Through her actions, it was argued that she afforded others with a service that enabled them "to obtain, read, listen to or look at a terrorist publication, by providing links to speeches and other propaganda, and at the time of doing so intended an effect of her conduct to be a direct or indirect encouragement or other inducement to the commission, preparation or instigation of acts of terrorism."[68]

Russia similarly has a law in place that deals with the dissemination of terrorist publications, namely, Federal Law No. 114 FZ on Counteraction of Extremist Activities of 2002. This law criminalizes **extremism**, which is defined as any "activities of organizations or physical persons in planning, organizing, and carrying out acts aimed at inciting national, racial, or religious hatred."[69] This law has been criticized for its use to combat the dissemination of material that *might* incite violence and hatred.[70] In the United States, Section 303 of the Antiterrorism and Effective Death Penalty Act of 1996 criminalizes providing "material support or resources" that are used for violent and nonviolent activities of a designated foreign terrorist organization under Section 302 of the act (see Table 14-1). Tarek Mehanna was charged and convicted under this act for providing material support to terrorists (by, for example, translating jihadi videos into English to reach a wider audience) and conspiracy to kill Americans, among other crimes.[71] His case centered on whether his translations of the jihadi videos could be viewed as an expression of sympathy for the terrorists, which would be protected under the First Amendment to the U.S. Constitution, or whether these translations were intended to provide material support or resources to the terrorists to assist them in their operations (e.g., gaining new recruits), which is not protected. His actions were ultimately viewed as occurring outside of the scope of protection of the U.S. Constitution, and as a result, he was charged and convicted for his crimes.[72]

Terrorists' use of the Internet has been erroneously labeled cyberterrorism. In reality, **cyberterrorism** refers to the use of the Internet to target critical infrastructure with the intention of provoking fear and causing damage, serious bodily harm, or death in order to effect some form of change in the government or population in furtherance of a political, religious, or ideological goal.[73] Pursuant to 42 U.S.C. § 5195c(e), critical infrastructure refers to "systems and assets, whether physical or virtual, so vital to the United States that the incapacity or destruction of such systems and assets would have a debilitating impact on security, national economic security, national public health or safety, or any combination of those matters." The sixteen designated critical infrastructure sectors in the United States are healthcare and public health; banking and finance; food and agriculture; critical manufacturing; transportation systems; nuclear reactors, materials, and waste; dams; defense and industrial bases; emergency services; energy; water; communications; information technology; chemical; government facilities; and even commercial facilities. Significant damage, bodily harm, and even death could occur from targeting any one of the critical infrastructures.

Some critical infrastructure systems are connected to administrative or corporate systems linked to the Internet. These systems are connected for convenience purposes, economic benefits, and to increase processing power capabilities. However, these connections come at a cost—namely, security. Without such connections, potential discussions about critical infrastructure protection would center on the physical security of facilities, the

Table 14-1 U.S. State Department List of Designated Foreign Terrorist Organizations

Abu Nidal Organization (ANO)	Ansar al-Islam (AAI)
Abu Sayyaf Group (ASG)	Continuity Irish Republican Army (CIRA)
Aum Shinrikyo (AUM)	Islamic State of Iraq and the Levant (formerly al-Qa'ida in Iraq)
Basque Fatherland and Liberty (ETA)	Islamic Jihad Union (IJU)
Gama'a al-Islamiyya (Islamic Group) (IG)	Harakat ul-Jihad-i-Islami/Bangladesh (HUJI-B)
HAMAS	al-Shabaab
Harakat ul-Mujahidin (HUM)	Revolutionary Struggle (RS)
Hizballah	Kata'ib Hizballah (KH)
Kahane Chai (Kach)	al-Qa'ida in the Arabian Peninsula (AQAP)
Kurdistan Workers Party (PKK) (Kongra-Gel)	Harakat ul-Jihad-i-Islami (HUJI)
Liberation Tigers of Tamil Eelam (LTTE)	Tehrik-e Taliban Pakistan (TTP)
National Liberation Army (ELN)	Jundallah
Palestine Liberation Front (PLF)	Army of Islam (AOI)
Palestinian Islamic Jihad (PIJ)	Indian Mujahedeen (IM)
Popular Front for the Liberation of Palestine (PFLP)	Jemaah Anshorut Tauhid (JAT)
PFLP-General Command (PFLP-GC)	Abdallah Azzam Brigades (AAB)
Revolutionary Armed Forces of Colombia (FARC)	Haqqani Network (HQN)
Revolutionary People's Liberation Party/Front (DHKP/C)	Ansar al-Dine (AAD)
Shining Path (SL)	Boko Haram
al-Qa'ida (AQ)	Ansaru
Islamic Movement of Uzbekistan (IMU)	al-Mulathamun Battalion
Real Irish Republican Army (RIRA)	Ansar al-Shari'a in Benghazi
Jaish-e-Mohammed (JEM)	Ansar al-Shari'a in Darnah
Lashkar-e Tayyiba (LeT)	Ansar al-Shari'a in Tunisia
Al-Aqsa Martyrs Brigade (AAMB)	ISIL Sinai Province (formally Ansar Bayt al-Maqdis)
Asbat al-Ansar (AAA)	al-Nusrah Front
al-Qaida in the Islamic Maghreb (AQIM)	Mujahidin Shura Council in the Environs of Jerusalem (MSC)
Communist Party of the Philippines/New People's Army (CPP/NPA)	Jaysh Rijal al-Tariq al Naqshabandi (JRTN)
Jemaah Islamiya (JI)	ISIL-Khorasan (ISIL-K)
Lashkar i Jhangvi (LJ)	Islamic State of Iraq and the Levant's Branch in Libya (ISIL-Libya)

Source: U.S. Department of State, *Foreign Terrorist Organizations*, accessed August 21, 2016, http://www.state.gov/j/ct/rls/other/des/123085.htm.

proper vetting of employees, restriction of employee access to systems, and the monitoring of such access. The current trend to connect critical infrastructure systems to administrative or corporate systems linked to the Internet exposes these critical infrastructure systems to unnecessary risks, risks that would not have been present had these systems been air gapped (i.e., physically isolated from unsecured networks, such as the Internet). These risks became evident when the Slammer worm infected a U.S. nuclear power plant in Ohio in 2003.[74]

Given that terrorists (even suicide bombers) have cited political reasons for engaging in terrorism, cyberterrorism is considered a political cybercrime.[75] Like terrorists, an individual, group, or government can engage in cyberterrorism. The determination of whether a person, group, or state engages in acts of cyberterrorism depends on who is classifying them. Unlike terrorism, cyberterrorism has not yet occurred. Although there have been numerous instances of cybertrespass involving critical infrastructure, those cybercrimes were not committed by terrorists. In 2000, a cyberattack by Vitek Boden on the industrial control system of a sewage treatment plant owned by the Maroochy Shire Council in Queensland, Australia, which resulted in hundreds of thousands of gallons of raw sewage leaking into rivers, parks, and grounds near the facility, was erroneously labeled cyberterrorism.[76] Despite Boden's having targeted critical infrastructure and intending to cause harm, his act cannot be labeled an act of cyberterrorism; he did not engage in the act to effect some change in the government or population or for some larger political, religious, or ideological purpose.[77] Instead, he was merely exacting revenge on Maroochy Shire Council for rejecting him for a job he applied for.

Other U.S. critical infrastructures have been targeted by cybercriminals, for example, the emergency services sector. In 2003, Rajib Mitra utilized radio and computer equipment to jam the emergency services radio system in Madison, Wisconsin.[78] Foreign states have also accessed key industrial control systems of the financial, dam, water, and other critical infrastructure sectors.[79] In addition to the direct attacks on these critical infrastructures, other sectors have been found to be vulnerable to cyberattacks, even nuclear facilities. A controlled hacking experiment known as Aurora targeted a replica of the control system of a power plant in Idaho to illustrate that the system's controls could be remotely accessed and altered.[80] Outside of the United States, nuclear facilities have been targeted by malware. Stuxnet, for instance, targeted the industrial control system of an Iranian nuclear facility. This malware enabled the remote control of operations and sought to damage nuclear centrifuges. The malware was distributed through the connection of a device by an employee to a system within the facility. In 2012, Stuxnet infected systems of the U.S. energy industry, particularly Chevron. Chevron did not report any damage because of Stuxnet's design. Specifically, the malware was designed to target the industrial control systems of Iran's nuclear facilities.

Furthermore, the transportation sector has been targeted by cybercriminals and found to be vulnerable to cyberattacks. In the 1990s and 2000s, systems of the Federal Aviation Administration (FAA) were hacked and data was stolen. For example, in 2002, hackers gained unauthorized access to the FAA system and stole airport passenger screening data.[81] The belief is that air traffic control systems are air gapped. However, reports in 2009 and 2010 illustrate that these systems are vulnerable to cyberattacks. In 2009, "a government audit found that some air traffic control systems were vulnerable to cyberattacks and that some support systems had been breached, allowing hackers to access personnel records and network services."[82] In 2010, the Department of Transportation Inspector General reported that not all air traffic control systems had been updated to detect cyberintrusions.[83] Reports have further revealed that airplanes are vulnerable to cyberattacks. Specifically, for certain airplane models (e.g., Boeing company 737), the FAA stated that additional safety standards are required:

> These airplanes will have novel or unusual design features associated with the architecture and connectivity capabilities of the airplanes' computer systems and networks, which may allow access to or by external computer systems and networks and may result in security vulnerabilities to the airplanes' systems. The applicable airworthiness regulations do not contain adequate or appropriate safety standards for this design feature.[84]

The onboard wireless systems on aircraft are also vulnerable to cyberattacks. Cybersecurity measures are needed to prevent aircraft onboard entertainment systems and wired and wireless electronic communications from being exploited by hackers. Others have claimed that airplanes could be subjected to a cyberattack due to a vulnerability in the automatic dependent surveillance–broadcast (ADS-B).[85] Moreover, one hacker, Hugo Teso, claimed at a conference in Amsterdam that he could exploit airline security software using a smartphone application, an Android app known as PlaneSploit.[86] The FAA responded to Teso's claim by stating "the described technique cannot engage or control the aircraft's autopilot system using the (Flight Management System) or prevent a pilot from overriding the autopilot . . . therefore, a hacker cannot obtain 'full control of an aircraft' as the technology consultant has claimed."[87]

CYBERWARFARE

> "[T]o gain a hundred victories in a hundred battles is not the highest excellence; to subjugate the enemy's army without doing battle is the highest of excellence. Warfare is the way of deception. Therefore, if able, appear unable, if active, appear not active, if near, appear far, if far, appear near."[88]
>
> Sun Tzu – *The Art of War*

Some authors believe that non-state actors can engage in **cyberwarfare**.[89] However, non-state actors, at least those without some form of connection or direction by a state, cannot engage in cyberwarfare, because they do not have the legal authority to declare a war. Similar to traditional war, cyberwarfare can only be commenced by legitimate authorities—a state, members of the state, or a state-sponsored individual or entity. Someone acting on his or her own accord or for criminal or terroristic reasons cannot engage in warfare.

The goals of those engaging in cyberwarfare include disrupting normal online operations and assuming the identity and privileges of another person through unauthorized access to systems with the intention of using these privileges to cause harm.[90] A cyberweapon can be used to achieve these goals. Some researchers have argued that to be classified as a cyberweapon, the intent of the perpetrator to use this must be malicious in nature, seeking specifically to cause harm and damage.[91] Cyberwarfare must include tactics that have some form of real-world effect. The tactics may also intend to (but not actually cause) real-world effects. If the effects do not occur because of some form of countermeasure, the actions themselves are still considered a form of cyberwarfare. Like traditional warfare, cyberwarfare is inconsistent and mutable, its effects vary depending on the countermeasures in place and the characteristics of the target and the target's vulnerabilities. That is, if the cyberweapons are dependent on exploiting vulnerabilities that have been fixed or patched by the target, then the cyberweapon is no longer viable. Adjustments need to be made to either bypass existing measures or find new vulnerabilities to exploit. Cyberweapon effects cannot thus be considered separate from adversarial vulnerabilities and the ability to recover from cyberthreats.[92]

A cyberattack conducted through the use of a cyberweapon could potentially amount to an act of war.[93] An act of war must be declared either through words, actions, or both. To amount to cyberwarfare, the provocation has to be hostile and directed at a country, its critical infrastructure, and citizens, and present an imminent likelihood of death or serious injury or damage that threatens national or economic security.

BOX 14-1 THE CASE FOR A CYBERARMS POLICY

Cyberarms control would be difficult with respect to international consensus on what should be classified as a cyberweapon, how cyberarm controls would be implemented, and determining who would be responsible for the control of cyberweapons. The Wassenaar Arrangement on Export Controls for Conventional Arms and Dual-Use Goods and Technologies of 1996 (a nonbinding multilateral agreement of participating states[94] on best practices) is one such attempt at cyberarms control. In 2013, the Wassenaar Arrangement was amended to include restrictions on the use of intrusion software, which is defined as

> software specially designed or modified to avoid detection by 'monitoring tools', or to defeat 'protective countermeasures', of a computer or network capable device, and performing any of the following: . . . a. The extraction of data or information, from a computer or network capable device, or the modification of system or user data; or . . . b. The modification of the standard execution path of a program or process in order to allow the execution of externally provided instructions.[95]

However, the amendment has been widely criticized because of its limitations on dual-use technologies.[96] Indeed, what complicates the development of a cyberarms control policy is the dual use of certain cyberweapons. For instance, keyloggers that can be used as a tool of cyberwarfare are of dual use. Keyloggers can be legally used in the workplace or unbeknownst to users to steal data in order to cause harm. DDoS attacks have also been used by companies to test their own systems' vulnerabilities. Overall, in cyberwarfare, apart from testing systems, some software programs that could be used as weapons in a cyberarsenal have been used for legitimate purposes. Accordingly, any cyberarms control policy would be difficult to enforce given the dual use and prevalence of cyberweapons and the resultant restrictions that would be placed on states to respond with retaliatory cyberattacks.[97] The number, acquisition, development, and testing of cyberweapons cannot be practically regulated.[98] What can be regulated is their use; specifically, restrictions can be made on the use of cyberweapons that do not discriminate and distinguish between civilian and military targets.[99]

Cyberwarfare has not yet occurred. Some researchers, like Thomas Rid, argue that it will not occur.[100] However, Rid's assertions in his book *Cyber War Will Not Take Place* do not adequately support his claim. As a matter of fact, cyberwar *could* take place.[101] Rid points to the consequences of cyberwarfare as a limiting factor in its taking place. This limiting factor has not prevented countries from preparing for such an event by building capacity and infrastructure to launch offensive and defensive tactics in cyberspace. Indeed, countries around the world have sought to bolster **cyberdefensive tactics** in response to cyberattacks on infrastructure or in anticipation of such attacks. Cyberdefense includes the ability to detect vulnerabilities and patch them and detect attempted cyberattacks and mitigate their impact with the necessary human and technical resources. **Cyberoffensive tactics** involve proactive responses designed to penetrate enemy systems and cause harm or damage. If a cyberoffensive is to be launched in response to a cyberattack, the source of the original cyberattack should first be identified. Active threat neutralization is the responsibility of the military.[102] This responsibility in the United States falls on the United States Cyber Command (USCYBERCOM). Each branch of U.S. Armed Forces has its own cybercommand: Fleet Cyber Command (FLTCYBERCOM); Marine Forces Cyber Command (MARFORCYBER); Air Forces Cyber (AFCYBER); and Army Cyber Command (ARCYBER).[103]

Cyberoffensive techniques would require a higher degree of certainty before actions are taken; that is, attribution must be established. This is particularly problematic with political cybercrimes, such as cyberwarfare, when a country is being blamed for an attack. In 2008, Georgia experienced military attacks from Russia, and cyberattacks, which were also believed to originate from Russia.[104] The cyberattacks against Georgia involved DDoS attacks against government, financial, and media websites. Before these attacks occurred, individuals online were encouraged to attack Georgia, and even the cybertools and instructions needed to engage in DDoS attacks were provided. Russia has not claimed responsibility for the cyberattacks on Georgia and has denied involvement in the cyberattacks.[105]

Without attribution, a cyberattack cannot be described as an act of cyberwarfare. If a particular cyberattack could be adequately attributed to a specific nation-state and the harmful intent of the state could be established, the targeted country could respond by contacting the United Nations Security Council and informing it of the incident. Pursuant to Article 36(1) of the UN Charter, the UN Security Council could recommend appropriate response strategies. Countries are obligated to prevent their territory from being used as a staging zone for cybercrime. The original application of this responsibility was in environmental law. Specifically, the International Court of Justice in the *Corfu Channel* case held that states are responsible for preventing transboundary harm from occurring from within their territory.[106] If countries cannot or will not intervene to prevent their country from being used as a safe harbor for cybercriminals, the international community can intervene.

Depending on the circumstances, retaliation may be authorized. Whom does one retaliate against? The only way to answer this question is to identify the perpetrator. If the perpetrators are non-state actors, retaliation on the part of a government outside of legal proceedings in accordance with the target country's laws, international laws, and any agreements with the perpetrator country, violates state sovereignty. Notwithstanding the legal implications, countries can and have turned to self-help measures to deal with political cybercrimes (although countries have not publicly accepted responsibility for these acts), namely, hackback. **Hackback** circumvents existing laws by gaining unauthorized access to third party systems. These actions occur outside of the purview of the criminal justice system. Hackbacks may not target those responsible or may impact more than those responsible. Depending on what and who is attacked, it may amount to **collective punishment**, whereby those targeted are not responsible for the illicit behavior that the hackback was in response to. Ultimately, hackback triggers national and international law violations.

Bolstering cyberdefensive and cyberoffensive capabilities can be seen as a form of self-help of a nation.[107] According to **realism**, states engage in self-help by continuously seeking power and security to advance their own national interests at the expense of other states due to the mistrust of other nations and their intentions.[108] Here, governments are driven to enhance their own cybersecurity capabilities owing to their uncertainty of the intentions of other states in the development of offensive and defensive cybersecurity capabilities. Disinformation can also be spread about cybercapabilities of countries to prevent adversaries from knowing each other's competencies. Tensions often arise between states with comprehensive cybersecurity offensive and defensive capabilities. Consider the following scenario: To enhance cyberoffensive and cyberdefensive capabilities, Country X and Country Y are increasing their cybersecurity infrastructure and human resources by creating new units within government and military organizations, calling for greater education in cyber-related disciplines among the populace, and hiring more individuals in these fields. Both countries are uncertain about the other country's intentions behind these actions and may misinterpret each other's actions as a threat. This state is known as the **security dilemma**, which ultimately holds that countries misinterpret the actions of another nation to improve security as a threat. This misinterpretation can have detrimental consequences if it leads to cyberwarfare.

Cyberwarfare can lead to quick escalation of conflict. Particularly, there is a danger that the use of cyberwarfare tactics may lead to mutually assured destruction and brinkmanship. **Mutually assured destruction** is the doctrine of military strategy holding that the full-scale use of force by two opposing sides effectively results in the destruction of both in an attack. Mutually assured destruction would involve a full-scale use of cyberweapons by defenders and attackers that would cause the annihilation of both parties. **Brinkmanship** refers to the process of engaging in continual escalation of actions to the point of a catastrophic outcome with the intention of gaining a favorable outcome. For this to occur, threats must be credible. In **game theory**, which focuses on elucidating agents' intentions and strategic decisions with respect to their preferences or the perceived utility and costs of particular actions,[109] the game of chicken is an example of brinkmanship:

> Two cars are driving along a single lane on a bridge heading in opposite directions. The best outcome of the game is for the player to continue driving straight ahead while the other player swerves (in order to avoid a crash). To obtain the optimal result, therefore, a grave risk must be taken. The worst case scenario is for neither player to swerve in order to yield the bridge to the other. This would result in a head on collision.[110]

Cyberwarfare can be understood through the lens of game theory. Indeed, cyberwarfare can be viewed as a game played between countries engaging in offensive and defensive tactics. A game that represents this is the Stag Hunt. Two hunters have a choice to hunt either a rabbit or stag in the forest. The rabbit provides a meal for only one of the hunters. If one of the hunters pursues the rabbit, he or she will have enough to eat. The stag cannot be hunted by one person alone. Both hunters can work together and hunt the stag, which will provide enough food for both of them. The best outcome for this particular game is for the two hunters to cooperate. Trust, however, is required. What prevents countries from cooperation is mistrust; this is what drives states to engage in self-help, bolstering their cyberdefensive and cyberoffensive capabilities at the expense of other states.

According to **liberalism**, the international system creates opportunities for states to both cooperate and engage in self-help.[111] It is up to the state to determine whether or not to take advantage of these opportunities. Even though a state prefers transnational security against political cybercrimes that traverse borders (hunting the stag together), it may be distracted on occasion to focus on its own state security (hunting the rabbit) if the intentions of other states are unclear. What one country does is heavily dependent on what the other country does. States are interdependent when it comes to cybersecurity. This requires actions by states that are mutually beneficial to other countries. Given the nature of this threat, mutual security and cooperation should be preferred. In fact, liberalism holds that the preferred strategy is mutual security and cooperation between nations and that international institutions (e.g., the United Nations) can assist in achieving this goal.

Laws of War: Can They Be Applied to Cyberspace?

Pursuant to laws of armed conflict, to be considered cyberwarfare, a cyberattack must be state sponsored and conducted in conjunction with real-world attacks that amount to an armed attack intentionally designed to cause injury, death, or destruction. Traditional warfare is guided by **just war theory**. The laws of war include the justifications that are legally acceptable to engage in war (i.e., the right to go to war, *jus ad bellum*) and the type of conduct in war that is considered acceptable during war (i.e., *jus in bello*). These principles provide guidance as to what justifies the right to go to war and what is ethical conduct during war.

With respect to *jus ad bellum*, to be a just war, a country must engage in it for permissible reasons. Under Article 2(4) of the United Nations Charter, "All Members shall refrain in their international relations from the threat or use of force against the territorial integrity or political independence of any state, or in any other manner inconsistent with the Purposes of the United Nations." States cannot use force against another state unless for self-defense purposes. The right to self-defense is included in Article 51 of the UN Charter:

> Nothing in the present Charter shall impair the inherent right of individual or collective self-defense if an armed attack occurs against a Member of the United Nations, until the Security Council has taken measures necessary to maintain international peace and security. Measures taken by Members in the exercise of this right of self-defense shall be immediately reported to the Security Council and shall not in any way affect the authority and responsibility of the Security Council under the present Charter to take at any time such action as it deems necessary in order to maintain or restore international peace and security.

Self-defense is only authorized for armed attacks.[112] In instances where actions by governments have caused harm but do not amount to an armed attack, a **retorsion** (i.e., legal acts by the harmed country in response to an incident) or a **reprisal** (i.e., illegal acts conducted by a state to obtain justice for an act committed against it) may be taken.[113]

In regard to *jus in bello*, to be a just war, a country must engage in the right conduct during war. Just wars are those in which force is utilized as a last resort. This means that a country should try to utilize other measures before resorting to a cyberattack on a country or at the very least determine that other measures are not viable before resorting to war. *Jus in bello* includes conduct during war that seeks to minimize casualties and suffering. Proportionality in the means used is critical to lessen the consequences of war. The means used are the tactics that a country uses during war. The extent of the force that is justified is directly related to proportionality. The actions taken in response to cyberwarfare must be limited to the actions necessary to stop the cyberattack(s) while minimizing impacts on nonmilitary computers. Discrimination in targets is also crucial; only legitimate targets should be subjected to cyberattacks. The acts of a state thus have to be discriminate and distinct. This means that they have to be designed to deal with a particular target and not targeted at the population as a whole. In cyberspace, it is difficult to distinguish between military and civilian targets.[114] The countermeasures used by a state as a form of self-defense, therefore, can only be directed at those responsible for the act; civilian casualties should be limited to the best of the country's ability.

Due to the need to engage in proportionate and discriminate cyberattacks, ethical guidelines for cyberwarfare are needed to control actions taken within cyberspace. Rules are needed to protect the civilian populations and noncombatants who are largely affected by these actions. An attempt to create these rules is the *Tallinn Manual* (originally titled *Tallinn Manual on the International Law Applicable to Cyber Warfare*). For instance, Rule 43 of the manual prohibits "means or methods of cyberwarfare that are indiscriminate by nature. Means or methods of cyberwarfare are indiscriminate when they cannot be: a) directed at a specific military objective or b) limited in their effects as required by the law of armed conflict and consequently are of a nature to strike military objectives and civilians or civilian objects without distinction." Articles 51(4)(b) and 51(4)(c) of the 1977 Additional Protocol I of the Geneva Convention serve as the legal basis for Rule 43. The *Tallinn Manual* includes a comprehensive analysis of existing laws and their application to cyberwarfare.

BOX 14-2 STUXNET: AN ACT OF CYBERWARFARE?

Some authors, such as Fanelli and Conti, have argued that Stuxnet meets the criteria of distinction of targets and proportionality in response because the malware targeted specific systems, and while causing them to fail, did so with limited, if any, collateral damage. Nonetheless, the spread of Stuxnet could not be controlled, and in the end, it infected computers beyond its intended target, including the computers of the American energy corporation Chevron in 2012. By contrast, what could be controlled was the harm it caused (in other cases, this, of course, depends on the goal of the creator and distributor of the cyberweapon). The issue at hand with Stuxnet is that this malware has not been attributed to a particular nation-state. Use of Stuxnet may well be considered an armed attack; however, the identity of the creators and distributors of this malware have not been established, so the action cannot be classified as an armed attack. Accordingly, the act itself cannot be described as cyberwarfare.

CONTROLLING POLITICAL CYBERCRIME

Political cybercriminals use similar tactics and may even target the same individuals, institutions, and governments; they differ in motive and intent. Critical infrastructure is also targeted by political cybercriminals. Critical infrastructure needs to be protected by both physical security and cybersecurity because it includes sectors so vital to the functioning of society that any damage or destruction to these sectors could have a debilitating impact on a nation. To minimize threats, some (but not all) public and private sectors have disabled users' ability to attach external drives or download items to external drives, revoked local administrator rights to system and data, and blocked access to file-sharing websites (e.g., Dropbox). The best approach, while considered undesirable by critical infrastructure sectors and at the moment unattainable, is to disconnect industrial control systems from other systems. Indeed, the impact of many political cybercrimes can be limited through air gapping. Currently, a more viable approach includes a combination of physical security, personnel security, and cybersecurity measures to protect critical infrastructure.

What should be practiced is what is known as defense in depth, which includes implementing access control systems, firewalls, intrusion detection and intrusion protection systems, and multifactor authentication. In addition to these measures, policies should be implemented and thorough employee background investigations and training should be conducted. Training on "cybersecurity conscious" behavior is particularly important (e.g., avoiding malware, watering hole attacks, and spearphishing). So too is preparedness for major cybersecurity incidents. This involves not only the creation and availability of a plan but also conducting drills and exercises that ensure that the plan is viable and any weaknesses identified are dealt with prior to an incident. The United States has run several preparedness exercises designed to deal with political cybercrimes, some conducted with other countries. For example, the Cyberstorm exercises (Cyberstorm I, II, III, IV, and V) were conducted by the U.S. Department of Homeland Security in order to strengthen the preparedness of the public and private sectors against cyberattacks.[115] These exercises also sought to enhance information sharing between the public sectors (i.e., state, federal, and international) and private sectors. Another exercise, known as Quantum Dawn 2.0, particularly involved the public sector and the financial sector. About fifty financial institutions and governmental organizations (e.g., Department of Homeland Security, Federal Bureau of Investigation, Securities and Exchange Commission, and Department of the Treasury) participated in this exercise.[116] The exercise was a simulated cyberattack on the U.S. financial system, and it provided the industry with an opportunity to run through its response procedures. This exercise demonstrated that information sharing between the private sector and government is one of the most effective ways to combat political and other forms of cybercrimes.

A trend in many organizations is allowing employees to bring their own devices (BYOD) to work for both personal and professional reasons (meaning a person can connect his or her devices to the organization's WiFi for official and unofficial purposes). This poses particular cybersecurity issues depending on the existing protective measures on these devices and employees' behavior when using the devices (i.e., are they cybersecurity conscious?). Another trend is the rapid deployment of Internet of Things (IoT) devices, which puts critical infrastructure sectors that utilize these technologies at risk of cyberthreats (see Chapter 11).

Overall, a sustainable coordinated effort among countries worldwide is needed to deal with political cybercrimes. This requires effective intelligence sharing between government, law enforcement agencies, and the private sector within and between countries. To accomplish this, international training and capacity building to protect against political cybercrimes should be emphasized. Ultimately, the interconnectedness of today's global society mandates a shared responsibility and necessity to collectively solve the cybersecurity issues that threaten U.S. national and economic security. Nowhere is this need more pronounced than in political cybercrime.

CASE STUDY

An attack on one North Atlantic Treaty Organization (NATO) state is considered an attack on all NATO states; "this principle is enshrined in Article 5 of the North Atlantic Treaty."[117] How does this work in cyberspace? What would be needed in order for NATO to retaliate?

REVIEW QUESTIONS

1. What is cybervigilantism? Please provide an example of this.
2. What are the ways in which hacktivism occurs?
3. Is hacktivism a legitimate form of political protest? Why do you think so?
4. Why is cyberespionage considered a political cybercrime?
5. Is terrorists' use of the Internet a form of cyberterrorism? Why do you think so?
6. What are the essential elements that must be present for an act to be considered cyberterrorism?
7. What type of act amounts to war in cyberspace?
8. What acts are considered legitimate during cyberwarfare?
9. What are cyberdefensive and cyberoffensive tactics? When are offensive cyberactions justified?
10. What are the ways in which political cybercrime can be combated?

LAWS

Additional Protocol I of the Geneva Convention of 1977
Antiterrorism and Effective Death Penalty Act of 1996 (United States)
Federal Law No. 114 FZ on Counteraction of Extremist Activities of 2002 (Russia)
First Amendment to the U.S. Constitution (United States)
North Atlantic Treaty of 1949
Terrorism Act of 2006 (United Kingdom)
UN Charter of 1945

DEFINITIONS

Advanced persistent threats. A group with both the capability and intent to persistently and effectively target a specific entity.

Brinkmanship. The process of engaging in continual escalation of actions to the point of a catastrophic outcome with the intention of gaining a favorable outcome.

Collective punishment. Punishment targeted against those who are not responsible for the illicit behavior.

Cyberdefensive tactics. Measures that can detect vulnerabilities and patch them and detect attempted cyberattacks and mitigate their impact with the necessary human and technical resources.

Cyberoffensive tactics. Cyberoffensive tactics involve proactive responses designed to penetrate enemy systems and cause harm or damage.

Cyberterrorism. Cyberterrorism refers to the use of the Internet, computers, and related technology to target critical infrastructure with the intention of provoking fear and causing damage, serious bodily harm, or death in order to effect some form of change in the government or population in furtherance of a political, religious, or ideological goal.

Cybervigilante. One who engages in cybercrime in furtherance of self-perceived justice to draw attention to his or her cause.

Cyberwarfare. Cyberattacks against another nation that amount to an act of force commenced by a country or by someone acting on behalf of the country.

Espionage. The practice of spying or using spies, typically by a government, to obtain economic, political, or military information.

Extremism. Any activity used to plan, organize, and execute acts aimed at inciting national, religious, or racial hatred.

Game theory. Theory focusing on elucidating agents' intentions and strategic decisions with respect to their preferences or the perceived utility and costs of particular actions.

Hackback. A cyberattack that circumvents existing laws by gaining unauthorized access to third party systems. This illicit act is committed in response to a cyberattack and may target parties not responsible for the initial attack.

Hacktivist. One who uses the Internet and digital devices to gain access or exceed authorized access to a system in order to modify, delete, or render temporarily or permanently unusable a system or website in furtherance of a political goal.

Incitement to violence. Speech directed to incite, or which is likely to incite, imminent lawless, violent action. This form of speech is not protected under the First Amendment to the U.S. Constitution.

Just war theory. Traditional warfare is guided by just war theory, which provides guidance to countries on legitimate justifications to go to war (i.e., *jus ad bellum*) and what constitutes ethical conduct during war (i.e., *jus in bello*).

Left-wing terrorism. The use of coercive tactics to provoke fear and cause harm or damage with the intention of replacing a capitalist regime with a socialist or communist regime.

Liberalism. Liberalism holds that the international system creates opportunities for states to both cooperate and engage in self-help and it is up to the state to determine whether or not to take advantage of these opportunities.

Mutually assured destruction. A doctrine of military strategy holding that the full-scale use of force by two opposing sides effectively results in the destruction of both in the attack.

Nationalist-separatist terrorism. The use of coercive tactics by an ethnic or religious group that believes it is persecuted, or actually is persecuted, by a majority in order to create an independent homeland.

Realism. Realism holds that states engage in self-help by continuously seeking power and security to advance their own national interests at the expense of other states due to mistrust of other nations and their intentions.

Religious terrorism. The use of coercive acts in pursuit of what individuals believe to be divinely commanded purposes, representing extremists' interpretations of their faith.

Reprisal. Illegal acts conducted by a state to obtain justice for an attack committed against it.

Retorsion. Legal acts conducted by a harmed country in response to an attack.

Right-wing terrorism. The use of threats or acts of violence against a particular group. Such groups are often motivated by notions of racial supremacy or antigovernment and antiregulatory beliefs.

Security dilemma. The security dilemma ultimately holds that countries misinterpret as a threat the actions of another nation to improve security.

Special-interest terrorism. The use of coercive tactics in order to resolve a specific issue that is believed to warrant immediate attention.

Terrorism. Engagement in coercive tactics in order to cause fear, destruction, harm, or death with the intention of effecting some form of change in the government or population in pursuit of a political, ideological, or religious goal.

Watering hole attack. An attack whereby a cybercriminal monitors and determines the websites most frequented by members of a particular organization and infects those sites with malware in an attempt to gain access to the organization's networks.

ENDNOTES

1. R. Schwartz, "U.S. Confirms Syrian Electronic Army Defaced Marines Website," *ABC News*, September 3, 2013, http://abcnews.go.com/blogs/headlines/2013/09/u-s-confirms-syrian-electronic-army-defaced-marines-com/.

2. J. Bacon, "Pro-Syrian Group Hacks U.S. Marines Website," *USA Today*, September 2, 2013, http://www.usatoday.com/story/news/nation/2013/09/02/marines-hackers-syrian-electronic-army/2755265/.

3. P. Mosendz, "Syrian Electronic Army Claims to Have Hacked U.S. Army Website," *Newsweek*, June 8, 2015, http://www.newsweek.com/syrian-electronic-army-claims-have-hacked-us-army-website-340874; G. Gross, "U.S. Army Website Defaced, and Brought Down," *Computerworld*, June 8, 2015, http://www.computerworld.com/article/2933016/cybercrime-hacking/us-army-website-defaced-and-brought-down.html.

4. J. Bacon, "Pro-Syrian Group Hacks U.S. Marines Website," *USA Today*, September 2, 2013, http://www.usatoday.com/story/news/nation/2013/09/02/marines-hackers-syrian-electronic-army/2755265/; L. Ryan, "Why Terrorists love Twitter," *National Journal*, June 2, 2014, http://www.nationaljournal.com/tech/why-terrorists-love-twitter-20140602.

5. Ryan, "Why Terrorists Love Twitter."

6. E. Lee, "AP Twitter Account Hacked in Market-Moving Attack," *Bloomberg News*, April 24, 2013, http://www.bloomberg.com/news/articles/2013-04-23/dow-jones-drops-recovers-after-false-report-on-ap-twitter-page.

7. M. Fisher, "Syrian Hackers Claim AP Hack That Tipped Stock Market by $136 Billion. Is It Terrorism?" *Washington Post*, April 23, 2013, https://www.washingtonpost.com/news/worldviews/wp/2013/04/23/syrian-hackers-claim-ap-hack-that-tipped-stock-market-by-136-billion-is-it-terrorism/.

8. A. W. Brugess, C. Regehr, and A. R. Roberts, A. R. *Victimology: Theories and Applications* (Burlington, MA: Jones and Bartlett, 2010), 59.

9. G. Coleman, *Hacker, Hoaxer, Whistleblower, Spy: The Many Faces of Anonymous* (New York: Verso, 2014).

10. This is the term used in the media to describe the decision not to indict the police officer responsible for the fatal shooting of Michael Brown. See, for example, E. Grinberg, "Ferguson Decision: What Witnesses Told the Grand Jury," *CNN*, November 26, 2014, http://www.cnn.com/2014/11/25/justice/ferguson-decision-michael-brown-witness-testimony/; BBC News, "Ferguson Decision: Darren Wilson's Testimony," November 25, 2014, http://www.bbc.com/news/world-us-canada-30189966; *Wall Street Journal*, "The Ferguson Decision," November 24, 2014, http://www.wsj.com/articles/the-ferguson-decision-1416890863.

11. J. Chasmar, "Anonymous Seizes KKK's Twitter Account over Ferguson Threats," *Washington Times*, November 17, 2014, http://www.washingtontimes.com/news/2014/nov/17/anonymous-seizes-kkks-twitter-account-over-ferguso/#ixzz3gTAgx7ea.

12. C. Fishwick, "Anonymous Takes Over Ku Klux Klan's Twitter Account," *Guardian*, November 17, 2014, http://www.theguardian.com/technology/2014/nov/17/anonymous-takes-over-ku-klux-klans-twitter-account.

13. L. Suhay, "After Ferguson Threat, Anonymous Removes the KKK's Hoods. Effective?" *Christian Science Monitor*, November 19, 2014," http://www.csmonitor.com/USA/2014/1119/After-Ferguson-threat-Anonymous-removes-the-KKK-s-hoods.-Effective-video.

14. Fishwick, "Anonymous Takes Over Ku Klux Klan's Twitter Account."

15. C. Altus, "#BBCTrending: Anonymous Takes on the Ku Klux Klan," *BBC News*, November 24, 2014, http://www.bbc.com/news/blogs-trending-30105412.

16. L. Goode, "Anonymous and the Political Ethos of Hacktivism," *Popular Communication: The International Journal of Media and Culture* 13, no. 1 (2015): 74–86.

17. T. M. Knapp, "Hacktivism: Political dissent in the final frontier," *New England Law Review* 49, no. 2 (2015): 259–295.

18. D. Denning, "Activism, Hacktivism, and Cyberterrorism: The Internet as a Tool for Influencing Foreign Policy," in *Networks and Netwars: The Future of Terror, Crime, and Militancy*, ed. J. Arquilla and D. Ronfeldt (Santa Monica, CA: Rand Corp., 2001), 264.

19. R. Dominguez, "Entr'actions: From Radical Transparency To Radical Translucency"; J. Geiger, *Entr'acte: Performing Publics, Pervasive Media, and Architecture* (New York: Palgrave-Macmillan, 2015), 73–84.
20. T. M. Knapp, "Hacktivism: Political Dissent in the Final Frontier."
21. A. Jauregui, "Anonymous DDoS Petition: Group Calls on White House to Recognize Distributed Denial of Service as Protest," *Huffington Post*, January 12, 2013, http://www.huffington post.com/2013/01/12/anonymous-ddos-petition-white-house_n_2463009.html.
22. K. Chamberlain, "Redefining Cyberactivism: The Future of Online Project," *Review of Communications* 4, nos. 3–4 (2004): 139–140.
23. Denning, "Activism, Hacktivism, and Cyberterrorism," 270.
24. Ibid., 278.
25. Ibid., 279.
26. N. Perlroth, "In Cyberattack on Saudi Firm, U.S. Sees Iran Firing Back," *New York Times*, October 23, 2012, http://www.nytimes.com/2012/10/24/business/global/cyberattack-on -saudi-oil-firm-disquiets-us.html?_r=0.
27. L. Constantin, "Kill Timer Found in Shamoon Malware Suggests Possible Connection to Saudi Aramco Attack," *ComputerWorld*, August 23, 2012, http://www.computerworld.com.au /article/434428/kill_timer_found_shamoon _malware_suggests_possible_connection_saudi _aramco_attack/.
28. K. Zetter, "Qatari Gas Company Hit with Virus in Wave of Attacks on Energy Companies," *Wired*, August 30, 2012," http://www.wired.com/2012/08/hack-attack-strikes-rasgas/.
29. S. Mansfield-Devine, "Hacktivism: Assessing the Damage," *Network Security* 2011, no. 8 (2011): 6.
30. M. J. Schwartz, "Operation Payback: Feds Charge 13 on Anonymous Attacks," *Information Week*, October 4, 2013, http://www.darkreading.com/attacks-and-breaches/operation -payback-feds-charge-13-on-anonymous-attacks/d/d-id/1111819?.
31. J. Finkle and M. Hosenball, "U.S. Undercover Investigators Among Those Exposed in Data Breach," *Reuters*, August 23, 2014, http://www.reuters.com/article/2014/08/23/us-usa -security-contractor-cyberattack-idUSKBN0GM1TZ20140823.
32. C. Davenport, "USIS Contracts for Federal Background Security Checks Won't Be Renewed," *Washington Post*, September 9, 2014, https://www.washingtonpost.com/business/economy /opm-to-end-usis-contracts-for-background-security-checks/2014/09/09/4fcd490a-3880-11e 4-9c9f-ebb47272e40e_story.html.
33. E. Nakashima, "Chinese Hack of Federal Personnel Files Included Security-Clearance Database," *Washington Post*, June 12, 2015, https://www.washingtonpost.com/world/national -security/chinese-hack-of-government-network-compromises-security-clearance-files/2015/ 06/12/9f91f146-1135-11e5-9726-49d6fa26a8c6_story.html; E. Nakashi, "Hacks of OPM Databases Compromised 22.1 Million People, Federal Authorities Say," *Washington Post*, July 9, 2015, https://www.washingtonpost.com/news/federal-eye/wp/2015/07/09/hack-of-security -clearance-system-affected-21-5-million-people-federal-authorities-say/.
34. E. Nakashima, "U.S. Decides against Publicly Blaming China for Data Hack," *Washington Post*, July 21, 2015, https://www.washingtonpost.com/world/national-security/us-avoids -blaming-china-in-data-theft-seen-as-fair-game-in-espionage/2015/07/21/03779096-2eee -11e5-8353-1215475949f4_story.html.
35. E. Perez and S. Prokupecz, "First on CNN: U.S. Data Hack May Be 4 Times Larger Than the Government Originally Said," *CNN*, June 23, 2015, http://www.cnn.com/2015/06/22/poli tics/ opm-hack-18-million/.
36. J. Ribeir, "OPM Hit by Class-Action Suit over Breach of Federal Employee Data," *Computer World*, June 30, 2015, http://www.computerworld.com/article/2942038/security/opm-hit-by -classac.

37. The White House, Office of the Press Secretary, "Press Briefing by Press Secretary Josh Earnest," September 24, 2105, https://www.whitehouse.gov/the-press-office/2015/09/25/press-briefing-press-secretary-josh-earnest-9242015.

38. J. Borger, M. Zonszein, and S. Siddiquiin, "US Accuses Israel of Spying on Nuclear Talks with Iran," *Guardian*, March 24, 2015, http://www.theguardian.com/world/2015/mar/24/israel-spied-on-us-over-iran-nuclear-talks.

39. FBI, "Cyber's Most Wanted," accessed August 17, 2016, https://www.fbi.gov/wanted/cyber.

40. E. Nakashima and W. Wan, "U.S. Announces First Charges against Foreign Country in Connection with Cyberspying," *Washington Post*, May 19, 2014, https://www.washingtonpost.com/world/national-security/us-to-announce-first-criminal-charges-against-foreign-country-for-cyberspying/2014/05/19/586c9992-df45-11e3-810f-764fe508b82d_story.html.

41. W. J. Lynn, "Defending a New Domain: The Pentagon's Cyberstrategy," *Foreign Affairs*, September/October 2010, https://www.foreignaffairs.com/articles/united-states/2010-09-01/defending-new-domain.

42. T. Erdbrink and J. Warric, "Iran: Country under Attack by Second Computer Virus," *Washington Post*, April 25, 2011, https://www.washingtonpost.com/world/iran-country-under-attack-by-second-computer-virus/2011/04/25/AFudkBjE_story.html.

43. K. Zetter, "Meet 'Flame,' the Massive Spy Malware Infiltrating Iranian Computers," *Wired*, May 28, 2012, http://www.wired.com/2012/05/flame/.

44. The P5+1 is made up of China, France, Russia, the United Kingdom, and the United States, plus Germany.

45. S. Gibbs, "Duqu 2.0: Computer Virus 'Linked to Israel' Found at Iran Nuclear Talks Venue," *Guardian*, June 11, 2015, http://www.theguardian.com/technology/2015/jun/11/duqu-20-computer-virus-with-traces-of-israeli-code-was-used-to-hack-iran-talks.

46. PBS, *Warnings? Cyberwar!*, April 24, 2003, http://www.pbs.org/wgbh/pages/frontline/shows/cyberwar/ warnings/.

47. N. Thornburgh, "Inside the Chinese Hack Attack," *Time*, August 25, 2005, http://content.time.com/time/nation/article/0,8599,1098371,00.html.

48. U.S. Attorney's Office, District of New Jersey, "Former Employee of New Jersey Defense Contractor Sentenced to 70 Months in Prison for Exporting Sensitive Military Technology to China," March 25, 2013, http://www.justice.gov/usao-nj/pr/former-employee-new-jersey-defense-contractor-sentenced-70-months-prison-exporting.

49. M. Apuzzo, "Chinese Businessman Is Charged in Plot to Steal U.S. Military Data," *New York Times*, July 11, 2014, http://www.nytimes.com/2014/07/12/business/chinese-businessman-is-charged-in-plot-to-steal-us-military-data.html?_r=0.

50. Office of the National Counterintelligence Executive, *Foreign Spies Stealing US Economic Secrets in Cyberspace: Report to Congress on Foreign Economic Collection and Industrial Espionage, 2009–2011*, October 2011, http://ncsc.gov/publications/reports/fecie_all/Foreign_Economic_Collection_2011.pdf.

51. Kaspersky, "Kaspersky Lab Uncovers 'Operation NetTraveler,' a Global Cyberespionage Campaign Targeting Government-Affiliated Organizations and Research Institutes," 2013, http://www.kaspersky.com/about/news/virus/2013/Kaspersky_Lab_Uncovers_Operation_NetTraveler_a_Global_Cyberespionage_Campaign_Targeting_Government_Affiliated_Organizations_and_Research_Institutes.

52. Office of the National Counterintelligence Executive, *Foreign Spies Stealing US Economic Secrets in Cyberspace*.

53. U.S. China Economic and Security Review Commission, *Report to Congress, One Hundred Thirteenth Congress, First Session* (Washington, DC: U.S. Government Printing Office, 2013), http://www.gpo.gov/fdsys/pkg/GPO-USCC-2013/html/GPO-USCC-2013-1.htm.

54. Ibid.
55. Mandiant, *APT1: Exposing One of China's Cyber Espionage Units*, 2013, 2, http://intelreport .mandiant.com/Mandiant_APT1_Report.pdf.
56. Office of the National Counterintelligence Executive, *Foreign Spies Stealing US Economic Secrets in Cyberspace*.
57. Ibid., B-2.
58. Executive Office of the President of the United States, *Administration Strategy on Mitigating the Theft of U.S. Trade Secrets*, 2013, https://www.whitehouse.gov/sites/default/files/omb/IPEC/ admin_strategy_on_mitigating_the_theft_of_u.s._trade_secrets.pdf.
59. Ibid.
60. M.-H. Maras, *Counterterrorism* (Burlington: MA: Jones and Bartlett, 2012), 7; M.-H. Maras, *Transnational Security* (Boca Raton, FL: CRC Press, 2014), 73.
61. Maras, *Counterterrorism*, 18; Maras, *Transnational Security*, 75.
62. Maras, *Counterterrorism*, 12; Maras, *Transnational Security*, 75.
63. Maras, *Counterterrorism*, 20; Maras, *Transnational Security*, 76.
64. M.-H. Maras, ed., *CRC Press Terrorism Reader* (Boca Raton, FL: CRC Press, 2013), 35.
65. Maras, *Counterterrorism*, 7; Maras, *Transnational Security*, 78–82.
66. *Brandenburg v. Ohio*, 395 U.S. 444 (1969).
67. K. Perry, "Woman Charged with Encouraging Terrorism on Twitter," *Telegraph*, November 27, 2014, http://www.telegraph.co.uk/news/uknews/terrorism-in-the-uk/11259426/Woman -charged-with-encouraging-terrorism-on-Twitter.html.
68. Ibid.
69. E. A. Pain, "Xenophobia and Ethnopolitical Extremism in Post-Soviet Russia: Dynamics and Growth Factors," *Nationalities Papers: The Journal of Nationalism and Ethnicity* 35, no. 5 (2007): 895.
70. S. N. Cross, "Russia and Countering Violent Extremism in the Internet and Social Media: Exploring Prospects for U.S.-Russia Cooperation Beyond the 'Reset,'" *Journal of Strategic Security* 6, no. 4 (2013): 13.
71. U.S. Attorney's Office, District of Massachusetts, "Tarek Mehanna Sentenced in Boston to 17 Years in Prison on Terrorism-Related Charges," April 12, 2012, https://www.fbi.gov/boston /press-releases/2012/tarek-mehanna-sentenced-in-boston-to-17-years-in-prison-on-terrorism -related-charges.
72. *United States v. Tarek Mehanna*, Superseding Indictment, Cr. No. 09-CR-I0017-GAO, District Court of Massachusetts, 2009; *United States v. Tarek Mehanna*, Second Superseding Indictment, Cr. No. 09-CR-10017-GAO, District Court of Massachusetts, 2010; *United States of America v. Tarek Mehanna* (2013), in the United States Court of Appeals for the First Circuit, on Appeal from the United States District Court, DOJ Appellate Brief on Conviction and Sentencing, No. 12-1461.
73. Maras, *Computer Forensics*, 183.
74. K. Poulsen, "Slammer Worm Crashed Ohio Nuke Plant Network," *Security Focus*, August 19, 2003, http://www.securityfocus.com/news/6767.
75. Maras, *Transnational Security*, 150.
76. Maras, *Computer Forensics*, 184.
77. Ibid.
78. *United States v. Mitra*, 405 F3d 492 at 494 (7th Cir. 2005).
79. B. Gertz, "FBI Eyes Chinese Hacking of Dams Database," *Washington Times*, January 6, 2015, http://www.washingtontimes.com/news/2015/jan/6/fbi-eyes-chinese-hacking-of-dams-database /?page=all.
80. C. A. Theohary and A. I. Harrington, *Cyber Operations in DOD Policy and Plans: Issues for Congress. Congressional Research Service, R43848*, January 5, 2015, http://fas.org/sgp/crs/natsec /R43848.pdf.

81. R. Abeyratne, "Cyber Terrorism and Aviation—National and International Responses," *Journal of Transportation Security* 4, no. 4 (2011): 337–349.

82. L. C. Baldor, "FAA Cyber System Vulnerable to Attack," *Huffington Post*, May 25, 2011, http://www.huffingtonpost.com/2010/08/12/faa-cyber-security-system_n_680257.html.

83. WPVI-TV Philadelphia, "FAA Computers Still Vulnerable to Cyberattack," April 13, 2010, http://6abc.com/archive/7609082/.

84. FAA, "Special Conditions: Boeing Model 777-200, -300, and -300ER Series Airplanes; Aircraft Electronic System Security Protection from Unauthorized External Access," *Federal Register*, November 18, 2013, https://www.federalregister.gov/articles/2013/11/18/2013-27342/special-conditions-boeing-model-777-200--300-and--300er-series-airplanes-aircraft-electronic-system.

85. D. Storm, "Hacker Uses an Android to Remotely Attack and Hijack an Airplane," *Computer World*, April 10, 2013, http://www.computerworld.com/article/2475081/cybercrime-hacking/hacker-uses-an-android-to-remotely-attack-and-hijack-an-airplane.html; M. Strohmeier, V. Lenders, and I. Martinovic, "On the Security of the Automatic Dependent Surveillance -Broadcast Protocol," *IEEE Communications Surveys & Tutorials* 17, no. 2 (2015): 1066.

86. D. Gross, "Hacker Says Phone App Could Hijack Plane," *CNN*, April 12, 2013, http://www.cnn.com/2013/04/11/tech/mobile/phone-hijack-plane/.

87. Ibid.

88. Sun Tzu, *The Art of War*, trans. L. Giles, The Internet Classics Archive, MIT, accessed August 15, 2016, http://classics.mit.edu/Tzu/artwar.html.

89. K. F. Rauscher and A. Korotkov, *Working Towards Rules for Governing Cyber Conflict: Rendering the Geneva and Hague Conventions in Cyberspace*, 2011, http://www.eastwest.ngo/sites/default/files/US-Russia%20%281%29.pdf.

90. R. Parks and D. Duggan, "Principles of Cyberwarfare, Security Privacy," *IEEE* 9, no. 5 (2011): 30–35.

91. L. Arimatsu, "A Treaty for Governing Cyber-Weapons: Potential Benefits and Practical Limitations," in *Cyber Conflict: Fourth International Conference on Cyber Conflict*, ed. C. Czosseck, R. Ottis, and K. Ziolkowski (Tallinn: NATO, 2012), 91–109; M. Robinson, K. Jones, and H. Janicke, "Cyber Warfare: Issues and Challenges," *Computers & Security* 49 (March 2015): 70–94.

92. N. Rowe, "The Ethics of Cyberweapons in Warfare," *International Journal of Cyberethics* 1, no. 1 (2010): 20–31.

93. J. Stone, "Cyber War Will Take Place!" *Journal of Strategic Studies* 36, no. 1 (2013): 101–108.

94. Participating states in the Wassenaar Arrangement include Argentina, Australia, Austria, Belgium, Bulgaria, Canada, Croatia, Czech Republic, Denmark, Estonia, Finland, France, Germany, Greece, Hungary, Ireland, Italy, Japan, Latvia, Lithuania, Luxembourg, Malta, Mexico, Netherlands, New Zealand, Norway, Poland, Portugal, Republic of Korea, Romania, Russian Federation, Slovakia, Slovenia, South Africa, Spain, Sweden, Switzerland, Turkey, Ukraine, United Kingdom and United States. The Wassenaar Arrangement, "About Us," accessed August 19, 2016, http://www.wassenaar.org/about-us/.

95. N. Cardozo and E. Galperin, "What Is the U.S. Doing about Wassenaar, and Why Do We Need to Fight It?" *Electronic Frontier Foundation*, May 28, 2015, https://www.eff.org/deeplinks/2015/05/we-must-fight-proposed-us-wassenaar-implementation.

96. J. A. Fleishman, "Commerce Dep't Struggles to Implement Anti-Cyberwar Regs," *North Carolina Journal of International Law*," February 17, 2016, http://blogs.law.unc.edu/ncilj/2016/02/17/commerce-dept-struggles-to-implement-anticyberwar-regs/; Cardozo and Galperin, "What Is the U.S. Doing about Wassenaar?"; E. Kovacs, "Experts Concerned about Effects of Proposed Wassenaar Cybersecurity Rules," *SecurityWeek*, May 26, 2015, http://www.securityweek.com/experts-concerned-about-effects-proposed-wassenaar-cybersecurity-rules; J. Granick, *Changes to Export Control Arrangement Apply to Computer Exploits and More*, Center for Internet

and Society, Stanford Law School, 2014, http://cyberlaw.stanford.edu/publications /changes-export-control-arrangement-apply-computer-exploits-and-more.

97. D. E. Denning, "Reflections on Cyberweapons Controls," *Computer Security Journal* 16, no. 4 (2000): 43–53.
98. Arimatsu, "A Treaty for Governing Cyber-Weapons."
99. Robinson, Jones, and Janicke, "Cyber Warfare: Issues and Challenges."
100. T. J. Junio, "How Probable Is Cyber War? Bringing IR Theory Back in to the Cyber Conflict Debate," *Journal of Strategic Studies* 36, no. 1 (2013): 125–133.
101. "Cyber War Will Take Place!"
102. W. A. Owens, K. W. Dam, and H. S. Lin, "Technology, Policy, Law, and Ethics Regarding U.S. Acquisition and Use of Cyberattack Capabilities," National Research Council (Washington, DC: National Academies Press, 2009), 54.
103. U.S. Strategic Command, "U.S. Cyber Command," August 2013, http://www.stratcom.mil /factsheets/Cyber_ Command/.
104. Maras, *Computer Forensics*, 181.
105. S. Gorman, "Georgia States Computers Hit by Cyberattack," *Wall Street Journal*, August 12, 2008, http://www.wsj.com/articles/SB121850756472932159.
106. *Corfu Channel* (U.K. v. Alb.), 1949 I.C.J. 4, 22 (Apr. 9).
107. *Report of the Group of Governmental Experts on Developments in the Field of Information & Tele-communications in the Context of International Security, 65th Session,* UN Doc A/65/201, July 30, 2010.
108. Maras, *Counterterrorism*, 18; Maras, *Transnational Security*, 23.
109. J. von Neumann and O. Morgenstern, *Theory of Games and Economic Behavior* (Princeton, NJ: Princeton University Press, 1944).
110. Maras, *Counterterrorism*, 18; Maras, *Transnational Security*, 68.
111. R. Jervis, "Realism, Neoliberalism, and Cooperation," *International Security* 24, no. 1 (1999): 51; K. N. Waltz, "Structural Realism after the Cold War," *International Security* 25, no. 1 (2000): 5–41.
112. M. N. Schmitt, "Classification of Cyber Conflict," *Journal of Conflict & Security Law* 17, no. 2 (2012): 245–260.
113. L. F. L. Oppenheim, *International Law: A Treatise,* 7th ed. (London: Longmans Green & Co, 1948).
114. N. Rowe, "The Ethics of Cyberweapons in Warfare," *International Journal of Cyberethics* 1, no. 1 (2010): 20–31.
115. U.S. Department of Homeland Security, *Cyber Storm: Securing Cyber Space,* last modified April 21, 2016, http://www.dhs.gov/cyber-storm-securing-cyber-space.
116. SIFMA, *Cybersecurity Exercise: Quantum Dawn 2,* accessed August 20, 2016, http://www.sifma .org/services/bcp/cybersecurity-exercise--quantum-dawn-2/.
117. NATO, Collective Defence—Article 5, updated March 22, 2016, http://www.nato.int/cps/en /natohq/topics_ 110496.htm.

TABLE OF LAWS

Act on Punishment of Activities Relating to Child Prostitution and Child Pornography, and the Protection of Children of 1999 (Japan)
Adam Walsh Child Protection and Safety Act of 2006 (United States)
Additional Protocol I of the Geneva Convention of 1977[1]
African Charter on the Rights and Welfare of the Child of 1990
African Youth Charter of 2006
Agreement on Cooperation in Combating Offences related to Computer Information of 2001 (Commonwealth of Independent States)
Agreement on Cooperation in the Field of Information Security of 2009 (Shanghai Cooperation Organization)
Agreement on Trade-Related Aspects of Intellectual Property Rights of 1994 (WTO)
Americans with Disabilities Act of 1990 (United States)
Animal Crush Video Prohibition Act of 2010 (United States)
Anticybersquatting Consumer Protection Act of 1999 (United States)
Antiterrorism and Effective Death Penalty Act of 1996 (United States)
Appendix I of the Convention on the International Trade in Endangered Species of Wild Fauna and Flora (CITES) of 1973
Appendix II of the Convention on the International Trade in Endangered Species of Wild Fauna and Flora (CITES) of 1973
Arab Convention on Combating Information Technology Offences of 2010 (Arab League)
Assembly Bill 2578 (New Jersey)
Berne Convention for the Protection of Literary and Artistic Works of 1886 (WIPO)
Child Online Protection Act of 1998 (United States)
Child Pornography Prevention Act of 1996 (United States)
Children's Internet Protection Act of 2000 (United States)
Communications of Decency Act of 1996 (United States)
Comprehensive Drug Abuse Prevention and Control Act of 1970 (United States)
Computer Fraud and Abuse Act of 1986 (United States)
Computer Misuse Act of 1990 (United Kingdom)
Controlled Substances Act of 1970 (United States)
Controlling the Assault of Non-Solicited Pornography and Marketing Act of 2003 (CAN-SPAM Act of 2003) (United States)

Convention on Action against Trafficking in Human Beings of 2005 (Council of Europe)
Convention on Cybercrime of 2001 (Council of Europe)
Convention on the Confidence and Security in Cyberspace of 2014 (African Union)
Convention on the International Trade in Endangered Species of Wild Fauna and Flora (CITES) of 1973
Copyright Treaty of 1996 (WIPO)
Coroner and Justice Act of 2009 (United Kingdom)
Criminal Justice and Courts Act of 2015 (United Kingdom)
Criminal Justice and Immigration Act of 2008 (United Kingdom)
Criminal Law (Sexual Offences) Act of 1993 (Ireland)
Criminal Law (Sexual Offences and Related Matters) Amendment Act of 2007 (South Africa)
Cyber Security Enhancement Act of 2002 (United States)
Cybercrime Convention of 2001 (Council of Europe)
Digital Millennium Copyright Act of 1998 (United States)
Directive 2001/29/EC on the Harmonisation of Certain Aspects of Copyright and Related Rights in the Information Society (European Union)
Disability Discrimination Act of 1995 (United Kingdom)
Economic Espionage Act of 1996 (United States)
Eighteenth Amendment to the U.S. Constitution (United States)
Electronic Funds Transfer Act of 1978 (United States)
Endangered Species Act of 1973 (United States)
Executive Order 13636 of 2013 (United States)
Fair and Accurate Credit Transactions Act of 2003 (United States)
Federal Food, Drug, and Cosmetic Act of 1938 (United States)
Federal Law No. 114 FZ on Counteraction of Extremist Activities of 2002 (Russia)
Firearm Owners' Protection Act of 1986 (United States)
First Amendment to the U.S. Constitution (United States)
Foreign Economic Espionage Penalty Enhancement Act of 2012 (United States)
Framework Convention on Tobacco Control of 2003 (World Health Organization)
Framework Decision on Combating the Sexual Exploitation of Children, including Child Pornography of 2004 (Council of the European Union)
Gambling Act of 2005 (Gibraltar)
Gambling Act of 2005 (United Kingdom)
General Agreement on Trade in Services of 1995 (WTO)
Gun Control Act of 1968 (United States)
Health Information Technology for Economic and Clinical Health Act of 2009 (HITECH Act of 2009) (United States)
Health Insurance Portability and Accountability Act of 1996 (United States)
Homeland Security Act of 2002 (United States)
Identity Theft and Assumption Deterrence Act of 1998 (United States)
Interstate Horseracing Act of 1978 (United States)
Interstate Wire Act of 1961 (United States)
Investment Advisors Act of 1940 (United States)
Jacob Wetterling Crimes Against Children and Sexually Violent Offender Registration Act of 1994 (United States)
Juvenile Protection Act of 2011 (South Korea)
Juvenile Sexual Protection Act of 2000 (South Korea)
Lacey Act of 1990 (United States)
Law 13/2011 on Gambling (Spain)
Law 4002/2011 (Greece)
Law Safeguarding Women's Rights and Interests of 1992 (People's Republic of China)

Law that Prohibits the Purchase of Sexual Services of 1999 (Sweden)
Malicious Communications Act of 1988 (United Kingdom)
Mann Act of 1910 (United States)
Money Laundering Control Act of 1986 (United States)
National Prohibition Act of 1919 (United States)
No Electronic Theft Act of 1997 (United States)
North Atlantic Treaty of 1949
Overseas Employment Act of 2013 (Bangladesh)
Patent Cooperation Treaty of 1970 (WIPO)
Patent Law Treaty of 2000 (WIPO)
Prevent All Cigarette Trafficking Act of 2009 (United States)
Prevention of Electronic Crimes Ordinance of 2007 (Pakistan)
Prosecutorial Remedies and Other Tools to End the Exploitation of Children Today Act of 2003 (United States)
Protection from Harassment Act of 2014 (Singapore)
Racketeer Influenced and Corrupt Organizations (RICO) Act of 1970 (United States)
Ryan Haight Online Pharmacy Consumer Protection Act of 2008 (United States)
Securities Act of 1933 (United States)
Securities Exchange Act of 1934 (United States)
Sex Offender Registration and Notification Act of 2006 (United States)
Sex Offenders Act of 1997 (United Kingdom)
Sexual Offences Act of 2003 (United Kingdom)
Singapore Treaty on the Law of Trademarks of 2006 (WIPO)
Terrorism Act of 2006 (United Kingdom)
Trademark Law Treaty of 1994 (WIPO)
Trafficking Victims Protection Act of 2000 (United States)
Truth in Lending Act of 1968 (United States)
Twenty-First Amendment to the U.S. Constitution (United States)
UN Charter of 1945
UN Convention against Transnational Organized Crime of 2000
UN Convention on the Rights of the Child of 1989
UN Optional Protocol to the Convention on the Rights of the Child on the Sale of Children, Child Prostitution and Child Pornography of 2000
UN Protocol against the Smuggling of Migrants by Land, Sea and Air of 2000
UN Protocol to Prevent, Suppress and Punish Trafficking in Persons of 2000
Uniting and Strengthening America by Providing Appropriate Tools Required to Intercept and Obstruct Terrorism Act of 2001 (USA Patriot Act of 2001) (United States)
Unlawful Internet Gambling Enforcement Act of 2006 (United States)
Volstead Act of 1919 (United States)
William Wilberforce Trafficking Victims Protection Reauthorization Act of 2008 (United States)

NOTES

1. Protocol Additional to the Geneva Conventions of 12 August 1949, and relating to the Protection of Victims of International Armed Conflicts (Protocol I), 8 June 1977.

INDEX